AFRICAN-AMERICAN PHILOSOPHY

Selected Readings

Tommy L. Lott
San José State University

UPPER SADDLE RIVER, NEW JERSEY 07458

Library of Congress Cataloging-in-Publication Data

African-American philosophy: selected readings / [edited by] TOMMY L. LOTT
   p. cm.
Includes bibliographical references.
ISBN 0-13-084696-1
   1. African Americans—Intellectual life—Sources. 2. African Americans—Social
conditions—Sources. 3. African Americans—Civil rights—History—Sources. 4. African
American philosophy—History—Sources. 5. United States—Race relations—Sources. 6.
United States—Intellectual life—Sources. I. Lott, Tommy Lee, [date]

E184.6 .A335   2002
191'.089'96073—dc21   2001036892

VP, Editorial Director: *Charlyce Jones Owen*
Acquisitions Editor: *Ross Miller*
Editorial Assistant: *Carla Worner*
Senior Managing Editor: *Jan Stephan*
Editorial/Production Supervisor: *Joanne Riker*
Prepress and Manufacturing Buyer: *Brian Mackey*
Director of Marketing: *Beth Gillett Mejia*
Marketing Manager: *Chris Ruel*
Cover Art Director: *Jayne Conte*
Cover Designer: *Bruce Kenselaar*

This book was set in 10/11 New Baskerville by East End Publishing Services, Inc.
and was printed and bound by Hamilton Printing Company. The cover was
printed by Phoenix Color Corp.

 © 2002 by Pearson Education, Inc.
Upper Saddle River, New Jersey 07458

Printed in the United States of America

10   9   8   7   6   5   4   3   2   1

ISBN 0-13-084696-1

Pearson Education LTD., London
Pearson Education Australia PTY, Limited, Sydney
Pearson Education Singapore, Pte. Ltd
Pearson Education North Asia Ltd, Hong Kong
Pearson Education Canada, Ltd., Toronto
Pearson Educación de Mexico, S.A. de C.V.
Pearson Education — Japan, Tokyo
Pearson Education Malaysia, Pte. Ltd
Pearson Education, Upper Saddle River, New Jersey

For
Saundria Lott
and
Jimmy Braswell

Contents

CHAPTER 3

Assimilation and Social Uplift   99

CHAPTER 4

Contemporary Black Feminist Thought   173

Preface

This anthology provides readings for use in courses designed to introduce students to African-American philosophy. Although recent debates regarding affirmative action, race, and racism are prominent in philosophy texts, a much broader perspective is needed to deal more adequately with issues of major concern to African-Americans. Indeed, this volume presents a wide range of issues that emanate from a history of African-American thought regarding social progress. I have based the selection on my experience teaching a variety of courses in philosophy departments, as well as in interdisciplinary studies programs, at several universities. In a philosophy course on African-American social and political thought that I taught at Stanford University the philosophical questions underlying the historical debates were the main focus with an eye to contemporary issues. When I taught a humanities course on philosophies of social change at Wheelock College, I emphasized the historical significance of the arguments within very specific social and political contexts, for in this interdisciplinary studies course, African-American philosophy was one of several components. Nonetheless, the reading for both courses included classic nineteenth-century texts and articles by twentieth-century writers.

Patterned along the same lines, this volume incorporates writings by historical and contemporary authors from many disciplines into a format that includes writings by philosophers, a format that opens dialog across disciplines. This serves a twofold objective. For the benefit of instructors and students who lack a background in African-American studies some of the basic ideas informing African-American thought are represented in many of the speeches and essays. There is also a benefit for students and instructors who lack a background in philosophy. In the essays by philosophers the style and method of philosophical analysis are given an application to questions that have a bearing on social policy regarding African-Americans. The references listed under Further Reading at the end of each chapter provide a guide to important books and articles on each topic.

I would like to thank the Prentice Hall reviewers for their valuable insight and comments about the manuscript: Rita Manning, San José State University; Jay M. Van Hook, Northwestern College; and David Theo Goldberg, University of California, Irvine.

I would also like to thank John Perry, Chair of Philosophy at Stanford University and Theresa Perry, Dean of Humanities at Wheelock College, for providing me the opportunity to teach courses on African-American Philosophy. I am deeply indebted to my graduate teachers at U.C.L.A., Angela Davis, Bernard Boxill, and Ronald Takaki, for introducing me to the history of African-American thought.

Tommy L. Lott

CHAPTER 1

Antebellum Critical Thought

Early in the nineteenth century black abolitionists in the North began to raise questions regarding slavery and freedom. In many cases they advocated resistance, including rebellion and violence. It remains an open empirical question as to how much influence the advocacy of resistance had on actual revolts. The philosophically interesting question is not so much whether Nat Turner's revolt was influenced by David Walker's pamphlet, but whether Walker's advocacy of revolt counts as a form of political resistance at par with Turner's.

The relatively few occurrences of slave revolts in the United States, in comparison with other parts of the New World, have led some historians to question whether there was much resistance by American slaves. Howard McGary argues that the focus by historians on rebellions involving violence is misguided. He insists that a more viable concept of resistance that applies to slavery must include more subtle forms such as sabotage, disruption, obstruction, noncooperation, ignorance, and illness. He proposes an alternative criterion by which to establish a more viable concept of the slave's resistance.

Nineteenth-century African-American critical thought appeared in different media. In addition to narratives advocating the abolition of slavery (written earlier by Mary Prince, Ottobah Cugiano, and Olaubah Equiano, later by Harriet Jacobs and Frederick Douglass) that appealed to the moral sentiments of white audiences in England and America, there were also occasions when black abolitionists appealed directly to black audiences, and sometimes directly to the slaves, to resist slavery.

David Walker, an outspoken black abolitionist, is well known for his pamphlet *An Appeal to the Colored Citizens of the World*. Accused by Garrison of using inflammatory rhetoric, Walker's publication was smuggled to port cities of the South and, within days, Southern governors and legislatures offered rewards for his capture, dead or alive. Walker is well known for his skillful use of Christian teachings to condemn slavery. He is less well known for his endeavor to organize free blacks in New England. As a leading activist in the antislavery crusade, he delivered an address at the First General Colored Association meeting in Boston in

1828. Geared toward an audience of free blacks in the North, the strong indictments of his *Appeal* are absent from his argument for a united front to fight slavery more effectively.

Following in Walker's footsteps, Maria Stewart, a close friend, also employed Christian theology to call for a unified effort to champion the rights and liberty of black people. She draws attention to her gendered standpoint by criticizing black male colleagues for not assuming more of a leadership role to speak out against racial injustice. Her religious orientation is also reflected in her condemnation of gambling and dancing. She frequently quotes the bible to advocate virtuous conduct. With regard to matters of public policy she criticizes the emigration scheme of the American Colonization Society as a misguided endeavor. Stewart points out that the funding required to relocate free blacks to Liberia would be better used to build a college that would benefit them here in America.

The tradition of employing Christian doctrine to argue for the abolition of slavery was well established among black abolitionists by the time of the Civil War. Henry Highland Garnet's sermon commemorating the passage of the Thirteenth Amendment in the hall of the House of Representatives represents a later stage of that tradition. Garnet relies on theology to argue that only the love of liberty is compatible with a true Christianity. Because slaves are reduced to degradation and sin, their actions can never be understood in the usual sense of "voluntary." From this Garnet concludes that the slave is morally obligated to use every means to get rid of the "diabological injustice" that denies liberty to slaves. He remarks, "Heaven would frown upon the men who would not resist such aggression." With explicit reference to slave rebellions led by Denmark Vesey, Toussaint L'Ouverture, Joseph Cinque, and Nat Turner, Garnet invokes an early version of what we now understand as liberation theology, in this case, informed by a tradition of rebellion.

Resistance and Slavery

Howard McGary

Historians have documented rebellions and revolts by blacks who were held as slaves.[1] There were violent confrontations between blacks and whites as slaves fought to break their bondage. These occurrences were rare, however, and this fact has led some scholars to question the extent and nature of slave resistance. My aim in this chapter is not to list or examine clear-cut cases of resistance by blacks held as slaves, but to argue that there were more subtle forms of resistance that are often overlooked by historians and other scholars interested in the issue of resistance to slavery. Historians who have endorsed what I have labeled subtle forms of resistance count such things as sabotage, disruption, obstruction, noncooperation, ignorance, illness, and the destruction of farm animals and tools as acts of resistance.[2] Other historians, like George Fredrickson, Christopher Lasch, and Lawrence Levine, have claimed that such acts should not qualify as acts of resistance.[3] For them, resistance is an act that requires planned action involving some actual or potential violence. I disagree, but before we can appreciate the subtle forms of defiance as genuine acts of resistance, we must be clear about what we mean by the concept "resistance."

In the narrative of Linda Brent, a North Carolina slave, we find an interesting account of how the refusal of women slaves to submit to sexual advances of the slaveholder can be seen as resistance to slavery.[4] Elsewhere, we find the refusal by slave women to bear children offered as a form of resistance.[5] According to some definitions, these actions cannot qualify as acts of resistance, but the account of resistance that I construct in this chapter will allow us to include these acts.

Source: Howard McGary, "Resistance and Slavery" in Howard McGary and Bill Lawson, *Between Slavery and Freedom* (Bloomington: Indiana University Press, 1993), 35–54.

There is a voluminous body of literature devoted to chattel slavery in the United States. Some of this literature focuses on the institution of slavery itself, while some focuses on the impact of the American slave system on slaves. In his controversial book *Slavery,* Stanley Elkins compares the American slave system to the Nazi concentration camps. He concludes by argument from analogy that the American slave system broke down the slave's adult personality and reduced him or her to a state of infantile dependency, a state similar to the condition of prisoners of Nazi concentration camps. Elkins calls this personality type a "Sambo." He concludes that one of the tests for the non-Sambo personality is resistance. According to Elkins, the lack of resistance by slaves is evidence that they were "Sambos."[6]

Even prior to Elkins's work, some scholars asserted that black slaves in America were docile and content, concluding that they did not resist slavery.[7] Others have argued strongly against this depiction of the American slave personality and the contention that slaves as a group did not resist slavery.[8]

From a careful reading of the arguments on both sides of the debate, one comes away convinced of the need for clarity concerning how to determine what constitutes "resistance." Merely pointing out instances where slaves acted in docile or aggressive ways does not settle whether such acts constitute acts of resistance. As I have noted, when some historians use the term "resistance" in relation to the actions of American slaves, they have counted a wide range of actions. These actions range from violent direct action against the slave system to slaves avoiding work by pretending to be sick.[9] If scholars are to correctly assess whether American slaves resisted slavery, or for that matter whether any oppressed group resisted its oppression, they first must be able to distinguish resistance from other distinct, but related notions, such as weak compliance.

An examination of resistance could be conceptual in nature or it could focus on actual methods and tactics employed by resisters. I shall not be concerned here with arguing for methods or tactics of resistance, but rather with determining how a third party evaluates whether a person is resisting. Toward this end, I shall raise objections to Roger Gottlieb's groundbreaking essay, "The Concept of Resistance: Jewish Resistance during the Holocaust,"[10] and then offer an alternative account of how we should evaluate whether a person is resisting. I will make use of examples and insights from the long period of slavery in America as well as examples from the civil rights movement.

Gottlieb teases out his account of resistance by focusing on Jewish resistance during the Holocaust. As we will see in the first section, Gottlieb's analysis centers on the beliefs of Holocaust victims about the reduction of their oppression—and by oppression he obviously means to "press down" or to harm. But the better description of the experiences of the victims of the Holocaust is genocide. The aim of the Nazis was not to subjugate Jews, but to eliminate them. In the case of slavery, however, slaves were an important part of the economy of the South and as such they were seen as necessary. So the aims of the Nazis were quite different from the aims of the slaveholders.[11]

Gottlieb's focus on beliefs and intentions is understandable given that he is concerned with an event that is part of fairly recent history. Some Holocaust victims are still alive and can be consulted about their beliefs about resistance to Nazi oppression in concentration camps. This is not the case with slavery. There are no living ex-slaves who can be consulted about day-to-day resistance to slavery.

If any action is to count as a paradigm case of resistance, it would have to be a slave revolt. But even here we discover that our intuitions may differ about what makes it a clear case of resistance. Do we want to count foolhardy self-sacrifice as a case of resistance? If not, why not? We also need to know to what extent a person's actions must be planned or

organized in order to qualify as resistance. For example, suppose the slavemaster attempted to march a group of slaves along a road and one person refused to go. He is warned once and then shot dead. Was his action an act of resistance? Does it matter that the person's action has little or no chance of reducing oppression? An adequate account of resistance should answer these questions.

The point of this discussion is not to prove that we can always give a correct judgment about whether certain acts constitute resistance, but to explore different conceptions of how we determine acts of resistance in order to see how they compare with one another, and to discover the consequences of adopting one criterion rather than another as an official account.

GOTTLIEB ON RESISTANCE

Scholars have offered a variety of reasons for why slavery lasted so long. Some incorrectly concluded that its longevity was due in part to a failure on the part of blacks to resist their oppression. Not only do these scholars indulge in blaming the victim; they also fail to appreciate the character of certain actions because of unclarity about the criteria for judging acts of resistance. Those who blame the victims fail to appreciate the destruction of farm tools, suicides, and the "Sambo" personality[12] as genuine acts of resistance. I hope to illustrate that actions and omissions such as these are erroneously seen as acts of contentment, weakness, and even compliance because of a failure by some historians to appreciate how these acts functioned within the slave system.

Philosophers and scholars from other disciplines have examined concepts like oppression, justice, and civil disobedience. Oddly enough, few analytic philosophers have analyzed the concept of resistance. Perhaps this is due to the fact that much of the literature on the topic has been descriptive rather than conceptual in nature. Because of this, philosophers may believe that an examination of questions concerning resistance is empirical and therefore best answered by inquirers from other fields.

Gottlieb is an exception. He contends that, unlike "the concepts of freedom, equality, political rights, and civil disobedience, the concept of resistance has not been analyzed in a manner to help us distinguish acts of resistance from those of passivity, compliance or collaboration."[13] In order to remedy this shortcoming, he concentrates on the state of mind of the person thought to be resisting, rather than the effects of the person's actions. This general strategy is not novel; it has been used to examine other concepts. We find it employed by some legal philosophers in their accounts of the notion of an attempt in criminal law. My examination of the criteria for determining acts of resistance will involve raising fundamental objections both to Gottlieb's conditions for describing an act as one of resistance, and to his general strategy.

A clear account of resistance would be of great value. Not only would it enable us to distinguish resistance from passivity and compliance, it would also help us to judge the legitimacy of the use of force by the state and other bodies. Such an account would also help us to distinguish politically significant acts from mere crimes. For example, we would be in a better position to determine whether blacks and whites who revolted in Watts, Detroit, Newark, and Miami in the 1960s were resisting racial oppression or merely looting and committing assault. Further, it would allow one to determine whether persons who work within an unjust system can ever be said to be resisting the evils of that system. Finally, if an action can be correctly described as an act of resistance, then this might influence the general population to have sympathy rather than contempt for those committing these acts.[14]

Gottlieb's account of resistance depends upon an account of intentional action. According to Gottlieb, the essential features for an action A to count as an act of resistance are as follows:

(a) Agent S is oppressed and S believes that he or she is oppressed;
(b) S intentionally does A and,
(c) S's intention in doing A involves two sorts of beliefs: (i) S believes that a part of him or her can be threatened, dominated or destroyed by the oppressive relationship, and (ii) S also has beliefs about how the oppressor is exercising the assault or domination, and
(d) either S believed that his or her doing A would directly reduce oppression or S believed that his or her intentionally doing A would set in motion those things that reduce oppression, and
(e) S's belief and desires caused S to do A.[15]

According to Gottlieb's account, if a person genuinely believes that he or she wants to reduce oppression and acts on that belief, then resistance is a correct description of that action even if it is impossible for the action to reduce oppression.

Note that we can separate the question "What makes an act intentional?" from the question, "What makes an intentional act an act of resistance?" My focus will be on the latter.

Gottlieb's account of resistance will not allow us to distinguish paradigm cases of resistance from: intransigence, where people strongly believe that they are resisting but they are not (e.g., a case where a slave's defiance is a personal strategy for self-gratification rather than an action that is intended to reduce oppression); cases of ineffectual resistance (like the slave's mistreatment of farm animals); and cases where one does not believe that one's action constitutes resistance, although functionally it reduces oppression (e.g., an "insider" subverts an unjust government because of agreement with the resistance, but feels that his actions are too insignificant to qualify as acts of resistance).

On Gottlieb's account, we cannot disqualify an act as resistance simply because it is nonaggressive or nonmilitant. Depending upon the person's intention, an extremely ineffective act could count as genuine resistance. For example, during the period of chattel slavery in this country some slaves were assigned jobs as slavedrivers.[16] Their function was to keep other slaves in line. Some of the slavedrivers rationalized their actions by claiming that their intent was to minimize the suffering of slaves, and thus they were reducing oppression. On Gottlieb's account, if their explanations were correct, they resisted, but in an ineffective way.

According to Gottlieb, the goal of an act of resistance must be to lessen oppression, not just to shift its effect or spread it around.[17] But given his condition (d), the agent can adopt quite unrealistic means for achieving his or her goal. Since Gottlieb's account rests on the beliefs of the agent, we must be able to verify the agent's beliefs, especially in odd cases like that of the slavedrivers. On Gottlieb's account, an observer must know the motives of S in order to correctly judge S's action as resistance, but empirically this is often impossible because mental states are not accessible to the observer.

It is understandable why one might want to focus on beliefs about intentions rather than effects or results; but such an exclusive focus is not acceptable. By concentrating on beliefs and intentions we may be better able to judge normative and descriptive concerns related to resistance, like courage and self-worth, but I do not believe we are better able to distinguish acts of resistance from those that are not. The final test of whether or not an act constitutes resistance should not rest solely on an agent's beliefs about intentions. A person's beliefs can be false even though they are firmly held.

Defining acts of resistance in terms of the beliefs of the agent allows a wide range of ineffectual acts to count as acts of resistance. It is important to recognize that it is one thing to define acts of resistance in terms of the agent's intentions and another to determine whether or not the agent has such intentions. Gottlieb's account of resistance places emphasis on intentions. Although he recognizes that the factual question bears on whether we may describe a person's action as resistance, Gottlieb does not give an adequate account of how we can settle whether or not the person has such intentions. Even if he is right that intent is a logically necessary condition for resistance, it is not sufficient for others to establish that a person is resisting.

Gottlieb gives further support for his focus on intention in two subsections of his paper, "Tacit Resistance" and "Unconscious or Self-Deceptive Non-Resistance." He claims that with some acts of resistance the beliefs and intentions that the agent has about reducing oppression are tacitly held. The person resists in such cases because of feelings of hatred or guilt rather than an intention to reduce oppression.[18] For Gottlieb these tacit beliefs not only imply that the person has the proper mental state, but that this mental state functioned as motivation for the act of resistance.

Such a reply does not meet my objection, however, although it does explain why unconscious beliefs, in some cases, can give us reason to think that an action is intentional. But it does not explain why we do not need a criterion for determining when a person has certain intentions and if these intentions led to the action in question.

CONSCIOUS AND UNCONSCIOUS RESISTANCE

There is an odd ring to the phrase "unconscious resistance." It is puzzling because resistance, like protest, is thought to be a conscious moral and political action, or to at least have a significant moral and political component. As Gottlieb points out, we do make judgments about the actions and characters of persons by virtue of their responses to such things as injustice or oppression. We would certainly like to think, in cases where such character judgments are made, that the actions which form the basis for our judgments are voluntary. In other words, we require that the agent's responses be intentional. If their actions are not intentional, we are inclined to conclude that the unjust or oppressive actions do not reflect on their characters save insofar as their unintentional actions are due to ignorance of things that they should have known about, such as ignorance of the fact that throwing a bomb into a crowded legislative chamber will cause harm to the persons assembled there.

Yet Gottlieb needs something like a concept of "unconscious resistance" if his account is to succeed. He wants to describe certain acts as acts of resistance that, on first glance, appear not to be. He cites some of the nonmilitant and nonaggressive actions of

Jews in Nazi concentration camps as resistance because these Jews were either consciously or unconsciously attempting to hold on to their humanity. This, in the context of Nazi concentration camps, constitutes intentional covert opposition to the oppressor and oppression. On the other hand, Gottlieb dismisses the efforts of the council of influential Jews (*Judenrats*) who appeared to cooperate with the Nazis and administered the Jewish ghettos created by the Nazis. Gottlieb denies that these councils were thereby resisting the Nazi oppression.

Gottlieb incorrectly assumes that cooperation with the oppressor is incompatible with intentionally reducing oppression. This general assumption is clearly false. Persons involved in counterintelligence activities often intentionally cooperate with an oppressive regime in order to eventually halt or reduce its damaging effects. When Gottlieb says that people often have the unconscious aim of reducing oppression, this casts doubt on his rejection of the actions of the *Judenrats* as resistance. The causal relationship in Gottlieb's account disallows accepting effective actions not caused by intent to resist (not just any intent to act).

In the case of unconscious resistance, the action that is done with an unconscious intent to resist is like effective acts not caused by the intent to resist, since unconsciousness implies that the intent is not presently active and, though potentially motivating, it is not presently functioning as a motivator. Put another way, counting unconscious intent is like counting an "almost" in horseshoes: the intent is near the action but not truly connected. True causal connections cannot involve reference to unconscious beliefs.

Gottlieb cannot simply point at the passive or apparent cooperative nature of the *Judenrats'* actions because these could be a part of a chosen strategy to achieve a desired end, namely to reduce oppression by limiting the severity of the punishments inflicted by the Nazis. Perhaps Gottlieb does not focus on the appearance of their actions, but on the actors' beliefs. But if he does, then he must have some satisfactory way of ascertaining whether or not the *Judenrats* had the appropriate intentions. If not, we are allowed to read our own beliefs into what the agent intended when he or she acted. This would violate condition (c) of his account of acts of resistance, which requires the agent to have certain beliefs about thwarting oppression, but does not require the beliefs to be true. Beliefs held with a great deal of conviction can be false or completely out of line with the beliefs of others in the community.

Gottlieb recognizes that beliefs and intentions are problematic criteria, but given his chosen strategy, he must employ them. He asserts that if we encounter entities who appear to be language speakers, but whose sentences translate into beliefs radically different from our own, we might revise our judgment that they were speaking a language. In an analogous fashion, he concludes that if a person's purported beliefs about how to resist in a given situation sufficiently differ from our own, we are justified in believing that this person does not intend to resist.[19]

I disagree. I doubt that we are justified in concluding, on the basis of Gottlieb's account, that a person did not resist. We are only justified in concluding that we have insufficient evidence as to what the person did and why, and thus that we have insufficient information to claim that he or she resisted. For an observer to correctly judge that an action is an act of resistance, it is not necessary for him to know the actor's intentions, or the exact effects of his action.

During the civil rights movement a number of Americans of good will, both black and white, pondered what they should do to reduce the oppression and discrimination experienced by black Americans. Some people adopted a strategy of direct confrontation with unjust governmental practices, including armed self-defense, sit-ins, and attempts to integrate schools, transportation systems, and places of public accommodation. Others used more subtle means, like public lectures exposing the evils of racism, to break down biased racial attitudes; some resolved to build defense mechanisms within themselves to enable them to tolerate oppression. Many of these same tactics were employed by blacks and whites during the antebellum period.

What their actions must all have in common if they are to qualify as acts of resistance on Gottlieb's model, however, is the intent to reduce the oppression of black people. Gottlieb assumes that if S intentionally acts to reduce oppression, then S has a general conception of oppression, but S must also have a specific conception of the particular oppressive system or practice. In the example of the civil rights movement, S must have some knowledge of the Jim Crow system and what is evil and unjust about it. To have the concept of oppression is different from having the concept of "tallness." One can understand what it is to be tall without being committed to any negative evaluative or normative stance, but this is not so with oppression. When one identifies someone's actions or a practice as oppressive, then one is also saying that person's actions or the practice is unacceptable.

Of course, it is debatable whether people who employed very subtle means intended to reduce oppression, but we can attempt to assess their intentions and their sincerity or dedication by determining whether their beliefs about what they intended to do to reduce oppression are consistent with their other beliefs. This will not, however, settle the question, "Are they resisting?" In such cases the person who is said to be intending to resist oppression might have to make a radical revision of his basic set of beliefs.

For example, some students who joined the Student Nonviolent Coordinating Committee in its militant but peaceful protest in the South willingly absorbed the violence directed toward the nonviolent protestors. Yet these students categorically rejected Martin Luther King's views on nonviolence.[20] Were their beliefs about why they were engaging in these nonviolent protests consistent with their other beliefs? In all cases I think not. Their actions could not be consistently described as "nonviolent protest" given their beliefs about self-respect and the nature of protest. One might conclude that the students felt the time for self-defensive violence had not yet come and that nonviolence for now was the most effective type of resistance. Such an explanation might explain the actions of some, but not of

those who categorically rejected the willing acceptance of violence at the hands of the oppressor. From the fact that a belief B is inconsistent with a person's basic beliefs, it would be deductively invalid to infer that he or she does not have belief B. We lack a failproof method for ascertaining the sincerity of a person's beliefs. This is why we focus on people's actions in order to get some evidence or assurance that their beliefs are, in fact, sincere.

What Gottlieb fails to fully appreciate is the fact that people can believe things that are false, but even more important they can intend to do what is impossible.[21] People with a great deal of sincerity can intend to reduce oppression by adopting such methods as wishing it away or calling on the spirits, and thus count their acts as acts of resistance. If I am right about this, Gottlieb needs a method for ascertaining the sincerity of the agent's beliefs and intentions. His proposal of disqualifying a person's beliefs because they are "radically different from our own" will not suffice. Gottlieb's account fails to provide adequate provisions for consistency and sincerity of belief. His assumption about the superiority of our way of thinking may be classist, racist, or sexist.

Gottlieb is right, however, that we would not do any better by simply focusing on the effects of the agent's action. For instance, during the Watts Riot of 1965 a number of persons engaged in rash, but understandable, actions (such as burning down needed facilities in their communities). They acted with the best of intentions, but the effects of their actions in the short run heightened oppression in Watts rather than reducing it. Denying the reliance on the effects of an action does raise questions about the scope of those who are affected by the reduction of oppression and about how far into the future we should look if we are to employ an analysis which examines effects. If we focus only on the short-term effects of actions and limit the scope to blacks in the Watts community, we would certainly conclude that they did not resist. Gottlieb fails to see that what is crucial when a third party determines whether an action counts as an act of resistance is not always what the agent actually believes and intends, but the circumstances the agent faced at the time of action.

In civil law a person can be justifiably held liable for an action he did not intend to commit and for consequences he did not expect. For example, in *Re Polemis and Furness, Withey and Co.* (3KB 560 [1921]), stevedores in the employ of Furness, Withey and Company knowingly carried planks near the hatch of a ship that their employer had chartered. They inadvertently dropped a plank into the hold, creating a spark and a fire because, unbeknownst to them, kerosene had been stored there and some gaseous fumes were still in the hold. The court ruled that Furness, Withey and Company were liable even though there was no intention to cause the fire or reason for the stevedores to anticipate that a fire would result from dropping a plank into the hold.

In a like manner, persons can be correctly said to have resisted oppression even though we lack reliable information about their beliefs or intentions when they acted. I believe that we may justifiably conclude that the slaves' practice of stealing from their masters was a form of resistance even though we do not have reliable information about what their actual intentions were when they stole or about the actual consequences of their acts on the slave system. The evidence for this interpretation is supported by the fact that slaves stole from slaveholders at great risk to themselves even when their survival needs were met. Orlando Patterson has argued that stealing by slaves was a way for them to assert their humanity.[22] I would add it was a way of resisting the oppressive characterization of themselves as nonpersons.

Even in the absence of open rebellion or evidence of a worked-out plan for resisting slavery, I believe we are warranted in concluding that stealing by slaves from their masters, under certain circumstances, counts as "day-to-day" resistance to slavery. These acts, in the context of slavery, can reasonably be seen as efforts to reduce oppression by frustrating the demands of the slave system. I disagree with those historians who claim that only the testimony of slaves themselves can tell us whether they resisted slavery.

If historians, sociologists, and other analysts are really to develop adequate criteria to distinguish acts of resistance from those that are not, they should not always give primacy to an agent's intentions. They should focus on the conditions that the agent faced when he or she acted or failed to act and the avenues available for reducing oppression. With this information, a better strategy to adopt in order to distinguish acts of resistance from those that are not would be one similar to the reasonable person test in the law. The reasonable person test denotes a hypothetical individual who possesses and exercises those qualities of attention, knowledge, intelligence, and judgment which a decent society requires of its members for the protection of their interests and the interests of others. A person's intentions and their effects are sometimes useful, but they are not always necessary in order to make a judgment about whether the act is an act of resistance.

One of my central points is to question how we assess the existence of an intent, a belief, and their connection to an action. Intents and beliefs are mental states, and hence not directly observable by a third party. At times they may not even be observable by the agent (we do not always know the causes of our actions). The reasonable person hypothesis seems to offer a workable solution. But the question remains: "Reasonable in what sense?" A solution may be formally reasonable or pragmatically reasonable. The former is theoretically elegant, but in practice it may be ineffective. The latter is relativistic, and thus we need greater detail of its operation if it is to prove helpful.

"Reasonable" in the context of the legal test is a culture-bound concept. It refers to the consensus of persons in the culture. My test for resistance will also be culture-bound, but this is as it should be. I should note that my account of how we determine whether or not an act counts as resistance recognizes the existence of belief and intent, but, as I have suggested, my mechanism differs from Gottlieb's because it does not depend upon assessing the sincerity of each. My account of resistance cannot tell us that resistance, in fact, has occurred, but only that it is likely that it did. When you deal in the empirical and practical, absolutes are often unattainable.

It might seem counterintuitive to accept an account of resistance that does not require the resister to intend to reduce oppression. But this is because we mistakenly believe that it is redundant to say that S intentionally resisted his oppressors. When we think of someone resisting, we assume that they intended their action to reduce oppression or set in motion those things that will lead to the reduction or the elimination of oppression. I believe, however, that we need to distinguish: (i) S intended to do A from (ii) S did A and S's action was intentional.

We should not assume that a correct analysis of how a third party identifies an act of resistance should have (i) as a necessary condition. We often perform an *action* intentionally with no intention of bringing about an important and reasonable *description* of that action. For example, one may intentionally eat sweets with no intention of ingesting food with a high caloric content. The actions of very young children can sometimes be correctly described as acts of resistance even though these children did not, under a description of their actions, have an intention to reduce what they perceived to be oppression.

In fact, in some cases of resistance the resisters have no clear conception that they are being oppressed. This is true with young children who have not formed a clear general conception of oppression, but it is also true of persons who have a clear conception of oppression in general terms but lack a full understanding of the particular nature of the oppression that they are experiencing. Such cases are graphically illustrated by examples drawn from the oppression of women. Housewives intentionally engage in actions that under an appropriate description can be said to reduce their oppression without having intended to do so under their own description of their actions.

Gottlieb wants to handle such cases by claiming that these women unconsciously intend to reduce their oppression. I think this assumes that certain beliefs are present in the mind, but that they have not yet been brought to the surface. I contend that there need not be such unconscious beliefs in such cases. A desire to ease a feeling of dissatisfaction is not always something that can be turned into beliefs about the specific nature of one's oppression and how to reduce it, even with a great deal of effort devoted to consciousness-raising.

It is my contention that many acts of resistance lacked the *mens rea* condition because they were behavior patterns that were passed down from generation to generation, having the consequence of reducing oppression or force without the resister having conscious or unconscious beliefs about the reduction of some force or oppression. Perhaps those slaves who originated the practice had the intention of reducing oppression by engaging in the acts that established it. For strategic reasons, they may have chosen to teach these practices to their children as routine behaviors.[23] This would have the effect of keeping the practices clandestine since even if slaves who acted in these ways were interrogated by the slaveholders, they could not reveal any intentions about reducing oppression because they did not have them.

Remember, on my account, the agent's beliefs are sufficient, but not necessary. Given that chattel slavery in the United States lasted so long and that the system had clearly established procedures for keeping slaves in check, it is not surprising to find that resistance took this form.

AN ALTERNATIVE ACCOUNT OF RESISTANCE

If the above observations are correct, then the features of action A that are essential for A to be judged by a third party as an act of resistance should be reformulated as follows:

(a)' The condition of constraint (positive or negative) exists against agent S and the group in which S is a member, and S has a general conception of these constraints, and

(b)' S's action A is intentional under S's description of A which may or may not be the same description under which S's action A reduces the constraint, and (c)' S's action A under an appropriate description is one that could reduce the constraint directed at the group of which S is a member, and

(d)' The causal process that S sets in motion with his action A is one that reasonable persons, who are similarly constrained and aware of their constraints, would also be likely to set in motion if they wanted to reduce these constrictions.

In the discussion above, I did not challenge Gottlieb's focus on oppression as the object of the resistance. But condition (a)' reflects my disagreement with Gottlieb's contention that resistance is always resistance to oppression. We can resist things that are not oppressive, even in the political context. By adopting the above conditions, we are still able to preserve an important feature of the act of resistance, namely the moral importance attached to an act that reduces oppression. At the same time, we avoid the difficulties raised to Gottlieb's account of resistance, because S can engage in an action that causally reduces or sets in motion those acts that will reduce oppression even though, at the time he or she acted, S may not have intended to reduce oppression.

From the point of view of a historian, this account of when a person can be said to have resisted focuses on the moral import of the action rather than the person. It does not attempt to identify the state of mind of the actor but rather focuses on the fact that the agent acted and that his action was judged from the perspective of the oppressed to be an important part of a causal process that could reasonably lead to the reduction of oppression.

The revised account of when some third party's action can correctly describe an act as resistance avoids counting conformist acts as resistance because the agent believed them to be so. It would not allow us to count as acts of resistance the actions of those slaves who sincerely believed that informing the slave masters of the efforts of fellow slaves would bring down the slave system. Allowing these conformist acts to count as resistance, because the agent intended them to be so, serves to hamper rather than to encourage political efforts to reduce oppression. Counting such actions as resistance allows too much room for misguided persons to self-deceptively ease their consciences by erroneously concluding that they had contributed to the reduction of oppression.[24]

It may seem that my adoption of the reasonable-person test makes me susceptible to the same criticism that was raised against Gottlieb. In other words, we allow the belief of others to be a substitute for the beliefs of those said to be resisting. This does not present a problem for my account, however, because I do not make the agent's beliefs about the reduction of oppression a necessary condition for describing an act as resistance.

It is incumbent upon me nevertheless to show why my account does not allow the oppressors or supporters of the status quo to use the reasonable-person test to discount legitimate acts of resistance. But remember that the reasonable-person test is culture-bound and, as such, subject to abuse by persons with power and influence. Therefore I would argue that the determination of what counts as resistance must involve a genuine public dialogue, with care taken to empower and acknowledge the voices of those who directly share the legacy of social practice like slavery and the Holocaust.[25]

What my account of resistance highlights is the fact that we should avoid the temptation to tailor our accounts to accommodate only cases of oppression in recent history. On the other hand, we do not want to focus solely on effect simply because there are no survivors who can be interviewed about their beliefs about the reduction of oppression. Hopefully, the account of resistance that I have sketched here suffers from neither of these shortcomings.

This account of resistance appreciates but rejects any account of resistance that makes beliefs about the intent to reduce oppression necessary for the identification of an act of resistance. In order to fully understand the wide range of acts of resistance, however, one must recognize that resistance to certain acts by victims of oppression is not directed at some generic, general condition of oppression, but to specific actions and practices. For example, the action and practices that make up the institution of slavery were not identical with those that define the Holocaust. As noted earlier, the slaveholder wanted to act to make the slave a profitable piece of human property, whereas the intent of the Nazis was the extermination of the Jews.

The means adopted to achieve these different goals may have been similar in certain respects, but there were some important differences. For example, in order to appreciate the refusal to work or the destruction of farm tools by slaves as acts of resistance, one must be knowledgeable about the specific nature of the practices on the plantation and the context in which these acts took place. It is my contention that those who wish to evaluate such actions would be better served in some cases by focusing on what slaves were up against instead of always trying to determine the slaves' actual beliefs about whether their actions were intended to reduce oppression. Remember, my disagreement with Gottlieb is not that the beliefs of slaves are never useful in determining acts of resistance, but rather than such beliefs are not necessary in order to describe an act as resistance.

It is important to note that a primary assault of chattel slavery was the attempt by slaveholders to get slaves to accept or rationalize their miserable predicament. It is clear from reading slave narratives that slaveholders were successful to some degree in achieving this desired result. People who have been indoctrinated from the time of birth to accept oppressive practices and lifestyles very often do not possess even unconscious beliefs about the specific nature of some of the oppressive practices to which they emotionally and physically react.

In fact, as the black liberation movement in the United States and the women's movement have shown us, it is not the case that oppressed people are always knowledgeable about their oppression. Black Americans and women did not always possess beliefs about their oppression. It is doubtful that these beliefs existed in their unconscious mind in the way that the truths of mathematics were said to exist in the mind of the slave boy in Plato's *Meno,* nor were they suppressed in the way

Freud described. The victims of certain types of oppression have to learn rather than recollect or cease to suppress their beliefs about oppression.

It is clear why Gottlieb wants to focus on unconscious beliefs. He adopts a Davidsonian account of reasons as causes of action.[26] So, in his mind, in order to say that S resisted W then S must have had certain beliefs which counted as his reasons for acting. For Gottlieb, even in those circumstances where the agent S does not acknowledge the requisite belief about the reduction of oppression, such beliefs have to exist and be operative, even if they exist in S's unconscious mind. As I said earlier, the move to the unconscious mind is crucial for Gottlieb because it allows him to expand the class of acts that can be said to qualify as acts of resistance.

My worry with this approach is that it fails to fully appreciate the far-reaching affects caused by prolonged oppression. Gottlieb assumes that people, for the most part, have a clear picture of what is oppressive in their lives and why. Given that his focus was the Holocaust, his adoption of this model is understandable.

Compared to slavery, the Holocaust lasted a relatively short period of time. Victims knew clearly what it meant to be free persons and what it meant in very specific terms to live a life free of Nazi oppression. Chattel slavery in the United States, on the other hand, lasted for several hundred years. Most slaves never knew what it meant to live lives free of the domination of slaveholders. This fact should not be ignored if one is to develop an adequate account of the role that beliefs about the nature of one's oppression play in my accounts of resistance to slavery.

It is important that we make it clear that my adoption of the reasonable-person test does not commit me to the counterintuitive result whereby a slave's actions count as resistance to slavery even if the slave did not see slavery as oppressive, but actually delighted in its existence. Consider the following hypothetical case:

Imagine the situation, on W*, where slaves played "the stealing game," the object of which was to see who could steal the most from his or her master without getting caught. These slaves, as it turns out, liked slavery and amused themselves by playing "the stealing game." Now, some slaves who put their hearts into the game exhibited great skill—so much so, that the "stealing game" had a negative impact on W*'s economy. But, except for the "stealing game," the slaves were otherwise obedient, loyal, and respectful.[27]

Does this case satisfy all of my conditions for resistance and thus serve as a counterexample to my account of resistance? I think not. An important feature of my account is that the person who is said to be resisting is dissatisfied or unhappy with their predicament. But from the fact they are unhappy with or frustrated with their situation, it does not follow that they believe that specific practices that caused their predicaments are oppressive. Unhappiness and frustration accompany oppression, but these states do not entail that one is oppressed or that one believes that one is oppressed.

The American slave experience, given its brutality and longevity, can tell us a great deal about extremely provocative questions concerning the nature of resistance. For example, is it fair to call an act resistance if one believes that the action will be ineffectual or foolish? It is also useful to know if every act of resistance is an act of courage.

Let us now turn to the first of these questions. When we say that an act is foolish, it is most often judged against the prevalent beliefs and standards of the time. Of course, sometimes we say that something is foolish if the action runs counter to what we take to be irrefutable facts, like the laws of nature. But in most instances, the claim that an action is foolish is judged relative to our existing norms and practices. We take these norms and practices to be true, but they are at best only contingently true. My contention is that when we examine the wisdom of most alleged acts of resistance in the case of slavery, we should recognize that what might be foolish or foolhardy for a white free person would not be foolish for a black person caught in the muck of slavery. We should also note that what might be foolish for persons struggling under a certain set of oppressive practices

may not be foolish for those struggling under a different set.

These are extremely important questions because, as many commentators on slavery have noted, slavery was an extremely complex institution in economic, psychological, and sociological terms. The relationships that existed between slaves and their owners were multidimensional. For example, slaves were dehumanized by their slaveholders but they were also involved in intimate relationships with them. So, the battle lines between slaves and slaveholders were not as clearly drawn as, say, in war-time situations, where the enemy is distinct and clearly identifiable. This is not to say that the majority of slaves did not see slaveowners as adversaries, but rather that the very nature of chattel slavery clouded some issues and caused slaves to act in ways that they would otherwise not have acted had they controlled their own destinies. When one makes an assessment of the behavior of a slave, one must keep these things in mind and not be too quick to accept what might seem like an obvious interpretation of a slave's behavior.

With consuming and tightly controlled institutions such as slavery, one should not expect each and every act of resistance to be efficacious. Some of the most effective acts of insurrection taken alone would have been judged as foolish or hopeless prior to the time of action. Some actions have a way of motivating other actions, but it is often impossible to predict with any certainty which actions will have this effect. Nonetheless, we still want to be able to distinguish acts by cowards that turn out to have positive results from actions by brave persons who intentionally act to thwart specific oppressive practices.

My account of resistance allows us to make such a distinction because the beliefs of the actor *can* be used as evidence but they *need* not be used. If, for example, a slave wishes to poison a rival for his girlfriend's affections, but inadvertently poisons a notoriously brutal slave overseer, should the slave's act qualify as an act of resistance? It might, and my account of resistance supports my thinking. My account allows us to examine and use the beliefs of the actor when they are readily apparent; when they are not, we can examine the action in its context, in the light of existing norms and practices, in order to make a judgment about whether or not the action qualifies as resistance.

In these cases, it might seem that my account completely ignores the motives of the actor in an assessment of the action. This view is mistaken. We make inferences about the agents' motives, but we do not assume that every act that qualifies as an act of resistance was performed by someone with a belief (conscious or unconscious) about the reduction of oppression. So, it is true that we sometimes call an act resistance even though we have to remain silent about such things as the courage of the actor. Is this an unacceptable consequence of my account? I think not.

We often associate acts of resistance with courage, but it would be a mistake to claim that every act of resistance is an act of courage. Aristotle wrote that courage is the proper mixture of fear and cheer.[28] By this he meant that a courageous person takes risk, but not to the point of being foolhardy. However, some risks are greater than others. For example, we all know that extending a pole to a drowning person involves some risk and that the results of such an action are clearly noble, but we would refrain from calling such an action courageous because the risk of harm to the rescuer is so slight. If I am right that courage involves taking risks that can not be described as minor, then clearly some acts of resistance will not qualify as courageous acts. When we are informed about the full range of acts of resistance to slavery, then we will see that in the day-to-day acts of resistance, courage was not always the issue.

NOTES

1. See, for instance, Herbert Aptheker, *American Negro Slave Revolts* (New York: Alfred A. Knopf, 1943).
2. See Raymond A. Bauer and Alice H. Bauer, "Day to Day Resistance to Slavery," *Journal of Negro History* 27: 4 (1942), 388–419.
3. See George M. Fredrickson and Christopher Lasch, "Resistance to Slavery," in Ann J. Lane, ed., *The Debate Over Slavery* (Urbana: University of Illinois Press, 1971), pp. 223–44 and

Lawrence Levine, *Black Culture and Black Consciousness: Afro-American Folk Thought from Slavery to Freedom* (New York, 1977).
4. Linda Brent, *Incidents in the Life of a Slave* (Boston: By the author, 1861), p. 26.
5. Herbert Gutman, *The Black Family in Slavery and Freedom, 1750–1925* (New York: Pantheon, 1976), p. 73.
6. Stanley Elkins, *Slavery: A Problem in American Institutional and Intellectual Life,* (1959; 3d rev. ed. Chicago: University of Chicago Press, 1976), chapter 3.
7. See, for example, Ulrich B. Phillips, *American Negro Slavery* (New York: D. Appleton, 1918; rpt. Baton Rouge: Louisiana State University Press, 1969).
8. See, for example, Kenneth Stampp, *The Peculiar Institution* (New York: Vantage Books, 1956).
9. A good example of the practice of pretending to be sick can be found in the narrative of William Grimes, *The Life of William Grimes* in William Loren Katz, ed., *Five Black Lives* (Middletown, Conn.: Wesleyan University Press, 1971), pp. 81–82.
10. Roger S. Gottlieb, "The Concept of Resistance: Jewish Resistance during the Holocaust," *Social Theory and Practice* 9: 1 (1983), 31–49.
11. Laurence Thomas, "American Slavery and the Holocaust: Their Ideologies Compared," *Public Affairs Quarterly* 5: 2 (1991), 191–207.
12. For accounts of the "Sambo" personality and its role in the slave community, see John W. Blassingame, *The Slave Community: Plantation Life in the Antebellum South* (New York: Oxford University Press, 1972), esp. pp. 200–16; and Orlando Patterson, "Towards a Future That Has No Past: Reflections on the Fate of Blacks in the Americas," *The Public Interest* 27 (1972), 43. For several excellent philosophical discussions of the consequences of the "Sambo" personality on the self-concept, see Thomas E. Hill, Jr., "Servility and Self-Respect," *The Monist* 57: 1 (1973), 87; Laurence Thomas, "Morality and Our Self-Concept," *Journal of Value Inquiry* 12: 4 (1978); and Bernard Boxill, "Self-Respect and Protest, *Philosophy and Public Affairs* 6: 1 (1976).
13. Gottlieb, "The Concept of Resistance," pp. 39–40.
14. See chapter 5 of this volume.
15. Gottlieb, "The Concept of Resistance," pp. 34–47.
16. See William L. Van Deburg, *The Slave Driver: Black Agricultural Labor Supervision in the Ante-*

bellum South (Westport, Conn.: Greenwood Press, 1979).

17. Gottlieb, "The Concept of Resistance," p. 34.
18. Ibid., p. 43.
19. Ibid., p. 45.
20. See Cleveland Sellars (with Robert Terrell), *The River of No Return: Autobiography of a Black Militant and the Life and Death of SNCC* (New York: Morrow, 1973), pp. 46–47.
21. For a good argument in support of the claim that people can intend to do what they believe to be impossible see Irving Thalberg, "Can One Intend the Impossible?" in *Enigmas of Agency* (New York: Allen and Unwin, 1972).
22. Orlando Patterson, "Towards a Future That Has No Past: Reflections on the Fate of Blacks in the Americas," *The Public Interest* 27 (1972), 43.
23. The play of slave children is an area that might prove extremely useful in spelling out the nature and extent of such behaviors. See, for example, David K. Wiggins, "The Play of Slave Children in the Plantation Communities of the Old South, 1820–1860," *Journal of Sport History* 7: 2 (1980), 21–39.
24. I would like to thank David Benfield, Douglas Husak, Walton Johnson, Brian McLaughlin, Kenneth Monteiro, Irving Thalberg, and members of the Society for the Study of Black Philosophy for their comments and criticisms of earlier drafts of this section.
25. Marilyn Friedman discusses the conditions for a genuine public dialogue in her paper "The Impracticality of Impartiality," *Journal of Philosophy* 86: 11 (1989), 645–56.
26. Donald Davidson, "Actions, Reasons and Causes," *Journal of Philosophy* 60: 23 (1963), 685–700.
27. I thank Laurence Thomas for this example and line of criticism.
28. Aristotle, *Nicomachean Ethics* 1115b7–1116a10.

Speech at the First General Colored Association

Boston, 1828

David Walker

WE MUST HAVE UNITY

Mr. President, I cannot but congratulate you, together with my brethren on this highly interesting occasion, the first semi-annual meeting of this Society. When I reflect upon the many impediments through which we have had to conduct its affairs, and see, with emotions of delight, the present degree of eminency to which it has arisen, I cannot, sir, but be of the opinion, that an invisible arm must have been stretched out in our behalf. From the very second conference, which was by us convened, to agitate the proposition respecting this society, to its final consolidation, we were by some, opposed, with an avidity and zeal, which, had it been on the opposite side, would have done great honor to themselves. And, sir, but for the undeviating, and truly patriotic exertions of those who were favorable to the formation of this institution, it might have been this day, in a yet unorganized condition. Did I say in an unorganized condition? Yea, had our opponents their way, the very notion of such an institution might have been obliterated from our minds. How strange it is,

Source: David Walker, "Speech at the First General Colored Association," *Freedom's Journal,* 19 December 1828.

to see men of sound sense, and of tolerably good judgment, act so diametrically in opposition to their interests; but I forbear making any further comments on this subject, and return to that for which we are convened.

First then, Mr. President, it is necessary to remark here, at once, that the primary object of this institution is, to unite the colored population, so far, through the United States of America, as may be practicable and expedient; forming societies, opening, extending, and keeping up correspondences, and not withholding anything which may have the least tendency to meliorate our miserable condition—with the restrictions, however, of not infringing on the articles of its constitution, or that of the United States of America. Now, that we are disunited is a fact, that no one of common sense will deny; and, that the cause of which, is a powerful auxiliary in keeping us from rising to the scale of reasonable and thinking beings, none but those who delight in our degradation will attempt to contradict. Did I say those who delight in our degradation? Yea, sir, glory in keeping us ignorant and miserable that we might be the better and the longer slaves. I was credibly informed by a gentleman of unquestionable veracity, that a slaveholder upon finding one of his young slaves with a small spelling book in his hand, fell upon and beat him almost to death, exclaiming, at the same time to the child, you will acquire better learning than I or any of my family.

I appeal to every candid and unprejudiced mind, do not all such men glory in our miseries and degradations; and are there not millions whose chief glory centers in this horrid wickedness? Now, Mr. President, those are the very humane, philanthropic, and charitable men who proclaim to the world, that the blacks are such a poor, ignorant and degraded species of beings, that, were they set at liberty, they would die for the want of something to subsist upon, and in consequence of which, they are compelled to keep them in bondage, to do them good.

O Heaven! What will not avarice and the love of despotic sway cause men to do with their fellow creatures, when actually in their power? But, to return whence I digressed; it has been asked in what way will the *General Colored Association* unite the colored population, so far, in the United States as may be practicable and expedient? to which enquiry! answer, by asking the following: Do not two hundred and eight years very intolerable sufferings teach us the actual necessity of a general union among us? Do we not know indeed, the horrid dilemma into which we are, and from which, we must exert ourselves, to be extricated? Shall we keep slumbering on, with our arms completely folded up, exclaiming every now and then, against our miseries, yet never to do the least thing to ameliorate our condition, or that of posterity? Shall we not, by such inactivity, leave or rather entail a hereditary degradation on our children, but a little, if at all, inferior to that which our fathers, under all their comparative disadvantages and privations, left on us? In time, shall we, while almost every other people under Heaven, are making such mighty efforts to better their condition, go around from house to house, enquiring what good associations and societies are going to do us? Ought we not to form ourselves into a general body, to protect, aid, and assist each other to the utmost of our power, with the beforementioned restrictions?

Yes, Mr. President, it is indispensably our duty to try every scheme that we think will have a tendency to facilitate our salvation, and leave the final result to that God, who holds the destinies of people in the hollow of his hand, and who ever has, and will, repay every nation according to its works.

Will any be so hardy as to say, or even to imagine, that we are incapable of effecting any object which may have a tendency to hasten our emancipation, in consequence of the prevalence of ignorance and poverty among us? That the major part of us are ignorant and poor, I am at this time unprepared to deny. —But shall this deter us from all lawful attempts to bring about the desired object? Nay, sir, it should rouse us to greater exertions: there ought to be a spirit of emulation and inquiry among us, a hungering and thirsting after religion; these are requisitions, which, if we ever be so happy as to acquire, will fit us for all the departments of life; and, in my humble opinion, ultimately result in rescuing us from an oppression, unparalleled, I had almost said, in the annals of the world.

But some may even think that our white brethren and friends are making such mighty efforts, for the amelioration of our condition, that we may stand as natural spectators of the work. That we have many good friends, yea, very good, among that body, perhaps none but a few of those who have ever read at all will deny; and that many of them have gone, and will go, all lengths for our good, is evident from the very works of the great, the good, and the godlike Granville Sharpe, Wilberforce, Lundy, and the truly patriotic and lamented Mr. Ashman, late Colonial Agent of Liberty, who, with a zeal which was only equaled by the goodness of his heart, has lost his life in our cause, and a host of others too numerous to mention; a number of private gentlemen too, who, though they say but little, are nevertheless, busily engaged for good. Now, all of those great, and indeed, good friends which God has given us I do humbly, and very gratefully acknowledge. But, that we should cooperate with them, as far as we are able by uniting and cultivating a spirit of friendship and of love among us, is obvious from the very exhibition of our miseries, under which we groan.

Two million and a half of colored people in these United States, more than five hundred thousand of whom are about two-thirds of the way free. Now, I ask, if no more than these last were united (which they must be, or always live as enemies) and resolved to aid and assist each other to the utmost of their power, what mighty deeds could be done by them for the good of our cause?

But, Mr. President, instead of a general compliance with these requisitions, which have a natural tendency to raise us in the estimation of the world, we see, to our sorrow, in the very midst of us a gang of villains, who, for the paltry sum of fifty or a hundred dollars, will kidnap and sell into perpetual slavery their fellow creatures! and, too, if one of their fellow sufferers, whose miseries are a little more enhanced by the scourges of a tyrant should abscond from his pretended owner, to take a little recreation, and unfortunately fall in their way, he is gone! for they will sell him for a glass of whiskey! Brethren and fellow sufferers, I ask you, in the name of God, and of Jesus Christ, shall we suffer such notorious villains to rest peaceably among us? Will they not take our wives and little ones, more particularly our little ones, when a convenient opportunity will admit, and sell them for money to slaveholders, who will doom them to chains, handcuffs, and even unto death? May God open our eyes on those children of the devil and enemies of all good!

But, sir, this wickedness is scarcely more infernal than that which was attempted a few months since, against the government of our brethren, the Haytians, by a consummate rogue, who ought to have long since been *haltered*, but who, I was recently informed, is nevertheless received into company among some of our most respectable men, with a kind of brotherly affection which ought to be shown only to a gentleman of honor.

Now, Mr. President, all such mean, and more than disgraceful actions as these are powerful auxiliaries, which work for our destruction, and which are abhorred in the sight of God and of good men.

But, sir, I cannot but bless God for the glorious anticipation of a not very distant period when these things which now help to degrade us will no more be practiced among the sons of Africa,—for, though this, and perhaps another generation may not experience the promised blessings of heaven, yet, the dejected, degraded, and now enslaved children of Africa will have, in spite of all their enemies, to take their stand among the nations of the earth. And, sir, I verily believe that God has something in reserve for us, which, when he shall have poured it upon us, will repay us for all our suffering and miseries.

An Address Delivered at the African Masonic Hall

Boston, February 27, 1833

Maria W. Stewart

African rights and liberty is a subject that ought to fire the breast of every free man of color in these United States, and excite in his bosom a lively, deep, decided and heart-felt interest. When I cast my eyes on the long list of illustrious names that are enrolled on the bright annals of fame among the whites, I turn my eyes within, and ask my thoughts, "Where are the names of our illustrious ones?" It must certainly have been for the want of energy on the part of the free people of color, that they have been long willing to bear the yoke of oppression. It must have been the want of ambition and force that has given the whites occasion to say that our natural abilities are not as good, and our capacities by nature inferior to theirs. They boldly assert that did we possess a natural independence of soul, and feel a love for liberty within our breasts, some one of our sable race, long before this, would have testified it, notwithstanding the disadvantages under which we labor. We have made ourselves appear altogether unqualified to speak in our own defence, and are therefore looked upon as objects of pity and commiseration. We have been imposed upon, insulted and derided on every side; and now, if we complain, it is considered as the height of impertinence. We have suffered ourselves to be considered as dastards, cowards, mean, faint-hearted wretches; and on this account (not because of our complexion) many despise us, and would gladly spurn us from their presence.

Source: Maria W. Stewart, "An Address Delivered at the African Masonic Hall" in *Productions of Mrs. Maria W. Stewart* (Boston: Friends of Freedom and Virtue, 1835).

These things have fired my soul with a holy indignation, and compelled me thus to come forward, and endeavor to turn their attention to knowledge and improvement; for knowledge is power. I would ask, is it blindness of mind, or stupidity of soul, or the want of education that has caused our men who are 60 or 70 years of age, never to let their voices be heard, nor their hands be raised in behalf of their color? Or has it been for the fear of offending the whites? If it has, O ye fearful ones, throw off your fearfulness, and come forth in the name of the Lord, and in the strength of the God of Justice, and make yourselves useful and active members in society; for they admire a noble and patriotic spirit in others; and should they not admire it in us? If you are men, convince them that you possess the spirit of men; and as your day, so shall your strength be. Have the sons of Africa no souls? Feel they no ambitious desires? Shall the chains of ignorance forever confine them? Shall the insipid appellation of "clever negroes," or "good creatures," any longer content them? Where can we find among ourselves the man of science, or a philosopher, or an able statesman, or a counsellor at law? Show me our fearless and brave, our noble and gallant ones. Where are our lecturers in natural history, and our critics in useful knowledge? There may be a few such men among us, but they are rare. It is true our fathers bled and died in the revolutionary war, and others fought bravely under the command of Jackson, in defence of liberty. But where is the man that has distinguished himself in these modern days by acting wholly in the defence of African rights and liberty? There was one, although he sleeps, his memory lives.

I am sensible that there are many highly intelligent men of color in these United States, in the force of whose arguments, doubtless, I should discover my inferiority; but if they are blessed with wit and talent, friends and fortune, why have they not made themselves men of eminence, by striving to take all the reproach that is cast upon the people of color, and in endeavoring to alleviate the woes of their brethren in bondage? Talk, without effort, is nothing; you are abundantly capable, gentlemen, of making yourselves men of distinction; and this gross neglect, on your part, causes my blood to boil within me. Here is the grand cause which hinders the rise and progress of people of color. It is their want of laudable ambition and requisite courage.

Individuals have been distinguished according to their genius and talents, ever since the first formation of man, and will continue to be while the world stands. The different grades rise to honor and respectability as their merits may deserve. History informs us that we sprung from one of the most learned nations of the whole earth; from the seat, if not the parent, of science. Yes, poor despised Africa was once the resort of sages and legislators of other nations, was esteemed the school for learning, and the most illustrious men in Greece flocked thither for instruction. But it was our gross sins and abominations that provoked the Almighty to frown thus heavily upon us, and give our glory unto others. Sin and prodigality have caused the downfall of nations, kings and emperors; and were it not that God in wrath remembers mercy, we might indeed despair; but a promise is left us; "Ethiopia shall again stretch forth her hands unto God."

But it is of no use for us to boast that we sprung from this learned and enlightened nation, for this day a thick mist of moral gloom hangs over millions of our race. Our condition as a people has been low for hundreds of years, and it will continue to be so, unless by true piety and virtue, we strive to regain that which we have lost. White Americans, by their prudence, economy, and exertions, have sprung up and become one of the most flourishing nations in the world, distinguished for their knowledge of the arts and sciences, for their polite literature. While our minds are vacant and starve for want of knowledge, theirs are filled to overflowing. Most of our color have been taught to stand in fear of the white man from their earliest infancy, to work as soon as they could walk, and to call "master" before they could scarce lisp the name of mother. Continual fear and laborious servitude have in some degree lessened in us that natural force and energy which belong to man; or else, in defiance of opposition, our men, before this, would have nobly and boldly contended for their rights. But give the man of color an equal opportunity with the white from the cradle to manhood, and from manhood to the grave, and you would discover the dignified statesman, the man of science, and the philosopher. But there is no such opportunity for the sons of Africa, and I fear that our powerful ones are fully determined that there never shall be. Forbid, ye Powers on high, that it should any longer be said that our men possess no force. O ye sons of Africa, when will your voices be heard in our legislative halls, in defiance of your enemies, contending for equal rights and liberty? How can you, when you reflect from what you have fallen, refrain from crying mightily unto God, to turn away from us the fierceness of his anger, and remember our transgressions against us no more forever? But a god of infinite purity will not regard the prayers of those who hold religion in one hand, and prejudice, sin and pollution in the other; he will not regard the prayers of self-righteousness and hypocrisy. Is it possible, I exclaim, that for the want of knowledge we have labored for hundreds of years to support others, and been content to receive what they chose to give us in return? Cast your eyes about, look as far as you can see; all, all is owned by the lordly white, except here and there a lowly dwelling which the man of color, midst deprivations, fraud, and opposition has been scarce able to procure. Like King Solomon, who put neither nail nor hammer to the temple, yet received the praise; so also have the white Americans gained themselves a name, like the names of the great men that are in the earth, while in reality we have been their principal foundation and support. We have pursued the shadow, they have obtained the substance; we have performed the labor, they have received the profits; we have planted the vines, they have eaten the fruits of them.

I would implore our men, and especially our rising youth, to flee from the gambling board and the dance-hall; for we are poor, and have no money to throw away. I do not consider dancing as criminal in itself, but it is astonishing to me that our fine young men are so blind to their own interest and the future welfare of their children as to spend their hard earnings for this frivolous amusement; for it has been carried on among us to such an unbecoming extent that it has become absolutely disgusting. "Faithful are the wounds of a friend, but the kisses of an enemy are deceitful [Proverbs 27:6]." Had those men among us who had an opportunity, turned their attention as assiduously to mental and moral improvement as they have to gambling and dancing, I might have remained quietly at home and they stood contending in my place. These polite accomplishments will never enroll your names on the bright annals of fame who admire the belle void of intellectual knowledge, or applaud the dandy that talks largely on politics, without striving to assist his fellow in the revolution, when the nerves and muscles of every other man forced him into the field of action. You have a right to rejoice, and to let your hearts cheer you in the days of your youth; yet remember that for all these things God will bring you into judgment. Then, O ye sons of Africa, turn your mind from these perishable objects, and contend for the cause of God and the rights of man. Form yourselves into temperance societies. There are temperate men among you; then why will you any longer neglect to strive, by your example, to suppress vice in all its abhorrent forms? You have been told repeatedly of the glorious results arising from temperance, and can you bear to see the whites arising in honor and respectability without endeavoring to grasp after that honor and respectability also?

But I forbear. Let our money, instead of being thrown away as heretofore, be appropriated for schools and seminaries of learning for our children and youth. We ought to follow the example of the whites in this respect. Nothing would raise our respectability, add to our peace and happiness, and reflect so much honor upon us, as to be ourselves the promoters of temperance, and the supporters, as far as we are able, of useful and scientific knowledge. The rays of light and knowledge have been hid from our view; we have been taught to consider ourselves as scarce superior to the brute creation; and have performed the most laborious part of American drudgery. Had we as a people received one-half the early advantages the whites have received, I would defy the government of these United States to deprive us any longer of our rights.

I am informed that the agent of the Colonization Society has recently formed an association of young men for the purpose of influencing those of us to go to Liberia who may feel disposed. The colonizationists are blind to their own interest, for should the nations of the earth make war with America, they would find their forces much weakened by our absence; or should we remain here, can our "brave soldiers" and "fellow citizens," as they were termed in time of calamity, condescend to defend the rights of whites and be again deprived of their own, or sent to Liberia in return? Or, if the colonizationists are the real friends to Africa, let them expend the money which they collect in erecting a college to educate her injured sons in this land of gospel, light, and liberty; for it would be most thankfully received on our part, and convince us of the truth of their professions, and save time, expense, and anxiety. Let them place before us noble objects worthy of pursuit, and see if we prove ourselves to be those unambitious negroes they term us. But, ah, methinks their hearts are so frozen toward us they had rather their money should be sunk in the ocean than to administer it to our relief: and I fear, if they dared, like Pharaoh, king of Egypt, they would order every male child among us to be drowned. But the most high God is still as able to subdue the lofty pride of these white Americans as He was the heart of that ancient rebel. They say, though we are looked upon as things, yet we sprang from a scientific people. Had our men the requisite force and energy they would soon convince them by their efforts, both in public and private, that they were men, or things in the shape of men. Well may the colonizationists laugh us to scorn for our negligence; well may they cry: "Shame to the sons of Africa." As the burden of the Israelites was too great for Moses to bear, so also is our burden too great for our noble advocate to bear. You must feel interested, my brethren, in what he undertakes, and hold up his hands by your good works, or in spite of himself his soul will become discouraged and his heart will die within him; for he has, as it were, the strong bulls of Bashan [Psalms 22:12] to contend with.

It is of no use for us to wait any longer for a generation of well educated men to arise. We have slumbered and slept too long already; the day is far spent; the night of death approaches; and you have sound sense and good judgment sufficient to begin with, if you feel disposed to make a right use of it. Let every man of color throughout the United States, who possesses the spirit and principles of a man, sign a petition to Congress to abolish slavery in the District of Columbia, and grant you the rights and privileges of common free citizens; for if you had had faith as a grain of mustard seed [Matthew 13:31], long before this the mountain of prejudice might have been removed. We are all sensible that the Anti-Slavery Society has taken hold of the arm of our whole population, in order to raise them out of the mire. Now all we have to do is, by a spirit of virtuous ambition, to strive to raise ourselves; and I am happy to have it in my power thus publicly to say that the colored inhabitants of this city, in some respects, are beginning to improve. Had the free people of color in these United States nobly and freely contended for their rights, and showed a natural genius and talent, although not so brilliant as some; had they held up, encouraged and patronized each other, nothing could have hindered us from being a thriving and flourishing people. There has been a fault among us. The reason why our distinguished men have not made themselves more influential, is because they fear that the strong current of opposition through which they must pass would cause their downfall and prove

their overthrow. And what gives rise to this opposition? Envy. And what has it amounted to? Nothing. And who are the cause of it? Our whited sepulchres [Matthew 23:27], who want to be great, and don't know how; who love to be called of men "Rabbi, Rabbi;" who put on false sanctity, and humble themselves to their brethren for the sake of acquiring the highest place in the synagogue and the uppermost seat at the feast. You, dearly beloved, who are the genuine followers of our Lord Jesus Christ—the salt of the earth, and the light of the world—are not so culpable. As I told you in the very first of my writing, I will tell you again, I am but as a drop in the bucket—as one particle of the small dust of the earth [Isaiah 40:15]. God will surely raise up those among us who will plead the cause of virtue and the pure principles of morality more eloquently than I am able to do.

It appears to me that America has become like the great city of Babylon, for she has boasted in her heart: "I sit a queen and am no widow, and shall se no sorrow [Revelation 18:7]!" She is, indeed, a seller of slaves and the souls of men; she has made the Africans drunk with the wine of her fornication; she has put them completely beneath her feet, and she means to keep them there; her right hand supports the reins of government and her left hand the wheel of power, and she is determined not to let go her grasp. But many powerful sons and daughters of Africa will shortly arise, who will put down vice and immorality among us, and declare by Him that sitteth upon the throne that they will have their rights; and if refused, I am afraid they will spread horror and devastation around. I believe that the oppression of injured Africa has come up before the majesty of Heaven; and when our cries shall have reached the ears of the Most High, it will be a tremendous day for the people of this land; for strong is the hand of the Lord God Almighty.

Life has almost lost its charms for me; death has lost its sting, and the grave its terrors [I Corinthians 15:55]; and at times I have a strong desire to depart and dwell with Christ, which is far better. Let me entreat my white brethren to awake and save our sons from dissipation and our daughters from ruin. Lend the hand of assistance to feeble merit; plead the cause of virtue among our sable race; so shall our curses upon you be turned into blessings; and though you should endeavor to drive us from these shores, still we will cling to you the more firmly; nor will we attempt to rise above you; we will presume to be called your equals only.

The unfriendly whites first drove the native American from his much loved home. Then they stole our fathers from their peaceful and quiet dwellings, and brought them hither, and made bond-men and bond-women of them and their little ones. They have obliged our brethren to labor; kept them in utter ignorance; nourished them in vice, and raised them in degradation; and now that we have enriched their soil, and filled their coffers, they say that we are not capable of becoming like white men, and that we can never rise to respectability in this country. They would drive us to a strange land. But before I go, the bayonet shall pierce me through. African rights and liberty is a subject that ought to fire the breast of every free man of color in these United States, and excite in his bosom a lively, deep, decided, and heartfelt interest.

An Address to the Slaves of the United States of America

Henry Highland Garnet

Brethren and fellow citizens: Your brethren of the North, East and West have been accustomed to meet together in national conventions, to sympathize with each other, and to weep over your unhappy condition. In these meetings we have addressed all classes of the free, but we have never, until this time, sent a word of consolation and advice to you. We have been contented in sitting still and mourning over your sorrows, earnestly hoping that before this day your sacred liberties would have been restored. But we have hoped in vain. Years have rolled on, and tens of thousands have been borne on streams of blood and tears to the shores of eternity. While you have been oppressed, we have also been partakers with you; nor can we be free while you are enslaved. We, therefore, write to you as being bound with you.

Many of you are bound to us, not only by the ties of a common humanity, but we are connected by the more tender relations of parents, wives, husbands and sisters and friends. As such we most affectionately address you.

Slavery has fixed a deep gulf between you and us, and while it shuts out from you the relief and consolation which your friends would willingly render, it afflicts and persecutes you with a fierceness which we might not expect to see in the fiends of hell. But still the Almighty Father of mercies has left to us a glimmering ray of hope, which shines out like a lone star in a cloudy sky. Mankind is becoming wiser, and better, the oppressor's power is

Source: Henry Highland Garnet, "An Address to the Slaves of the United States of America" [Pamphlet] published in *A Memorial Discourse by Rev. Henry Highland Garnet, Delivered in the Hall of the House of Representatives.* Washington, D.C., 12 February 1865, 44-51.

fading, and you every day are becoming better informed and more numerous. Your grievances, brethren, are many. We shall not attempt in this short address to present to the world all the dark catalogue of the nation's sins which have been committed upon an innocent people. Nor is it indeed necessary, for you feel them from day to day, and all the civilized world looks upon them with amazement.

Two hundred and twenty-seven years ago the first of our injured race were brought to the shores of America. They came not with glad spirits to select their homes in the New World. They came not with their own consent, to find an unmolested enjoyment of the blessings of this fruitful soil. The first dealings they had with men calling themselves Christians exhibited to them the worst features of corrupt and sordid hearts, and convinced them that no cruelty is too great, no villainy and no robbery too abhorrent for even enlightened men to perform, when influenced by avarice and lust. Neither did they come flying upon the wings of Liberty to a land of freedom. But they came with broken hearts from their beloved native land and were doomed to unrequited toil and deep degradation. Nor did the evil of their bondage end at their emancipation by death. Succeeding generations inherited their chains, and millions have come from eternity into time, and have returned again to the world of spirits, cursed and ruined by American slavery.

The propagators of the system, or their immediate successors, very soon discovered its growing evil and its tremendous wickedness, and secret promises were made to destroy it. The gross inconsistency of a people holding slaves, who had themselves "ferried o'er the wave" for freedom's sake, was too apparent to be entirely overlooked. The voice of Freedom cried, "Emancipate your slaves." Humanity supplicated with tears for the deliverance of the children of Africa. Wisdom urged her solemn plea. The bleeding captive pleaded his innocence and pointed to Christianity who stood weeping at the cross. Jehovah frowned upon the nefarious institution, and thunderbolts, red with vengeance, struggled to leap forth to blast the guilty wretches who

maintained it. But all was vain. Slavery had stretched its dark wings of death over the land, the Church stood silently by, the priests prophesied falsely, and the people loved to have it so. Its throne is established, and now it reigns triumphant.

Nearly three millions of your fellow citizens are prohibited by law and public opinion (which in this country is stronger than law) from reading the Book of Life. Your intellect has been destroyed as much as possible, and every ray of light they have attempted to shut out from your minds. The oppressors themselves have become involved in the ruin. They have become weak, sensual and rapacious; they have cursed you; they have cursed themselves; they have cursed the earth which they have trod.

The colonies threw the blame upon England. They said that the mother country entailed the evil upon them, and they would rid themselves of it if they could. The world thought they were sincere, and the philanthropic pitied them. But time soon tested their sincerity. In a few years the colonists grew strong and severed themselves from the British government. Their independence was declared, and they took their station among the sovereign powers of the earth. The declaration was a glorious document. Sages admired it, and the patriotic of every nation reverenced the Godlike sentiments which it contained. When the power of government returned to their hands, did they emancipate the slaves? No; they rather added new links to our chains. Were they ignorant of the principles of Liberty? Certainly they were not. The sentiments of their revolutionary orators fell in burning eloquence upon their hearts, and with one voice they cried, "Liberty or death." Oh, what a sentence was that! It ran from soul to soul like electric fire and nerved the arms of thousands to fight in the holy cause of Freedom. Among the diversity of opinions that are entertained in regard to physical resistance, there are but a few found to gainsay the stern declaration. We are among those who do not.

Slavery! How much misery is comprehended in that single word. What mind is there that does not shrink from its direful effects? Unless the image of God be obliterated from the soul, all men cherish the love of liberty. The nice discerning political economist does not regard the sacred right more than the untutored African who roams in the wilds of Congo. Nor has the one more right to the full enjoyment of his freedom than the other. In every man's mind the good seeds of liberty are planted, and he who brings his fellow down so low as to make him contented with a condition of slavery commits the highest crime against God and man. Brethren, your oppressors aim to do this. They endeavor to make you as much like brutes as possible. When they have blinded the eyes of your mind; when they have embittered the sweet waters of life; when they have shut out the light which shines from the word of God— then, and not till then, has American slavery done its perfect work.

To such degradation it is sinful in the extreme for you to make voluntary submission. The divine commandments you are in duty bound to reverence and obey. If you do not obey them, you will surely meet with the displeasure of the Almighty. He requires you to love Him supremely, and your neighbor as yourself, to keep the Sabbath day holy, to search the Scriptures, and bring up your children with respect for His laws, and to worship no other God but Him. But slavery sets all these at nought and hurls defiance in the face of Jehovah. The forlorn condition in which you are placed does not destroy your obligation to God. You are not certain of heaven, because you allow yourselves to remain in a state of slavery, where you cannot obey the commandments of the Sovereign of the universe. If the ignorance of slavery is a passport to heaven, then it is a blessing, and no curse, and you should rather desire its perpetuity than its abolition. God will not receive slavery, nor ignorance, nor any other state of mind, for love and obedience to Him. Your condition does not absolve you from your moral obligation. The diabolical injustice by which your liberties are cloven down, neither God nor angels, nor just men command you to suffer for a single moment. Therefore it is your solemn and imperative duty to use every means, both moral, intellectual and physical,

that promises success. If a band of heathen men should attempt to enslave a race of Christians, and to place their children under the influence of some false religion, surely Heaven would frown upon the men who would not resist such aggression, even to death. If, on the other hand, a band of Christians should attempt to enslave a race of heathen men, and to entail slavery upon them, and to keep them in heathenism in the midst of Christianity, the God of heaven would smile upon every effort which the injured might make to disenthral themselves.

Brethren, it is as wrong for your lordly oppressors to keep you in slavery as it was for the man thief to steal our ancestors from the coast of Africa. You should therefore now use the same manner of resistance as would have been just in our ancestors when the bloody footprints of the first remorseless soul thief was placed upon the shores of our fatherlands. The humblest peasant is as free in the sight of God as the proudest monarch that ever swayed a scepter. Liberty is a spirit sent out from God and, like its great Author, is no respecter of persons.

Brethren, the time has come when you must act for yourselves. It is an old and true saying that, "if hereditary bondmen would be free, they must themselves strike the blow." You can plead your own cause and do the work of emancipation better than any others. The nations of the Old World are moving in the great cause of universal freedom, and some of them at least will, ere long, do you justice. The combined powers of Europe have placed their broad seal of disapprobation upon the African slave trade. But in the slaveholding parts of the United States the trade is as brisk as ever. They buy and sell you as though you were brute beasts. The North has done much; her opinion of slavery in the abstract is known. But in regard to the South, we adopt the opinion of the *New York Evangelist*— "We have advanced so far, that the cause apparently waits for a more effectual door to be thrown open than has been yet." We are about to point you to that more effectual door. Look around you and behold the bosoms of your loving wives heaving with untold agonies! Hear the cries of your poor children!

Remember the stripes your fathers bore. Think of the torture and disgrace of your noble mothers. Think of your wretched sisters, loving virtue and purity, as they are driven into concubinage and are exposed to the unbridled lusts of incarnate devils. Think of the undying glory that hangs around the ancient name of Africa—and forget not that you are native-born American citizens, and as such you are justly entitled to all the rights that are granted to the freest. Think how many tears you have poured out upon the soil which you have cultivated with unrequited toil and enriched with your blood; and then go to your lordly enslavers and tell them plainly that you *are determined to be free.* Appeal to their sense of justice and tell them that they have no more right to oppress you than you have to enslave them. Entreat them to remove the grievous burdens which they have imposed upon you, and to remunerate you for your labor. Promise them renewed diligence in the cultivation of the soil, if they will render to you an equivalent for your services. Point them to the increase of happiness and prosperity in the British West Indies since the Act of Emancipation.* Tell them, in language which they cannot misunderstand, of the exceeding sinfulness of slavery and of a future judgment and of the righteous retributions of an indignant God. Inform them that all you desire is freedom, and that nothing else will suffice. Do this, and forever after cease to toil for the heartless tyrants, who give you no other reward but stripes and abuse. If they then commence work of death, they, and not you, will be responsible for the consequences. You had far better all die—*die immediately*—than live slaves and entail your wretchedness upon your posterity. If you would be free in this generation, here is your only hope. However much you and all of us may desire it, there is not much hope of redemption without the shedding of blood. If you must bleed, let it all come at once—rather *die freemen than live to be the slaves.* It is impossible, like the children of Israel, to make a grand exodus from the land of bondage. The Pharaohs are on both sides of the blood-red waters! You cannot move *en masse* to the dominions of the British Queen, nor can you pass through Florida and overrun Texas and at last find peace in Mexico. The propagators of American slavery are spending their blood and treasure that they may plant the black flag in the heart of Mexico and riot in the halls of the Montezumas.† In the language of the Reverend Robert Hall, when addressing the volunteers of Bristol who were rushing forth to repel the invasion of Napoleon, who threatened to lay waste the fair homes of England, "Religion is too much interested in your behalf not to shed over you her most gracious influences."

You will not be compelled to spend much time in order to become inured to hardships. From the first moment that you breathed the air of heaven, you have been accustomed to nothing else but hardships. The heroes of the American Revolution were never put upon harder fare than a peck of corn and few herrings per week. You have not become enervated by the luxuries of life. Your sternest energies have been beaten out upon the anvil of severe trial. Slavery has done this to make you subservient to its own purposes. But it has done more than this; it has prepared you for any emergency. If you receive good treatment, it is what you can hardly expect; if you meet with pain, sorrow, and even death, these are the common lot of the slaves.

Fellow men, patient sufferers, behold your dearest rights crushed to the earth! See your sons murdered, and your wives, mothers and sisters doomed to prostitution. In the name of the merciful God, and by all that life is worth, let it no longer be a debatable question, whether it is better to choose liberty or death.

---

*Slavery was abolished in the British West Indies by an act of Parliament in 1833.

†American-Mexican relations deteriorated after the annexation of Texas in December, 1845. American troops had moved into territory claimed by Mexico in July, 1845, and when the Mexicans entered this territory, President Polk requested a declaration of war, which Congress made on May 12, 1846. The war was basically the result of the drive by the slaveowners to acquire new land for cotton.

In 1822, Denmark Veazie, of South Carolina, formed a plan for the liberation of his fellow men.* In the whole history of human efforts to overthrow slavery, a more complicated and tremendous plan was never formed. He was betrayed by the treachery of his own people, and died a martyr to freedom. Many a brave hero fell, but history, faithful to her high trust, will transcribe his name on the same monument with Moses, Hampden, Tell, Bruce and Wallace, Toussaint L'Ouverture, Lafayette and Washington. That tremendous movement shook the whole empire of slavery. The guilty soul thieves were overwhelmed with fear. It is a matter of fact that at this time, and in consequence of the threatened revolution, the slave states talked strongly of emancipation. But they blew but one blast of the trumpet of freedom, and then laid it aside. As these men became quiet, the slaveholders ceased to talk about emancipation; and now behold your condition today! Angels sigh over it, and humanity has long since exhausted her tears in weeping on your account!

The patriotic Nathaniel Turner[†] followed Denmark Veazie. He was goaded to desperation by wrong and injustice. By despotism, his name has been recorded on the list of infamy, and future generations will remember him among the noble and brave.

Next arose the immortal Joseph Cinque, the hero of the *Amistad.*[‡] He was a native African, and by the help of God he emancipated a whole shipload of his fellow men on the high seas. And he now sings of liberty on the sunny hills of Africa and beneath his native palm trees, where he hears the lion roar and feels himself as free as the king of the forest.

Next arose Madison Washington, that bright star of freedom, and took his station in the constellation of true heroism.** He was a slave on board the brig *Creole*, of Richmond, bound to New Orleans, that great slave mart, with a hundred and four others. Nineteen struck for liberty or death. But one life was taken, and the whole were emancipated, and the vessel was carried into Nassau, New Providence.

Noble men! Those who have fallen in freedom's conflict, their memories will be cherished by the true-hearted and the God-fearing in all future generations; those who are living, their names are surrounded by a halo of glory.

Brethren, arise, arise! Strike for your lives and liberties. Now is the day and the hour. Let every slave throughout the land do this, and the days of slavery are numbered. You cannot be more oppressed than you have

---

*Denmark Vesey was a slave in Charleston, South Carolina, who bought his own liberty after he won a $1,500 raffle. Once free himself, he was determined to aid his people in gaining their freedom, and for four years he planned a vast slave plot. The slaves involved had hidden away weapons and ammunition. In 1822 the plot was uncovered when two house slaves turned informers, and the authorities arrested 131 suspects. Federal troops were present to protect Charleston against further revolts as the leaders of the revolt were hanged.

† The Nat Turner revolt in Virginia in 1831 was the greatest slave revolt in American history. At the head of a small band of slaves, Turner moved from plantation to plantation, murdering slaveholding families. Some sixty whites were killed, and in retaliation, more than one hundred Negroes, innocent and guilty, were murdered before the rebellion was crushed. Turner was later captured and executed.

‡In 1839, Joseph Cinque, son of an African king, led fifty-four slaves in a revolt aboard the *Amistad* off the coast of Cuba. Cinque and his men seized the ship and attempted to sail it back to Africa, but the slave dealers, whose lives had been spared, landed the vessel on the Connecticut coast. Defended by Abolitionists, the case went all the way up to the Supreme Court with ex-President John Quincy Adams acting as the lawyer for the Africans. On March 9, 1841, the Supreme Court ordered Cinque and his fellow Africans freed. They returned to Sierra Leone in 1842.

** In 1841 a mutiny broke out aboard the *Creole*, sailing from Virginia for New Orleans. On the high seas 130 slaves, led by Madison Washington, rebelled, killed a slaveowner and guided the ship into the harbor of Nassau, where, under British law, they would be free. Over the objections of the United States State Department, the British allowed the Negroes to go free, although the British government finally agreed to pay an indemnity for not returning the slaves.

been; you cannot suffer greater cruelties than you have already. *Rather die freemen than live to be slaves.* Remember that you are *four millions!*

It is in your power so to torment the God-cursed slaveholders that they will be glad to let you go free. If the scale was turned, and black men were the masters and white men the slaves, every destructive agent and element would be employed to lay the oppressor low. Danger and death would hang over their heads day and night. Yes, the tyrants would meet with plagues more terrible than those of Pharaoh. But you are a patient people. You act as though you were made for the special use of these devils. You act as though your daughters were born to pamper the lusts of your masters and overseers. And worse than all, you tamely submit while your lords tear your wives from your embraces and defile them before your eyes. In the name of God, we ask, are you men? Where is the blood of your fathers? Has it all run out of your veins? Awake, awake; millions of voices are calling you! Your dead fathers speak to you from their graves. Heaven, as with a voice of thunder, calls on you to arise from the dust.

Let your motto be Resistance! *Resistance!* RESISTANCE! No oppressed people have ever secured their liberty without resistance. What kind of resistance you had better make you must decide by the circumstances that surround you, and according to the suggestion of expediency. Brethren, adieu! Trust in the living God. Labor for the peace of the human race, and remember that you are *four millions!*

FURTHER READING

Aptheker, Herbert. 1948. *American Negro Slave Revolts.* New York: International Publishers, 1993.

Bauer, Raymond, and Alice Bauer. 1970. "Day to Day Resistance to Slavery." In Peter I. Rose, ed., *Old Memories, New Moods.* New York: Atherton.

Douglass, Frederick. 1848. *Narrative of the Life of A Slave.* In Anthony Appiah, ed., *Early African-American Classics.* New York: Bantam, 1990.

Harding, Vincent. 1969. "Religion and Resistance among Antebellum Negroes 1800–1860." In August Meier and Elliot Rudwick, eds., *The Making of Black America.* Vol. 1. New York: Atheneum.

Hartman, Saidiya V. 1997. *Scenes of Subjection: Terror, Slavery, and Self-making in Nineteenth-Century America* New York: Oxford University Press.

Jacobs, Harriet. 1863. *Incidents in the Life of A Slave Girl.* In Anthony Appiah, ed., *Early African-American Classics.* New York: Bantam, 1990.

James, C.L.R. 1943. *The Black Jacobins: Toussaint L'Ouerture and the San Domingo Revolution.* New York: Random House, 1963, reprint.

Lott, Tommy L., ed. 1998. *Subjugation and Bondage: Critical Essays on Slavery and Social Philosophy.* Lanham, MD: Rowman and Littlefield.

McGary, Howard, and Bill Lawson. 1992. *Between Slavery and Freedom: Philosophy and American Slavery.* Bloomington: Indiana University Press.

Patterson, Orlando. 1982. *Slavery and Social Death.* Cambridge, MA: Harvard University Press.

Rawick, George P. 1972. *From Sundown to Sunup: The Making of the Black Community.* Westport, CT: Greenwood.

Thomas, Laurence M. 1992. *Vessels of Evil: The Psychology of American Slavery and the Holocaust.* Philadelphia: Temple University Press.

Willett, Cynthia. 1995. *Maternal Ethics and Other Slave Moralities.* New York: Routledge.

CHAPTER 2

Emigration and Diaspora Thought

A lot of early black nationalism, as well as the more evolved turn-of-the-century pan-Africanism, was motivated by the racial degradation faced by free black people. Black abolitionists were concerned with the question of equal rights for exslaves. Prior to the Civil War black nationalist thought was dominated by the idea of emigration. As early as 1808 Paul Cuffee, an educated New England shipowner, championed repatriation. To demonstrate the feasibility of emigration, Cuffee made two trips to Sierra Leone, bringing 38 African-Americans on the second. Despite the efforts of Cuffee and his followers, the search for a place where black people could flourish as a group was not focused on Africa.

In *Notes of Canada West*, Mary Ann Shadd Carey, the publisher of Canada's first antislavery newspaper *The Provincial Freeman*, urges African-Americans to consider Canada as a place to settle. Educational opportunity, political rights, and the right to own property were the key elements in her recommendation of Canada as a site for African-American emigration. In 1861 the Haitian government extended free passage and a guarantee of freedom of worship, liberal political privileges, and access to the land to African-Americans interested in emigration. James Theodore Holly wrote *A Vindication of the Capacity of the Negro Race for Self Government and Civilized Progress* in favor of emigration to Haiti. Although he was against emigration, Frederick Douglass ran advertisements that promoted emigration to Haiti in his newspaper *The North Star*. Editorial debates between Douglass and his detractors over the question of emigration appeared as early as 1854, culminating in a National Convention at Cleveland. Along with Holly, who was the principal organizer, William Wells Brown, Henry Highland Garnet, Martin Delaney, and William Watkins were among the supporters. Africa was ruled out on the ground that a black nation in the New World could compete better with slavery. The rationale for emigration presented by these early nationalists portended Marcus Garvey's argument that the abuse of black people globally would stop only if there was a black nation powerful enough to take action.

Black nationalism in America is often associated with an anti-assimilationist view. However, if the term "assimilation" refers to the acquisition of European culture by black people, this was never rejected by any of the major thinkers who advocated emigration. Holly expressed a version of the Eurocentric doctrine of manifest destiny when advocating the development of a higher civilization for black people in the New World. None of the emigrationists who focused on Africa argued, for instance, that black people should leave the New World and return to Africa as a means of regaining their lost African cultural heritage. Rather, all were committed to the modernization of Africa on a Eurocentric model.

Martin Delany identified the plight of African-Americans with the situation of oppressed groups in Europe. He points out in *The Condition, Elevation, Emigration, and Destiny of the Colored People of the United States* that the idea of the natural inferiority of African people was recently advanced to justify slavery. Although Delany preferred the elevation of black people in the United States over emigration, he believed the question of emigration had to be considered given that African-Americans were not allowed to attain a respectable social position in this country.

Delany's argument for emigration was empirical. Hence, he was not conceptually constrained to prefer Africa to Central America, Haiti, or Canada. He insisted that the elevation of black people was an economic endeavor—a physical end requiring a physical means of attaining it. He opposed the idea promulgated by religious leaders that an oppressed people must pray for what they receive. Delany maintained that the remedy for the degradation and oppression of black people is not to moralize about equality, but to gain knowledge of all the various business enterprises, trades, professions, and sciences that are necessary to change physical *conditions*. Because of his belief that African-Americans have a right to citizenship based on birth, Delany's commitment to emigration was contingent. Nevertheless, this shift was not inconsistent with his earlier view that the passage of the Fugitive Slave Law in 1793 rendered emigration the best means of social and political elevation for African-Americans. Not only was his commitment to Africa as a site for emigration tentative, but so also was his commitment to emigration.

Delany's empirical perspective on the question of emigration contrasts sharply with the conceptual orientation of Edward Blyden. Unlike Delany, whose argument rests solely on the idea of autonomy and liberty, Blyden prefers to speak of African-Americans as "exiled Africans," a conceptual shift that added the appeal of African nationalism to the argument for emigration. In his essay "The Call of Providence to the Descendents of Africa in America," Blyden cites the degradation of slavery as a ground for the African-American's obligation to return to Africa. He presents a religious argument to explain God's purpose in allowing the enslavement of Africans. Drawing on the analogy between African slaves and Israelites—neither are inferior, only disadvantaged—he claims that God has spoken to African-Americans by His providence. Africa, the land of the African-American's forefathers, has been preserved from invasion and awaits the return of exiled Africans in America. Despite his belief that slavery is an outrage against humanity, Blyden views it as a civilizing force in history. Exslaves will bring the knowledge and skills of Western civilization to Africa. His religious argument aimed to show that African-Americans have a duty to go back and take possession of their ancestral homeland to fulfill this historical purpose.

The idea that Africa can provide a homeland for the black diaspora reaches fruition in the teachings of Marcus Garvey. Following Blyden, Garvey maintained that African-Americans and all people in the black diaspora are African. Drawing upon this common identification with Africa, he argued that what was needed for social uplift is nationhood. He founded the United Negro Improvement Association (U.N.I.A.), an organization devoted to the social uplift of black people. Although the bulk of the membership were African-Americans, it is worth noting that the U.N.I.A. had chapters in Canada and other countries in the Caribbean and Central and Latin America.

Garvey was opposed to the idea of assimilation. His argument focuses on antiblack racism as a barrier to the acceptance of black people by whites on equal terms. He cites the system of illegitimate assimilation under which mixed-race children are rejected by white parents as evidence that "to the white man the question of racial differences is eternal." Along with the idea of self-initiative he appropriates from the teachings of Booker T. Washington, Garvey asserts a view held by earlier emigrationists. In his speech "The True Solution of the Negro Problem" he maintains that black people can solve their own problems by redeeming Africa from European colonialism and building a nation strong enough to protect black people all over the world.

Garvey viewed antiblack racisim as a function of the economic condition of black people. He compares the economic status of black people with the social status of the leper. The prejudice against black people will continue until achievement and progress are demonstrated. Just as the American Jew fights for a homeland in Palestine, the Irish American fights for independence in Ireland, the African-American must fight for the freedom of Africa. By establishing a nation in Africa, black people will have a place to develop as a group without incurring the hatred and animosity of whites who are threatened by competition with blacks who seek higher, or better, positions in government and industry.

Garvey is well known for his advocacy of black separatism. In "Racial Ideals" he argues for a division of the world along racial lines—Ireland for the Irish, Palestine for the Jews, Egypt for the Egyptians, Asia for the Asiatics, and Africa for the Africans. His argument turns on a notion of cultural difference, but unlike Asiatic culture, which differs from European culture, Garvey does not draw a similar contrast between African and European cultures. Instead he speaks of the black person being allowed enough latitude "to develop a culture of his own." The particular nature of the culture black people will develop is never specified. Rather the parallel is stated in terms of race. Hence, Garvey held that there should be a "peaceful, prosperous and progressive" white race in America and Europe, yellow race in Asia, and black race in Africa. For Garvey, prosperity and progress had more to do with the issue of self-government and political independence than with the question of cultural development in Africa.

A Plea for Emigration, or Notes of Canada West

Mary Ann Shadd Carey

INTRODUCTORY REMARKS

The increasing desire on the part of the colored people, to become thoroughly informed respecting the Canadas, and particularly that part of the province called Canada West—to learn of the climate, soil and productions, and of the inducements offered generally to emigrants, and to them particularly, since that the passage of the odious Fugitive Slave Law has made a residence in the United States to many of them dangerous in the extreme,—this consideration, and the absence of condensed information accessible to all, is my excuse for offering this tract to the notice of the public. The people are in a strait,—on the one hand, a pro-slavery administration, with its entire controllable force, is bearing upon them with fatal effect: on the other, the Colonization Society, in the garb of *Christianity* and *Philanthropy*, is seconding the efforts of the first named power, by bringing into the lists a vast social and immoral influence, thus making more effective the agencies employed. Information is needed.—Tropical Africa, the land of promise of the colonizationists, teeming as she is with the breath of pestilence, a burning sun and fearful maladies, bids them welcome;—she feelingly invites to moral and physical death, under a voluntary escort of their most bitter enemies at home. Again, many look with dreadful forebodings to the probability of worse than inquisitorial inhumanity in the Southern States.

Source: Mary Ann Shadd Carey, *A Plea for Emigration, or Notes of Canada West,* [Pamphlet] (Detroit: G.W. Pattison, 1852).

BRITISH AMERICA

British America, it is well known, is a country equal in extent, at least, to the United States, extending on the north to the Arctic Ocean, from the Atlantic on the east, to the Pacific on the west, and the southern boundary of which is subject to the inequalities in latitude of the several Northern States and Territories belonging to the United States government. This vast country includes within its limits, some of the most beautiful lakes and rivers on the Western Continent. The climate, in the higher latitudes, is extremely severe, but for a considerable distance north of the settled districts, particularly in the western part, the climate is healthy and temperate: epidemics are not of such frequency as in the United States, owing to a more equable temperature, and local diseases are unknown. The province claiming especial attention, as presenting features most desirable in a residence, is Canada, divided into East and West; and of these Canada West is to be preferred. . . .

Prices of Land in the Country— City Property, & C.

The country in the vicinity of Toronto and to the eastward, being thickly settled, (farms being advertised "thirty miles on Yonge street,") the price of property is, of course, very much higher than in the western districts. City property varies according to location— two hundred dollars the foot, is the value of lots in good position in Toronto: in the suburbs very fine lots may be had at reasonable rates. Farms, at a few miles distant, range from thirty to fifty dollars the acre—fifty dollars being thought a fair price for the best quality of land with improvements; but in the western districts, farms may be bought for one thousand dollars, superior in every way, to farms near the city of Toronto, that are held at five thousand. Improved lands, near Chatham, London, Hamilton, and other towns west, may be bought at prices varying from ten up to one hundred: at a few miles distant, uncleared lands, belonging to Government, may be had by paying one dollar sixty-two cents, two, and two fifty, according to locality—well timbered and watered, near cultivated farms on the river and lake shore. Thousands of acres, of the very best land in the Province, are now in the market at the above prices, and either in the interior, or well situated as to prospect from the lakes, and near excellent markets. The land is laid out in what are called concessions, these concessions, or blocks, being sub-divided into lots. There is, therefore, a uniformity of appearance throughout in the farms, and no contest about roads on individual property can result—the roads being designed to benefit equally contiguous property, and under jurisdiction of Government. One hundred acres is the smallest quantity to be had of Government, but individual holders sell in quantities to suit purchasers. Large quantities of land are held by individuals, though at a higher rate generally than that held by Government; and their titles are said to be often defective. In every respect, the preference should be for purchases of Government—land is cheaper, as well situated, and below a specified number of acres, may not be bought; a prohibition of advantage to many who would buy, as there is induced a spirit of enterprise and competition, and a sense of responsibility. Too many are now *independently* dragging along miserably, on the few acres, ten, twenty, or such a matter, bought at the high rates of individual holders, in a country in which the prices must, for a long time, require more land in process of culture, to afford a comfortable support. There is every inducement to buy, near or in towns, as well as in the country, as land is cheap, business increasing, with the steady increase of population, no lack of employment at fair prices, and no complexional or other qualification in existence.

Labor—Trades

In Canada, as in other recently settled countries, there is much to do, and comparatively few for the work. The numerous towns and villages springing up, and the great demand for timber and agricultural products, make labor of every kind plenty: all trades that are practiced in the United States, are there patronized by whomsoever carried on—no man's complexion affecting his business. If a colored man understands his business, he receives the public patronage the same as a white man. He is not obliged to work a little better, and at a lower rate—there is no degraded class to identify him with, therefore every man's work stands or falls according to merit, not as is his color. Builders, and other tradesmen, of different complexions, work together on the same building and in the same shop, with perfect harmony, and often the proprietor of an establishment is colored, and the majority or all of the men employed are white. Businesses that in older communities have ceased to remunerate, yield a large percentage to the money invested.

The mineral resources of the Canadas not being developed, to any extent, for fuel wood is generally used, and a profitable trade in that commodity is carried on; and besides lumber for buildings, the getting out of materials for staves, coopers' stuff, and various purposes, affords steady employment and at fair prices, for cash. This state of things must increase, and assume more importance in Canada markets, as the increasing population of the western United States burn and otherwise appropriate their timber. Railroads are in process of construction—steamboats now ply between Toronto and the several towns on the lakes; and in process of time, iron and other works will be in operation, it is said, all requiring their quota, and of course keeping up the demand. Boards for home and foreign markets, are successfully manufactured, and numerous mill-sites are fast being appropriated to saw and grist mills. In some sections, colored men are engaged in saw mills on their own account. At Dawn, a settlement on the Suydenham, (of which hereafter,) and at other points, this trade is prosecuted with profit to them. To enumerate the different occupations in which colored persons are engaged, even in detail, would but fatigue, and would not further the end in view, namely: To set forth the advantage of a residence in a country, in which chattel slavery is not tolerated, and prejudice of *color* has no existence whatever—the adaptation of that country, by climate, soil, and political character, to their physical and political necessities; and the superiority of a residence there over their present position at *home*. It will suffice, that colored men prosecute all the different trades; are store keepers, farmers, clerks, and laborers; and are not only unmolested, but sustained and encouraged in any business for which their qualifications and means fit them; and as the resources of the country develop, new fields of enterprise will be opened to them, and consequently new motives to honorable effort.

Churches—Schools

In the large towns and cities, as in similar communities in other Christian countries, the means for religious instruction are ample. There are costly churches in which all classes and complexions worship, and no "negro pew," or other seat for colored persons, especially. I was forcibly struck, when at Toronto, with the contrast the religious community there presented, to our own large body of American Christians. In the churches, originally built by the white Canadians, the presence of colored persons, promiscuously seated, elicited no comment whatever. They are members, and visitors, and as such have their pews according to their inclination, near the door, or remote, or central, as best suits them. The number of colored persons, attending the churches with whites, constitutes a minority, I think. They have their "own churches." That that is the feature in their policy, which is productive of mischief to the entire body, is evident enough; and the opinion of the best informed and most influential among them, in Toronto and the large towns, is decided and universal. I have heard men of many years residence, and who have, in a

measure, been moulded by the better sentiment of society, express deep sorrow at the course of colored persons, in pertinaciously refusing overtures of religious fellowship from the whites; and in the face of all experience to the contrary, erecting Colored Methodist, and Baptist, and other Churches. This opinion obtains amongst many who, when in the United States, were connected with colored churches. Aside from their caste character, their influence on the colored people is fatal. The character of the exclusive church in Canada tends to perpetuate ignorance, both of their true position as British subjects, and of the Christian religion in its purity. It is impossible to observe thoughtfully the workings of that incipient Zion, (the Canadian African Church, of whatever denomination,) in its present imperfect state, without seriously regretting that it should have been thought necessary to call it into existence. In her bosom is nurtured the long-standing and rankling prejudices, and hatred against whites, without exception, that had their origin in American oppression, and that should have been left in the country in which they originated—'tis that species of animosity that is not bounded by geographical lines, nor suffers discrimination.

A goodly portion of the people in the western part of the Province, (for there are but few in the eastern,) are enjoying superior religious opportunities, but the majority greatly need active missionary effort: first, to teach them love to their neighbor; and, again, to give them an intelligent and correct understanding of the Sacred Scriptures. The missionary strength, at present, consists of but six preachers—active and efficient gentlemen, all of them, and self-sacrificing in the last degree; and several women engaged in teaching, under the same auspices. Much privation, suffering, opposition, and sorrow await the missionary in that field. If it were possible for him to foresee what is in store for him there, a mission to India, or the South Sea Islands, would be preferable; for, in that case, the sympathy of the entire community is enlisted, and his sojourn is made as pleasant as possible—the people to whom he is sent, are either as little children, simple and confiding, or out-right savages; and in that case, deadly enemies. In this less remote field—almost in speaking distance—neglect from friends, suspicion, abuse, misrepresentation, and a degrading surveillance, often of serious and abiding consequences, await him. Not directly from the fugitives—those designed primarily to be benefitted—may assaults be looked for, at first. They possess a desire for the light, and incline to cluster around the missionary invariably. There are those who pretend to have been enlightened, and to have at heart the common good, whose influence and operations, he will find designedly counteracting his conscientious efforts, the more effectively appealing to a common origin and kindred sufferings—secretly striking behind, and bringing his character as a missionary, and his operations, into discredit in the eyes of a sympathizing Christian community. This, and more, awaits those who may be called to the field; but the case is not a hopeless one. The native good sense of the fugitives, backed by proper schools, will eventually develop the real character of their operations and sacrifices. They and their families, of all others, should have the support of Christians.

The refugees express a strong desire for intellectual culture, and persons often begin their education at a time of life when many in other countries think they are too old. There are no separate schools: at Toronto and in many other places, as in the churches, the colored people avail themselves of existing schools; but in the western country, in some sections, there is a tendency to "exclusiveness." The colored people of that section petitioned, when the School Law was under revision, that they might have separate schools: there were counter petitions by those opposed, and to satisfy all parties, twelve freeholders among *them*, can, by following a prescribed form, demand a school for their children; but if other schools, under patronage of Government, exist, (as Catholic or Protestant,) they can demand admission into them, if they have not one. They are not compelled to have a colored school. The following is that portion of the school law that directly relates to them:

"And be it enacted, That it shall be the duty of the Municipal Council of any township, and of the Board of School Trustees of any city, town or incorporated village, on the application in writing of twelve or more resident heads of families, to authorize the establishment of one or more separate schools for Protestants, Roman Catholics or colored people, and, in such case, it shall prescribe the limits of the divisions or sections for such school, and shall make the same provisions for the holding of the first meeting for the election of Trustees of each such separate school or schools, as is provided in the fourth section of this Act for holding the first school meeting in a new school section: Provided always, that each separate school shall go into operation at the same time with alterations in school sections, and shall be under the same regulations in respect to the persons for whom such school is permitted to be established, as are common schools generally: Provided, secondly, that none but colored people shall be allowed to vote for the election of Trustees of the separate school for their children, and none but the parties petitioning for the establishment of, or sending children to a separate Protestant or Roman Catholic school, shall vote at the election of Trustees of such schools: Provided, thirdly, that each separate Protestant, or Roman Catholic, or colored school, shall be entitled to share in the school fund according to the average attendance of pupils attending each such separate school, (the mean attendance of pupils for both summer and winter being taken,) as compared with the average attendance of pupils attending the common schools in such city, town, village or township: Provided, fourthly, that no Protestant separate school shall be allowed in any school division, except when the teacher of the common school is a Roman Catholic, nor shall any Roman Catholic separate school be allowed except when the teacher of the common school is a Protestant."

As before said, the facilities for obtaining a liberal education, are ample in the large towns and cities. In Toronto, students of all complexions associate together, in the better class schools and colleges. The operations of missionaries being chiefly among colored people, they have established several schools in connection with their labors, yet they are open to children without exception. The colored common schools have more of a complexional character than the private, which, with no exception that I have heard of, are open to all. The Act of Parliament above referred to, was designed to afford the fullest and most equable facilities for instruction to all, and that particular clause was inserted with the view to satisfy them, though less objectionable to the body of them, than what they asked for.

The fugitives, in some instances, settled on Government land before it came into market, cleared away and improved it. Their friends established schools which were flourishing, when they were obliged to break up, and the people to disperse, because of inability to purchase and other persons buying. This cause has, in a measure, retarded the spread of general information amongst them.

Again, ten, twenty or more families are often settled near one another, or interspersed among the French, Dutch, Scotch, Irish and Indians, in the woodland districts: often, English is not spoken. There may not be an English school, and all revel together in happy ignorance. Nothing but the sound of the axe, and their own crude ideas of independence, to inspire them, unless it be an Indian camp fire occasionally. This may be rather an uninviting state of affairs to those living in crowded cities, but it is true there are numerous grown up families, of white and colored, who do not know B. But as uninteresting as is the detail, in this particular aspect of these affairs, the signs are encouraging. If they went to labor honestly, in a region semibarbarous, they have cut their way out, and are now able to make themselves heard in a demand for religious instructors of the right kind, and schools. Many efficient persons have devoted their time and talents to their instruction, but there has not been anything like an equal number to the work: neither are they often found to have materials to work with. Individuals in the United States often send books to those most needy, yet they are usually of such a character as to be utterly use-

less. I have often thought, if it is really a benevolent act to send old almanacs, old novels, and all manner of obsolete books to them what good purpose was accomplished, or even what sort of vanity was gratified, by emptying the useless contents of old libraries on destitute fugitives? It would be infinitely better not to give, it seems, though probably persons sending them think differently. The case is aggravated from the fact of a real desire, on the part of the recipients, to learn, and their former want of opportunity. Probably the propensity to give is gratified; but why not give, when gifts are *needed*, of that which is useful? But the question, if it is answering any good purpose to give such things as books even, has not been satisfactorily answered in the affirmative, to persons who have seen the fugitives in their Canadian homes. . . .

Political Rights—Election Law— Oath—Currency

There is no legal discrimination whatever effecting colored emigrants in Canada, nor from any cause whatever are their privileges sought to be abridged. On taking proper measures, the most ample redress can be obtained. The following "abstracts of acts," bearing equally on all, and observed fully by colored men qualified, will give an idea of the measures given them:[*]

"The qualifications of voters at municipal elections in townships, are freeholders and householders of the township or ward, entered on the roll for rateable real property, in their own right or that of their wives, as proprietors or tenants, and resident at the time in the township or ward."

"In towns, freeholders and householders for rateable real property in their own names or that of their wives, as proprietors or tenants to the amount of £5 per annum or upwards, resident at the time in the ward. The property qualification of town voters may consist partly of freehold and partly of leasehold."

In villages it is £3 and upwards, with freehold or leasehold; in cities £8.

---

[*] Scobies' Canadian Almanac for 1852.

The laws regulating elections, and relating to electors, are not similar in the two Canadas; but colored persons are not affected by them more than others.

"No person shall be entitled to vote at county elections, who has not vested in him, by legal title, real property in said county of the clear yearly value of forty-four shillings and five pence and one farthing, currency. Title to be in fee simple or freehold under tenure of free and common soccage, or in *fief* in *rature*, or in *franc allen*, or derived from the Governor and Council of the late Province of Quebec, or Act of Parliament. Qualificatiori, to be effective, requires actual and uninterrupted possession on the part of the elector, or that he should have been in receipt of the rents and profits of said property for his own use and benefit at least six months before the date of the writ of election. But the title will be good without such anterior possession, if the property shall have come by inheritance, devise, marriage or contract of marriage, and also if the deed or patent from the Crown on which he holds to claim such estate in Upper Canada, have been registered three calendar months before the date of the writ of election. In Lower Canada, possession of the property under a written promise of sale registered, if not a notarial deed, for twelve months before the election, to be sufficient title to vote. In Upper Canada, a conveyance to wife after marriage must have been registered three calendar months, or husband have been in possession of property six months before election."

"Only British subjects of the full age of twenty-one are allowed to vote. Electors may remove objection by producing certificate, or by taking the oath."

These contain no proscriptive provisions, and there are none. Colored men comply with these provisions and vote in the administration of affairs. There is no difference made whatever and even in the slight matter of taking the census it is impossible to get at the exact number of whites or colored, as they are not designated as such. There is, it is true, petty jealousy manifested at times by individuals, which is made use of by the designing; but impartiality and strict justice characterise proceedings at law, and the bearing of the laws. The oath, as prescribed by law, is as follows:

"I, A. B., do sincerely promise and swear, that I will bear faithful and true allegiance to Her Majesty Queen Victoria, as lawful Sovereign of the United Kingdom of Great Britian and Ireland, and of this Province of Canada, dependent on and belonging to the said United Kingdom, and that I will defend her to the uttermost of my power against all traitors, conspiracies and attempts whatever which shall be made against Her Person, Crown and Dignity, and that I will do my utmost endeavor to disclose and make known to Her Majesty, Her Heirs and Successors all treasons and traitorous conspiracies and attempts which I shall know to be against Her or any of them, and all this I do swear without any equivocation, mental evasion, or secret reservation, and, renouncing all pardons and dispensations from persons whatever, to the contrary. So help me God."

"The Deputy Returning Officer may administer oath of allegiance to persons who, according to provisions of any Act of Parliament, shall become, on taking such oath; entitled to the privileges of British birth in the Province."

"Persons knowing themselves not to be qualified, voting at elections, incur penalty of £10; and on action brought, the burden of proof shall be on the defendant. Such votes null and void."

"The qualifications of Municipal Councillors are as follows:—Township Councillor must be a freeholder or householder of the township or ward, * * * as proprietor or tenant rated on the roll, in case of a freeholder for £100 or upwards; householder for £200 or upwards: Village Councillor, in case of a freeholder, for £10 or upwards; a householder for £20 and upwards: Town Councillor, in case of a freeholder £20 per annum; if a householder to the amount of £40 and upwards. The property qualification of Town Councillors may be partly freehold and partly leasehold."

A tenant voter in town or city must have occupied by actual residence, as a separate tenant, a dwelling house or houses for twelve months, of the yearly value of £11 2s. 1½d. currency, and have paid a year's rent, or that amount of money for the twelve months immediately preceding the date of election writ. A person holding only a shop or place of business, but not actually residing therein, is not entitled to vote. And a voter having changed his residence within the town during the year, does not affect his right to vote, but must vote in the ward in which he resides on the day. . . .

"Seeds of all kinds, farming utensils and implements of husbandry, when specially imported in good faith by any society incorporated or established for the encouragement of agriculture."

"Wearing apparel in actual use, and other personal effects not merchandize; horses and cattle; implements and tools of trade of handicraftsmen."

* * * "Trees, shrubs, bulbs and roots; wheat and indian corn; animals specially imported for the improvement of stock; paintings, drawings, maps, busts, printed books, (not foreign reprints of British copy-right works,) ashes, pot and pearl, and soda."

CURRENCY OF CANADA.

GOLD.		*CURRENCY.*	
The British Sovereign when of full weight,{		£1	4s	4d.
U.S. Eagle, coined before 1st July 1834,		£1	13s	4d
U.S. Eagle, between 1st of July, 1834, and 1st of July, 1851,		£2	10s	0d

SILVER.		
British Crown,	6s	1d
Half crown,	3	0
Shilling,	1	2
Sixpence,	0	7¼
The dollar,	5	1
Half "	2	6½
U.S. quarter dollar,	1	3
Other " "	1	0
U.S. eighth "	0	7½
Other eighth silver dollar,	0s	6d
U.S. sixteenth dollar,	0	3½
Other " "	0	3
Five franc piece,	4	8

COPPER.		
British penny,	0	1
" half penny,	0	0½
" farthing,	0	0¼

*Abstract of Law of Succession in Upper Canada

* * * "Be it therefore enacted, &c., That whenever, on or after the first day of January, which will be in the year of our Lord one thousand eight hundred and fifty-two, any person shall die siezed in fee simple or for the life of another of any real estate in Upper Canada, without having lawfully devised the same, such real estate shall descend or pass by way of succession in manner following, that is to say:

Firstly—To his lineal descendants, and those claiming by or under them, *per stirpes.*

Secondly—To his father.

Thirdly—To his mother: and

Fourthly—To his collateral relatives.

Subject in all cases to the rules and regulations hereinafter prescribed.

2. "That if the intestate shall leave several descendants in the direct line of lineal descent, and all of equal degree of consanguinity to such intestate, the inheritance shall descend to such persons in equal parts, however remote from the intestate the common degree of consanguinity may be.

3. "That if any of the children of such intestate be living, and any be dead, the inheritance shall descend to the children who are living, and to the descendants of such children as shall have died, so that each child who shall be living shall inherit such share as would have descended to him if all the children of the intestate who shall have died, leaving issue, had been living, and so that the descendants of each child who shall be dead shall inherit the share which their parents would have received, if living, in equal shares.

18. "That children and relatives who are illegitimate shall not be entitled to inherit under any of the provisions of this Act."

The Thirty Thousand Colored Freemen of Canada

The colored subjects of her Majesty in the Canadas are, in the general, in good circumstances, that is, there are few cases of positive

---

* 14 and 15 Vic. Cap. 6—1851. Scobie.

destitution to be found among those permanently settled. They are settled promiscuously in cities, towns, villages, and the farming districts; and no equal number of colored men in the States, north or south, can produce more freeholders. They are settled on, and own portions of the best farming lands in the province, and own much valuable property in the several cities, etc. There is, of course, a difference in the relative prosperity and deportment in different sections, but a respect for, and observance of the laws, is conceded to them by all; indeed, much indifference on the part of whites has given place to genuine sympathy, and the active abolitionists and liberal men of the country, look upon that element in their character as affording ground for hope of a bright future for them, and as evidence that their sympathy for the *free* man is not misplaced, as more than compensation for their own exertions for those yet in bonds. I have said, there is but little actual poverty among them. They are engaged in the different trades and other manual occupations. They have a paper conducted by the Rev. Henry Bibb, and other able men, white and colored, are laboring among them, and in view of the protection afforded, there is no good reason why they should not prosper. After the passage of the fugitive law, the sudden emigration of several thousand in a few months, destitute as they necessarily were, from having, in many instances, to leave behind them all they possessed, made not a little suffering for a brief period, (only among them,) and the report of *their* condition had an injurious bearing upon all the colored settlers. Clothing, provisions, and other articles were sent them, but often so disposed of, or appropriated, as not to benefit those for whom intended. Distrust of agents, indiscriminately, and altogether but little real good has followed from the charity. The sensible men among them, seeing the bad results from a general character for poverty and degradation, have not been slow to express their disapprobation in the social circle, in meetings, and through the public papers. The following extracts express fully the sentiments of nine-tenths of the colored men of Canada; they think they are fully able to live without begging. There are others (very ignorant people,) who think differently, as there will be in all communities, though they are in the minority. There are those, also, and they are a respectable minority, (in point of numbers,) who are in favor of distinctive churches and schools, and of being entirely to themselves; they will come in for especial notice, but first, let us hear the people of Buxton and other places:

"If facts would bear out the statements made, the fugitives would have little to choose between slavery on one side of the line, and starvation on the other; but we rejoice that he is not reduced to the alternative. The man who is willing to work need not suffer, and unless a man supports himself he will neither be independent nor respectable in any country." * * * "The cry that has been often raised, that we could not support ourselves, is a foul slander, got up by our enemies, and circulated both on this and the other side of the line, to our prejudice. Having lived many years in Canada, we hesitate not to say that all who are able and willing to work, can make a good living." * * * It is time the truth should be known concerning the relief that has been sent to the "suffering fugitives in Canada," and to what extent it has been applied. The boxes of clothing and barrels of provisions which have been sent in, from time to time, by the praiseworthy, but misguided zeal of friends in the United States, has been employed to support the idle, who are too lazy to work, and who form but a small portion of the colored population in Canada. There are upwards of thirty thousand colored persons in Canada West, and not more than three thousand of them have ever received aid, and not more than half of them required it had they been willing to work. We do not think it right that twenty-seven thousand colored persons, who are supporting themselves by their own industry, should lie under the disgrace of being called public beggars, when they receive nothing, and don't want anything. * * * We wish the people of the United States to know that there is one portion of Canada West where the colored people are self-supporting, and they wish them to send neither petticoat nor pantaloons to the county of

Kent. ∗ ∗ ∗ The few cases of real want which arise from sickness or old age, can, with a trifling effort, be relieved here, without making it a pretext for a system of wholesale begging in the United States."

EDWARD R. GRANTS,
SAMUEL WICKHAM, } Committee.
ROBERT HARRIS,

"As to the state of things in Toronto and in Hamilton, I can say, from actual observation, that extreme suffering is scarcely known among the black people, while some who are far from being as industrious and deserving as they ought to be, receive aid to which they would hardly seem entitled."—*S. R. Ward's Letter to the Voice of the Fugitive.*

Notwithstanding the prosperity and liberal sentiment of the majority, there is yet a great deal of ignorance, bigotry, prejudice, and idleness. There are those who are only interested in education so far as the establishment of separate schools, churches, &c., tend to make broad the line of separation they wish to make between them and the whites; and they are active to increase their numbers, and to perpetuate, in the minds of the newly arrived emigrant or refugee, prejudices, originating in slavery, and as strong and objectionable in their manifestations as those entertained by whites towards them. Every casual remark by whites is tortured into a decided and effective negro hate. The expressions of an individual are made to infer the existence of prejudice on the part of the whites, and partiality by the administrators of public affairs. The recently arrived fugitives, unacquainted with the true state of things; are "*completely convinced* by the noisy philippic against all the "white folks," and all colored ones who think differently from them, and he is thus prepared to aid demagogues in preventing the adoption of proper measures for the spread of education and general intelligence, to maintain an ascendancy over the inferior minds around them, and to make the way of the missionary a path of thorns. Among that portion, generally, may those be found, who by their indolent habits, tend to give point to what of prejudice is lingering in the minds of the whites; and it is to be feared that they may take some misguided step now, the consequences of which will entail evil on the many who will hereafter settle in Canada. The only ground of hope is in the native good sense of those who are now making use of the same instrumentalities for improvement as are the whites around them.

The French and Foreign Population

The population of Canada consists of English, Scotch, French, Irish and Americans; and, including colored persons, numbers about 1,582,000. Of the whites, the French are in the majority, but the increasing emigration of Irish, Scotch, English and other Europeans, is fast bringing about an equality in point of numbers that will be felt in political circles. In Canada West the French are in the minority.

The disposition of the people generally towards colored emigrants, that is, so far as the opinions of old settlers may be taken, and my own observation may be allowed, is as friendly as could be looked for under the circumstances. The Yankees, in the country and in the States adjoining, leave no opportunity unimproved to embitter their minds against them. The result is, in some sections, a contemptible sort of prejudice, which, among English, is powerless beyond the individual entertaining it—not even affecting *his circle.* This grows out of the constitution of English society, in which people are not obliged to think as others do. There is more independent thought and free expression than among Americans. The affinity between the Yankees and French is strong; said to grow out of similar intentions with respect to political affairs: and they express most hostility, but it is not of a complexional character only, as that serves as a mark to identify men of a different policy. Leaving out Yankees—having but little practical experience of colored people—they, (the French,) are pre-disposed, from the influence alluded to, to deal roughly with them; but in the main benevolence and a sense of justice are elements in their character. They are not averse to truth. There is a prevailing hostility to chattel slavery, and an honest representation of the colored people: their aims and progressive character, backed by uniform good conduct on their part, would in a very short time destroy every vestige of prejudice in the Province.

"The public mind literally thirsts for the truth, and honest listeners, and anxious inquirers will travel many miles, crowd our country chapels, and remain for hours eagerly and patiently seeking the light. * * * Let the ignorance now prevalent on the subject of slavery be met by fair and full discussion, and open and thorough investigation, and the apathy and prejudice now existing will soon disappear."—*S. R. Ward.*

Colored persons have been refused entertainment in taverns, (invariably of an inferior class,) and on some boats distinction is made; but in all cases, it is that kind of distinction that is made between poor foreigners and other passengers, on the cars and steamboats of the Northern States. There are the emigrant train and the forward deck in the United States. In Canada, colored persons, holding the same relation to the Canadians, are in some cases treated similarly. It is an easy matter to make out a case of prejudice in any country. We naturally look for it, and the conduct of many is calculated to cause unpleasant treatment, and to make it difficult for well-mannered persons to get comfortable accommodations. There is a medium between servility and presumption, that recommends itself to all persons of common sense, of whatever rank or complexion; and if colored people would avoid the two extremes, there would be but few cases of prejudices to complain of in Canada. In cases in which tavern keepers and other public characters persist in refusing to entertain them, they can, in common with the traveling public generally, get redress at law.

Persons emigrating to Canada, need not hope to find the general state of society as it is in the States. There is as in the old country, a strong class feeling—lines are as completely drawn between the different classes, and aristocracy in the Canadas is the same in its manifestations as aristocracy in England, Scotland and elsewhere. There is no approach to Southern chivalry, nor the sensitive democra-

cy prevalent at the North; but there is an aristocracy of birth, not of skin, as with Americans. In the ordinary arrangements of society, from wealthy and titled immigrants and visitors from the mother country, down through the intermediate circles to Yankees and Indians, it appears to have been settled by common consent, that one class should not "see any trouble over another;" but the common ground on which all honest and respectable men meet, is that of innate hatred of American Slavery.

Recapitulation

The conclusion arrived at in respect to Canada, by an impartial person, is, that no settled country in America offers stronger inducements to colored people. The climate is healthy, and they enjoy as good health as other settlers, or as the natives; the soil is of the first quality; the laws of the country give to them, at first, the same protection and privileges as to other persons not born subjects; and after compliance with Acts of Parliament affecting them, as taking oath, &c., they may enjoy full "privileges of British birth in the Province." The general tone of society is healthy; vice is discountenanced, and infractions of the law promptly punished; and, added to this, there is an increasing anti-slavery sentiment, and a progressive system of religion.

THE BRITISH WEST INDIES—MEXICO— SOUTH AMERICA—AFRICA

Inducements have been held out by planters to colored men, to settle in the British West Indies, and agents have been sent particularly from Jamaica and Trinidad, from time to time, to confer with them on the subject. The most prominent feature in their efforts, has been the direct advantage to the planter from such emigration. The advantages to be derived by settlers, in a pecuniary point, from any system of emigration originating with proprietors of estates, will be doubtful, so long as the present mode of planting, managing and involving estates, continues, if the emigrants consent to be mere laborers instead of owners of the soil. But from a system of voluntary emigration to those islands, different results may be looked for. The former method would but degrade them, the latter materially elevate them. The vicinity of those islands to the southern United States makes it necessary that they should be peopled by colored men, and *under British protection;* in short, that they should be British subjects. The policy of the dominant party in the United States, is to drive *free* colored people out of the country, and to send them to Africa, only, and at the some time, to give the fullest guaranty to slaveholders, for the continuance of their system. To fulfil, to the letter, this latter, they make large calculations of a future interest in the West Indies, Honduras, and ultimately South America. They wish to consecrate to slavery and the slave power that portion of this continent; at the same time they deprecate the vicinity of freemen. To preserve those countries from the ravages of slavery, should be the motive to their settlement by colored men. Jamaica, with its fine climate and rich soil, is the key to the gulf of Mexico. It is not distant from the United States, Cuba, nor Hayti; but, as if providentially, is just so positioned that, if properly garrisoned by colored free men, may, under Britain, promptly and effectually check "foreign interference in its own policy, and any mischievous designs now in contemplation toward Cuba and Hayti. So of that portion of the Isthmus now under the protection of Great Britain. In view of the ultimate destiny of the southern portion of North America, it is of the first importance that colored men strengthen that and similar positions in that region. They are the natural protectors of the Isthmus and the contiguous country: it is said by medical men, that those of the human family, physically capable of resisting the influences of great heat, are also capable of enduring severe cold; and the varied experience of colored persons in America, proves that they live to as great age as whites, whether as whalemen in the northern seas, and settlers in the British provinces, (far north of the United States,) or in the West Indies. The question of availability, can never be raised, for at this time there are those who conduct with great ability the business of the Islands. Colored men are greatly in the majority, not more than one-sixth are whites. They are legislators, lawyers, physicians, ministers, planters, editors, merchants, and laborers; and they demonstrate clearly their capacity for self-government, and the various departments of civil life, by the great change in their condition since emancipation. The story of loss from the emancipation act, is a gross misrepresentation, gotten up by interested parties for the benefit of slavery. True there may not be so much exported as formerly, for the very good reason that there are more purchasers at home. The miserably fed slave of former days, is now the independent *free* man, with the ability to buy whatever his judgment prompts him to. Neither is the demand for laborers for large estates evidence that the peasantry are idle. There are more small farmers and cultivators on their own account, more store-keepers and traders, and they of the emancipated class. More attention is, of course, paid to education, and the children are thus relieved, in a measure, from out door duties. Much has been done by the colored people of those islands to improve their condition, and much more may be done conjointly with emigrants from the States, to perfect society, strengthen the British in that quarter, and thus keep up "the balance of power." It needs no prophet to foretell the establishment of an empire formed out of the southern United States and Mexico. The settlement by colored people of those countries, with their many sympathizers, is but a preparatory step: that step has been taken, slavery and republican rapacity will do the rest. Under what more favorable auspices could emigration to the West Indies be made than the present, now that a general welcome would be extended by the people to those who would like a milder climate than the States? What government so powerful and so thoroughly impartial, as Her Majesty's; so practically anti-slavery, and so protective! None. The objection that "we wish our own government, to demonstrate our capacity for self-government, is done away with at once, for there are colonies controlled, so far as their immediate affairs extend, by colored men. The assertion that white men universally degrade colored, is disproved by the facts. There is no aristocracy of skin; every incentive to honorable effort is kept before them. It is of the first importance, then, that the government of those islands should be anti-slavery, and that only governments, anti-slavery in spirit and tendency, and having a liberal religious policy, should be sought out by colored people from the United States. They, of all others on this continent, have drank plentifully of the cup of degradation, made more bitter from the never ending parade about freedom. They would be powerful auxiliaries of the present inhabitants, in forming a wall of defense, or available for offensive operations, as a *decided protest*, for instance, as the best interests and policy of the British government might demand. Those who oppose emigration from the United States, say, "you (colored people,) will not desire to be the laborers in other countries; to dig the canals, work on rail roads, ditch, and the like, but you will prefer to engage in trade, and that others will forestall you." Men who are honest in their desire for a change, who love liberty better than slavery, or who are unwilling to await the tedious process by which, in the United States, their rights will be given, if ever, will not be fastidious on emigrating to a country. Emigrants to any country, who should aim at a monopoly of the so called respectable occupations, exclusively, would be looked upon with *distrust*, as well as contempt, and the result to the emigrant would not be far different from a monopoly of menial employments. There will be no scarcity of land, and a medium, between the extensive operations of capitalists, and the degrading occupations of colored people, generally, in the crowded cities of the United States, thus opens to them a certain road to future eminence, in every way preferable to the sudden changes and chances of trade, exclusively.

Allusion is at times made to South America, and plans for a grant of territory from governments in that country, in which to form an "independent government," have been proposed. Others say, "unite with existing governments." Neither plan can recommend itself to prospective emigrants generally. In the first place, there is no precedent on record of a grant, similar to the one sought, and the policy of independent governments, with respect to each other, would always be opposed to unqualified grants. The great objection to uniting with those governments at present, would be their want of toleration in matters of religion; so long as the intimate connexion of the State with the Romish Church exists, those countries must be but a poor asylum for the oppressed. The liberals, with them, form a minority, struggling for life against the exactions of popery, and the ambition of military chiefs. Would colored men be prepared to adopt the religion of the country? That with them would be the only guaranty of protection, such "protection as vultures give to lambs.' 'Let us seize upon Africa, or some other, unappropriated territory while we may,' say others, 'and establish our own governments.' But Africa has already been seized upon; the English, French, Portuguese, Spanish and Turks, have long since shared her out among themselves, and little Liberia may yet revert to some heir-at-law, who has purposely been unmindful of her. There is yet Mexico, to be spoken of hereafter, and a southern continent, but that belongs to the United States, it may be by right of discovery; so there seems to be no safe alternative left but to be satisfied with that government now existing that is most reliable and most powerful. That government is Great Britain; her dependencies form a *secure* home for the American slave, and the disgraced *free* man. The last of her possessions to which I shall call attention in this place, is Vancouver's Island.

MEXICO

The vicinity of Mexico to the United States, and the known hostility of Mexicans to the institution of slavery, weigh strongly with some persons in favor of emigration to that country; but on careful consideration, it will be seen that that country does not present the features, in the main, that the States of South America do. The hankering of the old Castilians after lost power, is much greater in Mexico than farther south; and to regain that there would not be scruples about a coalition with American Slaveholders, even. The spirit of democracy has never so thoroughly pervaded that country, as those under the shadow of Simon Bolivar. Mexico was called New Spain. In her was remodelled the prominent features of Spanish policy in Europe. There was the grand centre point of Spanish dignity, religious intolerance, and regal domination, for the New World. In the States of South America, a change of policy was a necessity growing out of the relations of the Church of Rome in society generally. In Mexico, it was an earnest demand of the majority to throw off the Spanish yoke. This is shown in the relative position of the Church in those countries. In Mexico the Roman Catholic church is in undisputed supremacy, and the Pope is to them the ultimatum. In the states of South America, though that religion prevails, yet concession has been made, by Rome, in the person of a dignitary of equal powers there with the Pope elsewhere. With them the Pope is but little more respected than the Greek Patriarch. In those States, except Peru, (in which there is but one idea generally among Natives and Spanish,) there was no previously civilized class, continually brooding over Spanish wrongs: the natives came to terms, and they and Creoles combined to destroy Spanish tyranny backed by Rome; consequently, after victory over Spain was achieved by them, their remaining enemy was and is the Church in its modified form. It yet has, as before said, sufficient influence to make those countries undesirable for colored people from the United States in the present phase of things. We want a strong position; Mexico does not offer that, even though the majority are anti-slavery. The Southern United States have "marked her for their prey," which she will be for a time; and combining with the minority, the probability is a contest for the supremacy of slavery for a long time. If it were certain that slavery would not be tolerated but for a short period, still the move would be inexpedient, as direct contact with revolutionary movements, or other plans of progress, in her present state affecting it, would be inevitable. The position of

colored Americans must be a conservative one, for a time, in any foreign country, (from the very nature of their relations to foreign nations,) as well as for themselves in the United States; and it were folly in them to voluntarily enter the breach between any two hostile nations until stronger in position; their efforts, to be rational, should be to gain strength. People who love liberty do not emigrate to weak governments to embroil themselves in their quarrels with stronger ones, but to strong ones, to add to their strength and better their own condition, and foreigners fighting for others, are, generally, either hirelings, or isolated adventurers striving after fame. Whatever people go to Mexico and adopt her institutions, must calculate before hand, to set aside the habits of independent civil life—must for a long time repudiate the plough, the arts, and trade, with their concomitants, in a great country, or make them but secondary in importance to the, there, paramount idea of military life, and the certainty of frequent attacks from abroad and at home. The weakness, or rather the internal feuds of Mexico, invite attack from unscrupulous parties, is it meet then that emigrants of any nation should make haste to "settle there?" We look in vain for the precedent of emigration to a country, distracted even to bloodshed, with internal feuds, by any people; and we may look in vain for prosperity. In advocating this, we would leave out of sight, the check that a fortifying of the West Indies with our emigrants would give to depredations on the contiguous countries, and only gratify the love to fight, without immediate advantage. Let Mexico, at present, take care of herself, by the efforts of her own mixed population rightly directed, and let our emigrants so *abolitionize* and strengthen neighboring positions as to promote the prosperity and harmony of the whole. This can be done without compromising away honor; in fact, the sentiment "liberty or death," is never realized but by so proceeding as to secure the first permanently, and only courting the latter when life is no longer of utility. I know that the recollection of innumerable wrongs, makes the desire for payment in like coin the necessity of some men's natures, but no real end is attained after all: the Indians have learned sense from frequent defeat, the consequence of going to war before they were prepared, and whole tribes not cultivate the arts of peace and progress. Let us learn even of savages! We can get up a fight at any time, but who is the wiser for the sight? No one, honest men would but try to suppress it; so would a coalition with any nation, and especially a weak one, to carry out retaliatory measures, result.

The pro-slavery party of the United States is the aggressive party on this continent. It is the serpent that aims to swallow all others. It is meet then to make strongholds, and, if need be, defend them; that will be the most effective check to greediness of land [for] negroes.

VANCOUVER'S ISLAND— CONCLUDING REMARKS

This island is situated between 49° and 51° north latitude, or on the southern boundary of British America; and between 122° and 127° west longitude. It is about three hundred miles long, and between ninety and one hundred miles broad, and contains about twenty-eight thousand square miles. Though remotely situated, and comparatively uninhabited, (there being not more than twenty thousand persons on it,) it will, it is said, be the first island in importance on the globe. It has a fine climate, being in the same latitude as the south of England, Germany, and the north of France: the soil is also of the best description. But it is not as an agricultural island that it will surpass all others. The Western Continent, and particularly the northern part, say "wise men of the east," must eventually leave the eastern far in the distance, (a fact that should not be lost sight of by colored men,) and that over the Pacific will the trade with eastern nations be prosecuted. It is important now as a stopping place for whale ships visiting the Northern Seas, and is directly in the route to the East Indies, Japan Isles, and China, from Oregon and British America. The overland route to the Pacific terminating near that point, the great Atlantic trade of Western Europe and America will find there the most practicable outlet and the shortest distance to Eastern Asia; consequently the people there settled, of whatever complexion, will be the "merchant princes of the world," and under the protection of Great Britain. Now, there are two weighty reasons why the people settled there should be colored principally; the first, because by that means they would become more fully involved in the destiny of this Continent; any eastern move of magnitude, as for instance to Africa, if *possible*, would appear a retrograde step, now that the current of affairs is so clearly setting west: and, secondly, in no more effectual way could a check be given to the encroachments of slavery on free soil. The purely American sympathy for "kith and kin" only, would experience unmistakable obstacles to its free exercise, in the event of a contemplated annexation of that delightful Western country.

It will be seen, that the possibility of a pretty extensive emigration to those countries has been the prominent feature throughout this tract, and for that reason direct reference has been made to other points, under British jurisdiction, than Canada. The preference given to these, (Canada, West Indies, and Vancouver's Island,) over British Colonies elsewhere, has been because of their strong position and availability in every way. There would not be as in Africa, Mexico, or South America, hostile tribes to annoy the settler, or destroy at will towns and villages with their inhabitants: the strong arm of British power would summarily punish depredations made, of whatever character, and the emigrants would naturally assume the responsibility of British freemen.

The question whether or not an extensive emigration by the free colored people of the United States would affect the institution of slavery, would then be answered. I have here taken the affirmative of that question, because that view of the case seems to me most clear. The free colored people have steadily discountenanced any rational scheme of emigration, in the hope that by remaining in the States, a powerful miracle for the overthrow of slavery would be wrought. What are the facts. More territory has been given up to slavery, the Fugitive Law has passed, and a concert of measures, seriously affecting their personal liberty, has been entered into by several of the Free states; so subtle, unseen and effective have been their movements, that, were it not that we remember there is a Great Britain, we would be overwhelmed, powerless, from the force of such successive shocks; and the end may not be yet, if we persist in remaining for targets, while they are strengthening themselves in the Northwest, and in the Gulf. There would be more of the right spirit, and infinitely more of real manliness, in a peaceful but decided demand for freedom to the slave from the Gulf of Mexico, than in a miserable scampering from state to state, in a vain endeavor to gather the crumbs of freedom that a pro-slavery besom may sweep away at any moment. May a selection for the best be made, now that there are countries between which and the United States a comparison may be instituted. A little folding of the hands, and there can be no retreat from the clutches of the slave power.

The Condition, Elevation, Emigration, and Destiny of the Colored People of the United States

Martin R. Delany

CHAPTER I

Condition of Many Classes in Europe Considered

That there have been in all ages and in all countries, in every quarter of the habitable globe, especially among those nations laying the greatest claim to civilization and enlightenment, classes of people who have been deprived of equal privileges, political, religious and social, cannot be denied, and that this deprivation on the part of the ruling classes is cruel and unjust, is also equally true. Such classes have ever been looked upon as inferior to their oppressors, and have ever been mainly the domestics and menials of society, doing the low offices and drudgery of those among whom they lived, moving about and existing by mere sufferance, having no rights nor privileges but those conceded by the common consent of their political superiors. These are historical facts that cannot be controverted, and therefore proclaim in tones more eloquently than thunder, the listful attention of every oppressed man, woman, and child under the government of the people of the United States of America.

In past ages there were many such classes, as the Israelites in Egypt, the Gladiators in Rome, and similar classes in Greece; and in the present age, the Gipsies in Italy and Greece, the Cossacs in Russia and Turkey, the Sclaves and Croats in the Germanic States, and the Welsh and Irish among the British, to say nothing of various other classes among other nations.

Source: Martin R. Delany, *The Condition, Elevation, Emigration, and Destiny of the Colored People of the United States,* [Pamphlet] (Wilmington, DE: n.p., 1849 and Philadelphia: np.1852). Copyright ©1993, Black Classic Press, Baltimore, MD.

That there have in all ages, in almost every nation, existed a nation within a nation—a people who although forming a part and parcel of the population, yet were from force of circumstances, known by the peculiar position they occupied, forming in fact, by the deprivation of political equality with others, no part, and if any, but a restricted part of the body politic of such nations, is also true.

Such then are the Poles in Russia, the Hungarians in Austria, the Scotch, Irish, and Welsh in the United Kingdom, and such also are the Jews, scattered throughout not only the length and breadth of Europe, but almost the habitable globe, maintaining their national characteristics, and looking forward in high hopes of seeing the day when they may return to their former national position of self-government and independence, let that be in whatever part of the habitable world it may. This is the lot of these various classes of people in Europe, and it is not our intention here, to discuss the justice or injustice of the causes that have contributed to their degradation, but simply to set forth the undeniable facts, which are as glaring as the rays of a noon-day's sun, thereby to impress them indelibly on the mind of every reader of this pamphlet.

It is not enough, that these people are deprived of equal privileges by their rulers, but, the more effectually to succeed, the equality of these classes must be denied, and their inferiority by nature as distinct races, actually asserted. This policy is necessary to appease the opposition that might be interposed in their behalf. Wherever there is arbitrary rule, there must of necessity, on the part of the dominant classes, superiority be assumed. To assume superiority, is to deny the equality of others, and to deny their equality, is to premise their incapacity for self-government. Let this once be conceded, and there will be little or no sympathy for the oppressed, the oppressor being left to prescribe whatever terms at discretion for their government, suits his own purpose.

Such then is the condition of various classes in Europe: yes, nations, for centuries within nations, even without the hope of redemption among those who oppress them. And however unfavorable their condition, there is none more so than that of the colored people of the United States.

CHAPTER II

Comparative Condition of the Colored People of the United States

The United States, untrue to her trust and unfaithful to her professed principles of republican equality, has also pursued a policy of political degradation to a large portion of her native born countrymen, and that class is the Colored People. Denied an equality not only of political, but of natural rights, in common with the rest of our fellow citizens, there is no species of degradation to which we are not subject.

Reduced to abject slavery is not enough, the very thought of which should awaken every sensibility of our common nature; but those of their descendants who are freemen even in the non-slaveholding States, occupy the very same position politically, religiously, civilly and socially, (with but few exceptions,) as the bondman occupies in the slave States.

In those States, the bondman is disfranchised, and for the most part so are we. He is denied all civil, religious, and social privileges, except such as he gets by mere sufferance, and so are we. They have no part nor lot in the government of the country, neither have we. They are ruled and governed without representation, existing as mere nonentities among the citizens, and excrescences on the body politic—a mere dreg in community, and so are we. Where then is our political superiority to the enslaved? none, neither are we superior in any other relation to society, except that we are defacto masters of ourselves and joint rulers of our own domestic household, while the bondman's self is claimed by another, and his relation to his family denied him. What the unfortunate classes are in Europe, such are we in the United States, which is folly to deny, insanity not to understand, blindness not to see, and surely now full time that our eyes were opened to these startling truths, which for ages have stared us full in the face.

It is time that we had become politicians, we mean, to understand the political economy and domestic policy of nations; that we had become as well as moral theorists, also the practical demonstrators of equal rights and self-government. Except we do, it is idle to talk about rights, it is mere chattering for the sake of being seen and heard—like the slave, saying something because his so called "master" said it, and saying just what he told him to say. Have we not now sufficient intelligence among us to understand our true position, to realise our actual condition, and determine for ourselves what is best to be done? If we have not now, we never shall have, and should at once cease prating about our equality, capacity, and all that.

Twenty years ago, when the writer was a youth, his young and yet uncultivated mind was aroused, and his tender heart made to leap with anxiety in anticipation of the promises then held out by the prime movers in the cause of our elevation.

In 1830 the most intelligent and leading spirits among the colored men in the United States, such as James Forten, Robert Douglass, I. Bowers, A. D. Shadd, John Peck, Joseph Cassey, and John B. Vashon of Pennsylvania; John T. Hilton, Nathaniel and Thomas Paul, and James G. Barbodoes of Massachusetts; Henry Sipkins, Thomas Hamilton, Thomas L. Jennings, Thomas Downing, Samuel E. Cornish, and others of New York; R. Cooley and others of Maryland, and representatives from other States which cannot now be recollected, the data not being at hand, assembled in the city of Philadelphia, in the capacity of a National Convention, to "devise ways and means for the bettering of our condition." These Conventions determined to assemble annually, much talent, ability, and energy of character being displayed; when in 1831 at a sitting of the Convention in September, from their previous pamphlet reports, much interest having been created throughout the country, they were favored by the presence of a number of whites, some of whom were able and distinguished men, such as Rev. R. R. Gurley, Arthur Tappan, Elliot Cresson, John Rankin, Simeon Jocelyn and others, among them William Lloyd Garrison, then quite a young

man, all of whom were staunch and ardent Colonizationists, young Garrison at that time, doing his mightiest in his favorite work.

Among other great projects of interest brought before the convention at a previous sitting, was that of the expediency of a general emigration, as far as it was practicable, of the colored people to the British Provinces of North America. Another was that of raising sufficient means for the establishment and erection of a College for the proper education of the colored youth. These gentlemen long accustomed to observation and reflection on the condition of their people, saw at once, that there must necessarily be means used adequate to the end to be attained—that end being an unqualified equality with the ruling class of their fellow citizens. He saw that as a class, the colored people of the country were ignorant, degraded and oppressed, by far the greater portion of them being abject slaves in the South, the very condition of whom was almost enough, under the circumstances, to blast the remotest hope of success, and those who were freemen, whether in the South or North, occupied a subservient, servile, and menial position, considering it a favor to get into the service of the whites, and do their degrading offices. That the difference between the whites and themselves, consisted in the superior advantages of the one over the other, in point of attainments. That if a knowledge of the arts and sciences, the mechanical occupations, the industrial occupations, as farming, commerce, and all the various business enterprises, and learned professions were necessary for the superior position occupied by their rulers, it was also necessary for them. And very reasonably too, the first suggestion which occurred to them was, the advantages of a location, then the necessity of a qualification. They reasoned with themselves, that all distinctive differences made among men on account of their origin, is wicked, unrighteous, and cruel, and never shall receive countenance in any shape from us, therefore, the first acts of the measures entered into by them, was to protest, solemnly protest, against every unjust measure and policy in the country, having for its object the proscription of the colored people, whether state, national, municipal, social, civil, or religious.

But being far-sighted, reflecting, discerning men, they took a political view of the subject, and determined for the good of their people to be governed in their policy according to the facts as they presented themselves. In taking a glance at Europe, they discovered there, however unjustly, as we have shown in another part of this pamphlet, that there are and have been numerous classes proscribed and oppressed, and it was not for them to cut short their wise deliberations, and arrest their proceedings in contention, as to the cause, whether on account of language, the color of eyes, hair, skin, or their origin of country— because all this is contrary to reason, a contradiction to common sense, at war with nature herself, and at variance with facts as they stare us every day in the face, among all nations, in every country—this being made the pretext as a matter of *policy* alone—a fact worthy of observation, that wherever the objects of oppression are the most easily distinguished by any peculiar or general characteristics, these people are the more easily oppressed, because the war of oppression is the more easily waged against them. This is the case with the modern Jews and many other people who have strongly-marked, peculiar, or distinguishing characteristics. This arises in this wise. The policy of all those who proscribe any people, induces them to select as the objects of proscription, those who differed as much as possible, in some particulars, from themselves. This is to ensure the greater success, because it engenders the greater prejudice, or in other words, elicits less interest on the part of the oppressing class, in their favor. This fact is well understood in national conflicts, as the soldier or civilian, who is distinguished by his dress, mustache, or any other peculiar appendage, would certainly prove himself a madman, if he did not take the precaution to change his dress, remove his mustache, and conceal as much as possible his peculiar characteristics, to give him access among the repelling party. This is mere policy, nature having nothing to do with it. Still, it is a fact, a great truth well worthy of remark, and as such we adduce it for the benefit of those of our readers, unaccustomed to an enquiry into the policy of nations.

In view of these truths, our fathers and leaders in our elevation, discovered that as a policy, we the colored people were selected as the subordinate class in this country, not on account of any actual or supposed inferiority on their part, but simply because, in view of all the circumstances of the case, they were the very best class that could be selected. They would have as readily had any other class as subordinates in the country, as the colored people, but the condition of society *at the time,* would not admit of it. In the struggle for American Independence, there were among those who performed the most distinguished parts, the most common-place peasantry of the Provinces. English, Danish, Irish, Scotch, and others, were among those whose names blazoned forth as heroes in the American Revolution. But a single reflection will convince us, that no course of policy could have induced the proscription of the parentage and relatives of such men as Benjamin Franklin the printer, Roger Sherman the cobbler, the tinkers, and others of the signers of the Declaration of Independence. But as they were determined to have a subservient class, it will readily be conceived, that according to the state of society at the time, the better policy on their part was, to select some class, who from their political position—however much they may have contributed their aid as we certainly did, in the general struggle for liberty by force of arms—who had the least claims upon them, or who had the *least chance,* or was the *least potent* in urging their claims. This class of course was the colored people and Indians.

The Indians who in the early settlement of the continent, before an African captive had ever been introduced thereon, were reduced to the most abject slavery, toiling day and night in the mines, under the relentless hands of heartless Spanish taskmasters, but being a race of people raised to the sports of fishing, the chase, and of war, were wholly unaccustomed to labor, and therefore sunk under the insupportable weight, two millions and a half having fallen victims to the cruelty of oppression and toil suddenly placed upon their shoulders. And it was only this that prevented their farther enslavement as a class, after the provinces were absolved from the British Crown. It is true that their general enslavement took place on the islands and in the mining districts of South America, where indeed, the Europeans continued to enslave them, until a comparatively recent period; still, the design, the feeling, and inclination from policy, was the same to do so here, in this section of the continent.

Nor was it until their influence became too great, by the political position occupied by their brethren in the new republic, that the German and Irish peasantry ceased to be sold as slaves for a term of years fixed by law, for the repayment of their passage-money, the descendants of these classes of people for a long time being held as inferiors, in the estimation of the ruling class, and it was not until they assumed the rights and privileges guaranteed to them by the established policy of the country, among the leading spirits of whom were their relatives, that the policy towards them was discovered to be a bad one, and accordingly changed. Nor was it, as is frequently very erroneously asserted, by colored as well as white persons, that it was on account of hatred to the African, or in other words, on account of hatred to his color, that the African was selected as the subject of oppression in this country. This is sheer nonsense; being based on policy and nothing else, as shown in another place. The Indians, who being the most foreign to the sympathies of the Europeans on this continent, were selected in the first place, who, being unable to withstand the hardships, gave way before them.

But the African race had long been known to Europeans, in all ages of the world's history, as a long-lived, hardy race, subject to toil and labor of various kinds, subsisting mainly by traffic, trade, and industry, and consequently being as foreign to the sympathies of the invaders of the continent as the Indians, they were selected, captured, brought here as a laboring class, and as a matter of policy held as such. Nor was the absurd idea of natural inferiority of the African ever dreamed of, until recently adduced by the slave-holders and their abettors, in justification of their policy.

This, with contemptuous indignation, we fling back into their face, as a scorpion to a vulture. And so did our patriots and leaders in the cause of regeneration know better, and never for a moment yielded to the base doctrine. But they had discovered the great fact, that a cruel policy was pursued towards our people, and that they possessed distinctive characteristics which made them the objects of proscription. These characteristics being strongly marked in the colored people, as in the Indians, by color, character of hair and so on, made them the more easily distinguished from other Americans, and the policies more effectually urged against us. For this reason they introduced the subject of emigration to Canada, and a proper institution for the education of the youth.

At this important juncture of their proceedings, the afore named white gentlemen were introduced to the notice of the Convention, and after gaining permission to speak, expressed their gratification and surprise at the qualification and talent manifested by different members of the Convention, all expressing their determination to give the cause of the colored people more serious reflection. Mr. Garrison, the youngest of them all, and none the less honest on account of his youthfulness, being but 26 years of age at the time, (1831) expressed his determination to change his course of policy at once, and espouse the cause of the elevation of the colored people here in their own country. We are not at present well advised upon this point, it now having escaped our memory, but we are under the impression that Mr. Jocelyn also, at once changed his policy.

During the winter of 1832, Mr. Garrison issued his "Thoughts on African Colonization," and near about the same time or shortly after, issued the first number of the "Liberator," in both of which, his full convictions of the enormity of American slavery, and the wickedness of their policy towards the colored people, were fully expressed. At the sitting of the Convention in this year, a number, perhaps all of these gentlemen were present, and those who had denounced the Colonization scheme, and espoused the cause of the elevation of the colored people in this country, or the Anti-Slavery cause, as it was now termed, expressed themselves openly and without reserve.

Sensible of the high-handed injustice done to the colored people in the United States, and the mischief likely to emanate from the unchristian proceedings of the deceptious Colonization scheme, like all honest hearted penitents, with the ardor only known to new converts, they entreated the Convention, whatever they did, not to entertain for a moment, the idea of recommending emigration to their people, nor the establishment of separate institutions of learning. They earnestly contended, and doubtless honestly meaning what they said, that they (the whites) had been our oppressors and injurers, they had obstructed our progress to the high positions of civilization, and now, it was their bounden duty to make full amends for the injuries thus inflicted on an unoffending people. They exhorted the Convention to cease; as they had laid on the burden, they would also take it off; as they had obstructed our pathway, they would remove the hindrance. In a word, as they had oppressed and trampled down the colored people, they would now elevate them. These suggestions and promises, good enough to be sure, after they were made, were accepted by the Convention—though some gentlemen were still in favor of the first project as the best policy, Mr. A. D. Shadd of West Chester, Pa., as we learn from himself, being one among that number—ran through the country like wild-fire, no one thinking, and if he thought, daring to speak above his breath of going any where out of certain prescribed limits, or of sending a child to school, if it should but have the name of "colored" attached to it, without the risk of being termed a "traitor" to the cause of his people, or an enemy to the Anti-Slavery cause.

At this important point in the history of our efforts, the colored men stopped suddenly, and with their hands thrust deep in their breeches-pockets, and their mouths gaping open, stood gazing with astonishment, wonder, and surprise, at the stupendous moral colossal statues of our Anti-Slavery friends and brethren, who in the heat and zeal of honest hearts, from a desire to make atone-

ment for the many wrongs inflicted, promised a great deal more than they have ever been able half to fulfill, in thrice the period in which they expected it. And in this, we have no fault to find with our Anti-Slavery friends, and here wish it to be understood, that we are not laying any thing to their charge as blame, neither do we desire for a moment to reflect on them, because we heartily believe that all that they did at the time, they did with the purest and best of motives, and further believe that they now are, as they then were, the truest friends we have among the whites in this country. And hope, and desire, and request, that our people should always look upon *true* anti-slavery people, Abolitionists we mean, as their friends, until they have just cause for acting otherwise. It is true, that the Anti-Slavery, like all good causes, has produced some recreants, but the cause itself is no more to be blamed for that, than Christianity is for the malconduct of any professing hypocrite, nor the society of Friends, for the conduct of a broad-brimmed hat and shadbelly coated horse-thief, because he spoke *thee* and *thou* before stealing the horse. But what is our condition even amidst our Anti-Slavery friends? And here, as our sole intention is to contribute to the elevation of our people, we must be permitted to express our opinion freely, without being thought uncharitable.

In the first place, we should look at the objects for which the Anti-Slavery cause was commenced, and the promises or inducements it held out at the commencement. It should be borne in mind, that Anti-Slavery took its rise among *colored men*, just at the time they were introducing their greatest projects for their own elevation, and that our Anti-Slavery brethren were converts of the colored men, in behalf of their elevation. Of course, it would be expected that being baptized into the new doctrines, their faith would induce them to embrace the principles therein contained, with the strictest possible adherence.

The cause of dissatisfaction with our former condition, was, that we were proscribed, debarred, and shut out from every respectable position, occupying the places of inferiors and menials.

It was expected that Anti-Slavery, according to its professions, would extend to colored persons, as far as in the power of its adherents, those advantages nowhere else to be obtained among white men. That colored boys would get situations in their shops and stores, and every other advantage tending to elevate them as far as possible, would be extended to them. At least, it was expected, that in Anti-Slavery establishments, colored men would have the preference. Because, there was no other ostensible object in view, in the commencement of the Anti-Slavery enterprise, than the *elevation* of the *colored man,* by facilitating his efforts in attaining to equality with the white man. It was urged, and it was true, that the colored people were susceptible of all that the whites were, and all that was required was to give them a fair opportunity, and they would prove their capacity. That it was unjust, wicked, and cruel, the result of an unnatural prejudice, that debarred them from places of respectability, and that public opinion could and should be corrected upon this subject. That it was only necessary to make a sacrifice of feeling, and an innovation on the customs of society, to establish a different order of things,—that as Anti-Slavery men, they were willing to make these sacrifices, and determined to take the colored man by the hand, making common cause with him in affliction, and bear a part of the odium heaped upon him. That his cause was the cause of God— that "In as much as ye did it not unto the least of these my little ones, ye did it not unto me," and that as Anti-Slavery men, they would "do right if the heavens fell." Thus, was the cause espoused, and thus did we expect much. But in all this, we were doomed to disappointment, sad, sad disappointment. Instead of realising what we had hoped for, we find ourselves occupying the very same position in relation to our Anti-Slavery friends, as we do in relation to the pro-slavery part of the community—a mere secondary, underling position, in all our relations to them, and any thing more than this, is not a matter of course affair—it comes not by established anti-slavery custom or right, but like that which emanates from the proslavery portion of the community, by mere sufferance.

It is true, that the "Liberator" office, in Boston, has got Elijah Smith, a colored youth, at the cases—the "Standard," in New York, a young colored man, and the "Freeman," in Philadelphia, William Still, another, in the publication office, as "packing clerk;" yet these are but three out of the hosts that fill these offices in their various departments, all occupying places that could have been, and as we once thought, would have been, easily enough, occupied by colored men. Indeed, we can have no other idea about anti-slavery in this country, than that the legitimate persons to fill any and every position about an anti-slavery establishment are colored persons. Nor will it do to argue in extenuation, that white men are as justly entitled to them as colored men; because white men do not from *necessity* become anti-slavery men in order to get situations; they being white men, may occupy any position they are capable of filling—in a word, their chances are endless, every avenue in the country being opened to them. They do not therefore become abolitionists, for the sake of employment—at least, it is not the song that anti-slavery sung, in the first love of the new faith, proclaimed by its disciples.

And if it be urged that colored men are incapable as yet to fill these positions, all that we have to say is, that the cause has fallen far short; almost equivalent to a failure, of a tithe, of what it promised to do in half the period of its existence, to this time, if it have not as yet, now a period of twenty years, raised up colored men enough, to fill the offices within its patronage. We think it is not unkind to say, if it had been half as faithful to itself, as it should have been—its professed principles we mean; it could have reared and tutored from childhood, colored men enough by this time, for its own especial purpose. These we know could have been easily obtained, because colored people in general, are favorable to the anti-slavery cause, and wherever there is an adverse manifestation, it arises from sheer ignorance; and we have now but comparatively few such among us. There is one thing certain, that no colored person, except such as would reject education altogether, would be adverse to putting their child with an anti-slavery person, for educational advantages. This then, could have been done. But it has not been done, and let the cause of it be whatever it may, and let whoever may be to blame, we are willing to let all that pass, and extend to our anti-slavery brethren the right-hand of fellowship, bidding them God-speed in the propagation of good and wholesome sentiments—for whether they are practically carried out or not, the professions are in themselves all right and good. Like Christianity, the principles are holy and of divine origin. And we believe, if ever a man started right, with pure and holy motives, Mr. Garrison did; and that, had he the power of making the cause what it should be, it would all be right, and there never would have been any cause for the remarks we have made, though in kindness, and with the purest of motives. We are nevertheless, still occupying a miserable position in the community, wherever we live; and what we most desire is, to draw the attention of our people to this fact, and point out what, in our opinion, we conceive to be a proper remedy.

CHAPTER III

American Colonization

When we speak of colonization, we wish distinctly to be understood, as speaking of the "American Colonization Society"—or that which is under its influence—commenced in Richmond, Virginia, in 1817, under the influence of Mr. Henry Clay of Ky., Judge Bushrod Washington of Va., and other Southern slaveholders, having for their express object, as their speeches and doings all justify us in asserting in good faith, the removal of the free colored people from the end of their birth, for the security of the slaves, as property to the slave propagandists.

This scheme had no sooner been propagated, than the old and leading colored men of Philadelphia, Pa., with Richard Allen, James Forten, and others at their head, true to their trust and the cause of their brethren, summoned the colored people together, and then and there, in language and with voices pointed and loud, protested against the scheme as an outrage, having no other object in view, than the benefit of the slave-holding interests of the country, and that as freemen, they would never prove recreant to the cause of their brethren in bondage, by leaving them without hope of redemption from their chains. This determination of the colored patriots of Philadelphia was published in full, authentically, and circulated throughout the length and breadth of the country by the papers of the day. The colored people every where received the news, and at once endorsed with heart and soul, the doings of the Anti-Colonization Meeting of colored freemen. From that time forth, the colored people generally have had no sympathy with the colonization scheme, nor confidence in its leaders, looking upon them all, as arrant hypocrites, seeking every opportunity to deceive them. In a word, the monster was crippled in its infancy, and has never as yet recovered from the stroke. It is true, that like its ancient sire, that was "more subtile than all the beasts of the field," it has inherited a large portion of his most prominent characteristic—an idiosyncrasy with the animal—that enables him to entwine himself into the greater part of the Church and other institutions of the country, which having once entered there, leaves his venom, which put such a spell on the conductors of those institutions, that it is only on condition that a colored person consents to go to the neighborhood of his kindred brother monster the boa, that he may find admission in the one or the other. We look upon the American Colonization Society as one of the most arrant enemies of the colored man, ever seeking to discomfit him, and envying him of every privilege that he may enjoy. We believe it to be anti-Christian in its character, and misanthropic in its pretended sympathies. Because if this were not the case, men could not be found professing morality and Christianity—as to our astonishment we have found them—who unhesitatingly say, "I know it is right"—that is in itself—"to do" so and so, "and I am willing and ready to do it, but only on condition, that you go to Africa." Indeed, a highly talented clergyman, informed us in November last (three months ago) in the city of Philadelphia, that he was present when the Rev. Doctor J. P. Durbin, late President of Dickinson College, called on Rev. Mr. P. of B., to consult him about going to Liberia, to take charge of the literary department of an University in contemplation, when the following conversation ensued: Mr. P.—"Doctor, I have as much and more than I can do here, in educating the youth of our own country, and preparing them for usefulness here at home." Dr. D.—"Yes, but do as you may, you can never be elevated here." Mr. P.—"Doctor, do you not believe that the religion of our blessed Redeemer Jesus Christ, has morality, humanity, philanthropy, and justice enough in it to elevate us, and enable us to obtain our rights in this our own country?" Dr. D.—"No, indeed, sir, I do not, and if you depend upon that, your hopes are vain!" Mr. P.—Turning to Doctor Durbin, looking him solemnly, though affectionately in the face, remarked—"Well, Doctor Durbin, we both profess to be ministers of Christ; but dearly as I love the cause of my Redeemer, if for a moment, I could entertain the opinion you do about Christianity, I would not serve him another hour!" We do not know, as we were not advised, that the Rev. doctor added in fine,—"Well, you may quit now, for all your serving him will not avail against the power of the god (hydra) of Colonization." Will any one doubt for a single moment, the justice of our strictures on colonization, after reading the conversation between the Rev. Dr. Durbin and the colored clergyman? Surely not. We can therefore make no account of it, but that of setting it down as being the worst enemy of the colored people.

Recently, there has been a strained effort in the city of New York on the part of the Rev. J. B. Pinney and others, of the leading white colonizationists, to get up a movement among some poor pitiable colored men—we say pitiable, for certainly the colored persons who are at this period capable of loaning themselves to the enemies of their race, against the best interest of all that we hold sacred to that race, are pitiable in the lowest extreme, far beneath the dignity of an enemy, and therefore, we pass them by with the simple remark,

that this is the hobby that colonization is riding all over the country, as the "tremendous" access of colored people to their cause within the last twelve months. We should make another remark here perhaps, in justification of governor Pinney's New York allies—that is, report says, that in the short space of some three or five months, one of his confidants, benefited himself to the "reckoning" of from eleven to fifteen hundred dollars, or "such a matter, "while others were benefited in sums "pretty considerable" but of a less "reckoning." Well, we do not know after all, that they may not have quite as good a right, to pocket part of the spoils of this "grab game," as any body else. However, they are of little consequence, as the ever watchful eye of those excellent gentlemen and faithful guardians of their people's rights—the *Committee of Thirteen*, consisting of Messrs. John J. Zuille, *Chairman*, T. Joiner White, Philip A. Bell, *Secretaries*, Robert Hamilton, George T. Downing, Jeremiah Powers, John T. Raymond, Wm. Burnett, James McCuen Smith, Ezekiel Dias, Junius C. Morel, Thomas Downing, and Wm. J. Wilson, have properly chastised this petslave of Mr. Pinney, and made it "know its place," by keeping within the bounds of its master's enclosure.

In expressing our honest conviction of the designedly injurious character of the Colonization Society, we should do violence to our own sense of individual justice, if we did not express the belief, that there are some honest hearted men, who not having seen things in the proper light, favor that scheme, simply as a means of elevating the colored people. Such persons, so soon as they become convinced of their error, immediately change their policy, and advocate the elevation of the colored people, anywhere and everywhere, in common with other men. Of such were the early abolitionists as before stated; and the great and good Dr. F. J. Lemoyne, Gerrit Smith, and Rev. Charles Avery, and a host of others, who were Colonizationists, before espousing the cause of our elevation, here at home, and nothing but an honorable sense of justice, induces us to make these exceptions, as there are many good persons within our knowledge, whom we believe to be well wishers of the colored people, who may favor colonization.* But the animal itself is the same "hydra-headed monster," let whomsoever may fancy to pet it. A serpent is a serpent, and none the less a viper, because nestled in the bosom of an honest hearted man. This the colored people must bear in mind, and keep clear of the hideous thing, lest its venom may be tost upon them. But why deem any argument necessary to show the unrighteousness of colonization? Its very origin as before shown—the source from whence it sprung, being the offspring of slavery—is in itself, sufficient to blast it in the estimation of every colored person in the United States, who has sufficient intelligence to comprehend it.

We dismiss this part of the subject, and proceed to consider the mode and means of our elevation in the United States.

CHAPTER IV

Our Elevation in the United States

That very little comparatively as yet has been done, to attain a respectable position as a class in this country, will not be denied, and that the successful accomplishment of this

---

* Benjamin Coates, Esq., a merchant of Philadelphia, we believe to be an honest hearted man, and real friend of the colored people, and a true, though as yet, rather undecided philanthropist. Mr. Coates, to our knowledge, has supported three or four papers published by colored men, for the elevation of colored people in the United States, and given, as he continues to do, considerable sums to their support. We have recently learned from himself, that, though he still advocates Colonization, simply as a means of elevating the colored race of the United States, that he has *left* the Colonization Society, and prefers seeing colored people located on this continent, to going to Liberia, or elsewhere off of it—though his zeal for the enlightenment of Africa, is unabated, as every good man's should be; and we are satisfied, that Mr. Coates is neither well understood, nor rightly appreciated by the friends of our cause. One thing we do know, that he left the Colonization Society, because he could not conscientiously subscribe to its measures.

end is also possible, must also be admitted; but in what manner, and by what means, has long been, and is even now, by the best thinking minds among the colored people themselves, a matter of difference of opinion.

We believe in the universal equality of man, and believe in that declaration of God's word, in which it is there positively said, that "God has made of one blood all the nations that dwell on the face of the earth." Now of "the nations that dwell on the face of the earth," that is, all the people—there are one thousand millions of souls, and of this vast number of human beings, two-thirds are colored, from black, tending in complexion to the olive or that of the Chinese, with all the intermediate and admixtures of black and white, with the various "crosses" as they are physiologically, but erroneously termed, to white. We are thus explicit in stating these points, because we are determined to be understood by all. We have then, two colored to one white person throughout the earth, and yet, singular as it may appear, according to the present geographical and political history of the world, the white race predominates over the colored; or in other words, wherever there is one white person, that one rules and governs two colored persons. This is a living undeniable truth, to which we call the especial attention of the colored reader in particular. Now there is a cause for this, as there is no effect without a cause, a comprehensible remediable cause. We all believe in the justice of God, that he is impartial, "looking upon his children with an eye of care," dealing out to them all, the measure of his goodness; yet, how can we reconcile ourselves to the difference that exists between the colored and the white races, as they truthfully present themselves before our eyes? To solve this problem, is to know the remedy; and to know it, is but necessary, in order successfully to apply it. And we shall but take the colored people of the United States, as a fair sample of the colored races everywhere of the present age, as the arguments that apply to the one, will apply to the other, whether Christians, Mahomedans, or pagans.

The colored races are highly susceptible of religion; it is a constituent principle of their nature, and an excellent trait in their character. But unfortunately for them, they carry it too far. Their hope is largely developed, and consequently, they usually stand still—hope in God, and really expect Him to do that for them, which it is necessary they should do themselves. This is their great mistake, and arises from a misconception of the character and ways of Deity. We must know God, that is understand His nature and purposes, in order to serve Him; and to serve Him well, is but to know him rightly. To depend for assistance upon God, is a *duty* and right; but to know when, how, and in what manner to obtain it, is the key to this great Bulwark of Strength, and Depository of Aid.

God himself is perfect; perfect in all his works and ways. He has means for every end; and every means used must be adequate to the end to be gained. God's means are laws—fixed laws of nature, a part of His own being, and as immutable, as unchangeable as Himself. Nothing can be accomplished but through the medium of, and conformable to these laws.

They are *three*—and like God himself, represented in the three persons in the Godhead—the *Spiritual, Moral* and *Physical* Laws.

That which is Spiritual, can only be accomplished through the medium of the Spiritual law; that which is Moral, through the medium of the Moral law; and that which is Physical, through the medium of the Physical law. Otherwise than this, it is useless to expect any thing. Does a person want a spiritual blessing, he must apply through the medium of the spiritual law—*pray* for it in order to obtain it. If they desire to do a moral good, they must apply through the medium of the moral law—exercise their sense and feeling of *right* and *justice*, in order to effect it. Do they want to attain a physical end, they can only do so through the medium of the physical law—go to *work* with muscles, hands, limbs, might and strength, and this, and nothing else will attain it.

The argument that man must pray for what he receives, is a mistake, and one that is doing the colored people especially, incalculable injury. That man must pray in order to get to Heaven, every Christian will admit—but a great truth we have yet got to learn, that he can live on earth whether he is religious or not, so that he conforms to the great law of God, regulating the things of earth; the great physical laws. It is only necessary, in order to convince our people of their error and palpable mistake in this matter, to call their attention to the fact, that there are no people more religious in this Country, than the colored people, and none so poor and miserable as they. That prosperity and wealth, smiles upon the efforts of wicked white men, whom we know to utter the name of God with curses, instead of praises. That among the slaves, there are thousands of them religious, continually raising their voices, sending up their prayers to God, invoking His aid in their behalf, asking for a speedy deliverance; but they are still in chains, although they have thrice suffered out their three score years and ten. That "God sendeth rain upon the just and unjust," should be sufficient to convince us that our success in life, does not depend upon our religious character, but that the physical laws governing all earthly and temporary affairs, benefit equally the just and the unjust. Any other doctrine than this, is downright delusion, unworthy of a free people, and only intended for slaves. That all men and women, should be moral, upright, good and religious—we mean *Christians*—we would not utter a word against, and could only wish that it were so; but, what we here desire to do is, to correct the long standing error among a large body of the colored people in this country, that the cause of our oppression and degradation, is the displeasure of God towards us, because of our unfaithfulness to Him. This is not true; because if God is just—and he is—there could be no justice in prospering white men with his fostering care, for more than two thousand years, in all their wickedness, while dealing out to the colored people, the measure of his displeasure, for not half the wickedness as that of the whites. Here then is our mistake, and let it forever henceforth be corrected. We are no longer slaves, believing any interpretation that our oppressors may give the word of God, for the purpose of deluding us to the more easy subjugation; but freemen, comprising some of the first minds of intelligence and rudimental qualifications, in the country. What then is the remedy, for our degradation and oppression? This appears now to be the only remaining question —the means of successful elevation in this our own native land? This depends entirely upon the application of the means of Elevation.

CHAPTER V

Means of Elevation

Moral theories have long been resorted to by us, as a means of effecting the redemption of our brethren in bonds, and the elevation of the free colored people in this country. Experience has taught us, that speculations are not enough; that the *practical* application of principles adduced, the thing carried out, is the only true and proper course to pursue.

We have speculated and moralised much about equality—claiming to be as good as our neighbors, and every body else—all of which, may do very well in ethics—but not in politics. We live in society among men, conducted by men, governed by rules and regulations. However arbitrary, there are certain policies that regulate all well organized institutions and corporate bodies. We do not intend here to speak of the legal political relations of society, for those are treated on elsewhere. The business and social, or voluntary and mutual policies, are those that now claim our attention. Society regulates itself—being governed by mind, which like water, finds its own level. "Like seeks like," is a principle in the laws of matter, as well as of mind. There is such a thing as inferiority of things, and positions; at least society has made them so; and while we continue to live among men, we must agree to all *just* measures—all those we mean, that do not necessarily infringe on the rights of others. By the regulations of society, there is no equality of persons, where there is not an equality of attainments. By this, we do not wish to be understood as advocating the actual equal attainments of every individual; but we mean to say, that if these attainments be necessary for the elevation of the white man, they are necessary for the elevation of the colored man. That some colored men and women, in a like proportion to the whites,

should be qualified in all the attainments possessed by them. It is one of the regulations of society the world over, and we shall have to conform to it, or be discarded as unworthy of the associations of our fellows.

Cast our eyes about us and reflect for a moment, and what do we behold! every thing that presents to view gives evidence of the skill of the white man. Should we purchase a pound of groceries, a yard of linen, a vessel of crockeryware, a piece of furniture, the very provisions that we eat,—all, all are the products of the white man, purchased by us from the white man, consequently, our earnings and means, are all given to the white man.

Pass along the avenues of any city or town, in which you live—behold the trading shops—the manufactories—see the operations of the various machinery—see the stage-coaches coming in, bringing the mails of intelligence—look at the railroads interlining every section, bearing upon them their mighty trains, flying with the velocity of the swallow, ushering in the hundreds of industrious, enterprising travellers. Cast again your eyes widespread over the ocean—see the vessels in every direction with their white sheets spread to the winds of heaven, freighted with the commerce, merchandise and wealth of many nations. Look as you pass along through the cities, at the great and massive buildings—the beautiful and extensive structures of architecture—behold the ten thousand cupolas, with their spires all reared up towards heaven, intersecting the territory of the clouds—all standing as mighty living monuments, of the industry, enterprise, and intelligence of the white man. And yet, with all these living truths, rebuking us with scorn, we strut about, place our hands akimbo, straighten up ourselves to our greatest height, and talk loudly about being "as good as any body." How do we compare with them? Our fathers are their coach-men, our brothers their cook-men, and ourselves their waiting-men. Our mothers their nurse-women, our sisters their scrub-women, our daughters their maid-women, and our wives their washer-women. Until colored men, attain to a position above permitting their mothers, sisters, wives, and daughters, to do the drudgery and menial offices of other men's wives and daughters; it is useless, it is nonsense, it is pitiable mockery, to talk about equality and elevation in society. The world is looking upon us, with feelings of commisseration, sorrow, and contempt. We scarcely deserve sympathy, if we peremptorily refuse advice, bearing upon our elevation.

We will suppose a case for argument: In this city reside, two colored families, of three sons and three daughters each. At the head of each family, there is an old father and mother. The opportunities of these families, may or may not be the same for educational advantages—be that as it may, the children of the one go to school, and become qualified for the duties of life. One daughter becomes school-teacher, another a mantua-maker, and a third a fancy shop-keeper; while one son becomes a farmer, another a merchant, and a third a mechanic. All enter into business with fine prospects, marry respectably, and settle down in domestic comfort—while the six sons and daughters of the other family, grow up without educational and business qualifications, and the highest aim they have, is to apply to the sons and daughters of the first named family, to hire for domestics! Would there be an equality here between the children of these two families? Certainly not. This, then, is precisely the position of the colored people generally in the United States, compared with the whites. What is necessary to be done, in order to attain an equality, is to change the condition, and the person is at once changed. If, as before stated, a knowledge of all the various business enterprises, trades, professions, and sciences, is necessary for the elevation of the white, a knowledge of them also is necessary for the elevation of the colored man; and he cannot be elevated without them.

White men are producers—we are consumers. They build houses, and we rent them. They raise produce, and we consume it. They manufacture clothes and wares, and we garnish ourselves with them. They build coaches, vessels, cars, hotels, saloons, and other vehicles and places of accommodation, and we deliberately wait until they have got them in readiness, then walk in, and contend with as much assurance for a "right," as though the whole thing was bought by, paid for, and belonged to us. By

their literary attainments, they are the contributors to, authors and teachers of, literature, science, religion, law, medicine, and all other useful attainments that the world now makes use of. We have no reference to ancient times—we speak of modern things.

These are the means by which God intended man to succeed: and this discloses the secret of the white man's success with all of his wickedness, over the head of the colored man, with all of his religion. We have been pointed and plain, on this part of the subject, because we desire our readers to see persons and things in their true position. Until we are determined to change the condition of things, and raise ourselves above the position in which we are now prostrated, we must hang our heads in sorrow, and hide our faces in shame. It is enough to know that these things are so; the causes we care little about. Those we have been examining, complaining about, and moralising over, all our life time. This we are weary of. What we desire to learn now is, how to effect a *remedy*; this we have endeavored to point out. Our elevation must be the result of *self-efforts*, and work of our *own hands*. No other human power can accomplish it. If we but determine it shall be so, it will be so. Let each one make the case his own, and endeavor to rival his neighbor, in honorable competition.

These are the proper and only means of elevating ourselves and attaining equality in this country or any other, and it is useless, utterly futile, to think about going any where, except we are determined to use these as the necessary means of developing our manhood. The means are at hand, within our reach. Are we willing to try them? Are we willing to raise ourselves superior to the condition of slaves, or continue the meanest underlings, subject to the beck and call of every creature bearing a pale complexion? If we are, we had as well remained in the South, as to have come to the North in search of more freedom. What was the object of our parents in leaving the south, if it were not for the purpose of attaining equality in common with others of their fellow citizens, by giving their children access to all the advantages enjoyed by others? Surely this was their object. They heard of liberty and equality here, and they hastened on to enjoy it, and no people are more astonished and disappointed than they, who for the first time, on beholding the position we occupy here in the free north—what is called, and what they expect to find, the free States. They at once tell us, that they have as much liberty in the south as we have in the north—that there as free people, they are protected in their rights—that we have nothing more—that in other respects they have the same opportunity, indeed the preferred opportunity, of being their maids, servants, cooks, waiters, and menials in general, there, as we have here—that had they known for a moment, before leaving, that such was to be the only position they occupied here, they would have remained where they were, and never left. Indeed, such is the disappointment in many cases, that they immediately return back again, completely insulted at the idea, of having us here at the north, assume ourselves to be their superiors. Indeed, if our superior advantages of the free States, do not induce and stimulate us to the higher attainments in life, what in the name of degraded humanity will do it? Nothing, surely nothing. If, in fine, the advantages of free schools in Massachusetts, New York, Pennsylvania, Ohio, Michigan, and wherever else we may have them, do not give us advantages and pursuits superior to our slave brethren, then are the unjust assertions of Messrs. Henry Clay, John C. Calhoun, Theodore Frelinghuysen, late Governor Poindexter of Mississippi, George McDuffy, Governor Hammond of South Carolina, Extra Billy (present Governor) Smith, of Virginia, and the host of our oppressors, slaveholders and others, true, that we are insusceptible and incapable of elevation to the more respectable, honorable, and higher attainments among white men. But this we do not believe—neither do you, although our whole life and course of policy in this country are such, that it would seem to prove otherwise. The degradation of the slave parent has been entailed upon the child, induced by the subtle policy of the oppressor, in regular succession handed down from father to son—a system of regular submission and servitude, menialism and dependence, until it has be-

come almost a physiological function of our system, an actual condition of our nature. Let this no longer be so, but let us determine to equal the whites among whom we live, not by declarations and unexpressed self-opinion, for we have always had enough of that, but by actual proof in acting, doing, and carrying out practically, the measures of equality. Here is our nativity, and here have we the natural right to abide and be elevated through the measures of our own efforts.

CHAPTER VI

The United States Our Country

Our common country is the United States. Here were we born, here raised and educated; here are the scenes of childhood; the pleasant associations of our school going days; the loved enjoyments of our domestic and fireside relations, and the sacred graves of our departed fathers and mothers, and from here will we not be driven by any policy that may be schemed against us.

We are Americans, having a birthright citizenship—natural claims upon the country—claims common to all others of our fellow citizens—natural rights, which may, by virtue of unjust laws, be obstructed, but never can be annulled. Upon these do we place ourselves, as immovably fixed as the decrees of the living God. But according to the economy that regulates the policy of nations, upon which rests the basis of justifiable claims to all freemen's rights, it may be necessary to take another view of, and enquire into the political claims of colored men....

CHAPTER XXIII

Things as They Are

And if thou boast TRUTH to utter,
SPEAK, and leave the rest to God.

In presenting this work, we have but a single object in view, and that is, to inform the minds of the colored people at large, upon many things pertaining to their elevation, that but few among us are acquainted with. Unfortunately for us, as a body, we have been taught to believe, that we must have some person to think for us, instead of thinking for ourselves. So accustomed are we to submission and this kind of training, that it is with difficulty, even among the most intelligent of the colored people, an audience may be elicited for any purpose whatever, if the expounder is to be a colored person; and the introduction of any subject is treated with indifference, if not contempt, when the originator is a colored person. Indeed, the most ordinary white person, is almost revered, while the most qualified colored person is totally neglected. Nothing from them is appreciated.

We have been standing comparatively still for years, following in the footsteps of our friends, believing that what they promise us can be accomplished, just because they say so, although our own knowledge should long since, have satisfied us to the contrary. Because even were it possible, with the present hate and jealousy that the whites have towards us in this country, for us to gain equality of rights with them; we never could have an equality of the exercise and enjoyment of those rights—because, the great odds of numbers are against us. We might indeed, as some at present, have the right of the elective franchise—nay, it is not the elective franchise, because the *elective franchise* makes the enfranchised, *eligible* to any position attainable; but we may exercise the right of *voting* only, which to us, is but poor satisfaction; and we by no means care to cherish the privilege of voting somebody into office, to help to make laws to degrade us.

In religion—because they are both *translators* and *commentators*, we must believe nothing, however absurd, but what our oppressors tell us. In Politics, nothing but such as they promulge; in Anti-Slavery, nothing but what our white brethren and friends say we must; in the mode and manner of our elevation, we must do nothing, but that which may be laid down to be done by our white brethren from some quarter or other; and now, even on the subject of emigration, there are some colored people to be found, so lost to their own interest and self-respect, as to be gulled by slave owners and colonizationists, who are led to believe there is no other place in which they can become elevated, but Liberia, a government of American slave-holders, as we have shown—simply, because white men have told them so.

Upon the possibility, means, mode and manner, of our Elevation in the United States—Our Original Rights and Claims as Citizens—Our Determination not to be Driven from our Native Country—the Difficulties in the Way of our Elevation—Our Position in Relation to our Anti-Slavery Brethren—the Wicked Design and Injurious Tendency of the American Colonization Society—Objections to Liberia—Objections to Canada—Preferences to South America, &c., &c., all of which we have treated without reserve; expressing our mind freely, and with candor, as we are determined that as far as we can at present do so, the minds of our readers shall be enlightened. The custom of concealing information upon vital and important subjects, in which the interest of the people is involved, we do not agree with, nor favor in the least; we have therefore, laid this cursory treatise before our readers, with the hope that it may prove instrumental in directing the attention of our people in the right way, that leads to their Elevation. Go or stay—of course each is free to do as he pleases—one thing is certain; our Elevation is the work of our own hands. And Mexico, Central America, the West Indies, and South America, all present now, opportunities for the individual enterprise of our young men, who prefer to remain in the United States, in preference to going where they can enjoy real freedom, and equality of rights. Freedom of Religion, as well as of politics, being tolerated in all of these places.

Let our young men and women, prepare themselves for usefulness and business; that the men may enter into merchandise, trading, and other things of importance; the young women may become teachers of various kinds, and otherwise fill places of usefulness. Parents must turn their attention more to the education of their children. We mean, to educate them for useful practical business purposes. Educate them for the Store and the

Counting House—to do every-day practical business. Consult the children's propensities, and direct their education according to their inclinations. It may be, that there is too great a desire on the part of parents, to give their children a professional education, before the body of the people, are ready for it. A people must be a business people, and have more to depend upon than mere help in people's houses and Hotels, before they are either able to support, or capable of properly appreciating the services of professional men among them. This has been one of our great mistakes—we have gone in advance of ourselves. We have commenced at the superstructure of the building, instead of the foundation—at the top instead of the bottom. We should first be mechanics and common tradesmen, and professions as a matter of course would grow out of the wealth made thereby. Young men and women, must now prepare for usefulness—the day of our Elevation is at hand—all the world now gazes at us—and Central and South America, and the West Indies, bid us come and be men and women, protected, secure, beloved and Free.

The branches of Education most desirable for the preparation of youth, for practical useful every-day life, are Arithmetic and good Penmanship, in order to be Accountants; and a good rudimental knowledge of Geography—which has ever been neglected, and under estimated—and of Political Economy; which without the knowledge of the first, no people can ever become adventurous—nor of the second, never will be an enterprising people. Geography, teaches a knowledge of the world, and Political Economy, a knowledge of the wealth of nations; or how to make money. These are not abstruse sciences, or learning not easily acquired or understood; but simply, common School Primer learning, that every body may get. And, although it is the very Key to prosperity and success in common life, but few know any thing about it. Unfortunately for our people, so soon as their children learn to read a Chapter in the New Testament, and scribble a miserable hand, they are pronounced to have "Learning enough;" and taken away from School, no use to themselves, nor community. This is appar-

ent in our Public Meetings, and Official Church Meetings; of the great number of men present, there are but few capable of filling a Secretaryship. Some of the large cities may be an exception to this. Of the multitudes of Merchants, and Business men throughout this country, Europe, and the world, few are qualified, beyond the branches here laid down by us as necessary for business. What did John Jacob Astor, Stephen Girard, or do the millionaires and the greater part of the merchant princes, and mariners, know about Latin and Greek, and the Classics? Precious few of them know any thing. In proof of this, in 1841, during the Administration of President Tyler, when the mutiny was detected on board of the American Man of War Brig Somers, the names of the Mutineers, were recorded by young S—a Midshipman in Greek. Captain Alexander Slidell McKenzie, Commanding, was unable to read them; and in his despatches to the Government, in justification of his policy in executing the criminals, said that he "discovered some curious characters which he was unable to read," &c.; showing thereby, that that high functionary, did not understand even the Greek Alphabet, which was only necessary, to have been able to read proper names written in Greek.

What we most need then, is a good business practical Education; because, the Classical and Professional education of so many of our young men, before their parents are able to support them, and community ready to patronize them, only serves to lull their energy, and cripple the otherwise, praiseworthy efforts they would make in life. A Classical education, is only suited to the wealthy, or those who have a prospect of gaining a livelihood by it. The writer does not wish to be understood, as underrating a Classical and Professional education; this is not his intention; he fully appreciates them, having had some such advantages himself; but he desires to give a proper guide, and put a check to the extravagant idea that is fast obtaining, among our people especially, that a Classical, or as it is termed, a "finished education," is necessary to prepare one for usefulness in life. Let us have an education, that shall practically develope our thinking faculties and manhood; and then, and not until then, shall we be able to vie with our oppressors, go where we may. We as heretofore, have been on the extreme; either no qualification at all, or a Collegiate education. We jumped too far; taking a leap from the deepest abyss to the highest summit; rising from the ridiculous to the sublime; without medium or intermission.

Let our young women have an education; let their minds be well informed; well stored with useful information and practical proficiency, rather than the light superficial acquirements, popularly and fashionably called accomplishments. We desire accomplishments, but they must be *useful.*

Our females must be qualified, because they are to be the mothers of our children. As mothers are the first nurses and instructors of children; from them children consequently, get their first impressions, which being always the most lasting, should be the most correct. Raise the mothers above the level of degradation, and the offspring is elevated with them. In a word, instead of our young men, transcribing in their blank books, recipes for *Cooking;* we desire to see them making the transfer of *Invoices of Merchandise.* Come to our aid then; the *morning* of our *Redemption* from degradation, adorns the horizon.

In our selection of individuals, it will be observed, that we have confined ourself entirely to those who occupy or have occupied positions among the whites, consequently having a more general bearing as useful contributors to society at large. While we do not pretend to give all such worthy cases, we gave such as we possessed information of, and desire it to be understood, that a large number of our most intelligent and worthy men and women, have not been named, because from their more private position in community, it was foreign to the object and design of this work. If we have said aught to offend, "take the will for the deed," and be assured, that it was given with the purest of motives, and best intention, from a true hearted man and brother; deeply lamenting the sad fate of his race in this country, and sincerely desiring the elevation of man, and submitted to the serious consideration of all, who favor the promotion of the cause of God and humanity.

CHAPTER XXIV

A Glance at Ourselves—Conclusion

With broken hopes—sad devastation;
A race *resigned* to DEGRADATION!

We have said much to our young men and women, about their vocation and calling; we have dwelt much upon the menial position of our people in this country. Upon this point we cannot say too much, because there is a seeming satisfaction and seeking after such positions manifested on their part, unknown to any other people. There appears to be, a want of a sense of propriety or *self-respect,* altogether inexplicable; because young men and women among us, many of whom have good trades and homes, adequate to their support, voluntarily leave them, and seek positions, such as servants, waiting maids, coachmen, nurses, cooks in gentlemens' kitchen, or such like occupations, when they can gain a livelihood at something more respectable, or elevating in character. And the worse part of the whole matter is, that they have become so accustomed to it, it has become so "fashionable," that it seems to have become second nature, and they really become offended, when it is spoken against.

Among the German, Irish, and other European peasantry who come to this country, it matters not what they were employed at before and after they come; just so soon as they can better their condition by keeping shops, cultivating the soil, the young men and women going to night-schools, qualifying themselves for usefulness, and learning trades—they do so. Their first and last care, object and aim is, to better their condition by raising themselves above the condition that necessity places them in. We do not say too much, when we say, as an evidence of the deep degradation of our race, in the United States, that there are those among us, the wives and daughters, some of the *first ladies,* (and who dare say they are not the "first," because they belong to the "first class" and associate where any body among us can?) whose husbands are industrious, able and willing to support them, who voluntarily leave home, and become chamber-maids, and stewardesses, upon vessels and steamboats, in all probability, to enable them to obtain some more fine or costly article of dress or furniture.

We have nothing to say against those whom *necessity* compels to do these things, those who can do no better; we have only to do with those who can, and will not, or do not do better. The whites are always in the advance, and we either standing still or retrograding; as that which does not go forward, must either stand in one place or go back. The father in all probability is a farmer, mechanic, or man of some independent business; and the wife, sons and daughters, are chamber-maids, on vessels, nurses and waiting-maids, or coachmen and cooks in families. This is retrogradation. The wife, sons, and daughters should be elevated above this condition as a necessary consequence.

If we did not love our race superior to others, we would not concern ourself about their degradation; for the greatest desire of our heart is, to see them stand on a level with the most elevated of mankind. No people are ever elevated above the condition of their *females*; hence, the condition of the *mother* determines the condition of the child. To know the position of a people, it is only necessary to know the *condition* of their *females;* and despite themselves, they cannot rise above their level. Then what is our condition? Our *best ladies* being washerwomen, chamber-maids, children's traveling nurses, and common house servants, and menials, we are all a degraded, miserable people, inferior to any other people as a whole, on the face of the globe.

These great truths, however unpleasant, must be brought before the minds of our people in its true and proper light, as we have been too delicate about them, and too long concealed them for fear of giving offence. It would have been infinitely better for our race, if these facts had been presented before us half a century ago—we would have been now proportionably benefitted by it.

As an evidence of the degradation to which we have been reduced, we dare premise, that this chapter will give offence to many, very many, and why? Because they may say, "He dared to say that the occupation of a *servant* is a degradation." It is not necessarily degrading; it would not be, to one or a few people of a kind; but a *whole race of servants* are a degradation to that people.

Efforts made by men of qualifications for the toiling and degraded millions among the whites, neither gives offence to that class, nor is it taken unkindly by them; but received with manifestations of gratitude; to know that they are thought to be, equally worthy of, and entitled to stand on a level with the elevated classes; and they have only got to be informed of the way to raise themselves, to make the effort and do so as far as they can. But how different with us. Speak of our position in society, and it at once gives insult. Though we are servants; among ourselves we claim to be *ladies* and *gentlemen*, equal in standing, and as the popular expression goes, "Just as good as any body"—and so believing, we make no efforts to raise above the common level of menials; because the *best* being in that capacity, all are content with the position. We cannot at the same time, be domestic and lady; servant and gentleman. We must be the one or the other. Sad, sad indeed, is the thought, that hangs drooping in our mind, when contemplating the picture drawn before us. Young men and women, "we write these things unto you, because ye are strong," because the writer, a few years ago, gave unpardonable offence to many of the young people of Philadelphia and other places, because he dared tell them, that he thought too much of them, to be content with seeing them the servants of other people. Surely, she that could be the mistress, would not be the maid; neither would he that could be the master, be content with being the servant; then why be offended, when we point out to you, the way that leads from the menial to the mistress or the master. All this we seem to reject with fixed determination, repelling with anger, every effort on the part of our intelligent men and women to elevate us, with true Israelitish degradation, in reply to any suggestion or proposition that may be offered, "Who made thee a ruler and judge?"

The writer is no "Public Man," in the sense in which this is understood among our people, but simply an humble individual, endeavoring to seek a livelihood by a profession obtained entirely by his own efforts, without relatives and friends able to assist him; except such friends as he gained by the merit of his course and conduct, which he here gratefully acknowledges; and whatever he has accomplished, other young men may, by making corresponding efforts, also accomplish.

We have advised an emigration to Central and South America, and even to Mexico and the West Indies, to those who prefer either of the last named places, all of which are free countries, Brazil being the only real slaveholding State in South America—there being nominal slavery in Dutch Guiana, Peru, Buenos Ayres, Paraguay, and Uraguay, in all of which places colored people have equality in social, civil, political, and religious privileges; Brazil making it punishable with death to import slaves into the empire.

Our oppressors, when urging us to go to Africa, tell us that we are better adapted to the climate than they—that the physical condition of the constitution of colored people better endures the heat of warm climates than that of the whites; this we are willing to *admit,* without argument, without adducing the physiological reason why, that colored people can and do stand warm climates better than whites; and find an answer fully to the point in the fact, that they also stand *all other* climates, cold, temperate, and modified, that white people can stand; therefore, according to our oppressors' own showing, we are a *superior race,* being endowed with properties fitting us for *all parts* of the earth, while they are only adapted to *certain* parts. Of course, this proves our right and duty to live wherever we may *choose;* while the white race may only live where they *can.* We are content with the fact, and have ever claimed it. Upon this rock, they and we shall ever agree.

Of the West India Islands, Santa Cruz, belonging to Denmark; Porto Rico, and Cuba with its little adjuncts, belonging to Spain, are the only slave-holding Islands among them—three-fifths of the whole population of Cuba being colored people, who cannot and will not much longer endure the burden and the yoke. They only want intelligent leaders of their own color, when they are ready at any moment to charge to the conflict—to liberty

or death. The remembrance of the noble mulatto, Placido, the gentleman, scholar, poet, and intended Chief Engineer of the Army of Liberty and Freedom in Cuba; and the equally noble black, Charles Blair, who was to have been Commander-in-Chief, who were shamefully put to death in 1844, by that living monster, Captain General O'Donnell, is still fresh and indelible to the mind of every bondman of Cuba.

In our own country, the United States, there are *three million five hundred thousand slaves;* and we, the nominally free colored people, are *six hundred thousand* in number; estimating one-sixth to be men, we have *one hundred thousand* able bodied freemen, which will make a powerful auxiliary in any country to which we may become adopted—an ally not to be despised by any power on earth. We love our country, dearly love her, but she don't love us—she despises us, and bids us begone, driving us from her embraces; but we shall not go where she desires us; but when we do go, whatever love we have for her, we shall love the country none the less that receives us as her adopted children.

For the want of business habits and training, our energies have become paralyzed; our young men never think of business, any more than if they were so many bondmen, without the right to pursue any calling they may think most advisable. With our people in this country, dress and good appearances have been made the only test of gentleman and ladyship, and that vocation which offers the best opportunity to dress and appear well, has generally been preferred, however menial and degrading, by our young people, without even, in the majority of cases, an effort to do better; indeed, in many instances, refusing situations equally lucrative, and superior in position; but which would not allow as much display of dress and personal appearance. This, if we ever expect to rise, must be discarded from among us, and a high and respectable position assumed.

One of our great temporal curses is our consummate poverty. We are the poorest people, as a class, in the world of civilized mankind—abjectly, miserably poor, no one scarcely being able to assist the other. To this, of course, there are noble exceptions; but that which is common to, and the very process by which white men exist, and succeed in life, is unknown to colored men in general. In any and every considerable community may be found, some one of our white fellow-citizens, who is worth more than all the colored people in that community put together. We consequently have little or no efficiency. We must have means to be practically efficient in all the undertakings of life; and to obtain them, it is necessary that we should be engaged in lucrative pursuits, trades, and general business transactions. In order to be thus engaged, it is necessary that we should occupy positions that afford the facilities for such pursuits. To compete now with the mighty odds of wealth, social and religious preferences, and political influences of this country, at this advanced stage of its national existence, we never may expect. A new country, and new beginning, is the only true, rational, politic remedy for our disadvantageous position; and that country we have already pointed out, with triple golden advantages, all things considered, to that of any country to which it has been the province of man to embark.

Every other than we, have at various periods of necessity, been a migratory people; and all when oppressed, shown a greater abhorrence of oppression, if not a greater love of liberty, than we. We cling to our oppressors as the objects of our love. It is true that our enslaved brethren are here, and we have been led to believe that it is necessary for us to remain, on that account. Is it true, that all should remain in degradation, because a part are degraded? We believe no such thing. We believe it to be the duty of the Free, to elevate themselves in the most speedy and effective manner possible; as the redemption of the bondman depends entirely upon the elevation of the freeman; therefore, to elevate the free colored people of America, anywhere upon this continent; forebodes the speedy redemption of the slaves. We shall hope to hear no more of so fallacious a doctrine—the necessity of the free remaining in degradation, for the sake of the oppressed. Let us apply, first, the lever to ourselves; and the force that

elevates us to the position of manhood's considerations and honors, will cleft the manacle of every slave in the land.

When such great worth and talents—for want of a better sphere—of men like Rev. Jonathan Robinson, Robert Douglass, Frederick A. Hinton, and a hundred others that might be named, were permitted to expire in a barber-shop; and such living men as may be found in Boston, New York, Philadelphia, Baltimore, Richmond, Washington City, Charleston, (S.C.) New Orleans, Cincinnati, Louisville, St. Louis, Pittsburg, Buffalo, Rochester, Albany, Utica, Cleveland, Detroit, Milwaukie, Chicago, Columbus, Zanesville, Wheeling, and a hundred other places, confining themselves to Barber-shops and waiterships in Hotels; certainly the necessity of such a course as we have pointed out, must be cordially acknowledged; appreciated by every brother and sister of oppression; and not rejected as heretofore, as though they preferred inferiority to equality. These minds must become "unfettered," and have "space to rise." This cannot be in their present positions. A continuance in any position, becomes what is termed "Second Nature;" it begets an *adaptation*, and *reconciliation* of *mind* to such condition. It changes the whole physiological condition of the system, and adapts man and woman to a higher or lower sphere in the pursuits of life. The offsprings of slaves and peasantry, have the general characteristics of their parents; and nothing but a different course of training and education, will change the character.

The slave may become a lover of his master, and learn to forgive him for continual deeds of maltreatment and abuse; just as the Spaniel would couch and fondle at the feet that kick him; because he has been taught to reverence them, and consequently, becomes adapted in body and mind to his condition. Even the shrubbery-loving Canary, and lofty-soaring Eagle, may be tamed to the cage, and learn to love it from habit of confinement. It has been so with us in our position among our oppressors; we have been so prone to such positions, that we have learned to love them. When reflecting upon this all important, and to us, all absorbing subject; we feel in the agony and anxiety of the moment, as though we could cry out in the language of a Prophet of old: "Oh that my head were waters, and mine eyes a fountain of tears, that I might weep day and night for the" degradation "of my people! Oh that I had in the wilderness a lodging place of way-faring men; that I might leave my people, and go from them!"

The Irishman and German in the United States, are very different persons to what they were when in Ireland and Germany, the countries of their nativity. There their spirits were depressed and downcast; but the instant they set their foot upon unrestricted soil; free to act and untrammeled to move; their physical condition undergoes a change, which in time becomes physiological, which is transmitted to the offspring, who when born under such circumstances, is a decidedly different being to what it would have been, had it been born under different circumstances.

A child born under oppression, has all the elements of servility in its constitution; who when born under favorable circumstances, has to the contrary, all the elements of freedom and independence of feeling. Our children then, may not be expected, to maintain that position and manly bearing; born under the unfavorable circumstances with which we are surrounded in this country; that we so much desire. To use the language of the talented Mr. Whipper, "they cannot be raised in this country, without being stoop shouldered." Heaven's pathway stands unobstructed, which will lead us into a Paradise of bliss. Let us go on and possess the land, and the God of Israel will be our God.

The lessons of every schoolbook, the pages of every history, and columns of every newspaper, are so replete with stimuli to nerve us on to manly aspirations, that those of our young people, who will now refuse to enter upon this great theatre of Polynesian adventure, and take their position on the stage of Central and South America, where a brilliant engagement, of certain and most triumphant success, in the drama of human equality awaits them; then, with the blood of *slaves*, write upon the lintel of every door in sterling Capitals, to be gazed and hissed at by every passer by—

> Doomed by the Creator
> To servility and degradation;
> The SERVANT of the *white man,*
> And despised of every nation!

The Call of Providence to the Descendants of Africa in America

Edward W. Blyden

> Behold, the Lord thy God hath set the land before thee:
> go up and possess it, as the Lord God of thy fathers hath
> said unto thee; fear not, neither be discouraged.
>
> —Deuteronomy 1:21.

Among the descendants of Africa in this country the persuasion seems to prevail, though not now to the same extent as formerly, that they owe no special duty to the land of their forefathers; that their ancestors having been brought to this country against their will, and themselves having been born in the land, they are in duty bound to remain there and give their attention exclusively to the acquiring for themselves, and perpetuating to their posterity, social and political rights, notwithstanding the urgency of the call which their fatherland, by its forlorn and degraded moral condition, makes upon them for their assistance.

All other people feel a pride in their ancestral land, and do everything in their power to create for it, if it has not already, an honorable name. But many of the descendants of Africa, on the contrary, speak disparagingly of their country; are ashamed to acknowledge any connection with that land, and would turn indignantly upon any who would bid them go up and take possession of the land of their fathers.

It is a sad feature in the residence of Africans in this country, that it has begotten in them a forgetfulness of Africa—a want of sympathy with her in her moral and intellectual desolation, and a clinging to the land which

for centuries has been the scene of their thralldom. A shrewd European observer* of American society, says of the Negro in this country, that he "makes a thousand fruitless efforts to insinuate himself among men who repulse him; he conforms to the taste of his oppressors, adopts their opinions, and hopes by imitating them to form a part of their community. Having been told from infancy that his race is naturally inferior to that of the whites, he assents to the proposition, and is ashamed of his own nature. In each of his features he discovers a trace of slavery, and, if it were in his power, he would willingly rid himself of everything that makes him what he is."

It can not be denied that some very important advantages have accrued to the black man from his deportation to this land, but it has been at the expense of his manhood. Our nature in this country is not the same as it appears among the lordly natives of the interior of Africa, who have never felt the trammels of a foreign yoke. We have been dragged into depths of degradation. We have been taught a cringing servility. We have been drilled into contentment with the most undignified circumstances. Our finer sensibilities have been blunted. There has been an almost utter extinction of all that delicacy of feeling and sentiment which adorns character. The temperament of our souls has become harder or coarser, so that we can walk forth here, in this land of indignities, in ease and in complacen-

Source: Edward Wilmot Blyden, "The Call of Providence to the Descendents of Africa in America," in Edward W. Blyden, *Liberia's Offering* (New York: John A. Gray, 1862), 67–91.

*DeTocqueville, *Democracy in America* [Vol. I, p. 346].

cy, while our complexion furnishes ground for every species of social insult which an intolerant prejudice may choose to inflict.

But a change is coming over us. The tendency of events is directing the attention of the colored people to some other scene, and Africa is beginning to receive the attention, which has so long been turned away from her; and as she throws open her portals and shows the inexhaustible means of comfort and independence within, the black man begins to feel dissatisfied with the annoyances by which he is here surrounded, and looks with longing eyes to his fatherland. I venture to predict that, within a very brief period, that downtrodden land instead of being regarded with prejudice and distaste, will largely attract the attention and engage the warmest interest of every man of color. A few have always sympathized with Africa, but it has been an indolent and unmeaning sympathy—a sympathy which put forth no effort, made no sacrifices, endured no self-denial, braved no obloquy for the sake of advancing African interests. But the scale is turning, and Africa is becoming the all-absorbing topic.

It is my desire, on the present occasion, to endeavor to set before you the work which, it is becoming more and more apparent, devolves upon the black men of the United States; and to guide my thoughts, I have chosen the words of the text: "Behold, the Lord thy God hath set the land before thee: go up and possess it, as the Lord God of thy fathers hath said unto thee; fear not, neither be discouraged."

You will at once perceive that I do not believe that the work to be done by black men is in this country. I believe that their field of operation is in some other and distant scene. Their work is far nobler and loftier than that which they are now doing in this country. It is theirs to betake themselves to injured Africa, and bless those outraged shores, and quiet those distracted families with the blessings of Christianity and civilization. It is theirs to bear with them to that land the arts of industry and peace, and counteract the influence of those horrid abominations which an inhuman avarice has introduced—to roll back the appalling cloud of ignorance and superstition which overspreads the land, and to rear on the those shores an asylum of liberty for the down-trodden sons of Africa wherever found. This is the work to which Providence is obviously calling the black men of this country.

I am aware that some, against all experience, are hoping for the day when they will enjoy equal social and political rights in this land. We do not blame them for so believing and trusting. But we would remind them that there is a faith against reason, against experience, which consists in believing or pretending to believe very important propositions upon very slender proofs, and in maintaining opinions without any proper grounds. It ought to be clear to every thinking and impartial mind, that there can never occur in this country an equality, social or political, between whites and blacks. The whites have for a long time had the advantage. All the affairs of the country are in their hands. They make and administer the laws; they teach the schools; here, in the North, they ply all the trades, they own all the stores, they have possession of all the banks, they own all the ships and navigate them; they are the printers, proprietors, and editors of the leading newspapers, and they shape public opinion. Having always had the lead, they have acquired an ascendency they will ever maintain. The blacks have very few or no agencies in operation to counteract the ascendant influence of the Europeans. And instead of employing what little they have by a unity of effort to alleviate their condition, they turn all their power against themselves by their endless jealousies, and rivalries, and competition; everyone who is able to "pass" being emulous of a place among Europeans or Indians. This is the effect of their circumstances. It is the influence of the dominant class upon them. It argues no essential inferiority in them—no more than the disadvantages of the Israelites in Egypt argued their essential inferiority to the Egyptians. They are the weaker class overshadowed and depressed by the stronger. They are the feeble oak dwarfed by the overspreadings of a large tree, having not the advantage of rain, and sunshine, and fertilizing dews.

Before the weaker people God has set the land of their forefathers, and bids them go up and possess it without fear or discouragement. Before the tender plant he sets an open field, where, in the unobstructed air and sunshine, it may grow and flourish in all its native luxuriance.

There are two ways in which God speaks to men: one is by his word and the other by his providence. He has not sent any Moses, with signs and wonders, to cause an exodus of the descendants of Africa to their fatherland, yet he has loudly spoken to them as to their duty in the matter. He has spoken by his providence. First; By suffering them to be brought here and placed in circumstances where they could receive a training fitting them for the work of civilizing and evangelizing the land whence they were torn, and by preserving them under the severest trials and afflictions. Secondly; By allowing them, notwithstanding all the services they have rendered to this country, to be treated as strangers and aliens, so as to cause them to have anguish of spirit, as was the case with the Jews in Egypt, and to make them long for some refuge from their social and civil deprivations. Thirdly; By bearing a portion of them across the tempestuous seas back to Africa, by preserving them through the process of acclimation, and by establishing them in the land, despite the attempts of misguided men to drive them away. Fourthly; By keeping their fatherland in reserve for them in their absence.

The manner in which Africa has been kept from invasion is truly astounding. Known for ages, it is yet unknown. For centuries its inhabitants have been the victims of the cupidity of foreigners. The country has been rifled of its population. It has been left in some portions almost wholly unoccupied, but it has remained unmolested by foreigners. It has been very near the crowded countries of the world, yet none has relieved itself to any great extent of its overflowing population by seizing upon its domains. Europe, from the North, looks wishfully and with longing eyes across the narrow straits of Gilbraltar. Asia, with its teeming millions, is connected with us by an isthmus wide enough to admit of her throwing thousands into the country. But, notwithstanding the known wealth of the resources of the land, of which the report has gone into all the earth, there is still a terrible veil between us and our neighbors, the all-conquering Europeans, which they are only now essaying to lift; while the teeming millions of Asia have not even attempted to leave their boundaries to penetrate our borders. Neither alluring visions of glorious conquests, nor brilliant hopes of rapid enrichment, could induce them to invade the country. It has been preserved alike from the boastful civilization of Europe, and the effete and barbarous institutions of Asia. We call it, then, a Providential interposition, that while the owners of the soil have been abroad, passing through the fearful ordeal of a most grinding oppression, the land, though entirely unprotected, has lain uninvaded. We regard it as a providential call to Africans every where, to "go up and possess the land"; so that in a sense that is not merely constructive and figurative, but truly literal, God says to the black men of this country, with reference to Africa: "Behold, I set the land before you, go up and possess it."

Of course it can not be expected that this subject of the duty of colored men to go up and take possession of their fatherland, will be at once clear to every mind. Men look at objects from different points of view, and form their opinions according to the points from which they look, and are guided in their actions according to the opinions they form. As I have already said, the majority of exiled Africans do not seem to appreciate the great privilege of going and taking possession of the land. They seem to have lost all interest in that land, and to prefer living in subordinate and inferior positions in a strange land among oppressors, to encountering the risks involved in emigrating to a distant country. As I walk the streets of these cities, visit the hotels, go on board the steamboats, I am grieved to notice how much intelligence, how much strength and energy is frittered away in those trifling employments, which, if thrown into Africa, might elevate the millions of that land from their degradation, tribes at a time, and create an African power which would command the respect of the world, and place in the possession of Africans, its rightful owners, the wealth which is now diverted to other quarters. Most of the wealth that could be drawn from that land, during the last six centuries, has passed into the hands of Europeans, while many of Africa's own sons, sufficiently intelligent to control those immense resources, are sitting down in poverty and dependence in the land of strangers—exiles when they have so rich a domain from which they have never been expatriated, but which is willing, nay, anxious to welcome them home again.

We need some African power, some great center of the race where our physical, pecuniary, and intellectual strength may be collected. We need some spot whence such an influence may go forth in behalf of the race as shall be felt by the nations. We are now so scattered and divided that we can do nothing. The imposition begun last year by a foreign power upon Hayti, and which is still persisted in, fills every black man who has heard of it with indignation, but we are not strong enough to speak out effectually for that land. When the same power attempted an outrage upon the Liberians, there was no African power strong enough to interpose. So long as we remain thus divided, we may expect impositions. So long as we live simply by the sufferance of the nations, we must expect to be subject to their caprices.

Among the free portion of the descendants of Africa, numbering about four or five millions, there is enough talent, wealth, and enterprise, to form a respectable nationality on the continent of Africa. For nigh three hundred years their skill and industry have been expended in building up the southern countries of the New World, the poor, frail constitution of the Caucasian not allowing him to endure the fatigue and toil involved in such labors. Africans and their descendants have been the laborers, and the mechanics, and the artisans in the greater portion of this hemisphere. By the results of their labor the European countries have been sustained and enriched. All the cotton, coffee, indigo, sugar, tobacco, etc., which have formed the most important articles of European commerce, have been raised and prepared for market by the labor of the black man. Dr. Palmer of New-Orleans, bears the same testimony.* And all this labor they have done, for the most part not only without compensation, but with abuse, and contempt, and insult, as their reward.

Now, while Europeans are looking to our fatherland with such eagerness of desire, and are hastening to explore and take away its riches, ought not Africans in the Western hemisphere to turn their regards thither also? We need to collect the scattered forces of the race, and there is no rallying-ground more favorable than Africa. There

> No pent-up Utica contracts our powers,
> The whole boundless continent is ours.

Ours as a gift from the Almighty when he drove asunder the nations and assigned them their boundaries; and ours by peculiar physical adaptation.

An African nationality is our great need, and God tells us by his providence that he has set the land before us, and bids us go up and possess it. We shall never receive the respect of other races until we establish a powerful nationality. We should not content ourselves with living among other races, simply by their permission or their endurance, as Africans live in this country. We must build up Negro states; we must establish and maintain the various institutions; we must make and administer laws, erect and preserve churches, and support the worship of God; we must have governments; we must have legislation of our own; we must build ships and navigate them; we must ply the trades, instruct the schools, control the press, and thus aid in shaping the opinions and guiding the destinies of mankind. Nationality is an ordinance of Nature. The heart of every true Negro yearns after a distinct and separate nationality.

---

*In the famous sermon of this distinguished divine on *Slavery a Divine Trust*, he says: "The enriching commerce which has built the splendid cities and marble palaces of England as well as of America, has been largely established upon the products of Southern soil; and the blooms upon Southern fields, gathered by black hands, have fed the spindles and looms of Manchester and Birmingham not less than of Lawrence and Lowell."

Impoverished, feeble, and alone, Liberia is striving to establish and build up such a nationality in the home of the race. Can any descendant of Africa turn contemptuously upon a scene where such efforts are making? Would not every right-thinking Negro rather lift up his voice and direct the attention of his brethren to that land? Liberia, with outstretched arms, earnestly invites all to come. We call them forth out of all nations; we bid them take up their all and leave the countries of their exile, as of old the Israelites went forth from Egypt, taking with them their trades and their treasures, their intelligence, their mastery of arts, their knowledge of the sciences, their practical wisdom, and every thing that will render them useful in building up a nationality. We summon them from these States, from the Canadas, from the East and West-Indies, from South-America, from every where, to come and take part with us in our great work.

But those whom we call are under the influence of various opinions, having different and conflicting views of their relations and duty to Africa, according to the different stand-points they occupy. So it was with another people who, like ourselves, were suffering from the effects of protracted thralldom, when on the borders of the land to which God was leading them. When Moses sent out spies to search the land of Canaan, every man, on his return, seemed to be influenced in his report by his peculiar temperament, previous habits of thought, by the degree of his physical courage, or by something peculiar in his point of observation. All agreed, indeed, that it was an exceedingly rich land, "flowing with milk and honey," for they carried with them on their return, a proof of its amazing fertility. But a part, and a larger part, too, saw only giants and walled towns, and barbarians and cannibals. "Surely," said they, "it floweth with milk and honey. Nevertheless the people be strong that dwell in the land, and the cities are walled, and very great; and moreover we saw the children of Anak there. The land through which we have gone to search it, is a land that eateth up the inhabitants thereof; and all the people that we saw in it are men of a great stature. And there we saw the giants,

the sons of Anak, which come of the giants: and we were in our own sight as grasshoppers, and so we were in their sight." It was only a small minority of that company that saw things in a more favorable light. "Caleb stilled the people before Moses, and said, Let us go up at once and possess it; for we be well able to overcome it." (Numbers 13.)

In like manner there is division among the colored people of this country with regard to Africa, that land which the providence of God is bidding them go up and possess. Spies sent from different sections of this country by the colored people—and many a spy not commissioned—have gone to that land, and have returned and reported. Like the Hebrew spies, they have put forth diverse views. Most believe Africa to be a fertile and rich country, and an African nationality a desirable thing. But some affirm that the land is not fit to dwell in, for "it is a land that eateth up the inhabitants thereof," notwithstanding the millions of strong and vigorous aborigines who throng all parts of the country, and the thousands of colonists who are settled along the coast; some see in the inhabitants incorrigible barbarism, degradation, and superstition, and insuperable hostility to civilization; others suggest that the dangers and risks to be encountered, and the self-denial to be endured, are too great for the slender advantages which, as it appears to them, will accrue from immigration. A few only report that the land is open to us on every hand—that "every prospect pleases," and that the natives are so tractable that it would be a comparatively easy matter for civilized and Christianized black men to secure all the land to Christian law, liberty, and civilization.

I come to-day to defend the report of the minority. The thousands of our own race, emigrants from this country, settled for more than forty years in that land, agree with the minority report. Dr. Barth, and other travelers to the east and south-east of Liberia, indorse the sentiment of the minority, and testify to the beauty, and healthfulness, and productiveness of the country, and to the mildness and hospitality of its inhabitants. In Liberia we hear from natives, who are constantly coming to our settlements from the far interior, of land exuberantly fertile, of large, numerous, and wealthy tribes, athletic and industrious; not the descendants of Europeans—according to Bowen's insane theory—but *black* men, pure Negroes, who live in large towns, cultivate the soil, and carry on extensive traffic, maintaining amicable relations with each other and with men from a distance.

The ideas that formerly prevailed of the interior of Africa, which suited the purposes of poetry and sensation writing, have been proved entirely erroneous. Poets may no longer sing with impunity of Africa:

> A region of drought, where no river glides,
> Nor rippling brook with osiered sides;
> Where sedgy pool, nor bubbling fount,
> Nor tree, nor cloud, nor misty mount,
> Appears to refresh the aching eye,
> But barren earth and the burning sky,
> And the blank horizon round and round.

No; missionary and scientific enterprises have disproved such fallacies. The land possesses every possible inducement. That extensive and beauteous domain which God has given us appeals to us and to black men every where, by its many blissful and benignant aspects; by its flowery landscapes, its beautiful rivers, its serene and peaceful skies; by all that attractive and perennial verdure which overspreads the hills and valleys; by its every prospect lighted up by delightful sunshine; by all its natural charms, it calls upon us to rescue it from the grasp of remorseless superstition, and introduce the blessings of the Gospel.

But there are some among the intelligent colored people of this country who, while they profess to have great love for Africa, and tell us that their souls are kindled when they hear of their fatherland, yet object to going themselves, because, as they affirm, the black man has a work to accomplish in this land—he has a destiny to fulfill. He, the representative of Africa, like the representatives from various parts of Europe, must act his part in building up this great composite nation. It is not difficult to see what the work of the black man is in this land. The most inexperienced observer may at once read his destiny. Look at the various departments of society here in the *free* North; look at the different branches of industry, and see how the black man is aiding to build up this nation. Look at the hotels, the saloons, the steamboats, the barbershops, and see how successfully he is carrying out his destiny! And there is an extreme likelihood that such are forever to be the exploits which he is destined to achieve in this country until he merges his African peculiarities in the Caucasian.

Others object to the *climate* of Africa, first, that it is unhealthy, and secondly, that it is not favorable to intellectual progress. To the first, we reply that it is not more insalubrious than other new countries. Persons going to Africa, who have not been broken down as to their constitutions in this country, stand as fair a chance of successful acclimation as in any other country of large, unbroken forests and extensively uncleared lands. In all new countries there are sufferings and privations. All those countries which have grown up during the last two centuries, in this hemisphere, have had as a foundation the groans, and tears, and blood of the pioneers. But what are the sufferings of pioneers, compared with the greatness of the results they accomplish for succeeding generations? Scarcely any great step in human progress is made without multitudes of victims. Every revolution that has been effected, every nationality that has been established, every country that has been rescued from the abominations of savagism, every colony that has been planted, has involved perplexities and sufferings to the generation who undertook it. In the evangelization of Africa, in the erection of African nationalities, we can expect no exceptions. The man, then, who is not able to suffer and to die for his fellows when necessity requires it, is not fit to be a pioneer in this great work.

We believe, as we have said, that the establishment of an African nationality in Africa is the great need of the African race; and the men who have gone, or may hereafter go to assist in laying the foundations of empire, so far from being dupes, or cowards, or traitors, as some have ignorantly called them, are the truest heroes of the race. They are the soldiers rushing first into the breach—physicians who at the risk of their own lives are first to explore an infectious disease. How much more nobly do they act than those who have held for years that it is nobler to sit here and patiently suffer with our brethren! Such sentimental inactivity finds no respect in these days of rapid movement. The world sees no merit in mere innocence. The man who contents himself to sit down and exemplify the virtue of patience and endurance will find no sympathy from the busy, restless crowd that rush by him. Even the "sick man" must get out of the way when he hears the tramp of the approaching host, or be crushed by the heedless and massive car of progress. Blind Bartimeuses are silenced by the crowd. The world requires active service; it respects only productive workers. The days of hermits and monks have passed away. Action—work, work—is the order of the day. Heroes in the strife and struggle of humanity are the demand of the age.

> They who would be free, *themselves* must *strike* the blow.

With regard to the objection founded upon the unfavorableness of the climate to intellectual progress, I have only to say, that proper moral agencies, when set in operation, can not be overborne by physical causes. "We continually behold lower laws held in restraint by higher; mechanic by dynamic; chemical by vital; physical by moral."* It has not yet been proved that with the proper influences, the tropics will not produce men of "cerebral activity." Those races which have degenerated by a removal from the North to the tropics did not possess the proper moral power. They had in themselves the seed of degeneracy, and would have degenerated any where. It was not Anglo-Saxon blood, nor a temperate climate, that kept the first emigrants to this land from falling into the same indolence and inefficiency which have overtaken the European settlers in South-America, but the Anglo-Saxon Bible—the principles contained in that book, are the great conservative and elevating power. Man is the same, and the human mind is the same, whether existing beneath African suns or Arctic frosts. I can conceive of no difference. It is the moral influences brought to bear upon the man that make the difference in his progress.

"High degrees of moral sentiment," says a distinguished American writer,[†] "control the unfavorable influences of climate; and some of our grandest examples of men and of races come from the equatorial regions." Man is elevated by taking hold of that which is higher than himself. Unless this is done, climate, color, race, will avail nothing.

> —unless above himself he can
> Erect himself, how poor a thing is man!

For my own part, I believe that the brilliant world of the tropics, with its marvels of nature, must of necessity give to mankind a new career of letters, and new forms in the various arts, whenever the millions of men at present uncultivated shall enjoy the advantages of civilization.

Africa will furnish a development of civilization which the world has never yet witnessed. Its great peculiarity will be its moral element. The Gospel is to achieve some of its most beautiful triumphs in that land. "God shall enlarge Japheth, and he shall dwell in the tents of Shem," was the blessing upon the European and Asiatic races. Wonderfully have these predictions been fulfilled. The all-conquering descendants of Japheth have gone to every clime, and have planted themselves on almost every shore. By means fair and unfair, they have spread themselves, have grown wealthy and powerful. They have been truly "enlarged." God has "dwelt in the tents of Shem," for so some understand the passage. The Messiah—God manifest in the flesh—was of the tribe of Judah. He was born and dwelt in the tents of Shem. The promise to Ethiopia, or Ham, is like that to Shem, of a spiritual kind. It refers not to physical strength, not to large and extensive domains, not to foreign conquests, not to wide-spread domination, but to the possession of spiritual

---

* Dean Trench, quoted by Baden Powell in *Essays and Reviews*, 1861.

[†] R. W. Emerson, in the *Atlantic Monthly*, April, 1862.

qualities, to the elevation of the soul heavenward, to spiritual aspirations and divine communications. "Ethiopia shall stretch forth her hands unto God." Blessed, glorious promise! Our trust is not to be in chariots or horses, not in our own skill or power, but our help is to be in the name of the Lord. And surely, in reviewing our history as a people, whether we consider our preservation in the lands of our exile, or the preservation of our fatherland from invasion, we are compelled to exclaim: "Hitherto hath the Lord helped us!" Let us, then, fear not the influences of climate. Let us go forth stretching out our hands to God, and if it be as hot as Nebuchadnezzar's furnace, there will be one in the midst like unto the Son of God, counteracting its deleterious influences.

Behold, then, the Lord our God has set the land before us, with its burning climate, with its privations, with its moral, intellectual, and political needs, and by his providence he bids us go up and possess it without fear or discouragement. Shall we go up at his bidding? If the black men of this country, through unbelief or indolence, or for any other cause, fail to lay hold of the blessings which God is proffering to them, and neglect to accomplish the work which devolves upon them, the work will be done, but others will be brought in to do it, and to take possession of the country.

For while the colored people here are tossed about by various and conflicting opinions as to their duty to that land, men are going thither from other quarters of the globe. They are entering the land from various quarters with various motives and designs, and may eventually so preöccupy the land as to cut us off from the fair inheritance which lies before us, unless we go forth without further delay and establish ourselves.

The enterprise and energy manifested by white men who, with uncongenial constitutions, go from a distance to endeavor to open up that land to the world, are far from creditable to the civilized and enlightened colored men of the United States, when contrasted with their indifference in the matter. A noble army of self-expatriated evangelists have gone to that land from Europe and America; and, while anxious to extend the blessings of true religion, they have in no slight degree promoted the cause of science and commerce. Many have fallen, either from the effects of the climate or by the hands of violence;* still the interest in the land is by no means diminished. The enamored worshiper of science, and the Christian philanthropist, are still laboring to solve the problem of African geography, and to elevate its benighted tribes. They are not only disclosing to the world the mysteries of regions hitherto unexplored, but tribes whose very existence had not before been known to the civilized world have been brought, through their instrumentality, into contact with civilization and Christianity. They have discovered in the distant portions of that land countries as productive as any in Europe and America. They have informed the world of bold and lofty mountains, extensive lakes, noble rivers, falls rivaling Niagara, so that, as a result of their arduous, difficult, and philanthropic labors of exploration, the cause of Christianity, ethnology, geography, and commerce has been, in a very important degree, subserved.

Dr. Livingstone, the indefatigable African explorer, who, it is estimated, has passed over not less than eleven thousand miles of African ground, speaking of the motives which led him to those shores, and still keep him there in spite of privations and severe afflictions, says:

---

* The names of John Ledyard, Frederick Horneman, Dr. Walter Oudney, Captain Clapperton, Major Denman, John Richardson, and Dr. Overweg occur in the list of those who have fallen victims either to the climate of the hardships of their pilgrimage. But a more melancholy enumeration may be made. Major Houghton perished, or was murdered, in the basin of the Gambia. The truly admirable Mungo Park was killed in an attack of the natives, at a difficult passage of the Niger. The same fate befell Richard Lander in the lower course of the river. Major Laing was foully slain in his tent at a halting-place in the Sahara. John Davidson was assassinated soon after passing the fringe of the desert. Dr. Cowan and Captain Donovan disappeared in the wilds of South-Africa. Dr. Vogel was assassinated in the country about Lake Chad.—*Leisure Hour.*

I expect to find for myself no large fortune in that country; nor do I expect to explore any large portions of a new country; but I do hope to find a pathway, by means of the river Zambesi, which may lead to highlands, where Europeans may form a settlement, and where, by opening up communication and establishing commercial intercourse with the natives of Africa, they may slowly, but not the less surely, impart to the people of that country the knowledge and inestimable blessings of Christianity.

The recently formed Oxford, Cambridge, and Dublin Missionary Society state their object to be to spread Christianity among the untaught people of Central Africa, "so to operate among them as by mere teaching and influence to help *to build up native Christian states.*" The idea of building up "native Christian states" is a very important one, and is exactly such an idea as would be carried out if there were a large influx of civilized blacks from abroad.

I am sorry to find that among some in this country, the opinion prevails that in Liberia a distinction is maintained between the colonists and the aborigines, so that the latter are shut out from the social and political privileges of the former. No candid person who has read the laws of Liberia, or who has visited that country, can affirm or believe such a thing. The idea no doubt arises from the fact that the aborigines of a country generally suffer from the settling of colonists among them. But the work of Liberia is somewhat different from that of other colonies which have been planted on foreign shores. The work achieved by other emigrants has usually been—the enhancement of their own immediate interests; the increase of their physical comforts and conveniences; the enlargement of their borders by the most speedy and available methods, without regard to the effect such a course might have upon the aborigines. Their interests sometimes coming into direct contact with those of the owners of the soil, they have not unfrequently, by their superior skill and power, reduced the poor native to servitude or complete annihilation. The Israelites could live in peace in the land of Canaan only by ex-

terminating the indigenous inhabitants. The colony that went out from Phenicia, and that laid the foundations of empire on the northern shores of Africa, at first paid a yearly tax to the natives; with the increasing wealth and power of Carthage, however, the respective conditions of the Carthaginians and the natives were changed, and the Phenician adventurers assumed and maintained a dominion over the Lybians. The colonies from Europe which landed at Plymouth Rock, at Boston, and at Jamestown—which took possession of the West-India islands and of Mexico, treated the aborigines in the same manner. The natives of India, Australia, and New-Zealand are experiencing a similar treatment under the overpowering and domineering rule of the Anglo-Saxons. Eagerness for gain and the passion for territorial aggrandisement have appeared to the colonists necessary to their growth and progress.

The work of Liberia, as I have said, is different and far nobler. We, on the borders of our fatherland, can not, as the framers of our Constitution wisely intimated, allow ourselves to be influenced by "avaricious speculations," or by desires for "territorial aggrandisement." Our work there is moral and intellectual as well as physical. We have to work upon the *people,* as well as upon the *land*—upon *mind* as well as upon *matter.* Our prosperity depends as much upon the wholesome and elevating influence we exert upon the native population, as upon the progress we make in agriculture, commerce, and manufacture. Indeed the conviction prevails in Liberia among the thinking people that we can make no important progress in these things without the coöperation of the aborigines. We believe that no policy can be more suicidal in Liberia than that which would keep aloof from the natives around us. We believe that our life and strength will be to elevate and incorporate them among us as speedily as possible.

And, then, the aborigines are not a race alien from the colonists. We are a part of them. When alien and hostile races have come together, as we have just seen, one has had to succumb to the other; but when different peoples of the same family have been brought together, there has invariably been a fusion, and the result has been an improved and powerful class. When three branches of the great Teutonic family met on the soil of England, they united. It is true that at first there was a distinction of caste among them in consequence of the superiority in every respect of the great Norman people; but, as the others came up to their level, the distinctions were quietly effaced, and Norman, Saxon, and Dane easily amalgamated. Thus, "a people inferior to none existing in the world was formed by the mixture of three branches of the great Teutonic family with each other and the aboriginal Britons."*

In America we see how readily persons from all parts of Europe assimilate; but what great difficulty the Negro, the Chinese, and the Indian experience! We find here representatives from all the nations of Europe easily blending with each other. But we find elements that will not assimilate. The Negro, the Indian, and the Chinese, who do not belong to the same family, repel each other, and are repelled by the Europeans. "The antagonistic elements are in contact, but refuse to unite, and as yet no agent has been found sufficiently potent to reduce them to unity."

But the case with Americo-Liberians and the aborigines is quite different. We are all descendants of Africa. In Liberia there may be found persons of almost every tribe in West-Africa, from Senegal to Congo. And not only do we and the natives belong to the same race, but we are also of the same family. The two peoples can no more be kept from assimilating and blending than water can be kept from mingling with its kindred elements. The policy of Liberia is to diffuse among them as rapidly as possible the principles of Christianity and civilization, to prepare them to take an active part in the duties of the nationality which we are endeavoring to erect. Whence, then, comes the slander which represents Liberians as "maintaining a distance from the aborigines—a constant and uniform separation"?

To take part in the noble work in which they are engaged on that coast, the government and people of Liberia earnestly invite

*Macaulay's *History of England*, vol. i. chap. 1.

the descendants of Africa in this country.† In all our feebleness, we have already accomplished something; but very little in comparison of what has to be done. A beginning has been made, however—a great deal of preparatory work accomplished. And if the intelligent and enterprising colored people of this country would emigrate in large numbers, an important work would be done in a short time. And we know exactly the kind of work that would be done. We know that where now stand unbroken forests would spring up towns and villages, with their schools and churches—that the natives would be taught the arts of civilization—that their energies would be properly directed—that their prejudices would disappear—that there would be a rapid and important revulsion from the practices of heathenism, and a radical change in their social condition—that the glorious principles of a Christian civilization would diffuse themselves throughout those benighted communities. Oh! that our people would take this matter into serious consideration, and think of the great privilege of kindling in the depths of the moral and spiritual gloom of Africa a glorious light—of causing the wilderness and the solitary place to be glad—the desert to bloom and blossom as the rose—and the whole land to be converted into a garden of the Lord.

Liberia, then, appeals to the colored men of this country for assistance in the noble work which she has begun. She appeals to those who believe that the descendants of Africa live in the serious neglect of their duty if they fail to help to raise the land of their forefathers from her degradation. She appeals to those who believe that a well-established African nationality is the most direct and efficient means of securing respectability

†The Legislature of Liberia, at its last session, 1861–62, passed an Act authorizing the appointment of Commissioners to "itinerate among and lecture to the people of color in the United States of North-America, to present to them the claims of Liberia, and its superior advantages as a desirable home for persons of African descent." The President appointed for this work, Professors Crummell and Blyden and J. D. Johnson, Esq.

and independence for the African race. She appeals to those who believe that a rich and fertile country, like Africa, which has lain so long under the cheerless gloom of ignorance, should not be left any longer without the influence of Christian civilization—to those who deem it a far more glorious work to save extensive tracts of country from barbarism and continued degradation than to amass for themselves the means of individual comfort and aggrandizement—to those who believe that there was a providence in the deportation of our forefathers from the land of their birth, and that that same providence now points to a work in Africa to be done by us their descendants. Finally, Liberia appeals to all African patriots and Christians—to all lovers of order and refinement—to lovers of industry and enterprise—of peace, comfort, and happiness—to those who having felt the power of the Gospel in opening up to them life and immortality, are desirous that their benighted kindred should share in the same blessings. "Behold, the Lord thy God hath set the land before thee: go up and possess it, as the Lord God of thy fathers hath said unto thee; fear not, neither be discouraged"— 1862.

The African Problem and the Method of Its Solution

Edward W. Blyden

I am seriously impressed with a sense of the responsibility of my position to-night. I stand in the presence of the representatives of that great organization which seems first of all the associations in this country to have distinctly recognized the hand of God in the history of the Negro race in America—to have caught something of the meaning of the Divine purpose in permitting their exile to and bondage in this land. I stand also in the presence of what, for the time being at least, must be considered the foremost congregation of the land—the religious home of the President of the United States. There are present, also, I

Source: Edward W. Blyden "The African Problem and the Method of Its Solution" in annual discourse delivered at the seventy-third anniversary of the American Colonization Society Washington, D.C., 18 January 1890 (Washington, D.C.: n.p., 1890).

learn, on this occasion, some of the statesmen and lawmakers of the land.

My position, then, is one of honor as well as of responsibility, and the message I have to deliver, I venture to think, concerns directly or indirectly the whole human race. I come from that ancient country, the home of one of the great original races, occupied by the descendants of one of the three sons to whom, according to Biblical history, the whole world was assigned—a country which is now engaging the active attention of all Europe. I come, also, from the ancestral home of at least five millions in this land. Two hundred millions of people have sent me on an errand of invitation to their blood relations here. Their cry is, "Come over and help us." And I find among hundreds of thousands of the invited an eager and enthusiastic response. They tell me to wave the answer across the deep to the anxious and expectant hearts, which, during the long and weary night of separation, have been constantly watching and praying for the return—to the Rachels weeping for their children, and refusing to be comforted because they are not—they tell me, "Wave the answer back to our brethren to hold the fort for we are coming." They have for the last seventy years been returning through the agency of the Society whose anniversary we celebrate to-night. Some have gone every year during that period, but they have been few compared to the vast necessity. They have gone as they have been able to go, and are making an impression for good upon that continent. My subject to-night will be, The African Problem and the Method of its Solution.

This is no new problem. It is nearly as old as recorded history. It has interested thinking men in Europe and Asia in all ages. The imagination of the ancients peopled the interior of that country with a race of beings shut out from and needing no intercourse with the rest of mankind lifted by their purity and simplicity of character above the necessity of intercourse with other mortals—leading a blameless and protracted existence and producing in their sequestered, beautiful, and fertile home, from which flowed the wonderful Nile, the food of the Gods. Not milk and honey but nectar and ambrosia were supposed to abound there. The Greeks especially had very high conceptions of the sanctity and spirituality of the interior Africans. The greatest of their poets picture the Gods as vacating Olympus every year and proceeding to Ethiopia to be feasted by its inhabitants. Indeed, the religion of some portion of Greece is supposed to have been introduced from Africa. But leaving the region of mythology, we know that the three highest religions known to mankind—if they had not their origin in Africa—were domiciled there in the days of their feeble beginnings, Judaism, Christianity, and Mohammedanism.

A sacred mystery hung over that continent, and many were the aspirations of philosophers and poets for some definite knowledge of what was beyond the narrow fringe they saw. Julius Caesar, fascinated while listening to a tale of the Nile, lost the vision of military glory. The philosopher overcame the soldier and he declared himself ready to abandon for a time the alluring fields of politics in order to trace out the sources of that mysterious river which gave to mankind Egypt with her magnificent conceptions and splendid achievements.

The mystery still remains. The problem continues unsolved. The conquering races of the world stand perplexed and worried before the difficulties which beset their enterprise of reducing that continent to subjection. They have overcome the whole of the Western Hemisphere. From Behring Straits to Cape Horn America has submitted to their sway. The native races have almost disappeared from the mainland and the islands of the sea. Europe has extended her conquests to Australia, New Zealand, and the Archipelagos of the Pacific. But, for hundreds of years, their ships have passed by those tempting regions, where "Afric's sunny fountains roll down their golden sands," and though touching at different points on the coast, they have been able to acquire no extensive foothold in that country. Notwithstanding the reports we receive on every breeze that blows from the East, of vast "spheres of influence" and large European possessions, the points actually occupied by white men in the boundless equatorial regions of that immense continent may be accurately represented on the map only by microscopic dots. I wish that the announcements we receive from time to time with such a flourish of trumpets, that a genuine civilization is being carried into the heart of the Dark Continent, were true. But the fact is, that the bulk of Central Africa is being rapidly subjected to Mohammedanism. That system will soon be—or rather is now—knitting together the conquerors and the conquered into a harmonious whole; and unless Europe gets a thorough understanding of the situation, the gates of missionary enterprise will be closed; because, from all we can learn of the proceedings of some, especially in East Africa, the industrial *régime* is being stamped out to foster the militant. The current number of the *Fortnightly*, near the close of an interesting article on "Stanley's Expedition," has this striking sentence: "Stanley has triumphed, but Central Africa is darker than ever!"

It would appear that the world outside of Africa has not yet stopped to consider the peculiar conditions which lift that continent out of the range of the ordinary agencies by which Europe has been able to occupy other countries and subjugate or exterminate their inhabitants.

They have not stopped to ponder the providential lessons on this subject scattered through the pages of history, both past and contemporary.

First. Let us take the most obvious lesson as indicated in the climatic conditions. Perhaps in no country in the world is it so necessary (as in Africa) that the stranger or new comer should possess the *mens sana in corpore sano*—the sound mind in sound body; for the climate is most searching, bringing to the surface any and every latent physical or mental defect. If a man has any chronic or hereditary disease it is sure to be developed, and if wrong medical treatment is applied it is very apt to be exaggerated and often to prove fatal to the patient. And as with the body so with the mind. Persons of weak minds, either inherited or brought on by excessive mental application or troubles of any kind, are almost sure to develop an impatience or irritability, to the surprise and annoyance of their friends who knew them at home. The Negro immigrant from a temperate region sometimes suffers from these climatic inconveniences, only in his case, after a brief process of acclimatization, he becomes himself again, while the white man never regains his soundness in that climate, and can retain his mental equilibrium only by periodical visits to his native climate. The regulation of the British Government for West Africa is that their officials are allowed six months' leave of absence to return to Europe after fifteen month's residence at Sierra Leone and twelve months on the Gold Coast or Lagos; and for every three days during which they are kept on the coast after the time for their leave arrives, they are allowed one day in Europe. The neglect of this regulation is often attended with most serious consequences.

Second. When we come into the moral and intellectual world it would seem as if the Almighty several times attempted to introduce the foreigner and a foreign civilization into Africa and then changed his purpose. The Scriptures seem to warrant the idea that in some way inexplicable to us, and incompatible with our conception of the character of the Sovereign of the Universe, the unchangeable Being sometimes reverses His apparent plans. We read that, "it repented God," &c. For thousands of years the northeastern portion of Africa witnessed a wonderful development of civilization. The arts and sciences flourished in Egypt for generations, and that country was the centre of almost universal influence; but there was no effect produced upon the interior of Africa. So North Africa became the seat of a great military and commercial power which flourished for 700 years. After this the Roman Catholic Church constructed a mighty influence in the same region, but the interior of the continent received no impression from it.

In the fifteenth century the Congo country, of which we now hear so much, was the scene of extensive operations of the Roman Catholic Church. Just a little before the discovery of America thousands of the natives of the Congo, including the most influential families, were baptized by Catholic missionaries; and the Portuguese, for a hundred years, devoted themselves to the work of African evangelization and exploration. It would appear that they knew just as much of interior Africa as is known now after the great exploits of Speke and Grant and Livingstone, Baker and Cameron and Stanley. It is said that there is a map in the Vatican, three hundred years old, which gives all the general physical relief and the river and lake systems of Africa with more or less accuracy; but the Arab geographers of a century before had described the mountain system, the great lakes, and the course of the Nile.

Just about the time that Portugal was on the way to establish a great empire on that continent, based upon the religious system of Rome, America was discovered, and, instead of the Congo, the Amazon became the seat of Portuguese power. Neither Egyptian, Carthaginian, Persian, or Roman influence was allowed to establish itself on that continent. It would seem that in the providential purpose no solution of the African problem was to come from alien sources. Africans were not doomed to share the fate of some other dark races who have come in contact with the aggressive European. Europe was diverted to the Western Hemisphere. The energies of that conquering race, it was decreed, should be spent in building up a home for themselves on this side. Africa followed in chains.

The Negro race was to be preserved for a special and important work in the future. Of the precise nature of that work no one can form any definite conception. It is probable that if foreign races had been allowed to enter their country they would have been destroyed. So they were brought over to be helpers in this country and at the same time to be preserved. It was not the first time in the history of the world that a people have been preserved by subjection to another people. We know that God promised Abraham that his seed should inherit the land of Canaan; but when He saw that in their numerically weak condition they would have been destroyed in conflicts with the indigenous inhabitants, he took them down to Egypt and kept them there in bondage four hundred years that they might be fitted, both by discipline and numerical increase, for the work that would devolve upon them. Slavery would seem to be a strange school in which to preserve a people; but God has a way of salting as well as purifying by fire.

The Europeans, who were fleeing from their own country in search of wider areas of freedom and larger scope for development, found here an aboriginal race unable to cooperate with them in the labors required for the construction of the material framework of the new civilization. The Indians would not work, and they have suffered the consequences of that indisposition. They have passed away. To take their place as accessories in the work to be done God suffered the African to be brought hither, who could work and would work, and could endure the climatic conditions of a new southern country, which Europeans could not. Two currents set across the Atlantic towards the west for nigh three hundred years—the one from Europe, the other from Africa. The one from Africa had a crimson color. From that stream of human beings millions fell victims to the cruelties of the middle passage, and otherwise suffered from the brutal instincts of their kidnappers and enslavers. I do not know whether Africa has been invited to the celebration of the fourth centenary of the discovery of America; but she has quite as much reason, if not as much right, to participate in the demonstration of that occasion as the European nations. Englishman, Hollander, and Huguenot, Nigritian and Congo came together. If Europe brought the head, Africa furnished the hands for a great portion of the work which has been achieved here, though it was the opinion of an African chief that the man who discovered America ought to have been imprisoned for having uncovered one people for destruction and opened a field for the oppression and suffering of another.

But when the new continent was opened Africa was closed. The veil, which was being drawn aside, was replaced, and darkness once more enveloped the land, for then not the *country* but the *people* were needed. They were to do a work elsewhere, and meanwhile their country was to be shut out from the view of the outside world.

The first Africans landed in this country in the State of Virginia in the year 1619. Then began the first phase of what is called the Negro problem. These people did not come hither of their own accord. Theirs was not a voluntary but a compulsory expatriation. The problem, then, on their arrival in this country, which confronted the white people was how to reduce to effective and profitable servitude an alien race which it was neither possible nor desirable to assimilate. This gave birth to that peculiar institution, established in a country whose *raison d'être* was that all men might enjoy the "right to life, liberty, and the pursuit of happiness." Laws had to be enacted by Puritans, Cavaliers, and Roundheads for slaves, and every contrivance had to be devised for the safety of the institution. It was a difficult problem, in the effort to solve which both master and slave suffered.

It would seem, however, that in the first years of African slavery in this country, the masters upon many of whom the relationship was forced, understood its providential origin and purpose, until after a while, avarice and greed darkened their perceptions, and they began to invent reasons, drawn even from the Word of God, to justify their holding these people in perpetual bondage for the advantage of themselves and their children forever. But even after a blinding cupidity had captured the generality by its bewitching spell, there were those (far-sighted men, especially after the yoke of Great Britain had been thrown off) who saw that the abnormal relation could not be permanent under the democratic conditions established by the fundamental law of the land. It was Thomas Jefferson, the writer of the Declaration of Independence, who made the celebrated utterance: "Nothing is more clearly written in the Book of Destiny than the emancipation of the blacks; and it is equally certain that the two races will never live in a state of equal freedom under the same Government, so insurmountable are the barriers which nature, habit, and opinion have established between them."

For many years, especially in the long and weary period of the anti-slavery conflict, the latter part of this dictum of Jefferson was denounced by many good and earnest men. The most intelligent of the colored people resented it as a prejudiced and anti-Christian conception. But as the years go by and the Negroes rise in education and culture, and therefore in love and pride of race, and in proper conception of race gifts, race work and race destiny, the latter clause of that famous sentence is not only being shorn of its obscurity and repulsiveness, but is being welcomed as embodying a truth indispensable to the preservation and prosperity of both races, and as pointing to the regeneration of the African Fatherland. There are some others of the race who, recognizing Jefferson's principle, would make the races one by amalgamation.

It was under the conviction of the truth expressed by that statesman that certain gentlemen of all political shades and differing religious views, met together in this city in the winter of 1816–'17, and organized the American Colonization Society. Though friendly to the anti-slavery idea, and anxious for the extinction of the abnormal institution, these men did not make their views on that subject prominent in their published utterances. They were not Abolitionists in the political or technical sense of that phrase. But their labors furnished an outlet and encouragement for persons desiring to free their slaves, giving them the assurance that their freedmen would be returned to their Fatherland, carrying thither what light of Christianity and civilization they had received. It seems a pity that this humane, philanthropic, and far-seeing work should have met with organized opposition from another band of philanthropists, who, anxious for a speedy deliverance of the captives, thought they saw in the Colonization Society an agency for riveting instead of breaking the fetters of the slave, and they denounced it with all the earnestness and eloquence they could command, and they commanded, both among whites and blacks, some of the finest orators the country has ever produced. And they did a grand work, both directly and indirectly, for the Negro and for Africa. They did their work and dissolved their organization. But when their work was done the work of the Colonization Society really began.

In the development of the Negro question in this country the colonizationists might be called the prophets and philosophers; the abolitionists, the warriors and politicians. Colonizationists saw what was coming and patiently prepared for its advent. Abolitionists attacked the first phase of the Negro problem and labored for its immediate solution; colonizationists looked to the last phase of the problem and labored to get both the whites and blacks ready for it. They labored on two continents, in America and in Africa. Had they not begun as early as they did to take up lands in Africa for the exiles, had they waited for the abolition of slavery, it would now have been impossible to obtain a foothold in their fatherland for the returning hosts. The colonizationist, as prophet, looked at the State as it would be; the abolitionist, as politician, looked at the State as it was. The politician sees the present and is possessed by it. The prophet sees the future and gathers inspiration from it. The politician may influence legislation; the prophet, although exercising great moral influence, seldom has any legislative power. The agitation of the politician may soon culminate in legal enactments; the teachings of the prophet may require generations before they find embodiment in action. The politician has to-day; the prophet, to-morrow. The politician deals with facts, the prophet with ideas, and ideas take root very slowly. Though nearly three generations have passed away since Jefferson made his utterance, and more than two since the organization of the Colonization Society, yet the conceptions they put forward can scarcely be said to have gained maturity, much less currency, in the public mind. But the recent discussions in the halls of Congress show that the teachings of the prophet are now beginning to take hold of the politician. It may take many years yet before the people come up to these views, and, therefore, before legislation upon them may be possible, but there is evidently movement in that direction.

The first phase of the Negro problem was solved at Appomattox, after the battle of the warrior, with confused noise and garments rolled in blood. The institution of slavery, for which so many sacrifices had been made, so many of the principles of humanity had been violated, so many of the finer sentiments of the heart had been stifled, was at last destroyed by violence.

Now the nation confronts the second phase, the educational, and millions are being poured out by State governments and by individual philanthropy for the education of the freedmen, preparing them for the third and last phase of the problem, viz: EMIGRATION.

In this second phase, we have that organization, which might be called the successor of the old Anti-Slavery Society, taking most active and effective part. I mean the American Missionary Association. I have watched with constant gratitude and admiration the course and operations of that Society, especially when I remember that, organized in the dark days of slavery, twenty years before emancipation, it held aloft courageously the banner on

which was inscribed freedom for the Negro and no fellowship with his oppressors. And they, among the first, went South to lift the freedmen from the mental thraldom and moral degradation in which slavery had left him. They triumphed largely over the spirit of their opponents. They braved the dislike, the contempt, the apprehension with which their work was at first regarded, until they succeeded by demonstrating the advantages of knowledge over ignorance, to bring about that state of things to which Mr. Henry Grady, in his last utterances, was able to refer with such satisfaction, viz., that since the war the South has spent $122,000,000 in the cause of public education, and this year it is pledged to spend $37,000,000, in the benefits of which the Negro is a large participant.

It is not surprising that some of those who, after having been engaged in the noble labors of solving the first phase of the problem—in the great anti-slavery war—and are now confronting the second phase, should be unable to receive with patience the suggestion of the third, which is the emigration phase, when the Negro, freed in body and in mind, shall bid farewell to these scenes of his bondage and discipline and betake himself to the land of his fathers, the scene of larger opportunities and loftier achievements. I say it is not surprising that the veterans of the past and the present should be unable to give much enthusiasm to the work of the future. It is not often given to man to labor successfully in the land of Egypt, in the wilderness and across the Jordan. Some of the most effective workers, must often, with eyes undimmed and natural force unabated, lie down and die on the borders of full freedom, and if they live, life to them is like a dream. The young must take up the work. To old men the indications of the future are like a dream. Old men are like them that dream. Young men see visions. They catch the spirit of the future and are able to place themselves in accord with it.

But things are not yet ready for the solution of the third and last phase of the problem. Things are not ready in this country among whites or blacks. The industrial condition of the South is not prepared for it. Things are not yet ready in Africa for a complete exodus. Europe is not yet ready; she still thinks that she can take and utilize Africa for her own purposes. She does not yet understand that Africa is to be for the African or for nobody. Therefore she is taking up with renewed vigor, and confronting again, with determination, the African problem. Englishmen, Germans, Italians, Belgians, are taking up territory and trying to wring from the grey-haired mother of civilization the secret of the ages. Nothing has come down from Egypt so grand and impressive as the Sphinxes that look at you with calm and emotionless faces, guarding their secret to-day as they formerly guarded the holy temples. They are a symbol of Africa. She will not be forced. She only can reveal her secret. Her children trained in the house of bondage will show it to the world. Some have already returned and have constructed an independent nation as a beginning of this work on her western borders.

It is a significant fact that Africa was completely shut up until the time arrived for the emancipation of her children in the Western World. When Jefferson and Washington and Hamilton and Patrick Henry were predicting and urging the freedom of the slave, Mungo Park was beginning that series of explorations by English enterprise which has just ended in the expedition of Stanley. Just about the time that England proclaimed freedom throughout her colonies, the brothers Lander made the great discovery of the mouth of the Niger; and when Lincoln issued the immortal proclamation, Livingstone was unfolding to the world that wonderful region which Stanley has more fully revealed and which is becoming now the scene of the secular and religious activities of Christendom. The King of the Belgians has expended fortunes recently in opening the Congo and in introducing the appliances of civilization, and by a singular coincidence a bill has been brought forward in the U.S. Senate to assist the emigration of Negroes to the Fatherland just at the time when that philanthropic monarch has despatched an agent to this country to invite the co-operation in his great work of qualified freedmen. This is significant.

What the King of the Belgians has just done is an indication of what other European

Powers will do when they have exhausted themselves in costly experiments to utilize white men as colonists in Africa. They will then understand the purpose of the Almighty in having permitted the exile and bondage of the Africans, and they will see that for Africa's redemption the Negro is the chosen instrument. They will encourage the establishment and building up of such States as Liberia. They will recognize the scheme of the Colonization Society as the providential one.

The little nation which has grown up on that coast as a result of the efforts of this Society, is now taking hold upon that continent in a manner which, owing to inexperience, it could not do in the past. The Liberians have introduced a new article into the commerce of the world—the Liberian coffee. They are pushing to the interior, clearing up the forests, extending the culture of coffee, sugar, cocoa, and other tropical articles, and are training the aborigines in the arts of civilization and in the principles of Christianity. The Republic occupies five hundred miles of coast with an elastic interior. It has a growing commerce with various countries of Europe and America. No one who has visited that country and has seen the farms on the banks of the rivers and in the interior, the workshops, the schools, the churches, and other elements and instruments of progress will say that the United States, through Liberia, is not making a wholesome impression upon Africa—an impression which, if the members of the American Congress understood, they would not begrudge the money required to assist a few hundred thousand to carry on in that country the work so well begun. They would gladly spare them from the laboring element of this great nation to push forward the enterprises of civilization in their Fatherland, and to build themselves up on the basis of their race manhood.

If there is an intelligent Negro here tonight I will say to him, let me take you with me in imagination to witness the new creation or development on that distant shore; I will not paint you an imaginary picture, but will describe an historical fact; I will tell you of reality. Going from the coast, through those depressing alluvial plains which fringe the eastern and western borders of the continent, you reach, after a few miles' travel, the first high or undulating country, which, rising abruptly from the swamps, enchants you with its solidity, its fertility, its verdure, its refreshing and healthful breezes. You go further, and you stand upon a higher elevation where the wind sings more freshly in your ears, and your heart beats fast as you survey the continuous and unbroken forests that stretch away from your feet to the distant horizon. The melancholy cooing of the pigeons in some unseen retreat or the more entrancing music of livelier and picturesque songsters alone disturb the solemn and almost oppressive solitude. You hear no human sound and see the traces of no human presence. You decline to pursue your adventurous journey. You refuse to penetrate the lonely forest that confronts you. You return to the coast, thinking of the long ages which have elapsed, the seasons which, in their onward course, have come and gone, leaving those solitudes undisturbed. You wonder when and how are those vast wildernesses to be made the scene of human activity and to contribute to human wants and happiness. Finding no answer to your perplexing question you drop the subject from your thoughts. After a few years—a very few it may be—you return to those scenes. To your surprise and gratification your progress is no longer interrupted by the inconvenience of bridle-paths and tangled vines. The roads are open and clear. You miss the troublesome creeks and drains which, on your previous journey, harassed and fatigued you. Bridges have been constructed, and without any of the former weariness you find yourself again on the summit, where in loneliness you had stood sometime before. What do you now see? The gigantic trees have disappeared, houses have sprung up on every side. As far as the eye can see the roofs of comfortable and homelike cottages peep through the wood. The waving corn and rice and sugar-cane, the graceful and fragrant coffee tree, the unbrageous cocoa, orange, and mango plum have taken the place of the former sturdy denizens of the forest. What has brought about the change? The Negro emigrant has arrived from America, and, slender though his facilities have been, has produced these wonderful

revolutions. You look beyond and take in the forests that now appear on the distant horizon. You catch glimpses of native villages embowered in plantain trees, and you say these also shall be brought under civilized influences, and you feel yourself lifted into manhood, the spirit of the teacher and guide and missionary comes upon you, and you say, "There, below me and beyond lies the world into which I must go. There must I cast my lot. I feel I have a message to it, or a work in it"; and the sense that there are thousands dwelling there, some of whom you may touch, some of whom you may influence, some of whom may love you or be loved by you, thrills you with a strange joy and expectation, and it is a thrill which you can never forget; for ever and anon it comes upon you with increased intensity. In that hour you are born again. You hear forevermore the call ringing in your ears, "Come over and help us."

These are the visions that rise before the Liberian settler who has turned away from the coast. This is the view that exercises such an influence upon his imagination, and gives such tone to his character, making him an independent and productive man on the continent of his fathers.

As I have said, this is no imaginary picture, but the embodiment of sober history. Liberia, then, is a fact, an aggressive and progressive fact, with a great deal in its past and everything in its future that is inspiring and uplifting.

It occupies one of the most charming countries in the western portion of that continent. It has been called by qualified judges the garden spot of West Africa. I love to dwell upon the memories of scenes which I have passed through in the interior of that land. I have read of countries which I have not visited—the grandeur of the Rocky Mountains and the charms of the Yosemite Valley, and my imagination adds to the written description and becomes a gallery of delightful pictures. But of African scenes my memory is a treasure-house in which I delight to revel. I have distinctly before me the days and dates when I came into contact with their inexhaustible beauties. Leaving the coast line, the seat of malaria, and where are often seen the remains of the slaver's barracoons, which always give an impression of the deepest melancholy, I come to the high table-lands with their mountain scenery and lovely valleys, their meadow streams and mountain rivulets, and there amid the glories of a changeless and unchanging nature, I have taken off my shoes and on that consecrated ground adored the God and Father of the Africans.

This is the country and this is the work to which the American Negro is invited. This is the opening for him which, through the labors of the American Colonization Society, has been effected. This organization is more than a *colonization* society, more than an emigration society. It might with equal propriety and perhaps with greater accuracy be called the African *Repatriation* Society; or since the idea of planting towns and introducing extensive cultivation of the soil is included in its work, it might be called the African Repatriation and Colonization Society, for then you bring in a somewhat higher idea than mere colonization—the mere settling of a new country by strangers—you bring in the idea of restoration, of compensation to a race and country much and long wronged.

Colonizationists, notwithstanding all that has been said against them, have always recognized the manhood of the Negro and been willing to trust him to take care of himself. They have always recognized the inscrutable providence by which the African was brought to these shores. They have always taught that he was brought hither to be trained out of his sense of irresponsibility to a knowledge of his place as a factor in the great work of humanity; and that after having been thus trained he could find his proper sphere of action only in the land of his origin to make a way for himself. They have believed that it has not been given to the white man to fix the intellectual or spiritual status of this race. They have recognized that the universe is wide enough and God's gifts are varied enough to allow the man of Africa to find out a path of his own within the circle of genuine human interests, and to contribute from the field of his particular enterprise to the resources—material, intellectual, and moral—of the great human family.

But will the Negro go to do this work?

Is he willing to separate himself from a settled civilization which he has helped to build up to betake himself to the wilderness of his ancestral home and begin anew a career on his own responsibility?

I believe that he is. And if suitable provision were made for their departure to-morrow hundreds of thousands would avail themselves of it. The African question, or the Negro problem, is upon the country, and it can no more be ignored than any other vital interest. The chief reason, it appears to me, why it is not more seriously dealt with is because the pressure of commercial and political exigencies does not allow time and leisure to the stronger and richer elements of the nation to study it. It is not a question of color simply—that is a superficial accident. It lies deeper than color. It is a question of race, which is the outcome not only of climate, but of generations subjected to environments which have formed the mental and moral constitution.

It is a question in which two distinct races are concerned. This is not a question then purely of reason. It is a question also of instinct. Races feel; observers theorize.

The work to be done beyond the seas is not to be a reproduction of what we see in this country. It requires, therefore, distinct race perception and entire race devotion. It is not to be the healing up of an old sore, but the unfolding of a new bud, an evolution; the development of a new side of God's character and a new phase of humanity. God said to Moses, "I am that I am"; or, more exactly, "I shall be that I shall be." Each race sees from its own standpoint a different side of the Almighty. The Hebrews could not see or serve God in the land of the Egyptians; no more can the Negro under the Anglo-Saxon. He can serve *man* here. He can furnish the labor of the country, but to the inspiration of the country he must ever be an alien.

In that wonderful sermon of St. Paul on Mars Hill in which he declared that God hath made of one blood all nations of men to dwell on all the face of the earth and hath determined the bounds of their habitation, he also said, "In Him we live and move and have our being." Now it cannot be supposed that in the types and races which have already displayed themselves God has exhausted himself. It is by God in us, where we have freedom to act out ourselves, that we do each our several work and live out into action, through our work, whatever we have within us of noble and wise and true. What we do is, if we are able to be true to our nature, the representation of some phase of the Infinite Being. If we live and move and have our being in Him, God also lives, and moves and has His being in us. This is why slavery of any kind is an outrage. It spoils the image of God as it strives to express itself through the individual or the race. As in the Kingdom of Nature, we see in her great organic types of being, in the movement, changes, and order of the elements, those vast thoughts of God, so in the great types of man, in the various races of the world, as distinct in character as in work, in the great divisions of character, we see the will and character and consciousness of God disclosed to us. According to this truth a distinct phase of God's character is set forth to be wrought out into perfection in every separate character. As in every form of the inorganic universe we see some noble variation of God's thought and beauty, so in each separate man, in each separate race, something of the absolute is incarnated. The whole of mankind is a vast representation of the Deity. Therefore we cannot extinguish any race either by conflict or amalgamation without serious responsibility.

You can easily see then why one race overshadowed by another should long to express itself—should yearn for the opportunity to let out the divinity that stirs within it. This is why the Hebrews cried to God from the depths of their affliction in Egypt, and this is why thousands and thousands of Negroes in the South are longing to go to the land of their fathers. They are not content to remain where everything has been done on the line of another race. They long for the scenes where everything is to be done under the influence of a new racial spirit, under the impulse of new skies and the inspiration of a fresh development. Only those are fit for this new work who believe in the race—have faith in its future—a prophetic insight into its destiny from a consciousness of its possibilities. The inspiration of the race is in the race.

Only one race has furnished the prophets for humanity—the Hebrew race; and before they were qualified to do this they had to go down to the depths of servile degradation. Only to them were revealed those broad and pregnant principles upon which every race can stand and work and grow; but for the special work of each race the prophets arise among the people themselves.

What is pathetic about the situation is, that numbers among whites and blacks are disposed to ignore the seriousness and importance of the question. They seem to think it a question for political manipulation and to be dealt with by partisan statesmanship, not recognizing the fact that the whole country is concerned. I freely admit the fact, to which attention has been recently called, that there are many Afro-Americans who have no more to do with Africa than with Iceland, but this does not destroy the truth that there are millions whose life is bound up with that continent. It is to them that the message comes from their brethren across the deep, "Come over and help us"—1890.

Race Assimilation

Marcus Garvey

Some Negro leaders have advanced the belief that in another few years the white people will make up their minds to assimilate their black populations; thereby sinking all racial prejudice in the welcoming of the black race into the social companionship of the white. Such leaders further believe that by the amalgamation of black and white, a new type will spring up, and that type will become the American and West Indian of the future.

This belief is preposterous. I believe that white men should be white, yellow men should be yellow, and black men should be black in the great panorama of races, until each and every race by its own initiative lifts itself up to the common standard of humanity, as to compel the respect and appreciation of all, and so make it possible for each one to stretch out the hand of welcome without

being able to be prejudiced against the other because of any inferior and unfortunate condition.

The white man of America will not, to any organized extent, assimilate the Negro, because in so doing, he feels that he will be committing racial suicide. This he is not prepared to do. It is true he illegitimately carries on a system of assimilation; but such assimilation, as practised, is one that he is not prepared to support because he becomes prejudiced against his own offspring, if that offspring is the product of black and white; hence, to the white man the question of racial differences is eternal. So long as Negroes occupy an inferior position among the races and nations of the world, just so long will others be prejudiced against them, because it will be profitable for them to keep up their system of superiority. But when the Negro by his own initiative lifts himself from his low state to the highest human standard he will be in a position to stop begging and praying, and demand a place that no individual, race or nation will be able to deny him—1922.

Source: Marcus Garvey, "Race Assimilation," in Amy Jacques-Garvey, ed., *Philosophy and Opinions of Marcus Garvey* (New York: Universal Publishing House, 1923/25).

The True Solution of the Negro Problem

Marcus Garvey

As far as Negroes are concerned, in America we have the problem of lynching, peonage and dis-franchisement.

Source: Marcus Garvey, "The True Solution of the Negro Problem," in Amy Jacques-Garvey, ed., *Philosophy and Opinions of Marcus Garvey* (New York: Universal Publishing House, 1923/25).

In the West Indies, South and Central America we have the problem of peonage, serfdom, industrial and political governmental inequality.

In Africa we have, not only peonage and serfdom, but outright slavery, racial exploitation and alien political monopoly.

We cannot allow a continuation of these crimes against our race. As four hundred million men, women and children, worthy of the existence given us by the Divine Creator, we are determined to solve our own problem, by redeeming our Motherland Africa from the hands of alien exploiters and found there a government, a nation of our own, strong enough to lend protection to the members of our race scattered all over the world, and to compel the respect of the nations and races of the earth.

Do they lynch Englishmen, Frenchmen, Germans or Japanese? No. And Why? Because these people are represented by great governments, mighty nations and empires, strongly organized. Yes, and ever ready to shed the last drop of blood and spend the last penny in the national treasury to protect the honor and integrity of a citizen outraged anywhere.

Until the Negro reaches this point of national independence, all he does as a race will count for naught, because the prejudice that will stand out against him even with his ballot in his hand, with his industrial progress to show, will be of such an overwhelming nature as to perpetuate mob violence and mob rule, from which he will suffer, and which he will not be able to stop with his industrial wealth and with his ballot.

You may argue that he can use his industrial wealth and his ballot to force the government to recognize him, but he must understand that the government is the people. That the majority of the people dictate the policy of governments, and if the majority are against a measure, a thing, or a race, then the government is impotent to protect that measure, thing or race.

If the Negro were to live in this Western Hemisphere for another five hundred years he would still be outnumbered by other races who are prejudiced against him. He cannot resort to the government for protection for government will be in the hands of the majority of the people who are prejudiced against him, hence for the Negro to depend on the ballot and his industrial progress alone, will be hopeless as it does not help him when he is lynched, burned, jim-crowed and segregated. The future of the Negro therefore, outside of Africa, spells ruin and disaster—1922.

An Appeal to the Conscience of the Black Race to See Itself

Marcus Garvey

It is said to be a hard and difficult task to organize and keep together large numbers of the Negro race for the common good. Many have tried to congregate us, but have failed, the reason being that our characteristics are such as to keep us more apart than together.

Source: Marcus Garvey, "An Appeal to the Conscience of the Black Race to See Itself," in Amy Jacques-Garvey, ed., *Philosophy and Opinions of Marcus Garvey* (New York: Universal Publishing House, 1923/25).

The evil of internal division is wrecking our existence as a people, and if we do not seriously and quickly move in the direction of a readjustment it simply means that our doom becomes imminently conclusive.

For years the Universal Negro Improvement Association has been working for the unification of our race, not on domestic-national lines only, but universally. The success which we have met in the course of our effort is rather encouraging, considering the time consumed and the environment surrounding the object of our concern.

It seems that the whole world of sentiment is against the Negro, and the difficulty of our generation is to extricate ourselves from the prejudice that hides itself beneath, as well as above, the action of an international environment.

Prejudice is conditional on many reasons, and it is apparent that the Negro supplies, consciously or unconsciously, all the reasons by which the world seems to ignore and avoid him. No one cares for a leper, for lepers are infectious persons, and all are afraid of the disease, so, because the Negro keeps himself poor, helpless and undemonstrative, it is natural also that no one wants to be of him or with him.

PROGESS AND HUMANITY

Progress is the attraction that moves humanity, and to whatever people or race this "modern virtue" attaches itself, there will you find the splendor of pride and self-esteem that never fail to win the respect and admiration of all.

It is the progress of the Anglo-Saxons that singles them out for the respect of all the world. When their race had no progress or achievement to its credit, then, like all other inferior peoples, they paid the price in slavery, bondage, as well as through prejudice. We cannot forget the time when even the ancient Briton was regarded as being too dull to make a good Roman slave, yet today the influence of that race rules the world.

It is the industrial and commercial progress of America that causes Europe and the rest of the world to think appreciatively of the Anglo-American race. It is not because one hundred and ten million people live in the United States that the world is attracted to the republic with so much reverence and respect—a reverence and respect not shown to India with its three hundred millions, or to China with its four hundred millions. Progress of and among any people will advance them in the respect and appreciation of the rest of their fellows. It is such a progress that the Negro must attach to himself if he is to rise above the prejudice of the world.

The reliance of our race upon the progress and achievements of others for a consideration in sympathy, justice and rights is like a dependence upon a broken stick, resting upon which will eventually consign you to the ground.

SELF-RELIANCE AND RESPECT

The Universal Negro Improvement Association teaches our race self-help and self-reliance, not only in one essential, but in all those things that contribute to human happiness and well-being. The disposition of the many to depend upon the other races for a kindly and sympathetic consideration of their needs, without making the effort to do for themselves, has been the race's standing disgrace by which we have been judged and through which we have created the strongest prejudice against ourselves.

There is no force like success, and that is why the individual makes all efforts to surround himself throughout life with the evidence of it. As of the individual, so should it be of the race and nation. The glittering success of Rockefeller makes him a power in the American nation; the success of Henry Ford suggests him as an object of universal respect, but no one knows and cares about the bum or hobo who is Rockefeller's or Ford's neighbor. So, also, is the world attracted by the glittering success of races and nations, and pays absolutely no attention to the bum or hobo race that lingers by the wayside.

The Negro must be up and doing if he will break down the prejudice of the rest of the world. Prayer alone is not going to improve our condition, nor the policy of watchful waiting. We must strike out for ourselves in the course of material achievement, and by our own effort and energy present to the world those forces by which the progress of man is judged.

A NATION AND COUNTRY

The Negro needs a nation and a country of his own, where he can best show evidence of his own ability in the art of human progress. Scattered as an unmixed and unrecognized part of alien nations and civilizations is but to demonstrate his imbecility, and point him out as an unworthy derelict, fit neither for the society of Greek, Jew nor Gentile.

It is unfortunate that we should so drift apart, as a race, as not to see that we are but perpetuating our own sorrow and disgrace in failing to appreciate the first great requisite of all peoples—organization.

Organization is a great power in directing the affairs of a race or nation toward a given goal. To properly develop the desires that are uppermost, we must first concentrate through some system or method, and there is none better than organization. Hence, the Universal Negro Improvement Association appeals to each and every Negro to throw in his lot with those of us who, through organization, are working for the universal emancipation of our race and the redemption of our common country, Africa.

No Negro, let him be American, European, West Indian or African, shall be truly respected until the race as a whole has emancipated itself, through self-achievement and progress, from universal prejudice. The Negro will have to build his own government, industry, art, science, literature and culture, before the world will stop to consider him. Until then, we are but wards of a superior race and civilization, and the outcasts of a standard social system.

The race needs workers at this time, not plagiarists, copyists and mere imitators; but men and women who are able to create, to originate and improve, and thus make an independent racial contribution to the world and civilization.

MONKEY APINGS OF "LEADERS"

The unfortunate thing about us is that we take the monkey apings of our "so-called leading men" for progress. There is no progress in aping white people and telling us that they represent the best in the race, for in that respect any dressed monkey would represent the best of its species, irrespective of the creative matter of the monkey instinct. The best in a race is not reflected through or by the action of its apes, but by its ability to create of and by itself. It is such a creation that the Universal Negro Improvement Association seeks.

Let us not try to be the best or worst of others, but let us make the effort to be the best of ourselves. Our own racial critics criticise us as dreamers and "fanatics," and call us "benighted" and "ignorant," because they lack racial backbone. They are unable to see themselves creators of their own needs. The slave instinct has not yet departed from them. They still believe that they can only live or exist through the good graces of their "masters." The good slaves have not yet thrown off their shackles; thus, to them, the Universal Negro Improvement Association is an "impossibility."

It is the slave spirit of dependence that causes our "so-called leading men" (apes) to seek the shelter, leadership, protection and patronage of the "master" in their organization and so-called advancement work. It is the spirit of feeling secured as good servants of the master, rather than as independents, why our modern Uncle Toms take pride in laboring under alien leadership and becoming surprised at the audacity of the Universal Negro Improvement Association in proclaiming for racial liberty and independence.

But the world of white and other men, deep down in their hearts, have much more respect for those of us who work for our racial salvation under the banner of the Universal Negro Improvement Association, than they could ever have in all eternity for a group of helpless apes and beggars who make a monopoly of undermining their own race and belittling themselves in the eyes of self-respecting people, by being "good boys" rather than able men.

Surely there can be no good will between apes, seasoned beggars and independent minded Negroes who will at least make an effort to do for themselves. Surely, the "dependents" and "wards" (and may I not say racial imbeciles?) will rave against and plan the destruction of movements like the Universal Negro Improvement Association that expose them to the liberal white minds of the world as not being representative of the best in the Negro, but, to the contrary, the worst. The best of a race does not live on the patronage and philanthropy of others, but makes an effort to do for itself. The best of the great white race doesn't fawn before and beg black, brown or yellow men; they go out, create for self and thus demonstrate the fitness of the race to survive; and so the white race of America and the world will be informed that the best in the Negro race is not the class of beggars who send out to other races piteous appeals annually for donations to maintain their coterie, but the groups within us that are honestly striving to do for themselves with the voluntary help and appreciation of that class of other races that is reasonable, just and liberal enough to give to each and every one a fair chance in the promotion of those ideals that tend to greater human progress and human love.

The work of the Universal Negro Improvement Association is clear and clean-cut. It is that of inspiring an unfortunate race with pride in self and with the determination of going ahead in the creation of those ideals that will lift them to the unprejudiced company of races and nations. There is no desire for hate or malice, but every wish to see all mankind linked into a common fraternity of progress and achievement that will wipe away the odor of prejudice, and elevate the human race to the height of real godly love and satisfaction—1923.

The Negro's Place in World Reorganization

Marcus Garvey

Gradually we are approaching the time when the Negro peoples of the world will have either to consciously, through their own organization, go forward to the point of destiny as laid out by themselves, or must sit quiescently and see themselves pushed back into the mire of economic serfdom, to be ultimately crushed by the grinding mill of exploitation and be exterminated ultimately by the strong hand of prejudice.

There is no doubt about it that we are living in the age of world reorganization out of which will come a set program for the organized races of mankind that will admit of no sympathy in human affairs, in that we are

Source: Marcus Garvey, "The Negro's Place in World Reorganization," in Amy Jacques-Garvey, ed., *Philosophy and Opinions of Marcus Garvey* (New York: Universal Publishing House, 1923/25).

planning for the great gigantic struggle of the survival of the fittest group. It becomes each and every one engaged in this great race for place and position to use whatsoever influence possible to divert the other fellow's attention from the real object. In our own sphere in America and the western world we find that we are being camouflaged, not so much by those with whom we are competing for our economic, political existence, but by men from within our own race, either as agents of the opposition or as unconscious fools who are endeavoring to flatter us into believing that our future should rest with chance and with Providence, believing that through these agencies will come the solution of the restless problem. Such leadership is but preparing us for the time that is bound to befall us if we do not exert ourselves now toward our own creative purpose. The mission of the

Universal Negro Improvement Association is to arouse the sleeping consciousness of Negroes everywhere to the point where we will, as one concerted body, act for our own preservation. By laying the foundation for such we will be able to work toward the glorious realization of an emancipated race and a constructed nation. Nationhood is the strongest security of any people and it is for that the Universal Negro Improvement Association strives at this time. With the clamor of other peoples for a similar purpose, we raise a noise even to high heaven for the admission of the Negro into the plan of autonomy.

BLACK AFRICA

On every side we hear the cry of white supremacy—in America, Canada, Australia, Europe, and even South America. There is no white supremacy beyond the power and strength of the white man to hold himself against the others. The supremacy of any race is not permanent; it is a thing only of the time in which the race finds itself powerful. The whole world of white men is becoming nervous as touching its own future and that of other races. With the desire of self-preservation, which naturally is the first law of nature, they raise the hue and cry that the white race must be first in government and in control. What must the Negro do in the face of such a universal attitude but to align all his forces in the direction of protecting himself from the threatened disaster of race domination and ultimate extermination?

Without a desire to harm anyone, the Universal Negro Improvement Association feels that the Negro should without compromise or any apology appeal to the same spirit of racial pride and love as the great white race is doing for its own preservation, so that while others are raising the cry of a white America, a white Canada, a white Australia, we also without reservation raise the cry of a "Black Africa." The critic asks, "Is this possible?" and the four hundred million courageous Negroes of the world answer, "Yes."

Out of this very reconstruction of world affairs will come the glorious opportunity for Africa's freedom. Out of the present chaos and European confusion will come an opportunity for the Negro never enjoyed in any other age, for the expansion of himself and the consolidation of his manhood in the direction of building himself a national power in Africa.

The germ of European malice, revenge and antagonism is so deeply rooted among certain of the contending powers that in a short while we feel sure they will present to Negroes the opportunity for which we are organized.

DISABLEMENT OF GERMANY NOT PERMANENT

No one believes in the permanent disablement of Germany, but all thoughtful minds realize that France is but laying the foundation through revenge for a greater conflict than has as yet been seen. With such another upheaval, there is absolutely no reason why organized Negro opinion could not be felt and directed in the channel of their own independence in Africa.

To fight for African redemption does not mean that we must give up our domestic fights for political justice and industrial rights. It does not mean that we must become disloyal to any government or to any country wherein we were born. Each and every race outside of its domestic national loyalty has a loyalty to itself; therefore, it is foolish for the Negro to talk about not being interested in his own racial, political, social and industrial destiny. We can be as loyal American citizens or British subjects as the Irishman or the Jew, and yet fight for the redemption of Africa, a complete emancipation of the race.

Fighting for the establishment of Palestine does not make the American Jew disloyal; fighting for the independence of Ireland does not make the Irish-American a bad citizen. Why should fighting for the freedom of Africa make the Afro-American disloyal or a bad citizen?

The Universal Negro Improvement Association teaches loyalty to all governments outside of Africa; but when it comes to Africa, we feel that the Negro has absolutely no obligation to any one but himself.

Out of the unsettled state and condition of the world will come such revolutions that will give each and every race that is oppressed the opportunity to march forward. The last world war brought the opportunity to many heretofore subject races to regain their freedom. The next world war will give Africa the opportunity for which we are preparing. We are going to have wars and rumors of wars. In another twenty or thirty years we will have a changed world, politically, and Africa will not be one of the most backward nations, but African shall be, I feel sure, one of the greatest commonwealths that will once more hold up the torchlight of civilization and bestow the blessings of freedom, liberty and democracy upon all mankind—March 24, 1923.

Aims and Objects of Movement for Solution of Negro Problem

Marcus Garvey

Generally the public is kept misinformed of the truth surrounding new movements of reform. Very seldom, if ever, reformers get the truth told about them and their movements. Because of this natural attitude, the Universal Negro Improvement Association has been greatly handicapped in its work, causing thereby one of the most liberal and helpful human movements of the twentieth century to be held up to ridicule by those who take pride in poking fun at anything not already successfully established.

The white man of America has become the natural leader of the world. He, because of his exalted position, is called upon to help in all human efforts. From nations to individuals the appeal is made to him for aid in all things affecting humanity, so, naturally, there can be no great mass movement or change without first acquainting the leader on whose sympathy and advice the world moves.

It is because of this, and more so because of a desire to be Christian friends with the white race, why I explain the aims and objects of the Universal Negro Improvement Association.

The Universal Negro Improvement Association is an organization among Negroes that is seeking to improve the condition of the race, with the view of establishing a nation in Africa where Negroes will be given the opportunity to develop by themselves, without creating the hatred and animosity that now exist in countries of the white race through Negroes rivaling them for the highest and best positions in government, politics, society and industry. The organization believes in the rights of all men, yellow, white and black. To us, the white race has a right to the peaceful possession and occupation of countries of its own and in like manner the yellow and black races have their rights. It is

Source: Marcus Garvey, "Aims and Objects of Movement for Solution of Negro Problem," in Amy Jacques-Garvey, ed., *Philosophy and Opinions of Marcus Garvey* (New York: Universal Publishing House, 1923/25).

only by an honest and liberal consideration of such rights can the world be blessed with the peace that is sought by Christian teachers and leaders.

THE SPIRITUAL BROTHERHOOD OF MAN

The following preamble to the constitution of the organization speaks for itself:

> The Universal Negro Improvement Association and African Communities' League is a social, friendly, humanitarian, charitable, educational, institutional, constructive, and expansive society, and is founded by persons, desiring to the utmost to work for the general uplift of the Negro peoples of the world. And the members pledge themselves to do all in their power to conserve the rights of their noble race and to respect the rights of all mankind, believing always in the Brotherhood of Man and the Fatherhood of God. The motto of the organization is: One God! One Aim! One Destiny! Therefore, let justice be done to all mankind, realizing that if the strong oppresses the weak confusion and discontent will ever mark the path of man, but with love, faith and charity toward all the reign of peace and plenty will be heralded into the world and the generation of men shall be called Blessed.

The declared objects of the association are:

> To establish a Universal Confraternity among the race; to promote the spirit of pride and love; to reclaim the fallen; to administer to and assist the needy; to assist in civilizing the backward tribes of Africa; to assist in the development of Independent Negro Nations and Communities; to establish a central nation for the race; to establish Commissaries or Agencies in the principal countries and cities of the world for the representation of all Negroes; to promote a conscientious Spiritual worship among the native tribes of Africa; to establish Universities, Colleges, Academies and Schools for the racial education and culture of the people; to work for better conditions among Negroes everywhere.

SUPPLYING A LONG FELT WANT

The organization of the Universal Negro Improvement Association has supplied among Negroes a long-felt want. Hitherto the other Negro movements in America, with the exception of the Tuskegee effort of Booker T. Washington, sought to teach the Negro to aspire to social equality with the whites, meaning thereby the right to intermarry and fraternize in every social way. This has been the source of much trouble and still some Negro organizations continue to preach this dangerous "race destroying doctrine" added to a program of political agitation and aggression. The Universal Negro Improvement Association on the other hand believes in and teaches the pride and purity of race. We believe that the white race should uphold its racial pride and perpetuate itself, and that the black race should do likewise. We believe that there is room enough in the world for the various race groups to grow and develop by themselves without seeking to destroy the Creator's plan by the constant introduction of mongrel types.

The unfortunate condition of slavery, as imposed upon the Negro, and which caused the mongrelization of the race, should not be legalized and continued now to the harm and detriment of both races.

The time has really come to give the Negro a chance to develop himself to a moral-standard-man, and it is for such an opportunity that the Universal Negro Improvement Association seeks in the creation of an African nation for Negroes, where the greatest latitude would be given to work out this racial ideal.

There are hundreds of thousands of colored people in America who desire race amalgamation and miscegenation as a solution of the race problem. These people are, therefore, opposed to the race pride ideas of black and white; but the thoughtful of both races will naturally ignore the ravings of such persons and honestly work for the solution of a problem that has been forced upon us.

Liberal white America and race loving Negroes are bound to think at this time and thus evolve a program or plan by which there can be a fair and amicable settlement of the question.

We cannot put off the consideration of the matter, for time is pressing on our hands. The educated Negro is making rightful constitutional demands. The great white majority will never grant them, and thus we march on to danger if we do not now stop and adjust the matter.

The time is opportune to regulate the relationship between both races. Let the Negro have a country of his own. Help him to return to his original home, Africa, and there give him the opportunity to climb from the lowest to the highest positions in a state of his own. If not, then the nation will have to hearken to the demand of the aggressive, "social equality" organization, known as the National Association for the Advancement of Colored People, of which W.E.B. Du Bois is leader, which declares vehemently for social and political equality, viz.: Negroes and whites in the same hotels, homes, residential districts, public and private places, a Negro as president, members of the Cabinet, Governors of States, Mayors of cities, and leaders of society in the United States. In this agitation, Du Bois is ably supported by the "Chicago Defender," a colored newspaper published in Chicago. This paper advocated Negroes in the Cabinet and Senate. All these, as everybody knows, are the Negroes' constitutional rights, but reason dictates that the masses of the white race will never stand by the ascendancy of an opposite minority group to the favored positions in a government, society and industry that exist by the will of the majority, hence the demand of the Du Bois group of colored leaders will only lead, ultimately, to further disturbances in riots, lynching and mob rule. The only logical solution therefore, is to supply the Negro with opportunities and environments of his own, and there point him to the fullness of his ambition.

NEGROES WHO SEEK SOCIAL EQUALITY

The Negro who seeks the White House in America could find ample play for his ambition in Africa. The Negro who seeks the office of Secretary of State in America would have a fair chance of demonstrating his diplomacy in Africa. The Negro who seeks a seat in the Senate or of being governor of a State in America, would be provided with a glorious chance for statesmanship in Africa.

The Negro has a claim on American white sympathy that cannot be denied. The Negro has labored for 300 years in contributing to America's greatness. White America will not be unmindful, therefore, of this consideration, but will treat him kindly. Yet it is realized that all human beings have a limit to their humanity. The humanity of white America, we realize, will seek self-protection and self-preservation, and that is why the thoughtful and reasonable Negro sees no hope in America for satisfying the aggressive program of the National Association for the Advancement of Colored People, but advances the reasonable plan of the Universal Negro Improvement Association, that of creating in Africa a nation and government for the Negro race.

This plan when properly undertaken and prosecuted will solve the race problem in America in fifty years. Africa affords a wonderful opportunity at the present time for colonization by the Negroes of the Western world. There is Liberia, already established as an independent Negro government. Let white America assist Afro-Americans to go there and help develop the country. Then, there are the late German colonies; let white sentiment force England and France to turn them over to the American and West Indian Negroes who fought for the Allies in the World's War. Then, France, England and Belgium owe America billions of dollars which they claim they cannot afford to repay immediately. Let them compromise by turning over Sierra Leone and the Ivory Coast on the West Coast of Africa and add them to Liberia and help make Liberia a state worthy of her history.

The Negroes of Africa and America are one in blood. They have sprung from the same common stock. They can work and live together and thus make their own racial contribution to the world.

Will deep thinking and liberal white America help? It is a considerate duty.

It is true that a large number of self-seeking colored agitators and so-called political leaders, who hanker after social equality and fight for the impossible in politics and governments, will rave, but remember that the slave-holder raved, but the North said, "Let the slaves go free"; the British Parliament raved when the Colonists said, "We want a free and American nation"; the Monarchists of France raved when the people declared for a more liberal form of government.

The masses of Negroes think differently from the self-appointed leaders of the race. The majority of Negro leaders are selfish, self-appointed and not elected by the people. The people desire freedom in a land of their own, while the colored politician desires office and social equality for himself in America, and that is why we are asking white America to help the masses to realize their objective ... —1923.

Racial Ideals

Marcus Garvey

The coming together, all over this country, of fully six million people of Negro blood, to work for the creation of a nation of their own in their motherland, Africa, is no joke.

There is now a world revival of thought and action, which is causing peoples everywhere to bestir themselves towards their own security, through which we hear the cry of Ireland for the Irish, Palestine for the Jew, Egypt for the Egyptian, Asia for the Asiatic, and thus we Negroes raise the cry of Africa for the Africans, those at home and those abroad.

Some people are not disposed to give us credit for having feelings, passions, ambitions and desires like other races; they are satisfied to relegate us to the back-heap of human aspirations; but this is a mistake. The Almighty Creator made us men, not unlike others, but in His own image; hence, as a race, we feel that we, too, are entitled to the rights that are common to humanity.

The cry and desire for liberty is justifiable, and is made holy everywhere. It is sacred

Source: Marcus Garvey, "Racial Ideals," in Amy Jacques-Garvey, ed., *Philosophy and Opinions of Marcus Garvey* (New York: Universal Publishing House, 1923/25).

and holy to the Anglo-Saxon, Teuton and Latin; to the Anglo-American it precedes that of all religions, and now come the Irish, the Jew, the Egyptian, the Hindoo, and, last but not least, the Negro, clamoring for their share as well as their right to be free.

All men should be free—free to work out their own salvation. Free to create their own destinies. Free to nationally build up themselves for the upbringing and rearing of a culture and civilization of their own. Jewish culture is different from Irish culture. Anglo-Saxon culture is unlike Teutonic culture. Asiatic culture differs greatly from European culture; and, in the same way, the world should be liberal enough to allow the Negro latitude to develop a culture of his own. Why should the Negro be lost among the other races and nations of the world and to himself? Did nature not make of him a son of the soil? Did the Creator not fashion him out of the dust of the earth?—out of that rich soil to which he bears such a wonderful resemblance?—a resemblance that changes not, even though the ages have flown? No, the Ethiopian cannot change his skin; and so we appeal to the conscience of the white world to yield us a place of national freedom among the creatures of present-day temporal materialism.

We Negroes are not asking the white man to turn Europe and America over to us. We are not asking the Asiatic to turn Asia over for the accommodation of the blacks. But we are asking a just and righteous world to restore Africa to her scattered and abused children.

We believe in justice and human love. If our rights are to be respected, then, we, too, must respect the rights of all mankind; hence, we are ever ready and willing to yield to the white man the things that are his, and we feel that he, too, when his conscience is touched, will yield to us the things that are ours.

We should like to see a peaceful, prosperous and progressive white race in America and Europe; a peaceful, prosperous and progressive yellow race in Asia, and, in like manner, we want, and we demand, a peaceful, prosperous and progressive black race in Africa. Is that asking too much? Surely not. Humanity, without any immediate human hope of racial oneness, has drifted apart, and is now divided into separate and distinct groups, each with its own ideals and aspirations. Thus, we cannot expect any one race to hold a monopoly of creation and be able to keep the rest satisfied.

DISTINCT RACIAL GROUP IDEALISM

From our distinct racial group idealism we feel that no black man is good enough to govern the white man, and no white man good enough to rule the black man; and so of all races and peoples. No one feels that the other, alien in race, is good enough to govern or rule to the exclusion of native racial rights. We may as well, therefore, face the question of superior and inferior races. In twentieth century civilization there are no inferior and superior races. There are backward peoples, but that does not make them inferior. As far as humanity goes, all men are equal, and especially where peoples are intelligent enough to know what they want. At this time all peoples know what they want—it is liberty. When a people have sense enough to know that they ought to be free, then they naturally become

the equal of all, in the higher calling of man to know and direct himself. It is true that economically and scientifically certain races are more progressive than others; but that does not imply superiority. For the Anglo-Saxon to say that he is superior because he introduced submarines to destroy life, or the Teuton because he compounded liquid gas to outdo in the art of killing, and that the Negro is inferior because he is backward in that direction is to leave one's self open to the retort "Thou shalt not kill," as being the divine law that sets the moral standard of the real man. There is no superiority in the one race economically monopolizing and holding all that would end to the sustenance of life, and thus cause unhappiness and distress to others; for our highest purpose should be to love and care for each other, and share with each other the things that our Heavenly Father has placed at our common disposal; and even in this, the African is unsurpassed, in that he feeds his brother and shares with him the product of the land. The idea of race superiority is questionable; nevertheless, we must admit that from the white man's standard, he is far superior to the rest of us, but that kind of superiority is too inhuman and dangerous to be permanently helpful. Such a superiority was shared and indulged in by other races before, and even by our own, when we boasted of a wonderful civilization on the banks of the Nile, when others were still groping in darkness; but because of our unrighteousness it failed, as all such will. Civilization can only last when we have reached the point where we will be our brother's keeper. That is to say, when we feel it righteous to live and let live.

NO EXCLUSIVE RIGHT TO THE WORLD

Let no black man feel that he has the exclusive right to the world, and other men none, and let no white man feel that way, either. The world is the property of all mankind, and each and every group is entitled to a portion. The black man now wants his, and in terms uncompromising he is asking for it.

The Universal Negro Improvement Association represents the hopes and aspirations of the awakened Negro. Our desire is for a place in the world; not to disturb the tranquility of other men, but to lay down our burden and rest our weary backs and feet by the banks of the Niger, and sing our songs and chant our hymns to the God of Ethiopia. Yes, we want rest from the toil of centuries, rest of political freedom, rest of economic and industrial liberty, rest to be socially free and unmolested, rest from lynching and burning, rest from discrimination of all kinds.

Out of slavery we have come with our tears and sorrows, and we now lay them at the feet of American white civilization. We cry to the considerate white people for help, because in their midst we can scarce help ourselves. We are strangers in a strange land. We cannot sing, we cannot play on our harps, for our hearts are sad. We are sad because of the tears of our mothers and the cry of our fathers. Have you not heard the plaintive wail? It is your father and my father burning at stake; but, thank God, there is a larger humanity growing among the good and considerate white people of this country, and they are going to help. They will help us to recover our souls.

As children of captivity we look forward to a new day and a new, yet ever old, land of our fathers, the land of refuge, the land of the Prophets, the land of the Saints, and the land of God's crowning glory. We shall gather together our children, our treasures and our loved ones, and, as the children of Israel, by the command of God, faced the promised land, so in time we shall also stretch forth our hands and bless our country.

Good and dear America that has succored us for three hundred years knows our story. We have watered her vegetation with our tears for two hundred and fifty years. We have built her cities and laid the foundation of her imperialism with the mortar of our blood and bones for three centuries, and now we cry to her for help. Help us, America, as we helped you. We helped you in the Revolutionary War. We helped you in the Civil War, and, although Lincoln helped us, the price is not half paid. We helped you in the Spanish-American war. We died nobly and courageously in Mexico, and did we not leave behind us on the stained battlefields of France and Flanders our rich blood to mark the poppies' bloom, and to bring back to you the glory of the flag that never touched the dust? We have no regrets in service to America for three hundred years, but we pray that America will help us for another fifty years until we have solved the troublesome problem that now confronts us. We know and realize that two ambitious and competitive races cannot live permanently side by side, without friction and trouble, and that is why the white race wants a white America and the black race wants and demands a black Africa.

Let white America help us for fifty years honestly, as we have helped her for three hundred years, and before the expiration of many decades there shall be no more race problem. Help us to gradually go home, America. Help us as you have helped the Jews. Help us as you have helped the Irish. Help us as you have helped the Poles, Russians, Germans and Armenians.

The Universal Negro Improvement Association proposes a friendly cooperation with all honest movements seeking intelligently to solve the race problem. We are not seeking social equality; we do not seek intermarriage, nor do we hanker after the impossible. We want the right to have a country of our own, and there foster and re-establish a culture and civilization exclusively ours. Don't say it can't be done. The Pilgrims and colonists did it for America, and the new Negro, with sympathetic help, can do it for Africa.

BACK TO AFRICA

The thoughtful and industrious of our race want to go back to Africa, because we realize it will be our only hope of permanent existence. We cannot all go in a day or year, ten or twenty years. It will take time under the rule of modern economics, to entirely or largely depopulate a country of a people, who have been its residents for centuries, but we feel that, with proper help for fifty years, the problem can be solved. We do not want all the Negroes in Africa. Some are no good here, and naturally will be no good there. The no-good

Negro will naturally die in fifty years. The Negro who is wrangling about and fighting for social equality will naturally pass away in fifty years, and yield his place to the progressive Negro who wants a society and country of his own.

Negroes are divided into two groups, the industrious and adventurous, and the lazy and dependent. The industrious and adventurous believe that whatsoever others have done it can do. The Universal Negro Improvement Association belongs to this group, and so you find us working, six million strong, to the goal of an independent nationality. Who will not help? Only the mean and despicable "who never to himself hath said, this is my own, my native land." Africa is the legitimate, moral and righteous home of all Negroes, and now, that the time is coming for all to assemble under their own vine and fig tree, we feel it our duty to arouse every Negro to a consciousness of himself.

White and black will learn to respect each other when they cease to be active competitors in the same countries for the same things in politics and society. Let them have countries of their own, wherein to aspire and climb without rancor. The races can be friendly and helpful to each other, but the laws of nature separate us to the extent of each and every one developing by itself.

We want an atmosphere all our own. We would like to govern and rule ourselves and not be encumbered and restrained. We feel now just as the white race would feel if they were governed and ruled by the Chinese. If we live in our own districts, let us rule and govern those districts. If we have a majority in our communities, let us run those communities. We form a majority in Africa and we should naturally govern ourselves there. No man can govern another's house as well as himself. Let us have fair play. Let us have justice. This is the appeal we make to white America—1924.

FURTHER READING

Aptheker, Herbert, ed. 1951. *A Documentary History of the Negro People in the United States,* vol. 2. New York: Citadel Press.

Blyden, Edward W. 1887. *Christianity, Islam and the Negro Race.* Baltimore, MD: Black Classic Press, 1993.

Boxill, Bernard R. 1992. "Two Traditions in African American Philosophy." *Philosophical Forum* 24.1–3 (Fall–Spring 1992–1993). Reprinted in John P. Pittman, ed., *African-American Perspectives and Philosophical Traditions.* New York: Routledge, 1997.

Gilroy, Paul. 1993. *The Black Atlantic: Modernity and Double Consciousness.* Cambridge, MA: Harvard University Press.

Kelley, Robin D. G., and Sidney Lemelle, eds. 1994. *Imagining Home: Class, Culture and Nationalism in the African Diaspora.* London: Verso Books.

Moses, Wilson J. 1996. *Classical Black Nationalism: From the American Revolution to Marcus Garvey.* New York: New York University Press.

Mudimbe, V. Y. 1988. *The Invention of Africa: Gnosis, Philosophy and the Order of Knowledge.* Bloomington: University of Indiana Press.

Outlaw, Lucius. 1996. *On Race and Philosophy.* New York: Routledge.

Stuckey, Sterling. 1972. *The Ideological Origins of Black Nationalism.* Boston: Beacon Press.

Takaki, Ronald T. 1993. *Violence in the Black Imagination.* New York: Oxford.

Van De Burg, William L. 1997. *Modern Black Nationalism: From Marcus Garvey to Louis Farrakhan.* New York: New York University Press.

White, E. Frances. 1990. "Africa on My Mind: Gender, Counter Discourse and African American Nationalism." *Journal of Women's History* 2 (Spring).

CHAPTER 3

Assimilation and Social Uplift

The assimilationist doctrine represents another important strand of black abolitionist thought that opposed the separatist goals of nationalism and asserted the demand for full social and political rights for African-Americans. As noted in the previous section, there is little indication in the writings by emigrationists that their advocacy of repatriation to Africa was motivated by a desire to regain a lost African culture. Rather, the separation from whites sought by emigrationists was motivated by a desire for self-government—a decidedly *political* objective that must be distinguished from the anti-assimilationist doctrine that aims to promote *cultural* difference.

In 1900 the Pan-African Congress held its initial meeting in London. W. E. B. Du Bois and Anna Julia Cooper were among the black leaders who spoke to a gathering of representatives from the Caribbean and Africa. By the early twenties the concept of Pan-Africanism was virtually synonymous with Garveyism in the black popular imagination. From the inception of the movement, with Du Bois and Cooper as founding members, the agenda was focused primarily on the decolonization of Africa. The commonly held assumption that once independence was gained, Africa would have to modernize on the model of European culture yields a rarely noticed convergence of views held by emigrationists and assimilationists. Blyden's acknowledgment that Islam had been less disruptive of African life and culture than Christianity displays his awareness of the need to respect indigenous cultures. Nevertheless this observation did not inhibit his advocacy of modernization in Africa on the model of European Christianity. A concept of *cultural* pluralism that stands opposed to assimilation (and not simply a pluralism of races on the same path toward Western culture) is missing from the largely political agendas of nationalists and assimilationists alike.

Frederick Douglass's *Narrative of the Life of a Slave*, published in 1848, and his writings in *The North Star*, a newspaper he published for 16 years, propelled him into the forefront of the struggle against slavery. His abolitionist stance became increasingly militant, shifting from moral suasion to a more militant political action. In 1848 he visited John Brown at Springfield. He was later implicated in the raid on Harpers Ferry and had to flee to Canada. After Emancipation he visited Lincoln twice at the White House and became a recruiter for the military. After the war he served in several posts in government in Washington, D.C., including Minister to Haiti.

In his "Address to the Colored People of the United States," published in *The North Star,* Douglass urges northern blacks to join interracial coalitions to wage the struggle against slavery. Long before Booker T. Washington, Douglass advocated developing skills in the mechanical trades as a practical means of social elevation above menial labor. He presents an earlier version of the view, expressed later by Washington and Garvey, that respect will be accorded to black people when they take steps to move from a dependent to an interdependent status. His remark that African-Americans must learn to make the boots that they are presently only allowed to black captures his belief that, by establishing themselves in the more enduring vocations, African-Americans will transform present social relations with white Americans.

For Douglass, the struggle for African-American social equality amounts to a demand for full citizenship. In "The Present and Future of the Colored Race in America" he claims that the future of America will be determined by the future of African-Americans. Douglass is critical of the treatment of exslaves and refers to free blacks as "slaves of the community." He meant to draw attention to the fact that, as a degraded caste, slaves are freed only in form. He also meant to question the prevailing policy of granting slaves freedom, but not trusting them as social equals. Relying on a comparison with the rapid change in social status of the former oppressed Irish Americans, Douglass rejects the claim by ethnologists that black people are biologically inferior. He argues that such notions are employed to justify enslavement and oppression.

Douglass's commitment to assimilation is reflected in his debate with emigrationists. In "The African Civilization Society" Douglass responds to Garnet's inquiry as to why Douglass prefers America to Africa. He protests the idea fostered by the African Civilization Society that Africa, not America, is the true home of black people. According to Douglass, this idea endorses the assumption of the slaveholders who founded the American Colonization Society that white and black people can never live in the same land on terms of equality. He rejects as implausible the contention of emigrationists that the American planters will be destroyed through competition with the African production of cotton. Instead, he insists that the best way to end the slave trade and develop civilization in Africa is to stay in America and fight for abolition. Two important reasons are cited. First, the work of elevation must be done in America because there is no place on the globe where black people can speak to a larger audience than in the United States. Secondly, African-Americans ought to have a fair chance to work out their destiny in the country of their birth. It is important to note that Douglass did not oppose the right of African-Americans to emigrate as individuals. He was concerned with arguments presented by Blyden and other nationalists that emigration is a duty. This stronger claim renders the question less private and individual and more a matter of public policy.

In "The Lessons of the Hour" Douglass maintains that the fight for racial equality is here in America and that it would be wrong for the United States government to provide money for the return of black people to Africa. He feared that this government funding of expatriation would set the stage for a dangerous policy of compelling African-Americans to return to Africa. He dismisses what he calls "native land" talk as nonsense, insisting that the native land of African-Americans is America and that the "colonization scheme" supported by nationalists fosters the idea that African-Americans are forever doomed to be without citizenship in the land of their birth. Most of all it evades a solution to the race problem by denying equal rights as citizens to a group of people whose admixture of white and black ancestry would make it "difficult to find their native land outside of the United States."

Anna Julia Cooper is well known as an outspoken woman activist in the nineteenth century, but less well known as a first rate scholar who, in addition to writing a doctoral thesis in French on the Haitian revolution, also published in Paris a definitive modern French translation of the old French epic *Le Pelerinage de Chalemagne* (1925). Her early writings were collected in *A Voice from the South* published in 1892. Although she was prominent among the small group of nineteenth-century black intellectuals, Cooper's feminist views are rarely considered in the same context with the accommodationist view presented in Booker T. Washington's writings, or Du Bois's view of the role of a talented tenth. In different respects she compares with both Washington and Du Bois. Her family background of enslavement is similar to Washington's, yet her education at Oberlin College and Columbia University and subquently her doctorate from the Sorbonne at age 65 places her, along with Du Bois and Alain Locke, among the highest educated Americans. In a fashion similar to Washington, she argues that the so-called Negro question is a problem for the nation to solve. Going a step further, however, she adds that the status of black women is the only true measure of collective racial progress, given that black women are the least likely to be among the eminent and the most likely to be responsible for the raising of families.

The influence of the "cult of true womanhood" on Cooper's perspective of the plight of uneducated black women is evident in many of her writings. She was critical of black men for blocking the education of black women and critical of the white women's movement for excluding black women from its concerns. The major thrust of her argument in "Has American a Race Problem? If So, How Can It Best Be Solved?" is to advance the idea that the solution is good for America. Her rather conservative view of immigrants as less American than African-American is similar to the view held by Booker T. Washington. Anticipating later thinkers such as Du Bois and Alain Locke, she claims that each race has its "message" to contribute to the evolution of civilization.

Although supporters of Booker T. Washington would prefer to emphasize his philosophy of self-reliance, it is his accommodationist stance that provides a backdrop for many of the social movements that developed in the first quarter of the twentieth century. Garvey was a self-proclaimed follower of Washington. Du Bois's involvement in the Niagara movement, as well as Alain Locke's attempt to organize a cultural version of the labor-oriented New Negro movement were in different ways indebted to Washington's legacy. In his "Atlanta Exposition Address" delivered in 1895, Booker T. Washington uses the famous hand metaphor to represent his social philosophy. According to Washington, black and white Americans can be united as the hand in all things economic while remaining as separate as the five fingers in all things social. His call to the white Southern business community was to "cast down your buckets where you are." By this he meant that it is in the interest of the country for white businesses to hire and train black people rather than turn to immigrant labor. On the other side of the fence he encouraged black people to invest in social progress by learning to dignify and glorify common labor. Washington often presented the argument for incorporating African-Americans into the economic progress of the South in terms of the self-interest of whites in the North and South. America cannot prosper without the prosperity of the South and the South cannot prosper without the prosperity of black Southerners who constitute one-half of the "ignorance and crime." The compromise he insists upon in exchange for support of his education programs would be to give up all political agitation for the artificial forcing of social equality. Nevertheless, in "Our New Citizen" Washington adds two important stipulations to his appeal to whites in the North. He beckons them, along with white Southerners, to join hands with the Southern Negro to "stimulate him in self-help" and "give him the rights of man."

In "Democracy and Education" notions of self-support and industrial independence, the cornerstones of Washington's view of social uplift, are defined in terms of modernization. According to Washington, "You cannot graft a fifteenth-century civilization onto a twentieth-century civilization by the mere performance of gymnastics." He goes on to link education and economic dependency to questions regarding citizenship. The story of the black cadet at Annapolis (Henry Baker) is used to make the point that education is a failure when it does not give a person "moral courage to stand up in defense of right and justice." The education of whites must prepare them to overcome their prejudice toward black people. With deliberate irony Washington points out that in the long run whites also suffer harm from racial injustice. "It is for the white man to save himself from his degradation that I plead."

Washington's emphasis on economics is stated very forcefully in his "Address Delivered at Hampton Institute." When he tells us that respect will come from having the best farm or being the largest taxpayer, he suggests that present race relations are subject to economic influence. He argues that black labor has been crucial to the general welfare of the South, citing figures from his own research to dispel the myth of black people as a tax burden. His findings are used to show the relevance of education on the eradication of crime, poverty and unemployment.

W. E. B. Du Bois is famous for his proclamation in *The Souls of Black Folk* that the problem of the twentieth century is the problem of the color line. In his 1897 address, "The Conservation of Races," to the initial meeting of the Negro Academy, he proposed a sociohistorical definition of race that emphasized cultural and political loyalty. The idea that black people, as a group, have a unique cultural contribution to make to world civilization was linked with the African-American's political struggle for social equality. Although Du Bois argues for social development based on the cultural heritage of black people, he is not concerned, at this early stage of his career, with the redemption of an African past. The aim of his anti-assimilationist argument was to foster group pride and loyalty rather than promote separatism—although in a later section we shall see that he has special reasons for advocating this latter view as well. The view of race and group progress Du Bois advocates in 1897 is derived from his study of European history and sociology.

In his well-known essay "The Talented Tenth," Du Bois is concerned with the duty of the "college-bred Negro" for social leadership. The traditional black leader has been the, sometimes corrupt, preacher, while the majority of black college graduates have been teachers. Du Bois advocates the training of more college-educated preachers to replace those who are often "ignorant and immoral."

Unlike Washington, who bemoans the fact that educated blacks as a group had accumulated little capital, Du Bois stresses the importance of culture for social elevation and criticizes Washington's emphasis on material wealth. According to Du Bois, the history of human progress has taught us that culture filters from the top downward. The role of education cannot be limited to a curriculum of trade and industrial training, but must also be devoted to the transmission of knowledge and culture from generation to generation. An educated social leadership will fill in for a number of social factors affecting the group progress of black people—including no traditions to fall back on, no long established customs, no strong family ties, and no well-defined social classes. Du Bois wanted vocational education to teach trades and other mechanical skills, but he thought education must also "civilize a race of ex-slaves." To accomplish the latter the object of education cannot be only "to make men into carpenters," but rather must also be devoted to "make carpenters into men."

An Address to the Colored People of the United States

Frederick Douglass

Under a solemn sense of duty, inspired by our relation to you as fellow sufferers under the multiplied and grievous wrongs to which we as a people are universally subjected,—we, a portion of your brethren, assembled in National Convention, at Cleveland, Ohio, take the liberty to address you on the subject of our mutual improvement and social elevation.

The condition of our variety of the human family, has long been cheerless, if not hopeless, in this country. The doctrine perseveringly proclaimed in high places in church and state, that it is impossible for colored men to rise from ignorance and debasement, to intelligence and respectability in this country, has made a deep impression upon the public mind generally, and is not without its effect upon us. Under this gloomy doctrine, many of us have sunk under the pall of despondency, and are making no effort to relieve ourselves, and have no heart to assist others. It is from this despond that we would deliver you. It is from this slumber we would rouse you. The present, is a period of activity and hope. The heavens above us are bright, and much of the darkness that overshadowed us has passed away. We can deal in the language of brilliant encouragement, and speak of success with certainty. That our condition has been gradually improving, is evident to all, and that we shall yet stand on a common platform with our fellow countrymen, in respect to political and social rights, is certain. The spirit of the age—the voice of inspiration—the deep longings of the human soul—the conflict of right with wrong—the upward tendency of the oppressed throughout the world, abound with evidence complete and ample, of the final triumph of right over wrong, of freedom over slavery, and equality over caste. To doubt this, is to forget the past, and blind our eyes to the present, as well as to deny and oppose the great law of progress, written out by the hand of God on the human soul.

Great changes for the better have taken place and are still taking place. The last ten years have witnessed a mighty change in the estimate in which we as a people are regarded, both in this and other lands. England has given liberty to nearly one million, and France has emancipated three hundred thousand of our brethren, and our own country shakes with the agitation of our rights. Ten or twelve years ago, an educated colored man was regarded as a curiosity, and the thought of a colored man as an author, editor, lawyer or doctor, had scarce been conceived. Such, thank Heaven, is no longer the case. There are now those among us, whom we are not ashamed to regard as gentlemen and scholars, and who are acknowledged to be such, by many of the most learned and respectable in our land. Mountains of prejudice have been removed, and truth and light are dispelling the error and darkness of ages. The time was, when we trembled in the presence of a white man, and dared not assert, or even ask for our rights, but would be guided, directed, and governed, in any way we were demanded, without ever stopping to enquire whether we were right or wrong. We were not only slaves, but our ignorance made us willing slaves. Many of us uttered complaints against the faithful abolitionists, for the broad assertion of our rights; thought they went too far, and were only making our condition worse. This

Source: Frederick Douglass, "An Address to the Colored People of the United States," *The North Star,* 29 September 1848.

sentiment has nearly ceased to reign in the dark abodes of our hearts; we begin to see our wrongs as clearly, and comprehend our rights as fully, and as well as our white countrymen. This is a sign of progress; and evidence which cannot be gainsayed. It would be easy to present in this connection, a glowing comparison of our past with our present condition, showing that while the former was dark and dreary, the present is full of light and hope. It would be easy to draw a picture of our present achievements, and erect upon it a glorious future.

But, fellow countrymen, it is not so much our purpose to cheer you by the progress we have already made, as it is to stimulate you to still higher attainments. We have done much, but there is much more to be done.—While we have undoubtedly great cause to thank God, and take courage for the hopeful changes which have taken place in our condition, we are not without cause to mourn over the sad condition which we yet occupy. We are yet the most oppressed people in the world. In the Southern states of this Union, we are held as slaves. All over that wide region our paths are marked with blood. Our backs are yet scarred by the lash, and our souls are yet dark under the pall of slavery.—Our sisters are sold for purposes of pollution, and our brethren are sold in the market, with beasts of burden. Shut up in the prison-house of bondage—denied all rights, and deprived of all privileges, we are blotted from the page of human existence, and placed beyond the limits of human regard. Death, moral death, has palsied our souls in that quarter, and we are a murdered people.

In the Northern states, we are not slaves to individuals, not personal slaves, yet in many respects we are the slaves of the community. We are, however, far enough removed from the actual condition of the slave, to make us largely responsible for their continued enslavement, or their speedy deliverance from chains. For in the proportion which we shall rise in the scale of human improvement, in that proportion do we augment the probabilities of a speedy emancipation of our enslaved fellow-countrymen. It is more than a mere figure of speech to say, that we are as a people, chained together. We are one people—one in general complexion, one in a common degradation, one in popular estimation. As one rises, all must rise, and as one falls all must fall. Having now, our feet on the rock of freedom, we must drag our brethren from the slimy depths of slavery, ignorance, and ruin. Every one of us should be ashamed to consider himself free, while his brother is a slave.—The wrongs of our brethren, should be our constant theme. There should be no time too precious, no calling too holy, no place too sacred, to make room for this cause. We should not only feel it to be the cause of humanity, but the cause of christianity, and fit work for men and angels. We ask you to devote yourselves to this cause, as one of the first, and most successful means of self improvement. In the careful study of it, you will learn your own rights, and comprehend your own responsibilities, and, scan through the vista of coming time, your high, and God-appointed destiny. Many of the brightest and best of our number, have become such by their devotion to this cause, and the society of white abolitionists. The latter have been willing to make themselves of no reputation for our sake, and in return, let us show ourselves worthy of their zeal and devotion. Attend anti-slavery meetings, show that you are interested in the subject, that you hate slavery, and love those who are laboring for its overthrow.—Act with white Abolition societies wherever you can, and where you cannot, get up societies among yourselves, but without exclusiveness. It will be a long time before we gain all our rights; and although it may seem to conflict with our views of human brotherhood, we shall undoubtedly for many years be compelled to have institutions of a complexional character, in order to attain this very idea of human brotherhood. We would, however, advise our brethren to occupy memberships and stations among white persons, and in white institutions, just so fast as our rights are secured to us.

Never refuse to act with a white society or institution because it is white, or a black one, because it is black. But act with all men without distinction of color. By so acting, we shall find many opportunities for removing prejudices and establishing the rights of all men. We say avail yourselves of *white* institutions, not because they are white, but because they afford a more convenient means of improvement. But we pass from these suggestions, to others which may be deemed more important. In the Convention that now addresses you, there has been much said on the subject of labor, and especially those departments of it, with which we as a class have been long identified. You will see by the resolutions there adopted on that subject, that the Convention regarded those employments though right in themselves, as being nevertheless, degrading to us as a class, and therefore, counsel you to abandon them as speedily as possible, and to seek what are called the more respectable employments. While the Convention do not inculcate the doctrine that any kind of needful toil is in itself dishonorable, or that colored persons are to be exempt from what are called menial employments, they do mean to say that such employments have been so long and universally filled by colored men, as to become a badge of degradation, in that it has established the conviction that colored men are only fit for such employments. We therefore, advise you by all means, to cease from such employments, as far as practicable, by pressing into others. Try to get your sons into mechanical trades; press them into the blacksmith's shop, the machine shop, the joiner's shop, the wheelwright's shop, the cooper's shop, and the tailor's shop.

Every blow of the sledge hammer, wielded by a sable arm, is a powerful blow in support of our cause. Every colored mechanic, is by virtue of circumstances, an elevator of his race. Every house built by black men, is a strong tower against the allied hosts of prejudice. It is impossible for us to attach too much importance to this aspect of the subject. Trades are important. Wherever a man may be thrown by misfortune, if he has in his hands a useful trade, he is useful to his fellow man, and will be esteemed accordingly; and of all men in the world who need trades we are the most needy.

Understand this, that independence is an essential condition of respectability. To be dependent, is to be degraded. Men may indeed pity us, but they cannot respect us. We do not mean that we can become entirely independent of all men; that would be absurd and impossible, in the social state. But we mean that we must become equally independent with other members of the community. That other members of the community shall be as dependent upon us, as we upon them.—That such is not now the case, is too plain to need an argument. The houses we live in are built by white men—the clothes we wear are made by white tailors—the hats on our heads are made by white hatters, and the shoes on our feet are made by white shoe-makers, and the food that we eat, is raised and cultivated by white men. Now it is impossible that we should ever be respected as a people, while we are so universally and completely dependent upon white men for the necessaries of life. We must make white persons as dependent upon us, as we are upon them. This cannot be done while we are found only in two or three kinds of employments, and those employments have their foundation chiefly, if not entirely, in the pride and indolence of the white people. Sterner necessities, will bring higher respect.

The fact is, we must not merely make the white man dependent upon us to shave him but to feed him; not merely dependent upon us to black his boots, but to make them. A man is only in a small degree dependent on us when he only needs his boots blacked, or his carpet bag carried; as a little less pride, and a little more industry on his part, may enable him to dispense with our services entirely. As wise men it becomes us to look forward to a state of things, which appears inevitable. The time will come, when those menial employments will afford less means of living than they now do. What shall a large class of our fellow countrymen do, when white men find it economical to black their own boots, and shave themselves. What will they do when white men learn to wait on themselves? We warn you brethren, to seek other and more enduring vocations.

Let us entreat you to turn your attention to agriculture. Go to farming. Be tillers of the soil. On this point we could say much, but the time and space will not permit. Our cities are overrun with menial laborers, while the country is eloquently pleading for the hand of industry to till her soil, and reap the reward of honest labor. We beg and intreat you, to save your money—live economically—dispense with finery, and the gaities which have rendered us proverbial, and save your money. Not for the senseless purpose of being better off than your neighbor, but that you may be able to educate your children, and render your share to the common stock of prosperity and happiness around you. It is plain that the equality which we aim to accomplish, can only be achieved by us, when we can do for others, just what others can do for us. We should therefore, press into all the trades, professions and callings, into which honorable white men press.

We would in this connection, direct your attention to the means by which we have been oppressed and degraded. Chief among those means, we may mention the press. This engine has brought to the aid of prejudice, a thousand stings. Wit, ridicule, false philosophy, and an impure theology, with a flood of low black-guardism, come through this channel into the public mind; constantly feeding and keeping alive against us, the bitterest hate. The pulpit too, has been arrayed against us. Men with sanctimonious face, have talked of our being descendants of Ham—that we are under a curse, and to try to improve our condition, is virtually to counteract the purposes of God!

It is easy to see that the means which have been used to destroy us, must be used to save us. The press must be used in our behalf: aye! we must use it ourselves; we must take and read newspapers; we must read books, improve our minds, and put to silence and to shame, our opposers...

—September 29, 1848.

The Present and Future of the Colored Race in America

Frederick Douglass

I think that most of you will agree with me in respect to the surpassing importance of the subject we are here to consider this evening though you may differ from me in other respects. It seems to me that the relation subsisting between the white and colored people of this country, is of all other questions, the great, paramount, imperative, and all commanding question for this age and nation to solve.

Source: Frederick Douglass, "The Present and Future of the Colored Race in America," *Douglass' Monthly,* June 1863.

All the circumstances of the hour plead with an eloquence, equaled by no human tongue, for the immediate solution of this vital problem. 200,000 graves.—A distracted and bleeding country plead for this solution. It cannot be denied, nobody now even attempts to deny, that the question, what shall be done with the Negro, is the one grand cause of the tremendous war now upon us, and likely to continue upon us, until the country is united upon some wise policy concerning it. When the country was at peace and all appeared prosperous, there was something like a plausible argument in favor of leaving things to their own course. No such policy avails now. The question now stands before us as one of life and death. We are encompassed by it as by a wall of fire. The flames singe and burn us on all sides, becoming hotter every hour.

Men sneer at it as the "n—r question," endeavoring to degrade it by misspelling it. But they degrade nothing but themselves. They would much rather talk about the Constitution as it is, and the Union as it was, or about the Crittenden, or some other impossible compromise, but the Negro peeps out at every flash of their rhetorical pyrotechnics and utterly refuses to be hid by either fire, dust or smoke. The term, Negro, is at this hour the most pregnant word in the English language. The destiny of the nation has the Negro for its pivot, and turns upon the question as to what shall be done with him. Peace and war, union and disunion, salvation and ruin, glory and shame all crowd upon our thoughts the moment this vital word is pronounced.

You and I have witnessed many attempts to put this Negro question out of the pale of popular thought and discussion, and have seen the utter vanity of all such attempts.—It has baffled all the subtle contrivances of an ease loving and selfish priesthood, and has constantly refused to be smothered under the soft cushions of a canting and heartless religion. It has mocked and defied the compromising cunning of so called statesmen, who would have gladly postponed our present troubles beyond our allotted space of life and bequeath them as a legacy of sorrow to our children. But this wisdom of the crafty is confounded and their counsels brought to naught. A divine energy, omniscient and omnipotent, acting through the silent, solemn and all pervading laws of the universe, irresistible, unalterable and eternal, has ever more forced this mighty question of the Negro upon the attention of the country and the world.

What shall be done with the Negro? meets us not only in the street, in the Church, in the Senate, and in our State Legislatures; but in our diplomatic correspondence with foreign nations, and even on the field of bat-

tle, where our brave sons and brothers are striking for Liberty and country, or for honored graves.

This question met us before the war; it meets us during the war, and will certainly meet us after the war, unless we shall have the wisdom, the courage, and the nobleness of soul to settle the status of the Negro, on the solid and immovable bases of Eternal justice.

I stand here tonight therefore, to advocate what I conceive to be such a solid basis, one that shall fix our peace upon a rock. Putting aside all the hay, wood and stubble of expediency, I shall advocate for the Negro, his most full and complete adoption into the great national family of America. I shall demand for him the most perfect civil and political equality, and that he shall enjoy all the rights, privileges and immunities enjoyed by any other members of the body politic. I weigh my words and I mean all I say, when I contend as I do contend, that this is the *only solid, and final solution* of the problem before us. It is demanded not less by the terrible exigencies of the nation, than by the Negro himself for the Negro and the nation, are to rise or fall, be killed or cured, saved or lost together. Save the Negro and you save the nation, destroy the Negro and you destroy the nation, and to save both you must have but one great law of Liberty, Equality and Fraternity for all Americans without respect to color.

Already I am charged with treating this question, in the light of abstract ideas. I admit the charge, and would to heaven that this whole nation could now be brought to view it in the same calm, clear light. The failure so to view it is the one great national mistake. Our wise men and statesmen have insisted upon viewing the whole subject of the Negro upon what they are pleased to call practical and common sense principles, and behold the results of their so called practical wisdom and common sense! Behold, how all to the mocker has gone.

Under this so called practical wisdom and statesmanship, we have had sixty years of compromising servility on the part of the North to the slave power of the South. We have dishonored our manhood and lied in our throats to defend the monstrous abomination. Yet this greedy slave power, with every day of his shameless truckling on our part became more and more exacting, unreasonable, arrogant and domineering, until it has plunged the country into a war such as the world never saw before, and I hope never will see again.

Having now tried, with fearful results, the wisdom of reputed wise men, it is now quite time that the American people began to view this question in the light of other ideas than the cold and selfish ones which have hitherto enjoyed the reputation of being wise and practicable, but which are now proved to be entirely and absolutely impracticable.

The progress of the nation downward has been rapid as all steps downward are apt to be.

First. We found the Golden Rule impracticable.

Second. We found the Declaration of Independence very broadly impracticable.

Third. We found the Constitution of the United States, requiring that the majority shall rule, is impracticable.

Fourth. We found that the union was impracticable.

The golden rule did not hold the slave tight enough. The Constitution did not hold the slave tight enough. The Declaration of Independence did not hold the slave at all, and the union was a loose affair and altogether impracticable. Even the Democratic party bowed and squatted lower than all other parties, became at last weak and impracticable, and the slaveholders broke it up as they would an abolition meeting. Nevertheless: I am aware that there are such things as practicable and impracticable, and I will not ignore the objections, which may be raised against the policy which I would have the nation adopt and carry out toward my enslaved and oppressed fellow countrymen.

There are at least four answers, other than mine, floating about in the public mind, to the question what shall be done with the Negro.

First. It is said that the white race can, if they will, reduce the whole colored population to slavery, and at once make all the laws and institutions of the country harmonize with that state of facts and thus abolish at a blow, all distinctions and antagonisms. But this mode of settling the question, simple as it is, would not work well. It would create a class of tyrants in whose presence no man's Liberty, not even the white man's Liberty would be safe. The slaveholder would then be the only really free man of the country.—All the rest would be either slaves, or be poor white trash, to be kept from between the wind and our slaveholding nobility. The non-slaveholder would be the patrol, the miserable watch dog of the slave plantation.

Second. The next and best defined solution of our difficulties about the Negro, is colonization, which proposes to send the Negro back to Africa where his ancestors came from.—This is a singularly pleasing dream. But as was found in the case of sending missionaries to the moon, it was much easier to show that they might be useful there, than to show how they could be got there. It would take a larger sum of money than we shall have to spare at the close of this war, to send five millions of American born people, five thousand miles across the sea.

It may be safely affirmed that we shall hardly be in a condition at the close of this war to afford the money for such costly transportation, even if we could consent to the folly of sending away the only efficient producers in the largest half of the American union.

Third. It may be said as another mode of escaping the claims of absolute justice, the white people may Emancipate the slaves in form yet retain them as slaves in fact just as General Banks is now said to be doing in Louisiana, or then may free them from individual masters, only to make them slaves to the community. They can make of them a degraded caste. But this would be about the worst thing that could be done. It would make pestilence and pauperism, ignorance and crime, a part of American Institutions. It would be dooming the colored race to a condition indescribably wretched and the dreadful contagion of their vices and crimes would fly like cholera and small pox through all classes. Woe, woe! to this land, when it strips five millions of its people of all motives for cultivating an upright character. Such would be the effect of abolishing slavery, without conferring equal rights. It would be to lacerate and depress the spirit of the Negro, and make him a scourge and a curse to the country. Do anything else with us, but plunge us not into this hopeless pit.

Fourth. The white people of the country may trump up some cause of war against the colored people, and wage that terrible war of races which some men even now venture to predict, if not to desire, and exterminate the black race entirely. They would spare neither age nor sex.

But is there not some chosen curse, some secret thunder in the stores of heaven red with uncommon wrath to blast the men who harbor this bloody solution? The very thought is more worthy of demons than of men. Such a war would indeed remove the colored race from the country.—But it would also remove justice, innocence and humanity from the country. It would fill the land with violence and crime, and make the very name of America a stench in the nostrils of mankind. It would give you hell for a country and fiends for your countrymen.

Now, I hold that there is but one way of wisely disposing of the colored race, and that is to do them right and justice. It is not only to break the chains of their bondage and accord to them personal liberty, but it is to admit them to the full and complete enjoyment of civil and political Equality.

The mere abolition of slavery is not the end of the law for the black man, or for the white man. To emancipate the bondman from the laws that make him a chattel, and yet subject him to laws and deprivations which will inevitably break down his spirit, destroy his patriotism and convert him into a social pest, will be little gain to him and less gain to the country. One of the most plausible arguments ever made for slavery, is that which assumes that those who argue for the freedom of the Negro, do not themselves propose to treat him as an equal fellow citizen. The true course is to look this matter squarely in the face and determine to grant the entire claims

of justice and liberty keeping back no part of the price.

But the question comes not only from those who hate the colored race, but from some who are distinguished for their philanthropy: can this thing be done? can the white and colored people of America ever be blended into a common nationality under a system of equal Laws?

Mark, I state the question broadly and fairly. It respects civil and political equality, in its fullest and best sense: can such equality ever be practically enjoyed?

The question is not can there be social equality? That does not exist anywhere.— There have been arguments to show that no one man should own more property than another. But no satisfactory conclusion has been reached. So there are those who talk about social Equality, but nothing better on that subject than *"pursuit,"* the right of pursuit has been attained.

The question is not whether the colored man is mentally equal to his white brother, for in this respect there is no equality among white men themselves.

The question is not whether colored men will be likely to reach the Presidential chair. I have no trouble here: for a man may live quite a tolerable life without ever breathing the air of Washington.

But the question is: Can the white and colored people of this country be blended into a common nationality, and enjoy together, in the same country, under the same flag, the inestimable blessings of life, liberty and the pursuit of happiness, as neighborly citizens of a common country?

I answer most unhesitatingly, I believe they can. In saying this I am not blind to the past. I know it well. As a people we have moved about among you like dwarfs among giants—too small to be seen. We were morally, politically and socially dead. To the eye of doubt and selfishness we were far beyond the resurrection trump. All the more because I know the past. All the more, because I know the terrible experience of the slave, and the depressing power of oppression, do I believe in the possibility of a better future for the colored people of America.

Let me give a few of the reasons for the hope that is within me.

The first is, despite all theories and all disparagements, the Negro is a man. By every fact, by every argument, by every rule of measurement, mental, moral or spiritual, by everything in the heavens above and in the earth beneath which vindicates the humanity of any class of beings, the Negro's humanity is equally vindicated. The lines which separate him from the brute creation are as broad, distinct and palpable, as those which define and establish the very best specimens of the Indo-Caucasian race. I will not stop here to prove the manhood of the Negro. His virtues and his vices, his courage and his cowardice, his beauties and his deformities, his wisdom and his folly, everything connected with him, attests his manhood.

If the Negro were a horse or an ox, the question as to whether he can become a party to the American government, and member of the nation, could never have been raised. The very questions raised against him confirm the truth of what they are raised to disprove. We have laws forbidding the Negro to learn to read, others forbidding his owning a dog, others punishing him for using fire arms, and our Congress came near passing a law that a Negro should in no case be superior to a white man, thus admitting the very possibility of what they were attempting to deny.

The foundation of all governments and all codes of laws is in the fact that man is a rational creature, and is capable of guiding his conduct by ideas of right and wrong, of good and evil, by hope of reward and fear of punishment. Can any man doubt that the Negro answers this description? Do not all the laws ever passed concerning him imply that he is just such a creature? I defy the most malignant accuser to prove that there is a more law abiding people anywhere than are the colored people. I claim for the colored man that he possesses all the natural conditions and attributes essential to the character of a good citizen. He can understand the requirements of the law and the reason of the law. He can obey the law, and with his arm and life defend and execute the law. The preservation of society, the protection of persons and property are the simple and primary objects for which governments are instituted among men.

There certainly is nothing in the ends sought, nor in the character of the means by which they are to be attained, which necessarily excludes colored men. I see no reason why we may not, in time, co-operate with our white fellow-countrymen in all the labors and duties of upholding a common government, and sharing with them in all the advantages and glory of a common nationality.

That the interests of all the people would be promoted by the full participation of colored men in the affairs of government seems very plain to me. The American government rests for support, more than any other government in the world, upon the loyalty and patriotism of all its people. The friendship and affection of her black sons and daughters, as they increase in virtue and knowledge, will be an element of strength to the Republic too obvious to be neglected and repelled. I predict, therefore, that under an enlightened public sentiment, the American people will cultivate the friendship, increase the usefulness and otherwise advance the interests of the colored race. They will be as eager to extend the rights and dignity of citizenship as they have hitherto been eager to deny those rights.

But a word as to objections. The constitution is interposed. It always is.

Let me tell you something. Do you know that you have been deceived and cheated? You have been told that this government was intended from the beginning for white men, and for white men exclusively; that the men who formed the Union and framed the Constitution designed the permanent exclusion of the colored people from the benefits of those institutions. Davis, Taney and Yancey, traitors at the south, have propagated this statement, while their copperhead echoes at the north have repeated the same. There never was a bolder or more wicked perversion of the truth of history. So far from this purpose was the mind and heart of your fathers, that they desired and expected the abolition of slavery. They framed the Constitution plainly with a view to the speedy downfall of slavery. They carefully excluded from the

Constitution any and every word which could lead to the belief that they meant it for persons of only one complexion.

The Constitution, in its language and in its spirit, welcomes the black man to all the rights which it was intended to guarantee to any class of the American people. Its preamble tells us for whom and for what it was made.

But I am told that the ruling class in America being white, it is impossible for men of color ever to become a part of the "body politic." With some men this seems a final statement, a final argument, which it is utterly impossible to answer. It conveys the idea that the body politic is a rather fastidious body, from which everything offensive is necessarily excluded. I, myself, once had some high notions about this body politic and its high requirements, and of the kind of men fit to enter it and share its privileges. But a day's experience at the polls convinced me that the "body politic" is not more immaculate than many other bodies. That in fact it is a very mixed affair. I saw ignorance enter, unable to read the vote it cast. I saw the convicted swindler enter and deposit his vote. I saw the gambler, the horse jockey, the pugilist, the miserable drunkard just lifted from the gutter, covered with filth, enter and deposit his vote. I saw Pat, fresh from the Emerald Isle, requiring two sober men to keep him on his legs, enter and deposit his vote for the Democratic candidate amid the loud hurrahs of his fellow-citizens. The sight of these things went far to moderate my ideas about the exalted character of what is called the body politic, and convinced me that it could not suffer in its composition even should it admit a few sober, industrious and intelligent colored voters.

It is a fact, moreover, that colored men did at the beginning of our national history, form a part of the body politic, not only in what are now the free states, but also in the slave states. Mr. Wm. Goodell, to whom the cause of liberty in America is as much indebted as to any other one American citizen, has demonstrated that colored men formerly voted in eleven out of the thirteen original states.

The war upon the colored voters, and the war upon the Union, originated with the same parties, at the same time, and for the same guilty purpose of rendering slavery perpetual, universal and all controlling in the affairs of the nation.

Let this object be defeated and abandoned, let the country be brought back to the benign objects set forth in the preamble of the Constitution, and the colored man will easily find his way into the body politic, and be welcome in the jury box as well as at the ballot box. I know that prejudice largely prevails, and will prevail to some extent long after slavery shall be abolished in this country, but the power of prejudice will be broken when slavery is once abolished. There is not a black law on the statute book of a single free state that has not been placed there in deference to slavery existing in the slave states.

But it is said that the Negro belongs to an inferior race. Inferior race! This is the apology, the philosophical and ethnological apology for all the hell-black crimes ever committed by the white race against the blacks and the warrant for the repetition of those crimes through all times. Inferior race! It is an old argument. All nations have been compelled to meet it in some form or other since mankind have been divided into strong and weak, oppressors and oppressed. Whenever and wherever men have been oppressed and enslaved, their oppressors and enslavers have in every instance found a warrant for such oppression and enslavement in the alleged character of their victims. The very vices and crimes which slavery generates are usually charged as the peculiar characteristic of the race enslaved. When the Normans conquered the Saxons, the Saxons were a coarse, unrefined, inferior race. When the United States wants to possess herself of Mexican territory, the Mexicans are an inferior race. When Russia wants a share of the Ottoman Empire, the Turks are an inferior race, the sick man of Europe. So, too, when England wishes to impose some new burden on Ireland, or excuse herself for refusing to remove some old one, the Irish are denounced as an inferior race. But this is a monstrous argument. Now, suppose it were true that the Negro is inferior instead of being an apology for oppression and proscription, it is an appeal to all that is noble and magnanimous in the human soul against both. When

Douglass ▲ *The Present and Future of the Colored Race in America*   113

used in the service of oppression, it is as if one should say, "that man is weak; I am strong, therefore I will knock him down, and as far as I can I will keep him down. Yonder is an ignorant man. I am instructed, therefore I will do what I can to prevent his being instructed and to withhold from him the means of education. There is another who is low in his associations, rude in his manners, coarse and brutal in his appetites, therefore I will see to it that his degradation shall be permanent, and that society shall hold out to him no motives or incitements to a more elevated character." I will not stop here to denounce this monstrous excuse for oppression. That men can resort to it shows that when the human mind is once completely under the dominion of pride and selfishness, the reasoning faculties are inverted if not subverted.

I should like to know what constitutes inferiority and the standard of superiority. Must a man be as wise as Socrates, as learned as Humbolt, as profound as Bacon, or as eloquent as Charles Sumner, before he can be reckoned among superior men? Alas! if this were so, few even of the most cultivated of the white race could stand the test. Webster was white and had a large head, but all white men have not large heads. The Negro is black and has a small head, but all Negroes have not small heads. What rule shall we apply to all these heads? Why this: Give all an equal chance to grow.

But I am told that the Irish element in this country is exceedingly strong, and that that element will never allow colored men to stand upon an equal political footing with white men. I am pointed to the terrible outrages committed from time to time by Irishmen upon Negroes. The mobs at Detroit, Chicago, Cincinnati, and New York, are cited as proving the unconquerable aversion of the Irish towards the colored race.

Well, my friends, I admit that the Irish people are among our bitterest persecutors. In one sense it is strange, passing strange, that they should be such, but in another sense it is quite easily accounted for. It is said that a Negro always makes the most cruel Negro driver, a northern slaveholder the most rigorous master, and the poor man suddenly made

rich becomes the most haughty insufferable of all purse-proud fools.

Daniel O'Connell once said that the history of Ireland might be traced like a wounded man through a crowd—by the blood. The Irishman has been persecuted for his religion about as rigorously as the black man has been for his color. The Irishman has outlived his persecution, and I believe that the Negro will survive his.

But there is something quite revolting in the idea of a people lately oppressed suddenly becoming oppressors, that the persecuted can so suddenly become the persecutors.

Let us see a small sample of the laws by which our Celtic brothers have in other days been oppressed. Religion, not color, was the apology for this oppression, and the one apology is about as good as the other.

The following summary is by that life-long friend of the Irish—Sydney Smith:

In 1695, the Catholics were deprived of all means of educating their children, at home or abroad, and of all the privileges of being guardians to their own or to other persons' children. Then all the Catholics were disarmed, and then all the priests banished. After this (probably by way of joke) an act was passed to *confirm* the treaty of Limerick, the great and glorious King William, totally forgetting the contract he had entered into of recommending the religious liberties of the Catholics to the attention of Parliament.

On the 4th of March, 1704, it was enacted that any son of a Catholic who would turn Protestant should succeed to the family estate, which from that moment could no longer be sold, as charged with debt and legacy.

On the same day, Popish fathers were debarred, by a penalty of five hundred pounds, from being guardians to their own children. If the child, however young, declared himself a Protestant, he was to be delivered immediately to the custody of some Protestant relation.

No Protestant to marry a Papist. No Papist to purchase land or take a lease of land for more than thirty-one years. If the profits of the land so leased by the Catholic amounted to above a certain rate, settled by the act, *farm to belong to the first Protestant who made the discovery.* No Papist to be in a line of entail, but the estate to pass on to the next Protestant heir, as if the Papist were dead. If a Papist dies intestate, and no Protestant heir can be found, property to be equally divided among all the sons; or, if he has none, among all the daughters. By the 16th clause of this bill, no Papist to hold any office, civil or military. Not to dwell in Limerick or Galway, except on certain conditions. Not to vote at elections.

In 1709, Papists were prevented from holding an annuity for life. If any son of a Papist chose to turn Protestant and enroll the certificate of his conversion in the Court of Chancery, that court is empowered to compel his father to state the value of his property upon oath, and to make out of that property a competent allowance to the son, at their own discretion, not only for his present maintenance, but for his future portion after the death of his father. An increase of jointure to be enjoyed by Papist wives upon their conversion. Papists keeping schools to be prosecuted as convicts. Popish priests who are converted, to receive thirty pounds per annum.

Rewards are given by the same act for the discovery of Popish clergy—fifty pounds for discovering a Popish bishop, twenty pounds for a common Popish clergy, ten pounds for a Popish usher! Two justices of the peace can compel any Papist above 18 years of age to disclose every particular which has come to his knowledge respecting Popish priests, celebration of mass, or Papist schools. Imprisonment for a year if he refuses to answer. Nobody can hold property in trust for a Catholic. Juries in all trials growing out of these statutes to be Protestants. No Papist to take more than two apprentices, except in the linen trade. All the Catholic clergy to give in their names and places of abode at the quarter sessions, and to keep no curates. Catholics not to serve on grand juries. In any trial upon statutes for strengthening the Protestant interest, a Papist juror may be peremptorily challenged.

In the next reign, Popish horses were attached and allowed to be seized for the militia. Papists cannot be either high or petty constables. No Papists to vote at elections. Papists in towns to provide Protestant watchmen, and not to vote at vestries.

In the reign of George second, Papists were prohibited from being barristers. Barristers and solicitors marrying Papists, considered to be Papists, and subjected to all penalties as such. Persons robbed by privateers, during a war with a Popish Prince, to be indemnified by grand jury presentments, and the money to be levied on the *Catholics* only. No Papist to marry a Protestant; any priest celebrating such marriage *to be hanged.*

A full acount of the laws here referred to may be found in a book entitled, "History of the penal Laws against Irish Catholics," by Henry Parnell, member of Parliament.—They are about as harsh and oppressive, as some of the laws against the colored people in border and Western States.

These barbarous and inhuman laws were all swept away by the act of Catholic Emancipation, and the present barbarous laws against the free colored people, must share the same fate.

There are signs of this good time coming all around us. Slavery has overleapt itself.— Having taken the sword it is destined to perish by the sword, and the long despised Negro is to bear an honorable part in the salvation of himself and the country by the same blow. It has taken two years to convince the Washington Government, of the wisdom of calling the black man to participate in the gigantic effort now making to save the country. Even now they have not fully learned it—but learn it they will, and learn it they must before this tremendous war shall be ended.—Massachusetts, glorious old Massachusetts, has called the black man to the honor of bearing arms, and a thousand are already enrolled.

Now what will be the effect? Suppose colored men are allowed to fight the battles of the Republic. Suppose they do fight and win victories as I am sure they will, what will be the effect upon themselves? Will not the country rejoice in such victories? and will it not extend to the colored man the praise due to his bravery? Will not the colored man himself soon begin to take a more hopeful view of his own destiny?

The fact is, my friends, we are opening a new account with the American people and with the whole human family.

Hitherto we have been viewed and have viewed ourselves, as an impotent and spiritless race, having only a mission of folly and degradation before us. Tonight we stand at the portals of a new world, a new life and a new destiny.

We have passed through the furnace and have not been consumed. During more than two centuries and a half, we have survived contact with the white race. We have risen from the small number of twenty, to the large number of five millions, living and increasing, where other tribes are decreasing and dying. We have illustrated the fact, that the two most opposite races of men known to ethnological science, can live in the same latitudes, longitudes, and altitudes, and that so far as natural causes are concerned there is reason to believe that we may permanently live under the same skies, brave the same climates, and enjoy Liberty, equality and fraternity in a common country.   —June 1863.

The Lessons of the Hour

Frederick Douglass

Friends and Fellow Citizens: No man should come before an audience like the one by whose presence I am now honored, without a noble object and a fixed and earnest purpose. I think that, in whatever else I may be deficient, I have the qualifications indicated, to speak to you this evening. I am here to speak for, and to defend, so far as I can do so within the bounds of truth, a long-suffering people, and one just now subject to much misrepresentation and persecution. Charges are at this time preferred against them, more damaging and distressing than any which they have been called upon to meet since their emancipation.

I propose to give you a colored man's view of the unhappy relations at present existing between the white and colored people of the Southern States of our union. We have had the Southern white man's view of the sub-

ject. It has been presented with abundant repetition and with startling emphasis, colored by his peculiar environments. We have also had the Northern white man's view tempered by time, distance from the scene, and his higher civilization.

This kind of evidence may be considered by some as all-sufficient upon which to found an intelligent judgment of the whole matter in controversy, and that therefore my testimony is not needed. But experience has taught us that it is sometimes wise and necessary to have more than the testimony of two witnesses to bring out the whole truth, especially is this the case where one of the witnesses has a powerful motive for concealing or distorting the facts in any given case. You must not, therefore, be surprised if my version of the Southern question shall widely differ from both the North and the South, and yet I shall fearlessly submit my testimony to the candid judgment of all who hear me. I shall do so in the firm belief that my testimony is true.

Source: Frederick Douglass, "The Lessons of the Hour" [Pamphlet] (Baltimore: n.p., 1894).

There is one thing, however, in which I think we shall all agree at the start. It is that the so-called, but mis-called, negro problem is one of the most important and urgent subjects that can now engage public attention. It is worthy of the most earnest consideration of every patriotic American citizen. Its solution involves the honor or dishonor, glory or shame, happiness or misery of the whole American people. It involves more. It touches deeply not only the good name and fame of the Republic, but its highest moral welfare and its permanent safety. Plainly enough the peril it involves is great, obvious and increasing, and should be removed without delay.

The presence of eight millions of people in any section of this country constituting an aggrieved class, smarting under terrible wrongs, denied the exercise of the commonest rights of humanity, and regarded by the ruling class in that section, as outside of the government, outside of the law, and outside of society; having nothing in common with the people with whom they live, the sport of mob violence and murder is not only a disgrace and scandal to that particular section but a menace to the peace and security of the people of the whole country.

I have waited patiently but anxiously to see the end of the epidemic of mob law and persecution now prevailing at the South. But the indications are not hopeful, great and terrible as have been its ravages in the past, it now seems to be increasing not only in the number of its victims, but in its frantic rage and savage extravagance. Lawless vengeance is beginning to be visited upon white men as well as black. Our newspapers are daily disfigured by its ghastly horrors. It is no longer local, but national; no longer confined to the South, but has invaded the North. The contagion is spreading, extending and overleaping geographical lines and state boundaries, and if permitted to go on it threatens to destroy all respect for law and order not only in the South, but in all parts of our country—North as well as South. For certain it is, that crime allowed to go on unresisted and unarrested will breed crime. When the poison of anarchy is once in the air, like the pestilence that walketh in the darkness, the winds of heaven will take it up and favor its diffusion. Though it may strike down the weak to-day, it will strike down the strong to-morrow.

Not a breeze comes to us now from the late rebellious States that is not tainted and freighted with negro blood. In its thirst for blood and its rage for vengeance, the mob has blindly, boldly and defiantly supplanted sheriffs, constables and police. It has assumed all the functions of civil authority. It laughs at legal processes, courts and juries, and its red-handed murderers range abroad unchecked and unchallenged by law or by public opinion. Prison walls and iron bars are no protection to the innocent or guilty, if the mob is in pursuit of negroes accused of crime. Jail doors are battered down in the presence of unresisting jailors, and the accused, awaiting trial in the courts of law are dragged out and hanged, shot, stabbed or burned to death as the blind and irresponsible mob may elect.

We claim to be a Christian country and a highly civilized nation, yet, I fearlessly affirm that there is nothing in the history of savages to surpass the blood chilling horrors and fiendish excesses perpetrated against the colored people by the so-called enlightened and Christian people of the South. It is commonly thought that only the lowest and most disgusting birds and beasts, such as buzzards, vultures and hyenas, will gloat over and prey upon dead bodies, but the Southern mob in its rage feeds its vengeance by shooting, stabbing and burning when their victims are dead.

Now the special charge against the negro by which this ferocity is justified, and by which mob law is defended by good men North and South, is alleged to be assaults by negroes upon white women. This charge once fairly started, no matter by whom or in what manner, whether well or ill-founded, whether true or false, is certain to subject the accused to immediate death. It is nothing, that in the case there may be a mistake as to identity. It is nothing that the victim pleads "not guilty." It is nothing that he only asks for time to establish his innocence. It is nothing that the accused is of fair reputation and his accuser is of an abandoned character. It is nothing that the majesty of the law is defied and insulted;

no time is allowed for defence or explanation; he is bound with cords, hurried off amid the frantic yells and cursing of the mob to the scaffold and under its shadow he is tortured till by pain or promises, he is made to think he can possibly gain time or save his life by confession, and then whether innocent or guilty, he is shot, hanged, stabbed or burned to death amid the wild shouts of the mob. When the will of the mob has been accomplished, when its thirst for blood has been quenched, when its victim is speechless, silent and dead, his mobocratic accusers and murderers of course have the ear of the world all to themselves, and the world generally approves their verdict.

Such then is the state of Southern civilization in its relation to the colored citizens of that section and though the picture is dark and terrible I venture to affirm that no man North or South can deny the essential truth of the picture.

Now it is important to know how this state of affairs is viewed by the better classes of the Southern States. I will tell you, and I venture to say if our hearts were not already hardened by familiarity with such crimes against the negro, we should be shocked and astonished by the attitude of these so-called better classes of the Southern people and their lawmakers. With a few noble exceptions the upper classes of the South are in full sympathy with the mob and its deeds. There are few earnest words uttered against the mob or its deeds. Press, platform and pulpit are either generally silent or they openly apologize for the mob. The mobocratic murderers are not only permitted to go free, untried and unpunished, but are lauded and applauded as honorable men and good citizens, the guardians of Southern women. If lynch law is in any case condemned, it is only condemned in one breath, and excused in another.

The great trouble with the negro in the South is, that all presumptions are against him. A white man has but to blacken his face and commit a crime, to have some negro lynched in his stead. An abandoned woman has only to start the cry that she has been insulted by a black man, to have him arrested and summarily murdered by the mob. Fright-

ened and tortured by his captors, confused into telling crooked stories about his whereabouts at the time when the alleged crime was committed and the death penalty is at once inflicted, though his story may be but the incoherency of ignorance or distraction caused by terror.

Now in confirmation of what I have said of the better classes of the South, I have before me the utterances of some of the best people of that section, and also the testimony of one from the North, a lady, from whom, considering her antecedents, we should have expected a more considerate, just and humane utterance.

In a late number of the "Forum" Bishop Haygood, author of the "Brother in Black," says that "The most alarming fact is, that execution by lynching has ceased to surprise us. The burning of a human being for any crime, it is thought, is a horror that does not occur outside of the Southern States of the American Union, yet unless assaults by negroes come to an end, there will most probably be still further display of vengeance that will shock the world, and men who are just will consider the provocation."

In an open letter addressed to me by ex-Governor Chamberlain, of South Carolina, and published in the "Charleston News and Courier," a letter which I have but lately seen, in reply to an article of mine on the subject published in the "North American Review," the ex-Governor says: "Your denunciation of the South on this point is directed exclusively, or nearly so, against the application of lynch law for the punishment of one crime, or one sort of crime, the existence, I suppose, I might say the prevalence of this crime at the South is undeniable. But I read your (my) article in vain for any special denunciation of the crime itself. As you say your people are lynched, tortured and burned for assault on white women. As you value your own good fame and safety as a race, stamp out the infamous crime." He further says, the way to stop lynching is to stamp out the crime.

And now comes the sweet voice of a Northern woman, of Southern principles, in the same tone and the same accusation, the good Miss Frances Willard, of the W. C. T. U.

She says in a letter now before me, "I pity the Southerner. The problem on their hands is immeasurable. The colored race," she says, "multiplies like the locusts of Egypt. The safety of woman, of childhood, of the home, is menaced in a thousand localities at this moment, so that men dare not go beyond the sight of their own roof tree." Such then is the crushing indictment drawn up against the Southern negroes, drawn up, too, by persons who are perhaps the fairest and most humane of the negro's accusers. But even they paint him as a moral monster ferociously invading the sacred rights of women and endangering the homes of the whites.

The crime they allege against the negro, is the most revolting which men can commit. It is a crime that awakens the intensest abhorrence and invites mankind to kill the criminal on sight. This charge thus brought against the negro, and as constantly reiterated by his enemies, is not merely against the individual culprit, as would be in the case with an individual culprit of any other race, but it is in a large measure a charge against the colored race as such. It throws over every colored man a mantle of odium and sets upon him a mark for popular hate, more distressing than the mark set upon the first murderer. It points him out as an object of suspicion and avoidance. Now it is in this form that you and I, and all of us, are required to meet it and refute it, if that can be done. In the opinion of some of us, it is thought that it were well to say nothing about it, that the least said about it the better. In this opinion I do not concur. Taking this charge in its broad and comprehensive sense in which it is presented, and as now stated, I feel that it ought to be met, and as a colored man, I am grateful for the opportunity now afforded me to meet it. For I believe it can be met and successfully met. I am of opinion that a people too spiritless to defend themselves are not worth defending.

Without boasting, on this broad issue as now presented, I am ready to confront ex-Governor Chamberlain, Bishop Fitzgerald, Bishop Haygood, and Miss Frances Willard and all others, singly or altogether, without any doubt of the result.

But I want to be understood at the outset. I do not pretend that negroes are saints or angels. I do not deny that they are capable of committing the crime imputed to them, but I utterly deny that they are any more addicted to the commission of that crime than is true of any other variety of the human family. In entering upon my argument, I may be allowed to say, that I appear here this evening not as the defender of any man guilty of this atrocious crime, but as the defender of the colored people as a class.

In answer to the terrible indictment, thus read, and speaking for the colored people as a class, I, in their stead, here and now plead not guilty and shall submit my case with confidence of acquittal by good men and women North and South.

It is the misfortune of the colored people in this country that the sins of the few are visited upon the many, and I am here to speak for the many whose reputation is put in peril by the sweeping charge in question. With General Grant and every other honest man, my motto is, "Let no guilty man escape." But while I am here to say this, I am here also to say, let no innocent man be condemned and killed by the mob, or crushed under the weight of a charge of which he is not guilty.

You will readily see that the cause I have undertaken to support, is not to be maintained by any mere confident assertions or general denials. If I had no better ground to stand upon than this I would leave the field of controversy and give up the colored man's cause at once to his able accusers. I am aware, however, that I am here to do in some measure what the masters of logic say cannot be done,—prove a negative.

Of course, I shall not be able to succeed in doing the impossible, but this one thing I can and will do. I can and will show that there are sound reasons for doubting and denying this horrible and hell-black charge of rape as the peculiar crime of the colored people of the South. My doubt and denial are based upon two fundamental and invincible grounds.

The first is, the well established and well tested character of the negro on the very point upon which he is now violently and persistently accused. The second ground for my doubt and denial is based upon what I know of the character and antecedents of the men and women who bring this charge against him. I undertake to say that the strength of this position will become more manifest as I proceed with my argument.

At the outset I deny that a fierce and frenzied mob is or ought to be deemed a competent witness against any man accused of any crime whatever. The ease with which a mob can be collected and the slight causes by which it may be set in motion, and the elements of which it is composed, deprives its testimony of the qualities that should inspire confidence and command belief. It is moved by impulses utterly unfavorable to an impartial statement of the truth. At the outset, therefore, I challenge the credibility of the mob, and as the mob is the main witness in the case against the negro, I appeal to the common sense of mankind in support of my challenge. It is the mob that brings this charge, and it is the mob that arraigns, condemns and executes, and it is the mob that the country has accepted as its witness.

Again, I impeach and discredit the veracity of southern men generally, whether mobocrats or otherwise, who now openly and deliberately nullify and violate the provisions of the constitution of their country, a constitution, which they have solemnly sworn to support and execute. I apply to them the legal maxim, "False in one, false in all."

Again I arraign the negro's accuser on another ground, I have no confidence in the truthfulness of men who justify themselves in cheating the negro out of his constitutional right to vote. The men, who either by false returns, or by taking advantage of his illiteracy or surrounding the ballot-box with obstacles and sinuosities intended to bewilder him and defeat his rightful exercise of the elective franchise, are men who are not to be believed on oath. That this is done in the Southern States is not only admitted, but openly defended and justified by so-called honorable men inside and outside of Congress.

Just this kind of fraud in the South is notorious. I have met it face to face. It was boldly defended and advocated a few weeks ago in a solemn paper by Prof. Weeks, a learned North Carolinian, in my hearing. His paper was one of the able papers read before one of the World's Auxiliary Congresses at Chicago.

Now men who openly defraud the negro by all manner of artifice and boast of it in the face of the world's civilization, as was done at Chicago, I affirm that they are not to be depended upon for truth in any case whatever, where the rights of the negro are involved. Their testimony in the case of any other people than the negro, against whom they should thus commit fraud would be instantly and utterly discredited, and why not the same in this case? Every honest man will see that this point is well taken, and I defy any argument that would drive me from this just contention. It has for its support common sense, common justice, common honesty, and the best sentiment of mankind, and has nothing to oppose it but a vulgar popular prejudice against the colored people of our country, which prejudice strikes men with moral blindness and renders them incapable of seeing any distinction between right and wrong.

But I come to a stronger position. I rest my conclusion not merely upon general principles, but upon well known facts. I reject the charge brought against the negro as a class, but all through the late war, while the slave masters of the South were absent from their homes in the field of rebellion, with bullets in their pockets, treason in their hearts, broad blades in their blood stained hands, seeking the life of the nation, with the vile purpose of perpetuating the enslavement of the negro, their wives, their daughters, their sisters and their mothers were left in the absolute custody of these same negroes, and during all those long four years of terrible conflict, when the negro had every opportunity to commit the abominable crime now alleged against him, there was never a single instance of such crime reported or charged against him. He was never accused of assault, insult, or an attempt to commit an assault upon any white woman in the whole South. A fact like this, although negative, speaks volumes and ought to have some weight with the American people.

Then, again on general principles, I do not believe the charge because it implies an improbable, if not impossible, change in the mental and moral character and composition of the negro. It implies a change wholly inconsistent with well known facts of human nature. It is a contradiction to well known human experience. History does not present an example of such a transformation in the character of any class of men so extreme, so unnatural and so complete as is implied in this charge. The change is too great and the period too brief. Instances may be cited where men fall like stars from heaven, but such is not the usual experience. Decline in the moral character of a people is not sudden, but gradual. The downward steps are marked at first by degrees and by increasing momentum from bad to worse. Time is an element in such changes, and I contend that the negroes of the South have not had time to experience this great change and reach this lower depth of infamy. On the contrary, in point of fact, they have been and still are, improving and ascending to higher levels of moral and social worth.

Again, I do not believe it and utterly deny it, because those who bring the charge do not and dare not, give the negro a chance to be heard in his own defence. He is not allowed to explain any part of his alleged offense. He is not allowed to vindicate his own character or to criminate the character and motives of his accusers. Even the mobocrats themselves admit that it would be fatal to their purpose to have the character of his accusers brought into court. They pretend to a delicate regard for the feelings of the parties assaulted, and therefore object to giving a fair trial to the accused. The excuse in this case is contemptible. It is not only mock modesty but mob modesty. Men who can collect hundreds and thousands, if we may believe them, and can spread before them in the tempest and whirlwind of vulgar passion, the most disgusting details of crime with the names of women, with the alleged offense, should not be allowed to shelter themselves under any pretense of modesty. Such a pretense is absurd and shameless. Who does not know that the modesty of womanhood is always an object for

protection in a court of law? Who does not know that a lawless mob composed in part of the basest of men can have no such respect for the modesty of women as a court of law. No woman need be ashamed to confront one who has insulted or assaulted her in a court of law. Besides innocence does not hesitate to come to the rescue of justice.

Again, I do not believe it, and deny it because if the evidence were deemed sufficient to bring the accused to the scaffold, through the action of an impartial jury, there could be, and would be, no objection to having the alleged offender tried in conformity to due process of law.

Any pretence that a guilty negro, especially one guilty of the crime now charged, would in any case be permitted to escape condign punishment, is an insult to common sense. Nobody believes or can believe such a thing as escape possible, in a country like the South, where public opinion, the laws, the courts, the juries, and the advocates are all known to be against him, he could hardly escape if innocent. I repeat, therefore, I do not believe it, because I know, and you know, that a passionate and violent mob bent upon taking life, from the nature of the case, is not a more competent and trustworthy body to determine the guilt or innocence of a negro accused in such a case, than is a court of law. I would not, and you would not, convict a dog on such testimony.

But I come to another fact, and an all-important fact, bearing upon this case. You will remember that during all the first years of reconstruction and long after the war when the Southern press and people found it necessary to invent, adopt, and propagate almost every species of falsehood to create sympathy for themselves and to formulate an excuse for gratifying their brutal instincts, there was never a charge then made against a negro involving an assault upon any white woman or upon any little white child. During all this time the white women and children were absolutely safe. During all this time there was no call for Miss Willard's pity, or Bishop Haygood's defense of burning negroes to death.

You will remember also that during this time the justification for the murder of negroes was said to be negro conspiracies, insurrections, schemes to murder all the white people, to burn the town, and commit violence generally. These were the excuses then depended upon, but never a word was then said or whispered about negro outrages upon white women and children. So far as the history of that time is concerned, white women and children were absolutely safe, and husbands and fathers could leave home without the slightest anxiety on account of their families.

But when events proved that no such conspiracies; no such insurrections as were then pretended to exist and were paraded before the world in glaring head-lines, had ever existed or were even meditated; when these excuses had run their course and served their wicked purpose; when the huts of negroes had been searched, and searched in vain, for guns and ammunition to prove these charges, and no evidence was found, when there was no way open thereafter to prove these charges against the negro and no way to make the North believe in these excuses for murder, they did not even then bring forward the present allegation against the negro. They, however, went on harassing and killing just the same. But this time they based the right thus to kill on the ground that it was necessary to check the domination and supremacy of the negro and to secure the absolute rule of the Anglo-Saxon race.

It is important to notice that there has been three distinct periods of persecution of negroes in the South, and three distinct sets of excuses for persecution. They have come along precisely in the order in which they were most needed. First you remember it was insurrection. When that was worn out, negro supremacy became the excuse. When that is worn out, now it is assault upon defenseless women. I undertake to say, that this order and periodicity is significant and means something and should not be overlooked. And now that negro supremacy and negro domination are no longer defensible as an excuse for negro persecutions, there has come in due course, this heart-rending cry about the white women and little white children of the South.

Now, my friends, I ask what is the rational explanation of this singular omission of this charge in the two periods preceding the present? Why was not the charge made at that time as now? The negro was the same then as to-day. White women and children were the same then as to-day. Temptations to wrong doing were the same then as to-day. Why then was not this dreadful charge brought forward against the negro in war times and why was it not brought forward in reconstruction times?

I will tell you; or you, yourselves, have already answered the question. The only rational answer is that there was no foundation for such a charge or that the charge itself was either not thought of or was not deemed necessary to excuse the lawless violence with which the negro was then pursued and killed. The old charges already enumerated were deemed all sufficient. This new charge has now swallowed up all the old ones and the reason is obvious.

Things have changed since then, old excuses were not available and the negro's accusers have found it necessary to change with them. The old charges are no longer valid. Upon them the good opinion of the North and of mankind cannot be secured. Honest men no longer believe in the worn-out stories of insurrection. They no longer believe that there is just ground to apprehend negro supremacy. Time and events have swept away these old refuges of lies. They did their work in their day, and did it with terrible energy and effect, but they are now cast aside as useless. The altered times and circumstances have made necessary a sterner, stronger, and more effective justification of Southern barbarism, and hence, according to my theory, we now have to look into the face of a more shocking and blasting charge than either negro supremacy or insurrection or that of murder itself.

This new charge has come at the call of new conditions, and nothing could have been hit upon better calculated to accomplish its purpose. It clouds the character of the negro with a crime the most revolting, and is fitted to drive from him all sympathy and all fair play and all mercy. It is a crime that places him outside of the pale of the law, and settles upon his shoulders a mantle of wrath and fire that blisters and burns into his very soul.

It is for this purpose, as I believe, that this new charge unthought of in the times to which I have referred, has been largely invited, if not entirely trumped up. It is for this purpose that it has been constantly reiterated and adopted. It was to blast and ruin the negro's character as a man and a citizen.

I need not tell you how thoroughly it has already done its wonted work. You may feel its malign influence in the very air. You may read it in the faces of men. It has cooled our friends. It has heated our enemies, and arrested in some measure the efforts that good men were wont to make for the colored man's improvement and elevation. It has deceived our friends at the North and many good friends at the South, for nearly all have in some measure accepted the charge as true. Its perpetual reiteration in our newspapers and magazines has led men and women to regard us with averted eyes, increasing hate and dark suspicion.

Some of the Southern papers have denounced me for my unbelief, in their new departure, but I repeat I do not believe it and firmly deny it. I reject it because I see in it, evidence of an invention, called into being by a well defined motive, a motive sufficient to stamp it as a gross expedient to justify murderous assault upon a long enslaved and hence a hated people.

I do not believe it because it bears on its face, the marks of being a makeshift for a malignant purpose. I reject it not only because it was sprung upon the country simultaneously with well-known efforts now being industriously made to degrade the negro by legislative enactments, and by repealing all laws for the protection of the ballot, and by drawing the color line in all railroad cars and stations and in all other public places in the South; but because I see in it a means of paving the way for our entire disfranchisement.

Again, I do not believe it, and deny it, because the charge is not so much against the crime itself, as against the color of the man alleged to be guilty of it. Slavery itself, you will remember, was a system of legalized outrage upon the black women of the North, and no white man was ever shot, burned, or hanged

for availing himself of all the power that slavery gave him at this point.

Upon these grounds then—grounds which I believe to be solid and immovable—I dare here and now in the capital of the nation and in the presence of Congress to reject it, and ask you and all just men to reject this horrible charge so frequently made and construed against the negro as a class.

To sum up my argument on this lynching business. It remains to be said that I have shown that the negro's accusers in this case have violated their oaths and have cheated the negro out of his vote; that they have robbed and defrauded the negro systematically and persistently, and have boasted of it. I have shown that when the negro had every opportunity to commit the crime now charged against him he was never accused of it by his bitterest enemies. I have shown that during all the years of reconstruction, when he was being murdered at Hamburg, Yazoo, New Orleans, Copiah and elsewhere, he was never accused of the crime now charged against him. I have shown that in the nature of things no such change in the character and composition of a people as this charge implies could have taken place in the limited period allowed for it. I have shown that those who accuse him dare not confront him in a court of law and have their witnesses subjected to proper legal inquiry. And in showing all this, and more, I have shown that they who charge him with this foul crime may be justly doubted and deemed unworthy of belief.

But I shall be told by many of my Northern friends that my argument, though plausible, is not conclusive. It will be said that the charges against the negro are specific and positive, and that there must be some foundation for them, because as they allege men in their normal condition do not shoot and hang their fellowmen who are guiltless of crime. Well! This assumption is very just, very charitable. I only ask something like the same justice and charity could be shown to the negro as well as to the mob. It is creditable to the justice and humanity of the good people of the North by whom it is entertained. They rightly assume that men do not shoot and hang their fellowmen without just cause. But the vice of their argument is in their assumption that the lynchers are like other men. The answer to that argument is what may be truly predicated of human nature under one condition is not what may be true of human nature under another. Uncorrupted human nature may shudder at the commission of such crimes as those of which the Southern mob is guilty.

But human nature uncorrupted is one thing and human nature corrupted and perverted by long abuse of irresponsible power, is quite another and different thing. No man can reason correctly on this question who reasons on the assumption that the lynchers are like ordinary men.

We are not, in this case, dealing with men in their natural condition, but with men brought up in the exercise of arbitrary power. We are dealing with men whose ideas, habits and customs are entirely different from those of ordinary men. It is, therefore, quite gratuitous to assume that the principles that apply to other men apply to the Southern murderers of the negro, and just here is the mistake of the Northern people. They do not see that the rules resting upon the justice and benevolence of human nature do not apply to the mobocrats, or to those who were educated in the habits and customs of a slave-holding community. What these habits are I have a right to know, both in theory and in practice.

I repeat: The mistake made by those who on this ground object to my theory of the charge against the negro, is that they overlook the natural effect and influence of the life, education and habits of the lynchers. We must remember that these people have not now and have never had any such respect for human life as is common to other men. They have had among them for centuries a peculiar institution, and that peculiar institution has stamped them as a peculiar people. They were not before the war, they were not during the war and have not been since the war in their spirit or in their civilization, a people in common with the people of the North. I will not here harrow up your feelings by detailing their treatment of Northern prisoners during the war. Their institutions have taught them no respect for human life and especially the life of the negro. It has in fact taught them absolute contempt for his life. The sacredness of life which ordinary men feel does not touch them anywhere. A dead negro is with them a common jest.

They care no more for a negro's right to live than they care for his rights to liberty, or his rights to the ballot. Chief Justice Taney told the exact truth about these people when he said: "They did not consider that the black man had any rights which the white men were bound to respect." No man of the South ever called in question that statement and they never will. They could always shoot, stab and burn the negro without any such remorse or shame as other men would feel after committing such a crime. Any Southern man who is honest and is frank enough to talk on the subject, will tell you that he has no such ideas as we have of the sacredness of human life and especially, as I have said, of the life of the negro. Hence it is absurd to meet my arguments with the facts predicated on our common human nature.

I know I shall be charged with apologizing for criminals. Ex-Governor Chamberlain has already virtually done as much. But there is no foundation for any such charge. I affirm that neither I nor any other colored man of like standing with myself, has ever raised a finger or uttered a word in defense of any one really guilty of the dreadful crime now in question.

But, what I contend for, and what every honest man, black or white should contend for, is that when any man is accused of this or any other crime, of whatever name, nature, or extent, he shall have the benefit of a legal investigation; that he shall be confronted by his accusers; and that he shall through proper counsel, be able to question his accusers in open court and in open day-light so that his guilt or his innocence may be duly proved and established.

If this is to make me liable to the charge of apologizing for crime, I am not ashamed to be so charged. I dare to contend for the colored people of the United States that they are a law-abiding people, and I dare to insist upon it that they or any man, black or white, accused of crime, shall have a fair trial before he is punished.

Again, I cannot dwell too much upon the fact that colored people are much damaged by this charge. As an injured class we have a right to appeal from the judgment of the mob to the judgment of the law and the American people. Our enemies have known well where to strike and how to stab us most fatally. Owing to popular prejudice it has become the misfortune of the colored people of the South and of the North as well, to have as I have said, the sins of the few visited upon the many. When a white man steals, robs or murders, his crime is visited upon his own head alone. but not so with the black man. When he commits a crime the whole race is made to suffer. The cause before us is an example. This unfairness confronts us not only here, but it confronts us everywhere else.

Even when American art undertakes to picture the types of the two races it invariably places in comparison not the best of both races as common fairness would dictate, but it puts side by side in glaring contrast the lowest type of the negro with the highest type of the white man and calls upon you to "look upon this picture then upon that."

When a black man's language is quoted, in order to belittle and degrade him, his ideas are put into the most grotesque and unreadable English, while the utterances of negro scholars and authors are ignored. A hundred white men will attend a concert of white negro minstrels with faces blackened with burnt cork, to one who will attend a lecture by an intelligent negro.

On this ground I have a criticism to make, even of the late World's Columbian Exposition. While I join with all other men in pronouncing the Exposition itself one of the grandest demonstrations of civilization that the world has ever seen, yet great and glorious as it was, it was made to show just this kind of unfairness and discrimination against the negro.

As nowhere else in the world it was hoped that here the idea of human brotherhood would have been fully recognized and most gloriously illustrated. It should have been, and would have been, had it been what it professed to be, a World's Exposition. It was, however, in a marked degree an American Exposition. The spirit of American caste made itself conspicuously felt against the educated American negro, and to this extent, the Exposition was made simply an American Exposition and that in one of America's most illiberal features.

Since the day of Pentecost, there has never assembled in any one place or on any one occasion, a larger variety of peoples of all forms, features and colors, and all degrees of civilization, than was assembled at this World's Exposition. It was a grand ethnological lesson, a chance to study all likenesses and differences. Here were Japanese, Soudanese, Chinese, Cingalese, Syrians, Persians, Tunisians, Algerians, Egyptians, East Indians, Laplanders, Esquimaux, and as if to shame the educated negro of America, the Dahomeyans were there to exhibit their barbarism, and increase American contempt for the negro intellect. All classes and conditions were there save the educated American negro. He ought to have been there if only to show what American slavery and freedom have done for him. The fact that all other nations were there and there at their best, made his exclusion the more marked, and the more significant. People from abroad noticed the fact that while we have eight millions of colored people in the United States, many of them gentlemen and scholars, not one of them was deemed worthy to be appointed a Commissioner, or a member of an important committee, or a guide, or a guard on the Exposition grounds. What a commentary is this upon our boasted American liberty and American equality! It is a silence to be sure, but it is a silence that speaks louder than words. It says to the world that the colored people of America are deemed by Americans not within the compass of American law and of American civilization. It says to the lynchers and mobocrats of the South, go on in your hellish work of negro persecution. What you do to their bodies, we do to their souls.

I come now to the question of negro suffrage. It has come to be fashionable of late to ascribe much of the trouble at the South to ignorant negro suffrage. The great measure according suffrage to the negro recommended by General Grant and adopted by the loyal nation is now denounced as a blunder and a failure. They would, therefore, in some way abridge and limit this right by imposing upon it an educational or some other qualification. Among those who take this view are Mr. John J. Ingalls, and Mr. John M. Langston. They are both eloquent, both able, and both wrong. Though they are both Johns neither of them is to my mind a "St. John" and not even a "John the Baptist." They have taken up an idea which they seem to think quite new, but which in reality is as old as despotism and about as narrow and selfish. It has been heard and answered a thousand times over. It is the argument of the crowned heads and privileged classes of the world. It is as good against our Republican form of government as it is against the negro. The wonder is that its votaries do not see its consequences. It does away with that noble and just idea of Abraham Lincoln, that our government should be a government of the people, by the people, and for the people, and for *all* the people.

These gentlemen are very learned, very eloquent and very able, but I cannot follow them. Much learning has made them mad. Education is great, but manhood is greater. The one is the principle, the other is the accident. Man was not made as an attribute to education, but education is an attribute to man. I say to these gentlemen, first protect the man and you will thereby protect education. I would not make illiteracy a bar to the ballot, but would make the ballot a bar to illiteracy. Take the ballot from the negro and you take from him the means and motives that make for education. Those who are already educated and are vested with political power and have thereby an advantage, will have a strong motive for refusing to divide that advantage with others, and least of all will they divide it with the negro to whom they would deny all right to participate in the government.

I, therefore, cannot follow these gentlemen in their proposition to limit suffrage to the educated alone. I would not make suffrage more exclusive, but more inclusive. I

would not have it embrace merely the elite, but would include the lowly. I would not only include the men, I would gladly include the women, and make our government in reality as in name a government of the people and of the whole people.

But manifestly suffrage to the colored people is not the cause of the failure of good government, or the cause of trouble in the Southern States, but it is the lawless limitations of suffrage that makes the trouble.

Much thoughtless speech is heard about the ignorance of the negro in the South. But plainly enough it is not the ignorance of the negro, but the malevolence of his accusers, which is the real cause of Southern disorder. The illiteracy of the negro has no part or lot in the disturbances there. They who contend for disfranchisement on this ground know, and know very well, that there is no truth whatever in their contention. To make out their case they must show that some oppressive and hurtful measure has been imposed upon the country by negro voters. But they cannot show any such thing.

The negro has never set up a separate party, never adopted a negro platform, never proclaimed or adopted a separate policy for himself or for the country. His assailants know that he has never acted apart from the whole American people. They know that he has never sought to lead, but has always been content to follow. They know that he has not made his ignorance the rule of his political conduct, but the intelligence of white people has always been his guide. They know that he has simply kept pace with the average intelligence of his age and country. They know that he has gone steadily along in the line of his politics with the most enlightened citizens of the country. They know that he has always voted with one or the other of the two great political parties. They know that if the votes of these parties have been guided by intelligence and patriotism, the same may be said for the vote of the negro. They ought to know, therefore, that it is a shame and an outrage upon common sense and common fairness to make the negro responsible, or his ignorance responsible, for any disorder and confusion that may reign in the Southern

States. Yet, while any lie may be safely told against the negro and be credited, this lie will find eloquent mouths bold enough to tell it, and pride themselves upon their superior wisdom in denouncing the ignorant negro voter.

It is true that the negro once voted solidly for the candidates of the Republican party, but what if he did? He then only voted with John Mercer Langston, John J. Ingalls, John Sherman, General Harrison, Senator Hoar, Henry Cabot Lodge, and Governor McKinley, and many of the most intelligent statesmen and patriots of whom this country can boast. The charge against him at this point is, therefore, utterly groundless. It is a mere pretense, a sham, an excuse for fraud and violence, for persecution and a cloak for popular prejudice.

The proposition to disfranchise the colored voter of the South in order to solve the race problem I hereby denounce as a mean and cowardly proposition, utterly unworthy of an honest, truthful and grateful nation. It is a proposition to sacrifice friends in order to conciliate enemies; to surrender the constitution to the late rebels for the lack of moral courage to execute its provisions. It says to the negro citizens, "The Southern nullifiers have robbed you of a part of your rights, and as we are powerless and cannot help you, and wish to live on good terms with our Southern brethren, we propose to join your oppressors so that our practice shall be consistent with their theories. Your suffrage has been practically rendered a failure by violence, we now propose to make it a failure by law. Instead of conforming our practice to the theory of our government and the genius of our institutions, we now propose, as means of conciliation, to conform our practice to the theory of your oppressors."

Than this, was there ever a surrender more complete, more cowardly or more base? Upon the statesmen, black or white, who could dare to hint such a scheme of national debasement as a means of settling the race problem, I should inflict no punishment more severe than to keep him at home, and deprived of all legislative trusts forever.

Do not ask me what will be the final result of the so-called negro problem. I cannot tell you. I have sometimes thought that the American people are too great to be small, too just and magnanimous to oppress the weak, too brave to yield up the right to the strong, and too grateful for public services ever to forget them or fail to reward them. I have fondly hoped that this estimate of American character would soon cease to be contradicted or put in doubt. But the favor with which this cowardly proposition of disfranchisement has been received by public men, white and black, by Republicans as well as Democrats, has shaken my faith in the nobility of the nation. I hope and trust all will come out right in the end, but the immediate future looks dark and troubled. I cannot shut my eyes to the ugly facts before me.

Strange things have happened of late and are still happening. Some of these tend to dim the lustre of the American name, and chill the hopes once entertained for the cause of American liberty. He is a wiser man than I am, who can tell how low the moral sentiment of this republic may yet fall. When the moral sense of a nation begins to decline and the wheel of progress to roll backward, there is no telling how low the one will fall or where the other may stop. The downward tendency already manifest has swept away some of the most important safeguards. The Supreme Court has surrendered. State sovereignty is restored. It has destroyed the [C]ivil [R]ights Bill, and converted the Republican party into a party of money rather than a party of morals, a party of things rather than a party of humanity and justice. We may well ask what next?

The pit of hell is said to be bottomless. Principles which we all thought to have been firmly and permanently settled by the late war, have been boldly assaulted and overthrown by the defeated party. Rebel rule is now nearly complete in many States and it is gradually capturing the nation's Congress. The cause lost in the war, is the cause regained in peace, and the cause gained in war, is the cause lost in peace.

There was a threat made long ago by an American statesman, that the whole body of legislation enacted for the protection of American liberty and to secure the results of the war for the Union, should be blotted from the national statute book. The threat is now being sternly pursued, and may yet be fully re-alized. The repeal of the laws intended to pro-tect the elective franchise has heightened the suspicion that Southern rule may yet become complete, though I trust, not permanent. There is no denying that the trend is in the wrong way at present. The late election, how-ever, gives us hope that the loyal Republican party may return to its first born.

But I come now to another proposition held up just now as a solution of the race problem, and this I consider equally unwor-thy with the one just disposed of. The two be-long to the same low-bred family of ideas.

This proposition is to colonize the col-ored people of America in Africa, or some-where else. Happily this scheme will be defeated, both by its impolicy and its imprac-ticability. It is all nonsense to talk about the removal of eight millions of the American people from their homes in America to Africa. The expense and hardships, to say nothing of the cruelty of such a measure, would make success to such a measure impos-sible. The American people are wicked, but they are not fools, they will hardly be disposed to incur the expense, to say nothing of the in-justice which this measure demands. Never-theless, this colonizing scheme, unworthy as it is, of American statesmanship and American honor, and though full of mischief to the col-ored people, seems to have a strong hold on the public mind and at times has shown much life and vigor.

The bad thing about it is that it has now begun to be advocated by colored men of ac-knowledged ability and learning, and every little while some white statesman becomes its advocate. Those gentlemen will doubtless have their opinion of me; I certainly have mine of them. My opinion of them is that if they are sensible, they are insincere, and if they are sincere they are not sensible. They know, or they ought to know, that it would take more money than the cost of the late war, to transport even one-half of the colored people of the United States to Africa. Whether intentionally or not they are, as I think, simply trifling with an afflicted people. They urge them to look for relief, where they ought to know that relief is impossible. The

only excuse they can make is that there is no hope for the negro here and that the colored people in America owe something to Africa.

This last sentimental idea makes coloniza-tion very fascinating to dreamers of both col-ors. But there is really for it no foundation.

They tell us that we owe something to our native land. But when the fact is brought to view, which should never be forgotten, that a man can only have one native land, and that is the land in which he was born, the bottom falls entirely out of this sentimental argu-ment.

Africa, according to her advocates, is by no means modest in her demand upon us. She calls upon us to send her only our best men. She does not want our riff raff, but our best men. But these are just the men we want at home. It is true we have a few preachers and laymen with a missionary turn of mind who might be easily spared. Some who would possibly do as much good by going there as by staying here. But this is not the only coloniza-tion idea. Its advocates want not only the best, but millions of the best. They want the money to be voted by the United States Government to send them there.

Now I hold that the American negro owes no more to the negroes in Africa than he owes to the negroes in America. There are millions of needy people over there, but there are also millions of needy people over here as well, and the millions here need intelligent men of their numbers to help them, as much as intelligent men are needed in Africa. We have a fight on our hands right here, a fight for the whole race, and a blow struck for the negro in America is a blow struck for the negro in Africa. For until the negro is respect-ed in America, he need not expect considera-tion elsewhere. All this native land talk is nonsense. The native land of the American negro is America. His bones, his muscles, his sinews, are all American. His ancestors for two hundred and seventy years have lived, and la-bored, and died on American soil, and mil-lions of his posterity have inherited Caucasian blood.

It is competent, therefore, to ask, in view of this admixture, as well as in view of other facts, where the people of this mixed race are to go, for their ancestors are white and black, and it will be difficult to find their native land anywhere outside of the United States.

But the worse thing, perhaps, about this colonization nonsense is, that it tends to throw over the negro a mantle of despair. It leads him to doubt the possibility of his progress as an American citizen. It also encourages popular prejudice with the hope that by persecution or persuasion the negro can finally be driven from his natural home, while in the nature of the case, he must stay here, and will stay here and cannot well get away.

It tends to weaken his hold on one country while it can give him no rational hope of another. Its tendency is to make him despondent and doubtful, where he should be made to feel assured and confident. It forces upon him the idea that he is forever doomed to be a stranger and sojourner in the land of his birth, and that he has no permanent abiding place here.

All this is hurtful, with such ideas constantly flaunted before him he cannot easily set himself to work to better his condition in such ways as are open to him here. It sets him to groping everlastingly after the impossible.

Every man who thinks at all must know that home is the fountain head, the inspiration, the foundation and main support not only of all social virtue, but of all motives to human progress and that no people can prosper or amount to much without a home. To have a home, the negro must have a country, and he is an enemy to the moral progress of the negro, whether he knows it or not, who calls upon him to break up his home in this country for an uncertain home in Africa.

But the agitation of this subject has a darker side still. It has already been given out that we may be forced to go at the point of the bayonet. I cannot say we shall not, but badly as I think of the tendency of our times, I do not think that American sentiment will ever reach a condition which will make the expulsion of the negro from the United States by such means possible.

Colonization is no solution of the race problem. It is an evasion. It is not repenting

of wrong but putting out of sight the people upon whom wrong has been inflicted. Its reiteration and agitation only serve to fan the flame of popular prejudice and encourage the hope that in some way or other, in time or in eternity, those who hate the negro will get rid of him.

If the American people could endure the negro's presence while a slave, they certainly can and ought to endure his presence as a freeman. If they could tolerate him when he was a heathen, they might bear with him when he is a Christian, a gentleman and a scholar.

But woe to the South when it no longer has the strong arm of the negro to till its soil! And woe to the nation if it shall ever employ the sword to drive the negro from his native land!

Such a crime against justice, such a crime against gratitude, should it ever be attempted, would certainly bring a national punishment which would cause the earth to shudder. It would bring a stain upon the nation's honor, like the blood on Lady Macbeth's hand. The waters of all the oceans would not suffice to wash out the infamy that such an act of ingratitude and cruelty would leave on the character of the American people.

Another mode of impeaching the wisdom of emancipation, and one that seems to give pleasure to our enemies, is, as they say, that the condition of the colored people of the South has been made worse; that freedom has made their condition worse.

The champions of this idea are the men who glory in the good old times when the slaves were under the lash and were bought and sold in the market with horses, sheep and swine. It is another way of saying that slavery is better than freedom; that darkness is better than light and that wrong is better than right. It is the American method of reasoning in all matters concerning the negro. It inverts everything; turns truth upside down and puts the case of the unfortunate negro wrong end foremost every time. There is, however, always some truth on their side.

When these false reasoners assert that the condition of the emancipated is wretched and deplorable, they tell in part the truth, and I agree with them. I even concur with them that the negro is in some respects, and in some localities, in a worse condition to-day than in the time of slavery, but I part with these gentlemen when they ascribe this condition to emancipation.

To my mind, the blame for this condition does not rest upon emancipation, but upon slavery. It is not the work of the spirit of liberty, but the work of the spirit of bondage, and of the determination of slavery to perpetuate itself, if not under one form, then under another. It is due to the folly of endeavoring to retain the new wine of liberty in the old bottles of slavery. I concede the evil but deny the alleged cause.

The land owners of the South want the labor of the negro on the hardest possible terms. They once had it for nothing. They now want it for next to nothing and they have contrived three ways of thus obtaining it. The first is to rent their land to the negro at an exorbitant price per annum, and compel him to mortgage his crop in advance. The laws under which this is done are entirely in the interest of the landlord. He has a first claim upon everything produced on the land. The negro can have nothing, can keep nothing, can sell nothing, without the consent of the landlord. As the negro is at the start poor and empty handed, he has to draw on the landlord for meat and bread to feed himself and family while his crop is growing. The landlord keeps books; the negro does not; hence, no matter how hard he may work or how saving he may be, he is, in most cases, brought in debt at the end of the year, and once in debt, he is fastened to the land as by hooks of steel. If he attempts to leave he may be arrested under the law.

Another way, which is still more effective, is the payment of the labor with orders on stores instead of in lawful money. By this means money is kept entirely out of the hands of the negro. He cannot save money because he has no money to save. He cannot seek a better market for his labor because he has no money with which to pay his fare and because he is, by that vicious order system, already in debt, and therefore already in bondage. Thus

he is riveted to one place and is, in some sense, a slave; for a man to whom it can be said, "You shall work for me for what I shall choose to pay you and how I shall choose to pay you," is in fact a slave though he may be called a free man.

We denounce the landlord and tenant system of England, but it can be said of England as cannot be said of our free country, that by law no laborer can be paid for labor in any other than lawful money. England holds any other payment to be a penal offense and punishment by fine and imprisonments. The same should be the case in every State in the Union.

Under the mortgage system, no matter how industrious or economical the negro may be, he finds himself at the end of the year in debt to the landlord, and from year to year he toils on and is tempted to try again and again, seldom with any better result.

With this power over the negro, this possession of his labor, you may easily see why the South sometimes brags that it does not want slavery back. It had the negro's labor heretofore for nothing, and now it has it for next to nothing, and at the same time is freed from the obligation to take care of the young and the aged, the sick and decrepit.

I now come to the so-called, but mis-called "Negro Problem," as a characterization of the relations existing in the Southern States.

I say at once, I do not like or admit the justice or propriety of this formula. Words are things. They certainly are such in this case, and I may say they are a very bad thing in this case, since they give us a misnomer and one that is misleading. It is a formula of Southern origin, and has a strong bias against him. It has been accepted by the good people of the North, as I think, without investigation. It is a crafty invention and is in every way, worthy of its inventors.

The natural effect and purpose on its face of this formula is to divert attention from the true issue now before the American people. It does this by holding up and preoccupying the public mind with an issue entirely different from the real one in question. That which really is a great national problem and which ought to be so considered, dwarfs into a "negro problem."

The device is not new. It is an old trick. It has been oft repeated, and with a similar purpose and effect. For truth, it gives us false-hood. For innocence, it gives us guilt. It removes the burden of proof from the old master class, and imposes it upon the negro. It puts upon a race a work which belongs to the nation. It belongs to that craftiness often displayed by disputants, who aim to make the worse appear the better reason. It gives bad names to good things, and good names to bad things.

The negro has often been the victim of this kind of low cunning. You may remember that during the late war, when the South fought for the perpetuity of slavery, it called the slaves "domestic servants," and slavery "a domestic institution." Harmless names, in-deed, but the things they stood for were far from harmless.

The South has always known how to have a dog hanged by giving him a bad name. When it prefixed "negro" to the national problem, it knew that the device would awak-en and increase a deep-seated prejudice at once, and that it would repel fair and candid investigation. As it stands, it implies that the negro is the cause of whatever trouble there is in the South. In old slave times, when a little white child lost his temper, he was given a lit-tle whip and told to go and whip "Jim" or "Sal" and thus regained his temper. The same is true, to-day on a larger scale.

I repeat, and my contention is, that this negro problem formula lays the fault at the door of the negro, and removes it from the door of the white man, shields the guilty, and blames the innocent. Makes the negro re-sponsible and not the nation.

Now the real problem is, and ought to be regarded by the American people, a great na-tional problem. It involves the question, whether, after all, with our Declaration of In-dependence, with our glorious free constitu-tion, whether with our sublime Christianity, there is enough of national virtue in this great nation to solve this problem, in accordance with wisdom and justice.

The marvel is that this old trick of mis-naming things, so often played by Southern politicians, should have worked so well for the bad cause in which it is now employed,—for the Northern people have fallen in with it. It is still more surprising that the colored press of the country, and some of the colored ora-tors of the country, insist upon calling it a "negro problem," or a Race problem, for by it they mean the negro Race. Now—there is nothing the matter with the negro. He is all right. Learned or ignorant, he is all right. He is neither a Lyncher, a Mobocrat, or an Anar-chist. He is now, what he has ever been, a loyal, law-abiding, hard working, and peace-able man; so much so, that men have thought him cowardly and spiritless. They say that any other people would have found some violent way in which to resent their wrongs. If this problem depended upon *his* character and conduct, there would be no problem to solve; there would be no menace to the peace and good order of Southern society. He makes no unlawful fight between labor and capital. That problem which often makes the Ameri-can people thoughtful, is not of his bring-ing—though he may some day be compelled to talk, and on this tremendous problem.

He has as little to do with the cause of Southern trouble as he has with its cure. There is no reason, therefore, in the world, why he should give a name to this problem, and this lie, like all other lies, must eventually come to naught. A lie is worth nothing when it has lost its ability to deceive, and if it is at all in my power, this lie shall lose its power to de-ceive.

I well remember that this same old false-hood was employed and used against the negro, during the late war. He was then charged and stigmatized with being the cause of the war, on the principle that there would be no highway robbers if there were nobody on the road to be robbed. But as absurd as this pretense was, the color prejudice of the country was stimulated by it and joined in the accusation, and the negro has to bear the brunt of it.

Even at the North, he was hated and hunt-ed on account of it. In the great city of New

York, his houses were burned, his children were hunted down like wild beasts, and his people were murdered in the streets, because "they were the cause of the war." Even the noble and good Mr. Lincoln, one of the best men that ever lived, told a committee of negroes who waited upon him at Washington, that "they were the cause of the war." Many were the men who accepted this theory, and wished the negro in Africa, or in a hotter climate, as some do now.

There is nothing to which prejudice is not equal in the way of perverting the truth and inflaming the passions of men.

But call this problem what you may, or will, the all important question is: How can it be solved? How can the peace and tranquility of the South, and of the country, be secured and established?

There is nothing occult or mysterious about the answer to this question. Some things are to be kept in mind when dealing with this subject and never be forgotten. It should be remembered that in the order of Divine Providence the man who puts one end of a chain around the ankle of his fellow man will find the other end around his own neck. And it is the same with a nation. Confirmation of this truth is as strong as thunder. "As we sow, we shall reap," is a lesson to be learned here as elsewhere. We tolerated slavery, and it cost us a million graves, and it may be that lawless murder, if permitted to go on, may yet bring vengeance, not only on the reverend head of age and upon the heads of helpless women, but upon the innocent babe in the cradle.

But how can this problem be solved? I will tell you how it can *not* be solved. It cannot be solved by keeping the negro poor, degraded, ignorant and half-starved, as I have shown is now being done in the Southern States.

It cannot be solved by keeping the wages of the laborer back by fraud, as is now being done by the landlords of the South.

It cannot be done by ballot-box stuffing, by falsifying election returns, or by confusing the negro voter by cunning devices.

It cannot be done by repealing all federal laws enacted to secure honest elections.

It can, however, be done, and very easily done, for where there's a will, there's a way!

Let the white people of the North and South conquer their prejudices.

Let the great Northern press and pulpit proclaim the gospel of truth and justice against war now being made upon the negro.

Let the American people cultivate kindness and humanity.

Let the South abandon the system of "mortgage" labor, and cease to make the negro a pauper, by paying him scrip for his labor.

Let them give up the idea that they can be free, while making the negro a slave. Let them give up the idea that to degrade the colored man, is to elevate the white man.

Let them cease putting new wine into old bottles, and mending old garments with new cloth.

They are not required to do much. They are only required to undo the evil that they have done, in order to solve this problem.

In old times when it was asked, "How can we abolish slavery?" the answer was "Quit stealing."

The same is the solution of the Race problem to-day. The whole thing can be done by simply no longer violating the amendments of the Constitution of the United States, and no longer evading the claims of justice. If this were done, there would be no negro problem to vex the South, or to vex the nation.

Let the organic law of the land be honestly sustained and obeyed.

Let the political parties cease to palter in a double sense and live up to the noble declarations we find in their platforms.

Let the statesmen of the country live up to their convictions.

In the language of Senator Ingalls: "Let the nation try justice and the problem will be solved."

Two hundred and twenty years ago, the negro was made the subject of a religious problem, one which gave our white forefathers much perplexity and annoyance. At that time the problem was in respect of what relation a negro would sustain to the Christian

Church, whether he was a fit subject for baptism, and Dr. Godwin, a celebrated divine of his time, and one far in advance of his brethren, was at the pains of writing a book of two hundred pages, or more, containing an elaborate argument to prove that it was not a sin in the sight of God to baptize a negro.

His argument was very able, very learned, very long. Plain as the truth may now seem, there were at that time very strong arguments against the position of the learned divine.

As usual, it was not merely the baptism of the negro that gave trouble, but it was what might follow his baptism. The sprinkling him with water was a very simple thing, but the slave holders of that day saw in the innovation something more dangerous than water. They said that to baptize the negro and make him a member of the Church of Christ, was to make him an important person—in fact, to make him an heir of God and a joint heir of Jesus Christ. It was to give him a place at the Lord's supper. It was to take him out [of] the category of heathenism, and make it inconsistent to hold him as a slave; for the Bible made only the heathen a proper subject for slavery.

These were formidable consequences, certainly, and it is not strange that the Christian slave holders of that day viewed these consequences with immeasurable horror. It was something more terrible and dangerous than the fourteenth and fifteenth amendments to our Constitution. It was a difficult thing, therefore, at that day to get the negro in the water.

Nevertheless, our learned Doctor of Divinity, like many of the same class in our day, was quite equal to the emergency. He was able to satisfy all the important parties to the problem, except the negro, and him it did not seem necessary to satisfy.

The Doctor was [a] skilled dialectician. He did not only divide the word with skill, but he could divide the negro in two parts. He argued that the negro had a soul as well as a body, and insisted that while his body rightfully belonged to his master on earth, his soul belonged to his Master in heaven. By this convenient arrangement, somewhat metaphysical, to be sure, but entirely evangelical and logical, the problem of negro baptism was solved.

But with the negro in the case, as I have said, the argument was not entirely satisfactory. The operation was much like that by which the white man got the turkey and the Indian got the crow. When the negro looked around for his body, that belonged to his earthly master. When he looked around for his soul, that had been appropriated by his Heavenly Master. And when he looked around for something that really belonged to himself, he found nothing but his shadow, and that vanished in the shade.

One thing, however, is to be noticed with satisfaction, it is this: Something was gained to the cause of righteousness by this argument. It was a contribution to the cause of liberty. It was largely in favor of the negro. It was recognition of his manhood, and was calculated to set men to thinking that the negro might have some other important rights, no less than the religious right to baptism.

Thus with all its faults, we are compelled to give the pulpit the credit of furnishing the first important argument in favor of the religious character and manhood rights of the negro. Dr. Godwin was undoubtedly a good man. He wrote at a time of much moral darkness, and property in man was nearly everywhere recognized as a rightful institution. He saw only a part of the truth. He saw that the negro had a right to be baptized, but he could not all at once see that he had a paramount right to himself.

But this was not the only problem slavery had in store for the negro. Time and events brought another and it was this very important one:

Can the negro sustain the legal relation of a husband to a wife? Can he make a valid marriage contract in this Christian country?

This problem was solved by the same slave holding authority, entirely against the negro. Such a contact, it was argued, could only be binding upon men providentially enjoying the right to life, liberty, and the pursuit of happiness, and, since the negro is a slave, and slavery a divine institution, legal marriage was wholly inconsistent with the institution of slavery.

When some of us at the North questioned the ethics of this conclusion, we were told to mind our business, and our Southern brethren asserted, as they assert now, that they alone are competent to manage this, and all other questions relating to the negro.

In fact, there has been no end to the problems of some sort or other, involving the negro in difficulty.

Can the negro be a citizen? was the question of the Dred Scott decision.

Can the negro be educated? Can the negro be induced to work for himself, without a master? Can the negro be a soldier? Time and events have answered these and all other like questions. We have amongst us, those who have taken the first prizes as scholars; those who have won distinction for courage and skill on the battlefield; those who have taken rank as lawyers, doctors and ministers of the gospel; those who shine among men in every useful calling; and yet we are called "a problem;" "a tremendous problem;" a mountain of difficulty; a constant source of apprehension; a disturbing force, threatening destruction to the holiest and best interests of society. I declare this statement concerning the negro, whether by Miss Willard, Bishop Haygood, Bishop Fitzgerald, ex-Governor Chamberlain or by any and all others as false and deeply injurious to the colored citizen of the United States.

But, my friends, I must stop. Time and strength are not equal to the task before me. But could I be heard by this great nation, I would call to mind the sublime and glorious truths with which, at its birth, it saluted a listening world. Its voice then, was as the trump of an archangel, summoning hoary forms of oppression and time honored tyranny, to judgment. Crowned heads heard it and shrieked. Toiling millions heard it and clapped their hands for joy. It announced the advent of a nation, based upon human brotherhood and the self-evident truths of liberty and equality. Its mission was the redemption of the world from the bondage of ages. Apply these sublime and glorious truths to the situation now before you. Put away your race prejudice. Banish the idea that one class must rule over another. Recognize the fact that the rights of the humblest citizen are as worthy of protection as are those of the highest, and your problem will be solved; and, whatever may be in store for it in the future, whether prosperity, or adversity; whether it shall have foes without, or foes within, whether there shall be peace, or war; based upon the eternal principles of truth, justice and humanity, and with no class having any cause of complaint or grievance, your Republic will stand and flourish forever.

Has America a Race Problem?
If So, How Can It Best Be Solved?

Anna Julia Cooper

There are two kinds of peace in this world. The one produced by suppression, which is the passivity of death; the other brought about by a proper adjustment of living, acting forces. A nation or an individual may be at peace because all opponents have been killed or crushed; or, nation as well as individual may have found the secret of true harmony in the determination to live and let live.

A harmless looking man was once asked how many there were in his family.

"Ten," he replied grimly; "my wife's a one and I a zero." In that family there was harmony, to be sure, but it was the harmony of a despotism—it was the quiet of a muzzled mouth, the smoldering peace of a volcano crusted over.

Now I need not say that peace produced by suppression is neither natural nor desirable. Despotism is not one of the ideas that man has copied from nature. All through God's universe we see eternal harmony and symmetry as the unvarying result of the equilibrium of opposing forces. Fair play in an equal fight is the law written in Nature's book. And the solitary bully with his foot on the breast of his last antagonist has no warrant in any fact of God.

The beautiful curves described by planets and suns in their courses are the resultant of conflicting forces. Could the centrifugal force for one instant triumph, or should the centripetal grow weary and give up the struggle, immeasurable disaster would ensue—earth, moon, sun would go spinning off at a tangent or must fall helplessly into its master sphere. The acid counterbalances and keeps in order the alkali; the negative, the positive electrode. A proper equilibrium between a most inflammable explosive and the supporter of combustion, gives us water, the bland fluid that we cannot dispense with. Nay, the very air we breathe, which seems so calm, so peaceful, is rendered innocuous only by the constant conflict of opposing gases. Were the fiery, never-resting, all-corroding oxygen to gain the mastery we should be burnt to cinders in a trice. With the sluggish, inert nitrogen triumphant, we should die of inanition.

These facts are only a suggestion of what must be patent to every student of history. Progressive peace in a nation is the result of conflict; and conflict, such as is healthy, stimulating, and progressive, is produced through the co-existence of radically opposing or racially different elements. Bellamy's ox-like men pictured in *Looking Backward*, taking their daily modicum of provender from the grandmotherly government, with nothing to struggle for, no wrong to put down, no reform to push through, no rights to vindicate and uphold, are nice folks to read about; but they are not natural; they are not progressive. God's world is not governed that way. The child can never gain strength save by resistance, and there can be no resistance if all movement is in one direction and all opposition made forever an impossibility.

I confess I can see no deeper reason than this for the specializing of racial types in the world. Whatever our theory with reference to the origin of species and the unity of mankind, we cannot help admitting the fact that no sooner does a family of the human race take up its abode in some little nook between mountains, or on some plain walled in

Source: Anna Julia Cooper, "Has America a Race Problem? If So, How Can It Best Be Solved?" in Anna Julia Cooper, *A Voice from the South by a Black Woman of the South* (Xenia, Ohio: The Aldine Printing House, 1892), Chapter 7.

by their own hands, no sooner do they begin in earnest to live their own life, think their own thoughts, and trace out their own arts, than they begin also to crystallize some idea different from and generally opposed to that of other tribes or families.

Each race has its badge, its exponent, its message, branded in its forehead by the great Master's hand which is its own peculiar keynote, and its contribution to the harmony of nations.

Left entirely alone,—out of contact, that is with other races and their opposing ideas and conflicting tendencies, this cult is abnormally developed and there is unity without variety, a predominance of one tone at the expense of moderation and harmony, and finally a sameness, a monotonous dullness which means stagnation,—death.

It is this of which M. Guizot complains in Asiatic types of civilization; and in each case he mentions I note that there was but one race, one free force predominating. In Lect. II *History of Civilization* he says:

In Egypt the theocratic principle took possession of society and showed itself in its manners, its monuments and in all that has come down to us of Egyptian civilization. In India the same phenomenon occurs—a repetition of the almost exclusively prevailing influence of theocracy. In other regions the domination of a conquering caste; where such is the case the principle of force takes entire possession of society. In another place we discover society under the entire influence of the democratic principle. Such was the case in the commercial republics which covered the coasts of Asia Minor and Syria, in Ionia and Phoenicia. In a word whenever we contemplate the civilization of the ancients, we find them all impressed with *one ever prevailing character of unity*, visible in their institutions, their ideas and manners; *one sole influence seems to govern and determine all things*... . In one nation, as in Greece, the unity of the social principle led to a development of wonderful rapidity; no other people ever ran so brilliant a career in so short a time. But Greece had hardly become glorious before she appeared worn out. Her decline was as sudden as her rise had been rapid.

It seems as if the principle which called Greek civilization into life was exhausted. No other came to invigorate it or supply its place. In India and Egypt where again only one principle of civilization prevailed [*one race predominant you see*] society became stationary. Simplicity produced monotony. Society continued to exist, but there was no progression. It remained torpid and inactive.

Now I beg you to note that in none of these systems was a RACE PROBLEM possible. The dominant race had settled that matter forever. Asiatic society was fixed in cast iron molds. Virtually there was but one race inspiring and molding the thought, the art, the literature, the government. It was against this shriveling caste prejudice and intolerance that the zealous Buddha set his face like a flint. And I do not think it was all blasphemy in Renan when he said Jesus Christ was first of democrats, i.e., a believer in the royalty of the individual, a preacher of the brotherhood of man through the fatherhood of God, a teacher who proved that the lines on which worlds are said to revolve are *imaginary*, that for all the distinctions of blue blood and black blood and red blood—*a man's a man for a' that.* Buddha and the Christ, each in his own way, wrought to rend asunder the clamps and bands of caste, and to thaw out the ice of race tyranny and exclusiveness. The Brahmin, who was Aryan, spurned a suggestion even, from the Sudra, who belonged to the hated and proscribed Turanian race. With a Pariah he could not eat or drink. They were to him outcasts and unclean. Association with them meant contamination; the hint of their social equality was blasphemous. Respectful consideration for their rights and feelings was almost a physical no less than a moral impossibility.

No more could the Helots among the Greeks have been said to contribute anything to the movement of their times. The dominant race had them effectually under its heel. It was the tyranny and exclusiveness of these nations, therefore, which brought about their immobility and resulted finally in the barrenness of their one idea. From this came the poverty and decay underlying their civilization, from this the transitory, ephemeral character of its brilliancy.

To quote Guizot again:

> Society belonged to *one exclusive* power which could bear with no other. Every principle of a different tendency was proscribed. The governing principle would nowhere suffer by its side the manifestation and influence of a rival principle. This character of unity in their civilization is equally impressed upon their literature and intellectual productions. Those monuments of Hindoo literature lately introduced into Europe seem all struck from the same die. They all seem the result of one same fact, the expression of one idea. Religious and moral treatises, historical traditions, dramatic poetry, epics, all bear the same physiognomy. The same character of unity and monotony shines out in these works of mind and fancy, as we discover in their life and institutions.

Not even Greece with all its classic treasures is made an exception from these limitations produced by exclusiveness.

But the course of empire moves one degree westward. Europe becomes the theater of the leading exponents of civilization, and here we have a *Race Problem,*—if, indeed, the confused jumble of races, the clash and conflict, the din and devastation of those stormy years can be referred to by so quiet and so dignified a term as "problem." Complex and appalling it surely was. Goths and Huns, Vandals and Danes, Angles, Saxons, Jutes—could any prophet foresee that a vestige of law and order, of civilization and refinement would remain after this clumsy horde of wild barbarians had swept over Europe?

"Where is somebody'll give me some white for all this yellow?" cries one with his hands full of the gold from one of those magnificent monuments of antiquity which he and his tribe had just pillaged and demolished. Says the historian: "Their history is like a history of kites and crows." Tacitus writes: "To shout, to drink, to caper about, to feel their veins heated and swollen with wine, to hear and see around them the riot of the orgy, this was the first need of the barbarians. The heavy human brute gluts himself with sensations and with noise." Taine[3] describes them as follows:

> Huge white bodies, cool-blooded, with fierce blue eyes, reddish flaxen hair; ravenous stomachs, filled with meat and cheese, heated by strong drinks. Brutal drunken pirates and robbers, they dashed to sea in their two-sailed barks, landed anywhere, killed everything; and, having sacrificed in honor of their gods the tithe of all their prisoners, leaving behind the red light of their burning, went farther on to begin again.

A certain litany of the time reads: "From the fury of the Jutes, Good Lord deliver us." "Elgiva, the wife of one of their kings," says a chronicler of the time, "they hamstrung and subjected to the death she deserved"; and their heroes are frequently represented as tearing out the heart of their human victim and eating it while it still quivered with life.

A historian of the time, quoted by Taine, says it was the custom to buy men and women in all parts of England and to carry them to Ireland for sale. The buyers usually made the women pregnant and took them to market in that condition to ensure a better price. "You might have seen," continues the historian, "long files of young people of both sexes and of great beauty, bound with ropes and daily exposed for sale. They sold as slaves in this manner, their nearest relatives and even their own children."

What could civilization hope to do with such a swarm of sensuous, bloodthirsty vipers? Assimilation was horrible to contemplate. They will drag us to their level, quoth the culture of the times. Deportation was out of the question; and there was no need to talk of their emigrating. The fact is, the barbarians were in no hurry about moving. They didn't even care to colonize. They had come to stay. And Europe had to grapple with her race problem till time and God should solve it.

And how was it solved, and what kind of civilization resulted?

Once more let us go to Guizot. "Take ever so rapid a glance," says he, at modern Europe and it strikes you at once as diversified, confused, and stormy. All the principles of social organization are found existing together within it; powers temporal, and powers spiritual, the theocratic, monarchic, aristocratic, and democratic elements, all classes of society *in a state of continual struggle* without any one having sufficient force to master the others and take sole possession of society.

Then as to the result of this conflict of forces:

Incomparably more rich and diversified than the ancient, European civilization has within it the promise of *perpetual progress*. It has now endured more than fifteen centuries and in all that time has been in a state of progression, not so rapidly as the Greek nor yet so ephemeral. While in other civilizations the exclusive domination of a principle [*or race*] led to tyranny, in Europe the diversity of social elements [*growing out of the contact of different races*] the incapability of any one to exclude the rest, gave birth to the LIBERTY which now prevails. This inability of the various principles to exterminate one another compelled each to endure the others and made it necessary for them in order to live in common to enter into a sort of mutual understanding. Each consented to have only that part of civilization which equitably fell to its share. Thus, while everywhere else the predominance of one principle produced tyranny, the variety and warfare of the elements of European civilization gave birth to *reciprocity and liberty.*

There is no need to quote further. This is enough to show that the law holds good in sociology as in the world of matter, *that equilibrium, not repression among conflicting forces is the condition of natural harmony, of permanent progress, and of universal freedom.* That exclusiveness and selfishness in a family, in a community, or in a nation is suicidal to progress. Caste and prejudice mean immobility. One race predominance means death. The community that closes its gates against foreign talent can never hope to advance beyond a certain point. Resolve to keep out foreigners and you keep out progress. Home talent develops its one idea and then dies. Like the century plant it produces its one flower, brilliant and beautiful it may be, but it lasts only for a night. Its forces have exhausted themselves in that one effort. Nothing remains but to wither and to rot.

It was the Chinese wall that made China in 1800 A.D. the same as China in the days of Confucius. Its women have not even yet learned that they need not bandage their feet if they do not relish it. The world has rolled on, but within that wall the thoughts, the fashions, the art, the tradition, and the beliefs are those of a thousand years ago. Until very recently, the Chinese were wholly out of the current of human progress. They were like gray headed infants—a man of eighty years with the concepts and imaginings of a babe of eight months. A civilization measured by thousands of years with a development that might be comprised within as many days—arrested development due to exclusive living.

But European civilization, rich as it was compared to Asiatic types, was still not the consummation of the ideal of human possibilities. One more degree westward the hand on the dial points. In Europe there was conflict, but the elements crystallized out in isolated nodules, so to speak. Italy has her dominant principle, Spain hers, France hers, England hers, and so on. The proximity is close enough for interaction and mutual restraint, though the acting forces are at different points. To preserve the balance of power, which is nothing more than the equilibrium of warring elements, England can be trusted to keep an eye on her beloved step-relation-in-law, Russia,—and Germany no doubt can be relied on to look after France and some others. It is not, however, till the scene changes and America is made the theater of action, that the interplay of forces narrow[s] down to a single platform.

Hither came Cavalier and Roundhead, Baptist and Papist, Quaker, Ritualist, Freethinker and Mormon, the conservative Tory, the liberal Whig, and the radical Independent,—the Spaniard, the Frenchman, the Englishman, the Italian, the Chinaman, the African, Swedes, Russians, Huns, Bohemians,

Gypsies, Irish, Jews. Here surely was a seething caldron of conflicting elements. Religious intolerance and political hatred, race prejudice and caste pride—

> Double, double, toil and trouble;
> Fire burn and cauldron bubble.

Conflict, Conflict, Conflict.

America for Americans! This is the white man's country! The Chinese must go, shrieks the exclusionist. Exclude the Italians! Colonize the blacks in Mexico or deport them to Africa. Lynch, suppress, drive out, kill out! America for Americans!

"*Who are Americans?*" comes rolling back from ten million throats. Who are to do the packing and delivering of the goods? Who are the homefolks and who are the strangers? Who are the absolute and original tenants in fee-simple?

The red men used to be owners of the soil,—but they are about to be pushed over into the Pacific Ocean. They, perhaps, have the best right to call themselves "Americans" by law of primogeniture. They are at least the oldest inhabitants of whom we can at present identify any traces. If early settlers from abroad merely are meant and it is only a question of squatters' rights—why, the Mayflower, a pretty venerable institution, landed in the year of Grace 1620, and the first delegation from Africa just one year ahead of that,—in 1619. The first settlers seem to have been almost as much mixed as we are on this point; and it does not seem at all easy to decide just what individuals we mean when we yell "America for the Americans." At least the cleavage cannot be made by hues and noses, if we are to seek for the genuine F. F. V.'s as the inhabitants best entitled to the honor of that name.

The fact is this nation was foreordained to conflict from its incipiency. Its elements were predestined from their birth to an irrepressible clash followed by the stable equilibrium of opposition. Exclusive possession belongs to none. There never was a point in history when it did. There was never a time since America became a nation when there were not more than one race, more than one party, more than one belief contending for

supremacy. Hence no one is or can be supreme. All interests must be consulted, all claims conciliated. Where a hundred free forces are lustily clamoring for recognition and each wrestling mightily for the mastery, individual tyrannies must inevitably be chiselled down, individual bigotries worn smooth and malleable, individual prejudices either obliterated or concealed. America is not from choice more than of necessity republic in form and democratic in administration. The will of the majority must rule simply because no class, no family, no individual has ever been able to prove sufficient political legitimacy to impose [its] yoke on the country. All attempts at establishing oligarchy must be made by wheedling and cajoling, pretending that not supremacy but service is sought. The nearest approach to outspoken self-assertion is in the conciliatory tones of candid compromise. "I will let you enjoy that if you will not hinder me in the pursuit of this" has been the American sovereign's home policy since his first Declaration of Independence was inscribed as his policy abroad. Compromise and concession, liberality and toleration were the conditions of the nation's birth and are the *sine qua non* of its continued existence. A general amnesty and universal reciprocity are the only *modus vivendi* in a nation whose every citizen is his own king, his own priest and his own pope.

Tocqueville, years ago, predicted that republicanism must fail in America. But if republicanism fails, America fails, and somehow I can not think this colossal stage was erected for a tragedy. I must confess to being an optimist on the subject of my country. It is true we are too busy making history, and have been for some years past, to be able to write history yet, or to understand and interpret it. Our range of vision is too short for us to focus and image our conflicts. Indeed Von Holtz, the clearest headed of calm spectators, says he doubts if the history of American conflict can be written yet even by a disinterested foreigner. The clashing of arms and the din of battle, the smoke of cannon and the heat of combat, are not yet cleared away sufficiently for us to have the judicial vision of historians. Our jottings are like newspaper reports written in the saddle, mid prancing steeds and roaring artillery.

But of one thing we may be sure: the God of battles is in the conflicts of history. The evolution of civilization is His care, eternal progress His delight. As the European was higher and grander than the Asiatic, so will American civilization be broader and deeper and closer to the purposes of the Eternal than any the world has yet seen. This the last page is to mark the climax of history, the bright consummate flower unfolding *charity toward all and malice toward none,*—the final triumph of universal reciprocity born of universal conflict with forces that cannot be exterminated. Here at last is an arena in which every agony has a voice and free speech. Not a spot where no wrong can exist, but where each feeblest interest can cry with Themistocles, *"Strike, but hear me!"* Here you will not see as in Germany women hitched to a cart with donkeys; not perhaps because men are more chivalrous here than there, but because woman can speak. Here labor will not be starved and ground to powder, because the laboring man can make himself heard. Here races that are weakest can, *if they so elect*, make themselves felt.

The supremacy of one race,—the despotism of a class or the tyranny of an individual can not ultimately prevail on a continent held in equilibrium by such conflicting forces and by so many and such strong fibred races as there are struggling on this soil. Never in America shall one man dare to say as Germany's somewhat bumptious emperor is fond of proclaiming: "There is only one master in the country and I am he. I shall suffer no other beside me. Only to God and my conscience am I accountable." The strength of the opposition tones down and polishes off all such ugly excrescencies as that. "I am the State," will never be proclaimed above a whisper on a platform where there is within arm's length another just as strong, possibly stronger, who holds, or would like to hold that identical proposition with reference to himself. In this arena then is to be the last death struggle of political tyranny, of religious bigotry, and intellectual intolerance, of caste illiberality and class exclusiveness. And the last monster that shall be throttled forever

methinks is race prejudice. Men will here learn that a race, as a family, may be true to itself without seeking to exterminate all others. That for the note of the feeblest there is room, nay a positive need, in the harmonies of God. That the principles of true democracy are founded in universal reciprocity, and that "A man's a man" was written when God first stamped His own image and superscription on His child and breathed into his nostrils the breath of life. And I confess I can pray for no nobler destiny for my country than that it may be the stage, however far distant in the future, whereon these ideas and principles shall ultimately mature; and culminating here at whatever cost of production shall go forth hence to dominate the world.

Methought I saw a mighty conflagration, plunging and heaving, surging and seething, smoking and rolling over this American continent. Strong men and wise men stand helpless in mute consternation. Empty headed babblers add the din of their bray to the crashing and crackling of the flames. But the hungry flood rolls on. The air is black with smoke and cinders. The sky is red with lurid light. Forked tongues of fiery flame dart up and lick the pale stars, and seem to laugh at men's feebleness and frenzy. As I look on I think of Schiller's sublime characterization of fire: "Frightful becomes this God-power, when it snatches itself free from fetters and stalks majestically forth on its own career—the free daughter of Nature." Ingenuity is busy with newly patented snuffers all warranted to extinguish the flame. The street gamin with a hooked wire pulls out a few nuggets that chanced to be lying on the outskirts where they were cooked by the heat; and gleefully cries "What a nice fire to roast my chestnuts," and like little Jack Horner, "what a nice boy am I!"

Meantime this expedient, that expedient, the other expedient is suggested by thinkers and theorizers hoping to stifle the angry, roaring, devouring demon and allay the mad destruction.

Wehe wenn sie losgelassen,
Wachsend ohne Widerstand,
Durch die volkbelebten Gassen
Walzt den ungeheuren Brand!

But the strength of the Omnipotent is in it. The hand of God is leading it on. It matters not whether you and I in mad desperation cast our quivering bodies into it as our funeral pyre; or whether, like the street urchins, we pull wires to secure the advantage of the passing moment. We can neither help it nor hinder; only

> Let thy gold be cast in the furnace,
> Thy red gold, precious and bright.
> Do not fear the hungry fire
> With its caverns of burning light.

If it takes the dearest idol, the pet theory or the darling "ism," the pride, the selfishness, the prejudices, the exclusiveness, the bigotry and intolerance, the conceit of self, of race, or of family superiority,—nay, if it singe from thee thy personal gratifications in thy distinction by birth, by blood, by sex—everything,—and leave thee nothing but thy naked manhood, solitary and unadorned,—let them go—let them go!

> And thy gold shall return more precious,
> Free from every spot and stain,
> For gold must be tried by fire.

And the heart of nations must be tried by pain; and their polish, their true culture must be wrought in through conflict.

Has America a Race Problem?

Yes.

What are you going to do about it?

Let it alone and mind my own business. It is God's problem and He will solve it in time. It is deeper than Gehenna. What can you or I do!

Are there then no duties and special lines of thought growing out of the present conditions of this problem?

Certainly there are. *Imprimis;* let every element of the conflict see that it represent a positive force so as to preserve a proper equipoise in the conflict. No shirking, no skulking, no masquerading in another's uniform. Stand by your guns. And be ready for the charge. The day is coming, and now is, when America must ask each citizen not "who was your grandfather and what the color of

his cuticle," but *"What can you do?"* Be ready each individual element,—each race, each class, each family, each man to reply *"I engage to undertake an honest man's share."*

God and time will work the problem. You and I are only to stand for the quantities *at their best*, which he means us to represent.

Above all, for the love of humanity stop the mouth of those learned theorizers, the expedient mongers, who come out annually with their new and improved method of getting the answer and clearing the slate: amalgamation, deportation, colonization and all the other "ations" that were ever devised or dreamt of. If Alexander wants to be a god, let him; but don't have Alexander hawking his patent plan for universal deification. If all could or would follow Alexander's plan, just the niche in the divine cosmos meant for man would be vacant. And we think that men have a part to play in this great drama no less than gods, and so if a few are determined to be white—amen, so be it; but don't let them argue as if there were no part to be played in life by black men and black women, and as if to become white were the sole specific and panacea for all the ills that flesh is heir to— the universal solvent for all America's irritations. And again, if an American family of whatever condition or hue takes a notion to reside in Africa or in Mexico, or in the isles of the sea, it is most un-American for any power on this continent to seek to gainsay or obstruct their departure; but on the other hand, no power or element of power on this continent, least of all a self-constituted tribunal of "recent arrivals," possesses the right to begin figuring beforehand to calculate what it would require *to send* ten millions of citizens, whose ancestors have wrought here from the planting of the nation, to the same places at so much per head—at least till some one has consulted those heads.

We would not deprecate the fact, then, that America has a Race Problem. It is guaranty of the perpetuity and progress of her institutions, and insures the breadth of her culture and the symmetry of her development. More than all, let us not disparage the factor which the Negro is appointed to contribute to that problem. America needs the

Negro for ballast if for nothing else. His tropical warmth and spontaneous emotionalism may form no unseemly counterpart to the cold and calculating Anglo-Saxon. And then his instinct for law and order, his inborn respect for authority, his inaptitude for rioting and anarchy, his gentleness and cheerfulness as a laborer, and his deep-rooted faith in God will prove indispensable and invaluable elements in a nation menaced as America is by anarchy, socialism, communism, and skepticism poured in with all the jail birds from the continents of Europe and Asia. I believe with our own Dr. Crummell that "the Almighty does not preserve, rescue, and build up a lowly people merely for ignoble ends." And the historian of American civilization will yet congratulate this country that she has had a Race Problem and that descendants of the black race furnished one of its largest factors.

The Conservation of Races

W. E. B. Du Bois

The American Negro has always felt an intense personal interest in discussions as to the origins and destinies of races: primarily because back of most discussions of race with which he is familiar, have lurked certain assumptions as to his natural abilities, as to his political, intellectual and moral status, which he felt were wrong. He has, consequently, been led to deprecate and minimize race distinctions, to believe intensely that out of one blood God created all nations, and to speak of human brotherhood as though it were the possibility of an already dawning to-morrow.

Nevertheless, in our calmer moments we must acknowledge that human beings are divided into races: that in this country the two most extreme types of the world's races have met, and the resulting problem as to the future relations of these types is not only of intense and living interest to us, but forms an epoch in the history of mankind.

It is necessary, therefore, in planning our movements, in guiding our future development, that at times we rise above the pressing, but smaller questions of separate schools and cars, wage-discrimination and lynch law, to

Source: W. E. B. Du Bois, "The Conservation of Races" in The American Negro Academy, *Occasional Papers*, No. 2 (Washington, D.C., 1897).

survey the whole question of race in human philosophy and to lay, on a basis of broad knowledge and careful insight, those large lines of policy and higher ideals which may form our guiding lines and boundaries in the practical difficulties of every day. For it is certain that all human striving must recognize the hard limits of natural law, and that any striving, no matter how intense and earnest, which is against the constitution of the world, is vain. The question, then, which we must seriously consider is this: What is the real meaning of Race; what has, in the past, been the law of race development, and what lessons has the past history of race development to teach the rising Negro people?

When we thus come to inquire into the essential difference of races we find it hard to come at once to any definite conclusion. Many criteria of race differences have in the past been proposed, as color, hair, cranial measurements and language. And manifestly, in each of these respects, human beings differ widely. They vary in color, for instance, from the marble-like pallor of the Scandinavian to the rich, dark brown of the Zulu, passing by the creamy Slav, the yellow Chinese, the light brown Sicilian and the brown Egyptian. Men vary, too, in the texture of hair from the obstinately straight hair of the Chinese to the obstinately tufted and frizzled hair of the Bushman. In measurement of heads, again, men vary; from the broad-headed Tartar to the medium-headed European and the narrow-headed Hottentot; or, again in language, from the highly-inflected Roman tongue to the monosyllabic Chinese. All these physical characteristics are patent enough, and if they agreed with each other it would be very easy to classify mankind. Unfortunately for scientists, however, these criteria of race are most exasperatingly intermingled. Color does not agree with texture of hair, for many of the dark races have straight hair; nor does color agree with the breadth of the head, for the yellow Tartar has a broader head than the German; nor, again, has the science of language as yet succeeded in clearing up the relative authority of these various and contradictory criteria. The final word of sci-

ence, so far, is that we have at least two, perhaps three, great families of human beings— the whites and Negroes, possibly the yellow race. That other races have arisen from the intermingling of the blood of these two. This broad division of the world's races which men like Huxley and Raetzel have introduced as more nearly true than the old five-race scheme of Blumenbach, is nothing more than an acknowledgment that, so far as purely physical characteristics are concerned, the differences between men do not explain all the differences of their history. It declares, as Darwin himself said, that great as is the physical unlikeness of the various races of men their likenesses are greater, and upon this rests the whole scientific doctrine of Human Brotherhood.

Although the wonderful developments of human history teach that the grosser physical differences of color, hair and bone go but a short way toward explaining the different roles which groups of men have played in Human Progress, yet there are differences— subtle, delicate and elusive, though they may be—which have silently but definitely separated men into groups. While these subtle forces have generally followed the natural cleavage of common blood, descent and physical peculiarities, they have at other times swept across and ignored these. At all times, however, they have divided human beings into races, which, while they perhaps transcend scientific definition, nevertheless, are clearly defined to the eye of the Historian and Sociologist.

If this be true, then the history of the world is the history, not of individuals, but of groups, not of nations, but of races, and he who ignores or seeks to override the race idea in human history ignores and overrides the central thought of all history. What, then, is a race? It is a vast family of human beings, generally of common blood and language, always of common history, traditions and impulses, who are both voluntarily and involuntarily striving together for the accomplishment of certain more or less vividly conceived ideals of life.

Turning to real history, there can be no doubt, first, as to the widespread, nay, universal, prevalence of the race idea, the race spirit, the race ideal, and as to its efficiency as the vastest and most ingenious invention for human progress. We, who have been reared and trained under the individualistic philosophy of the Declaration of Independence and the laisser-faire philosophy of Adam Smith, are loath to see and loath to acknowledge this patent fact of human history. We see the Pharaohs, Caesars, Toussaints and Napoleons of history and forget the vast races of which they were but epitomized expressions. We are apt to think in our American impatience, that while it may have been true in the past that closed race groups made history, that here in conglomerate America *nous avons changer tout cela*—we have changed all that, and have no need of this ancient instrument of progress. This assumption of which the Negro people are especially fond, can not be established by a careful consideration of history.

We find upon the world's stage today eight distinctly differentiated races, in the sense in which History tells us the word must be used. They are, the Slavs of eastern Europe, the Teutons of middle Europe, the English of Great Britain and America, the Romance nations of Southern and Western Europe, the Negroes of Africa and America, the Semitic people of Western Asia and Northern Africa, the Hindoos of Central Asia and the Mongolians of Eastern Asia. There are, of course, other minor race groups, as the American Indians, the Esquimaux and the South Sea Islanders; these larger races, too, are far from homogeneous; the Slav includes the Czech, the Magyar, the Pole and the Russian; the Teuton includes the German, the Scandinavian and the Dutch; the English include the Scotch, the Irish and the conglomerate American. Under Romance nations the widely-differing Frenchman, Italian, Sicilian and Spaniard are comprehended. The term Negro is, perhaps, the most indefinite of all, combining the Mulattoes and Zamboes of America and the Egyptians, Bantus and Bushmen of Africa. Among the Hindoos are traces of widely differing nations, while the great Chinese, Tartar, Corean and Japanese families fall under the one designation—Mongolian.

The question now is: What is the real distinction between these nations? Is it the physical differences of blood, color and cranial measurements? Certainly we must all acknowledge that physical differences play a great part, and that, with wide exceptions and qualifications, these eight great races of today follow the cleavage of physical race distinctions; the English and Teuton represent the white variety of mankind; the Mongolian, the yellow; the Negroes, the black. Between these are many crosses and mixtures, where Mongolian and Teuton have blended into the Slav, and other mixtures have produced the Romance nations and the Semites. But while race differences have followed mainly physical race lines, yet no mere physical distinctions would really define or explain the deeper differences—the cohesiveness and continuity of these groups. The deeper differences are spiritual, psychical, differences—undoubtedly based on the physical, but infinitely transcending them. The forces that bind together the Teuton nations are, then, first, their race identity and common blood; secondly, and more important, a common history, common laws and religion, similar habits of thought and a conscious striving together for certain ideals of life. The whole process which has brought about these race differentiations has been a growth, and the great characteristic of this growth has been the differentiation of spiritual and mental differences between great races of mankind and the integration of physical differences.

The age of nomadic tribes of closely related individuals represents the maximum of physical differences. They were practically vast families, and there were as many groups as families. As the families came together to form cities the physical differences lessened, purity of blood was replaced by the requirement of domicile, and all who lived within the city bounds became gradually to be regarded as members of the group; *i.e.*, there was a slight and slow breaking down of physical barriers. This, however, was accompanied by an increase of the spiritual and social differences between cities. This city became husbandmen, this, merchants, another warriors, and so on. The *ideals of life* for which the different cities struggled were different. When at last cities began to coalesce into nations there was another breaking down of barriers which separated groups of men. The larger and broader differences of color, hair and physical proportions were not by any means ignored, but myriads of minor differences disappeared, and the sociological and historical races of men began to approximate the present division of races as indicated by physical researches. At the same time the spiritual and physical differences of race groups which constituted the nations became deep and decisive. The English nation stood for constitutional liberty and commercial freedom; the German nation for science and philosophy; the Romance nations stood for literature and art, and the other race groups are striving, each in its own way, to develope for civilization its particular message, its particular ideal, which shall help to guide the world nearer and nearer that perfection of human life for which we all long, that

one far off Divine event.

This has been the function of race differences up to the present time. What shall be its function in the future? Manifestly some of the great races of today—particularly the Negro race—have not as yet given to civilization the full spiritual message which they are capable of giving. I will not say that the Negro race has as yet given no message to the world, for it is still a mooted question among scientists as to just how far Egyptian civilization was Negro in its origin; if it was not wholly Negro, it was certainly very closely allied. Be that as it may, however, the fact still remains that the full, complete Negro message of the whole Negro race has not as yet been given to the world: that the messages and ideal of the yellow race have not been completed, and that the striving of the mighty Slavs has but begun. The question is, then: How shall this message be delivered: how shall these various ideals be realized? The answer is plain: By the development of these race groups, not as individuals, but as races. For the development of Japanese

genius, Japanese literature and art, Japanese spirit, only Japanese, bound and welded together, Japanese inspired by one vast ideal, can work out in its fullness the wonderful message which Japan has for the nations of the earth. For the development of Negro genius, of Negro literature and art, of Negro spirit, only Negroes bound and welded together, Negroes inspired by one vast ideal, can work out in its fullness the great message we have for humanity. We cannot reverse history; we are subject to the same natural laws as other races, and if the Negro is ever to be a factor in the world's history—if among the gaily-colored banners that deck the broad ramparts of civilization is to hang one uncompromising black, then it must be placed there by black hands, fashioned by black heads and hallowed by the travail of 200,000,000 black hearts beating in one glad song of jubilee.

For this reason, the advance guard of the Negro people—the 8,000,000 people of Negro blood in the United States of America—must soon come to realize that if they are to take their just place in the van of Pan-Negroism, then their destiny is *not* absorption by the white Americans. That if in America it is to be proven for the first time in the modern world that not only Negroes are capable of evolving individual men like Toussaint, the Saviour, but are a nation stored with wonderful possibilities of culture, then their destiny is not a servile imitation of Anglo-Saxon culture, but a stalwart originality which shall unswervingly follow Negro ideals.

It may, however, be objected here that the situation of our race in America renders this attitude impossible; that our sole hope of salvation lies in our being able to lose our race identity in the commingled blood of the nation; and that any other course would merely increase the friction of races which we call race prejudice, and against which we have so long and so earnestly fought.

Here, then, is the dilemma, and it is a puzzling one. I admit. No Negro who has given earnest thought to the situation of his people in America has failed, at some time in life, to find himself at these cross-roads; has failed to ask himself at some time: What, after all, am I? Am I an American or am I a Negro? Can I be both? Or is it my duty to cease to be a Negro as soon as possible and be an American? If I strive as a Negro, am I not perpetuating the very cleft that threatens and separates Black and White America? Is not my only possible practical aim the subduction of all that is Negro in me to the American? Does my black blood place upon me any more obligation to assert my nationality than German, or Irish or Italian blood would?

It is such incessant self-questioning and the hesitation that arises from it, that is making the present period a time of vacillation and contradiction for the American Negro; combined race action is stifled, race responsibility is shirked, race enterprises languish, and the best blood, the best talent, the best energy of the Negro people cannot be marshalled to do the bidding of the race. They stand back to make room for every rascal and demagogue who chooses to cloak his selfish deviltry under the veil of race pride.

Is this right? Is it rational? Is it good policy? Have we in America a distinct mission as a race—a distinct sphere of action and an opportunity for race development, or is self-obliteration the highest end to which Negro blood dare aspire?

If we carefully consider what race prejudice really is, we find it, historically, to be nothing but the friction between different groups of people; it is the difference in aim, in feeling, in ideals of two different races; if, now, this difference exists touching territory, laws, language, or even religion, it is manifest that these people cannot live in the same territory without fatal collision; but if, on the other hand, there is substantial agreement in laws, language and religion; if there is a satisfactory adjustment of economic life, then there is no reason why, in the same country and on the same street, two or three great national ideals might not thrive and develop, that men of different races might not strive together for their race ideals as well, perhaps even better, than in isolation. Here, it seems to me, is the reading of the riddle that puzzles so many of us. We are Americans, not only by birth and by citizenship, but by our political ideals, our language, our religion. Farther than that, our Americanism does not go. At that point, we are Negroes, members of a vast historic race that from the very dawn of creation has slept, but half awakening in the dark forests of its African fatherland. We are the first fruits of this new nation, the harbinger of that black to-morrow which is yet destined to soften the whiteness of the Teutonic to-day. We are that people whose subtle sense of song has given America its only American music, its only American fairy tales, its only touch of pathos and humor amid its mad money-getting plutocracy. As such, it is our duty to conserve our physical powers, our intellectual endowments, our spiritual ideals; as a race we must strive by race organization, by race solidarity, by race unity to the realization of that broader humanity which freely recognizes differences in men, but sternly deprecates inequality in their opportunities of development.

For the accomplishment of these ends we need race organizations: Negro colleges, Negro newspapers, Negro business organizations, a Negro school of literature and art, and an intellectual clearing house, for all these products of the Negro mind, which we may call a Negro Academy. Not only is all this necessary for positive advance, it is absolutely imperative for negative defense. Let us not deceive ourselves at our situation in this country. Weighted with a heritage of moral iniquity from our past history, hard pressed in the economic world by foreign immigrants and native prejudice, hated here, despised there and pitied everywhere; our one haven of refuge is ourselves, and but one means of advance, our own belief in our great destiny, our own implicit trust in our ability and worth. There is no power under God's high heaven that can stop the advance of eight thousand thousand honest, earnest, inspired and united people. But—and here is the rub—they *must* be honest, fearlessly criticising their own faults, zealously correcting them; they must be *earnest*. No people that laughs at itself, and ridicules itself, and wishes to God it was anything but itself ever wrote its name in history; it *must* be inspired with the Divine faith of our black mothers, that out of the blood and dust of battle will march a victorious host, a mighty nation, a peculiar people, to speak to the nations of earth a Divine truth that shall make them free. And such a people must be united; not merely united for the organized theft of political spoils, not united to disgrace religion with whoremongers and ward-heelers; not united merely to protest and pass resolutions, but united to stop the ravages of consumption among the Negro people, united to keep black boys from loafing, gambling and crime; united to guard the purity of black women and to reduce that vast army of black prostitutes that is today marching to hell: and united in serious organizations, to determine by careful conference and thoughtful interchange of opinion the broad lines of policy and action for the American Negro.

This, is the reason for being which the American Negro Academy has. It aims at once to be the epitome and expression of the intellect of the black-blooded people of America, the exponent of the race ideals of one of the world's great races. As such, the Academy must, if successful, be

(a). Representative in character.
(b). Impartial in conduct.
(c). Firm in leadership.

It must be representative in character; not in that it represents all interests or all factions, but in that it seeks to comprise something of the *best* thought, the most unselfish striving and the highest ideals. There are scattered in forgotten nooks and corners throughout the land, Negroes of some considerable training, of high minds, and high motives, who are unknown to their fellows, who exert far too little influence. These the Negro Academy should strive to bring into touch with each other and to give them a common mouthpiece.

The Academy should be impartial in conduct; while it aims to exalt the people it should aim to do so by truth—not by lies, by honesty—not by flattery. It should continually impress the fact upon the Negro people that they must not expect to have things done for them—they MUST DO FOR THEMSELVES;

that they have on their hands a vast work of self-reformation to do, and that a little less complaint and whining, and a little more dogged work and manly striving would do us more credit and benefit than a thousand Force or Civil Rights bills.

Finally, the American Negro Academy must point out a practical path of advance to the Negro people; there lie before every Negro today hundreds of questions of policy and right which must be settled and which each one settles now, not in accordance with any rule, but by impulse or individual preference; for instance: What should be the attitude of Negroes toward the educational qualification for voters? What should be our attitude toward separate schools? How should we meet discriminations on railways and in hotels? Such questions need not so much specific answers for each part as a general expression of policy, and nobody should be better fitted to announce such a policy than a representative honest Negro Academy.

All this, however, must come in time after careful organization and long conference. The immediate work before us should be practical and have direct bearing upon the situation of the Negro. The historical work of collecting the laws of the United States and of the various States of the Union with regard to the Negro is a work of such magnitude and importance that no body but one like this could think of undertaking it. If we could accomplish that one task we would justify our existence.

In the field of Sociology an appalling work lies before us. First, we must unflinchingly and bravely face the truth, not with apologies, but with solemn earnestness. The Negro Academy ought to sound a note of warning that would echo in every black cabin in the land: *Unless we conquer our present vices they will conquer us ;* we are diseased, we are developing criminal tendencies, and an alarmingly large percentage of our men and women are sexually impure. The Negro Academy should stand and proclaim this over the housetops, crying with Garrison: *I will not equivocate, I will not retreat a single inch, and I will be heard.* The Academy should seek to gather about it the talented, unselfish men, the pure and noble-minded women, to fight an army of devils that disgraces our manhood and our womanhood. There does not stand today upon God's earth a race more capable in muscle, in intellect, in morals, than the American Negro, if he will bend his energies in the right direction; if he will

> Burst his birth's invidious bar
> And grasp the skirts of happy chance,
> And breast the blows of circumstance,
> And grapple with his evil star.

In science and morals, I have indicated two fields of work for the Academy. Finally, in practical policy, I wish to suggest the following *Academy Creed:*

1. We believe that the Negro people, as a race, have a contribution to make to civilization and humanity, which no other race can make.

2. We believe it the duty of the Americans of Negro descent, as a body, to maintain their race identity until this mission of the Negro people is accomplished, and the ideal of human brotherhood has become a practical possibility.

3. We believe that, unless modern civilization is a failure, it is entirely feasible and practicable for two races in such essential political, economic and religious harmony as the white and colored people of America, to develop side by side in peace and mutual happiness, the peculiar contribution which each has to make to the culture of their common country.

4. As a means to this end we advocate, not such social equality between these races as would disregard human likes and dislikes, but such a social equilibrium as would, throughout all the complicated relations of life, give due and just consideration to culture, ability, and moral worth, whether they be found under white or black skins.

5. We believe that the first and greatest step toward the settlement of the present friction between the races—commonly called the Negro Problem—lies in the correction of the immorality, crime and laziness among the Negroes themselves, which still remains as a heritage from slavery. We believe that only earnest and long continued efforts on our own part can cure these social ills.

6. We believe that the second great step toward a better adjustment of the relations between the races, should be a more impartial selection of ability in the economic and intellectual world, and a greater respect for personal liberty and worth, regardless of race. We believe that only earnest efforts on the part of the white people of this country will bring much needed reform in these matters.

7. On the basis of the foregoing declaration, and firmly believing in our high destiny, we, as American Negroes, are resolved to strive in every honorable way for the realization of the best and highest aims, for the development of strong manhood and pure womanhood, and for the rearing of a race ideal in America and Africa, to the glory of God and the uplifting of the Negro people.

The Talented Tenth

W.E.B. Du Bois

The Negro race, like all races, is going to be saved by its exceptional men. The problem of education, then, among Negroes must first of all deal with the Talented Tenth; it is the problem of developing the Best of this race that they may guide the Mass away from the contamination and death of the Worst, in their own and other races. Now the training of men is a difficult and intricate task. Its technique is a matter for educational experts, but its object is for the vision of seers. If we make money the object of man-training, we shall develop money-makers but not necessarily men; if we make technical skill the object of education, we may posses artisans but not, in nature, men. Men we shall have only as we make manhood the object of the work of the schools—intelligence, broad sympathy, knowledge of the world that was and is, and of the relation of men to it—this is the curriculum of that Higher Education which must underlie true life. On this foundation we may build bread winning, skill of hand and quickness of brain, with never a fear lest the child and man mistake the means of living for the object of life.

If this be true—and who can deny it— three tasks lay before me; first to show from the past that the Talented Tenth as they have risen among American Negroes have been worthy of leadership; secondly, to show how these men may be educated and developed; and thirdly, to show their relation to the Negro problem.

You misjudge us because you do not know us. From the very first it has been the educated and intelligent of the Negro people that have led and elevated the mass, and the sole obstacles that nullified and retarded their efforts were slavery and race prejudice; for what is slavery but the legalized survival of the unfit and the nullification of the work of natural internal leadership? Negro leadership, therefore, sought from the first to rid the race of this awful incubus that it might make way for natural selection and the survival of the fittest. In colonial days came Phillis Wheatley and Paul Cuffe striving against the bars of prejudice; and Benjamin Banneker, the almanac maker, voiced their longings when he said to Thomas Jefferson, "I freely and cheerfully acknowledge that I am of the African race, and in colour which is natural to them, of the deepest dye; and it is under a sense of the most profound gratitude to the Supreme Ruler of the Universe, that I now confess to you that I am not under that state of tyrannical thraldom and inhuman captivity to which too many of my brethren are doomed, but that I have abundantly tasted of the fruition of those blessings which proceed from that free and unequalled liberty with which you are favored, and which I hope you will willingly allow, you have mercifully received from the immediate hand of that Being from whom proceedeth every good and perfect gift.

"Suffer me to recall to your mind that time, in which the arms of the British crown were exerted with every powerful effort, in order to reduce you to a state of servitude; look back, I entreat you, on the variety of dangers to which you were exposed; reflect on that period in which every human aid appeared unavailable, and in which even hope and fortitude wore the aspect of inability to the conflict, and you cannot but be led to a serious and grateful sense of your miraculous and providential preservation, you cannot but acknowledge, that the present freedom and tranquility which you enjoy, you have mercifully received, and that a peculiar blessing of heaven.

Source: W. E. B. Du Bois, "The Talented Tenth" in Booker T. Washington, et al., *The Negro Problem* (New York: James Pott & Co., 1903), 33–75.

"This, sir, was a time when you clearly saw into the injustice of a state of Slavery, and in which you had just apprehensions of the horrors of its condition. It was then that your abhorrence thereof was so excited, that you publicly held forth this true and invaluable doctrine, which is worthy to be recorded and remembered in all succeeding ages: 'We hold these truths to be self-evident, that all men are created equal; that they are endowed with certain inalienable rights, and that among these are life, liberty and the pursuit of happiness.'"

Then came Dr. James Derham, who could tell even the learned Dr. Rush something of medicine, and Lemuel Haynes, to whom Middlebury College gave an honorary A.M. in 1804. These and others we may call the Revolutionary group of distinguished Negroes—they were persons of marked ability, leaders of a Talented Tenth, standing conspicuously among the best of their time. They strove by word and deed to save the color line from becoming the line between the bond and free, but all they could do was nullified by Eli Whitney and the Curse of Gold. So they passed into forgetfulness.

But their spirit did not wholly die; here and there in the early part of the century came other exceptional men. Some were natural sons of unnatural fathers and were given often a liberal training and thus a race of educated mulattoes sprang up to plead for black men's rights. There was Ira Aldridge, whom all Europe loved to honor; there was that Voice crying in the Wilderness, David Walker, and saying:

"I declare it does appear to me as though some nations think God is asleep, or that he made the Africans for nothing else but to dig their mines and work their farms, or they cannot believe history, sacred or profane. I ask every man who has a heart, and is blessed with the privilege of believing—Is not God a God of justice to all his creatures? Do you say he is? Then if he gives peace and tranquility to tyrants and permits them to keep our fathers, our mothers, ourselves and our children in eternal ignorance and wretchedness to support them and their families, would he be to us a God of Justice? I ask, O, ye Christians, who hold us and our children in the most abject ignorance and degradation that ever a people were afflicted with since the world began—I say if God gives you peace and tranquility, and suffers you thus to go on afflicting us, and our children, who have never given you the least provocation—would He be to us a God of Justice? If you will allow that we are men, who feel for each other, does not the blood of our fathers and of us, their children, cry aloud to the Lord of Sabaoth against you for the cruelties and murders with which you have and do continue to afflict us?"

This was the wild voice that first aroused Southern legislators in 1829 to the terrors of abolitionism.

In 1831 there met that first Negro convention in Philadelphia, at which the world gaped curiously but which bravely attacked the problems of race and slavery, crying out against persecution and declaring that "Laws as cruel in themselves as they were unconstitutional and unjust, have in many places been enacted against our poor, unfriended and unoffending brethren (without a shadow of provocation on our part), at whose bare recital the very savage draws himself up for fear of contagion—looks noble and prides himself because he bears not the name of Christian." Side by side this free Negro movement, and the movement for abolition, strove until they merged into one strong stream. Too little notice has been taken of the work which the Talented Tenth among Negroes took in the great abolition crusade. From the very day that a Philadelphia colored man became the first subscriber to Garrison's "Liberator," to the day when Negro soldiers made the Emancipation Proclamation possible, black leaders worked shoulder to shoulder with white men in a movement, the success of which would have been impossible without them. There was Purvis and Remond, Pennington and Highland Garnett, Sojourner Truth and Alexander Crummel, and above all, Frederick Douglass—what would the abolition movement have been without them? They stood as living examples of the possibilities of the Negro race, their own hard experiences and well wrought culture said silently more than all the drawn periods of orators—

they were the men who made American slavery impossible. As Maria Weston Chapman once said, from the school of anti-slavery agitation "a throng of authors, editors, lawyers, orators and accomplished gentlemen of color have taken their degree! It has equally implanted hopes and aspirations, noble thoughts, and sublime purposes, in the hearts of both races. It has prepared the white man for the freedom of the black man, and it has made the black man scorn the thought of enslavement, as does a white man, as far as its influence has extended. Strengthen that noble influence! Before its organization, the country only saw here and there in slavery some faithful Cudjoe or Dinah, whose strong natures blossomed even in bondage, like a fine plant beneath a heavy stone. Now, under the elevating and cherishing influence of the American Anti-slavery Society, the colored race, like the white, furnishes Corinthian capitals for the noblest temples."

Where were these black abolitionists trained? Some, like Frederick Douglass, were self-trained, but yet trained liberally; others, like Alexander Crummell and McCune Smith, graduated from famous foreign universities. Most of them rose up through the colored schools of New York and Philadelphia and Boston, taught by college-bred men like Russworm, of Dartmouth, and college-bred white men like Neau and Benezet.

After emancipation came a new group of educated and gifted leaders: Langston, Bruce and Elliot, Greener, Williams and Payne. Through political organization, historical and polemic writing and moral regeneration, these men strove to uplift their people. It is the fashion of to-day to sneer at them and to say that with freedom Negro leadership should have begun at the plow and not in the Senate—a foolish and mischievous lie; two hundred and fifty years that black serf toiled at the plow and yet that toiling was in vain till the Senate passed the war amendments; and two hundred and fifty years more the half-free serf of to-day may toil at his plow, but unless he have political rights and righteously guarded civic status, he will still remain the poverty-stricken and ignorant plaything of rascals,

that he now is. This all sane men know even if they dare not say it.

And so we come to the present—a day of cowardice and vacillation, of strident wide-voiced wrong and faint hearted compromise; of double-faced dallying with Truth and Right. Who are to-day guiding the work of the Negro people? The "exceptions" of course. And yet so sure as this Talented Tenth is pointed out, the blind worshippers of the Average cry out in alarm: "These are exceptions, look here at death, disease and crime—these are the happy rule." Of course they are the rule, because a silly nation made them the rule: Because for three long centuries this people lynched Negroes who dared to be brave, raped black women who dared to be virtuous, crushed dark-hued youth who dared to be ambitious, and encouraged and made to flourish servility and lewdness and apathy. But not even this was able to crush all manhood and chastity and aspiration from black folk. A saving remnant continually survives and persists, continually aspires, continually shows itself in thrift and ability and character. Exceptional it is to be sure, but this is its chiefest promise; it shows the capability of Negro blood, the promise of black men. Do Americans ever stop to reflect that there are in this land a million men of Negro blood, well-educated, owners of homes, against the honor of whose womanhood no breath was ever raised, whose men occupy positions of trust and usefulness, and who, judged by any standard, have reached the full measure of the best type of modern European culture? Is it fair, is it decent, is it Christian to ignore these facts of the Negro problem, to belittle such aspiration, to nullify such leadership and seek to crush these people back into the mass out of which by toil and travail, they and their fathers have raised themselves?

Can the masses of the Negro people be in any possible way more quickly raised than by the effort and example of this aristocracy of talent and character? Was there ever a nation on God's fair earth civilized from the bottom upward? Never; it is, ever was and ever will be from the top downward that culture filters. The Talented Tenth rises and pulls all that are worth the saving up to their vantage ground. This is the history of human progress; and the two historic mistakes which have hindered that progress were the thinking first that no more could ever rise save the few already risen; or second, that it would better the unrisen to pull the risen down.

How then shall the leaders of a struggling people be trained and the hands of the risen few strengthened? There can be but one answer: The best and most capable of their youth must be schooled in the colleges and universities of the land. We will not quarrel as to just what the university of the Negro should teach or how it should teach it—I willingly admit that each soul and each race-soul needs its own peculiar curriculum. But this is true: A university is a human invention for the transmission of knowledge and culture from generation to generation, through the training of quick minds and pure hearts, and for this work no other human invention will suffice, not even trade and industrial schools.

All men cannot go to college but some men must; every isolated group or nation must have its yeast, must have for the talented few centers of training where men are not so mystified and befuddled by the hard and necessary toil of earning a living, as to have no aims higher than their bellies, and no God greater than Gold. This is true training, and thus in the beginning were the favored sons of the freedmen trained. Out of the colleges of the North came, after the blood of war, Ware, Cravath, Chase, Andrews, Bumstead and Spence to build the foundations of knowledge and civilization in the black South. Where ought they to have begun to build? At the bottom, of course, quibbles the mole with his eyes in the earth. Aye! truly at the bottom, at the very bottom; at the bottom of knowledge, down in the very depths of knowledge there where the roots of justice strike into the lowest soil of Truth. And so they did begin; they founded colleges, and up from the colleges shot normal schools, and out from the normal schools went teachers, and around the normal teachers clustered other teachers to teach the public schools; the college trained in Greek and Latin and mathematics,

2,000 men; and these men trained full 50,000 others in morals and manners, and they in turn taught thrift and the alphabet to nine millions of men, who to-day hold $300,000,000 of property. It was a miracle—the most wonderful peace-battle of the 19th century, and yet to-day men smile at it, and in fine superiority tell us that it was all a strange mistake; that a proper way to found a system of education is first to gather the children and buy them spelling books and hoes; afterward men may look about for teachers, if haply they may find them; or again they would teach men Work, but as for Life—why, what has Work to do with Life, they ask vacantly.

Was the work of these college founders successful; did it stand the test of time? Did the college graduates, with all their fine theories of life, really live? Are they useful men helping to civilize and elevate their less fortunate fellows? Let us see. Omitting all institutions which have not actually graduated students from a college course, there are to-day in the United States thirty-four institutions giving something above high school training to Negroes and designed especially for this race.

Three of these were established in border States before the War; thirteen were planted by the Freedmen's Bureau in the years 1864–1869; nine were established between 1870 and 1880 by various church bodies; five were established after 1881 by Negro churches, and four are state institutions supported by United States' agricultural funds. In most cases the college departments are small adjuncts to high and common school work. As a matter of fact six institutions—Atlanta, Fisk, Howard, Shaw, Wilberforce and Leland, are the important Negro colleges so far as actual work and number of students are concerned. In all these institutions, seven hundred and fifty Negro college students are enrolled. In grade the best of these colleges are about a year behind the smaller New England colleges and a typical curriculum is that of Atlanta University. Here students from the grammar grades, after a three years' high school course, take a college course of 136 weeks. One-fourth of this time is given to Latin and Greek; one-fifth, to English and modern languages; one-sixth, to history and social science; one-seventh, to natural science; one-eighth to mathematics, and one-eighth to philosophy and pedagogy.

In addition to these students in the South, Negroes have attended Northern colleges for many years. As early as 1826 one was graduated from Bowdoin College, and from that time till to-day nearly every year has seen elsewhere, other such graduates. They have, of course, met much color prejudice. Fifty years ago very few colleges would admit them at all. Even to-day no Negro has ever been admitted to Princeton, and at some other leading institutions they are rather endured than encouraged. Oberlin was the great pioneer in the work of blotting out the color line in colleges, and has more Negro graduates by far than any other Northern college.

The total number of Negro college graduates up to 1899, (several of the graduates of that year not being reported), was as follows:

	Negro Colleges	*White Colleges*
Before '76	137	75
'75–80	143	22
'80–85	250	31
'85–90	413	43
'90–95	465	66
'95–99	475	88
Class Unknown	57	64
Total	1,914	390

Of these graduates 2,079 were men and 252 were women; 50 per cent. of Northern-born college men come South to work among the masses of their people, at a sacrifice which few people realize; nearly 90 per cent. of the Southern-born graduates instead of seeking that personal freedom and broader intellectual atmosphere which their training has led them, in some degree, to conceive, stay and labor and wait in the midst of their black neighbors and relatives.

The most interesting question, and in many respects the crucial question, to be asked concerning college-bred Negroes, is: Do they earn a living? It has been intimated more than once that the higher training of

Negroes has resulted in sending into the world of work, men who could find nothing to do suitable to their talents. Now and then there comes a rumor of a colored college man working at menial service, etc. Fortunately, returns as to occupations of college-bred Negroes, gathered by the Atlanta conference, are quite full—nearly sixty per cent. of the total number of graduates.

This enables us to reach fairly certain conclusions as to the occupations of all college-bred Negroes. Of 1,312 persons reported, there were:

	Per Cent.
Teachers,	53.4
Clergymen,	16.8
Physicians, etc.,	6.3
Students,	5.6
Lawyers,	4.7
In Govt. Service,	4.0
In Business,	3.6
Farmers and Artisans,	2.7
Editors, Secretaries and Clerks,	2.4
Miscellaneous.	.5

Over half are teachers, a sixth are preachers, another sixth are students and professional men; over 6 per cent. are farmers, artisans and merchants, and 4 per cent. are in government service. In detail the occupations are as follows:

Occupations of College-Bred Men

Teachers:		
Presidents and Deans,	19	
Teachers of Music,	7	
Professors, Principals and Teachers,	675	Total 701
Clergymen:		
Bishop,	1	
Chaplains U.S. Army,	2	
Missionaries,	9	
Presiding Elders,	12	
Preachers,	197	Total 221
Physicians:		
Doctors of Medicine,	76	
Druggists,	4	
Dentists,	3	Total 83
Students,	74	
Lawyers,	62	
Civil Service:		
U.S. Minister Plenipotentiary,	1	

U.S. Consul,	1	
U.S. Deputy Collector,	1	
U.S. Gauger,	1	
U.S. Postmasters,	2	
U.S. Clerks,	44	
State Civil Service,	2	
City Civil Service,	1	Total 53
Business Men:		
Merchants, etc.,	30	
Managers,	13	
Real Estate Dealers,	4	Total 47
Farmers,	26	
Clerks and Secretaries:		
Secretary of National		
Societies,	7	
Clerks, etc.,	15	Total 22
Artisans,	9	
Editors,	9	
Miscellaneous,	5	

These figures illustrate vividly the function of the college-bred Negro. He is, as he ought to be, the group leader, the man who sets the ideals of the community where he lives, directs its thoughts and heads its social movements. It need hardly be argued that the Negro people need social leadership more than most groups; that they have no traditions to fall back upon, no long established customs, no strong family ties, no well defined social classes. All these things must be slowly and painfully evolved. The preacher was, even before the war, the group leader of the Negroes, and the church their greatest social institution. Naturally this preacher was ignorant and often immoral, and the problem of replacing the older type by better educated men has been a difficult one. Both by direct work and by direct influence on other preachers, and on congregations, the college-bred preacher has an opportunity for reformatory work and moral inspiration, the value of which cannot be overestimated.

It has, however, been in the furnishing of teachers that the Negro college has found its peculiar function. Few persons realized how vast a work, how mighty a revolution has been thus accomplished. To furnish five millions and more of ignorant people with teachers of their own race and blood, in one generation, was not only a very difficult undertaking, but a very important one, in that, it placed before the eyes of almost every Negro child an attainable ideal. It brought the masses of the blacks in contact with modern civilization, made black men the leaders of their communities and trainers of the new generation. In this work college-bred Negroes were first teachers, and then teachers of teachers. And here it is that the broad culture of college work has been of peculiar value. Knowledge of life and its wider meaning, has been the point of the Negro's deepest ignorance, and the sending out of teachers whose training has not been simply for bread winning, but also for human culture, has been of inestimable value in the training of these men.

In earlier years the two occupations of preacher and teacher were practically the only ones open to the black college graduate. Of later years a larger diversity of life among his people, has opened new avenues of employment. Nor have these college men been paupers and spendthrifts; 557 college-bred Negroes owned in 1899, $1,342,862.50 worth of real estate, (assessed value) or $2,411 per family. The real value of the total accumulations of the whole group is perhaps about $10,000,000, or $5,000 a piece. Pitiful, is it not, beside the fortunes of oil kings and steel trusts, but after all is the fortune of the millionaire the only stamp of true and successful living? Alas! it is, with many, and there's the rub.

The problem of training the Negro is to-day immensely complicated by the fact that the whole question of the efficiency and appropriateness of our present systems of education, for any kind of child, is a matter of active debate, in which final settlement seems still afar off. Consequently it often happens that persons arguing for or against certain systems of education for Negroes, have these controversies in mind and miss the real question at issue. The main question, so far as the Southern Negro is concerned, is: What under the present circumstance, must a system of education do in order to raise the Negro as quickly as possible in the scale of civilization? The answer to this question seems to me clear: It must strengthen the Negro's character, increase his knowledge and teach him to earn a living. Now it goes without saying, that it is hard to do all these things simultaneously or suddenly, and that at the same time it will not do to give all the attention to one and neglect the others; we could give black boys trades, but that alone will not civilize a race of ex-slaves; we might simply increase their knowledge of the world, but this would not necessarily make them wish to use this knowledge honestly; we might seek to strengthen character and purpose, but to what end if this people have nothing to eat or to wear? A system of education is not one thing, nor does it have a single definite object, nor is it a mere matter of schools. Education is that whole system of human training within and without the school house walls, which molds and develops men. If then we start out to train an ignorant and unskilled people with a heritage of bad habits, our system of training must set before itself two great aims—the one dealing with knowledge and character, the other part seeking to give the child the technical knowledge necessary for him to earn a living under the present circumstances. These objects are accomplished in part by the opening of the common schools on the one, and of the industrial schools on the other. But only in part, for there must also be trained those who are to teach these schools—men and women of knowledge and culture and technical skill who understand modern civilization, and have the training and aptitude to impart it to the children under them. There must be teachers, and teachers of teachers, and to attempt to establish any sort of a system of common and industrial school training, without *first* (and I say *first* advisedly) without *first* providing for the higher training of the very best teachers, is simply throwing your money to the winds. School houses do not teach themselves—piles of brick and mortar and machinery do not send out *men*. It is the trained, living human soul, cultivated and strengthened by long study and thought, that breathes the real breath of life into boys and girls and makes them human, whether they be black or white, Greek, Russian or American. Nothing, in these latter days, has so dampened the faith of thinking Negroes in recent educational movements, as the fact that such movements

have been accompanied by ridicule and denouncement and decrying of those very institutions of higher training which made the Negro public school possible, and make Negro industrial schools thinkable. It was Fisk, Atlanta, Howard and Straight, those colleges born of the faith and sacrifice of the abolitionists, that placed in the black schools of the South the 30,000 teachers and more, which some, who depreciate the work of these higher schools, are using to teach their own new experiments. If Hampton, Tuskegee and the hundred other industrial schools prove in the future to be as successful as they deserve to be, then their success in training black artisans for the South, will be due primarily to the white colleges of the North and the black colleges of the South, which trained the teachers who to-day conduct these institutions. There was a time when the American people believed pretty devoutly that a log of wood with a boy at one end and Mark Hopkins at the other, represented the highest ideal of human training. But in these eager days it would seem that we have changed all that and think it necessary to add a couple of saw-mills and a hammer to this outfit, and, at a pinch, to dispense with the services of Mark Hopkins.

I would not deny, or for a moment seem to deny, the paramount necessity of teaching the Negro to work, and to work steadily and skillfully; or seem to depreciate in the slightest degree the important part industrial schools must play in the accomplishment of these ends, but I *do* say, and insist upon it, that it is industrialism drunk with its vision of success, to imagine that its own work can be accomplished without providing for the training of broadly cultured men and women to teach its own teachers, and to teach the teachers of the public schools.

But I have already said that human education is not simply a matter of schools; it is much more a matter of family and group life—the training of one's home, of one's daily companions, of one's social class. Now the black boy of the South moves in a black world—a world with its own leaders, its own thoughts, its own ideals. In this world he gets by far the larger part of his life training, and through the eyes of this dark world he peers into the veiled world beyond. Who guides and determines the education which he receives in his world? His teachers here are the group-leaders of the Negro people—the physicians and clergymen, the trained fathers and mothers, the influential and forceful men about him of all kinds; here it is, if at all, that the culture of the surrounding world trickles through and is handed on by the graduates of the higher schools. Can such culture training of group leaders be neglected? Can we afford to ignore it? Do you think that if the leaders of thought among Negroes are not trained and educated thinkers, that they will have no leaders? On the contrary a hundred half-trained demagogues will still hold the places they so largely occupy now, and hundreds of vociferous busy-bodies will multiply. You have no choice; either you must help furnish this race from within its own ranks with thoughtful men of trained leadership, or you must suffer the evil consequences of a headless misguided rabble.

I am an earnest advocate of manual training and trade teaching for black boys, and for white boys, too. I believe that next to the founding of Negro colleges the most valuable addition to Negro education since the war, has been industrial training for black boys. Nevertheless, I insist that the object of all true education is not to make men carpenters, it is to make carpenters men; there are two means of making the carpenter a man, each equally important: the first is to give the group and community in which he works, liberally trained teachers and leaders to teach him and his family what life means; the second is to give him sufficient intelligence and technical skill to make him an efficient workman; the first object demands the Negro college and college-bred men—not a quantity of such colleges, but a few of excellent quality; not too many college-bred men, but enough to leaven the lump, to inspire the masses, to raise the Talented Tenth to leadership; the second object demands a good system of common schools, well-taught, conveniently located and properly equipped.

The Sixth Atlanta Conference truly said in 1901:

> We call the attention of the Nation to the fact that less than one million of the three million Negro children of school age, are at present regularly attending school, and these attend a session which lasts only a few months.
>
> We are to-day deliberately rearing millions of our citizens in ignorance, and at the same time limiting the rights of citizenship by educational qualifications. This is unjust. Half the black youth of the land have no opportunities open to them for learning to read, write and cipher. In the discussion as to the proper training of Negro children after they leave the public schools, we have forgotten that they are not yet decently provided with public schools.
>
> Propositions are beginning to be made in the South to reduce the already meagre school facilities of Negroes. We congratulate the South on resisting, as much as it has, this pressure, and on the many millions it has spent on Negro education. But it is only fair to point out that Negro taxes and the Negroes' share of the income from indirect taxes and endowments have fully repaid this expenditure, so that the Negro public school system has not in all probability cost the white taxpayers a single cent since the war.
>
> This is not fair. Negro schools should be a public burden, since they are a public benefit. The Negro has a right to demand good common school training at the hands of the States and the Nation since by their fault he is not in position to pay for this himself.

What is the chief need for the building up of the Negro public school in the South? (The Negro race in the South needs teachers to-day above all else. This is the concurrent testimony of all who know the situation. For the supply of this great demand two things are needed—institutions of higher education and money for school houses and salaries.) It is usually assumed that a hundred or more institutions for Negro training are to-day turning out so many teachers and college-bred men that the race is threatened with an over-supply. This is sheer nonsense. There are to-day less than 3,000 living Negro college graduates in the United States, and less than 1,000 Negroes in college. Moreover, in the 164 schools for Negroes, 95 per cent. of their students are doing elementary and secondary work, work which should be done in the public schools. Over half the remaining 2,157 students are taking high school studies. The mass of so-called "normal" schools for the Negro, are simply doing elementary common school work, or, at most, high school work, with a little instruction in methods. The Negro colleges and the postgraduate courses at other institutions are the only agencies for the broader and more careful training of teachers. The work of these institutions is hampered for lack of funds. It is getting increasingly difficult to get funds for training teachers in the best modern methods, and yet all over the South, from State Superintendents, county officials, city boards and school principals comes the wail, "We need TEACHERS!" and teachers must be trained. As the fairest minded of all white Southerners, Atticus G. Haygood, once said: "The defects of colored teachers are so great as to create an urgent necessity for training better ones. Their excellencies and their successes are sufficient to justify the best hopes of success in the effort, and to vindicate the judgment of those who make large investments of money and service, to give to colored students opportunity for thoroughly preparing themselves for the work of teaching children of their people."

The truth of this has been strikingly shown in the marked improvement of white teachers in the South. Twenty years ago the rank and file of white public school teachers were not as good as the Negro teachers. But they, by scholarships and good salaries, have been encouraged to thorough normal and collegiate preparation, while the Negro teachers have been discouraged by starvation wages and the idea that any training will do for a black teacher. If carpenters are needed it is well and good to train men as carpenters. But to train men as carpenters, and then set them to teaching is wasteful and criminal; and to train men as teachers and then refuse them living wages, unless they become carpenters, is rank nonsense.

The United States Commissioner of Education says in his report for 1900: "For comparison between the white and colored enrollment in secondary and higher education, I have added together the enrollment in high schools and secondary schools, with the attendance on colleges and universities, not being sure of the actual grade of work done in the colleges and universities. The work done in the secondary schools is reported in such detail in this office, that there can be no doubt of its grade."

He then makes the following comparisons of persons in every million enrolled in secondary and higher education:

	Whole Country	Negroes
1880	4,362	1,289
1900	10,743	2,061

And he concludes: "While the number in colored high schools and colleges had increased somewhat faster than the population, it had not kept pace with the average of the whole country, for it had fallen from 30 per cent to 24 per cent of the average quota. Of all colored pupils, one (1) in one hundred was engaged in secondary and higher work, and that ratio has continued substantially for the past twenty years. If the ratio of colored population in secondary and higher education is to be equal to the average for the whole country, it must be increased to five times its present average." And if this be true of the secondary and higher education, it is safe to say that the Negro has not one-tenth his quota in college studies. How baseless, therefore, is the charge of too much training! We need Negro teachers for the Negro common schools, and we need first-class normal schools and colleges to train them. This is the work of higher Negro education and it must be done.

Further than this, after being provided with group leaders of civilization, and a foundation of intelligence in the public schools, the carpenter, in order to be a man, needs technical skill. This calls for trade schools. Now trade schools are not nearly such simple things as people once thought. The original idea was that the "Industrial" school was to furnish education, practically free, to those willing to work for it; it was to "do" things— i.e.: become a center of productive industry, it was to be partially, if not wholly, self-supporting, and it was to teach trades. Admirable as were some of the ideas underlying this scheme, the whole thing simply would not work in practice; it was found that if you were to use time and material to teach trades thoroughly, you could not at the same time keep the industries on a commercial basis and make them pay. Many schools started out to do this on a large scale and went into virtual bankruptcy. Moreover, it was found also that it was possible to teach a boy a trade mechanically, without giving him the full educative benefit of the process, and, vice versa, that there was a distinctive educative value in teaching a boy to use his hands and eyes in carrying out certain physical processes, even though he did not actually learn a trade. It has happened, therefore, in the last decade, that a noticeable change has come over the industrial schools. In the first place the idea of commercially remunerative industry in a school is being pushed rapidly to the background. There are still schools with shops and farms that bring an income, and schools that use student labor partially for the erection of their buildings and the furnishing of equipment. It is coming to be seen, however, in the education of the Negro, as clearly as it has been seen in the education of the youths the world over, that it is the *boy* and not the material product, that is the true object of education. Consequently the object of the industrial school came to be the thorough training of boys regardless of the cost of the training, so long as it was thoroughly well done.

Even at this point, however, the difficulties were not surmounted. In the first place modern industry has taken great strides since the war, and the teaching of trades is no longer a simple matter. Machinery and long processes of work have greatly changed the work of the carpenter, the ironworker and the shoemaker. A really efficient workman must be to-day an intelligent man who has had good technical training in addition to

thorough common school, and perhaps even higher training. To meet this situation the industrial schools began a further development; they established distinct Trade Schools for the thorough training of better class artisans, and at the same time they sought to preserve for the purposes of general education, such of the simpler processes of elementary trade learning as were best suited therefor. In this differentiation of the Trade School and manual training, the best of the industrial schools simply followed the plain trend of the present educational epoch. A prominent educator tells us that, in Sweden, "In the beginning the economic conception was generally adopted, and everywhere manual training was looked upon as a means of preparing the children of the common people to earn their living. But gradually it came to be recognized that manual training has a more elevated purpose, and one, indeed, more useful in the deeper meaning of the term. It came to be considered as an educative process for the complete moral, physical and intellectual development of the child."

Thus, again, in the manning of trade schools and manual training schools we are thrown back upon the higher training as its source and chief support. There was a time when any aged and wornout carpenter could teach in a trade school. But not so to-day. Indeed the demand for college-bred men by a school like Tuskegee, ought to make Mr. Booker T. Washington the firmest friend of higher training. Here he has as helpers the son of a Negro senator, trained in Greek and the humanities, and graduated at Harvard; the son of a Negro congressman and lawyer, trained in Latin and mathematics, and graduated at Oberlin; he has as his wife, a woman who read Virgil and Homer in the same class room with me; he has as college chaplain, a classical graduate of Atlanta University; as teacher of science, a graduate of Fisk; as teacher of history, a graduate of Smith,—indeed some thirty of his chief teachers are college graduates, and instead of studying French grammars in the midst of weeds, or buying pianos for dirty cabins, they are at Mr. Washington's right hand helping him in a noble work. And yet one of the effects of Mr. Washington's propaganda has been to throw doubt upon the expediency of such training for Negroes, as these persons have had.

Men of America, the problem is plain before you. Here is a race transplanted through the criminal foolishness of your fathers. Whether you like it or not the millions are here, and here they will remain. If you do not lift them up, they will pull you down. Education and work are the levers to uplift a people. Work alone will not do it unless inspired by the right ideals and guided by intelligence. Education must not simply teach work—it must teach Life. The Talented Tenth of the Negro race must be made leaders of thought and missionaries of culture among their people. No others can do this work and Negro colleges must train men for it. The Negro race, like all other races, is going to be saved by its exceptional men—1903.

Atlanta Exposition Address

Booker T. Washington

One third of the population of the South is of the Negro race. No enterprise seeking the material, civil, or moral welfare of this section can disregard this element of our population and reach the highest success. I but convey to you, Mr. President and Directors, the sentiment of the masses of my race when I say that in no way have the value and manhood of the American Negro been more fittingly and generously recognized than by the managers of this magnificent exposition at every stage of its progress. It is a recognition that will do more to cement the friendship of the two races than any occurrence since the dawn of our freedom.

Not only this, but the opportunity here afforded will awaken among us a new era of industrial progress. Ignorant and inexperienced, it is not strange that in the first years of our new life we began at the top instead of at the bottom; that a seat in Congress or the State Legislature was more sought than real estate or industrial skill; that the political convention or stump-speaking had more attraction than starting a dairy farm or truck garden.

A ship lost at sea for many days suddenly sighted a friendly vessel. From the mast of the unfortunate vessel was seen a signal: "Water, water; we die of thirst!" The answer from the friendly vessel at once came back: "Cast down your bucket where you are." A second time the signal, "Water, water; send us water!" ran up from the distressed vessel, and was answered: "Cast down your bucket where you are." And a third and fourth signal for water was answered, "Cast down your bucket where you are." The captain of the distressed vessel, at last heeding the injunction, cast down his bucket, and it came up full of fresh, sparkling water from the mouth of the Amazon River. To those of my race who depend upon bettering their condition in a foreign land, or who underestimate the importance of cultivating friendly relations with the Southern white man who is their next-door neighbor, I would

Source: Booker T. Washington, "Atlanta Exposition Address" delivered at International Exposition at Atlanta, Georgia, 18 September 1895.

say: "Cast down your bucket where you are"— cast it down in making friends, in every manly way, of the people of all races by whom we are surrounded.

Cast it down in agriculture, mechanics, in commerce, in domestic service, and in the professions. And in this connection it is well to bear in mind that whatever other sins the South may be called to bear, when it comes to business, pure and simple, it is in the South that the Negro is given a man's chance in the commercial world, and in nothing is this Exposition more eloquent than in emphasizing this chance. Our greatest danger is that in the great leap from slavery to freedom we may overlook the fact that the masses of us are to live by the productions of our hands, and fail to keep in mind that we shall prosper in proportion as we learn to dignify and glorify common labor, and put brains and skill into the common occupations of life; shall prosper in proportion as we learn to draw the line between the superficial and the substantial, the ornamental gew-gaws of life and the useful. No race can prosper till it learns that there is as much dignity in tilling a field as in writing a poem. It is at the bottom of life we must begin, and not at the top. Nor should we permit our grievances to overshadow our opportunities.

To those of the white race who look to the incoming of those of foreign birth and strange tongue and habits for the prosperity of the South, were I permitted, I would repeat what I say to my own race, "Cast down your bucket where you are." Cast it down among the eight million Negroes whose habits you know, whose fidelity and love you have tested in days when to have proved treacherous meant the ruin of your firesides. Cast down your bucket among these people who have without strikes and labor wars tilled your fields, cleared your forests, builded your railroads and cities, brought forth treasures from the bowels of the earth, and helped make possible this magnificent representation of the progress of the South. Casting down your bucket among my people, helping and encouraging them as you are doing on these grounds, and, with education of head, hand, and heart, you will find that they will buy your surplus land, make blossom the waste places in your fields, and run your factories. While doing this, you can be sure in the future, as in the past, that you and your families will be surrounded by the most patient, faithful, law-abiding, and unresentful people that the world has seen. As we have proved our loyalty to you in the past, in nursing your children, watching by the sick bed of your mothers and fathers, and often following them with tear-dimmed eyes to their graves, so in the future, in our humble way, we shall stand by you with a devotion that no foreigner can approach, ready to lay down our lives, if need be, in defense of yours, interlacing our industrial, commercial, civil, and religious life with yours in a way that shall make the interests of both races one. In all things that are purely social we can be as separate as the fingers, yet one as the hand in all things essential to mutual progress.

There is no defense or security for any of us except in the highest intelligence and development of all. If anywhere there are efforts tending to curtail the fullest growth of the Negro, let these efforts be turned into stimulating, encouraging, and making him the most useful and intelligent citizen. Effort or means so invested will pay a thousand per cent interest. These efforts will be twice blessed—"Blessing him that gives and him that takes."

There is no escape through law of man or God from the inevitable:

> The laws of changeless justice bind
> Oppressor with oppressed;
> And close as sin and suffering joined
> We march to fare abreast.

Nearly sixteen millions of hands will aid you in pulling the load upward, or they will pull, against you, the load downward. We shall constitute one third and more of the ignorance and crime of the South, or one third its intelligence and progress; we shall contribute one third to the business and industrial prosperity of the South, or we shall prove a veritable body of death, stagnating, depressing, retarding every effort to advance the body politic.

Gentlemen of the Exposition, as we present to you our humble effort at an exhibition of our progress, you must not expect overmuch. Starting thirty years ago with ownership here and there in a few quilts and pumpkins and chickens (gathered from miscellaneous sources), remember, the path that has led from these to the inventions and production of agricultural implements, buggies, steam engines, newspapers, books, statuary carving, paintings, the management of drugstores and banks, has not been trodden without contact with thorns and thistles. While we take pride in what we exhibit as a result of our independent efforts, we do not for a moment forget that our part in this exhibition would fall far short of your expectations but for the constant help that has come to our educational life, not only from the Southern states, but especially from Northern philanthropists, who have made their gifts a constant stream of blessing and encouragement.

The wisest among my race understand that the agitation of questions of social equality is the extremest folly, and that progress in the enjoyment of all the privileges that will come to us must be the result of severe and constant struggle rather than of artificial forcing. No race that has anything to contribute to the markets of the world is long, in any degree, ostracized. It is important and right that all privileges of the law be ours, but it is vastly more important that we be prepared for the exercise of those privileges. The opportunity to earn a dollar in a factory just now is worth infinitely more than the opportunity to spend a dollar in an opera house.

In conclusion, may I repeat that nothing in thirty years has given us more hope and encouragement, and drawn us so near to you of the white race, as this opportunity offered by the Exposition; and here bending, as it were, over the altar that represents the results of the struggles of your race and mine, both starting practically empty-handed three decades ago, I pledge that, in your effort to work out the great and intricate problem which God has laid at the doors of the South, you shall have at all times the patient, sympathetic help of my race; only let this be constantly in mind, that while, from representations in these buildings of the product of field, of forest, of mine, of factory, letters, and art, much good will come, yet far above and beyond material benefits will be that higher good, that, let us pray God, will come in a blotting out of sectional differences and racial animosities and suspicions, in a determination to administer absolute justice, in a willing obedience among all classes to the mandates of law. This, coupled with our material prosperity, will bring into our beloved South a new heaven and a new earth—September 18, 1895.

Our New Citizen

Booker T. Washington

From whence came our new citizen? Who is he? And what is his mission? It is interesting to note that the Negro is the only citizen of this country who came here by special invitation and by reason of special provision. The Caucasian came here against the protest of the leading citizens of this country in 1492. We were so important to the prosperity of this country that special vessels were sent to convey us hither.

Shall we be less important in the future than in the past? The Negroes are one eighth of your population. Our race is larger than the population of the Argentine Republic, larger than Chile, larger than Peru and Venezuela combined—nearly as large as Mexico.

Whether the call has come for us to clear the forests of your country, to make your cotton, rice, and sugar cane, build houses or railroads, or to shoulder arms in defense of our country, have we not answered that call? When the call has come to educate our children, to teach them thrift, habits of industry, have we not filled every school that has been opened for us? When with others there have been labor wars, strikes, and destruction of property, have we not set the world an example in each one quietly attending to his own business? When, even here in the North, the shop, the factory, the trades have closed against us, have we not patiently, faithfully gone on taking advantage of our disadvantages, and through it all have we not continued to rise, to increase in numbers and prosperity? If in the past we have thus proven our right to your respect and confidence, shall it be less so in the future? If in proportion as we contribute, by the exercise of the higher virtues, by the product of brain and skilled hand, to the common prosperity of our country, shall we not receive all the privileges of any other citizen, whether born out of this country or under the Stars and Stripes?

You of the great and prosperous North still owe a serious and uncompleted duty to your less fortunate brothers of the white race South who suffered and are still suffering the consequences of American slavery. What was the task you asked them to perform? Returning to their destitute homes after years of war, to face blasted hopes, devastation, a shattered industrial system, you asked them to add to their burdens that of preparing in education, politics, and economics, in a few short years, for citizenship four or five millions of former slaves. That the South, staggering under the burden, made blunders, that in some measure there has been disappointment, no one need be surprised.

And yet, taking it all in all, we may, I think, safely challenge history to find a case where two races, but yesterday master and slave, today citizen and citizen, have made such marvelous progress in the adjustment of themselves to new conditions, where each has traveled so fast in the divine science of forgetting and forgiving; and yet do not misunderstand me that all is done or that there are not serious wrongs yet to be blotted out.

In making these observations I do not, I cannot, forget as an humble representative of my race the vacant seat, the empty sleeve, the lives offered up on Southern battlefields, that we might have a united country and that our flag should shelter none save freemen, nor do I forget the millions of dollars that have gone into the South from the hands of philanthropic individuals and religious organizations.

Nor are we of the black race leaving the work alone to your race in the North or your race in the South—mark what this new citizen is doing. Go with me tonight to the Tuskegee Institute in the Black Belt of Alabama, in an

Source: Booker T. Washington, "Our New Citizen" address delivered before the Hamilton Club, Chicago Illinois, 31 January 1896.

old slave plantation where a few years ago my people were bought and sold, and I will show you an industrial village, which is an example of others, with nearly eight hundred young men and women working with head and hand by night and by day, preparing themselves, in literature, in science, in agriculture, in dairying, in fruit-growing, in stock-raising, in brick-making, in brick masonry, in woodwork, in ironwork, in tinwork, in leatherwork, in cloth, in cooking, in laundrying, in printing, in household science—in the duties of Christian citizenship—preparing themselves that they may prepare thousands of others of our race that they may contribute their full quota of virtue, of thrift and intelligence to the prosperity of our beloved country. It is said that we will be hewers of wood and drawers of water, but we shall be more, we shall turn the wood into houses, into machinery, into implements of commerce and civilization. We shall turn the water into steam, into electricity, into dairy and agricultural products, into food and raiment—and thus wind our life about yours, thus knit our civil and commercial interests into yours in a way that shall make us all realize anew that "of one blood hath God made all men to dwell and prosper on the face of the earth."

But when all this is said, I repeat, gentlemen of the club, that you of this generation owe to the South, not less than to yourselves, an unfulfilled duty. Surely, surely, if the Negro, with all that is behind him, can forget the past, you ought to rise above him in this regard. When the South is poor you are poor, when the South commits crime you commit crime, when the South prospers you prosper.

There is no power that can separate our destiny. Let us ascend in this matter above color or race or party or sectionalism into the region of duty of man to man, American to American, Christian to Christian. If the Negro who has been oppressed, ostracized, denied rights in a Christian land, can help you, North and South, to rise, can be the medium of your rising to these sublime heights of unselfishness and self-forgetfulness, who may say that the Negro, this new citizen, will not see in it a recompense for all that he has suffered and will have performed a mission that will be placed beside that of the lowly Nazarine?

Let the Negro, the North, and the South do their duty with a new spirit and a new determination during this, the dawning of a new century, and at the end of fifty years a picture will be painted—what is it? A race dragged from its native land in chains, three hundred years of slavery, years of fratricidal war, thousands of lives laid down, freedom for the slave, reconstruction, blunders, bitterness between North and South. The South staggers under the burden; the North forgets the past and comes to the rescue; the Negro, in the midst, teaching North and South patience, forbearance, long-suffering, obedience to law, developing in intellect, character and property, skill and habits of industry. The North and South, joining hands with the Negro, take him whom they have wronged, help him, encourage him, stimulate him in self-help, give him the rights of man, and, in lifting up the Negro, lift themselves up into that atmosphere where there is a new North, a new South—a new citizen—a new republic—January 31, 1896.

Democracy and Education

Booker T. Washington

It is said that the strongest chain is no stronger than its weakest link. In the Southern part of our country there are twenty-two millions of your brethren who are bound to you by ties which you cannot tear asunder if you would. The most intelligent man in your community has his intelligence darkened by the ignorance of a fellow citizen in the Mississippi bottoms. The most wealthy in your city would be more wealthy but for the poverty of a fellow being in the Carolina rice swamps. The most moral and religious among you has his religion and morality modified by the degradation of the man in the South whose religion is a mere matter of form or emotionalism.

The vote in your state that is cast for the highest and purest form of government is largely neutralized by the vote of the man in Louisiana whose ballot is stolen or cast in ignorance. When the South is poor, you are poor; when the South commits crime, you commit crime. My friends, there is no mistake; you must help us to raise the character of our civilization or yours will be lowered. No member of your race in any part of our country can harm the weakest and meanest member of mine without the proudest and bluest blood in the city of Brooklyn being degraded. The central ideal which I wish you to help me consider is the reaching and lifting up of the lowest, most unfortunate, negative element that occupies so large a proportion of our territory and composes so large a percentage of our population. It seems to me that there never was a time in the history of our country when those interested in education should more earnestly consider to what extent the mere acquiring of a knowledge of literature

Source: Booker T. Washington, "Democracy and Education" address delivered before the Institute of the Arts and Sciences, Brooklyn, New York, 30 September 1896.

and science makes producers, lovers of labor, independent, honest, unselfish, and, above all, supremely good. Call education by what name you please, and if it fails to bring about these results among the masses it falls short of its highest end. The science, the art, the literature that fails to reach down and bring the humblest up to the fullest enjoyment of the blessings of our government is weak, no matter how costly the buildings or apparatus used, or how modern the methods in instruction employed. The study of arithmetic that does not result in making someone more honest and self-reliant is defective. The study of history that does not result in making men conscientious in receiving and counting the ballots of their fellow men is most faulty. The study of art that does not result in making the strong less willing to oppress the weak means little. How I wish that from the most humble log cabin schoolhouse in Alabama we could burn it, as it were, into the hearts and heads of all, that usefulness, service to our brother, is the supreme end of education. Putting the thought more directly as it applies to conditions in the South: Can you make your intelligence affect us in the same ratio that our ignorance affects you? Let us put a not improbable case. A great national question is to be decided, one that involves peace or war, the honor or dishonor of our nation—yea, the very existence of the government. The North and West are divided. There are five million votes to be cast in the South, and of this number one half are ignorant. Not only are one half the voters ignorant, but, because of this ignorant vote, corruption, dishonesty in a dozen forms have crept into the exercise of the political franchise, to the extent that the conscience of the intelligent class is soured in its attempts to defeat the will of the ignorant voters. Here, then, on the one hand you have an ignorant vote, and on the other hand an intelligent vote minus a conscience.

The time may not be far off when to this kind of jury we shall have to look for the verdict that is to decide the course of our democratic institutions.

When a great national calamity stares us in the face, we are, I fear, too much given to depending on a short campaign of education to do on the hustings what should have been accomplished in the schoolroom. With this preliminary survey, let us examine with more care the work to be done in the South before all classes will be fit for the highest duties of citizenship. In reference to my own race I am confronted with some embarrassment at the outset because of the various and conflicting opinions as to what is to be its final place in our economic and political life. Within the last thirty years—and, I might add, within the last three months—it has been proven by eminent authority that the Negro is increasing in numbers so fast that it is only a question of a few years before he will far outnumber the white race in the South, and it has also been proven that the Negro is fast dying out and it is only a question of a few years before he will have completely disappeared. It has also been proven that crime among us is on the increase and that crime is on the decrease; that education helps the Negro, that education also hurts him; that he is fast leaving the South and taking up his residence in the North and West, and that the tendency of the Negro is to drift to the lowlands of the Mississippi bottoms. It has been proven that as a slave laborer he produced less cotton than a free man. It has been proven that education unfits the Negro for work, and that education also makes him more valuable as a laborer; that he is our greatest criminal and that he is our most law-abiding citizen. In the midst of these opinions, in the words of a modern statesman, "I hardly know where I am at." I hardly know whether I am myself or the other fellow. But in the midst of this confusion there are a few things of which I feel certain that furnish a basis for thought and action. I know that, whether we are increasing or decreasing, whether we are growing better or worse, whether we are valuable or valueless, a few years ago fourteen of us were brought into this country and now there are eight million of us. I know that, whether in slavery or freedom, we have always been loyal to the Stars and Stripes, that no schoolhouse has been opened for us that has not been filled; that 1,500,000 ballots that we have the right to cast are as potent for weal and woe as the ballot cast by the whitest and most influential man in your commonwealth. I know that wherever our life touches yours we help or hinder; that wherever your life touches ours you make us stronger or weaker. Further I know that almost every other race that tried to look the white man in the face has disappeared. With all the conflicting opinions, and with the full knowledge of all our weaknesses, I know that only a few centuries ago in this country we went into slavery pagans: we came out Christians; we went into slavery pieces of property: we came out American citizens; we went into slavery without a language: we came out speaking the proud Anglo-Saxon tongue; we went into slavery with the slave chains clanking about our wrists: we came out with the American ballot in our hands. My friends, I submit it to your sober and candid judgment, if a race that is capable of such a test, such a transformation, is not worth saving and making a part, in reality as well as in name, of our democratic government. It is with an ignorant race as it is with a child: it craves at first the superficial, the ornamental, the signs of progress rather than the reality. The ignorant race is tempted to jump, at one bound, to the position that it has required years of hard struggle for others to reach. It seems to me that the temptation in education and missionary work is to do for a people a thousand miles away without always making a careful study of the needs and conditions of the people whom we are trying to help. The temptation is to run all people through a certain educational mold regardless of the condition of the subject or the end to be accomplished. Unfortunately for us as a race, our education was begun, just after the war, too nearly where New England education ended. We seemed to overlook the fact that we were dealing with a race that has little love for labor in their native land and consequently brought little love for labor with them to America. Added to this was the fact that they had been forced for two hundred and fifty years to labor without compensation under circumstances that were calculated to do anything but teach them the dignity, beauty, and civilizing power of intelligent labor. We forgot the industrial education that was given the Pilgrim Fathers of New England in clearing and planting its cold, bleak, and snowy hills and valleys, in providing shelter, founding the small mills and factories, in supplying themselves with homemade products, thus laying the foundation of an industrial life that now keeps going a large part of the colleges and missionary effort of the world. May I be tempted one step further in showing how prone we are to make our education formal, technical, instead of making it meet the needs of conditions regardless of formality and technicality? At least eighty per cent of my pupils in the South are found in the rural districts, and they are dependent on agriculture in some form for their support. Notwithstanding in this instance we have a whole race depending upon agriculture, and notwithstanding thirty years have passed since our freedom, aside from what we have done at Hampton and Tuskegee and one or two other institutions, not a thing has been attempted by state or philanthropy in the way of educating the race in this industry on which their very existence depends. Boys have been taken from the farms and educated in law, theology, Hebrew, and Greek—educated in everything else but the very subject they should know the most about. I question whether or not among all the educated colored people in the United States you can find six, if we except the institutions named, that have received anything like a thorough training in agriculture. It would have seemed, since self-support and industrial independence are the first conditions for lifting up any race, that education in theoretical and practical agriculture, horticulture, dairying, and stock-raising should have occupied the first place in our system. Some time ago when we decided to make tailoring a part of our training at the Tuskegee Institute, I was amazed to find that it was almost impossible to find in

the whole country an educated colored man who could teach the making of clothing. I could find them by the score who could teach astronomy, theology, Greek, or Latin, but almost none who could instruct in the making of clothing, something that has to be used by every one of us every day in the year. How often has my heart been made to sink as I have gone through the South and into the homes of the people and found women who could converse intelligently on Grecian history, who had studied geometry, could analyze the most complex sentences, and yet could not analyze the poorly cooked and still more poorly served bread and fat meat that they and their families were eating three times a day. It is little trouble to find girls who can locate Pekin and the Desert of Sahara on an artificial globe; but seldom can you find one who can locate on an actual dinner table the proper place for the carving knife and fork or the meat and vegetables. A short time ago, in one of our Southern cities, a colored man died who had received training as a skilled mechanic during the days of slavery. By his skill and industry he had built up a great business as a house contractor and builder. In this same city there are thirty-five thousand colored people, among them young men who have been well educated in languages and literature, but not a single one could be found who had been trained in architectural and mechanical drawing that could carry on the business which this ex-slave had built up, and so it was soon scattered to the wind. Aside from the work done in the institutions that I have mentioned, you will find no colored men who have been trained in the principles of architecture, notwithstanding the vast majority of the race is without homes. Here, then, are the three prime conditions for growth, for civilization—food, clothing, shelter—yet we have been the slaves of form and custom to such an extent that we have failed in a large measure to look matters squarely in the face and meet actual needs. You cannot graft a fifteenth-century civilization onto a twentieth-century civilization by the mere performance of mental gymnastics. Understand, I speak in no fault-finding spirit, but with a feeling of deep regret for what has been done; but the future must be an improvement on the past.

I have endeavored to speak plainly in regard to the past, because I fear that the wisest and most interested have not fully comprehended the task which American slavery has laid at the doors of the Republic. Few, I fear, realize what is to be done before the seven million of my people in the South can be made a safe, helpful, progressive part of our institutions. The South, in proportion to its ability, has done well, but this does not change facts. Let me illustrate what I mean by a single example. In spite of all that has been done, I was in a county in Alabama a few days ago where there are some thirty thousand colored people and about seven thousand whites; in this county not a single public school for Negroes has been open this year longer than three months, not a single colored teacher has been paid more than fifteen dollars a month for his teaching. Not one of these schools was taught in a building worthy of the name of schoolhouse. In this county the state or public authorities do not own a dollar's worth of school property—not a schoolhouse, a blackboard, or a piece of crayon. Each colored child had spent on him this year for his education about fifty cents, while one of your children had spent on him this year for education not far from twenty dollars. And yet each citizen of this county is expected to share the burdens and privileges of our democratic form of government just as intelligently and conscientiously as the citizens of your beloved Kings County. A vote in this county means as much to the nation as a vote in the city of Boston. Crime in this country is as truly an arrow aimed at the heart of the government as crime committed in your own streets. Do you know that a single schoolhouse built this year in a town near Boston to shelter about three hundred students has cost more for building alone than will be spent for the education, including buildings, apparatus, teachers, of the whole colored school population of Alabama? The commissioner of education for the state of Georgia recently reported to the state legislature that in the state

there were two hundred thousand children that had entered no school the past year, and one hundred thousand more who were in school but a few days, making practically three hundred thousand children between six and sixteen years of age that are growing up in ignorance in one Southern state. The same report states that outside of the cities and towns, while the average number of schoolhouses in a county is sixty, all of these sixty schoolhouses are worth in a lump sum less than $2,000, and the report further adds that many of the schoolhouses in Georgia are not fit for horse stables. These illustrations, my friends, as far as concerns the Gulf states, are not exceptional cases or overdrawn.

I have referred to industrial education as a means of fitting the millions of my people in the South for the duties of citizenship. Until there is industrial independence it is hardly possible to have a pure ballot. In the country districts of the Gulf states it is safe to say that not more than one black man in twenty owns the land he cultivates. Where so large a proportion of the people are dependent, live in other people's houses, eat other people's food, and wear clothes they have not paid for, it is a pretty hard thing to tell how they are going to vote. My remarks thus far have referred mainly to my own race. But there is another side. The longer I live and the more I study the question, the more I am convinced that it is not so much a problem as to what you will do with the Negro as what the Negro will do with you and your civilization. In considering this side of the subject, I thank God that I have grown to the point where I can sympathize with a white man as much as I can sympathize with a black man. I have grown to the point where I can sympathize with a Southern white man as much as I can sympathize with a Northern white man. To me "a man's a man for a' that and a' that." As bearing upon democracy and education, what of your white brethren in the South, those who suffered and are still suffering the consequences of American slavery for which both you and they are responsible? You of the great and prosperous North still owe to your unfortunate brethren of the Caucasian race in the

South, not less than to yourselves, a serious and uncompleted duty. What was the task you asked them to perform? Returning to their destitute homes after years of war to face blasted hopes, devastation, a shattered industrial system, you asked them to add to their own burdens that of preparing in education, politics, and economics in a few short years, for citizenship, four millions of former slaves. That the South, staggering under the burden, made blunders, and that in a measure there has been disappointment, no one need be surprised.

The educators, the statesmen, the philanthropists have never comprehended their duty toward the millions of poor whites in the South who were buffeted for two hundred years between slavery and freedom, between civilization and degradation, who were disregarded by both master and slave. It needs no prophet to tell the character of our future civilization when the poor white boy in the country districts of the South receives one dollar's worth of education and your boy twenty dollars' worth, when one never enters a library or reading room and the other has libraries and reading rooms in every ward and town. When one hears lectures and sermons once in two months and the other can hear a lecture or sermon every day in the year. When you help the South you help yourselves. Mere abuse will not bring the remedy. The time has come, it seems to me, when in this matter we should rise above party or race or sectionalism into the region of duty of man to man, citizen to citizen, Christian to Christian, and if the Negro who has been oppressed and denied rights in a Christian land can help you North and South to rise, can be the medium of your rising into this atmosphere of generous Christian brotherhood and self-forgetfulness, he will see in it a recompense for all that he has suffered in the past. Not very long ago a white citizen of the South boastingly expressed himself in public to this effect: "I am now forty-six years of age, but have never polished my own boots, have never saddled my own horse, have never built a fire in my own room, have never hitched a horse." He was asked a short time since by a lame man to

hitch his horse, but refused and told him to get a Negro to do it. Our state law requires that a voter is required to read the constitution before voting, but the last clause of the constitution is in Latin and the Negroes cannot read Latin, and so they are asked to read the Latin clause and are thus disfranchised, while the whites are permitted to read the English portion of the constitution. I do not quote these statements for the purpose of condemning the individual or the South, for though myself a member of a despised and unfortunate race, I pity from the bottom of my heart any of God's creatures whence such a statement can emanate. Evidently here is a man who, as far as mere book training is concerned, is educated, for he boasts of his knowledge of Latin, but, so far as the real purpose of education is concerned—the making of men useful, honest, and liberal—this man has never been touched. Here is a citizen in the midst of our republic, clothed in a white skin, with all the technical signs of education, but who is as little fitted for the highest purpose of life as any creature found in Central Africa. My friends, can we make our education reach down far enough to touch and help this man? Can we so control science, art, and literature as to make them to such an extent a means rather than an end; that the lowest and most unfortunate of God's creatures shall be lifted up, ennobled and glorified; shall be a freeman instead of a slave of narrow sympathies and wrong customs? Some years ago a bright young man of my race succeeded in passing a competitive examination for a cadetship at the United States naval academy at Annapolis. Says the young man, Mr. Henry Baker, in describing his stay at this institution: "I was several times attacked with stones and was forced finally to appeal to the officers, when a marine was detailed to accompany me across the campus and from the mess hall at meal times. My books were mutilated, my clothes were cut and in some instances destroyed, and all the petty annoyances which ingenuity could devise were inflicted upon me daily, and during seamanship practice aboard the *Dale* attempts were often made to do me personal injury while I would be aloft in the rigging. No one ever addressed me by name. I was called the Moke usually, the Nigger for variety. I was shunned as if I were a veritable leper and received curses and blows as the only method my persecutors had of relieving the monotony." Not once during the two years, with one exception, did any one of the more than four hundred cadets enrolled ever come to him with a word of advice, counsel, sympathy, or information, and he never held conversation with any one of them for as much as five minutes during the whole course of his experience at the academy, except on occasions when he was defending himself against their assaults. The one exception where the departure from the rule was made was in the case of a Pennsylvania boy, who stealthily brought him a piece of his birthday cake at twelve o'clock one night. The act so surprised Baker that his suspicions were aroused, but these were dispelled by the donor, who read to him a letter which he had received from his mother, from whom the cake came, in which she requested that a slice be given to the colored cadet who was without friends. I recite this incident and not for the purpose merely of condemning the wrong done a member of my race; no, no, not that. I mention the case, not for the one cadet, but for the sake of the four hundred cadets, for the sake of the four hundred American families, the four hundred American communities whose civilization and Christianity these cadets represented. Here were four hundred and more picked young men representing the flower of our country, who had passed through our common schools and were preparing themselves at public expense to defend the honor of our country. And yet, with grammar, reading, and arithmetic in the public schools, and with lessons in the arts of war, the principles of physical courage at Annapolis, both systems seemed to have utterly failed to prepare a single one of these young men for real life, that he could be brave enough, Christian enough, American enough, to take this poor defenseless black boy by the hand in open daylight and let the world know that he was his friend. Education, whether of black man or white man, that gives one physical

courage to stand in front of the cannon and fails to give him moral courage to stand up in defense of right and justice is a failure. With all that the Brooklyn Institute of Arts and Sciences stands for in its equipment, its endowment, its wealth and culture, its instructors, can it produce a mother that will produce a boy that will not be ashamed to have the world know that he is a friend to the most unfortunate of God's creatures? Not long ago a mother, a black mother, who lived in one of your Northern states, had heard it whispered around in her community for years that the Negro was lazy, shiftless, and would not work. So when her boy grew to sufficient size, at considerable expense and great self-sacrifice, she had her boy thoroughly taught the machinist's trade. A job was secured in a neighboring shop. With dinner bucket in hand and spurred on by the prayers of the now happy mother, the boy entered the shop to begin his first day's work. What happened? Had any one of the twenty white Americans been so educated that he gave this stranger a welcome into their midst? No, not this. Every one of the twenty white men threw down his tools and deliberately walked out, swearing that he would not give a black man an opportunity to earn an honest living. Another shop was tried, with the same result, and still another and the same. Today this promising and ambitious black man is a wreck—a confirmed drunkard, with no hope, no ambition. My friends, who blasted the life of this young man? On whose hands does his blood rest? Our system of education, or want of education, is responsible. Can our public schools and colleges turn out a set of men that will throw open the doors of industry to all men everywhere, regardless of color, so all shall have the same opportunity to earn a dollar that they now have to spend a dollar? I know a good many species of cowardice and prejudice, but I know none equal to this. I know not who is the worst, the ex-slaveholder who perforce compelled his slave to work without compensation, or the man who perforce compels the Negro to refrain from working for compensation. My friends, we are one in this country. The question of the highest citizenship and the complete education of all concerns nearly ten million of my own people and over sixty million of yours. We rise as you rise; when we fall you fall. When you are strong we are strong; when we are weak you are weak. There is no power that can separate our destiny. The Negro can afford to be wronged; the white man cannot afford to wrong him. Unjust laws or customs that exist in many places regarding the races injure the white man and inconvenience the Negro. No race can wrong another race simply because it has the power to do so without being permanently injured in morals. The Negro can endure the temporary inconvenience, but the injury to the white man is permanent. It is for the white man to save himself from his degradation that I plead. If a white man steals a Negro's ballot it is the white man who is permanently injured. Physical death comes to the one Negro lynched in a county, but death of the morals—death of the soul—comes to the thousands responsible for the lynching. We are a patient, humble people. We can afford to work and wait. There is plenty in this country for us to do. Away up in the atmosphere of goodness, forbearance, patience, long-suffering, and forgiveness the workers are not many or overcrowded. If others would be little we can be great. If others would be mean we can be good. If others would push us down we can help push them up. Character, not circumstances, makes the man. It is more important that we be prepared for voting than that we vote, more important that we be prepared to hold office than that we hold office, more important that we be prepared for the highest recognition than that we be recognized. Those who fought and died on the battlefield performed

their duty heroically and well, but a duty remains for you and me. The mere fiat of law could not make an ignorant voter an intelligent voter; could not make one citizen respect another; these results come to the Negro, as to all races, by beginning at the bottom and working up to the highest civilization and accomplishment. In the economy of God, there can be but one standard by which an individual can succeed—there is but one for a race. This country demands that every race measure itself by the American standard. By it a race must rise or fall, succeed or fail, and in the last analysis mere sentiment counts but little. During the next half-century and more my race must continue passing through the severe American crucible.

We are to be tested in our patience, in our forbearance, our power to endure wrong, to withstand temptation, to succeed, to acquire and use skill, our ability to complete, to succeed in commerce; to disregard the superficial for the real, the appearance for the substance; to be great and yet the servant of all. This, this is the passport to all that is best in the life of our republic, and the Negro must possess it or be debarred. In working out our destiny, while the main burden and center of activity must be with us, we shall need in a large measure the help, the encouragement, the guidance that the strong can give the weak. Thus helped, we of both races in the South shall soon throw off the shackles of racial and sectional prejudice and rise above the clouds of ignorance, narrowness, and selfishness into that atmosphere, that pure sunshine, where it will be our highest ambition to serve man, our brother, regardless of race or past conditions—September 30, 1896.

Address Delivered at Hampton Institute

Booker T. Washington

Few, if any, occasions within the past thirty years have meant more to the Negro race than that which calls us here. The Negro has been a laborer in this country nearly three hundred years, but with few exceptions he has been a forced laborer, an unskilled laborer, or an ignorant laborer; but here at the mouth of the James, but a few miles distant from where we entered this country as slaves, we have inaugurated today the largest and most complete attempt in this country to make the Negro an intelligent, conscientious, skillful producer, and to have him appreciate the dignity, beauty, and civilizing power that there is in labor. For this magnificent opportunity, not only the Hampton Institute but the Negro race bows in thanks to Mr. Morris K. Jesup, the generous helper, who has made what we see here possible; Dr. J. L. M. Curry, the farseeing agent of the John F. Slater Fund; as well as all the trustees and generous friends who have united in the opening of this new door. Coming as it does on the heels of the decision of the great American Jury, that our own country is to go forward and not backward in its business and commercial life, this enterprise means much, not alone to the Negro, but to the entire nation. Within the two decades it will be decided whether the Negro, by discarding ante-bellum ideas and methods, by putting brains and skill into the common occupations that lie at his door, will be able to lift labor out of toil, drudgery, and degradation into that which is dignified, beautiful, and glorified. Further, it will be decided within this time whether the Negro is to be replaced, crushed out as a helpful industrial factor by the fast-spreading trades unions, in connection with thousands of foreign skilled laborers, that even now press hard and

Source: Booker T. Washington, "Address Delivered at Hampton Institute" delivered 18 November 1896.

fast upon his heels and seem to press him into the very death. This question is for such unselfish members of the Anglo-Saxon race as are gathered here to help decide—and in deciding, not alone for the Negro, but whether you will have eight million people in this country, a nation within a nation, that will be a burden, a menace to your civilization and commercial life.

The Negro in slavery was tied to the white man through the bill of sale. In freedom he must tie himself to the white man through the bonds of commerce and the cultivation of the sympathetic good will of his white neighbor. When a black man has the best farm to be found in his country, every white man will respect him. A white man knows the Negro that lives in a two-story brick house whether he wants to or not. When a black man is the largest taxpayer in a community, his neighbors will not object very long to his voting and having his vote honestly counted. In the future there must be a more vital and practical connection between the Negro's educated brain and his means of earning a living.

But what has all this to do with the higher interests—the moral and religious side? I answer: Show me a race that is living on the outer edges of the industrial world, on the skimmed milk of business, and I will show you a race that is the football for political parties, and a race that cannot be what it should be in morals, and religion. I may be accused of wrong interpretation, but when the Bible says, "Work out your salvation with fear and trembling," I am tempted to believe that it means what it says. In the past we have had the fear and trembling. As a race I believe we are to work out our salvation, work it out with pen and ink, work it out with rule and compass, work it out with horsepower and steam power, work it out on the farm, in the shop, schoolroom, sewing room, the office, and in all life's callings. Here on these consecrated grounds I believe that we have a movement today that means the salvation of the Negro race, and as my people are taught in these classrooms, in these shops, on this farm from year to year to mix up with their religion zeal and habits of thrift, economy, carpentry, and blacksmithing with farming and sewing, with printing and house-building, and then as this influence penetrates the hills and valleys, the rice swamps, the Virginia tobacco fields, the Louisiana sugar bottoms, every hamlet and city, we shall agree that it is most possible for a race as for an individual to actually work out its salvation.

In attempting to elevate a race that has been in the position of the Negro race, nothing is so hard to avoid as extremes. It is not always easy to make a race, as well as its friends, see that on growth and development must we hang the line of certain well-defined and natural laws; that when there is artificial forcing, we have the superficial and deceptive signs of progress, but the real and permanent growth is wanting. The past history and present environment of the Negro lead him too often to imitate the white man at certain superficial points without stopping to count the steps, the years that it has taken the white man to reach his present position, or to note the foundations upon which his progress rests. Here at Hampton we have not alone the signs of progress but the reality. There is no position, however high, in science, or letters, or politics, that I would withhold from any race, but I would have the foundation sure—November 18, 1895.

FURTHER READING

Aptheker, Herbert. 1973. *Annotated Bibliography of the Published Writings of W.E.B. Du Bois.* Millwood, NY: Kraus-Thomson.

Blassingame, John et al., eds. 1979–94. *The Frederick Douglass Papers,* vols. 1–5. New Haven, CT: Yale University Press.

Rogers, William R. 1995. "We Are All Together Now:" *Frederick Douglass, William Lloyd Garrison, and The Prophetic Tradition.* New York: Garland Press.

Boxill, Bernard R. 1992. *Blacks and Social Justice.* Lanham, MD: Rowman and Littlefield Publishers.

Lemert, Charles, and Esme Bhan, eds. 1998. *The Voice of Anna Julia Cooper.* Lanham, MD: Rowman and Littlefield Publishers.

Gaines, Kevin. 1996. *Uplifting the Race: Black Leadership, Politics, and Culture in the Twentieth Century.* Chapel Hill: University of North Carolina Press.

Harlan, Louis R., ed. 1975. *The Booker T. Washington Papers.* Urbana: University of Illinois Press.

Lawson, Bill, and Frank Kirkland, eds. 1999. *Frederick Douglass: A Critical Reader.* Oxford: Blackwell Publishers.

Takaki, Ronald T. 1979. *Iron Cages: Race and Culture in Nineteenth-Century America.* New York: Knopf/Random House.

CHAPTER 4

Contemporary Black Feminist Thought

Many nineteenth-century black women activists, such as Mary Ann Shadd Carey, Maria Stewart, Sojourner Truth, and Harriet Jacobs, held feminist views that have been overshadowed by their involvement in the abolitionist movement. Contemporary black feminists begin with the recognition that the black women's struggle for equality has always been a twofold endeavor, requiring them to lift the race as they strive to overcome their subordination based on gender. In "The Social Construction of Black Feminist Thought" Patricia Hill Collins maintains that, because of racial discrimination, black women occupy a different standpoint than white women. She draws upon Karl Mannheim's account of the sociology of knowledge to argue that the black feminist standpoint reflects an Afrocentric concern with racial issues, as well as a feminist concern with issues related to gender.

Collins insists that lived experience is the criterion of meaning that grounds the perspective of black feminism. Hence, the positivist model that deems emotional life irrelevant to establishing claims must be modified to include criteria used by black women. These criteria include the use of dialogue to assess knowledge claims, a practice consistent with relying on lived experience as a criterion of meaning. There is also an ethics of caring and personal accountability entailed by the Afrocentric view. According to Collins, black academics are under obligation to give up the Eurocentric quest for a universal model; otherwise they will fail to provide black women the tools needed for resisting subordination.

As a means of incorporating the standpoint of black women into feminist theory, some black feminists have sought to raise the awareness of white feminists regarding important differences in values and interests. In "Black Women: Shaping Feminist Theory" bell hooks criticizes Betty Friedan's perspective (*The Feminine Mystique*) that focuses on the interests of college-educated white women who were compelled to remain in the home. She points out that the problems and dilemmas specific to this "leisure class" of white housewives were not the pressing concerns of the masses of women—especially black women facing racial discrimination and economic survival.

hooks challenges a commonly held tenent of feminist thought that "all women are oppressed." She points out that this assertion implies that women share a common lot, but in fact, it overlooks important factors such as race, religion, and sexual preference. Do these differences create a diversity of experience that determines the extent to which individual women are subjected to gender-based discrimination? hooks claims that the extent to which there is an absence of choice is the criterion we should use to gauge women's oppression. Because, for some women, sexism has not entailed an absolute absence of choice; they have been in a position to "ignore" many areas in which less fortunate women face discrimination and exploitation. hooks cites the tendency of white feminists to focus exclusively on gender as the sole determinant of women's fate. Her criticism is that it is easier for women who do not experience class or racial oppression to focus exclusively on gender. She calls for a more radical feminism that does not succumb to promoting merely the class interests of well-off conservative and liberal white women.

A major concern of contemporary black feminism has been the creation of a model to conceptualize the dual experience of gender and racial oppression. Kimberle Crenshaw proposes an intersectionist model that considers the standpoint of black women with regard to gender, race, and class in antidiscrimination legal cases. She is concerned with the ambivalence hindering social action that arises when challenging gender barriers might conflict with the antiracist agenda. Because race, and not gender, has figured directly into analyses of subordination as the primary oppositional force in black lives, it has become the commonly accepted criterion of group identity.

In "Demarginalizing the Intersection of Race and Sex: A Black Feminist Critique of Antidiscrimination Doctrine, Feminist Theory and Antiracist Politics," Crenshaw points out the consequences of social policy of treating race and gender as mutually exclusive categories for experience and analysis. She criticizes the legal doctrine as well as the social practices that reflect a single-axis analysis that distorts the multidimensionality of black women's experience. She analyzes several legal cases involving the intersection of race and gender to show that the dominant conception of discrimination assumes that subordination is a disadvantage that occurs only along a single categorical axis. In race discrimination cases discrimination is viewed only in terms of a category or group identity that includes middle-class blacks and black men. In sex discrimination cases discrimination is viewed only in terms that include middle-class white women. The net effect of this doctrine is to marginalize those who are multiply burdened.

When the operative concepts of race and sex are grounded in experiences that actually represent only a subset of a more complex phenomenon, the result can be to exclude black women from feminist theory and the discourse on antiracist policy. The lived experience of the intersection of race and gender amounts to something greater than the sum of racism and sexism and requires a recasting of the entire framework of legal and social practices. By reflecting on cases involving intersectionality, Crenshaw illustrates a broad range of issues that arise in connection with feminist critiques of rape and public policy debates concerning black female-headed households.

Crenshaw acknowledges that sometimes black women experience discrimination similiar to that experienced by white women and black men. Nonetheless, they also experience discrimination that is unique to black women and cannot be specified in terms of the general categories provided by discrimination policy. To avoid marginalizing those whose experience cannot be described within the parameters imposed by this policy, both feminist theory, as well as antiracist politics, will have to be reorganized around a view that more adequately addresses problems of intersectionality.

Questions regarding the intersection of race, class, and gender in the lived-experience of black women are expanded by Audre Lorde to include differences related to sexuality. Just as nonwhites can play an important role in educating whites regarding the humanity of nonwhites, women can carry out a similar function educating men and gays and lesbians educating the heterosexual community. She proposes replacing our talk of deviance with a practice of using difference "as a springboard for creative change within our lives." The first step will be to give up the mythical norm defined in America as white, thin, male, young, heterosexual, Christian, and financially secure. Lorde believes this norming process is carried into feminist discourse where there is a "pretense" to a homogeneity of experience under the rubric of "sisterhood." The norm for "sisterhood" is also amenable to distortion around difference when this is identified as *one way* of being different. Lorde maintains that women are as different among themselves as those who stand outside the mythical norm.

The notion of difference advanced by Lorde is the basis for her critical stance on a variety of issues. She critizes women's studies curricula for excluding literature by black women as too exotic for white women students and treating it as a subject that should only be taught by a black woman. Lorde rejects this practice as tokenism that should not be confused with a genuine invitation to share power. She also critizes the call for "unity" in black communities when this is a disguise for a homogeneity that treats a black feminist vision as a betrayal of the common interests of black people. Invoking racial unity can plaster over problems that need to be addressed. Lorde critizes Jomo Kenyatta's endorsement of female circumcision, insisting that this practice be viewed as a crime against humanity. According to Lorde, it is the responsibility of black men to stop such oppressive practices. Lorde believes that the true focus of revitalizing change is never merely the oppressive situations, but the piece of the oppressor planted deep inside each of us. Relying on a notion of "multiple selves," she points out that the black community is threatened by the idea of an openly woman-identified black woman, for the presence of black women not dependent on men will require a reordering of our view of social relationships.

The Social Construction of Black Feminist Thought

Patricia Hill Collins

Sojourner Truth, Anna Julia Cooper, Ida Wells-Barnett, and Fannie Lou Hamer are but a few names from a growing list of distinguished African American women activists. Although their sustained resistance to black women's victimization within interlocking systems of race, gender, and class oppression is well known, these women did not act alone.[1] Their actions were nurtured by the support of countless, ordinary African American women who, through strategies of everyday resistance, created a powerful foundation for this more visible black feminist activist tradition.[2] Such support has been essential to the shape and goals of black feminist thought.

The long-term and widely shared resistance among African American women can only have been sustained by an enduring and shared standpoint among black women about the meaning of oppression and the actions that black women can and should take to resist it. Efforts to identify the central concepts of this black women's standpoint figure prominently in the works of contemporary black feminist intellectuals.[3] Moreover, political and epistemological issues influence the social construction of black feminist thought. Like other subordinate groups, African American women not only have developed distinctive interpretations of black women's oppression, but have done so by using alternative ways of producing and validating knowledge itself.

Source: Patricia Hill Collins, "The Social Construction of Black Feminist Thought," *Signs* 14.4 (Summer, 1989): 745–73. Published by the University of Chicago Press.

A BLACK WOMEN'S STANDPOINT

The Foundation of Black Feminist Thought

Black women's everyday acts of resistance challenge two prevailing approaches to studying the consciousness of oppressed groups.[4] One approach claims that subordinate groups identify with the powerful and have no valid independent interpretation of their own oppression.[5] The second approach assumes that the oppressed are less human than their rulers and, therefore, are less capable of articulating their own standpoints.[6] Both approaches see any independent consciousness expressed by an oppressed group as being not of the group's own making and/or inferior to the perspective of the dominant group.[7] More important, both interpretations suggest that oppressed groups lack the motivation for political activism because of their flawed consciousness of their own subordination.

Yet African American women have been neither passive victims of nor willing accomplices to their own domination. As a result, emerging work in black women's studies contends that black women have a self-defined standpoint on their own oppression.[8] Two interlocking components characterize this standpoint. First, black women's political and economic status provides them with a distinctive set of experiences that offers a different view of material reality than that available to other groups. The unpaid and paid work that black women perform, the types of communities in which they live, and the kinds of relationships they have with others suggest that African American women, as a group, experience a different world than those who are not black and female.[9] Second, these experiences stimulate a distinctive black feminist consciousness concerning that material reality.[10] In brief, a subordinate group not only experiences a different reality than a group that rules, but a subordinate group may interpret that reality differently than a dominant group.

Many ordinary African American women have grasped this connection between what one does and how one thinks. Hannah Nelson, an elderly black domestic worker, discusses how work shapes the standpoints of African American and white women: "Since I have to work, I don't really have to worry about most of the things that most of the white women I have worked for are worrying about. And if these women did their own work, they would think just like I do – about this, anyway."[11] Ruth Shays, a black inner city resident, points out how variations in men's and women's experiences lead to differences in perspective: "The mind of the man and the mind of the woman is the same. But this business of living makes women use their minds in ways that men don't even have to think about."[12] Finally, elderly domestic worker Rosa Wakefield assesses how the standpoints of the powerful and those who serve them diverge: "If you eats these dinners and don't cook 'em, if you wears these clothes and don't buy or iron them, then you might start thinking that the good fairy or some spirit did all that.... Black folks don't have no time to be thinking like that.... But when you don't have anything else to do, you can think like that. It's bad for your mind, though."[13]

While African American women may occupy material positions that stimulate a unique standpoint, expressing an independent black feminist consciousness is problematic precisely because more powerful groups have a vested interest in suppressing such thought. As Hannah Nelson notes, "I have grown to womanhood in a world where the saner you are, the madder you are made to appear."[14] Nelson realizes that those who control the schools, the media, and other cultural institutions are generally skilled in establishing their view of reality as superior to alternative interpretations. While an oppressed group's experiences may put them in a position to see things differently, their lack of

control over the apparatuses of society that sustain ideological hegemony makes the articulation of their self-defined standpoint difficult. Groups unequal in power are correspondingly unequal in their access to the resources necessary to implement their perspectives outside their particular group.

One key reason that standpoints of oppressed groups are discredited and suppressed by the more powerful is that self-defined standpoints can stimulate oppressed groups to resist their domination. For instance, Annie Adams, a southern black woman, describes how she became involved in civil rights activities.

> When I first went into the mill we had segregated water fountains.... Same thing about the toilets. I had to clean the toilets for the inspection room and then when I got ready to go to the bathroom, I had to go all the way to the bottom of the stairs to the cellar. So I asked my boss man, "What's the difference? If I can go in there and clean them toilets, why can't I use them?" Finally, I started to use that toilet. I decided I wasn't going to walk a mile to go to the bathroom.[15]

In this case, Adams found the standpoint of the "boss man" inadequate, developed one of her own, and acted upon it. In doing so, her actions exemplify the connections between experiencing oppression, developing a self-defined standpoint on that experience, and resistance.

The Significance of Black Feminist Thought

The existence of a distinctive black women's standpoint does not mean that it has been adequately articulated in black feminist thought. Peter Berger and Thomas Luckmann provide a useful approach to clarifying the relationship between a black women's standpoint and black feminist thought with the contention that knowledge exists on two levels.[16] The first level includes the everyday, taken-for-granted knowledge shared by members of a given group, such as the ideas expressed by Ruth

Shays and Annie Adams. Black feminist thought, by extension, represents a second level of knowledge, the more specialized knowledge furnished by experts who are part of a group and who express the group's standpoint. The two levels of knowledge are interdependent; while black feminist thought articulates the taken-for-granted knowledge of African American women, it also encourages all black women to create new self-definitions that validate a black women's standpoint.

Black feminist thought's potential significance goes far beyond demonstrating that black women can produce independent, specialized knowledge. Such thought can encourage collective identity by offering black women a different view of themselves and their world than that offered by the established social order. This different view encourages African American women to value their own subjective knowledge base.[17] By taking elements and themes of black women's culture and traditions and infusing them with new meaning, black feminist thought rearticulates a consciousness that already exists.[18] More important, this rearticulated consciousness gives African American women another tool of resistance to all forms of their subordination.[19]

Black feminist thought, then, specializes in formulating and rearticulating the distinctive, self-defined standpoint of African American women. One approach to learning more about a black women's standpoint is to consult standard scholarly sources for the ideas of specialists on black women's experiences.[20] But investigating a black women's standpoint and black feminist thought requires more ingenuity than that required in examining the standpoints and thought of white males. Rearticulating the standpoint of African American women through black feminist thought is much more difficult since one cannot use the same techniques to study the knowledge of the dominated as one uses to study the knowledge of the powerful. This is precisely because subordinate groups have long had to use alternative ways to create an independent consciousness and to rearticulate it through specialists validated by the oppressed themselves.

THE EUROCENTRIC MASCULINIST KNOWLEDGE-VALIDATION PROCESS[21]

All social thought, including white masculinist and black feminist, reflects the interests and standpoint of its creators. As Karl Mannheim notes, "If one were to trace in detail ... the origin and ... diffusion of a certain thought-model, one would discover the affinity it has to the social position of given groups and their manner of interpreting the world."[22] Scholars, publishers, and other experts represent specific interests and credentialing processes and their knowledge claims must satisfy the epistemological and political criteria of the contexts in which they reside.[23]

Two political criteria influence the knowledge-validation process. First, knowledge claims must be evaluated by a community of experts whose members represent the standpoints of the groups from which they originate. Second, each community of experts must maintain its credibility as defined by the larger group in which it is situated and from which it draws its basic, taken-for-granted knowledge.

When white males control the knowledge-validation process, both political criteria can work to suppress black feminist thought. Since the general culture shaping the taken-for-granted knowledge of the community of experts is one permeated by widespread notions of black and female inferiority,[24] new knowledge claims that seem to violate these fundamental assumptions are likely to be viewed as anomalies.[25] Moreover, specialized thought challenging notions of black and female inferiority is unlikely to be generated from within a white-male-controlled academic community because both the kinds of questions that could be asked and the explanations that would be found satisfying would necessarily reflect a basic lack of familiarity with black women's reality.[26]

The experiences of African American women scholars illustrate how individuals who wish to rearticulate a black women's standpoint through black feminist thought can be suppressed by a white-male-controlled knowledge-validation process. Exclusion from basic literacy, quality educational experiences, and faculty and administrative positions has limited black women's access to influential academic positions.[27] Thus, while black women can produce knowledge claims that contest those advanced by the white male community, this community does not grant that black women scholars have competing knowledge claims based in another knowledge validation process. As a consequence, any credentials controlled by white male academicians can be denied to black women producing black feminist thought on the grounds that it is not credible research.

Those black women with academic credentials who seek to exert the authority that their status grants them to propose new knowledge claims about African American women face pressures to use their authority to help legitimate a system that devalues and excludes the majority of black women.[28] One way of excluding the majority of black women from the knowledge-validation process is to permit a few black women to acquire positions of authority in institutions that legitimate knowledge and to encourage them to work within the taken-for-granted assumptions of black female inferiority shared by the scholarly community and the culture at large. Those black women who accept these assumptions are likely to be rewarded by their institutions, often at significant personal cost. Those challenging the assumptions run the risk of being ostracized.

African American women academicians who persist in trying to rearticulate a black women's standpoint also face potential rejection of their knowledge claims on epistemological grounds. Just as the material realities of the powerful and the dominated produce separate standpoints, each group may also have distinctive epistemologies, or theories of knowledge. It is my contention that black female scholars may know that something is true but be unwilling or unable to legitimate their claims using Eurocentric masculinist criteria for consistency with substantiated knowledge and Eurocentric masculinist criteria for methodological adequacy.

For any particular interpretive context, new knowledge claims must be consistent with an existing body of knowledge that the group controlling the interpretive context accepts as true. The methods used to validate knowledge claims must also be acceptable to the group controlling the knowledge-validation process.

The criteria for the methodological adequacy of positivism illustrate the epistemological standards that black women scholars would have to satisfy in legitimating alternative knowledge claims.[29] Positivist approaches aim to create scientific descriptions of reality by producing objective generalizations. Since researchers have widely differing values, experiences, and emotions, genuine science is thought to be unattainable unless all human characteristics except rationality are eliminated from the research process. By following strict methodological rules, scientists aim to distance themselves from the values, vested interests, and emotions generated by their class, race sex, or unique situation and in so doing become detached observers and manipulators of nature.[30]

Several requirements typify positivist methodological approaches. First, research methods generally require a distancing of the researcher from her/his "object" of study by defining the researcher as a "subject" with full human subjectivity and objectifying the "object" of study.[31] A second requirement is the absence of emotions from the research process.[32] Third, ethics and values are deemed inappropriate in the research process, either as the reason for scientific inquiry or as part of the research process itself.[33] Finally, adversarial debates, whether written or oral, become the preferred method of ascertaining truth—the arguments that can withstand the greatest assault and survive intact become the strongest truths.[34]

Such criteria ask African American women to objectify themselves, devalue their emotional life, displace their motivations for furthering knowledge about black women, and confront, in an adversarial relationship, those who have more social, economic, and professional power than they. It seems unlikely, therefore, that black women would use a positivist epistemological stance in rearticulating a black women's standpoint. Black women are more likely to choose an alternative epistemology for assessing knowledge claims, one using standards that are consistent with black women's criteria for substantiated knowledge and with black women's criteria for methodological adequacy. If such an epistemology exists, what are its contours? Moreover, what is its role in the production of black feminist thought?

THE CONTOURS OF AN AFROCENTRIC FEMINIST EPISTEMOLOGY

Africanist analyses of the black experience generally agree on the fundamental elements of an Afrocentric standpoint. In spite of varying histories, black societies reflect elements of a core African value system that existed prior to and independently of racial oppression.[35] Moreover, as a result of colonialism, imperialism, slavery, apartheid, and other systems of racial domination, blacks share a common experience of oppression. These similarities in material conditions have fostered shared Afrocentric values that permeate the family structure, religious institutions, culture, and community life of blacks in varying parts of Africa, the Caribbean, South America, and North America.[36] This Afrocentric consciousness permeates the shared history of people of African descent through the framework of a distinctive Afrocentric epistemology.[37]

Feminist scholars advance a similar argument. They assert that women share a history of patriarchal oppression through the political economy of the material conditions of sexuality and reproduction.[38] These shared material conditions are thought to transcend divisions among women created by race, social class, religion, sexual orientation, and ethnicity and to form the basis of a women's standpoint with its corresponding feminist consciousness and epistemology.[39]

Since black women have access to both the Afrocentric and the feminist standpoints, an alternative epistemology used to rearticulate a black women's standpoint reflects elements of both traditions.[40] The search for the distinguishing features of an alternative epistemology used by African American women reveals that values and ideas that Africanist scholars identify as being characteristically "black" often bear remarkable resemblance to similar ideas claimed by feminist scholars as being characteristically "female."[41] This similarity suggests that the material conditions of oppression can vary dramatically and yet generate some uniformity in the epistemologies of subordinate groups. Thus, the significance of an Afrocentric feminist epistemology may lie in its enrichment of our understanding of how subordinate groups create knowledge that enables them to resist oppression.

The parallels between the two conceptual schemes raise a question: Is the worldview of women of African descent more intensely infused with the overlapping feminine/Afrocentric standpoints than is the case for either African American men or white women?[42] While an Afrocentric feminist epistemology reflects elements of epistemologies used by blacks as a group and women as a group, it also paradoxically demonstrates features that may be unique to black women. On certain dimensions, black women may more closely resemble black men, on others, white women, and on still others, black women may stand apart from both groups. Black feminist sociologist Deborah K. King describes this phenomenon as a "both/or" orientation, the act of being simultaneously a member of a group and yet standing apart from it. She suggests that multiple realities among black women yield a "multiple consciousness in black women's politics" and that this state of belonging yet not belonging forms an integral part of black women's oppositional consciousness.[43] Bonnie Thornton Dill's analysis of how black women live with contradictions, a situation she labels the "dialectics of black womanhood," parallels King's assertions that this "both/or" orientation is central to an Afrocentric feminist consciousness.[44] Rather than emphasizing how a black women's standpoint and its accompanying epistemology are different from those in Afrocentric and feminist analyses, I use black women's experiences as a point of contact between the two.

Viewing an Afrocentric feminist epistemology in this way challenges analyses claiming that black women have a more accurate view of oppression than do other groups. Such approaches suggest that oppression can be quantified and compared and that adding layers of oppression produces a potentially clearer standpoint. While it is tempting to claim that black women are more oppressed than everyone else and therefore have the best standpoint from which to understand the mechanisms, processes, and effects of oppression, this simply may not be the case.[45]

African American women do not uniformly share an Afrocentric feminist epistemology since social class introduces variations among black women in seeing, valuing, and using Afrocentric feminist perspectives. While a black women's standpoint and its accompanying epistemology stem from black women's consciousness of race and gender oppression, they are not simply the result of combining Afrocentric and female values—standpoints are rooted in real material conditions structured by social class.[46]

Concrete Experience as a Criterion of Meaning

Carolyn Chase, a thirty-one-year-old inner city black woman, notes, "My aunt used to say, 'A heap see, but a few know.'"[47] This saying depicts two types of knowing, knowledge and wisdom, and taps the first dimension of an Afrocentric feminist epistemology. Living life as black women requires wisdom since knowledge about the dynamics of race, gender, and class subordination has been essential to black women's survival. African American women give such wisdom high credence in assessing knowledge.

Allusions to these two types of knowing pervade the words of a range of African American women. In explaining the tenacity of racism, Zilpha Elaw, a preacher of the mid-1800s, noted: "The pride of a white skin is a bauble of great value with many in some parts of the United States, who readily sacrifice their intelligence to their prejudices, and pos-

sess more knowledge than wisdom."[48] In describing differences separating African American and white women, Nancy White invokes a similar rule: "When you come right down to it, white women just *think* they are free. Black women *know* they ain't free."[49] Geneva Smitherman, a college professor specializing in African American linguistics, suggests that "from a black perspective, written documents are limited in what they can teach about life and survival in the world. Blacks are quick to ridicule 'educated fools,' ... they have 'book learning,' but no 'mother wit,' knowledge, but not wisdom."[50] Mabel Lincoln eloquently summarizes the distinction between knowledge and wisdom: "To black people like me, a fool is funny—you know, people who love to break bad, people you can't tell anything to, folks that would take a shotgun to a roach."[51]

Black women need wisdom to know how to deal with the "educated fools" who would "take a shotgun to a roach." As members of a subordinate group, black women cannot afford to be fools of any type, for their devalued status denies them the protections that white skin, maleness, and wealth confer. This distinction between knowledge and wisdom, and the use of experience as the cutting edge dividing them, has been key to black women's survival. In the context of race, gender, and class oppression, the distinction is essential since knowledge without wisdom is adequate for the powerful, but wisdom is essential to the survival of the subordinate.

For ordinary African American women, those individuals who have lived through the experiences about which they claim to be experts are more believable and credible than those who have merely read or thought about such experiences. Thus, concrete experience as a criterion for credibility frequently is invoked by black women when making knowledge claims. For instance, Hannah Nelson describes the importance that personal experience has for her: "Our speech is most directly personal, and every black person assumes that every other black person has a right to a personal opinion. In speaking of grave matters, your personal experience is considered very good evidence. With us, distant statistics are certainly not as important as the actual experience of a sober person."[52] Similarly, Ruth Shays uses her concrete experiences to challenge the idea that formal education is the only route to knowledge: "I am the kind of person who doesn't have a lot of education, but both my mother and my father had good common sense. Now, I think that's all you need. I might not know how to use thirty-four words where three would do, but that does not mean that I don't know what I'm talking about ... I know what I'm talking about because I'm talking about myself. I'm talking about what I have lived."[53] Implicit in Shays's self-assessment is a critique of the type of knowledge that obscures the truth, the "thirty-four words" that cover up a truth that can be expressed in three.

Even after substantial mastery of white masculinist epistemologies, many black women scholars invoke their own concrete experiences and those of other black women in selecting topics for investigation and methodologies used. For example, Elsa Barkley Brown subtitles her essay on black women's history, "how my mother taught me to be a historian in spite of my academic training."[54] Similarly, Joyce Ladner maintains that growing up as a black woman in the South gave her special insights in conducting her study of black adolescent women.[55]

Henry Mitchell and Nicholas Lewter claim that experience as a criterion of meaning with practical images as its symbolic vehicles is a fundamental epistemological tenet in African American thought-systems.[56] Stories, narratives, and Bible principles are selected for their applicability to the lived experiences of African Americans and become symbolic representations of a whole wealth of experience. For example, Bible tales are told for their value to common life, so their interpretation involves no need for scientific historical verification. The narrative method requires that the story be "told, not torn apart in analysis, and trusted as core belief, not admired as science."[57] Any biblical story contains more than characters and a plot—it presents key ethical issues salient in African American life.

June Jordan's essay about her mother's suicide exemplifies the multiple levels of meaning that can occur when concrete experiences are used as a criterion of meaning. Jordan describes her mother, a woman who literally died trying to stand up, and the effect that her mother's death had on her own work:

> I think all of this is really about women and work. Certainly this is all about me as a woman and my life work. I mean I am not sure my mother's suicide was something extraordinary. Perhaps most women must deal with a similar inheritance, the legacy of a woman whose death you cannot possibly pinpoint because she died so many, many times and because, even before she became your mother, the life of that woman was taken.... I came too late to help my mother to her feet. By way of everlasting thanks to all of the women who have helped me to stay alive, I am working never to be late again.[58]

While Jordan has knowledge about the concrete act of her mother's death, she also strives for wisdom concerning the meaning of that death.

Some feminist scholars offer a similar claim that women, as a group, are more likely than men to use concrete knowledge in assessing knowledge claims. For example, a substantial number of the 135 women in a study of women's cognitive development were "connected knowers" and were drawn to the sort of knowledge that emerges from firsthand observation. Such women felt that since knowledge comes from experience, the best way of understanding another person's ideas was to try to share the experiences that led the person to form those ideas. At the heart of the procedures used by connected knowers is the capacity for empathy.[59]

In valuing the concrete, African American women may be invoking not only an Afrocentric tradition, but a women's tradition as well. Some feminist theorists suggest that women are socialized in complex relational nexuses where contextual rules take priority over abstract principles in governing behavior. This socialization process is thought to stimulate characteristic ways of knowing.[60] For example, Canadian sociologist Dorothy Smith maintains that two modes of knowing exist, one located in the body and the space it occupies and the other passing beyond it. She asserts that women, through their child-rearing and nurturing activities, mediate these two modes and use the concrete experiences of their daily lives to assess more abstract knowledge claims.[61]

Amanda King, a young black mother, describes how she used the concrete to assess the abstract and points out how difficult mediating these two modes of knowing can be:

> The leaders of the ROC [a labor union] lost their jobs too, but it just seemed like they were used to losing their jobs.... This was like a lifelong thing for them, to get out there and protest. They were like, what do you call them—intellectuals.... You got the ones that go to the university that are supposed to make all the speeches, they're the ones that are supposed to lead, you know, put this little revolution together, and then you got the little ones ... that go to the factory everyday, they be the ones that have to fight. I had a child, and I thought I don't have the time to be running around with these people ... I mean I understand some of that stuff they were talking about, like the bourgeoisie, the rich and the poor and all that, but I had surviving on my mind for me and my kid.[62]

For King, abstract ideals of class solidarity were mediated by the concrete experience of motherhood and the connectedness it involved.

In traditional African American communities, black women find considerable institutional support for valuing concrete experience. Black extended families and black churches are two key institutions where black women experts with concrete knowledge of what it takes to be self-defined black women share their knowledge with their younger, less experienced sisters. This relationship of sisterhood among black women can be seen as a model for a whole series of relationships that African American women have with each other, whether it is networks among women in extended families, among women in the black church, or among women in the African American community at large.[63]

Since the black church and the black family are both woman-centered and Afrocentric institutions, African American women traditionally have found considerable institutional support for this dimension of an Afrocentric feminist epistemology in ways that are unique to them. While white women may value the concrete, it is questionable whether white families, particularly middle-class nuclear ones, and white community institutions provide comparable types of support. Similarly, while black men are supported by Afrocentric institutions, they cannot participate in black women's sisterhood. In terms of black women's relationships with one another then, African American women may indeed find it easier than others to recognize connectedness as a primary way of knowing, simply because they are encouraged to do so by black women's tradition of sisterhood.

EPISTEMOLOGY AND BLACK FEMINIST THOUGHT

Living life as an African American woman is a necessary prerequisite for producing black feminist thought because within black women's communities thought is validated and produced with reference to a particular set of historical, material, and epistemological conditions.[64] African American women who adhere to the idea that claims about black women must be substantiated by black women's sense of their own experiences, and who anchor their knowledge claims in an Afrocentric feminist epistemology, have produced a rich tradition of black feminist thought.

Traditionally, such women were blues singers, poets, autobiographers, storytellers, and orators validated by the larger community of black women as experts on a black women's standpoint. Only a few unusual

African American feminist scholars have been able to defy Eurocentric masculinist epistemologies and explicitly embrace an Afrocentric feminist epistemology. Consider Alice Walker's description of Zora Neale Hurston: "In my mind, Zora Neale Hurston, Billie Holiday, and Bessie Smith form a sort of unholy trinity. Zora *belongs* in the tradition of black women singers, rather than 'the literati.'... Like Billie and Bessie she followed her own road, believed in her own gods, pursued her own dreams, and refused to separate herself from 'common' people."[65]

Zora Neale Hurston is an exception for, prior to 1950, few black women earned advanced degrees, and most of those who did complied with Eurocentric masculinist epistemologies. While these women worked on behalf of black women, they did so within the confines of pervasive race and gender oppression. Black women scholars were in a position to see the exclusion of black women from scholarly discourse, and the thematic content of their work often reflected their interest in examining a black women's standpoint. However, their tenuous status in academic institutions led them to adhere to Eurocentric masculinist epistemologies so that their work would be accepted as scholarly. As a result, while they produced black feminist thought, those black women most likely to gain academic credentials were often least likely to produce black feminist thought that used an Afrocentric feminist epistemology.

As more black women earn advanced degrees, the range of black feminist scholarship is expanding. Increasing numbers of African American women scholars are explicitly choosing to ground their work in black women's experiences, and, by doing so, many implicitly adhere to an Afrocentric feminist epistemology. Rather than being restrained by their "both/ and" status of marginality, these women make creative use of their outsider-within status and produce innovative black feminist thought. The difficulties these women face lie less in demonstrating the technical components of white male epistemologies than in resisting the hegemonic nature of these patterns of thought in order to

see, value, and use existing alternative Afrocentric feminist ways of knowing.

In establishing the legitimacy of their knowledge claims, black women scholars who want to develop black feminist thought may encounter the often conflicting standards of three key groups. First, black feminist thought must be validated by ordinary African American women who grow to womanhood "in a world where the saner you are, the madder you are made to appear."[66] To be credible in the eyes of this group, scholars must be personal advocates for their material, be accountable for the consequences of their work, have lived or experienced their material in some fashion, and be willing to engage in dialogues about their findings with ordinary, everyday people. Second, if it is to establish its legitimacy, black feminist thought also must be accepted by the community of black women scholars. These scholars place varying amounts of importance on rearticulating a black women's standpoint using an Afrocentric feminist epistemology. Third, black feminist thought within academia must be prepared to confront Eurocentric masculinist political and epistemological requirements.

The dilemma facing black women scholars engaged in creating black feminist thought is that a knowledge claim that meets the criteria of adequacy for one group and thus is judged to be an acceptable knowledge claim may not be translatable into the terms of a different group. Using the example of Black English, June Jordan illustrates the difficulty of moving among epistemologies: "You cannot 'translate' instances of Standard English preoccupied with abstraction or with nothing/nobody evidently alive into Black English. That would warp the language into uses antithetical to the guiding perspective of its community of users. Rather you must first change those Standard English sentences themselves into ideas consistent with the person-centered assumptions of Black English."[67] While the worldviews share a common vocabulary, the ideas themselves defy direct translation.

Once black feminist scholars face the notion that, on certain dimensions of a black women's standpoint, it may be fruitless to try to translate ideas from an Afrocentric feminist epistemology into a Eurocentric masculinist epistemology, then the choices become clearer. Rather than trying to uncover universal knowledge claims that can withstand the translation from one epistemology to another, time might be better spent rearticulating a black women's standpoint in order to give African American women the tools to resist their own subordination. The goal here is not one of integrating black female "folk culture" into the substantiated body of academic knowledge, for that substantiated knowledge is, in many ways, antithetical to the best interests of black women. Rather, the process is one of rearticulating a preexisting black women's standpoint and recentering the language of existing academic discourse to accommodate these knowledge claims. For those black women scholars engaged in this rearticulation process, the social construction of black feminist thought requires the skill and sophistication to decide which knowledge claims can be validated using the epistemological assumptions of one but not both frameworks, which claims can be generated in one framework and only partially accommodated by the other, and which claims can be made in both frameworks without violating the basic political and epistemological assumptions of either.

Black feminist scholars offering knowledge claims that cannot be accommodated by both frameworks face the choice between accepting the taken-for-granted assumptions that permeate white-male-controlled academic institutions or leaving academia. Those black women who choose to remain in academia must accept the possibility that their knowledge claims will be limited to their claims about black women that are consistent with a white male worldview. And yet those African American women who leave academia may find their work is inaccessible to scholarly communities.

Black feminist scholars offering knowledge claims that can be partially accommodated by both epistemologies can create a body of thought that stands outside of either.

Rather than trying to synthesize competing worldviews that, at this point in time, defy reconciliation, their task is to point out common themes and concerns. By making creative use of their status as mediators, their thought becomes an entity unto itself that is rooted in two distinct political and epistemological contexts.[68]

Those black feminists who develop knowledge claims that both epistemologies can accommodate may have found a route to the elusive goal of generating so-called objective generalizations that can stand as universal truths. Those ideas that are validated as true by African American women, African American men, white men, white women, and other groups with distinctive standpoints, with each group using the epistemological approaches growing from its unique standpoint, thus become the most objective truths.[69]

Alternative knowledge claims, in and of themselves, are rarely threatening to conventional knowledge. Such claims are routinely ignored, discredited, or simply absorbed and marginalized in existing paradigms. Much more threatening is the challenge that alternative epistemologies offer to the basic process used by the powerful to legitimate their knowledge claims. If the epistemology used to validate knowledge comes into question, then all prior knowledge claims validated under the dominant model become suspect. An alternative epistemology challenges all certified knowledge and opens up the question of whether what has been taken to be true can stand the test of alternative ways of validating truth. The existence of an independent black women's standpoint using an Afrocentric feminist epistemology calls into question the content of what currently passes as truth and simultaneously challenges the process of arriving at that truth.

NOTES

1. For analyses of how interlocking systems of oppression affect black women, see Frances Beale, "Double Jeopardy: To Be Black and Female," in *The Black Woman: An Anthology*, ed.

Toni Cade (New York: Signet, 1970); Angela Y. Davis, *Women, Race, and Class* (New York: Random House, 1981); Bonnie Thornton Dill, "Race, Class, and Gender: Prospects for an All-Inclusive Sisterhood," *Feminist Studies* 9, no. 1 (1983), 13–50; bell hooks, *Ain't I a Woman? Black Women and Feminism* (Boston: South End Press, 1981); Diane Lewis, "A Response to Inequality: Black Women, Racism, and Sexism," *Signs: Journal of Women in Culture and Society* 3, no. 2 (Winter 1977), 339–61; Pauli Murray, "The Liberation of Black Women," in *Voices of the New Feminism*, ed. Mary Lou Thompson (Boston: Beacon Press, 1970), 87–102; and the introduction in Filomina Chioma Steady, *The Black Woman Cross-Culturally* (Cambridge, MA: Schenkman, 1981), 7–41.

2. See the introduction in Steady, *The Black Woman*, for an overview of black women's strengths. This strength-resiliency perspective has greatly influenced empirical work on African American women. See e.g. Joyce Ladner's study of low-income black adolescent girls, *Tomorrow's Tomorrow* (New York: Doubleday, 1971); and Lena Wright Myers's work on black women's self-concept, *Black Women: Do They Cope Better?* (Englewood Cliffs, NJ: Prentice-Hall, 1980). For discussions of black women's resistance, see Elizabeth Fox-Genovese, "Strategies and Forms of Resistance: Focus on Slave Women in the United States," in *In Resistance: Studies in African, Caribbean and Afro-American History*, ed. Gary Y. Okihiro (Amherst: University of Massachusetts Press, 1986), 143–65; and Rosalyn Terborg-Penn, "Black Women in Resistance: A Cross-Cultural Perspective," in Okihiro, *In Resistance*, 188–209. For a comprehensive discussion of everyday resistance, see James C. Scott, *Weapons of the Weak: Everyday Forms of Peasant Resistance* (New Haven, CT: Yale University Press, 1985).

3. See Patricia Hill Collins's analysis of the substantive content of black feminist thought in "Learning from the Outsider Within: The Sociological Significance of Black Feminist Thought," *Social Problems* 33, no. 6 (1986), 14–32.

4. Scott describes consciousness as the meaning that people give to their acts through the symbols, norms, and ideological forms they create.

5. This thesis is found in scholarship of varying theoretical perspectives. For example, Marxist analyses of working-class consciousness claim that "false consciousness" makes the working class unable to penetrate the hegemony of ruling-class ideologies. See Scott's critique of this literature.

6. For example, in Western societies, African Americans have been judged as being less capable of intellectual excellence, more suited to manual labor, and therefore less human than whites. Similarly, white women have been assigned roles as emotional, irrational creatures ruled by passions and biological urges. They too have been stigmatized as being less than fully human, as being objects. For a discussion of the importance that objectification and dehumanization play in maintaining systems of domination, see Arthur Brittan and Mary Maynard, *Sexism, Racism and Oppression* (New York: Basil Blackwell, 1984).

7. The tendency for Western scholarship to assess black culture as pathological and deviant illustrates this process. See Rhett S. Jones, "Proving Blacks Inferior: The Sociology of Knowledge," in *The Death of White Sociology*, ed. Joyce Ladner (New York: Vintage, 1973), 114–35.

8. The presence of an independent standpoint does not mean that it is uniformly shared by all black women or even that black women fully recognize its contours. By using the concept of standpoint, I do not mean to minimize the rich diversity existing among African American women. I use the phrase "black women's standpoint" to emphasize the plurality of experiences within the overarching term "standpoint." For discussions of the concept of standpoint, see Nancy M. Hartsock, "The Feminist Standpoint: Developing the Ground for a Specifically Feminist Historical Materialism," in *Discovering Reality*, ed. Sandra Harding and Merrill Hintikka (Boston: D. Reidel, 1983), 283–310, and *Money, Sex, and Power* (Boston: Northeastern University Press, 1983); and Alison M. Jaggar, *Feminist Politics and Human Nature* (Totowa, NJ: Rowman & Allanheld, 1983), 377–89. My use of the standpoint epistemologies as an organizing concept in this essay does not mean that the concept is problem-free. For a helpful critique of standpoint epistemologies, see Sandra Harding, *The Science Question in Feminism* (Ithaca, NY: Cornell University Press, 1986).

9. One contribution of contemporary black women's studies is its documentation of how race, class, and gender have structured these differences. For representative works surveying African American women's experiences, see Paula Giddings, *When and Where I Enter: The Im-*

pact of Black Women on Race and Sex in America (New York: William Morrow, 1984); and Jacqueline Jones, *Labor of Love, Labor of Sorrow: Black Women, Work, and the Family from Slavery to the Present* (New York: Basic Books, 1985).

10. For example, Judith Rollins, *Between Women: Domestics and their Employers* (Philadelphia: Temple University Press, 1985); and Bonnie Thornton Dill, " 'The Means to Put My Children Through': Child-Rearing Goals and Strategies among Black Female Domestic Servants," in *The Black Woman*, ed. LaFrances Rodgers-Rose (Beverly Hills, CA: Sage Publications, 1980), 107 23, report that black domestic workers do not see themselves as being the devalued workers that their employers perceive and construct their own interpretations of the meaning of their work. For additional discussions of how black women's consciousness is shaped by the material conditions they encounter, see Ladner, *Tomorrow's Tomorrow;* Myers, *Black Women;* and Cheryl Townsend Gilkes, " 'Together and in Harness': Women's Traditions in the Sanctified Church," *Signs*, no. 4 (Summer 1985), 678–99. See also Marcia Westkott's discussion of consciousness as a sphere of freedom for "Feminist Criticism of the Social Sciences," *Harvard Educational Review* 49, no. 4 (1979), 422–30.

11. John Langston Gwaltney, *Drylongso: A Self-Portrait of Black America* (New York: Vintage, 1980), 4–12.

12. Ibid., 33.

13. Ibid., 88.

14. Ibid., 7.

15. Victoria Byerly, *Hard Times Cotton Mill Girls: Personal Histories of Womanhood and Poverty in the South* (New York: ILR Press, 1986), 134.

16. See Peter L. Berger and Thomas Luckmann, *The Social Construction of Reality* (New York: Doubleday, 1966), for a discussion of everyday thought and the role of experts in articulating specialized thought.

17. See Michael Omi and Howard Winant, *Racial Formation in the United States* (New York: Routledge & Kegan Paul, 1986), especially 93.

18. In discussing standpoint epistemologics, Hartsock, in *Money, Sex, and Power*, notes that a standpoint is "achieved rather than obvious, a mediated rather than immediate understanding" (132).

19. See Scott, *Weapons of the Weak;* and Hartsock, *Money, Sex, and Power.*

20. Some readers may question how one determines whether the ideas of any given African American woman are "feminist" and "Afrocen-

tric." I offer the following working definitions. I agree with the general definition of feminist consciousness provided by black feminist sociologist Deborah K. King: "Any purposes, goals, and activities that seek to enhance the potential of women, to ensure their liberty, afford them equal opportunity, and to permit and encourage their self-determination represent a feminist consciousness, even if they occur within a racial community" (in "Race, Class and Gender Salience in Black Women's Womanist Consciousness," typescript, Dartmouth College, Department of Sociology, Hanover, NH, 1987, 22). To be black or Afrocentric, such thought must not only reflect a similar concern for the self-determination of African American people, but must in some way draw upon key elements of an Afrocentric tradition as well.

21. The Eurocentric masculinist process is defined here as the institutions, paradigms, and any elements of the knowledge-validation procedure controlled by white males and whose purpose is to represent a white male standpoint. While this process represents the interests of powerful white males, various dimensions of the process are not necessarily managed by white males themselves.

22. Karl Mannheim, *Ideology and Utopia: An Introduction to the Sociology of Knowledge* (1936; reprint, New York: Harcourt, Brace & Co., 1954), 276.

23. The knowledge-validation model used in this essay is taken from Michael Mulkay, *Science and the Sociology of Knowledge* (Boston: Allen & Unwin, 1979). For a general discussion of the structure of knowledge, see Thomas Kuhn, *The Structure of Scientific Revolutions* (Chicago: University of Chicago Press, 1962).

24. For analyses of the content and functions of images of black female inferiority, see Mae King, "The Politics of Sexual Stereotypes," *Black Scholar* 4, nos. 6–7 (1973), 12–23; Cheryl Townsend Gilkes, "From Slavery to Social Welfare: Racism and the Control of Black Women," in *Class, Race, and Sex: The Dynamics of Control*, eds. Amy Smerdlow and Helen Lessinger (Boston: G. K. Hall, 1981), 288–300; and Elizabeth Higginbotham, "Two Representative Issues in Contemporary Sociological Work on Black Women," in *All the Women Are White, All the Blacks Are Men, But Some of Us Are Brave*, eds. Gloria T. Hull, Patricia Bell Scott, and Barbara Smith (Old Westbury, NY: Feminist Press, 1982).

25. Kuhn, *The Structure.*

26. Evelyn Fox Keller, *Reflections on Gender and Science* (New Haven, CT: Yale University Press, 1985), 167.

27. Maxine Baca Zinn, Lynn Weber Cannon, Elizabeth Higginbotham, and Bonnie Thornton Dill, "The Cost of Exclusionary Practices in Women's Studies," *Signs* 1, no. 2 (Winter 1986), 290–303.

28. Berger and Luckmann (in *The Social Construction of Reality*) note that if an outsider group, in this case African American women, recognizes that the insider group, namely, white men, requires special privileges from the larger society, a special problem arises of keeping the outsiders out and at the same time having them acknowledge the legitimacy of this procedure. Accepting a few "safe" outsiders is one way of addressing this legitimation problem. Collins's discussion (in "Learning from the Outsider Within") of black women as "outsiders within" addresses this issue. Other relevant works include Frantz Fanon's analysis of the role of the national middle class in maintaining colonial systems, in *The Wretched of the Earth* (New York: Grove, 1963); and William Tabb's discussion of the use of "bright natives" in controlling African American communities, *The Political Economy of the Black Ghetto* (New York: W. W. Norton, 1970).

29. While I have been describing Eurocentric masculinist approaches as a single process, there are many schools of thought or paradigms subsumed under this one process. Positivism represents one such paradigm. See Harding, *The Science Question*, for an overview and critique of this literature. The following discussion depends heavily on Jaggar, *Feminist Politics*, 355–8.

30. Jaggar, *Feminist Politics*, 356.

31. See Keller, *Reflections on Gender*, 67–126, especially her analysis of static autonomy and its relation to objectivity.

32. Ironically, researchers must "objectify" themselves to achieve this lack of bias. See Arlie Russell Hochschild, "The Sociology of Feeling and Emotion: Selected Possibilities," in *Another Voice: Feminist Perspectives on Social Life and Social Science*, eds. Marcia Millman and Rosabeth Kanter (Garden City, NY: Anchor, 1975), 280–307. Also, see Jaggar, *Feminist Politics*.

33. See *Social Science as Moral Inquiry*, eds. Norma Haan, Robert Bellah, Paul Rabinow, and William Sullivan (New York: Columbia University Press, 1983), especially Michelle Z. Rosaldo's "Moral/Analytic Dilemmas Posed by the Intersection of Feminism and Social Science," 76–96; and Robert Bellah's "The Ethical Aims of Social Inquiry," 360–81.

34. Janice Moulton, "A Paradigm of Philosophy: The Adversary Method," in Harding and Hintikka, *Discovering Reality*, 149–64.

35. For detailed discussions of the Afrocentric worldview, see John S. Mbiti, *African Religions and Philosophy* (London: Heinemann, 1969); Dominique Zahan, *The Religion, Spirituality, and Thought of Traditional Africa* (Chicago: University of Chicago Press, 1979); and Mechal Sobel, *Travelin' On': The Slave Journey to an Afro-Baptist Faith* (Westport, CT: Greenwood Press, 1979), 1–76.

36. For representative works applying these concepts to African American culture, see Niara Sudarkasa, "Interpreting the African Heritage in Afro-American Family Organization," in *Black Families*, ed. Harriette Pipes McAdoo (Beverly Hills, CA: Sage Publications, 1981); Henry H. Mitchell and Nicholas Cooper Lewter, *Soul Theology: The Heart of American Black Culture* (San Francisco: Harper & Row, 1986); Robert Farris Thompson, *Flash of the Spirit: African and Afro-American Art and Philosophy* (New York: Vintage, 1983); and Ortiz M. Walton, "Comparative Analysis of the African and the Western Aesthetics," in *The Black Aesthetic*, ed. Addison Gayle (Garden City, NY: Doubleday, 1971), 154–64.

37. One of the best discussions of an Afrocentric epistemology is offered by James E. Turner, "Foreword: Africana Studies and Epistemology; a Discourse in the Sociology of Knowledge," in *The Next Decade: Theoretical and Research Issues in Africana Studies*, ed. James E. Turner (Ithaca, NY: Cornell University Africana Studies and Research Center, 1984), v-xxv. See also Vernon Dixon, "World Views and Research Methodology," summarized in Harding, *The Science Question*, 170.

38. See Hester Eisenstein, *Contemporary Feminist Thought* (Boston: G. K. Hall, 1983). Nancy Hartsock's *Money, Sex, and Power*, 145–209, offers a particularly insightful analysis of women's oppression.

39. For discussions of feminist consciousness, see Dorothy Smith, "A Sociology for Women," in *The Prism of Sex: Essays in the Sociology of Knowledge*, eds. Julia A. Sherman and Evelyn T. Beck (Madison: University of Wisconsin Press, 1979); and Michelle Z. Rosaldo, "Women, Culture, and Society: A Theoretical Overview," in *Woman, Culture, and Society*, eds. Michelle Z. Rosaldo and

Louise Lamphere (Stanford, CA: Stanford University Press, 1974), 17–42. Feminist epistemologies are surveyed by Jaggar, *Feminist Politics.*

40. One significant difference between Afrocentric and feminist standpoints is that much of what is termed women's culture is, unlike African American culture, treated in the context of and produced by oppression. Those who argue for a women's culture are electing to value, rather than denigrate, those traits associated with females in white patriarchal societies. While this choice is important, it is not the same as identifying an independent, historical culture associated with a society. I am indebted to Deborah K. King for this point.

41. Critiques of the Eurocentric masculinist knowledge-validation process by both Africanist and feminist scholars illustrate this point. What one group labels "white" and "Eurocentric," the other describes as "male-dominated" and "masculinist." Although he does not emphasize its patriarchal and racist features, Morris Berman's *The Reenchantment of the World* (New York: Bantam Books, 1981) provides a historical discussion of Western thought. Afrocentric analyses of this same process can be found in Molefi Kete Asante, "International/Intercultural Relations," in *Contemporary Black Thought*, eds. Molefi Kete Asante and Abdulai S. Vandi (Beverly Hills, CA: Sage Publications, 1980), 43–58; and Dona Richards, "European Mythology: The Ideology of 'Progress,'" in Asante and Vandi, *Contemporary Black Thought*, 59–79. For feminist analyses, see Hartsock, *Money, Sex, and Power*. Harding also discusses this similarity (see ch. 7, "Other 'Others' and Fractured Identities: Issues for Epistemologists," 63–96).

42. Harding, *The Science Question*, 166.

43. King, "Race, Class and Gender Salience."

44. Bonnie Thornton Dill, "The Dialectics of Black Womanhood," *Signs* 4, no. 3 (Spring 1979), 543–55.

45. One implication of standpoint approaches is that the more subordinate the group, the purer the vision of the oppressed group. This is an outcome of the origins of standpoint approaches in Marxist social theory, itself a dualistic analysis of social structure. Because such approaches rely on quantifying and ranking human oppressions—familiar tenets of positivist approaches—they are rejected by blacks and feminists alike. See Harding, *The Science Question*, for a discussion of this point. See also Elizabeth V. Spelman's discussion of the falla-

cy of additive oppression in "Theories of Race and Gender: The Erasure of Black Women," *Quest* 5, no. 4 (1982), 36–62.

46. Class differences among black women may be marked. For example, see Paula Giddings's analysis (in *When and Where I Enter*) of the role of social class in shaping black women's political activism; or Elizabeth Higginbotham's study of the effects of social class in black women's college attendance in "Race and Class Barriers to Black Women's College Attendance," *Journal of Ethnic Studies* 13, no. 1 (1985), 89–107. Those African American women who have experienced the greatest degree of convergence of race, class, and gender oppression may be in a better position to recognize and use an alternative epistemology.

47. Gwaltney, *Drylongso*, 83.

48. William L. Andrews, *Sisters of the Spirit: Three Black Women's Autobiographies of the Nineteenth Century* (Bloomington: Indiana University Press, 1986), 85.

49. Gwaltney, *Drylongso*, 147.

50. Geneva Smitherman, *Talkin and Testifyin: The Language of Black America* (Detroit: Wayne State University Press, 1986), 76.

51. Gwaltney, *Drylongso*, 68.

52. Ibid., 7.

53. Ibid., 27, 33.

54. Elsa Barkley Brown, "Hearing Our Mothers' Lives" (paper presented at the Fifteenth Anniversary Faculty Lecture Series, African American and African Studies, Emory University, Atlanta, 1986).

55. Ladner, *Tomorrow's Tomorrow*.

56. Mitchell and Lewter, *Soul Theology*. The use of the narrative approach in African American theology exemplifies an inductive system of logic alternately called "folk wisdom" or a survival-based, need-oriented method of assessing knowledge claims.

57. Ibid., 8.

58. June Jordan, *On Call: Political Essays* (Boston: South End Press, 1985), 26.

59. Mary Belenky, Blythe Clinchy, Nancy Goldberger, and Jill Tarule, *Women's Ways of Knowing* (New York: Basic Books, 1986), 113.

60. Hartsock, *Money, Sex, and Power*, 237; and Nancy Chodorow, *The Reproduction of Mothering* (Berkeley and Los Angeles: University of California Press, 1978).

61. Dorothy Smith, *The Everyday World as Problematic* (Boston: Northeastern University Press, 1987).

62. Byerly, *Hard Times Cotton Mill Girls*, 198.

63. For black women's centrality in the family, see Steady, *The Black Woman*; Ladner, *Tomorrow's Tomorrow*; Brown, "Hearing Our Mothers' Lives"; and McAdoo, *Black Families*. See Gilkes, "'Together and in Harness,'" for black women in the church; and chapter 4 of Deborah Gray White, *Arn't I a Woman? Female Slaves in the Plantation South* (New York: W. W. Norton, 1985). See also Gloria Joseph, "Black Mothers and Daughters: Their Roles and Functions in American Society," in *Common Differences: Conflicts in Black and White Feminist Perspectives*, eds. Gloria Joseph and Jill Lewis (Garden City, NY: Anchor, 1981), 75–126. Even though black women play essential roles in black families

and black churches, these institutions are not free from sexism.

64. Black men, white women, and members of other race, class, and gender groups should be encouraged to interpret, teach, and critique the black feminist thought produced by African American women.

65. Alice Walker, *In Search of Our Mothers' Gardens* (New York: Harcourt Brace Jovanovich, 1974), 91.

66. Gwaltney, *Drylongso.*

67. Jordan, *On Call*, 130.

68. Collins, "Learning from the Outsider Within."

69. This point addresses the question of relativity in the sociology of knowledge and offers a way of regulating competing knowledge claims.

Black Women

Shaping Feminist Theory

bell hooks

Feminism in the United States has never emerged from the women who are most victimized by sexist oppression; women who are daily beaten down, mentally, physically, and spiritually—women who are powerless to change their condition in life. They are a silent majority. A mark of their victimization is that they accept their lot in life without visible question, without organized protest, without collective anger or rage. Betty Friedan's *The Feminine Mystique* is still heralded as having paved the way for contemporary feminist movement—it was written as if these women did not exist. Friedan's famous phrase, "the problem that has no name," often quoted to

describe the condition of women in this society, actually referred to the plight of a select group of college-educated, middle and upper class, married white women—housewives bored with leisure, with the home, with children, with buying products, who wanted more out of life. Friedan concludes her first chapter by stating: "We can no longer ignore that voice within women that says: 'I want something more than my husband and my children and my house.'" That "more" she defined as careers. She did not discuss who would be called in to take care of the children and maintain the home if more women like herself were freed from their house labor and given equal access with white men to the professions. She did not speak of the needs of women without men, without children, without homes. She ignored the existence of all non-white women and poor white women.

Source: bell hooks, "Black Women Shaping Feminist Theory" in bell hooks, *Feminist Theory: From Margin to Center* (Boston: South End Press), 1–15. Footnotes omitted.

She did not tell readers whether it was more fulfilling to be a maid, a babysitter, a factory worker, a clerk, or a prostitute, than to be a leisure class housewife.

She made her plight and the plight of white women like herself synonymous with a condition affecting all American women. In so doing, she deflected attention away from her classism, her racism, her sexist attitudes towards the masses of American women. In the context of her book, Friedan makes clear that the women she saw as victimized by sexism were college-educated, white women who were compelled by sexist conditioning to remain in the home. She contends:

> It is urgent to understand how the very condition of being a housewife can create a sense of emptiness, non-existence, nothingness in women. There are aspects of the housewife role that make it almost impossible for a woman of adult intelligence to retain a sense of human identity, the firm core of self or "I" without which a human being, man or woman, is not truly alive. For women of ability, in America today, I am convinced that there is something about the housewife state itself that is dangerous.

Specific problems and dilemmas of leisure class white housewives were real concerns that merited consideration and change but they were not the pressing political concerns of masses of women. Masses of women were concerned about economic survival, ethnic and racial discrimination, etc. When Friedan wrote *The Feminine Mystique,* more than one third of all women were in the work force. Although many women longed to be housewives, only women with leisure time and money could actually shape their identities on the model of the feminine mystique. They were women who, in Friedan's words, were "told by the most advanced thinkers of our time to go back and live their lives as if they were Noras, restricted to the doll's house by Victorian prejudices."

From her early writing, it appears that Friedan never wondered whether or not the plight of college-educated, white housewives was an adequate reference point by which to gauge the impact of sexism or sexist oppression on the lives of women in American society. Nor did she move beyond her own life experience to acquire an expanded perspective on the lives of women in the United States. I say this not to discredit her work. It remains a useful discussion of the impact of sexist discrimination on a select group of women. Examined from a different perspective, it can also be seen as a case study of narcissism, insensitivity, sentimentality, and self-indulgence which reaches its peak when Friedan, in a chapter titled "Progressive Dehumanization," makes a comparison between the psychological effects of isolation on white housewives and the impact of confinement on the self-concept of prisoners in Nazi concentration camps.

Friedan was a principal shaper of contemporary feminist thought. Significantly, the one-dimensional perspective on women's reality presented in her book became a marked feature of the contemporary feminist movement. Like Friedan before them, white women who dominate feminist discourse today rarely question whether or not their perspective on women's reality is true to the lived experiences of women as a collective group. Nor are they aware of the extent to which their perspectives reflect race and class biases, although there has been a greater awareness of biases in recent years. Racism abounds in the writings of white feminists, reinforcing white supremacy and negating the possibility that women will bond politically across ethnic and racial boundaries. Past feminist refusal to draw attention to and attack racial hierarchies suppressed the link between race and class. Yet class structure in American society has been shaped by the racial politic of white supremacy; it is only by analyzing racism and its function in capitalist society that a thorough understanding of class relationships can emerge. Class struggle is inextricably bound to the struggle to end racism. Urging women to explore the full implication of class in an early essay, "The Last Straw," Rita Mae Brown explained:

> Class is much more than Marx's definition of relationship to the means of production. Class

involves your behavior, your basic assumptions about life. Your experience (determined by your class) validates those assumptions, how you are taught to behave, what you expect from yourself and from others, your concept of a future, how you understand problems and solve them, how you think, feel, act. It is these behavioral patterns that middle class women resist recognizing although they may be perfectly willing to accept class in Marxist terms, a neat trick that helps them avoid really dealing with class behavior and changing that behavior in themselves. It is these behavioral patterns which must be recognized, understood, and changed.

White women who dominate feminist discourse, who for the most part make and articulate feminist theory, have little or no understanding of white supremacy as a racial politic, of the psychological impact of class, of their political status within a racist, sexist, capitalist state.

It is this lack of awareness that, for example, leads Leah Fritz to write in *Dreamers and Dealers*, a discussion of the current women's movement published in 1979:

> Women's suffering under sexist tyranny is a common bond among all women, transcending the particulars of the different forms that tyranny takes. *Suffering cannot be measured and compared quantitatively.* Is the enforced idleness and vacuity of a "rich" woman, which leads her to madness and/or suicide, greater or less than the suffering of a poor woman who barely survives on welfare but retains somehow her spirit? There is no way to measure such difference, but should these two women survey each other without the screen of patriarchal class, they may find a commonality in the fact that they are both oppressed, both miserable.

Fritz's statement is another example of wishful thinking, as well as the conscious mystification of social divisions between women, that has characterized much feminist expression. While it is evident that many women suffer from sexist tyranny, there is little indication that this forges "a common bond among all women." There is much evidence substantiat-

ing the reality that race and class identity creates differences in quality of life, social status, and lifestyle that take precedence over the common experience women share—differences which are rarely transcended. The motives of materially privileged, educated, white women with a variety of career and lifestyle options available to them must be questioned when they insist that "suffering cannot be measured." Fritz is by no means the first white feminist to make this statement. It is a statement that I have never heard a poor woman of any race make. Although there is much I would take issue with in Benjamin Barber's critique of the women's movement, *Liberating Feminism*, I agree with his assertion:

> Suffering is not necessarily a fixed and universal experience that can be measured by a single rod: it is related to situations, needs, and aspirations. But there must be some historical and political parameters for the use of the term so that political priorities can be established and different forms and degrees of suffering can be given the most attention.

A central tenet of modern feminist thought has been the assertion that "all women are oppressed." This assertion implies that women share a common lot, that factors like class, race, religion, sexual preference, etc. do not create a diversity of experience that determines the extent to which sexism will be an oppressive force in the lives of individual women. Sexism as a system of domination is institutionalized but it has never determined in an absolute way the fate of all women in this society. Being oppressed means the *absence of choices*. It is the primary point of contact between the oppressed and the oppressor. Many women in this society do have choices, (as inadequate as they are) therefore exploitation and discrimination are words that more accurately describe the lot of women collectively in the United States. Many women do not join organized resistance against sexism precisely because sexism has not meant an absolute lack of choices. They may know they are discriminated against on the basis of sex, but they do not equate this with oppression. Under capitalism, patriarchy is structured so that sexism restricts women's behavior in some realms even as freedom from limitations is allowed in other spheres. The absence of extreme restrictions leads many women to ignore the areas in which they are exploited or discriminated against; it may even lead them to imagine that no women are oppressed.

There are oppressed women in the United States, and it is both appropriate and necessary that we speak against such oppression. French feminist Christine Delphy makes the point in her essay, "For a Materialist Feminism," that the use of the term oppression is important because it places feminist struggle in a radical political framework:

> The rebirth of feminism coincided with the use of the term "oppression." The ruling ideology, i.e. common sense, daily speech, does not speak about oppression but about a "feminine condition." It refers back to a naturalist explanation: to a constraint of nature, exterior reality out of reach and not modifiable by human action. The term "oppression," on the contrary, refers back to a choice, an explanation, a situation that is political. "Oppression" and "social oppression" are therefore synonyms or rather social oppression is a redundance: the notion of a political origin, i.e. social, is an integral part of the concept of oppression.

However, feminist emphasis on "common oppression" in the United States was less a strategy for politicization than an appropriation by conservative and liberal women of a radical political vocabulary that masked the extent to which they shaped the movement so that is addressed and promoted their class interests.

Although the impulse towards unity and empathy that informed the notion of common oppression was directed at building solidarity, slogans like "organize around your own oppression" provided the excuse many privileged women needed to ignore the differences between their social status and the status of masses of women. It was a mark of race and class privilege, as well as the expression of freedom from the many constraints sexism places on working class women, that

middle class white women were able to make their interests the primary focus of feminist movement and employ a rhetoric of commonality that made their condition synonymous with "oppression." Who was there to demand a change in vocabulary? What other group of women in the United States had the same access to universities, publishing houses, mass media, money? Had middle class black women begun a movement in which they had labeled themselves "oppressed," no one would have taken them seriously. Had they established public forums and given speeches about their "oppression," they would have been criticized and attacked from all sides. This was not the case with white bourgeois feminists for they could appeal to a large audience of women, like themselves, who were eager to change their lot in life. Their isolation from women of other class and race groups provided no immediate comparative base by which to test their assumptions of common oppression.

Initially, radical participants in women's movement demanded that women penetrate that isolation and create a space for contact. Anthologies like *Liberation Now, Women's Liberation: Blueprint for the Future, Class and Feminism, Radical Feminism,* and *Sisterhood Is Powerful,* all published in the early 1970s, contain articles that attempted to address a wide audience of women, an audience that was not exclusively white, middle class, college-educated, and adult (many have articles on teenagers). Sookie Stambler articulated this radical spirit in her introduction to *Women's Liberation: Blueprint for the Future:*

> Movement women have always been turned off by the media's necessity to create celebrities and superstars. This goes against our basic philosophy. We cannot relate to women in our ranks towering over us with prestige and fame. We are not struggling for the benefit of the one woman or for one group of women. We are dealing with issues that concern all women.

These sentiments, shared by many feminists early in the movement, were not sustained. As more and more women acquired prestige, fame, or money from feminist writings or from gains from feminist movement for equality in the work-force, individual opportunism undermined appeals for collective struggle. Women who were not opposed to patriarchy, capitalism, classism, or racism labeled themselves "feminist." Their expectations were varied. Privileged women wanted social equality with men of their class; some women wanted equal pay for equal work; others wanted an alternative lifestyle. Many of these legitimate concerns were easily co-opted by the ruling capitalist patriarchy. French feminist Antoinette Fouque states:

> The actions proposed by the feminist groups are spectacular, provoking. But provocation only brings to light a certain number of social contradictions. It does not reveal radical contradictions within society. The feminists claim that they do not seek equality with men, but their practice proves the contrary to be true. Feminists are a bourgeois avant-garde that maintains, in an inverted form, the dominant values. Inversion does not facilitate the passage to another kind of structure. Reformism suits everyone! Bourgeois order, capitalism, phallocentrism are ready to integrate as many feminists as will be necessary. Since these women are becoming men, in the end it will only mean a few more men. The difference between the sexes is not whether one does or doesn't have a penis, it is whether or not one is an integral part of a phallic masculine economy.

Feminists in the United States are aware of the contradictions. Carol Ehrlich makes the point in her essay, "The Unhappy Marriage of Marxism and Feminism: Can It Be Saved?," that "feminism seems more and more to have taken on a blind, safe, nonrevolutionary outlook" as "feminist radicalism loses ground to bourgeois feminism," stressing that "we cannot let this continue":

> Women need to know (and are increasingly prevented from finding out) that feminism is *not* about dressing for success, or becoming a corporate executive, or gaining elective office; it is *not* being able to share a two career mar-

riage and take skiing vacations and spend huge amounts of time with your husband and two lovely children because you have a domestic worker who makes all this possible for you, but who hasn't the time or money to do it for herself; it is *not* opening a Women's Bank, or spending a weekend in an expensive workshop that guarantees to teach you how to become assertive (but not aggressive); it is most emphatically *not* about becoming a police detective or CIA agent or marine corps general.

But if these distorted images of feminism have more reality than ours do, it is partly our own fault. We have not worked as hard as we should have at providing clear and meaningful alternative analyses which relate to people's lives, and at providing active, accessible groups in which to work.

It is no accident that feminist struggle has been so easily co-opted to serve the interests of conservative and liberal feminists since feminism in the United States has so far been a bourgeois ideology. Zillah Eisenstein discusses the liberal roots of North American feminism in *The Radical Future of Liberal Feminism*, explaining in the introduction:

> One of the major contributions to be found in this study is the role of the ideology of liberal individualism in the construction of feminist theory. Today's feminists either do not discuss a theory of individuality or they unself-consciously adopt the competitive, atomistic ideology of liberal individualism. There is much confusion on this issue in the feminist theory we discuss here. Until a conscious differentiation is made between a theory of individuality that recognizes the importance of the individual within the social collectivity and the ideology of individualism that assumes a competitive view of the individual, there will not be a full accounting of what a feminist theory of liberation must look like our Western society.

The ideology of "competitive, atomistic liberal individualism" has permeated feminist thought to such an extent that it undermines the potential radicalism of feminist struggle. The usurpation of feminism by bourgeois women to support their class interests has been to a very grave extent justified by feminist theory as it has so far been conceived. (For example, the ideology of "common oppression.") Any movement to resist the co-optation of feminist struggle must begin by introducing a different feminist perspective—a new theory—one that is not informed by the ideology of liberal individualism.

The exclusionary practices of women who dominate feminist discourse have made it practically impossible for new and varied theories to emerge. Feminism has its party line and women who feel a need for a different strategy, a different foundation, often find themselves ostracized and silenced. Criticisms of or alternatives to established feminist ideas are not encouraged, e.g. recent controversies about expanding feminist discussions of sexuality. Yet groups of women who feel excluded from feminist discourse and praxis can make a place for themselves only if they first create, via critiques, an awareness of the factors that alienate them. Many individual white women found in the women's movement a liberatory solution to personal dilemmas. Having directly benefited from the movement, they are less inclined to criticize it or to engage in rigorous examination of its structure than those who feel it has not had a revolutionary impact on their lives or the lives of masses of women in our society. Non-white women who feel affirmed within the current structure of feminist movement (even though they may form autonomous groups) seem to also feel that their definitions of the party line, whether on the issue of black feminism or on other issues, is the only legitimate discourse. Rather than encourage a diversity of voices, critical dialogue, and controversy, they, like some white women, seek to stifle dissent. As activists and writers whose work is widely known, they act as if they are best able to judge whether other women's voices should be heard. Susan Griffin warns against this overall tendency towards dogmatism in her essay, "The Way of All Ideology":

> ... when a theory is transformed into an ideology, it begins to destroy the self and self-knowledge. Originally born of feeling, it pretends to float above and around feeling. Above sensation. It organizes experience according to itself, without touching experience. By virtue of being itself, it is supposed to know. To invoke the name of this ideology is to confer truthfulness. No one can tell it anything new. Experience ceases to surprise it, inform it, transform it. It is annoyed by any detail which does not fit into its world view. Begun as a cry against the denial of truth, now it denies any truth which does not fit into its scheme. Begun as a way to restore one's sense of reality, now it attempts to discipline real people, to remake natural beings after its own image. All that it fails to explain it records as its enemy. Begun as a theory of liberation, it is threatened by new theories of liberation; it builds a prison for the mind.

We resist hegemonic dominance of feminist thought by insisting that it is a theory in the making, that we must necessarily criticize, question, re-examine, and explore new possibilities. My persistent critique has been informed by my status as a member of an oppressed group, experience of sexist exploitation and discrimination, and the sense that prevailing feminist analysis has not been the force shaping my feminist consciousness. This is true for many women. There are white women who had never considered resisting male dominance until the feminist movement created an awareness that they could and should. My awareness of feminist struggle was stimulated by social circumstance. Growing up in a Southern, black, father-dominated, working class household, I experienced (as did my mother, my sisters, and my brother) varying degrees of patriarchal tyranny and it made me angry—it made us all angry. Anger led me to question the politics of male dominance and enabled me to resist sexist socialization. Frequently, white feminists act as if black women did not know sexist oppression existed until they voiced feminist sentiment. They believe they are providing black women with "the" analysis and "the" program for liberation. They do not understand, cannot even imagine, that black women, as well as other groups of women who live daily in oppressive situations, often acquire an awareness of patriarchal politics from their lived experience, just as they develop strategies of resistance (even though they may not resist on a sustained or organized basis).

These black women observed white feminist focus on male tyranny and women's oppression as if it were a "new" revelation and felt such a focus had little impact on their lives. To them it was just another indication of the privileged living conditions of middle and upper class white women that they would need a theory to inform them that they were "oppressed." The implication being that people who are truly oppressed know it even though they may not be engaged in organized resistance or are unable to articulate in written form the nature of their oppression. These black women saw nothing liberatory in party line analyses of women's oppression. Neither the fact that black women have not organized collectively in huge numbers around the issues of "feminism" (many of us do not know or use the term) nor the fact that we have not had access to the machinery of power that would allow us to share our analyses or theories about gender with the American public negate its presence in our lives or place us in a position of dependency in relationship to those white and non-white feminists who address a larger audience.

The understanding I had by age thirteen of patriarchal politics created in me expectations of the feminist movement that were quite different from those of young, middle class, white women. When I entered my first women's studies class at Stanford University in the early 1970s, white women were revelling in the joy of being together—to them it was an important, momentous occasion. I had not known a life where women had not been together, where women had not helped, protected, and loved one another deeply. I had not known white women who were ignorant of the impact of race and class on their social status and consciousness (Southern white women often have a more realistic perspective on racism and classism than white women in other areas of the United States.) I did not feel sympathetic to white peers who maintained that I could not expect them to have knowledge of or understand the life experi-

ences of black women. Despite my background (living in racially segregated communities) I knew about the lives of white women, and certainly no white women lived in our neighborhood, attended our schools, or worked in our homes.

When I participated in feminist groups, I found that white women adopted a condescending attitude towards me and other non-white participants. The condescension they directed at black women was one of the means they employed to remind us that the women's movement was "theirs"—that we were able to participate because they allowed it, even encouraged it; after all, we were needed to legitimate the process. They did not see us as equals. They did not treat us as equals. And though they expected us to provide first hand accounts of black experience, they felt it was their role to decide if these experiences were authentic. Frequently, college-educated black women (even those from poor and working class backgrounds) were dismissed as mere imitators. Our presence in movement activities did not count, as white women were convinced that "real" blackness meant speaking the patois of poor black people, being uneducated, streetwise, and a variety of other stereotypes. If we dared to criticize the movement or to assume responsibility for reshaping feminist ideas and introducing new ideas, our voices were tuned out, dismissed, silenced. We could be heard only if our statements echoed the sentiments of the dominant discourse.

Attempts by white feminists to silence black women are rarely written about. All too often they have taken place in conference rooms, classrooms, or the privacy of cozy living room settings, where one lone black woman faces the racist hostility of a group of white women. From the time the women's liberation movement began, individual black women went to groups. Many never returned after a first meeting. Anita Cornwall is correct in "Three for the Price of One: Notes from a Gay Black Feminist," when she states, "... sadly enough, fear of encountering racism seems to be one of the main reasons that so many black women refuse to join the women's movement." Recent focus on the issue of racism has generated discourse but has had little impact on the behavior of white feminists towards black women. Often the white women who are busy publishing papers and books on "unlearning racism" remain patronizing and condescending when they relate to black women. This is not surprising given that frequently their discourse is aimed solely in the direction of a white audience and the focus solely on changing attitudes rather than addressing racism in a historical and political context. They make us the "objects" of their privileged discourse on race. As "objects," we remain unequals, inferiors. Even though they may be sincerely concerned about racism, their methodology suggests they are not yet free of the type of paternalism endemic to white supremacist ideology. Some of these women place themselves in the position of "authorities" who must mediate communication between racist white women (naturally they see themselves as having come to terms with their racism) and angry black women whom they believe are incapable of rational discourse. Of course, the system of racism, classism, and educational elitism remain intact if they are to maintain their authoritative positions.

In 1981, I enrolled in a graduate class on feminist theory where we were given a course reading list that had writings by white women and men, one black man, but no material by or about black, Native American Indian, Hispanic, or Asian women. When I criticized this oversight, white women directed an anger and hostility at me that was so intense I found it difficult to attend the class. When I suggested that the purpose of this collective anger was to create an atmosphere in which it would be psychologically unbearable for me to speak in class discussions or even attend class, I was told that they were not angry. *I* was the one who was angry. Weeks after class ended, I received an open letter from one white female student acknowledging her anger and expressing regret for her attacks. She wrote:

I didn't know you. You were black. In class after a while I noticed myself, that I would always be the one to respond to whatever you said. And usually it was to contradict. Not that

the argument was always about racism by any means. But I think the hidden logic was that if I could prove you wrong about one thing, then you might not be right about anything at all.

And in another paragraph:

I said in class one day that there were some people less entrapped than others by Plato's picture of the world. I said I thought we, after fifteen years of education, courtesy of the ruling class, might be more entrapped than others who had not received a start in life so close to the heart of the monster. My classmate, once a close friend, sister, colleague, has not spoken to me since then. I think the possibility that we were not the best spokespeople for all women made her fear for her self-worth and for her Ph.D.

Often in situations where white feminists aggressively attacked individual black women, they saw themselves as the ones who were under attack, who were the victims. During a heated discussion with another white female student in a racially mixed women's group I had organized, I was told that she had heard how I had "wiped out" people in the feminist theory class, that she was afraid of being "wiped out" too. I reminded her that I was one person speaking to a large group of angry, aggressive people; I was hardly dominating the situation. It was I who left the class in tears, not any of the people I had supposedly "wiped out."

Racist stereotypes of the strong, superhuman black woman are operative myths in the minds of many white women, allowing them to ignore the extent to which black women are likely to be victimized in this society and the role white women may play in the maintenance and perpetuation of that victimization. In Lillian Hellman's autobiographical work *Pentimento*, she writes, "All my life, beginning at birth, I have taken orders from black women, wanting them and resenting them, being superstitious the few times I disobeyed." The black women Hellman describes worked in her household as family servants and their status was never that of an equal. Even as a child, she was always in the dominant position as they questioned, advised, or guided her; they were free to exercise these rights because she or another white authority figure allowed it. Hellman places power in the hands of these black women rather than acknowledge her own power over them; hence she mystifies the true nature of their relationship. By projecting onto black women a mythical power and strength, white women both promote a false image of themselves as powerless, passive victims and deflect attention away from their aggressiveness, their power, (however limited in a white supremacist, male-dominated state) their willingness to dominate and control others. These unacknowledged aspects of the social status of many white women prevent them from transcending racism and limit the scope of their understanding of women's overall social status in the United States.

Privileged feminists have largely been unable to speak to, with, and for diverse groups of women because they either do not understand fully the inter-relatedness of sex, race, and class oppression or refuse to take this inter-relatedness seriously. Feminist analyses of woman's lot tend to focus exclusively on gender and do not provide a solid foundation on which to construct feminist theory. They reflect the dominant tendency in Western patriarchal minds to mystify woman's reality by insisting that gender is the sole determinant of woman's fate. Certainly it has been easier for women who do not experience race or class oppression to focus exclusively on gender. Although socialist feminists focus on class and gender, they tend to dismiss race or they make a point of acknowledging that race is important and then proceed to offer an analysis in which race is not considered.

As a group, black women are in an unusual position in this society, for not only are we collectively at the bottom of the occupational ladder, but our overall social status is lower than that of any other group. Occupying such a position, we bear the brunt of sexist, racist, and classist oppression. At the same time, we are the group that has not been socialized to assume the role of exploiter/oppressor in

that we are allowed no institutionalized "other" that we can exploit or oppress. (Children do not represent an institutionalized other even though they may be oppressed by parents.) White women and black men have it both ways. They can act as oppressor or be oppressed. Black men may be victimized by racism, but sexism allows them to act as exploiters and oppressors of women. White women may be victimized by sexism, but racism enables them to act as exploiters and oppressors of black people. Both groups have led liberation movements that favor their interests and support the continued oppression of other groups. Black male sexism has undermined struggles to eradicate racism just as white female racism undermines feminist struggle. As long as these two groups or any group defines liberation as gaining social equality with ruling class white men, they have a vested interest in the continued exploitation and oppression of others.

Black women with no institutionalized "other" that we may discriminate against, exploit, or oppress often have a lived experience that directly challenges the prevailing classist, sexist, racist social structure and its concomitant ideology. This lived experience may shape our consciousness in such a way that our world view differs from those who have a degree of privilege (however relative within the existing system). It is essential for continued feminist struggle that black women recognize the special vantage point our marginality gives us and make use of this perspective to criticize the dominant racist, classist, sexist hegemony as well as to envision and create a counter-hegemony. I am suggesting that we have a central role to play in the making of feminist theory and a contribution to offer that is unique and valuable. The formation of a liberatory feminist theory and praxis is a collective responsibility, one that must be shared. Though I criticize aspects of feminist movement as we have known it so far, a critique which is sometimes harsh and unrelenting, I do so not in an attempt to diminish feminist struggle but to enrich, to share in the work of making a liberatory ideology and a liberatory movement.

Demarginalizing the Intersection of Race and Sex

A Black Feminist Critique of Antidiscrimination Doctrine, Feminist Theory, and Antiracist Politics

Kimberle Crenshaw

One of the very few Black women's studies books is entitled *All the Women Are White, All the Blacks Are Men, But Some of Us are Brave.*[1] I have chosen this title as a point of departure in my efforts to develop a Black feminist criticism[2] because it sets forth a problematic consequence of the tendency to treat race and gender as mutually exclusive categories of experience and analysis.[3] In this talk, I want to examine how this tendency is perpetuated by a single-axis framework that is dominant in antidiscrimination law and that is also reflected in feminist theory and antiracist politics.

I will center Black women in this analysis in order to contrast the multidimensionality of Black women's experience with the single-axis analysis that distorts these experiences. Not only will this juxtaposition reveal how Black women are theoretically erased, it will also illustrate how this framework imports its own theoretical limitations that undermine efforts to broaden feminist and antiracist analyses. With Black women as the starting point, it becomes more apparent how dominant conceptions of discrimination condition us to think about subordination as disadvantage occurring along a single categorical axis. I want to suggest further that this single-axis framework erases Black women in the conceptualization, identification and remediation of race and sex discrimination by limiting inquiry to the experiences of otherwise-privi-

Source: Kimberle Crenshaw, "Demarginalizing the Intersection of Race and Sex: A Black Feminist Critique of Antidiscrimination Doctrine, Feminist Theory, and Antiracist Politics," *University of Chicago Legal Forum* (1989): 139–167.

leged members of the group. In other words, in race discrimination cases, discrimination tends to be viewed in terms of sex- or class-privileged Blacks; in sex discrimination cases, the focus is on race- and class-privileged women.

This focus on the most privileged group members marginalizes those who are multiply-burdened and obscures claims that cannot be understood as resulting from discrete sources of discrimination. I suggest further that this focus on otherwise-privileged group members creates a distorted analysis of racism and sexism because the operative conceptions of race and sex become grounded in experiences that actually represent only a subset of a much more complex phenomenon.

After examining the doctrinal manifestations of this single-axis framework, I will discuss how it contributes to the marginalization of Black women in feminist theory and in antiracist politics. I argue that Black women are sometimes excluded from feminist theory and antiracist policy discourse because both are predicated on a discrete set of experiences that often does not accurately reflect the interaction of race and gender. These problems of exclusion cannot be solved simply by including Black women within an already established analytical structure. Because the intersectional experience is greater than the sum of racism and sexism, any analysis that does not take intersectionality into account cannot sufficiently address the particular manner in which Black women are subordinated. Thus, for feminist theory and antiracist policy discourse to embrace the experiences and concerns of Black women, the entire framework that has been used as a basis for translating "women's experience" or "the Black experience" into concrete policy demands must be rethought and recast.

As examples of theoretical and political developments that miss the mark with respect to Black women because of their failure to consider intersectionality, I will briefly discuss the feminist critique of rape and separate spheres ideology, and the public policy debates concerning female-headed households within the Black community.

I. THE ANTIDISCRIMINATION FRAMEWORK

A. The Experience of Intersectionality and the Doctrinal Response

One way to approach the problem of intersectionality is to examine how courts frame and interpret the stories of Black women plaintiffs. While I cannot claim to know the circumstances underlying the cases that I will discuss, I nevertheless believe that the way courts interpret claims made by Black women is itself part of Black women's experience and, consequently, a cursory review of cases involving Black female plaintiffs is quite revealing. To illustrate the difficulties inherent in judicial treatment of intersectionality, I will consider three Title VII[4] cases: *DeGraffenreid v General Motors,*[5] *Moore v Hughes Helicopter*[6] and *Payne v Travenol.*[7]

1. DeGraffenreid v General Motors. In *DeGraffenreid,* five Black women brought suit against General Motors, alleging that the employer's seniority system perpetuated the effects of past discrimination against Black women. Evidence adduced at trial revealed that General Motors simply did not hire Black women prior to 1964 and that all of the Black women hired after 1970 lost their jobs in a seniority-based layoff during a subsequent recession. The district court granted summary judgment for the defendant, rejecting the plaintiffs' attempt to bring a suit not on be-

half of Blacks or women, but specifically on behalf of Black women. The court stated:

> [P]laintiffs have failed to cite any decisions which have stated that Black women are a special class to be protected from discrimination. The Court's own research has failed to disclose such a decision. The plaintiffs are clearly entitled to a remedy if they have been discriminated against. However, they should not be allowed to combine statutory remedies to create a new 'super-remedy' which would give them relief beyond what the drafters of the relevant statutes intended. Thus, this lawsuit must be examined to see if it states a cause of action for race discrimination, sex discrimination, or alternatively either, but not a combination of both.[8]

Although General Motors did not hire Black women prior to 1964, the court noted that "General Motors has hired ... female employees for a number of years prior to the enactment of the Civil Rights Act of 1964."[9] Because General Motors did hire women—albeit *white women*—during the period that no Black women were hired, there was, in the court's view, no sex discrimination that the seniority system could conceivably have perpetuated.

After refusing to consider the plaintiff's sex discrimination claim, the court dismissed the race discrimination complaint and recommended its consolidation with another case alleging race discrimination against the same employer.[10] The plaintiffs responded that such consolidation would defeat the purpose of their suit since theirs was not purely a race claim, but an action brought specifically on behalf of Black women alleging race *and* sex discrimination. The court, however, reasoned:

> The legislative history surrounding Title VII does not indicate that the goal of the statute was to create a new classification of 'black women' who would have greater standing than, for example, a black male. The prospect of the creation of new classes of protected minorities, governed only by the mathematical principles of permutation and combination,

clearly raises the prospect of opening the hackneyed Pandora's box.[11]

Thus, the court apparently concluded that Congress either did not contemplate that Black women could be discriminated against as "Black women" or did not intend to protect them when such discrimination occurred.[12] The court's refusal in *DeGraffenreid* to acknowledge that Black women encounter combined race and sex discrimination implies that the boundaries of sex and race discrimination doctrine are defined respectively by white women's and Black men's experiences. Under this view, Black women are protected only to the extent that their experiences coincide with those of either of the two groups.[13] Where their experiences are distinct, Black women can expect little protection as long as approaches, such as that in *DeGraffenreid*, which completely obscure problems of intersectionality prevail.

2. Moore v Hughes Helicopter, Inc.   *Moore v Hughes Helicopter, Inc.*[14] presents a different way in which courts fail to understand or recognize Black women's claims. *Moore* is typical of a number of cases in which courts refused to certify Black females as class representatives in race *and* sex discrimination actions.[15] In *Moore*, the plaintiff alleged that the employer, Hughes Helicopter, practiced race and sex discrimination in promotions to upper-level craft positions and to supervisory jobs. Moore introduced statistical evidence establishing a significant disparity between men and women, and somewhat less of a disparity between Black and white men in supervisory jobs.[16]

Affirming the district court's refusal to certify Moore as the class representative in the sex discrimination complaint on behalf of all women at Hughes, the Ninth Circuit noted approvingly:

> ... Moore had never claimed before the EEOC that she was discriminated against as a female, *but only* as a Black female.... [T]his raised serious doubts as to Moore's ability to adequately represent white female employees.[17]

The curious logic in *Moore* reveals not only the narrow scope of antidiscrimination doctrine and its failure to embrace intersectionality, but also the centrality of white female experiences in the conceptualization of gender discrimination. One inference that could be drawn from the court's statement that Moore's complaint did not entail a claim of discrimination "against females" is that discrimination against Black females is something less than discrimination against females. More than likely, however, the court meant to imply that Moore did not claim that *all* females were discriminated against *but only* Black females. But even thus recast, the court's rationale is problematic for Black women. The court rejected Moore's bid to represent all females apparently because her attempt to specify her race was seen as being at odds with the standard allegation that the employer simply discriminated "against females."

The court failed to see that the absence of a racial referent does not necessarily mean that the claim being made is a more inclusive one. A white woman claiming discrimination against females may be in no better position to represent all women than a Black woman who claims discrimination as a Black female and wants to represent all females. The court's preferred articulation of "against females" is not necessarily more inclusive—it just appears to be so because the racial contours of the claim are not specified.

The court's preference for "against females" rather than "against Black females" reveals the implicit grounding of white female experiences in the doctrinal conceptualization of sex discrimination. For white women, claiming sex discrimination is simply a statement that but for gender, they would not have been disadvantaged. For them there is no need to specify discrimination as *white* females because their race does not contribute to the disadvantage for which they seek redress. The view of discrimination that is derived from this grounding takes race privilege as a given.

Discrimination against a white female is thus the standard sex discrimination claim;

claims that diverge from this standard appear to present some sort of hybrid claim. More significantly, because Black females' claims are seen as hybrid, they sometimes cannot represent those who may have "pure" claims of sex discrimination. The effect of this approach is that even though a challenged policy or practice may clearly discriminate against all females, the fact that it has particularly harsh consequences for Black females places Black female plaintiffs at odds with white females.

Moore illustrates one of the limitations of antidiscrimination law's remedial scope and normative vision. The refusal to allow a multiply-disadvantaged class to represent others who may be singularly-disadvantaged defeats efforts to restructure the distribution of opportunity and limits remedial relief to minor adjustments within an established hierarchy. Consequently, "bottom-up" approaches, those which combine all discriminatees in order to challenge an entire employment system, are foreclosed by the limited view of the wrong and the narrow scope of the available remedy. If such "bottom-up" intersectional representation were routinely permitted, employees might accept the possibility that there is more to gain by collectively challenging the hierarchy rather than by each discriminatee individually seeking to protect her source of privilege within the hierarchy. But as long as antidiscrimination doctrine proceeds from the premise that employment systems need only minor adjustments, opportunities for advancement by disadvantaged employees will be limited. Relatively privileged employees probably are better off guarding their advantage while jockeying against others to gain more. As a result, Black women—the class of employees which, because of its intersectionality, is best able to challenge all forms of discrimination—are essentially isolated and often required to fend for themselves.

In *Moore*, the court's denial of the plaintiffs' bid to represent all Blacks and females left Moore with the task of supporting her race and sex discrimination claims with statistical evidence of discrimination against Black females alone.[18] Because she was unable to represent white women or Black men, she

could not use overall statistics on sex disparity at Hughes, nor could she use statistics on race. Proving her claim using statistics on Black women alone was no small task, due to the fact that she was bringing the suit under a disparate impact theory of discrimination.[19]

The court further limited the relevant statistical pool to include only Black women who it determined were qualified to fill the openings in upper-level labor jobs and in supervisory positions.[20] According to the court, Moore had not demonstrated that there were any qualified Black women within her bargaining unit or the general labor pool for either category of jobs.[21] Finally, the court stated that even if it accepted Moore's contention that the percentage of Black females in supervisory positions should equal the percentage of Black females in the employee pool, it still would not find discriminatory impact.[22] Because the promotion of only two Black women into supervisory positions would have achieved the expected mean distribution of Black women within that job category, the court was "unwilling to agree that a prima facie case of disparate impact ha[d] been proven."[23]

The court's rulings on Moore's sex and race claim left her with such a small statistical sample that even if she had proved that there were qualified Black women, she could not have shown discrimination under a disparate impact theory. *Moore* illustrates yet another way that antidiscrimination doctrine essentially erases Black women's distinct experiences and, as a result, deems their discrimination complaints groundless.

3. Payne v Travenol Black female plaintiffs have also encountered difficulty in their efforts to win certification as class representatives in some race discrimination actions. This problem typically arises in cases where statistics suggest significant disparities between Black and white workers and further disparities between Black men and Black women. Courts in some cases[24] have denied certification based on logic that mirrors the rationale in *Moore*. The sex disparities between Black men and Black women created such conflicting interests that Black women could not possibly represent Black men adequately. In one such case, *Payne v Travenol*,[25] two Black female plaintiffs alleging race discrimination brought a class action suit on behalf of all Black employees at a pharmaceutical plant.[26] The court refused, however, to allow the plaintiffs to represent Black males and granted the defendant's request to narrow the class to Black women only. Ultimately, the district court found that there had been extensive racial discrimination at the plant and awarded back pay and constructive seniority to the class of Black female employees. But, despite its finding of general race discrimination, the court refused to extend the remedy to Black men for fear that their conflicting interests would not be adequately addressed;[27] the Fifth Circuit affirmed.[28]

Notably, the plaintiffs in *Travenol* fared better than the similarly-situated plaintiff in *Moore.* They were not denied use of meaningful statistics showing an overall pattern of race discrimination simply because there were no men in their class. The plaintiffs' bid to represent all Black employees, however, like Moore's attempt to represent all women employees, failed as a consequence of the court's narrow view of class interest.

Even though *Travenol* was a partial victory for Black women, the case specifically illustrates how antidiscrimination doctrine generally creates a dilemma for Black women. It forces them to choose between specifically articulating the intersectional aspects of their subordination, thereby risking their ability to represent Black men, or ignoring intersectionality in order to state a claim that would not lead to the exclusion of Black men. When one considers the political consequences of this dilemma, there is little wonder that many people within the Black community view the specific articulation of Black women's interests as dangerously divisive.

In sum, several courts have proved unable to deal with intersectionality, although for contrasting reasons. In *DeGraffenreid*, the court refused to recognize the possibility of compound discrimination against Black women and analyzed their claim using the employment of white women as the historical base. As a consequence, the employment ex-

periences of white women obscured the distinct discrimination that Black women experienced.

Conversely, in *Moore,* the court held that a Black woman could not use statistics reflecting the overall sex disparity in supervisory and upper-level labor jobs because she had not claimed discrimination as a woman, but "only" as a Black woman. The court would not entertain the notion that discrimination experienced by Black women is indeed sex discrimination—provable through disparate impact statistics on women.

Finally, courts, such as the one in *Travenol*, have held that Black women cannot represent an entire class of Blacks due to presumed class conflicts in cases where sex additionally disadvantaged Black women. As a result, in the few cases where Black women are allowed to use overall statistics indicating racially disparate treatment Black men may not be able to share in the remedy.

Perhaps it appears to some that I have offered inconsistent criticisms of how Black women are treated in antidiscrimination law: I seem to be saying that in one case, Black women's claims were rejected and their experiences obscured because the court refused to acknowledge that the employment experience of Black women can be distinct from that of white women, while in other cases, the interests of Black women were harmed because Black women's claims were viewed as so distinct from the claims of either white women or Black men that the court denied to Black females representation of the larger class. It seems that I have to say that Black women are the same and harmed by being treated differently or that they are different and harmed by being treated the same. But I cannot say both.

This apparent contradiction is but another manifestation of the conceptual limitations of the single-issue analyses that intersectionality challenges. The point is that Black women can experience discrimination in any number of ways and that the contradiction arises from our assumptions that their claims of exclusion must be unidirectional. Consider an analogy to traffic in an intersection, coming and going in all four directions. Discrimination, like traffic through an intersection, may flow in one direction, and it may flow in another. If an accident happens in an intersection, it can be caused by cars traveling from any number of directions and, sometimes, from all of them. Similarly, if a Black woman is harmed because she is in the intersection, her injury could result from sex discrimination or race discrimination.

Judicial decisions which premise intersectional relief on a showing that Black women are specifically recognized as a class are analogous to a doctor's decision at the scene of an accident to treat an accident victim only if the injury is recognized by medical insurance. Similarly, providing legal relief only when Black women show that their claims are based on race or on sex is analogous to calling an ambulance for the victim only after the driver responsible for the injuries is identified. But it is not always easy to reconstruct an accident: Sometimes the skid marks and the injuries simply indicate that they occurred simultaneously, frustrating efforts to determine which driver caused the harm. In these cases the tendency seems to be that no driver is held responsible, no treatment is administered, and the involved parties simply get back in their cars and zoom away.

To bring this back to a non-metaphorical level, I am suggesting that Black women can experience discrimination in ways that are both similar to and different from those experienced by white women and Black men. Black women sometimes experience discrimination in ways similar to white women's experiences; sometimes they share very similar experiences with Black men. Yet often they experience double-discrimination—the combined effects of practices which discriminate on the basis of race, and on the basis of sex. And sometimes, they experience discrimination as Black women—not the sum of race and sex discrimination, but as Black women.

Black women's experiences are much broader than the general categories that discrimination discourse provides. Yet the continued insistence that Black women's demands and needs be filtered through categorical analyses that completely obscure their experiences guarantees that their needs will seldom be addressed.

B. The Significance of Doctrinal Treatment of Intersectionality

DeGraffenreid, Moore and *Travenol* are doctrinal manifestations of a common political and theoretical approach to discrimination which operates to marginalize Black women. Unable to grasp the importance of Black women's intersectional experiences, not only courts, but feminist and civil rights thinkers as well have treated Black women in ways that deny both the unique compoundedness of their situation and the centrality of their experiences to the larger classes of women and Blacks. Black women are regarded either as too much like women or Blacks and the compounded nature of their experience is absorbed into the collective experiences of either group or as too different, in which case Black women's Blackness or femaleness sometimes has placed their needs and perspectives at the margin of the feminist and Black liberationist agendas.

While it could be argued that this failure represents an absence of political will to include Black women, I believe that it reflects an uncritical and disturbing acceptance of dominant ways of thinking about discrimination. Consider first the definition of discrimination that seems to be operative in antidiscrimination law: Discrimination which is wrongful proceeds from the identification of a specific class or category; either a discriminator intentionally identifies this category, or a process is adopted which somehow disadvantages all members of this category.[29] According to the dominant view, a discriminator treats all people within a race or sex category similarly. Any significant experiential or statistical variation within this group suggests either that the group is not being discriminated against or that conflicting interests exist which defeat any attempts to bring a common claim.[30] Consequently, one generally cannot combine these categories. Race and sex, moreover, become significant only when they operate to explicitly *disadvantage* the victims; because the *privileging* of whiteness or maleness is implicit, it is generally not perceived at all.

Underlying this conception of discrimination is a view that the wrong which antidiscrimination law addresses is the use of race or gender factors to interfere with decisions that would otherwise be fair or neutral. This process-based definition is not grounded in a bottom-up commitment to improve the substantive conditions for those who are victimized by the interplay of numerous factors. Instead, the dominant message of antidiscrimination law is that it will regulate only the limited extent to which race or sex interferes with the process of determining outcomes. This narrow objective is facilitated by the top-down strategy of using a singular "but for" analysis to ascertain the effects of race or sex. Because the scope of antidiscrimination law is so limited, sex and race discrimination have come to be defined in terms of the experiences of those who are privileged *but for* their racial or sexual characteristics. Put differently, the paradigm of sex discrimination tends to be based on the experiences of white women; the model of race discrimination tends to be based on the experiences of the most privileged Blacks. Notions of what constitutes race and sex discrimination are, as a result, narrowly tailored to embrace only a small set of circumstances, none of which include discrimination against Black women.

To the extent that this general description is accurate, the following analogy can be useful in describing how Black women are marginalized in the interface between antidiscrimination law and race and gender hierarchies: Imagine a basement which contains all people who are disadvantaged on the basis of race, sex, class, sexual preference, age and/or physical ability. These people are stacked—feet standing on shoulders—with those on the bottom being disadvantaged by the full array of factors, up to the very top, where the heads of all those disadvantaged by a singular factor brush up against the ceiling. Their ceiling is actually the floor above which only those who are *not* disadvantaged in any way reside. In efforts to correct some aspects of

domination, those above the ceiling admit from the basement only those who can say that "but for" the ceiling, they too would be in the upper room. A hatch is developed through which those placed immediately below can crawl. Yet this hatch is generally available only to those who—due to the singularity of their burden and their otherwise privileged position relative to those below—are in the position to crawl through. Those who are multiply-burdened are generally left below unless they can somehow pull themselves into the groups that are permitted to squeeze through the hatch.

As this analogy translates for Black women, the problem is that they can receive protection only to the extent that their experiences are recognizably similar to those whose experiences tend to be reflected in antidiscrimination doctrine. If Black women cannot conclusively say that "but for" their race or "but for" their gender they would be treated differently, they are not invited to climb through the hatch but told to wait in the unprotected margin until they can be absorbed into the broader, protected categories of race and sex.

Despite the narrow scope of this dominant conception of discrimination and its tendency to marginalize those whose experiences cannot be described within its tightly-drawn parameters, this approach has been regarded as the appropriate framework for addressing a range of problems. In much of feminist theory and, to some extent, in antiracist politics, this framework is reflected in the belief that sexism or racism can be meaningfully discussed without paying attention to the lives of those other than the race, gender- or class-privileged. As a result, both feminist theory and antiracist politics have been organized, in part, around the equation of racism with what happens to the Black middle-class or to Black men, and the equation of sexism with what happens to white women.

Looking at historical and contemporary issues in both the feminist and the civil rights communities, one can find ample evidence of how both communities' acceptance of the dominant framework of discrimination has hindered the development of an adequate theory and praxis to address problems of intersectionality. This adoption of a single-issue framework for discrimination not only marginalizes Black women within the very movements that claim them as part of their constituency but it also makes the illusive goal of ending racism and patriarchy even more difficult to attain.

II. FEMINISM AND BLACK WOMEN: "AIN'T WE WOMEN?"

Oddly, despite the relative inability of feminist politics and theory to address Black women substantively, feminist theory and tradition borrow considerably from Black women's history. For example, "Ain't I a Woman" has come to represent a standard refrain in feminist discourse.[31] Yet the lesson of this powerful oratory is not fully appreciated because the context of the delivery is seldom examined. I would like to tell part of the story because it establishes some themes that have characterized feminist treatment of race and illustrates the importance of including Black women's experiences as a rich source for the critique of patriarchy.

In 1851, Sojourner Truth declared "Ain't I a Woman?" and challenged the sexist imagery used by male critics to justify the disenfranchisement of women.[32] The scene was a Women's Rights Conference in Akron, Ohio; white male hecklers, invoking stereotypical images of "womanhood," argued that women were too frail and delicate to take on the responsibilities of political activity. When Sojourner Truth rose to speak, many white women urged that she be silenced, fearing that she would divert attention from women's suffrage to emancipation. Truth, once permitted to speak, recounted the horrors of slavery, and its particular impact on Black women:

> Look at my arm! I have ploughed and planted and gathered into barns, and no man could head me—and ain't I a woman? I could work as much and eat as much as a man—when I could get it—and bear the lash as well! And

ain't I a woman? I have born thirteen children, and seen most of 'em sold into slavery, and when I cried out with my mother's grief, none but Jesus heard me—and ain't I a woman?[33]

By using her own life to reveal the contradiction between the ideological myths of womanhood and the reality of Black women's experience, Truth's oratory provided a powerful rebuttal to the claim that women were categorically weaker than men. Yet Truth's personal challenge to the coherence of the cult of true womanhood was useful only to the extent that white women were willing to reject the racist attempts to rationalize the contradiction—that because Black women were something less than real women, their experiences had no bearing on true womanhood. Thus, this 19th-century Black feminist challenged not only patriarchy, but she also challenged white feminists wishing to embrace Black women's history to relinquish their vestedness in whiteness.

Contemporary white feminists inherit not the legacy of Truth's challenge to patriarchy but, instead, Truth's challenge to their forbearers. Even today, the difficulty that white women have traditionally experienced in sacrificing racial privilege to strengthen feminism renders them susceptible to Truth's critical question. When feminist theory and politics that claim to reflect *women*'s experience and *women*'s aspirations do not include or speak to Black women, Black women must ask: "Ain't *We* Women?" If this is so, how can the claims that "women are," "women believe" and "women need" be made when such claims are inapplicable or unresponsive to the needs, interests and experiences of Black women?

The value of feminist theory to Black women is diminished because it evolves from a white racial context that is seldom acknowledged. Not only are women of color in fact overlooked, but their exclusion is reinforced when *white* women speak for and as *women*. The authoritative universal voice—usually white male subjectivity masquerading as non-racial, non-gendered objectivity[34]—is merely transferred to those who, but for gender, share many of the same cultural, economic and social characteristics. When feminist theory attempts to describe women's experiences through analyzing patriarchy, sexuality, or separate spheres ideology, it often overlooks the role of race. Feminists thus ignore how their own race functions to mitigate some aspects of sexism and, moreover, how it often privileges them over and contributes to the domination of other women.[35] Consequently, feminist theory remains *white*, and its potential to broaden and deepen its analysis by addressing non-privileged women remains unrealized.

An example of how some feminist theories are narrowly constructed around white women's experiences is found in the separate spheres literature. The critique of how separate spheres ideology shapes and limits women's roles in the home and in public life is a central theme in feminist legal thought.[36] Feminists have attempted to expose and dismantle separate spheres ideology by identifying and criticizing the stereotypes that traditionally have justified the disparate societal roles assigned to men and women.[37] Yet this attempt to debunk ideological justifications for *women's* subordination offers little insight into the domination of *Black* women. Because the experiential base upon which many feminist insights are grounded is white, theoretical statements drawn from them are overgeneralized at best, and often wrong.[38] Statements such as "men and women are taught to see men as independent, capable, powerful; men and women are taught to see women as dependent, limited in abilities, and passive,"[39] are common within this literature. But this "observation" overlooks the anomalies created by crosscurrents of racism and sexism. Black men and women live in a society that creates sex-based norms and expectations which racism operates simultaneously to deny; Black men are not viewed as powerful, nor are Black women seen as passive. An effort to develop an ideological explanation of gender domination in the Black community should proceed from an understanding of how crosscutting forces establish gender norms and how the conditions of Black subordination wholly frustrate access to these

norms. Given this understanding, perhaps we can begin to see why Black women have been dogged by the stereotype of the pathological matriarch[40] or why there have been those in the Black liberation movement who aspire to create institutions and to build traditions that are intentionally patriarchal.[41]

Because ideological and descriptive definitions of patriarchy are usually premised upon white female experiences, feminists and others informed by feminist literature may make the mistake of assuming that since the role of Black women in the family and in other Black institutions does not always resemble the familiar manifestations of patriarchy in the white community, Black women are somehow exempt from patriarchal norms. For example, Black women have traditionally worked outside the home in numbers far exceeding the labor participation rate of white women.[42] An analysis of patriarchy that highlights the history of white women's exclusion from the workplace might permit the inference that Black women have not been burdened by this particular gender-based expectation. Yet the very fact that Black women must work conflicts with norms that women should not, often creating personal, emotional and relationship problems in Black women's lives. Thus, Black women are burdened not only because they often have to take on responsibilities that are not traditionally feminine but, moreover, their assumption of these roles is sometimes interpreted within the Black community as either Black women's failure to live up to such norms or as another manifestation of racism's scourge upon the Black community.[43] This is one of the many aspects of intersectionality that cannot be understood through an analysis of patriarchy rooted in white experience.

Another example of how theory emanating from a white context obscures the multidimensionality of Black women's lives is found in feminist discourse on rape. A central political issue on the feminist agenda has been the pervasive problem of rape. Part of the intellectual and political effort to mobilize around this issue has involved the development of a historical critique of the role that law has played in establishing the bounds of normative sexuality and in regulating female sexual behavior.[44] Early carnal knowledge statutes and rape laws are understood within this discourse to illustrate that the objective of rape statutes traditionally has not been to protect women from coercive intimacy but to protect and maintain a property-like interest in female chastity.[45] Although feminists quite rightly criticize these objectives, to characterize rape law as reflecting male control over female sexuality is for Black women an oversimplified account and an ultimately inadequate account.

Rape statutes generally do not reflect *male* control over *female* sexuality, but *white* male regulation of *white* female sexuality.[46] Historically, there has been absolutely no institutional effort to regulate Black female chastity.[47] Courts in some states had gone so far as to instruct juries that, unlike white women, Black women were not presumed to be chaste.[48] Also, while it was true that the attempt to regulate the sexuality of white women placed unchaste women outside the law's protection, racism restored a fallen white woman's chastity where the alleged assailant was a Black man.[49] No such restoration was available to Black women.

The singular focus on rape as a manifestation of male power over female sexuality tends to eclipse the use of rape as a weapon of racial terror.[50] When Black women were raped by white males, they were being raped not as women generally, but as Black women specifically: Their femaleness made them sexually vulnerable to racist domination, while their Blackness effectively denied them any protection.[51] This white male power was reinforced by a judicial system in which the successful conviction of a white man for raping a Black woman was virtually unthinkable.[52]

In sum, sexist expectations of chastity and racist assumptions of sexual promiscuity combined to create a distinct set of issues confronting Black women.[53] These issues have seldom been explored in feminist literature nor are they prominent in antiracist politics. The lynching of Black males, the institutional practice that was legitimized by the regulation of white women's sexuality, has historically and contemporaneously oc-cupied the Black agenda on sexuality and violence. Consequently, Black women are caught between a Black community that, perhaps understandably, views with suspicion attempts to litigate questions of sexual violence, and a feminist community that reinforces those suspicions by focusing on white female sexuality.[54] The suspicion is compounded by the historical fact that the protection of white female sexuality was often the pretext for terrorizing the Black community. Even today some fear that antirape agendas may undermine antiracist objectives. This is the paradigmatic political and theoretical dilemma created by the intersection of race and gender: Black women are caught between ideological and political currents that combine first to create and then to bury Black women's experiences.

III. WHEN AND WHERE I ENTER: INTEGRATING AN ANALYSIS OF SEXISM INTO BLACK LIBERATION POLITICS

Anna Julia Cooper, a 19th-century Black feminist, coined a phrase that has been useful in evaluating the need to incorporate an explicit analysis of patriarchy in any effort to address racial domination.[55] Cooper often criticized Black leaders and spokespersons for claiming to speak for the race, but failing to speak for Black women. Referring to one of Martin Delaney's public claims that where he was allowed to enter, the race entered with him, Cooper countered: "Only the Black Woman can say, when and where I enter ... then and there the whole Negro race enters with me."[56]

Cooper's words bring to mind a personal experience involving two Black men with whom I had formed a study group during our first year of law school. One of our group members, a graduate from Harvard College, often told us stories about a prestigious and exclusive men's club that boasted memberships of several past United States presidents and other influential white males. He was one of its very few Black members. To celebrate completing our first-year exams, our friend invited us to join him at the club for drinks.

Anxious to see this fabled place, we approached the large door and grasped the brass door ring to announce our arrival. But our grand entrance was cut short when our friend sheepishly slipped from behind the door and whispered that he had forgotten a very important detail. My companion and I bristled, our training as Black people having taught us to expect yet another barrier to our inclusion; even an informal one-Black-person quota at the establishment was not unimaginable. The tension broke, however, when we learned that *we* would not be excluded because of our race, but that *I* would have to go around to the back door because I was a female. I entertained the idea of making a scene to dramatize the fact that my humiliation as a female was no less painful and my exclusion no more excusable than had we all been sent to the back door because we were Black. But, sensing no general assent to this proposition, and also being of the mind that due to our race a scene would in some way jeopardize all of us, I failed to stand my ground. After all, the Club was about to entertain its first Black guests—even though one would have to enter through the back door.[57]

Perhaps this story is not the best example of the Black community's failure to address problems related to Black women's intersectionality seriously. The story would be more apt if Black women, and only Black women, had to go around to the back door of the club and if the restriction came from within, and not from the outside of the Black community. Still this story does reflect a markedly decreased political and emotional vigilance toward barriers to Black women's enjoyment of privileges that have been won on the basis of race but continue to be denied on the basis of sex.[58]

The story also illustrates the ambivalence among Black women about the degree of political and social capital that ought to be expended toward challenging gender barriers, particularly when the challenges might conflict with the antiracism agenda. While there are a number of reasons—including antifeminist ones—why gender has not figured directly in analyses of the subordination of Black Americans, a central reason is that race is still

seen by many as the primary oppositional force in Black lives.[59] If one accepts that the social experience of race creates both a primary group identity as well as a shared sense of being under collective assault, some of the reasons that Black feminist theory and politics have not figured prominently in the Black political agenda may be better understood.[60]

The point is not that African Americans are simply involved in a more important struggle. Although some efforts to oppose Black feminism are based on this assumption, a fuller appreciation of the problems of the Black community will reveal that gender subordination does contribute significantly to the destitute conditions of so many African Americans and that it must therefore be addressed. Moreover, the foregoing critique of the single-issue framework renders problematic the claim that the struggle against racism is distinguishable from, much less prioritized over, the struggle against sexism. Yet it is also true that the politics of racial otherness that Black women experience along with Black men prevent Black feminist consciousness from patterning the development of white feminism. For white women, the creation of a consciousness that was distinct from and in opposition to that of white men figured prominently in the development of white feminist politics. Black women, like Black men, live in a community that has been defined and subordinated by color and culture.[61] Although patriarchy clearly operates within the Black community, presenting yet another source of domination to which Black women are vulnerable, the racial context in which Black women find themselves makes the creation of a political consciousness that is oppositional to Black men difficult.

Yet while it is true that the distinct experience of racial otherness militates against the development of an oppositional feminist consciousness, the assertion of racial community sometimes supports defensive priorities that marginalize Black women. Black women's particular interests are thus relegated to the periphery in public policy discussions about the presumed needs of the Black community. The controversy over the movie *The Color Purple* is illustrative. The animating fear behind much of the publicized protest was that by portraying domestic abuse in a Black family, the movie confirmed the negative stereotypes of Black men.[62] The debate over the propriety of presenting such an image on the screen overshadowed the issue of sexism and patriarchy in the Black community. Even though it was sometimes acknowledged that the Black community was not immune from domestic violence and other manifestations of gender subordination, some nevertheless felt that in the absence of positive Black male images in the media, portraying such images merely reinforced racial stereotypes.[63] The struggle against racism seemed to compel the subordination of certain aspects of the Black female experience in order to ensure the security of the larger Black community.

The nature of this debate should sound familiar to anyone who recalls Daniel Moynihan's diagnosis of the ills of Black America.[64] Moynihan's report depicted a deteriorating Black family, foretold the destruction of the Black male householder and lamented the creation of the Black matriarch. His conclusions prompted a massive critique from liberal sociologists[65] and from civil rights leaders.[66] Surprisingly, while many critics characterized the report as racist for its blind use of white cultural norms as the standard for evaluating Black families, few pointed out the sexism apparent in Moynihan's labeling Black women as pathological for their "failure" to live up to a white female standard of motherhood.[67]

The latest versions of a Moynihanesque analysis can be found in the Moyers televised special, *The Vanishing Black Family*,[68] and, to a lesser extent, in William Julius Wilson's *The Truly Disadvantaged*.[69] In *The Vanishing Black Family*, Moyers presented the problem of female-headed households as a problem of irresponsible sexuality, induced in part by government policies that encouraged family breakdown.[70] The theme of the report was that the welfare state reinforced the deterioration of the Black family by rendering the Black male's role obsolete. As the argument goes, because Black men know that someone will take care of their families, they are free to make babies and leave them. A corollary to the Moyers view is that welfare is also dysfunc-

tional because it allows poor women to leave men upon whom they would otherwise be dependent.

Most commentators criticizing the program failed to pose challenges that might have revealed the patriarchal assumptions underlying much of the Moyers report. They instead focused on the dimension of the problem that was clearly recognizable as racist.[71] White feminists were equally culpable. There was little, if any, published response to the Moyers report from the white feminist community. Perhaps feminists were under the mistaken assumption that since the report focused on the Black community, the problems highlighted were racial, not gender based. Whatever the reason, the result was that the ensuing debates over the future direction of welfare and family policy proceeded without significant feminist input. The absence of a strong feminist critique of the Moynihan/Moyers model not only impeded the interests of Black women, but it also compromised the interests of growing numbers of white women heads of household who find it difficult to make ends meet.[72]

William Julius Wilson's *The Truly Disadvantaged* modified much of the moralistic tone of this debate by reframing the issue in terms of a lack of marriageable Black men.[73] According to Wilson, the decline in Black marriages is not attributable to poor motivation, bad work habits or irresponsibility but instead is caused by structural economics which have forced Black unskilled labor out of the work force. Wilson's approach represents a significant move away from that of Moynihan/Moyers in that he rejects their attempt to center the analysis on the morals of the Black community. Yet, he too considers the proliferation of female-headed households as dysfunctional *per se* and fails to explain fully why such households are so much in peril. Because he incorporates no analysis of the way the structure of the economy and the workforce subordinates the interests of women, especially childbearing Black women, Wilson's suggested reform begins with finding ways to put Black men back in the family.[74] In Wilson's view, we must change the economic structure with an eye toward providing more Black jobs for Black men. Because he offers no critique of sexism, Wilson fails to consider economic or social reorganization that directly empowers and supports these single Black mothers.[75]

My criticism is not that providing Black men with jobs is undesirable; indeed, this is necessary not only for the Black men themselves, but for an entire community, depressed and subject to a host of sociological and economic ills that accompany massive rates of unemployment. But as long as we assume that the massive social reorganization Wilson calls for is possible, why not think about it in ways that maximize the choices of Black women?[76] A more complete theoretical and political agenda for the Black underclass must take into account the specific and particular concerns of Black women; their families occupy the bottom rung of the economic ladder, and it is only through placing them at the center of the analysis that their needs and the needs of their families will be directly addressed.[77]

IV. EXPANDING FEMINIST THEORY AND ANTIRACIST POLITICS BY EMBRACING THE INTERSECTION

If any real efforts are to be made to free Black people of the constraints and conditions that characterize racial subordination, then theories and strategies purporting to reflect the Black community's needs must include an analysis of sexism and patriarchy. Similarly, feminism must include an analysis of race if it hopes to express the aspirations of non-white women. Neither Black liberationist politics nor feminist theory can ignore the intersectional experiences of those whom the movements claim as their respective constituents. In order to include Black women, both movements must distance themselves from earlier approaches in which experiences are relevant only when they are related to certain clearly identifiable causes (for example, the oppression of Blacks is significant when based on race, of women when based on gender). The praxis of both should be centered on the life chances and life situations of people who should be cared about without regard to the source of their difficulties.

I have stated earlier that the failure to embrace the complexities of compoundedness is not simply a matter of political will, but is also due to the influence of a way of thinking about discrimination which structures politics so that struggles are categorized as singular issues. Moreover, this structure imports a descriptive and normative view of society that reinforces the status quo.

It is somewhat ironic that those concerned with alleviating the ills of racism and sexism should adopt such a top-down approach to discrimination. If their efforts instead began with addressing the needs and problems of those who are most disadvantaged and with restructuring and remaking the world where necessary, then others who are singularly disadvantaged would also benefit. In addition, it seems that placing those who currently are marginalized in the center is the most effective way to resist efforts to compartmentalize experiences and undermine potential collective action.

It is not necessary to believe that a political consensus to focus on the lives of the most disadvantaged will happen tomorrow in order to recenter discrimination discourse at the intersection. It is enough, for now, that such an effort would encourage us to look beneath the prevailing conceptions of discrimination and to challenge the complacency that accompanies belief in the effectiveness of this framework. By so doing, we may develop language which is critical of the dominant view and which provides some basis for unifying activity. The goal of this activity should be to facilitate the inclusion of marginalized groups for whom it can be said: "When they enter, we all enter."

NOTES

1. Gloria T. Hull, et al., eds. (The Feminist Press, 1982).
2. For other work setting forth a Black feminist perspective on law, see Judy Scales-Trent, *Black Women and the Constitution: Finding Our Place, Asserting Our Rights (Voices of Experience:*

New Responses to Gender Discourse), 24 Harv CR-CL L Rev 9 (1989); Regina Austin, *Sapphire-Bound!* forthcoming in Wisc Women's L J (1989); Angela Harris, *Race and Essentialism in Feminist Legal Theory* (unpublished manuscript on file with author); and Paulette M. Caldwell, *A Hair Piece* (unpublished manuscript on file with author).

3. The most common linguistic manifestation of this analytical dilemma is represented in the conventional usage of the term "Blacks and women." Although it may be true that some people mean to include Black women in either "Blacks" or "women," the context in which the term is used actually suggests that often Black women are not considered. See, for example, Elizabeth Spelman, *The Inessential Woman* 114–15 (Beacon Press, 1988) (discussing an article on Blacks and women in the military where "the racial identity of those identified as 'women' does not become explicit until reference is made to Black women, at which point it also becomes clear that the category of women excludes Black women"). It seems that if Black women were explicitly included, the preferred term would be either "Blacks and white women" or "Black men and all women."

4. Civil Rights Act of 1964, 42 USC § 2000e, et seq as amended (1982).

5. 413 F Supp 142 (E D Mo 1976).

6. 708 F2d 475 (9th Cir 1983).

7. 673 F2d 798 (5th Cir 1982).

8. *DeGraffenreid*, 413 F Supp at 143.

9. Id at 144.

10. Id at 145. In *Mosley v General Motors*, 497 F Supp 583 (E D Mo 1980), plaintiffs, alleging broad-based racial discrimination at General Motors' St. Louis facility, prevailed in a portion of their Title VII claim. The seniority system challenged in *DeGraffenreid*, however, was not considered in *Mosley*.

11. Id at 145.

12. Interestingly, no case has been discovered in which a court denied a white male's attempt to bring a reverse discrimination claim on similar grounds—that is, that sex and race claims cannot be combined because Congress did not intend to protect compound classes. White males in a typical reverse discrimination case are in no better position than the frustrated plaintiffs in *DeGraffenreid*: If they are required to make their claims separately, white males cannot prove race discrimination because white women are not discriminated against, and they cannot prove sex discrimina-

tion because Black males are not discriminated against. Yet it seems that courts do not acknowledge the compound nature of most reverse discrimination cases. That Black women's claims automatically raise the question of compound discrimination and white males' "reverse discrimination" cases do not suggest that the notion of compoundedness is somehow contingent upon an implicit norm that is not neutral but is white male. Thus, Black women are perceived as a compound class because they are two steps removed from a white male norm, while white males are apparently not perceived to be a compound class because they somehow represent the norm.

13. I do not mean to imply that all courts that have grappled with this problem have adopted the *DeGraffenreid* approach. Indeed, other courts have concluded that Black women are protected by Title VII. See, for example, *Jefferies v Harris Community Action Ass'n.*, 615 F2d 1025 (5th Cir 1980). I do mean to suggest that the very fact that the Black women's claims are seen as aberrant suggests that sex discrimination doctrine is centered in the experiences of white women. Even those courts that have held that Black women are protected seem to accept that Black women's claims raise issues that the "standard" sex discrimination claims do not. See Elaine W. Shoben, *Compound Discrimination: The Interaction of Race and Sex in Employment Discrimination*, 55 NYU L Rev 793, 803–04 (1980) (criticizing the *Jefferies* use of a sex-plus analysis to create a subclass of Black women).

14. 708 F2d 475.

15. See also *Moore v National Association of Securities Dealers*, 27 EPD (CCH) ¶ 32,238 (D DC 1981); but see *Edmondson v Simon*, 86 FRD 375 (N D Ill 1980) (where the court was unwilling to hold as a matter of law that no Black female could represent without conflict the interests of both Blacks and females).

16. 708 F2d at 479. Between January 1976 and June 1979, the three years in which Moore claimed that she was passed over for promotion, the percentage of white males occupying first-level supervisory positions ranged from 70.3 to 76.8%; Black males from 8.9 to 10.9%; white women from 1.8 to 3.3%; and Black females from 0 to 2.2%. The overall male/female ratio in the top five labor grades ranged from 100/0% in 1976 to 98/1.8% in 1979. The white/Black ratio was 85/3.3% in 1976 and 79.6/8% in 1979. The overall ratio of men to women in supervisory positions was

98.2 to 1.8% in 1976 to 93.4 to 6.6% in 1979; the Black to white ratio during the same time period was 78.6 to 8.9% and 73.6 to 13.1%.

For promotions to the top five labor grades, the percentages were worse. Between 1976 and 1979, the percentage of white males in these positions ranged from 85.3 to 77.9%; Black males 3.3 to 8%; white females from 0 to 1.4%, and Black females from 0 to 0%. Overall, in 1979, 98.2% of the highest level employees were male; 1.8% were female.

17. 708 F2d at 480 (emphasis added).
18. Id at 484–86.
19. Under the disparate impact theory that prevailed at the time, the plaintiff had to introduce statistics suggesting that a policy or procedure disparately affects the members of a protected group. The employer could rebut that evidence by showing that there was a business necessity supporting the rule. The plaintiff then countered the rebuttal by showing that there was a less discriminatory alternative. See, for example, *Griggs v Duke Power*, 401 US 424 (1971); *Connecticut v Teal*, 457 US 440 (1982).

    A central issue in a disparate impact case is whether the impact proved is statistically significant. A related issue is how the protected group is defined. In many cases a Black female plaintiff would prefer to use statistics which include white women and/or Black men to indicate that the policy in question does in fact disparately affect the protected class. If, as in *Moore*, the plaintiff may use only statistics involving Black women, there may not be enough Black women employees to create a statistically significant sample.

20. Id at 484.
21. The court buttressed its finding with respect to the upper-level labor jobs with statistics for the Los Angeles Metropolitan Area which indicated that there were only 0.2% Black women within comparable job categories. Id at 485 n 9.
22. Id at 486.
23. Id.
24. See *Strong v Arkansas Blue Cross & Blue Shield, Inc.*, 87 FRD 496 (E D Ark 1980); *Hammons v Falzer Coffee Co.*, 87 FRD 600 (W D Mo 1980); *Edmondson v Simon*, 86 FRD 375 (N D Ill 1980); *Vuyanich v Republic National Bank of Dallas*, 82 FRD 420 (N D Tex 1979); *Colston v Maryland Cup Corp.*, 26 Fed Rules Serv 940 (D Md 1978).
25. 416 F Supp 248 (N D Miss 1976).
26. The suit commenced on March 2, 1972, with the filing of a complaint by three employees seeking to represent a class of persons allegedly subjected to racial discrimination at the hands of the defendants. Subsequently, the plaintiffs amended the complaint to add an allegation of sex discrimination. Of the original named plaintiffs, one was a Black male and two were Black females. In the course of the three-year period between the filing of the complaint and the trial, the only named male plaintiff received permission of the court to withdraw for religious reasons. Id at 250.
27. As the dissent in *Travenol* pointed out, there was no reason to exclude Black males from the scope of the remedy *after* counsel had presented sufficient evidence to support a finding of discrimination against Black men. If the rationale for excluding Black males was the potential conflict between Black males and Black females, then "[i]n this case, to paraphrase an old adage, the proof of plaintiffs' ability to represent the interests of Black males was in the representation thereof." 673 F2d at 837–38.
28. 673 F2d 798 (5th Cir 1982).
29. In much of antidiscrimination doctrine, the presence of intent to discriminate distinguishes unlawful from lawful discrimination. See *Washington v Davis*, 426 US 229, 239–45 (1976) (proof of discriminatory purpose required to substantiate Equal Protection violation). Under Title VII, however, the Court has held that statistical data showing a disproportionate impact can suffice to support a finding of discrimination. See *Griggs*, 401 US at 432. Whether the distinction between the two analyses will survive is an open question. See *Wards Cove Packing Co., Inc. v Atonio*, 109 S Ct 2115, 2122–23 (1989) (plaintiffs must show more than mere disparity to support a prima facie case of disparate impact). For a discussion of the competing normative visions that underlie the intent and effects analyses, see Alan David Freeman, *Legitimizing Racial Discrimination Through Antidiscrimination Law: A Critical Review of Supreme Court Doctrine*, 62 Minn L Rev 1049 (1978).
30. See, for example, *Moore*, 706 F2d at 479.
31. See Phyliss Palmer, *The Racial Feminization of Poverty: Women of Color as Portents of the Future for All Women*, Women's Studies Quarterly 11:3–4 (Fall 1983) (posing the question of why "white women in the women's movement had not created more effective and continuous alliances with Black women" when "simultaneously ... Black women [have] become heroines for the women's movement, a posi-

tion symbolized by the consistent use of So-journer Truth and her famous words, "Ain't I a Woman?").

32. See Paula Giddings, *When and Where I Enter: The Impact of Black Women on Race and Sex in America* 54 (William Morrow and Co, Inc, 1st ed 1984).

33. Eleanor Flexner, *Century of Struggle: The Women's Rights Movement in the United States* 91 (Belknap Press of Harvard University Press, 1975). See also bell hooks, *Ain't I a Woman* 159–60 (South End Press, 1981).

34. "'Objectivity' is itself an example of the reification of white male thought." Hull et al., eds., *But Some of Us Are Brave* at XXV (cited in note 1).

35. For example, many white females were able to gain entry into previously all white male enclaves not through bringing about a fundamental reordering of male versus female work, but in large part by shifting their "female" responsibilities to poor and minority women.

36. Feminists often discuss how gender-based stereotypes and norms reinforce the subordination of women by justifying their exclusion from public life and glorifying their roles within the private sphere. Law has historically played a role in maintaining this subordination by enforcing the exclusion of women from public life and by limiting its reach into the private sphere. See, for example, Deborah L. Rhode, *Association and Assimilation*, 81 Nw U L Rev 106 (1986); Frances Olsen, *From False Paternalism to False Equality: Judicial Assaults on Feminist Community, Illinois 1869–95*, 84 Mich L Rev 1518 (1986); Martha Minow, *Foreword: Justice Engendered*, 101 Harv L Rev 10 (1987); Nadine Taub and Elizabeth M. Schneider, *Perspectives on Women's Subordination and the Role of Law*, in David Kairys, ed., *The Politics of Law* 117–39 (Pantheon Books, 1982).

37. See works cited in note 36.

38. This criticism is a discrete illustration of a more general claim that feminism has been premised on white middle-class women's experience. For example, early feminist texts such as Betty Friedan's *The Feminine Mystique* (W. W. Norton, 1963), placed white middle-class problems at the center of feminism and thus contributed to its rejection within the Black community. See hooks, *Ain't I a Woman* at 185–96 (cited in note 33) (noting that feminism was eschewed by Black women because its white middle-class agenda ignored Black women's concerns).

39. Richard A. Wasserstrom, *Racism, Sexism and Preferential Treatment: An Approach to the Topics*, 24 UCLA L Rev 581, 588 (1977). I chose this phrase not because it is typical of most feminist statements of separate spheres; indeed, most discussions are not as simplistic as the bold statement presented here. See, for example, Taub and Schneider, *Perspectives on Women's Subordination and the Role of Law* at 117–39 (cited in note 36).

40. For example, Black families have sometimes been cast as pathological largely because Black women's divergence from the white middle-class female norm. The most infamous rendition of this view is found in the Moynihan report which blamed many of the Black community's ills on a supposed pathological family structure. For a discussion of the report and its contemporary reincarnation, see pp 163–165.

41. See hooks, *Ain't I a Woman* at 94–99 (cited in note 33) (discussing the elevation of sexist imagery in the Black liberation movement during the 1960s).

42. See generally Jacqueline Jones, *Labor of Love, Labor of Sorrow; Black Women, Work, and the Family from Slavery to the Present* (Basic Books, 1985); Angela Davis, *Women, Race and Class* (Random House, 1981).

43. As Elizabeth Higginbotham noted, "women, who often fail to conform to 'appropriate' sex roles, have been pictured as, and made to feel, inadequate—even though as women, they possess traits recognized as positive when held by men in the wider society. Such women are stigmatized because their lack of adherence to expected gender roles is seen as a threat to the value system." Elizabeth Higginbotham, *Two Representative Issues in Contemporary Sociological Work on Black Women*, in Hull, et al., eds., *But Some of Us Are Brave* at 95 (cited in note 1).

44. See generally Susan Brownmiller, *Against Our Will* (Simon and Schuster, 1975); Susan Estrich, *Real Rape* (Harvard University Press, 1987).

45. See Brownmiller, *Against Our Will* at 17; see generally Estrich, *Real Rape*.

46. One of the central theoretical dilemmas of feminism that is largely obscured by universalizing the white female experience is that experiences that are described as a manifestation of male control over females can be instead a manifestation of dominant group control over all subordinates. The significance is that other nondominant men may not share in, participate in or connect

with the behavior, beliefs or actions at issue, and may be victimized themselves by "male" power. In other contexts, however, "male authority" might include nonwhite men, particularly in private sphere contexts. Efforts to think more clearly about when Black women are dominated as *women* and when they are dominated as *Black women* are directly related to the question of when power is *male* and when it is *white male*.

47. See Note, *Rape, Racism and the Law*, 6 Harv Women's L J 103, 117–23 (1983) (discussing the historical and contemporary evidence suggesting that Black women are generally not thought to be chaste). See also hooks, *Ain't I a Woman* at 54 (cited in note 33) (stating that stereotypical images of Black womanhood during slavery were based on the myth that "all black women were immoral and sexually loose"); Beverly Smith, *Black Women's Health: Notes for a Course*, in Hull et al., eds., *But Some of Us Are Brave* at 110 (cited in note 1) (noting that "... white men for centuries have justified their sexual abuse of Black women by claiming that we are licentious, always 'ready' for any sexual encounter").

48. The following statement is probably unusual only in its candor: "What has been said by some of our courts about an unchaste female being a comparatively rare exception is no doubt true where the population is composed largely of the Caucasian race, but we would blind ourselves to actual conditions if we adopted this rule where another race that is largely immoral constitutes an appreciable part of the population." *Dallas v State*, 76 Fla 358, 79 So 690 (1918), quoted in Note, 6 Harv Women's L J at 121 (cited in note 47).

Espousing precisely this view, one commentator stated in 1902: "I sometimes hear of a virtuous Negro woman but the idea is so absolutely inconceivable to me ... I cannot imagine such a creature as a virtuous Negro woman." Id at 82. Such images persist in popular culture. See Paul Grein, *Taking Stock of the Latest Pop Record Surprises*, LA Times § 6 at 1 (July 7, 1988) (recalling the controversy in the late 70s over a Rolling Stones recording which included the line "Black girls just wanna get fucked all night").

Opposition to such negative stereotypes has sometimes taken the form of sexual conservatism. "A desperate reaction to this slanderous myth is the attempt ... to conform to the strictest versions of patriarchal morality." Smith, *Black Women's Health*, in Hull et al.,

eds., *But Some of Us Are Brave* at 111 (cited in note 1). Part of this reaction is reflected in the attitudes and policies of Black schools which have been notoriously strict in regulating the behavior of female students. See Gail Elizabeth Wyatt, *The Sexual Experience of Afro-American Women*, in Martha Kirkpatrick, ed., *Women's Sexual Experience: Exploration of the Dark Continent* 24 (Plenum, 1982) (noting "the differences between the predominantly Afro-American universities, where there was far more supervision regarding sexual behavior, and the majority of white colleges, where there were fewer curfews and restrictions placed on the resident"). Any attempt to understand and critique the emphasis on Black virtue without focusing on the racist ideology that places virtue beyond the reach of Black women would be incomplete and probably incorrect.

49. Because of the way the legal system viewed chastity, Black women could not be victims of forcible rape. One commentator has noted that "[a]ccording to governing sterotypes [sic], chastity could not be possessed by Black women. Thus, Black women's rape charges were automatically discounted, and the issue of chastity was contested only in cases where the rape complainant was a white woman." Note, 6 Harv Women's L J at 126 (cited in note 47). Black women's claims of rape were not taken seriously regardless of the offender's race. A judge in 1912 said: "This court will never take the word of a nigger against the word of a white man [concerning rape]." Id at 120. On the other hand, lynching was considered an effective remedy for a Black man's rape of a white woman. Since rape of a white woman by a Black man was "a crime more horrible than death," the only way to assuage society's rage and to make the woman whole again was to brutally murder the Black man. Id at 125.

50. See *The Rape of Black Women as a Weapon of Terror*, in Garda Lerner, ed., *Black Women in White America* 172–93 (Pantheon Books, 1972). See also Brownmiller, *Against Our Will* (cited in note 44). Even where Brownmiller acknowledges the use of rape as racial terrorism, she resists making a "special case" for Black women by offering evidence that white women were raped by the Klan as well. Id at 139. Whether or not one considers the racist rape of Black women a "special case," such experiences are probably different. In any case, Brownmiller's treatment of the issue raises se-

rious questions about the ability to sustain an analysis of patriarchy without understanding its multiple intersections with racism.

51. Lerner, *Black Women in White America* at 173.
52. See generally, Note, 6 Harv Women's L J at 103 (cited in note 47).
53. Paula Giddings notes the combined effect of sexual and racial stereotypes: "Black women were seen having all of the inferior qualities of white women without any of their virtues." Giddings, *When and Where I Enter* at 82 (cited in note 32).
54. Susan Brownmiller's treatment of the Emmett Till case illustrates why antirape politicization makes some African Americans uncomfortable. Despite Brownmiller's quite laudable efforts to discuss elsewhere the rape of Black women and the racism involved in much of the hysteria over the Black male threat, her analysis of the Till case places the sexuality of white women, rather than racial terrorism, at center stage. Brownmiller states: "Rarely has one single case exposed so clearly as Till's the underlying group-male antagonisms over access to women, for what began in Bryant's store should not be misconstrued as an innocent flirtation .... In concrete terms, the accessibility of all white women was on review." Brownmiller, *Against Our Will* at 272 (cited in note 44).

Later, Brownmiller argues:

And what of the wolf whistle, Till's 'gesture of adolescent bravado'? We are rightly aghast that a whistle could be cause for murder but we must also accept that Emmett Till and J. W. Millam shared something in common. They both understood that the whistle was no small tweet of hubba-hubba or melodious approval for a well-turned ankle. Given the deteriorated situation ... it was a deliberate insult just short of physical assault, a last reminder to Carolyn Bryant that this black boy, Till, had a mind to possess her.

Id at 273.

While Brownmiller seems to categorize the case as one that evidences a conflict over possession, it is regarded in African American history as a tragic dramatization of the South's pathological hatred and fear of African Americans. Till's body, mutilated beyond recognition, was viewed by thousands so that, in the words of Till's mother, "the world could see what they did to my boy." Juan Williams, *Standing for Justice*, in *Eyes on the Prize* 44

(Viking, 1987). The Till tragedy is also regarded as one of the historical events that bore directly on the emergence of the Civil Rights movement. "[W]ithout question it moved black America in a way the Supreme Court ruling on school desegregation could not match." Id. As Williams later observed, "the murder of Emmitt Till had a powerful impact on a generation of blacks. It was this generation, those who were adolescents when Till was killed, that would soon demand justice and freedom in a way unknown in America before." Id at 57. Thus, while Brownmiller looks at the Till case and sees the vicious struggle over the possession of a white woman, African Americans see the case as a symbol of the insane degree to which whites were willing to suppress the Black race. While patriarchal attitudes toward women's sexuality played a supporting role, to place white women center stage in this tragedy is to manifest such confusion over racism as to make it difficult to imagine that the white antirape movement could be sensitive to more subtle racial tensions regarding Black women's participation in it.

55. See Anna Julia Cooper, *A Voice from the South* (Negro Universities Press, 1969 reprint of the Aldine Printing House, Ohio, 1892).
56. Id at 31.
57. In all fairness, I must acknowledge that my companion accompanied me to the back door. I remain uncertain, however, as to whether the gesture was an expression of solidarity or an effort to quiet my anger.
58. To this one could easily add class.
59. An anecdote illustrates this point. A group of female law professors gathered to discuss "Isms in the Classroom." One exercise led by Pat Cain involved each participant listing the three primary factors that described herself. Almost without exception, white women in the room listed their gender either primarily or secondarily; none listed their race. All of the women of color listed their race first, and then their gender. This seems to suggest that identity descriptions seem to begin with the primary source of opposition with whatever the dominant norm is. See Pat Cain, *Feminist Jurisprudence: Grounding the Theories* 19–20 (unpublished manuscript on file with author) (explaining the exercise and noting that "no white woman ever mentions race, whereas every woman of color does" and that, similarly, "straight women do not include 'heterosexual' ... whereas lesbians who are open always include 'lesbian'").

60. For a comparative discussion of Third World feminism paralleling this observation, see Kumari Jayawardena, *Feminism and Nationalism in the Third World* 1–24 (Zed Books Ltd, 1986). Jayawardena states that feminism in the Third World has been "accepted" only within the central struggle against international domination. Women's social and political status has improved most when advancement is necessary to the broader struggle against imperialism.

61. For a discussion of how racial ideology creates a polarizing dynamic which subordinates Blacks and privileges whites, see Kimberle Crenshaw, *Race, Reform and Retrenchment: Transformation and Legitimation in Antidiscrimination Law*, 101 Harv L Rev 1331, 1371–76 (1988).

62. Jack Matthews, *Three Color Purple Actresses Talk About Its Impact*, LA Times § 6 at 1 (Jan 31, 1986); Jack Matthews, *Some Blacks Critical of Spielberg's Purple*, LA Times § 6 at 1 (Dec 20, 1985). But see Gene Siskel, *Does Purple Hate Men?*, Chicago Tribune § 13 at 16 (Jan 5, 1986); Clarence Page, *Toward a New Black Cinema*, Chicago Tribune § 5 at 3 (Jan 12, 1986).

63. A consistent problem with any negative portrayal of African Americans is that they are seldom balanced by positive images. On the other hand, most critics overlooked the positive transformation of the primary male character in *The Color Purple*.

64. Daniel P. Moynihan, *The Negro Family: The Case for National Action* (Office of Policy Planning and Research, United States Department of Labor, 1965).

65. See Lee Rainwater and William L. Yancey, *The Moynihan Report and the Politics of Controversy* 427–29 (MIT Press, 1967) (containing criticisms of the Moynihan Report by, among others, Charles E. Silberman, Christopher Jencks, William Ryan, Laura Carper, Frank Riessman and Herbert Gans).

66. Id at 395–97 (critics included Martin Luther King, Jr., Benjamin Payton, James Farmer, Whitney Young, Jr. and Bayard Rustin).

67. One of the notable exceptions is Jacquelyne Johnson Jackson, *Black Women in a Racist Society*, in *Racism and Mental Health* 185–86 (University of Pittsburg Press, 1973).

68. *The Vanishing Black Family* (PBS Television Broadcast, January 1986).

69. William Julius Wilson, *The Truly Disadvantaged: The Inner City, The Underclass and Public Policy* (The University of Chicago Press, 1987).

70. Columnist Mary McGrory, applauding the show, reported that Moyers found that sex was as common in the Black ghetto as a cup of coffee. McGrory, *Moynihan was Right 21 Years Ago*, The Washington Post B1 and B4 (Jan 26, 1986). George Will argued that oversexed Black men were more of a menace than Bull Conner, the Birmingham Police Chief who in 1968 achieved international notoriety by turning fire hoses on protesting school children. George Will, *Voting Rights Won't Fix It*, The Washington Post A23 (Jan 23, 1986).

My guess is that the program has influenced the debate about the so-called underclass by providing graphic support to pre-existing tendencies to attribute poverty to individual immorality. During a recent and memorable discussion on the public policy implications of poverty in the Black community, one student remarked that nothing can be done about Black poverty until Black men stop acting like "roving penises," Black women stop having babies "at the drop of a hat," and they all learn middle-class morality. The student cited the Moyers report as her source.

71. Although the nearly exclusive focus on the racist aspects of the program poses both theoretical and political problems, it was entirely understandable given the racial nature of the subsequent comments that were sympathetic to the Moyers view. As is typical in discussions involving race, the dialogue regarding the Moyers program covered more than just the issue of Black families; some commentators took the opportunity to indict not only the Black underclass, but the Black civil rights leadership, the war on poverty, affirmative action and other race-based remedies. See, for example, Will, *Voting Rights Won't Fix It* at A23 (cited in note 70).

72. Their difficulties can also be linked to the prevalence of an economic system and family policy that treat the nuclear family as the norm and other family units as aberrant and unworthy of societal accommodation.

73. Wilson, *The Truly Disadvantaged* at 96 (cited in note 69).

74. Id at 154 (suggestions include macroeconomic policies which promote balanced economic growth, a nationally-oriented labor market strategy, a child support assurance program, a child care strategy, and a family allowances program which would be both means tested and race specific).

75. Nor does Wilson include an analysis of the impact of gender on changes in family patterns. Consequently, little attention is paid to the conflict that may result when gender-based ex-

pectations are frustrated by economic and demographic factors. This focus on demographic and structural explanations represent an effort to regain the high ground from the Moyers/Moynihan approach which is more psycho-social. Perhaps because psycho-social explanations have come dangerously close to victim-blaming, their prevalence is thought to threaten efforts to win policy directives that might effectively address deteriorating conditions within the working class and poor Black communities. See Kimberle Crenshaw, *A Comment on Gender, Difference, and Victim Ideology in the Study of the Black Family,* in *The Decline of Marriage Among African Americans: Causes, Con-*

sequences and Policy Implications (forthcoming 1989).
76. For instance, Wilson only mentions in passing the need for day care and job training for single mothers. Wilson at 153 (cited in note 69). No mention at all is made of other practices and policies that are racist and sexist, and that contribute to the poor conditions under which nearly half of all Black women must live.
77. Pauli Murray observes that the operation of sexism is at least the partial cause of social problems affecting Black women. See Murray, *The Liberation of Black Women,* in Jo Freeman, ed., *Women: A Feminist Perspective* 351–62 (Mayfield Publishing Co, 1975).

The Master's Tools Will Never Dismantle the Master's House

Audre Lorde

I agreed to take part in a New York University Institute for the Humanities conference a year ago, with the understanding that I would be commenting upon papers dealing with the role of difference within the lives of american women: difference of race, sexuality, class, and age. The absence of these considerations weakens any feminist discussion of the personal and the political.

It is a particular academic arrogance to assume any discussion of feminist theory without examining our many differences, and

Source: Audre Lorde, "The Master's Tools Will Never Dismantle the Master's House" in Audre Lorde, *Sister Outsider: Essays and Speeches* (Freedom, CA: The Crossing Press), 110–23. Comments at "The Personal and the Political Panel," Second Sex Conference, New York, September 29, 1979.

without a significant input from poor women, Black and Third World women, and lesbians. And yet, I stand here as a Black lesbian feminist, having been invited to comment within the only panel at this conference where the input of Black feminists and lesbians is represented. What this says about the vision of this conference is sad, in a country where racism, sexism, and homophobia are inseparable. To read this program is to assume that lesbian and Black women have nothing to say about existentialism, the erotic, women's culture and silence, developing feminist theory, or heterosexuality and power. And what does it mean in personal and political terms when even the two Black women who did present here were literally found at the last hour? What does it mean when the tools of a racist partriarchy are used to examine the fruits of that same patriarchy? It means that only the most narrow perimeters of change are possible and allowable.

The absence of any consideration of lesbian consciousness or the consciousness of Third World women leaves a serious gap within this conference and within the papers presented here. For example, in a paper on material relationships between women, I was conscious of an either/or model of nurturing which totally dismissed my knowledge as a Black lesbian. In this paper there was no examination of mutuality between women, no systems of shared support, no interdependence as exists between lesbians and women-identified women. Yet it is only in the patriarchal model of nurturance that women "who attempt to emancipate themselves pay perhaps too high a price for the results," as this paper states.

For women, the need and desire to nurture each other is not pathological but redemptive, and it is within that knowledge that our real power is rediscovered. It is this real connection which is so feared by a patriarchal world. Only within a patriarchal structure is maternity the only social power open to women.

Interdependency between women is the way to a freedom which allows the *I* to *be*, not in order to be used, but in order to be creative. This is a difference between the passive *be* and the active *being*.

Advocating the mere tolerance of difference between women is the grossest reformism. It is a total denial of the creative function of difference in our lives. Difference must be not merely tolerated, but seen as a fund of necessary polarities between which our creativity can spark like a dialectic. Only then does the necessity for interdependency become unthreatening. Only within that interdependency of different strengths, acknowledged and equal, can the power to seek new ways of being in the world generate, as well as the courage and sustenance to act where there are no charters.

Within the interdependence of mutual (nondominant) differences lies that security which enables us to descend into the chaos of knowledge and return with true visions of our future, along with the concomitant power to effect those changes which can bring that future into being. Difference is that raw and powerful connection from which our personal power is forged.

As women, we have been taught either to ignore our differences, or to view them as causes for separation and suspicion rather than as forces for change. Without community there is no liberation, only the most vulnerable and temporary armistice between an individual and her oppression. But community must not mean a shedding of our differences, nor the pathetic pretense that these differences do not exist.

Those of us who stand outside the circle of this society's definition of acceptable women; those of us who have been forged in the crucibles of difference—those of us who are poor, who are lesbians, who are Black, who are older—know that *survival is not an academic skill.* It is learning how to stand alone, unpopular and sometimes reviled, and how to make common cause with those others identified as outside the structures in order to define and seek a world in which we can all flourish. It is learning how to take our differences and make them strengths. *For the master's tools will never dismantle the master's house.* They may allow us temporarily to beat him at his own game, but they will never enable us to bring about genuine change. And this fact is only threatening to those women who still define the master's house as their only source of support.

Poor women and women of Color know there is a difference between the daily manifestations of marital slavery and prostitution because it is our daughters who line 42nd Street. If white american feminist theory need not deal with the differences between us, and the resulting difference in our oppressions, then how do you deal with the fact that the women who clean your houses and tend your children while you attend conferences on feminist theory are, for the most part, poor women and women of Color? What is the theory behind racist feminism?

In a world of possibility for us all, our personal visions help lay the groundwork for political action. The failure of academic feminists to recognize difference as a crucial strength is a failure to reach beyond the first patriarchal lesson. In our world, divide and conquer must become define and empower.

Why weren't other women of Color found to participate in this conference? Why were two phone calls to me considered a consultation? Am I the only possible source of names of Black feminists? And although the Black panelist's paper ends on an important and powerful connection of love between women, what about interracial cooperation between feminists who don't love each other?

In academic feminist circles, the answer to these questions is often, "We did not know who to ask." But that is the same evasion of responsibility, the same cop-out, that keeps Black women's art out of women's exhibitions, Black women's work out of most feminist publications except for the occasional "Special Third World Women's Issue," and Black women's texts off your reading lists. But as Adrienne Rich pointed out in a recent talk, white feminists have educated themselves about such an enormous amount over the past ten years, how come you haven't also educated yourselves about Black women and the differences between us—white and Black— when it is key to our survival as a movement?

Women of today are still being called upon to stretch across the gap of male ignorance and to educate men as to our existence and our needs. This is an old and primary tool of all oppressors to keep the oppressed occupied with the master's concerns. Now we hear that it is the task of women of Color to educate white women—in the face of tremendous resistance—as to our existence, our differences, our relative roles in our joint survival. This is a diversion of energies and a tragic repetition of racist patriarchal thought.

Simone de Beauvoir once said: "It is in the knowledge of the genuine conditions of our lives that we must draw our strength to live and our reasons for acting."

Racism and homophobia are real conditions of all our lives in this place and time. *I urge each one of us here to reach down into that deep place of knowledge inside herself and touch that terror and loathing of any difference that lives there. See whose face it wears.* Then the personal as the political can begin to illuminate all our choices.

Age, Race, Class, and Sex

Women Redefining Difference

Audre Lorde

Much of western European history conditions us to see human differences in simplistic opposition to each other: dominant/subordinate, good/bad, up/down, superior/inferior. In a society where the good is defined in terms of profit rather than in terms of human need, there must always be some group of people who, through systematized oppression, can be made to feel surplus, to occupy the place of the dehumanized inferior. Within this society, that group is made up of Black and Third World people, working-class people, older people, and women.

As a forty-nine-year-old Black lesbian feminist socialist mother of two, including one boy, and a member of an interracial couple, I usually find myself a part of some group defined as other, deviant, inferior, or just plain wrong. Traditionally, in american society, it is the members of oppressed, objectified groups who are expected to stretch out and bridge the gap between the actualities of our lives and the consciousness of our oppressor. For in order to survive, those of us for whom oppression is as american as apple pie have always had to be watchers, to become familiar with the language and manners of the oppressor, even sometimes adopting them for some illusion of protection. Whenever the need for some pretense of communication arises, those who profit from our oppression call upon us to share our knowledge with them. In other words, it is the responsibility of the oppressed to teach the oppressors their mistakes. I am responsible for educating teachers

Source: Audre Lorde, "Age, Race, Class, and Sex: Women Redefining Difference" in Audre Lorde, *Sister Outsider: Essays and Speeches* (Freedom, CA: The Crossing Press), 110-123. Paper delivered at the Copeland Colloquium, Amherst College, April 1980.

who dismiss my children's culture in school. Black and Third World people are expected to educate white people as to our humanity. Women are expected to educate men. Lesbians and gay men are expected to educate the heterosexual world. The oppressors maintain their position and evade responsibility for their own actions. There is a constant drain of energy which might be better used in redefining ourselves and devising realistic scenarios for altering the present and constructing the future.

Institutionalized rejection of difference is an absolute necessity in a profit economy which needs outsiders as surplus people. As members of such an economy, we have *all* been programmed to respond to the human differences between us with fear and loathing and to handle that difference in one of three ways: ignore it, and if that is not possible, copy it if we think it is dominant, or destroy it if we think it is subordinate. But we have no patterns for relating across our human differences as equals. As a result, those differences have been misnamed and misused in the service of separation and confusion.

Certainly there are very real differences between us of race, age, and sex. But it is not those differences between us that are separating us. It is rather our refusal to recognize those differences, and to examine the distortions which result from our misnaming them and their effects upon human behavior and expectation.

Racism, the belief in the inherent superiority of one race over all others and thereby the right to dominance. Sexism, the belief in the inherent superiority of one sex over the other and thereby the right to dominance. Ageism. Heterosexism. Elitism. Classism.

It is a lifetime pursuit for each one of us to extract these distortions from our living at the same time as we recognize, reclaim, and define those differences upon which they are imposed. For we have all been raised in a society where those distortions were endemic within our living. Too often, we pour the energy needed for recognizing and exploring difference into pretending those differences are insurmountable barriers, or that they do not exist at all. This results in a voluntary isolation, or false and treacherous connections. Either way, we do not develop tools for using human difference as a springboard for creative change within our lives. We speak not of human difference, but of human deviance.

Somewhere, on the edge of consciousness, there is what I call a *mythical norm*, which each one of us within our hearts knows "that is not me." In america, this norm is usually defined as white, thin, male, young, heterosexual, christian, and financially secure. It is with this mythical norm that the trappings of power reside within this society. Those of us who stand outside that power often identify one way in which we are different, and we assume that to be the primary cause of all oppression, forgetting other distortions around difference, some of which we ourselves may be practising. By and large within the women's movement today, white women focus upon their oppression as women and ignore differences of race, sexual preference, class, and age. There is a pretense to a homogeneity of experience covered by the word *sisterhood* that does not in fact exist.

Unacknowledged class differences rob women of each others' energy and creative insight. Recently a women's magazine collective made the decision for one issue to print only prose, saying poetry was a less "rigorous" or "serious" art form. Yet even the form our creativity takes is often a class issue. Of all the art forms, poetry is the most economical. It is the one which is the most secret, which requires the least physical labor, the least material, and the one which can be done between shifts, in the hospital pantry, on the subway, and on scraps of surplus paper. Over the last few years, writing a novel on tight finances, I came to appreciate the enormous differences in the material demands between poetry and prose.

As we reclaim our literature, poetry has been the major voice of poor, working class, and Colored women. A room of one's own may be a necessity for writing prose, but so are reams of paper, a typewriter, and plenty of time. The actual requirements to produce the visual arts also help determine, along class lines, whose art is whose. In this day of inflated prices for material, who are our sculptors, our painters, our photographers? When we speak of a broadly based women's culture, we need to be aware of the effect of class and economic differences on the supplies available for producing art.

As we move toward creating a society within which we can each flourish, ageism is another distortion of relationship which interferes without vision. By ignoring the past, we are encouraged to repeat its mistakes. The "generation gap" is an important social tool for any repressive society. If the younger members of a community view the older members as contemptible or suspect or excess, they will never be able to join hands and examine the living memories of the community, nor ask the all important question, "Why?" This gives rise to a historical amnesia that keeps us working to invent the wheel every time we have to go to the store for bread.

We find ourselves having to repeat and relearn the same old lessons over and over that our mothers did because we do not pass on what we have learned, or because we are unable to listen. For instance, how many times has this all been said before? For another, who would have believed that once again our daughters are allowing their bodies to be hampered and purgatoried by girdles and high heels and hobble skirts?

Ignoring the differences of race between women and the implications of those differences presents the most serious threat to the mobilization of women's joint power.

As white women ignore their built-in privilege of whiteness and define *woman* in terms of their own experience alone, then women of Color become "other," the outsider whose experience and tradition is too "alien" to comprehend. An example of this is the signal absence of the experience of women of Color as a resource for women's studies courses. The literature of women of Color is seldom included in women's literature courses and almost never in other literature courses, nor in women's studies as a whole. All too often, the excuse given is that the literatures of women of Color can only be taught by Colored women, or that they are too difficult to understand, or that classes cannot "get into" them because they come out of experiences that are "too different." I have heard this argument presented by white women of otherwise quite clear intelligence, women who seem to have no trouble at all teaching and reviewing work that comes out of the vastly different experiences of Shakespeare, Molière, Dostoyefsky, and Aristophanes. Surely there must be some other explanation.

This is a very complex question, but I believe one of the reasons white women have such difficulty reading Black women's work is because of their reluctance to see Black women as women and different from themselves. To examine Black women's literature effectively requires that we be seen as whole people in our actual complexities—as individuals, as women, as human—rather than as one of those problematic but familiar stereotypes provided in this society in place of genuine images of Black women. And I believe this holds true for the literatures of other women of Color who are not Black.

The literatures of all women of Color recreate the textures of our lives, and many white women are heavily invested in ignoring the real differences. For as long as any difference between us means one of us must be inferior, then the recognition of any difference must be fraught with guilt. To allow women of Color to step out of stereotypes is too guilt provoking, for it threatens the complacency of those women who view oppression only in terms of sex.

Refusing to recognize difference makes it impossible to see the different problems and pitfalls facing us as women.

Thus, in a patriarchal power system where whiteskin privilege is a major prop, the entrapments used to neutralize Black women

and white women are not the same. For example, it is easy for Black women to be used by the power structure against Black men, not because they are men, but because they are Black. Therefore, for Black women, it is necessary at all times to separate the needs of the oppressor from our own legitimate conflicts within our communities. This same problem does not exist for white women. Black women and men have shared racist oppression and still share it, although in different ways. Out of that shared oppression we have developed joint defenses and joint vulnerabilities to each other that are not duplicated in the white community, with the exception of the relationship between Jewish women and Jewish men.

On the other hand, white women face the pitfall of being seduced into joining the oppressor under the pretense of sharing power. This possibility does not exist in the same way for women of Color. The tokenism that is sometimes extended to us is not an invitation to join power; our racial "otherness" is a visible reality that makes that quite clear. For white women there is a wider range of pretended choices and rewards for identifying with patriarchal power and its tools.

Today, with the defeat of ERA, the tightening economy, and increased conservatism, it is easier once again for white women to believe the dangerous fantasy that if you are good enough, pretty enough, sweet enough, quiet enough, teach the children to behave, hate the right people, and marry the right men, then you will be allowed to co-exist with patriarchy in relative peace, at least until a man needs your job or the neighborhood rapist happens along. And true, unless one lives and loves in the trenches it is difficult to remember that the war against dehumanization is ceaseless.

But Black women and our children know the fabric of our lives is stitched with violence and with hatred, that there is no rest. We do not deal with it only on the picket lines, or in dark midnight alleys, or in the places where we dare to verbalize our resistance. For us, increasingly, violence weaves through the daily tissues of our living—in the supermarket, in the classroom, in the elevator, in the clinic and the schoolyard, from the plumber, the baker, the saleswoman, the bus driver, the bank teller, the waitress who does not serve us.

Some problems we share as women, some we do not. You fear your children will grow up to join the patriarchy and testify against you, we fear our children will be dragged from a car and shot down in the street, and you will turn your backs upon the reasons they are dying.

The threat of difference has been no less blinding to people of Color. Those of us who are Black must see that the reality of our lives and our struggle does not make us immune to the errors of ignoring and misnaming difference. Within Black communities where racism is a living reality, differences among us often seem dangerous and suspect. The need for unity is often misnamed as a need for homogeneity, and a Black feminist vision mistaken for betrayal of our common interests as a people. Because of the continuous battle against racial erasure that Black women and Black men share, some Black women still refuse to recognize that we are also oppressed as women, and that sexual hostility against Black women is practiced not only by the white racist society, but implemented within our Black communities as well. It is a disease striking the heart of Black nationhood, and silence will not make it disappear. Exacerbated by racism and the pressures of powerlessness, violence against Black women and children often becomes a standard within our communities, one by which manliness can be measured. But these woman-hating acts are rarely discussed as crimes against Black women.

As a group, women of Color are the lowest paid wage earners in america. We are the primary targets of abortion and sterilization abuse, here and abroad. In certain parts of Africa, small girls are still being sewed shut between their legs to keep them docile and for men's pleasure. This is known as female circumcision, and it is not a cultural affair as the late Jomo Kenyatta insisted, it is a crime against Black women.

Black women's literature is full of the pain of frequent assault, not only by a racist patriarchy, but also by Black men. Yet the necessity for and history of shared battle have made us, Black women, particularly vulnerable to the false accusation that anti-sexist is anti-Black. Meanwhile, womanhating as a recourse of the powerless is sapping strength from Black communities, and our very lives. Rape is on the increase, reported and unreported, and rape is not aggressive sexuality, it is sexualized aggression. As Kalamu ya Salaam, a Black male writer points out, "As long as male domination exists, rape will exist. Only women revolting and men made conscious of their responsibility to fight sexism can collectively stop rape."*

Differences between ourselves as Black women are also being misnamed and used to separate us from one another. As a Black lesbian feminist comfortable with the many different ingredients of my identity, and a woman committed to racial and sexual freedom from oppression, I find I am constantly being encouraged to pluck out some one aspect of myself and present this as the meaningful whole, eclipsing or denying the other parts of self. But this is a destructive and fragmenting way to live. My fullest concentration of energy is available to me only when I integrate all the parts of who I am, openly, allowing power from particular sources of my living to flow back and forth freely through all my different selves, without the restrictions of externally imposed definition. Only then can I bring myself and my energies as a whole to the service of those struggles which I embrace as part of my living.

A fear of lesbians, or of being accused of being a lesbian, has led many Black women into testifying against themselves. It has led some of us into destructive alliances, and others into despair and isolation. In the white women's communities, heterosexism is sometimes a result of identifying with the white patriarchy, a rejection of that interdependence between women-identified women which allows the self to be, rather than to be used in the service of men. Sometimes it reflects a diehard belief in the protective coloration of het-

---

*From "Rape: A Radical Analysis, An African-American Perspective" by Kalamu ya Salaam in *Black Books Bulletin*, vol. 6, no. 4 (1980).

erosexual relationships, sometimes a self-hate which all women have to fight against, taught us from birth.

Although elements of these attitudes exist for all women, there are particular resonances of heterosexism and homophobia among Black women. Despite the fact that woman-bonding has a long and honorable history in the African and African-american communities, and despite the knowledge and accomplishments of many strong and creative women-identified Black women in the political, social and cultural fields, heterosexual Black women often tend to ignore or discount the existence and work of Black lesbians. Part of this attitude has come from an understandable terror of Black male attack within the close confines of Black society, where the punishment for any female self-assertion is still to be accused of being a lesbian and therefore unworthy of the attention or support of the scarce Black male. But part of this need to misname and ignore Black lesbians comes from a very real fear that openly women-identified Black women who are no longer dependent upon men for their self-definition may well reorder our whole concept of social relationships.

Black women who once insisted that lesbianism was a white woman's problem now insist that Black lesbians are a threat to Black nationhood, are consorting with the enemy, are basically un-Black. These accusations, coming from the very women to whom we look for deep and real understanding, have served to keep many Black lesbians in hiding, caught between the racism of white women and the homophobia of their sisters. Often, their work has been ignored, trivialized, or misnamed, as with the work of Angelina Grimke, Alice Dunbar-Nelson, Lorraine Hansberry. Yet women-bonded women have always been some part of the power of Black communities, from our unmarried aunts to the amazons of Dahomey.

And it is certainly not Black lesbians who are assaulting women and raping children and grandmothers on the streets of our communities.

Across this country, as in Boston during the spring of 1979 following the unsolved murders of twelve Black women, Black lesbians are spearheading movements against violence against Black women.

What are the particular details within each of our lives that can be scrutinized and altered to help bring about change? How do we redefine difference for all women? It is not our differences which separate women, but our reluctance to recognize those differences and to deal effectively with the distortions which have resulted from the ignoring and misnaming of those differences.

As a tool of social control, women have been encouraged to recognize only one area of human difference as legitimate, those differences which exist between women and men. And we have learned to deal across those differences with the urgency of all oppressed subordinates. All of us have had to learn to live or work or coexist with men, from our fathers on. We have recognized and negotiated these differences, even when this recognition only continued the old dominant/subordinate mode of human relationship, where the oppressed must recognize the masters' difference in order to survive.

But our future survival is predicated upon our ability to relate within equality. As women, we must root out internalized patterns of oppression within ourselves if we are to move beyond the most superficial aspects of social change. Now we must recognize differences among women who are our equals, neither inferior nor superior, and devise ways to use each others' difference to enrich our visions and our joint struggles.

The future of our earth may depend upon the ability of all women to identify and develop new definitions of power and new patterns of relating across difference. The old definitions have not served us, nor the earth that supports us. The old patterns, no matter how cleverly rearranged to imitate progress, still condemn us to cosmetically altered repetitions of the same old exchanges, the same old guilt, hatred, recrimination, lamentation, and suspicion.

For we have, built into all of us, old blueprints of expectation and response, old structures of oppression, and these must be altered at the same time as we alter the living conditions which are a result of those structures. For the master's tools will never dismantle the master's house.

As Paulo Freire shows so well in *The Pedagogy of the Oppressed*, [Seabury Press, New York, 1970] the true focus of revolutionary change is never merely the oppressive situations which we seek to escape, but that piece of the oppressor which is planted deep within each of us, and which knows only the oppressors' tactics, the oppressors' relationships.

Change means growth, and growth can be painful. But we sharpen self-definition by exposing the self in work and struggle together with those whom we define as different from ourselves, although sharing the same goals. For Black and white, old and young, lesbian and heterosexual women alike, this can mean new paths to our survival.

> We have chosen each other
> and the edge of each others battles
> the war is the same
> if we lose
> someday women's blood will congeal
> upon a dead planet
> if we win
> there is no telling
> we seek beyond history
> for a new and more possible meeting.

[From "Outlines," unpublished poem.]

FURTHER READING

Bambara, Toni Cade, ed. 1970. *The Black Woman: An Anthology.* New York: New American Library.

Collins, Patricia Hill. 1998. *Fighting Words: Black Women and the Search for Justice.* Minneapolis: University of Minnesota Press.

Davis, Angela. 1982. *Women, Race and Class.* New York: Random House.

hooks, bell. 1981. *Ain't I a Woman.* Boston: South End Press.

James, Joy. 1999. *Shadowboxing: Representations of Black Feminist Politics.* New York: St. Martin's Press.

Rollins, Judith. 1985. *Between Women: Domestics and Their Employers.* Philadelphia: Temple University Press.

Sharpley, T. Denean, and Joy James, eds. 2000. *The Black Feminist Reader.* Oxford: Blackwell Publishers.

White, Deborah Gray. 1985. *Ar'n't I a Woman?* New York: W.W. Norton.

CHAPTER 5

Civil Rights and Civil Disobedience

The postwar civil rights movement in the United States provides a historical model of a social action with goals that pertained to matters of public concern. These goals were collective in the sense that they can be attained only through the cooperative endeavor of a large group of supporters. The civil rights movement involved a wide range of Americans who saw it rational to take social action to bring about certain public goods. The following selections focus on the intersection of self-interest and morality as a pragmatic concern underlying the philosophy of nonviolent direct action.

These two dimensions of social action highlight the discussion of rights by Richard Wasserstrom and A. Philip Randolph. Wasserstrom reflects on the simple assertion of the wrongness of denying that black people are humans—a racist view that was the starting point for many activists involved in the civil rights movement. Recognizing that this view of black people is the basis for not granting them the same rights as whites, he argues that racial discrimination will end only when replaced with a system of human rights.

Wasserstrom explores the differences between rights and duties to show that rights entail certain entitlements by reflecting on the system of racial discrimination in the South. He maintains that there is an equally important psychological dimension to living in a society in which there are rights. In such a society everyone can count on receiving and enjoying objects of value. Wasserstrom wants to establish that human rights are the "strongest of all moral claims." Following Gregory Vlastos, he endorses the principle that no persons should be treated differently from any other persons unless there is some relevant reason that justifies this difference in treatment. He disagrees with Vlastos's view of the connection between a person's well-being and the preconditions of a person's well-being. Wasserstrom wants to defend the plausibility of ascribing equal intrinsic value to each person's well-being and freedom.

He admits that it may not be possible to show that all people are capable of enjoying any of the same goods; nonetheless it is much less difficult to establish that the denial of opportunity to enjoy these goods makes it impossible to live a full satisfying life as a human. Wasserstrom criticizes strategies that aim to show the relevance of racial differences that would justify a denial of equal treatment based on race. He explains the logic used to justify racial discrimination by reference to the white Southerner's moral universe. This universe affords racist whites a *way of conceiving* and is the source of the denial of human rights, as well as the "opportunity to assert claims as a matter of right." Wasserstrom concludes that a society that simply lacks any conception of human rights is less offensive than one that has this conception but denies human rights to some persons. The inconsistency of the American creed of equal rights and the existence of legally sanctioned racial discrimination produced a tension in American society that the civil rights movement sought to resolve.

Wasserstrom speaks of a second-order right to demand basic human rights. This very notion has been a cornerstone of black social movements. The role of organized black labor in mass action to express dissent regarding the injustice of racial discrimination is represented in A. Philip Randolph's call for a march on Washington in June 1940. It is worth noting that at the march on Washington 25 years later Randolph introduced Martin Luther King, Jr. to the mass of demonstrators at that historic event. The success of Gandhi in India influenced Randolph, like King, to consider mass action as a strategy of protest. He refers to the independence movement in India led by Gandhi as a model for the effectiveness of mass action. In addition to expressing the will of the masses of African-Americans, the purpose of the march was to publicize the cause of racial justice to the world and to influence public opinion in America.

In his famous "Letter from Birmingham City Jail" Martin Luther King, Jr. articulates his vision of the goals and strategy of the civil rights movement. He points out that the recent demonstrations in Birmingham were a last resort taken only after the African-American community was left with no other alternative. All four steps of the practice of nonviolence had been followed in this case: collection of facts, negotiation, self-purification, and direct action. The role of conscience is highlighted by means of an analogy with Socrates. He speaks of the protester as "nonviolent gadflies" who create the tensions necessary for social change. The end result of direct action is to open the door to negotiation and dialogue. King points out that this claim regarding direct action presupposes that "freedom is never voluntarily given by the oppressor, it must be demanded by the oppressed."

The direct action King advocates seems inconsistent with the movement's basic commitment to the rule of law—especially with regard to the *Brown* decision. King addresses this charge of inconsistency by interpreting it as a challenge to explain the difference between just and unjust laws. He appeals to Aquinas's natural law theory, according to which any law that degrades humans is unjust. To indicate what makes them unjust, King cites the harm caused by segregation laws. He rejects the criticism that the protesters are moving too fast. Comparing the struggle for civil rights in America with liberation movements in Africa, Asia, South America, and the Caribbean, he asserts that African-Americans are moving "with a sense of cosmic urgency toward the promised land of racial justice."

King maintains that the discontent expressed by black America is a healthy sign of social change that he wants to channel into nonviolent direct action.

In his address to the Clergy and Laymen Concerned about Vietnam at the Riverside Church on April 4, 1967, King expresses his agreement with their motto: "A time comes when silence is betrayal." He immediately confronts the claim made by his detractors that peace and civil rights do not mix. This question is not one of foreign policy in Vietnam, but rather whether his speaking out against the Vietnam war will hurt the progress made by the civil rights movement. There are several considerations King brings to bear on the relationship between the war and his role as a civil rights leader. The economic cost of the war drains the public resources available to deal with poverty at home. There is also a great cost in human lives on all sides. King cites, as the ultimate irony, the fact that young black men are sent thousands of miles away to guarantee liberties in Southeast Asia that they are denied in America. "So we watch them [black and white boys] in brutal solidarity burning the huts of a poor village, but we realize that they would never live on the same block in Detroit. I could not be silent in the face of such cruel manipulation of the poor." His bold call for an end to the bombing and a date for troop withdrawal was made in recognition of the fact that the soldiers had been placed in a hopeless situation. In addition to the brutalizing process of war is the cynicism of knowing they are not fighting for any of the things the American policymakers claim.

In his discussion of the press reaction to King's Riverside Church address, Bayard Rustin notes that almost all of the criticism was concerned with questioning King's right to speak on American policy rather than with providing an evaluation of his proposals. Pointing to the fact that twice as many black soldiers proportionately are involved in Vietnam, Rustin maintains that King and all other black leaders have a duty to address foreign policy. Moreover, as King states in his address, his status as winner of a Nobel Peace Prize imposes a special duty to speak out. Although Rustin defends King's right to speak out on issues of peace, he argues that this dissent should not be organized within the civil rights movement. His reason for siding with those who criticized King for mixing the peace and civil rights movements is that it would be suicidal for the latter. He had in mind the widely held belief that the goals of the civil rights struggle would be compromised by opposing President Johnson's foreign policy. As a civil rights leader, King was faced with the dilemma of remaining silent on the Vietnam war to preserve executive and legislative support for domestic programs to end poverty and racial discrimination, or speaking out against the war and risk losing this support.

Rights, Human Rights, and Racial Discrimination

Richard Wasserstrom

The subject of natural, or human, rights is one that has recently come to enjoy a new-found intellectual and philosophical respectability. This has come about in part, I think, because of a change in philosophical mood—in philosophical attitudes and opinions toward topics in moral and political theory. And this change in mood has been reflected in a renewed interest in the whole subject of rights and duties. In addition, though, this renaissance has been influenced, I believe, by certain events of recent history—notably the horrors of Nazi Germany and the increasingly obvious injustices of racial discrimination in both the United States and Africa. For in each case one of the things that was or is involved is a denial of certain human rights.

This concern over the subject of natural rights, whatever the causes may be, is, however, in the nature of a reinstatement. Certainly there was, just a relatively few years ago, fairly general agreement that the doctrine of natural rights had been thoroughly and irretrievably discredited. Indeed, this was sometimes looked upon as the paradigm case of the manner in which a moral and political doctrine could be both rhetorically influential and intellectually inadequate and unacceptable. A number of objections, each deemed absolutely dispositive, had been put forward: the vagueness of almost every formulation of a set of natural rights, the failure of persons to agree upon what one's natural rights are, the case with which almost everyone would ac-

knowledge the desirability of overriding or disregarding any proffered natural rights in any one of a variety of readily familiar circumstances, the lack of any ground or argument for any doctrine of natural rights.

Typical is the following statement from J. B. Mabbott's little book, *The State and the Citizen*:[1]

> [T]he niceties of the theory [of natural rights] need not detain us if we can attack it at its roots, and there it is most clearly vulnerable. Natural rights must be self-evident and they must be absolute if they are to be rights at all. For if a right is derivative from a more fundamental right, then it is not natural in the sense intended; and if a right is to be explained or defended by reference to the good of the community or of the individual concerned, then these "goods" are the ultimate values in the case, and their pursuit may obviously infringe or destroy the "rights" in question. Now the only way in which to demonstrate the absurdity of a theory which claims self-evidence for every article of its creed is to make a list of the articles....
>
> Not only are the lists indeterminate and capricious in extent, they are also confused in content.... [T]here is no single "natural right" which is, in fact, regarded even by its own supporters as sacrosanct. Every one of them is constantly invaded in the public interest with universal approval (57–58).

Mabbott's approach to the problem is instructive both as an example of the ease with which the subject has been taken up and dismissed, and more importantly, as a reminder of the fact that the theory of natural rights has not been a single coherent doctrine. Instead,

Source: Richard Wasserstrom, "Rights, Human Rights and Racial Discrimination." Presented in a symposium on "Human Rights" at the sixty-first annual meeting of the American Philosophical Association, Eastern Division, December 27, 1964. Used with the permission of *The Journal of Philosophy* and the author.

[1] London: Arrow, 1958.

it has served, and doubtless may still serve; as a quite indiscriminate collection of a number of logically independent propositions. It is, therefore, at least as necessary here as in many other situations that we achieve considerable precision in defining and describing the specific subject of inquiry.

This paper is an attempt to delineate schematically the form of one set of arguments for natural, or human rights.[2] I do this in the following fashion. First, I consider several important and distinctive features and functions of rights in general. Next, I describe and define certain characteristics of human rights and certain specific functions and attributes that they have. Then, I delineate and evaluate one kind of argument for human rights, as so described and defined. And finally, I analyze one particular case of a denial of human rights—that produced by the system of racial discrimination as it exists in the South today.

I

If there are any such things as human rights, they have certain important characteristics and functions just because rights themselves are valuable and distinctive moral "commodities." This is, I think, a point that is all too often overlooked whenever the concept of a right is treated as a largely uninteresting, derivative notion—one that can be taken into account in wholly satisfactory fashion through an explication of the concepts of duty and obligation.[3]

Now, it is not my intention to argue that there can be rights for which there are no correlative duties, nor that there can be duties

for which there are no correlative rights—although I think that there are, e.g., the duty to be kind to animals or the duty to be charitable. Instead, what I want to show is that there are important differences between rights and duties, and, in particular, that rights fulfill certain functions that neither duties (even correlative duties) nor any other moral or legal concepts can fulfill.

Perhaps the most obvious thing to be said about rights is that they are constitutive of the domain of entitlements. They help to define and serve to protect those things concerning which one can make a very special kind of claim—a claim of right. To claim or to acquire anything as a matter of right is crucially different from seeking or obtaining it as through the grant of a privilege, the receipt of a favor, or the presence of a permission. To have a right to something is, typically, to be entitled to receive or possess or enjoy it now,[4] and to do so without securing the consent of another. As long as one has a right to anything, it is beyond the reach of another properly to withhold or deny it. In addition, to have a right is to be absolved from the obligation to weigh a variety of what would in other contexts be relevant considerations; it is to be entitled to the object of the right—at least *prima facie*—without any more ado. To have a right to anything is, in short, to have a very strong moral or legal claim upon it. It is the strongest kind of claim that there is.

Because this is so, it is apparent, as well, that the things to which one is entitled as a matter of right are not usually trivial or insignificant. The objects of rights are things that matter.

Another way to make what are perhaps some of the same points is to observe that rights provide special kinds of grounds or reasons for making moral judgments of at least two kinds. First, if a person has a right to something, he can properly cite that right as the *justification* for having acted in accordance with or in the exercise of that right. If a per-

[2] Because the phrase "natural rights" is so encrusted with certain special meanings, I shall often use the more neutral phrase "human rights." For my purposes there are no differences in meaning between the two expressions.

[3] See, for example, S. I. Benn and R. S. Peters, *Social Principles and the Democratic State*, p. 89: "Right and duty are different names for the same normative relation, according to the point of view from which it is regarded."

[4] There are some rights as to which the possession of the object of the right can be claimed only at a future time, e.g., the right (founded upon a promise) to be repaid next week.

son has acted so as to exercise his right, he has, without more ado, acted rightly—at least *prima facie.* To exercise one's right is to act in a way that gives appreciable assurance of immunity from criticism. Such immunity is far less assured when one leaves the areas of rights and goes, say, to the realm of the permitted or the nonprohibited.

And second, just as exercising or standing upon one's rights by itself needs no defense, so invading or interfering with or denying another's rights is by itself appropriate ground for serious censure and rebuke. Here there is a difference in emphasis and import between the breach or neglect of a duty and the invasion of or interference with a right. For to focus upon duties and their breaches is to concentrate necessarily upon the person who has the duty; it is to invoke criteria by which to make moral assessments of his conduct. Rights, on the other hand, call attention to the injury inflicted; to the fact that the possessor of the right was adversely affected by the action. Furthermore, the invasion of a right constitutes, as such, a special and independent injury, whereas this is not the case with less stringent claims.

Finally, just because rights are those moral commodities which delineate the areas of entitlement, they have an additional important function: that of defining the respects in which one can reasonably entertain certain kinds of expectations. To live in a society in which there are rights and in which rights are generally respected is to live in a society in which the social environment has been made appreciably more predictable and secure. It is to be able to count on receiving and enjoying objects of value. Rights have, therefore, an obvious psychological, as well as moral, dimension and significance.

II

If the above are some of the characteristics and characteristic functions of rights in general, what then can we say about human rights? More specifically, what is it for a right to be a human right, and what special role might human rights play?

Probably the simplest thing that might be said of a human right is that it is a right possessed by human beings. To talk about human rights would be to distinguish those rights which humans have from those which nonhuman entities, e.g., animals or corporations, might have.

It is certain that this is not what is generally meant by human rights. Rather than constituting the genus of all particular rights that humans have, human rights have almost always been deemed to be one species of these rights. If nothing else about the subject is clear, it is evident that one's particular legal rights, as well as some of one's moral rights, are not among one's human rights. If any right is a *human* right, it must, I believe, have at least four very general characteristics. First, it must be possessed by all human beings, as well as only by human beings. Second, because it is the same right that all human beings possess, it must be possessed equally by all human beings. Third, because human rights are possessed by all human beings, we can rule out as possible candidates any of those rights which one might have in virtue of occupying any particular status or relationship, such as that of parent, president, or promisee. And fourth, if there are any human rights, they have the additional characteristic of being assertable, in a manner of speaking, "against the whole world." That is to say, because they are rights that are not possessed in virtue of any contingent status or relationship, they are rights that can be claimed equally against any and every other human being.

Furthermore, to repeat, if there are any human *rights,* they also have certain characteristics as rights. Thus, if there are any human rights, these constitute the strongest of all moral claims that all men can assert. They serve to define and protect those things which all men are entitled to have and enjoy. They indicate those objects toward which and those areas within which every human being is entitled to act without securing further permission or assent. They function so as to put certain matters beyond the power of anyone else to grant or to deny. They provide every human being with a ready justification for acting in certain ways, and they provide each person with ready grounds upon which to condemn any interference or invasion. And they operate, as well, to induce well-founded confidence that the values or objects protected by them will be readily and predictably obtainable. If there are any human rights, they are powerful moral commodities.

Finally, it is, perhaps, desirable to observe that there are certain characteristics I have not ascribed to these rights. In particular, I have not said that human rights need have either of two features: absoluteness and self-evidence, which Mabbott found to be most suspect. I have not said that human rights are absolute in the sense that there are no conditions under which they can properly be overridden, although I have asserted—what is quite different—that they are absolute in the sense that they are possessed equally without any special, additional qualification by all human beings.[5]

Neither have I said (nor do I want to assert) that human rights are self-evident in any sense. Indeed, I want explicitly to deny that a special manner of knowing or a specific epistemology is needed for the development of a theory of human rights. I want to assert that there is much that can be said in defense or support of the claim that a particular right is a human right. And I want to insist, as well, that to adduce reasons for human rights is consistent with their character as human, or natural, rights. Nothing that I have said about human rights entails a contrary conclusion.

III

To ask whether there are any human, or natural rights is to pose a potentially misleading question. Rights of any kind, and particularly natural rights, are not like chairs or trees. One cannot simply look and see whether they are there. There are, though, at least two senses in which rights of all kinds can be said to exist. There is first the sense in which we can ask and answer the empirical question of whether in a given society there is intellectual or conceptual acknowledgment of the fact that persons or other entities have rights at all. We can ask, that is, whether the persons in that society "have" the concept of a right (or a human right), and whether they regard that concept as meaningfully applicable to persons or other entities in that society. And there is, secondly, the sense in which we can ask the question, to what extent, in a society that acknowledges the existence of rights, is there general respect for, protection of, or noninterference with the exercise of those rights.[6]

These are not, though, the only two questions that can be asked. For we can also seek to establish whether any rights, and particularly human rights, ought to be both acknowledged and respected. I want now to begin to do this by considering the way in which an argument for human rights might be developed.

It is evident, I think, that almost any argument for the acknowledgment of any rights as human rights starts with the factual assertion that there are certain respects in which all persons are alike or equal. The argument moves typically from that assertion to the conclusion that there are certain human rights. What often remains unclear, however, is the precise way in which the truth of any proposition about the respects in which persons are alike advances an argument for the acknowledgment of human rights. And what must be supplied, therefore, are the plausible intermediate premises that connect the initial premise with the conclusion.

---

[5] For the purposes of this paper and the points I wish here to make, I am not concerned with whether human rights are *prima facie* or absolute. I do not think that anything I say depends significantly upon this distinction. Without analyzing the notion, I will assume, though, that they are *prima facie* rights in the sense that there may be cases in which overriding a human right would be less undesirable than protecting it.

[6] This is an important distinction. Incontinence in respect to rights is a fairly common occurrence. In the South, for example, many persons might acknowledge that Negroes have certain rights while at the same time neglecting or refusing (out of timidity, cowardice, or general self-interest) to do what is necessary to permit these rights to be exercised.

One of the most careful and complete illustrations of an argument that does indicate some of these intermediate steps is that provided by Gregory Vlastos in an article entitled, "Justice and Equality."[7] Our morality, he says, puts an equal intrinsic value on each person's well-being and freedom. In detail, the argument goes like this:

There is, Vlastos asserts, a wide variety of cases in which all persons are capable of experiencing the same values.

> Thus, to take a perfectly clear case, no matter how A and B might differ in taste and style of life, they would both crave relief from acute physical pain. In that case we would put the same value on giving this to either of them, regardless of the fact that A might be a talented, brilliantly successful person, B "a mere nobody".... [I]n all cases where human beings are capable of enjoying the same goods, we feel that the intrinsic value of their enjoyment is the same. In just this sense we hold that (1) one man's well-being is as valuable as any other's.... [Similarly] we feel that choosing for oneself what one will do, believe, approve, say, read, worship, has its own intrinsic value, the same for all persons, and quite independently of the value of the things they happen to choose. Naturally we hope that all of them will make the best possible use of their freedom of choice. But we value their exercise of the freedom, regardless of the outcome; and we value it equally for all. For us (2) one man's freedom is as valuable as any other's.... [Thus], since we do believe in equal value as to human well-being and freedom, we should also believe in the prima facie equality of men's right to well-being and to freedom (51–52).

As it is stated, I am not certain that this argument answers certain kinds of attack. In particular, there are three questions that merit further attention. First, why should anyone have a right to the enjoyment of any goods at all, and, more specifically, well-being and freedom? Second, for what reasons might we be warranted in believing that the intrinsic

value of the enjoyment of such goods is the same for all persons? And third, even if someone ought to have a right to well-being and freedom and even if the intrinsic value of each person's enjoyment of these things is equal, why should all men have the equal right—and hence the human right—to secure, obtain, or enjoy these goods?

I think that the third question is the simplest of the three to answer. If anyone has a right to well-being and freedom and if the intrinsic value of any person's enjoyment of these goods is equal to that of any other's, then all men do have an equal right—and hence a human right—to secure, obtain, or enjoy these goods, just because it would be irrational to distinguish among persons as to the possession of these rights. That is to say, the principle that no person should be treated differently from any or all other persons unless there is some general and relevant reason that justifies this difference in treatment is a fundamental principle of morality, if not of rationality itself. Indeed, although I am not certain how one might argue for this, I think it could well be said that all men do have a "second-order" human right—that is, an absolute right—to expect all persons to adhere to this principle.

This principle, or this right, does not by itself establish that there are any specific human rights. But either the principle or the right does seem to establish that well-being and freedom are human rights if they are rights at all and if the intrinsic value of each person's enjoyment is the same. For, given these premises, it does appear to follow that there is no relevant and general reason to differentiate among persons as to the possession of this right.

I say "seem to" and "appear to" because this general principle of morality may not be strong enough. What has been said so far does not in any obvious fashion rule out the possibility that there is some general and relevant principle of differentiation. It only, apparently, rules out possible variations in intrinsic value as a reason for making differentiations.

The requirement of *relevance* does, I think, seem to make the argument secure.

---

[7] In Richard B. Brandt, ed., *Social Justice* (Englewood Cliffs, N.J.: Prentice Hall, 1962), pp. 31–72.

For, if *the reason* for acknowledging in a person a right to freedom and well-being is the intrinsic value of his enjoyment of these goods, then the nature of the intrinsic value of any other person's enjoyment is the only relevant reason for making exceptions or for differentiating among persons as to the possession of these rights.[8]

As to the first question, that of whether a person has a right to well-being and freedom, I am not certain what kind of answer is most satisfactory. If Vlastos is correct in asserting that these enjoyments are *values*, then that is, perhaps, answer enough. That is to say, if enjoying well-being is something *valuable*—and especially if it is intrinsically valuable—then it seems to follow that this is the kind of thing to which one ought to have a right. For if anything ought to be given the kind of protection afforded by a right, it ought surely be that which is valuable. Perhaps, too, there is nothing more that need be said other than to point out that we simply do properly value well-being and freedom.

I think that another, more general answer is also possible. Here I would revert more specifically to my earlier discussion of some of the characteristics and functions of rights. There are two points to be made. First, if we are asked, why ought anyone have a right to anything? or why not have a system in which there are not rights at all? the answer is that such a system would be a morally impoverished one. It would prevent persons from asserting those kinds of claims, it would preclude persons from having those types of expectations, and it would prohibit persons from making those kinds of judgments which a system of rights makes possible.

---

[8] See, e.g., Bernard Williams, "The Idea of Equality," in P. Laslett and W. G. Runciman, eds., *Philosophy, Politics and Society*, II (Oxford: Basil Blackwell, 1962), pp. 111–113.

Professor Vlastos imposes a somewhat different requirement which, I think, comes to about the same thing: "An equalitarian concept of justice may admit just inequalities without inconsistency if, and only if, it provides grounds for equal human rights *which are also grounds for unequal rights of other sorts*" (Vlastos, *op. cit.*, p. 40; italics in text).

Thus, if we can answer the question of why have rights at all, we can then ask and answer the question of what things—among others—ought to be protected by *rights*. And the answer, I take it, is that one ought to be able to claim as entitlements those minimal things without which it is impossible to develop one's capabilities and to live a life as a human being. Hence, to take one thing that is a precondition of well-being, the relief from acute physical pain, this is the kind of enjoyment that ought to be protected as a right of some kind just because without such relief there is precious little that one can effectively do or become. And similarly for the opportunity to make choices, examine beliefs, and the like.

To recapitulate. The discussion so far has indicated two things: (1) the conditions under which any specific right would be a human right, and (2) some possible grounds for arguing that certain values or enjoyments ought to be regarded as matters of right. The final question that remains is whether there are any specific rights that satisfy the conditions necessary to make them human rights. Or, more specifically, whether it is plausible to believe that there are no general and relevant principles that justify making distinctions among persons in respect to their rights to well-being and freedom.

Vlastos has it that the rights to well-being and freedom do satisfy these conditions, since he asserts that we, at least, do regard each person's well-being and freedom as having equal intrinsic value. If this is correct, if each person's well-being and freedom do have *equal* intrinsic value, then there is no general and relevant principle for differentiating among persons as to these values and, hence, as to their rights to secure these values. But this does not seem wholly satisfactory. It does not give us any reason for supposing that it is plausible to ascribe equal intrinsic value to each person's well-being and freedom.

The crucial question, then, is the plausibility of ascribing equal intrinsic value to each person's well-being and freedom. There are, I think, at least three different answers that might be given.

First, it might be asserted that this ascription simply constitutes another feature of our morality. The only things that can be done are to point out that this is an assumption that we do make and to ask persons whether they would not prefer to live in a society in which such an assumption is made.

While perhaps correct and persuasive, this does not seem to me to be all that can be done. In particular, there are, I think, two further arguments that may be made.

The first is that there are cases in which all human beings *equally* are capable of enjoying the same goods, e.g., relief from acute physical pain,[9] or that they are capable of deriving equal enjoyment from the same goods. If this is true, then if anyone has a right to this enjoyment, that right is a human right just because there is no rational ground for preferring one man's enjoyment to another's. For, if all persons do have equal capacities of these sorts and if the existence of these capacities is the reason for ascribing these rights to anyone, then all persons ought to have the right to claim equality of treatment in respect to the possession and exercise of these rights.

The difficulty inherent in this argument is at the same time the strength of the next one. The difficulty is simply that it does seem extraordinarily difficult to know how one would show that all men are equally capable of enjoying any of the same goods, or even how one might attempt to gather or evaluate relevant evidence in this matter. In a real sense, interpersonal comparisons of such a thing as the ability to bear pain seem to be logically as well as empirically unobtainable. Even more unobtainable, no doubt, is a measure of the comparative enjoyments derivable from choosing for oneself.[10] These are simply

---

[9] See Williams, *op. cit.*, p. 112: "These respects [in which men are alike] are notably the capacity to feel pain, both from immediate physical causes and from various situations represented in perception and in thought; and the capacity to feel affection for others, and the consequences of this, connected with the frustration of this affection, loss of its objects, etc."

[10] At times, Vlastos seems to adopt this view as well as the preceding one. See, e.g., Vlastos, *op. cit.*, p. 49: "So understood a person's well-being and freedom are aspects of his individual existence as unique and unrepeatable as is that existence itself...."

enjoyments the comparative worths of which, as possessed by different persons, there is no way to assess. If this is so, then this fact gives rise to an alternative argument.

We do know, through inspection of human history as well as of our own lives, that the denial of the opportunity to experience the enjoyment of these goods makes it impossible to live either a full or a satisfying life. In a real sense, the enjoyment of these goods differentiates human from nonhuman entities. And therefore, even if we have no meaningful or reliable criteria for comparing and weighing capabilities for enjoyment or for measuring their quantity or quality, we probably know all we need to know to justify our refusal to attempt to grade the value of the enjoyment of these goods. Hence, the dual grounds for treating their intrinsic values as equal for all persons: either these values are equal for all persons, or, if there are differences, they are not in principle discoverable or measurable. Hence, the argument, or an argument, for the human rights to well-being and freedom.

Because the foregoing discussion has been quite general and abstract, I want finally to consider briefly one illustration of a denial of human rights and to delineate both the several ways in which such a denial can occur and some of the different consequences of that denial. My example is that of the way in which Negro persons are regarded and treated by many whites in the South.

The first thing that is obvious is that many white Southerners would or might be willing to accept all that has been said so far and yet seek to justify their attitudes and behavior toward Negroes.

They might agree, for example, that all persons do have a right to be accorded equal treatment unless there is a general and relevant principle of differentiation. They would also surely acknowledge that some persons do have rights to many different things, including most certainly well-being and freedom. But they would insist, nonetheless, that there exists a general and relevant principle of differentiation, namely, that some persons are Negroes and others are not.

Now, those who do bother to concern themselves with arguments and with the need to give reasons would not, typically, assert that the mere fact of color difference does constitute a general and relevant reason. Rather, they would argue that this color difference is correlated with certain other characteristics and attitudes that are relevant.[11] In so doing, they invariably commit certain logical and moral mistakes.

First, the purported differentiating characteristic is usually not relevant to the differentiation sought to be made; e.g., none of the characteristics that supposedly differentiate Negroes from whites has any relevance to the capacity to bear acute physical pain or to the strength of the desire to be free from it. Indeed, almost all arguments neglect the fact that the capacities to enjoy those things which are constitutive of well-being and freedom are either incommensurable among persons or alike in all persons.

Second, the invocation of these differentiating characteristics always violates the requirement of relevance in another sense. For, given the typical definition of a Negro (in Alabama the legal definition is any person with "a drop of Negro blood"), it is apparent that there could not—under any plausible scientific theory—be good grounds for making any differentiations between Negroes and whites.[12]

Third, and related to the above, any argument that makes distinctions as to the possession of human rights in virtue of the truth of certain empirical generalizations invariably produces some unjust denials of those rights. That is to say, even if some of the generalizations about Negroes are correct, they are correct only in the sense that the distinguishing characteristics ascribed to Negroes are possessed by some or many Negroes but not by all Negroes. Yet, before any reason for differentiating among persons as to the possession of human rights can be a relevant reason, that reason must be relevant in respect to *each person* so affected or distinguished. To argue otherwise is to neglect the fact, among other

things, that human rights are personal and of at least *prima facie* equal importance to each possessor of those rights.

A different reaction or argument of white Southerners in respect to recent events in the South is bewilderment. Rather than (or in addition to) arguing for the existence of principles of differentiation, the white Southerner will say that he simply cannot understand the Negro's dissatisfaction with his lot. This is so because he, the white Southerner, has always treated his Negroes very well. With appreciable sincerity, he will assert that he has real affection for many Negroes. He would never needlessly inflict pain or suffering upon them. Indeed, he has often assumed special obligations to make certain that their lives were free from hunger, pain, and disease.

Now of course, this description of the facts is seldom accurate at all. Negroes have almost always been made to endure needless and extremely severe suffering in all too many obvious ways for all too many obviously wrong reasons. But I want to assume for my purposes the accuracy of the white Southerner's assertions. For these assertions are instructive just because they reveal some of the less obvious effects of a denial of human rights.

What is wholly missing from this description of the situation is the ability and inclination to conceptualize the Negro—any Negro—as the possible possessor of rights of any kind, and *a fortiori* of any human rights. And this has certain especially obnoxious consequences.

In the first place, the white Southerner's moral universe illustrates both the fact that it is possible to conceive of duties without conceiving of their correlative rights and the fact that the mistakes thereby committed are not chiefly mistakes of logic and definition. The mistakes matter morally. For what this way of conceiving most denies to any Negro is the opportunity to assert claims as a matter of right. It denies him the standing to protest against the way he is treated. If the white Southerner fails to do his duty, that is simply a matter between him and his conscience.

In the second place, it requires of any Negro that *he* make out his case for the enjoyment of any goods. It reduces all of *his* claims

---

[11] See Williams, *op. cit.*, p. 113.

[12] This is to say nothing, of course, of the speciousness of any principle of differentiation that builds upon inequalities that are themselves produced by the unequal and unjust distribution of *opportunities*.

to the level of requests, privileges, and favors. But there are simply certain things, certain goods, that nobody ought to have to request of another. There are certain things that no one else ought to have the power to decide to refuse or to grant. To observe what happens to any person who is required to adopt habits of obsequious, deferential behavior in order to minimize the likelihood of physical abuse, arbitrary treatment, or economic destitution is to see most graphically how important human rights are and what their denial can mean. To witness what happens to a person's own attitudes, aspirations, and conceptions of himself[13] when he must request or petition for the opportunity to voice an opinion, to consult with a public official, or to secure the protection of the law is to be given dramatic and convincing assurance of the moral necessity of a conception of human rights.

And there is one final point. In a real sense, a society that simply lacks any conception of human rights is less offensive than one which has such a conception but denies that some persons have these rights. This is so not just because of the inequality and unfairness involved in differentiating for the wrong reasons among persons. Rather, a society based on such denial is especially offensive because it implicitly, if not explicitly, entails that there are some persons who do not and would not desire or need or enjoy those minimal goods which all men do need and desire and enjoy. It is to read certain persons, all of whom are most certainly human beings, out of the human race. This is surely among the greatest of all moral wrongs.

I know of no better example of the magnitude of this evil than that provided by a lengthy account in a Southern newspaper about the high school band program in a certain city. The article described fully the magnificence of the program and emphasized especially the fact that it was a program in which *all high school students* in the city participated.

Negro children neither were nor could be participants in the program. The article, however, saw no need to point this out. I submit that it neglected to do so not because everyone knew the fact, but because in a real sense the writer and the newspaper do not regard Negro high school students as children—persons, human beings—at all.

What is the Negro parent who reads this article to say to his children? What are his children supposed to think? How does a Negro parent even begin to demonstrate to the world that his children are really children, too? These are burdens no civilized society ought ever to impose. These are among the burdens that an established and acknowledged system of human rights helps to eliminate.

---

[13] Vlastos puts what I take to be the same point this way: "Any practice which tends to so weaken and confuse the personal esteem of a group of persons—slavery, serfdom or, in our own time racial segregation—may be morally condemned on this one ground, even if there were no other for indicting it" (Vlastos, *op. cit.*, p. 71).

A Call for Mass Action

A. Philip Randolph

Fellow Marchers and delegates to the Policy Conference of the March on Washington Movement and friends: We have met at an hour when the sinister shadows of war are lengthening and becoming more threatening. As one of the sections of the oppressed darker races, and representing a part of the exploited millions of the workers of the world, we are deeply concerned that the totalitarian legions of Hitler, Hirohito and Mussolini do not batter the last bastions of democracy. We know that our fate is tied up with the fate of the democratic way of life. And so, out of the depth of our hearts, a cry goes up for the triumph of the United Nations. But we would not be honest with ourselves were we to stop with a call for a victory of arms alone. We know this is not enough. We fight that the democratic faiths, values, heritages and ideals may prevail.

Unless this war sounds the death knell to the old Anglo-American empire systems, the hapless story of which is one of exploitation for the profit and power of a monopoly-capitalist economy, it will have been fought in vain. Our aim, then, must not only be to defeat Nazism, fascism and militarism on the battlefield but to win the peace, for democracy, for freedom and the Brotherhood of Man without regard to his pigmentation, land of his birth or the God of his fathers.

We therefore sharply score the Atlantic Charter* as expressing a vile and hateful racism and a manifestation of the tragic and utter collapse of an old, decadent democratic political liberalism which worshiped at the shrine of a world-conquering monopoly capitalism. This system grew fat and waxed powerful off the flesh, blood, sweat and tears of the tireless toilers of the human race and the sons and daughters of color in the under-developed lands of the world.

When this war ends, the people want something more than the dispersal of equality and power among individual citizens in a liberal, political, democratic system. They demand with striking comparability the dispersal of equality and power among the citizen-workers in an economic democracy that will make certain the assurance of the good life—the more abundant life—in a warless world.

But, withal this condition of freedom, equality and democracy is not the gift of the Gods. It is the task of men—yes, men—brave men, honest men, determined men....

Thus our feet are set in the path toward equality—economic, political and social and racial. Equality is the heart and essence of democracy, freedom and justice. Without equality of opportunity in industry, in labor unions, schools and colleges, government, politics and before the law, without equality in social relations and in all phases of human endeavor, the Negro is certain to be consigned to an inferior status. There must be no dual standards of justice, no dual rights, privileges, duties or responsibilities of citizenship. No dual forms of freedom....

Source: A. Philip Randolph, "A Call for Mass Action" from March on Washington Movement: Proceedings of Policy Conference held in Detroit, 26–27 September, 1942, (pp. 4–11) copy in Schomburg Library, New York City.

*In the Atlantic Charter of 1941, Franklin D. Roosevelt and Winston Churchill endorsed the goals in the war against the fascist Axis powers. Among the principles enunciated were: no territorial aggrandizement; no changes of territory against the wishes of the people concerned; and self-government for all peoples. Nothing, however, was said about the African or Asian colonies held by the Allied Powers.

But our nearer goals include the abolition of discrimination, segregation and Jim Crow in the government, the Army, Navy, Air Corps, U. S. Marine, Coast Guard, Women's Auxiliary Army Corps and the Waves, and defense industries; the elimination of discrimination in hotels, restaurants, on public transportation conveyances, in educational, recreational, cultural, and amusement and entertainment places such as theaters, beaches and so forth.

We want the full works of citizenship with no reservations. We will accept nothing less.

But goals must be achieved. They are not secured because it is just and right that they be possessed by Negro or white people. Slavery was not abolished because it was bad and unjust. It was abolished because men fought, bled and died on the battlefield.

Therefore, if Negroes secure their goals, immediate and remote, they must win them and to win them they must fight, sacrifice, suffer, go to jail and, if need be, die for them. These rights will not be given. They must be taken.

Democracy was fought for and taken from political royalists—the kings. Industrial democracy, the rights of the workers to organize and designate the representatives of their own choosing to bargain collectively is being won and taken from the economic royalists—big business.

Now, the realization of goals and rights by a nation, race or class requires belief in and loyalty to principles and policies.... Policies rest upon principles. Concretely, a policy sets forth one's position on vital public questions such as political affiliations, religious alliances. The March on Washington Movement must be opposed to partisan political commitments, religious or denominational alliances. We cannot sup with the Communists, for they rule or ruin any movement. This is their policy. Our policy must be to shun them. This does not mean that Negro Communists may not join the March on Washington Movement.

As to the composition of our movement. Our policy is that it be all-Negro, and pro-Negro but not anti-white, or anti-Semitic or antilabor, or anti-Catholic. The reason for this policy is that all oppressed people must assume the responsibility and take the initiative to free themselves. Jews must wage their battle to abolish anti-Semitism. Catholics must wage their battle to abolish anti-Catholicism. The workers must wage their battle to advance and protect their interests and rights.

The essential value of an all-Negro movement such as the March on Washington is that it helps to create faith by Negroes in Negroes. It develops a sense of self-reliance with Negroes depending on Negroes in vital matters. It helps to break down the slave psychology and inferiority complex in Negroes which comes and is nourished with Negroes relying on white people for direction and support. This inevitably happens in mixed organizations that are supposed to be in the interest of the Negro....

Therefore, while the March on Washington Movement is interested in the general problems of every community and will lend its aid to help solve them, it has as its major interest and task the liberation of the Negro people, and this is sound social economy. It is in conformity with the principle of the division of labor. No organization can do everything. Every organization can do something, and each organization is charged with the social responsibility to do that which it can do, is built to do.

I have given quite some time to the discussion of this question of organizational structure and function and composition, because the March on Washington Movement is a mass movement of Negroes which is being built to achieve a definite objective, and is a departure from the usual pattern of Negro efforts and thinking. As a rule, Negroes do not choose to be to themselves in anything, they are only to themselves as a result of compulsive segregation. Negroes are together voluntarily for the same reason the workers join voluntarily into a trade-union. But because workers only join trade-unions, does not mean that the very same workers may not join organizations composed of some nonworkers, such as art museums or churches or fraternal lodges that have varying purposes. This same thing is true of Negroes. Because Negroes only can join the March on Washington Movement, does not indicate that Negroes in the M.O.W.M. may not join an interracial golf club or church or Elks Lodge or debating society or trade-union.

No one would claim that a society of Filipinos is undemocratic because it does not take in Japanese members, or that Catholics are anti-Jewish because the Jesuits won't accept Jews as members or that trade-unions are illiberal because they deny membership to employers. Neither is the March on Washington Movement undemocratic because it confines its members to Negroes. Now this reasoning would not apply to a public school or a Pullman car, because these agencies are public in nature and provide a service which is necessary to all of the people of a community.

Now, the question of policy which I have been discussing involves, for example, the March on Washington Movement's position on the war. We say that the Negro must fight for his democratic rights now, for after the war it may be too late. This is our policy on the Negro and the war. But this policy raises the question of method, programs, strategy and tactics—namely, how is this to be done. It is not sufficient to say that Negroes must fight for their rights now, during the war. Some methods must be devised, program set up, and strategy outlined.

This Policy Conference is designed to do this very thing. The first requirement to executing the policies of the March on Washington Movement is to have something to execute them with. This brings me to the consideration of organization. Organization supplies the power. The formulation of policies and the planning process furnish direction. Now, there is organization and organization. Some people say, for instance, Negroes are already organized, and they cite The Sisters of the Mysterious Ten, The Sons and Daughters of I Will Arise, the Holy Rollers, the social clubs, and so forth. But these organizations are concerned about the individual interest of helping the sick and funeralizing the dead or providing amusement and recreation. They deal with no social or racial problem which

concerns the entire people. The Negro people as a whole is not interested in whether Miss A. plays Contract Bridge on Friday or not, or whether the deacon of the Methodist Church has a 200- or 500-dollar casket when he dies. These are personal questions. But the Negro race is concerned about Negroes being refused jobs in defense plants, or whether a Negro can purchase a lower in a Pullman car, or whether the United States Treasury segregates Negro girls. Thus, while it is true Negroes are highly organized, the organizations are not built to deal with and manipulate the mechanics of power. Nobody cares how many Whist Clubs or churches or secret lodges Negroes establish, because they are not compulsive or coercive. They don't seek to transform the socioeconomic racial milieu. They accept and do not challenge conditions with an action program.

Hence, it is apparent that the Negro needs more than organization. He needs mass organization with an action program, aggressive, bold and challenging in spirit. Such a movement is our March on Washington.

Our first job, then, is actually to organize millions of Negroes and build them into block systems, with captains, so that they may be summoned to action overnight and thrown into physical motion. Without this type of organization, Negroes will never develop mass power, which is the most effective weapon a minority people can wield. Witness the strategy and maneuver of the people of India with mass civil disobedience and noncooperation and the marches to the sea to make salt. It may be said that the Indian people have not won their freedom. This is so, but they will win it. The central principle of the struggle of oppressed minorities like the Negro, labor, Jews, and others is not only to develop mass-demonstration maneuvers, but to repeat and continue them. The workers don't picket firms today and quit. They don't strike today and fold up. They practice the principle of repetition....

We must develop huge demonstrations, because the world is used to big dramatic affairs.... Besides, the unusual attracts. We must develop a series of marches of Negroes at a given time in a hundred or more cities throughout the country, or stage a big march of a hundred thousand Negroes on Washington to put our cause into the mainstream of public opinion and focus the attention of world interests. This is why India is in the news.

Therefore, our program is in part as follows:

1. A national conference for the integration and expression of the collective mind and will of the Negro masses.

2. The mobilization and proclamation of a nationwide series of mass marches on the city halls and city councils to awaken the Negro masses and center public attention upon the grievances and goals of the Negro people and serve as training and discipline of the Negro masses for the more strenuous struggle of a March on Washington, if, as, and when an affirmative decision is made thereon by the Negro masses of the country through our national conference.

3. A march on Washington as an evidence to white America that black America is on the march for its rights and means business.

4. The picketing of the White House following the March on Washington and maintaining the said picket line until the country and the world recognize the Negro has become of age and will sacrifice his all to be counted as men, free men.

This program is drastic and exacting. It will test our best mettle and stamina and courage. Let me warn you that in these times of storm and stress, this program will be opposed. Our Movement, therefore, must be well knit together. It must have moral and spiritual vision, understanding, and wisdom.

How can we achieve this?

Our Movement must be blueprinted. Our forces must be marshaled, with block captains to provide immediate and constant contact. Our block captains must hold periodic meetings for their blocks to develop initiative and the capacity to make decisions and move in relation to direction from the central organization of the division.

Our educational program must be developed around the struggle of the Negro masses.

This can be done by developing mass plans to secure mass registration of the Negro people for the primaries and elections. Through this program the Negro masses can be given a practical and pragmatic view of the mechanics and function of our government and the significance of mass political pressure.

Plans should be mapped by the various divisions to fight for Negro integration in the public utilities as motormen and conductors. During the war women may be placed on these jobs. We must make a drive now to see to it that Negro men and women receive their appropriate consideration in every important field of American industry from which Negroes are now generally barred.

Our day-to-day exercise of our civil rights is a constant challenge. In theaters, hotels, restaurants, amusement places, even in the North, now there is discrimination against Negroes. This is true in every large city. Negroes have the moral obligation to demand the right to enjoy and make use of their civil and political privileges. If we don't, we will lose the will to fight for our citizenship rights, and the public will consider that we don't want them and should not have them. This fight to break down these barriers in every city should be carefully and painstakingly organized. By fighting for these civil rights the Negro masses will be disciplined in struggle. Some of us will be put in jail, and court battles may ensue, but this will give the Negro masses a sense of their importance and value as citizens and as fighters in the Negro liberation movement and the cause for democracy as a whole. It will make white people in high places and the ordinary white man understand that Negroes have rights that they are bound to respect.

The giant public protest meetings must continue. They are educative and give moral strength to our movement and the Negro masses.

For this task we need men and women who will dedicate and consecrate their life, spirit, mind and soul to the great adventure of Negro freedom and justice.

Our divisions must serve as Negro mass parliaments where the entire community may debate the day-to-day issues such as police brutality, high rents, and other questions and make judgments and take action in the interest of the community. These divisions should hold meetings at least twice a month. In them every Negro should be made to feel his importance as a factor in the Negro liberation movement. We must have every Negro realize his leadership ability, the educated and uneducated, the poor and wealthy. In the March on Washington Movement the highest is as low as the lowest and the lowest is as high as the highest. Numbers in mass formation is our key, directed, of course, by the collective intelligence of the people.

Let us put our weight behind the fight to abolish the poll tax. This will give the black and white workers of the South new hope. But the Negro people are not the only oppressed section of mankind. India is now waging a world-shaking, history-making fight for independence. India's fight is the Negro's fight.

Now, let us be unafraid. We are fighting for big stakes. Our stakes are liberty, justice and democracy. Every Negro should hang his head in shame who fails to do his part now for freedom. This is the hour of the Negro. It is the hour of the common man. May we rise to the challenge to struggle for our rights. Come what will or may, let us never falter.

Letter from Birmingham City Jail

Martin Luther King, Jr.

My Dear Fellow Clergymen,

While confined here in the Birmingham city jail, I came across your recent statement calling our present activities "unwise and untimely." Seldom, if ever, do I pause to answer criticism of my work and ideas. If I sought to answer all of the criticisms that cross my desk, my secretaries would be engaged in little else in the course of the day, and I would have no time for constructive work. But since I feel that you are men of genuine good will and your criticisms are sincerely set forth, I would like to answer your statement in what I hope will be patient and reasonable terms.

I think I should give the reason for my being in Birmingham, since you have been influenced by the argument of "outsiders coming in." I have the honor of serving as president of the Southern Christian Leadership Conference, an organization operating in every southern state, with headquarters in Atlanta, Georgia. We have some eighty-five affiliate organizations all across the South—one being the Alabama Christian Movement for Human Rights. Whenever necessary and possible we share staff, educational and financial resources with our affiliates. Several months ago our local affiliate here in Birmingham invited us to be on call to engage in a nonviolent direct-action program if such were deemed necessary. We readily consented and when the hour came we lived up to our promises. So I am here, along with several members of my staff, because we were invited here.

Source: Reprinted by arrangement with the Estate of Martin Luther King Jr., c/o Writers House as agent for the proprietor. Copyright © Martin Luther King, Jr. 1968, copyright renewed 1991 Coretta Scott King.

I am here because I have basic organizational ties here.

Beyond this, I am in Birmingham because injustice is here. Just as the eighth century prophets left their little villages and carried their "thus saith the Lord" far beyond the boundaries of their hometowns; and just as the Apostle Paul left his little village of Tarsus and carried the gospel of Jesus Christ to practically every hamlet and city of the Graeco-Roman world, I too am compelled to carry the gospel of freedom beyond my particular hometown. Like Paul, I must constantly respond to the Macedonian call for aid.

Moreover, I am cognizant of the interrelatedness of all communities and states. I cannot sit idly by in Atlanta and not be concerned about what happens in Birmingham. Injustice anywhere is a threat to justice everywhere. We are caught in an inescapable network of mutuality, tied in a single garment of destiny. Whatever affects one directly affects all indirectly. Never again can we afford to live with the narrow, provincial "outside agitator" idea. Anyone who lives in the United States can never be considered an outsider anywhere in this country.

You deplore the demonstrations that are presently taking place in Birmingham. But I am sorry that your statement did not express a similar concern for the conditions that brought the demonstrations into being. I am sure that each of you would want to go beyond the superficial social analyst who looks merely at effects, and does not grapple with underlying causes. I would not hesitate to say that it is unfortunate that so-called demonstrations are taking place in Birmingham at this time, but I would say in more emphatic terms that it is even more unfortunate that the white power structure of this city left the Negro community with no other alternative.

In any nonviolent campaign there are four basic steps: (1) collection of the facts to determine whether injustices are alive, (2) negotiation, (3) self-purification, and (4) direct action. We have gone through all of these steps in Birmingham. There can be no gainsaying of the fact that racial injustice engulfs this community.

Birmingham is probably the most thoroughly segregated city in the United States. Its ugly record of police brutality is known in every section of this country. Its injust treatment of Negroes in the courts is a notorious reality. There have been more unsolved bombings of Negro homes and churches in Birmingham than any city in this nation. These are the hard, brutal and unbelievable facts. On the basis of these conditions Negro leaders sought to negotiate with the city fathers. But the political leaders consistently refused to engage in good faith negotiation.

Then came the opportunity last September to talk with some of the leaders of the economic community. In these negotiating sessions certain promises were made by the merchants—such as the promise to remove the humiliating racial signs from the stores. On the basis of these promises Rev. Shuttlesworth and the leaders of the Alabama Christian Movement for Human Rights agreed to call a moratorium on any type of demonstrations. As the weeks and months unfolded we realized that we were the victims of a broken promise. The signs remained. Like so many experiences of the past we were confronted with blasted hopes, and the dark shadow of a deep disappointment settled upon us. So we had no alternative except that of preparing for direct action, whereby we would present our very bodies as a means of laying our case before the conscience of the local and national community. We were not unmindful of the difficulties involved. So we decided to go through a process of self-purification. We started having workshops on nonviolence and repeatedly asked ourselves the questions, "Are you able to accept blows without retaliating?" "Are you able to endure the ordeals of jail?" We decided to set our direct action program around the Easter season, realizing that with the exception of Christmas, this was the largest shopping period of the year. Knowing that a strong economic withdrawal program would be the by-product of direct action, we felt that this was the best time to bring pressure on the merchants for the needed changes. Then it occurred to us that the March election was ahead and so we speedily decided to postpone action until after election day. When we discovered that Mr. Connor was in the run-off, we decided again to postpone action so that the demonstrations could not be used to cloud the issues. At this time we agreed to begin our nonviolent witness the day after the run-off.

This reveals that we did not move irresponsibly into direct action. We too wanted to see Mr. Connor defeated; so we went through postponement after postponement to aid in this community need. After this we felt that direct action could be delayed no longer.

You may well ask, "Why direct action? Why sit-ins, marches, etc.? Isn't negotiation a better path?" You are exactly right in your call for negotiation. Indeed, this is the purpose of direct action. Nonviolent direct action seeks to create such a crisis and establish such creative tension that a community that has constantly refused to negotiate is forced to confront the issue. It seeks so to dramatize the issue that it can no longer be ignored. I just referred to the creation of tension as a part of the work of the nonviolent resister. This may sound rather shocking. But I must confess that I am not afraid of the word tension. I have earnestly worked and preached against violent tension, but there is a type of constructive nonviolent tension that is necessary for growth. Just as Socrates felt that it was necessary to create a tension in the mind so that individuals could rise from the bondage of myths and half-truths to the unfettered realm of creative analysis and objective appraisal, we must see the need of having nonviolent gadflies to create the kind of tension in society that will help men to rise from the dark depths of prejudice and racism to the majestic heights of understanding and brotherhood. So the purpose of the direct action is to create a situation so crisis-packed that it will inevitably open the door to negotiation. We, therefore, concur with you in your call for negotiation. Too long has our beloved Southland been bogged down in the tragic attempt to live in monologue rather than dialogue.

One of the basic points in your statement is that our acts are untimely. Some have asked, "Why didn't you give the new administration time to act?" The only answer that I can give to this inquiry is that the new administration must be prodded about as much as the outgoing one before it acts. We will be sadly mistaken if we feel that the election of Mr. Boutwell will bring the millennium to Birmingham. While Mr. Boutwell is much more articulate and gentle than Mr. Connor, they are both segregationists, dedicated to the task of maintaining the status quo. The hope I see in Mr. Boutwell is that he will be reasonable enough to see the futility of massive resistance to desegregation. But he will not see this without pressure from the devotees of civil rights. My friends, I must say to you that we have not made a single gain in civil rights without determined legal and nonviolent pressure. History is the long and tragic story of the fact that privileged groups seldom give up their privileges voluntarily. Individuals may see the moral light and voluntarily give up their unjust posture; but as Reinhold Niebuhr has reminded us, groups are more immoral than individuals.

We know through painful experience that freedom is never voluntarily given by the oppressor; it must be demanded by the oppressed. Frankly, I have never yet engaged in a direct action movement that was "well-timed," according to the timetable of those who have not suffered unduly from the disease of segregation. For years now I have heard the words "Wait!" It rings in the ear of every Negro with a piercing familiarity. This "Wait" has almost always meant "Never." It has been a tranquilizing thalidomide, relieving the emotional stress for a moment, only to give birth to an ill-formed infant of frustration. We must come to see with the distinguished jurist of yesterday that "justice too long delayed is justice denied." We have waited for more than 340 years for our constitu-

tional and God-given rights. The nations of Asia and Africa are moving with jetlike speed toward the goal of political independence, and we still creep at horse and buggy pace toward the gaining of a cup of coffee at a lunch counter. I guess it is easy for those who have never felt the stinging darts of segregation to say, "Wait." But when you have seen vicious mobs lynch your mothers and fathers at will and drown your sisters and brothers at whim; when you have seen hate-filled policemen curse, kick, brutalize and even kill your black brothers and sisters with impunity; when you see the vast majority of your twenty million Negro brothers smothering in an airtight cage of poverty in the midst of an affluent society; when you suddenly find your tongue twisted and your speech stammering as you seek to explain to your six-year-old daughter why she can't go to the public amusement park that has just been advertised on television, and see tears welling up in her little eyes when she is told that Funtown is closed to colored children, and see the depressing clouds of inferiority begin to form in her little mental sky, and see her begin to distort her little personality by unconsciously developing a bitterness toward white people; when you have to concoct an answer for a five-year-old son asking in agonizing pathos: "Daddy, why do white people treat colored people so mean?"; when you take a cross-country drive and find it necessary to sleep night after night in the uncomfortable corners of your automobile because no motel will accept you; when you are humiliated day in and day out by nagging signs reading "white" and "colored"; when your first name becomes "nigger" and your middle name becomes "boy" (however old you are) and your last name becomes "John," and when your wife and mother are never given the respected title "Mrs."; when you are harried by day and haunted by night by the fact that you are a Negro, living constantly at tiptoe stance never quite knowing what to expect next, and plagued with inner fears and outer resentments; when you are forever fighting a degenerating sense of "nobodiness"; then you will understand why we find it difficult to wait. There comes a time when the cup of endurance runs over, and men are no longer willing to be plunged into an abyss of injustice where they experience the blackness of corroding despair. I hope, sirs, you can understand our legitimate and unavoidable impatience.

You express a great deal of anxiety over our willingness to break laws. This is certainly a legitimate concern. Since we so diligently urge people to obey the Supreme Court's decision of 1954 outlawing segregation in the public schools, it is rather strange and paradoxical to find us consciously breaking laws. One may well ask, "How can you advocate breaking some laws and obeying others?" The answer is found in the fact that there are two types of laws: there are *just* and there are *unjust* laws. I would agree with Saint Augustine that "An unjust law is no law at all."

Now what is the difference between the two? How does one determine when a law is just or unjust? A just law is a man-made code that squares with the moral law or the law of God. An unjust law is a code that is out of harmony with the moral law. To put it in the terms of Saint Thomas Aquinas, an unjust law is a human law that is not rooted in eternal and natural law. Any law that uplifts human personality is just. Any law that degrades human personality is unjust. All segregation statutes are unjust because segregation distorts the soul and damages the personality. It gives the segregator a false sense of superiority, and the segregated a false sense of inferiority. To use the words of Martin Buber, the great Jewish philosopher, segregation substitutes an "I-it" relationship for the "I-thou" relationship, and ends up relegating persons to the status of things. So segregation is not only politically, economically and sociologically unsound, but it is morally wrong and sinful. Paul Tillich has said that sin is separation. Isn't segregation an existential expression of man's tragic separation, an expression of his awful estrangement, his terrible sinfulness? So I can urge men to disobey segregation ordinances because they are morally wrong.

Let us turn to a more concrete example of just and unjust laws. An unjust law is a code that a majority inflicts on a minority that is not binding on itself. This is difference made legal. On the other hand a just law is a code that a majority compels a minority to follow that it is willing to follow itself. This is sameness made legal.

Let me give another explanation. An unjust law is a code inflicted upon a minority which that minority had no part in enacting or creating because they did not have the unhampered right to vote. Who can say that the legislature of Alabama which set up the segregation laws was democratically elected? Throughout the state of Alabama all types of conniving methods are used to prevent Negroes from becoming registered voters and there are some counties without a single Negro registered to vote despite the fact that the Negro constitutes a majority of the population. Can any law set up in such a state be considered democratically structured?

These are just a few examples of unjust and just laws. There are some instances when a law is just on its face and unjust in its application. For instance, I was arrested Friday on a charge of parading without a permit. Now there is nothing wrong with an ordinance which requires a permit for a parade, but when the ordinance is used to preserve segregation and to deny citizens the First Amendment privilege of peaceful assembly and peaceful protest, then it becomes unjust.

I hope you can see the distinction I am trying to point out. In no sense do I advocate evading or defying the law as the rabid segregationist would do. This would lead to anarchy. One who breaks an unjust law must do it *openly, lovingly* (not hatefully as the white mothers did in New Orleans when they were seen on television screaming, "nigger, nigger, nigger"), and with a willingness to accept the penalty. I submit that an individual who breaks a law that conscience tells him is unjust, and willingly accepts the penalty by staying in jail to arouse the conscience of the community over its injustice, is in reality expressing the very highest respect for law.

Of course, there is nothing new about this kind of civil disobedience. It was seen sublimely in the refusal of Shadrach, Meshach and Abednego to obey the laws of Nebuchadnezzar because a higher moral law was involved. It was practiced superbly by the early Christians who were willing to face hungry lions and the excruciating pain of chopping blocks, before submitting to certain unjust laws of the Roman Empire. To a degree academic freedom is a reality today because Socrates practiced civil disobedience.

We can never forget that everything Hitler did in Germany was "legal" and everything the Hungarian freedom fighters did in Hungary was "illegal." It was "illegal" to aid and comfort a Jew in Hitler's Germany. But I am sure that if I had lived in Germany during that time I would have aided and comforted my Jewish brothers even though it was illegal. If I lived in a Communist country today where certain principles dear to the Christian faith are suppressed, I believe I would openly advocate disobeying these anti-religious laws. I must make two honest confessions to you, my Christian and Jewish brothers. First, I must confess that over the last few years I have been gravely disappointed with the white moderate. I have almost reached the regrettable conclusion that the Negro's great stumbling block in the stride toward freedom is not the White Citizen's Counciler or the Ku Klux Klanner, but the white moderate who is more devoted to "order" than to justice; who prefers a negative peace which is the absence of tension to a positive peace which is the presence of justice; who constantly says, "I agree with you in the goal you seek, but I can't agree with your methods of direct action"; who paternalistically feels that he can set the timetable for another man's freedom; who lives by the myth of time and who constantly advised the Negro to wait until a "more convenient season." Shallow understanding from people of good will is more frustrating than absolute misunderstanding from people of ill will. Lukewarm acceptance is much more bewildering than outright rejection.

I had hoped that the white moderate would understand that law and order exist for the purpose of establishing justice, and that when they fail to do this they become dangerously structured dams that block the flow of social progress. I had hoped that the white

moderate would understand that the present tension of the South is merely a necessary phase of the transition from an obnoxious negative peace, where the Negro passively accepted his unjust plight, to a substance-filled positive peace, where all men will respect the dignity and worth of human personality. Actually, we who engage in nonviolent direct action are not the creators of tension. We merely bring to the surface the hidden tension that is already alive. We bring it out in the open where it can be seen and dealt with. Like a boil that can never be cured as long as it is covered up but must be opened with all its pus-flowing ugliness to the natural medicines of air and light, injustice must likewise be exposed, with all of the tension its exposing creates, to the light of human conscience and the air of national opinion before it can be cured.

In your statement you asserted that our actions, even though peaceful, must be condemned because they precipitate violence. But can this assertion be logically made? Isn't this like condemning the robbed man because his possession of money precipitated the evil act of robbery? Isn't this like condemning Socrates because his unswerving commitment to truth and his philosophical delvings precipitated the misguided popular mind to make him drink the hemlock? Isn't this like condemning Jesus because His unique God-consciousness and never-ceasing devotion to his will precipitated the evil act of crucifixion? We must come to see, as federal courts have consistently affirmed, that it is immoral to urge an individual to withdraw his efforts to gain his basic constitutional rights because the quest precipitates violence. Society must protect the robbed and punish the robber.

I had also hoped that the white moderate would reject the myth of time. I received a letter this morning from a white brother in Texas which said: "All Christians know that the colored people will receive equal rights eventually, but it is possible that you are in too great of a religious hurry. It has taken Christianity almost two thousand years to accomplish what it has. The teachings of Christ take time to come to earth." All that is said here grows out of a tragic misconception of time. It is the strangely irrational notion that there is something in the very flow of time that will inevitably cure all ills. Actually time is neutral. It can be used either destructively or constructively. I am coming to feel that the people of ill will have used time much more effectively than the people of good will. We will have to repent in this generation not merely for the vitriolic words and actions of the bad people, but for the appalling silence of the good people. We must come to see that human progress never rolls in on wheels of inevitability. It comes through the tireless efforts and persistent work of men willing to be co-workers with God, and without this hard word time itself becomes an ally of the forces of social stagnation. We must use time creatively, and forever realize that the time is always ripe to do right. Now is the time to make real the promise of democracy, and transform our pending national elegy into a creative psalm of brotherhood. Now is the time to lift our national policy from the quicksand of racial injustice to the solid rock of human dignity.

You spoke of our activity in Birmingham as extreme. At first I was rather disappointed that fellow clergymen would see my nonviolent efforts as those of the extremist. I started thinking about the fact that I stand in the middle of two opposing forces in the Negro community. One is a force of complacency made up of Negroes who, as a result of long years of oppression, have been so completely drained of self-respect and a sense of "somebodiness" that they have adjusted to segregation, and, of a few Negroes in the middle class who, because of a degree of academic and economic security, and because at points they profit by segregation, have unconsciously become insensitive to the problems of the masses. The other force is one of bitterness and hatred, and comes perilously close to advocating violence. It is expressed in the various black nationalist groups that are springing up over the nation, the largest and best known being Elijah Muhammad's Muslim movement. This movement is nourished by the contemporary frustration over the continued existence of racial discrimination. It is made up of people who have lost faith in America, who have absolutely repudiated Christianity, and who have concluded that the white man is an incurable "devil." I have tried to stand between these two forces, saying that we need not follow the "do-nothingism" of the complacent or the hatred and despair of the black nationalist. There is the more excellent way of love and nonviolent protest. I'm grateful to God that, through the Negro church, the dimension of nonviolence entered our struggle. If this philosophy had not emerged, I am convinced that by now many streets of the South would be flowing with floods of blood. And I am further convinced that if our white brothers dismiss us as "rabble-rousers" and "outside agitators" those of us who are working through the channels of nonviolent direct action and refuse to support our nonviolent efforts, millions of Negroes, out of frustration and despair, will seek solace and security in black nationalist ideologies, a development that will lead inevitably to a frightening racial nightmare.

Oppressed people cannot remain oppressed forever. The urge for freedom will eventually come. This is what happened to the American Negro. Something within has reminded him of his birthright of freedom; something without has reminded him that he can gain it. Consciously and unconsciously, he has been swept in by what the Germans call the *Zeitgeist*, and with his black brothers of Africa, and his brown and yellow brothers of Asia, South America and the Caribbean, he is moving with a sense of cosmic urgency toward the promised land of racial justice. Recognizing this vital urge that has engulfed the Negro community, one should readily understand public demonstrations. The Negro has many pent-up resentments and latent frustrations. He has to get them out. So let him march sometime; let him have his prayer pilgrimages to the city hall; understand why he must have sit-ins and freedom rides. If his repressed emotions do not come out in these nonviolent ways, they will come out in ominous expressions of violence. This is not a threat; it is a fact of history. So I have not said to my people "get rid of your discontent." But I have tried to say that this normal and healthy discontent can be channelized through the creative outlet of nonviolent direct action. Now this approach is being dismissed as extremist. I must admit that I was initially disappointed in being so categorized.

But as I continued to think about the matter I gradually gained a bit of satisfaction from being considered an extremist. Was not Jesus an extremist in love—"Love your enemies, bless them that curse you, pray for them that despitefully use you." Was not Amos an extremist for justice—"Let justice roll down like waters and righteousness like a mighty stream." Was not Paul an extremist for the gospel of Jesus Christ—"I bear in my body the marks of the Lord Jesus." Was not Martin Luther an extremist—"Here I stand; I can do none other so help me God." Was not John Bunyan an extremist—"I will stay in jail to the end of my days before I make a butchery of my conscience." Was not Abraham Lincoln an extremist—"This nation cannot survive half slave and half free." Was not Thomas Jefferson an extremist—"We hold these truths to be self-evident, that all men are created equal." So the question is not whether we will be extremist but what kind of extremist will we be. Will we be extremists for hate or will we be extremists for love? Will we be extremists for the preservation of injustice—or will we be extremists for the cause of justice? In that dramatic scene on Calvary's hill, three men were crucified. We must not forget that all three were crucified for the same crime—the crime of extremism. Two were extremists for immorality, and thusly fell below their environment. The other, Jesus Christ, was an extremist for love, truth and goodness, and thereby rose above his environment. So, after all, maybe the South, the nation and the world are in dire need of creative extremists.

I had hoped that the white moderate would see this. Maybe I was too optimistic. Maybe I expected too much. I guess I should have realized that few members of a race that has oppressed another race can understand or appreciate the deep groans and passionate yearnings of those that have been oppressed and still fewer have the vision to see that injustice must be rooted out by strong, persistent and determined action. I am thankful, however, that some of our white brothers have grasped the meaning of this social revolution and committed themselves to it. They are still all too small in quantity, but they are big in quality. Some like Ralph McGill, Lillian Smith, Harry Golden and James Dabbs have written about our struggle in eloquent, prophetic and understanding terms. Others have marched with us down nameless streets of the South. They have languished in filthy roach-infested jails, suffering the abuse and brutality of angry policemen who see them as "dirty nigger-lovers." They, unlike so many of their moderate brothers and sisters, have recognized the urgency of the moment and sensed the need for powerful "action" antidotes to combat the disease of segregation.

Let me rush on to mention my other disappointment. I have been so greatly disappointed with the white church and its leadership. Of course, there are some notable exceptions. I am not unmindful of the fact that each of you has taken some significant stands on this issue. I commend you, Rev. Stallings, for your Christian stance on this past Sunday, in welcoming Negroes to your worship service on a non-segregated basis. I commend the Catholic leaders of this state for integrating Springhill College several years ago.

But despite these notable exceptions I must honestly reiterate that I have been disappointed with the church. I do not say that as one of the negative critics who can always find something wrong with the church. I say it as a minister of the gospel, who loves the church; who was nurtured in its bosom: who has been sustained by its spiritual blessings and who will remain true to it as long as the cord of life shall lengthen.

I had the strange feeling when I was suddenly catapulted into the leadership of the bus protest in Montgomery several years ago that we would have the support of the white church. I felt that the white ministers, priests and rabbis of the South would be some of our strongest allies. Instead, some have been outright opponents, refusing to understand the freedom movement and misrepresenting its leaders; all too many others have been more cautious than courageous and have remained silent behind the anesthetizing security of the stained-glass windows.

In spite of my shattered dreams of the past, I came to Birmingham with the hope that the white religious leadership of this community would see the justice of our cause, and with deep moral concern, serve as the channel through which our just grievances would get to the power structure. I had hoped that each of you would understand. But again I have been disappointed. I have heard numerous religious leaders of the South call upon their worshippers to comply with a desegregation decision because it is the *law*, but I have longed to hear white ministers say, "Follow this decree because integration is morally *right* and the Negro is your brother." In the midst of blatant injustices inflicted upon the Negro, I have watched white churches stand on the sideline and merely mouth pious irrelevancies and sanctimonious trivialities. In the midst of a mighty struggle to rid our nation of racial and economic injustice, I have heard so many ministers say, "Those are social issues with which the gospel has no real concern," and I have watched so many churches commit themselves to a completely otherworldly religion which made a strange distinction between body and soul, the sacred and the secular.

So here we are moving toward the exit of the twentieth century with a religious community largely adjusted to the status quo, standing as a taillight behind other community agencies rather than a headlight leading men to higher levels of justice.

I have traveled the length and breadth of Alabama, Mississippi and all the other southern states. On sweltering summer days and crisp autumn mornings I have looked at her beautiful churches with their lofty spires pointing heavenward. I have beheld the impressive outlay of her massive religious education buildings. Over and over again I have

found myself asking: "What kind of people worship here? Who is their God? Where were their voices when the lips of Governor Barnett dripped with words of interposition and nullification? Where were they when Governor Wallace gave the clarion call for defiance and hatred? Where were their voices of support when tired, bruised and weary Negro men and women decided to rise from the dark dungeons of complacency to the bright hills of creative protest?"

Yes, these questions are still in my mind. In deep disappointment, I have wept over the laxity of the church. But be assured that my tears have been tears of love. There can be no deep disappointment where there is not deep love. Yes, I love the church: I love her sacred walls. How could I do otherwise? I am in the rather unique position of being the son, the grandson and the great-grandson of preachers. Yes, I see the church as the body of Christ. But, oh! How we have blemished and scarred that body through social neglect and fear of being nonconformists.

There was a time when the church was very powerful. It was during that period when the early Christians rejoiced when they were deemed worthy to suffer for what they believed. In those days the church was not merely a thermometer that recorded the ideas and principles of popular opinion; it was a thermostat that transformed the mores of society. Wherever the early Christians entered a town the power structure got disturbed and immediately sought to convict them for being "disturbers of the peace" and "outside agitators." But they went on with the conviction that they were "a colony of heaven," and had to obey God rather than man. They were small in number but big in commitment. They were too God-intoxicated to be "astronomically intimidated." They brought an end to such ancient evils as infanticide and gladiatorial contest.

Things are different now. The contemporary church is often a weak, ineffectual voice with an uncertain sound. It is so often the arch-supporter of the status quo. Far from being disturbed by the presence of the church, the power structure of the average community is consoled by the church's silent and often vocal sanction of things as they are.

But the judgment of God is upon the church as never before. If the church of today does not recapture the sacrificial spirit of the early church, it will lose its authentic ring, forfeit the loyalty of millions, and be dismissed as an irrelevant social club with no meaning for the twentieth century. I am meeting young people every day whose disappointment with the church has risen to outright disgust.

Maybe again, I have been too optimistic. Is organized religion too inextricably bound to the status quo to save our nation and the world? Maybe I must turn my faith to the inner spiritual church, the church within the church, as the true *ecclesia* and the hope of the world. But again I am thankful to God that some noble souls from the ranks of organized religion have broken loose from the paralyzing chains of conformity and joined us as active partners in the struggle for freedom. They have left their secure congregations and walked the streets of Albany, Georgia, with us. They have gone through the highways of the South on tortuous rides for freedom. Yes, they have gone to jail with us. Some have been kicked out of their churches, and lost support of their bishops and fellow ministers. But they have gone with the faith that right defeated is stronger than evil triumphant. These men have been the leaven in the lump of the race. Their witness has been the spiritual salt that has preserved the true meaning of the gospel in these troubled times. They have carved a tunnel of hope through the dark mountain of disappointment.

I hope the church as a whole will meet the challenge of this decisive hour. But even if the church does not come to the aid of justice, I have no despair about the future. I have no fear about the outcome of our struggle in Birmingham, even if our motives are presently misunderstood. We will reach the goal of freedom in Birmingham and all over the nation, because the goal of America is freedom. Abused and scorned though we may be, our destiny is tied up with the destiny of America. Before the Pilgrims landed at Plymouth we were here. Before the pen of Jefferson etched across the pages of history the majestic words of the Declaration of Independence, we were here. For more than two centuries our foreparents labored in this country without wages; they made cotton king; and they built the homes of their masters in the midst of brutal injustice and shameful humiliation—and yet out of a bottomless vitality they continued to thrive and develop. If the inexpressible cruelties of slavery could not stop us, the opposition we now face will surely fail. We will win our freedom because the sacred heritage of our nation and the eternal will of God are embodied in our echoing demands.

I must close now. But before closing I am impelled to mention one other point in your statement that troubled me profoundly. You warmly commended the Birmingham police force for keeping "order" and "preventing violence." I don't believe you would have so warmly commended the police force if you had seen its angry violent dogs literally biting six unarmed, nonviolent Negroes. I don't believe you would so quickly commend the policemen if you would observe their ugly and inhuman treatment of Negroes here in the city jail; if you would watch them push and curse old Negro women and young Negro girls; if you would see them slap and kick old Negro men and young boys; if you will observe them, as they did on two occasions, refuse to give us food because we wanted to sing our grace together. I'm sorry that I can't join you in your praise for the police department.

It is true that they have been rather disciplined in their public handling of the demonstrators. In this sense they have been rather publicly "nonviolent." But for what purpose? To preserve the evil system of segregation. Over the last few years I have consistently preached that nonviolence demands that the means we use must be as pure as the ends we seek. So I have tried to make it clear that it is wrong to use immoral means to attain moral ends. But now I must affirm that it is just as wrong, or even more so, to use moral means to preserve immoral ends. Maybe Mr. Connor and his policemen have been rather publicly nonviolent, as Chief Pritchett was in Albany,

Georgia, but they have used the moral means of nonviolence to maintain the immoral end of flagrant racial injustice. T. S. Eliot has said that there is no greater treason than to do the right deed for the wrong reason.

I wish you had commended the Negro sit-inners and demonstrators of Birmingham for their sublime courage, their willingness to suffer and their amazing discipline in the midst of the most inhuman provocation. One day the South will recognize its real heroes. They wil[l] be the James Merediths, courageously and with a majestic sense of purpose facing jeering and hostile mobs and the agonizing loneliness that characterizes the life of the pioneer. They will be old, oppressed, battered Negro women, symbolized in a seventy-two-year-old woman of Montgomery, Alabama, who rose up with a sense of dignity and with her people decided not to ride the segregated buses, and responded to one who inquired about her tiredness with ungrammatical profundity: "My feet is tired, but my soul is rested." They will be the young high school and college students, young ministers of the gospel and a host of their elders courageously and nonviolently sitting-in at lunch counters and willingly going to jail for conscience's sake. One day the South will know that when these disinherited children of God sat down at lunch counters they were in reality standing up for the best in the American dream and the most sacred values in our Judeo-Christian heritage, and thusly, carrying our whole nation back to those great wells of democracy which were dug deep by the Founding Fathers in the formulation of the Constitution and the Declaration of Independence.

Never before have I written a letter this long (or should I say a book?). I'm afraid that it is much too long to take your precious time. I can assure you that it would have been much shorter if I had been writing from a comfortable desk, but what else is there to do when you are alone for days in the dull monotony of a narrow jail cell other than write long letters, think strange thoughts, and pray long prayers?

If I have said anything in this letter that is an overstatement of the truth and is indicative of an unreasonable impatience, I beg you to forgive me. If I have said anything in this letter that is an understatement of the truth and is indicative of my having a patience that makes me patient with anything less than brotherhood, I beg God to forgive me.

I hope this letter finds you strong in the faith. I also hope that circumstances will soon make it possible for me to meet each of you, not as an integrationist or a civil rights leader, but as a fellow clergyman and a Christian brother. Let us all hope that the dark clouds of racial prejudice will soon pass away and the deep fog of misunderstanding will be lifted from our fear-drenched communities and in some not too distant tomorrow the radiant stars of love and brotherhood will shine over our great nation with all of their scintillating beauty.

Yours for the Cause of Peace
and Brotherhood,
Martin Luther King, Jr.

A Time to Break Silence

Martin Luther King, Jr.

I come to this magnificent house of worship tonight, because my conscience leaves me no other choice. I join with you in this meeting because I am in deepest agreement with the aims and work of the organization which has brought us together: Clergy and Laymen Concerned About Vietnam. The recent statement of your executive committee is the sentiment of my own heart, and I found myself in full accord when I read its opening lines: "A time comes when silence is betrayal." That time has come for us in relation to Vietnam.

The truth of these words is beyond doubt, but the mission to which they call us is a most difficult one. Even when pressed by the demands of inner truth, men do not easily assume the task of opposing their government's policy, especially in time of war. Nor does the human spirit move without great difficulty against all the apathy of conformist thought within one's own bosom and in the surrounding world. Moreover, when the issues at hand seem as perplexed as they often do in the case of this dreadful conflict, we are always on the verge of being mesmerized by uncertainty; but we must move on.

Some of us who have already begun to break the silence of the night have found that the calling to speak is often a vocation of agony, but we must speak. We must speak with all the humility that is appropriate to our limited vision, but we must speak. And we must rejoice as well, for surely this is the first time in our nation's history that a significant number of its religious leaders have chosen to move beyond the prophesying of smooth patriotism to the high grounds of a firm dissent based upon the mandates of conscience and the reading of history. Perhaps a new spirit is rising among us. If it is, let us trace its movements well and pray that our own inner being may be sensitive to its guidance, for we are deeply in need of a new way beyond the darkness that seems so close around us.

Over the past two years, as I have moved to break the betrayal of my own silences and to speak the burnings of my own heart, as I have called for radical departures from the destruction of Vietnam, many persons have questioned me about the wisdom of my path. At the heart of their concerns this query has often loomed large and loud: Why are *you* speaking about the war, Dr. King? Why are *you* joining the voices of dissent? Peace and civil rights don't mix, they say. Aren't you hurting the cause of your people? they ask. And when I hear them, though I often understand the source of their concern, I am nevertheless greatly saddened, for such questions mean that the inquirers have not really known me, my commitment or my calling. Indeed, their questions suggest that they do not know the world in which they live.

In the light of such tragic misunderstanding, I deem it of signal importance to try to state clearly, and I trust concisely, why I believe that the path from Dexter Avenue Baptist Church—the church in Montgomery, Alabama, where I began my pastorate—leads clearly to this sanctuary tonight.

I come to this platform tonight to make a passionate plea to my beloved nation. This speech is not addressed to Hanoi or to the National Liberation Front. It is not addressed to China or to Russia.

Nor is it an attempt to overlook the ambiguity of the total situation and the need for a collective solution to the tragedy of Vietnam. Neither is it an attempt to make North Vietnam or the National Liberation Front paragons of

Source: Reprinted by arrangement with the Estate of Martin Luther King Jr, c/o Writers House as agent for the proprietor. Copyright © Martin Luther King, Jr. 1968, copyright renewed 1991 Coretta Scott King.

virtue, nor to overlook the role they can play in a successful resolution of the problem. While they both may have justifiable reason to be suspicious of the good faith of the United States, life and history give eloquent testimony to the fact that conflicts are never resolved without trustful give and take on both sides.

Tonight, however, I wish not to speak with Hanoi and the N.L.F., but rather to my fellow Americans who, with me, bear the greatest responsibility in ending a conflict that has exacted a heavy price on both continents.

Since I am a preacher by trade, I suppose it is not surprising that I have seven major reasons for bringing Vietnam into the field of my moral vision. There is at the outset a very obvious and almost facile connection between the war in Vietnam and the struggle I and others have been waging in America. A few years ago there was a shining moment in that struggle. It seemed as if there was a real promise of hope for the poor—both black and white—through the Poverty Program. There were experiments, hopes, new beginnings. Then came the buildup in Vietnam and I watched the program broken and eviscerated as if it were some idle political plaything of a society gone mad on war, and I knew that America would never invest the necessary funds or energies in rehabilitation of its poor so long as adventures like Vietnam continued to draw men and skills and money like some demonic destructive suction tube. So I was increasingly compelled to see the war as an enemy of the poor and to attack it as such.

Perhaps the more tragic recognition of reality took place when it became clear to me that the war was doing far more than devastating the hopes of the poor at home. It was sending their sons and their brothers and their husbands to fight and to die in extraordinarily high proportions relative to the rest of the population. We were taking the black young men who had been crippled by our society and sending them eight thousand miles away to guarantee liberties in Southeast Asia which they had not found in Southwest Georgia and East Harlem. So we have been repeatedly faced with the cruel irony of watching Negro and white boys on TV screens as they

kill and die together for a nation that has been unable to seat them together in the same schools. So we watch them in brutal solidarity burning the huts of a poor village, but we realize that they would never live on the same block in Detroit. I could not be silent in the face of such cruel manipulation of the poor.

My third reason moves to an even deeper level of awareness, for it grows out of my experience in the ghettos of the North over the last three years—especially the last three summers. As I have walked among the desperate, rejected and angry young men I have told them that Molotov cocktails and rifles would not solve their problems. I have tried to offer them my deepest compassion while maintaining my conviction that social change comes most meaningfully through nonviolent action. But they asked—and rightly so—what about Vietnam? They asked if our own nation wasn't using massive doses of violence to solve its problems, to bring about the changes it wanted. Their questions hit home, and I knew that I could never again raise my voice against the violence of the oppressed in the ghettos without having first spoken clearly to the greatest purveyor of violence in the world today—my own government. For the sake of those boys, for the sake of this government, for the sake of the hundreds of thousands trembling under our violence, I cannot be silent.

For those who ask the question, "Aren't you a civil-rights leader?" and thereby mean to exclude me from the movement for peace, I have this further answer. In 1957 when a group of us formed the Southern Christian Leadership Conference, we chose as our motto: "To save the soul of America." We were convinced that we could not limit our vision to certain rights for black people, but instead affirmed the conviction that America would never be free or saved from itself unless the descendants of its slaves were loosed completely from the shackles they still wear....

Now, it should be incandescently clear that no one who has any concern for the integrity and life of America today can ignore the present war. If America's soul becomes totally poisoned, part of the autopsy must read

Vietnam. It can never be saved so long as it destroys the deepest hopes of men the world over. So it is that those of us who are yet determined that America *will* be are led down the path of protest and dissent, working for the health of our land.

As if the weight of such a commitment to the life and health of America were not enough, another burden of responsibility was placed upon me in 1964; and I cannot forget that the Nobel Prize for Peace was also a commission—a commission to work harder than I had ever worked before for "the brotherhood of man." This is a calling that takes me beyond national allegiances, but even if it were not present I would yet have to live with the meaning of my commitment to the ministry of Jesus Christ. To me the relationship of this ministry to the making of peace is so obvious that I sometimes marvel at those who ask me why I am speaking against the war. Could it be that they do not know that the good news was meant for all men—for communist and capitalist, for their children and ours, for black and for white, for revolutionary and conservative? Have they forgotten that my ministry is in obedience to the one who loved his enemies so fully that he died for them? What, then, can I say to the Viet Cong or to Castro or to Mao as a faithful minister of this one? Can I threaten them with death, or must I not share with them my life?

Finally, as I try to delineate for you and for myself the road that leads from Montgomery to this place I would have offered all that was most valid if I simply said that I must be true to my conviction that I share with all men the calling to be a son of the Living God. Beyond the calling of race or nation or creed is this vocation of sonship and brotherhood, and because I believe that the Father is deeply concerned especially for his suffering and helpless and outcast children, I come tonight to speak for them.

This I believe to be the privilege and the burden of all of us who deem ourselves bound by allegiances and loyalties which are broader and deeper than nationalism and which go beyond our nation's self-defined goals and positions. We are called to speak for the weak, for the voiceless, for victims of our nation and for those it calls enemy, for no document from human hands can make these humans any less our brothers.

And as I ponder the madness of Vietnam and search within myself for ways to understand and respond to compassion my mind goes constantly to the people of that peninsula. I speak now not of the soldiers of each side, not of the junta in Saigon, but simply of the people who have been living under the curse of war for almost three continuous decades now. I think of them too because it is clear to me that there will be no meaningful solution there until some attempt is made to know them and hear their broken cries.

They must see Americans as strange liberators. The Vietnamese people proclaimed their own independence in 1945 after a combined French and Japanese occupation, and before the Communist revolution in China. They were led by Ho Chi Minh. Even though they quoted the American Declaration of Independence in their own document of freedom, we refused to recognize them.[*] Instead, we decided to support France in its reconquest of her former colony.

Our government felt then that the Vietnamese people were not "ready" for independence, and we again fell victim to the deadly Western arrogance that has poisoned the international atmosphere for so long. With that tragic decision we rejected a revolutionary government seeking self-determination, and a government that had been established not by China (for whom the Vietnamese have no great love) but by clearly indigenous forces that included some Communists. For the peasants this new government meant real land reform, one of the most important needs in their lives.

For nine years following 1945 we denied the people of Vietnam the right of independ-

---

[*]In September, 1945, the Republic of Vietnam was established. The Constitution proclaimed its independence from all colonial rule and incorporated the famous principle of the American Declaration of Independence—the "self-evident" truths that "all men are created equal," and are endowed with "certain inalienable rights; that among these are life, liberty, and the pursuit of happiness."

ence. For nine years we vigorously supported the French in their abortive effort to recolonize Vietnam.

Before the end of the war we were meeting 80 percent of the French war costs. Even before the French were defeated at Dien Bien Phu, they began to despair of the reckless action, but we did not. We encouraged them with our huge financial and military supplies to continue the war even after they had lost the will. Soon we would be paying almost the full costs of this tragic attempt at recolonization.

After the French were defeated it looked as if independence and land reform would come again through the Geneva agreements.* But instead there came the United States, determined that Ho should not unify the temporarily divided nation, and the peasants watched again as we supported one of the most vicious modern dictators—our chosen man, Premier Diem. The peasants watched and cringed as Diem ruthlessly routed out all opposition, supported their extortionist landlords and refused even to discuss reunification with the North. The peasants watched as all this was presided over by United States influence and then by increasing numbers of United States troops who came to help quell the insurgency that Diem's methods had aroused. When Diem was overthrown they may have been happy, but the long line of military dictatorships seemed to offer no real change—especially in terms of their need for land and peace.

The only change came from America as we increased our troop commitments in support of governments which were singularly corrupt, inept and without popular support. All the while the people read our leaflets and received regular promises of peace and

*The Geneva Conference ended the war between France and the Republic of Vietnam. At Geneva, Vietnam was clearly established as a single sovereign nation, temporarily divided into regrouping zones for truce purposes. While the United States refused to sign the Agreement, it did pledge that it would "refrain from use of force to upset the agreement," and it acknowledged its U. N. obligation to respect Vietnam's territorial integrity and independence.

democracy—and land reform. Now they languish under our bombs and consider *us*—not their fellow Vietnamese—the real enemy. They move sadly and apathetically as we herd them off the land of their fathers into concentration camps where minimal social needs are rarely met. They know they must move or be destroyed by our bombs. So they go—primarily women and children and the aged.

They watch as we poison their water, as we kill a million acres of their crops. They must weep as the bulldozers roar through their areas preparing to destroy the precious trees. They wander into the hospitals, with at least twenty casualties from American firepower for one Vietcong-inflicted injury. So far we may have killed a million of them—mostly children. They wander into the towns and see thousands of the children, homeless, without clothes, running in packs on the streets like animals. They see the children degraded by our soldiers as they beg for food. They see the children selling their sisters to our soldiers, soliciting for their mothers.

What do the peasants think as we ally ourselves with the landlords and as we refuse to put any action into our many words concerning land reform? What do they think as we test out our latest weapons on them, just as the Germans tested out new medicine and new tortures in the concentration camps of Europe? Where are the roots of the independent Vietnam we claim to be building? Is it among these voiceless ones?

We have destroyed their two most cherished institutions: the family and the village. We have destroyed their land and their crops. We have cooperated in the crushing of the nation's only non-Communist revolutionary political force—the unified Buddhist Church. We have supported the enemies of the peasants of Saigon. We have corrupted their women and children and killed their men. What liberators!

Now there is little left to build on—save bitterness. Soon the only solid physical foundations remaining will be found at our military bases and in the concrete of the concentration camps we call fortified hamlets. The peasants may well wonder if we plan to build our new Vietnam on such grounds as these? Could we blame them for such thoughts? We must speak for them and raise the questions they cannot raise. These too are our brothers.

Perhaps the more difficult, but no less necessary, task is to speak for those who have been designated as our enemies. What of the National Liberation Front—that strangely anonymous group we call V.C. or Communists? What must they think of us in America when they realize that we permitted the repression and cruelty of Diem which helped to bring them into being as a resistance group in the South? What do they think of our condoning the violence which led to their own taking-up of arms? How can they believe in our integrity when now we speak of "aggression from the North" as if there were nothing more essential to the war? How can they trust us when now we charge them with violence after the murderous reign of Diem and charge them with violence while we pour every new weapon of death into their land? Surely we must understand their feelings even if we do not condone their actions. Surely we must see that the men we supported pressed them to their violence. Surely we must see that our own computerized plans of destruction simply dwarf their greatest acts.

How do they judge us when our officials know that their membership is less than 25 percent Communist and yet insist on giving them the blanket name? What must they be thinking when they know that we are aware of their control of major sections of Vietnam and yet we appear to allow national elections in which this highly organized political parallel government will have no part? They ask how we can speak of free elections when the Saigon press is censored and controlled by the military junta. And they are surely right to wonder what kind of new government we plan to help form without them—the only party in real touch with the peasants. They question our political goals and they deny the reality of a peace settlement from which they will be excluded. Their questions are frighteningly relevant. Is our nation planning to build on political myth again and then shore it up with the power of new violence?

Here is the true meaning and value of compassion and non-violence when it helps us to see the enemy's point of view, to hear his questions, to know his assessment of ourselves. For from his view we may indeed see the basic weaknesses of our own condition, and if we are mature, we may learn and grow and profit from the wisdom of the brothers who are called the opposition.

So, too, with Hanoi. In the North, where our bombs now pummel the land and our mines endanger the waterways, we are met by a deep but understandable mistrust. To speak for them is to explain this lack of confidence in Western words, and especially their distrust of American intentions now. In Hanoi are the men who led the nation to independence against the Japanese and the French, the men who sought membership in the French commonwealth and were betrayed by the weakness of Paris and the willfulness of the colonial armies. It was they who led a second struggle against French domination at tremendous costs, and then were persuaded to give up the land they controlled between the 13th and 17th parallels as a temporary measure at Geneva. After 1954 they watched us conspire with Diem to prevent elections which would have surely brought Ho Chi Minh to power over a United Vietnam,[*] and they realized they had been betrayed again....

At this point I should make it clear that while I have tried in these last few minutes to give a voice to the voiceless on Vietnam and to understand the arguments of those who are called enemy, I am as deeply concerned about our own troops there as anything else. For it occurs to me that what we are submitting them to in Vietnam is not simply the brutalizing process that goes on in any war where armies face each other and seek to destroy. We are adding cynicism to the process of death, for they must know after a short period there that none of the things we claim to be

---

[*]With the backing of the United States, President Ngo Dihn Diem of South Vietnam refused to allow the people of South Vietnam to vote in the elections scheduled under the Geneva Agreement to be held in 1956. The reason was clear to all. As President Eisenhower later conceded, "possibly 80 percent of the population would have voted for the Communist Ho Chi Minh."

fighting for are really involved. Before long they must know that their government has sent them into a struggle among Vietnamese, and the more sophisticated surely realize that we are on the side of the wealthy and the secure, while we create a hell for the poor.

Somehow this madness must cease. We must stop now. I speak as a child of God and brother to the suffering poor of Vietnam. I speak for those whose land is being laid waste, whose homes are being destroyed, whose culture is being subverted. I speak for the poor of America who are paying the double price of smashed hopes at home and death and corruption in Vietnam. I speak as a citizen of the world, for the world as it stands aghast at the path we have taken. I speak as an American to the leaders of my own nation. The great initiative in this war is ours. The initiative to stop it must be ours....

If we continue there will be no doubt in my mind and in the mind of the world that we have no honorable intentions in Vietnam. It will become clear that our minimal expectation is to occupy it as an American colony and men will not refrain from thinking that our maximum hope is to goad China into a war so that we may bomb her nuclear installations. If we do not stop our war against the people of Vietnam immediately the world will be left with no other alternative than to see this as some horribly clumsy and deadly game we have decided to play.

The world now demands a maturity of America that we may not be able to achieve. It demands that we admit that we have been wrong from the beginning of our adventure in Vietnam, that we have been detrimental to the life of the Vietnamese people. The situation is one in which we must be ready to turn sharply from our present ways.

In order to atone for our sins and errors in Vietnam, we should take the initiative in bringing a halt to this tragic war. I would like to suggest five concrete things that our government should do immediately to begin the long and difficult process of extricating ourselves from this nightmarish conflict:

1. End all bombing in North and South Vietnam.
2. Declare a unilateral cease-fire in the hope that such action will create the atmosphere for negotiation.
3. Take immediate steps to prevent other battlegrounds in Southeast Asia by curtailing our military buildup in Thailand and our interference in Laos.
4. Realistically accept the fact that the National Liberation Front has substantial support in South Vietnam and must thereby play a role in any meaningful negotiations and in any future Vietnam government.
5. Set a date that we will remove all foreign troops from Vietnam in accordance with the 1954 Geneva Agreement.

Part of our ongoing commitment might well express itself in an offer to grant asylum to any Vietnamese who fears for his life under a new regime which included the Liberation Front. Then we must make what reparations we can for the damage we have done. We must provide the medical aid that is badly needed, making it available in this country if necessary.

Meanwhile we in the churches and synagogues have a continuing task while we urge our government to disengage itself from a disgraceful commitment. We must continue to raise our voices if our nation persists in its perverse ways in Vietnam. We must be prepared to match actions with words by seeking out every creative means of protest possible.

As we counsel young men concerning military service we must clarify for them our nation's role in Vietnam and challenge them with the alternative of conscientious objection. I am pleased to say that this is the path now being chosen by more than seventy students at my own Alma Mater, Morehouse College, and I recommend it to all who find the American course in Vietnam a dishonorable and unjust one. Moreover I would encourage all ministers of draft age to give up their ministerial exemptions and seek status as conscientious objectors. These are the times for real choices and not false ones. We are at the moment when our lives must be placed on the line if our nation is to survive its own folly. Every man of humane convictions must decide on the protest that best suits his convictions, but we must all protest....

Dr. King's Painful Dilemma

Bayard Rustin

One of the undertones of the attacks in the white press on Dr. Martin Luther King's recent statements on Vietnam may well reveal that America really does not believe that Negroes, as citizens, have yet come of age. Like children, we should be seen but not heard.

I say this because the criticism of Dr. King was not limited to an evaluation of his proposals and his strategy for ending the war. It was, by and large, an attack on his right to debate, or even to discuss, Vietnam. In substance, many editorials seemed to be asking, "What is Dr. King doing discussing Vietnam?" or "Who gave him the right to make proposals about our [meaning white America's] foreign policy?"

In a democracy all citizens have not only a right but also a solemn duty to vote, to advise on domestic affairs, and to address themselves to all aspects of foreign policy. As Americans, Dr. King and all other Negroes have such a duty. First, it is their duty as citizens. Second, it is their duty as black citizens, considering that twice as many Negroes proportionately are fighting and dying in Vietnam.

Equally compelling, for Dr. King, is the fact that he is a Nobel Peace Prize winner. As such he has a moral obligation to speak out for peace according to his insight as a man of God and in keeping with his conscience as a free man.

On the other hand, however, if Dr. King makes proposals that others disagree with, they have the duty to differ with him on the merits or demerits of his proposals. Dr. King knows this, and he will expect no less. Such honest differences may encourage Dr. King to embark upon a reexamination of his position. Such honest discussion will encourage all of us to keep the vexing problem of Vietnam in constant review.

This process might very well turn out to be as illuminating for Dr. King as for the rest of us. But to assume that any individual (particularly any civil rights worker) does not have the right to discuss any problem that affects his nation is to propose that such an individual is still a second-class citizen.

The Negro community should, and I hope will, continue to enter all discussions relative to their experience as Americans. We must, of course, be prepared to accept the political consequences and responsibilities that result from taking such a position.

Perhaps the real question is this: How should Negroes who have a concern for peace organize to express these sentiments? Should they organize through the existing peace organizations, or should they organize within the civil rights movement? I must say that I would consider the involvement of the civil rights organizations as such in peace activities distinctly unprofitable and perhaps even suicidal.

Yet there must be an opportunity for Negroes to work for peace. For many Negroes do take a deep and genuine interest in the problems of war and peace, if for no other reason than because of the disproportionate number of Negroes in Vietnam.

This is not to say that there is going to be any tremendous onrush of Negroes into the peace movement. The immediate problems facing Negroes are so vast and crushing that they have little time or energy to focus upon international crises.

Nevertheless, when Dr. King speaks out as he recently did, we are forced to recognize and clarify the problems of strategy, tactics, and philosophy that confront the Negro freedom movement in a time of war. Dr. King is, no doubt, more aware today of the subtleties of these conflicts than he was before he made his statement.

Source: From the *New York Amsterdam News*, March 3, 1967.

FURTHER READING

Aptheker, Herbert. 1994. *A Documentary History of the Negro People in the United States, 1960–1968*, Vol 7. New York: Citadel Press.

Antczak, Frederick J. "When 'Silence Is Betrayal': An Ethical Criticism of the Revolution of Values in the Speech at Riverside Church." In Carolyn Calloway-Thomas and John Louis Lucaites, eds., *Martin Luther King, Jr., and the Sermonic Power of Public Discourse.* Tuscaloosa: University of Alabama Press.

Carson, Clayborne. 1981. *In Struggle: SNCC and the Black Awakening of the 1960s.* Cambridge, MA: Harvard University Press.

Chong, Dennis. 1991. *Collective Action and the Civil Rights Movement.* Chicago: University of Chicago Press.

Cone, James H. 1969. *Black Theology and Black Power.* New York: Seabury Press.

Fairclough, Adam. 1984. "Martin Luther King, Jr. and the War in Vietnam." *Phylon* 45 (July): 19–39.

Hughes, Langston. 1962. *Fight for Freedom: The Story of the NAACP.* New York: Norton.

Meier, August, and Elliot Rudwick. 1973. *CORE: A Study in the Civil Rights Movement, 1942–1968.* New York: Oxford University Press.

Moses, Greg. 1997. *Revolution and Conscience: Martin Luther King, Jr. and the Philosophy of Nonviolence.* New York: Guilford Press.

Rustin, Bayard. 1971. *Down the Line.* Chicago: Quadrangle Books.

Taylor, Clyde. 1973. *Vietnam and Black America: An Anthology of Protest and Resistance.* Garden City, NY: Anchor.

Walton, Jr., Hans. 1971. *The Political Philosophy of Martin Luther King, Jr.* Westport, CT: Greenwood Press.

CHAPTER 6

Marxism and Social Progress

Questions regarding the relative strength of race and class as dominate factors influencing the social progress of African Americans are prominent in debates among Marxists, as well as in debates between Marxists and nationalists. A major source of dissatisfaction for African-American Marxists is the racial discrimination practiced by unions and the general exclusion of African-American workers from the labor movement. The optimism displayed in the selections by Lucy Parsons and Ralph Bunche have to be considered within the sobering context of the problematic issues raised by W. E. B. Du Bois, E. Franklin Frazier, and Cornel West.

In 1905 the first convention of the Industrial Workers of the World was held in Chicago. Lucy Parsons, a black socialist activist, and Mother Jones were among the few women speakers on the program. Parsons was a well-known speaker in her own right, yet her notoriety was further augmented because she was the wife of martyred Haymarket anarchist Albert Parsons. She addressed the convention as a crusader for human rights without any special appeal to racial injustice, although she often spoke out against crimes against black people. Although she does not take the floor as a black person, Parsons chooses an interesting image to speak of herself as a "pigmy" among "intellectual giants." She speaks from the standpoint of labor when she claims that if wage labor has been slavery for men, it has been worse for women "for she has been the slave of a slave." With no racial connotation intended, she uses Babel's image of the woman wage slave to support her claim that women have a vital role to play in the organization of the labor movement. She further highlights the plight of women workers when she points out that the consumer practice of buying cheap bargains harms workers' interests and fastens "the chains of slavery upon our sisters."

Revolutionary socialism is defined by Parsons in terms of ownership of property and the means of production. Her socialist vision was that someday, "the land shall belong to the landless, the tools to the toiler, and the products to the producers." What she means by "revolution" is the turning over of wealth to the producers of that wealth. The purpose of political organizing is to raise the consciousness of workers to take possession of that which they have produced. Parsons maintains that the future method of seeking this goal will be the general strike.

Referring to current events occurring in Russia, Parsons champions the labor movement as a human manifestation of resistance to capitalism. She speaks of workers belonging to a global human family as a basis for recognizing their common interest. Differences of nationality, religion, and politics are overshadowed by membership in "the industrial republic of labor."

The issue of social equality for African-Americans was often framed by Marxists as "the Negro question." Ralph Bunche maintains that communists and the American working class must raise the public consciousness regarding this issue. He criticizes the international for going astray with the "national minority" theory. According to Bunche, the situation of African-Americans is unlike the situation of other colonial people. African-Americans are not seeking independence from United States imperialism. Bunche believes that Lenin's slogan of "self-determination" has a dangerous application in the American context, for it serves the aims of segregationists.

In a more favorable light Bunche cites Lenin's claim that African-Americans are a racialized caste subjected to inferior economic, social, and political status. He remarks that the first problem facing a Marxist view of racial inequality is to account for the existence of this "remnant of feudalism" in the highly developed American capitalist system. He traces the roots of the present status of African-Americans to slavery and, especially the failure of reconstruction. Bunche cites, in particular, the rejection of the radical plan that would transform slaves into free peasant-proprietors. He sees the caste status of African-Americans as a precapitalist survival and adds Lenin's insight regarding the bourgeois interest being served by maintaining this form of backwardness. By supplying a sense of white superiority, the caste status of African-Americans functions ideologically as a rationale for domination.

Bunche points to the shameful history of discrimination in trade unions to indicate why the sudden influx of thousands of black workers into Northern industry has aggravated anti-Negro prejudice. Despite these factors Bunche predicts a slow, but inevitable deepening of the class consciousness of the white proletariat, a growing ideological liberation from the bourgeoisie. This will lead to the submergence of national and racial differences and the revolutionary struggle against capitalism, eliminating race prejudice as a result of the elimination of the bourgeois ideology of class.

When comparing the African-American situation with "the liberation of subject nations of colonies," Bunche insists that the social and political liberation of African-Americans is a democratic task. For Bunche the similarity of these struggles derives from the fact that the revolution he envisions occurring in America is "an uncompleted bourgeois revolution." The completion of this revolution requires the elimination of the underlying economic conditions on the basis of which the American Negro is subordinated. Semifeudal forms of exploitation, such as peonage, tenancy, and sharecropping must be overturned and replaced with a nationalization of the land and its distribution among the cultivators.

Bunche believes this can be done without the socialization of all the means of production. These demands are not even socialist; rather they are the demands of a consistent democracy. The real struggle is the "class war of labor against capital." Hence, the emancipation of African-Americans cannot be the result of any "purely racial" movement.

W.E.B. Du Bois was much more critical of the labor movement than Bunche. He wrote "Socialism and the Negro Problem" in 1913, long before his own Marxist views began to take shape. With apparent distrust of the Socialist Party, he raises the question of whether African-Americans can be left off the socialist agenda. He asks whether socialists can exclude the Negro and still push Socialism forward. Du Bois draws in question the practice by the Socialist Party of going along with the segregation of white and black workers in the South. "After you have gotten the radical South and paid the price which they demand, will the result be Socialism?"

By the early thirties Du Bois had begun work on *Black Reconstruction*, a shorter version of which he had written for Alain Locke's Bronze Booklet series. Locke's attempt to tone down Du Bois's radical critique was fiercely resisted and in the end that version was never published. A major theme in *Black Reconstruction* is Du Bois's criticisms of the white working class. He presents some of these criticisms in "Marxism and the Negro Problem" written in 1933. Pointing to the fact that less than 150 African-Americans belong to any class that could possibly be considered bourgeois, he emphasizes the fact that this small elite is no more a part of the class of exploiters of wage labor than the black proletariat is a part of the white proletariat. Indeed, according to Du Bois, the bulk of the suffering of Negro labor comes not from capitalists, but from the white working class. Holding labor leaders responsible for the racism in unions, he claims that white workers deny African-Americans the right to vote, education, decent housing, affiliation with trade unions and heaps public insults upon them. The point Du Bois seeks to establish is that the exploitation of the Negro comes from white capitalists and equally the white proletariat, *not* from a black capitalist class.

E. Franklin Frazier ponders the question of why African-Americans have steadily refused to become allies with the radical groups in America. Despite the fact that race consciousness has "efaced" class consciousness, Frazier notes that black aristocrats in South Carolina do not relate to poor whites as equals. Frazier believes there is a class factor influencing the African-American's devotion to the present economic order. He presents the Pullman porters as a case in point. As a better situated group among the black middle class, they are wedded to bourgeois ideals—"an aristocratic laboring group." In line with some of Du Bois's observations, Frazier remarks that the white working class has taken over the tradition of the slaveholding aristocracy. He criticizes the intellectuals involved in the New Negro movement for their lack of political engagement. With the goal of transmitting middle-class values, the aim of this movement was only to acquire a bourgeois culture. Frazier questions this goal: Shouldn't this "most civilized" class within the group be "leading the revolt"?

Cornel West tackles the question of the role of race and class in the Marxist conception of African-American oppression. He discusses four basic views. The first is illustrated by the position adopted by the Socialist Party in its resolution on the Negro question in 1903. He criticizes the fact that strategies to confront racism were downplayed. The reductionist line taken by the Socialist Party subsumes African-American oppression under working-class exploitation. The second view recognizes that African-American oppression goes beyond economics. What West calls a "superexploitation thesis" was added to deal with racial discrimination in the workplace. The third view is most influential among African-American Marxists. According to this view African-Americans constitute an oppressed nation. Sometimes stated as a national minority thesis, this idea was rejected by Bunche, although it has been embraced by other African-American Marxists. The fourth view maintains that African-American oppression is general working-class exploitation and racial oppression. This view was held by Oliver Cox and other Marxists who saw African-Americans as a racially coerced sector of labor.

West insists that a new conception of African-American oppression is required that avoids the objections that stem from the above views all being presented at the macrostructural level. West proposes cultural phenomena as a site of white hegemony and the level at which oppression is experienced on an everyday basis. He believes that this kind of analysis is consistent with the antiracist position of Marxism.

Address to the First Convention of the Industrial Workers of the World

Lucy E. Parsons

Del. Lucy E. Parsons: I can assure you that after the intellectual feast that I have enjoyed immensely this afternoon, I feel fortunate to appear before you now in response to your call. I do not wish you to think that I am here to play upon words when I tell you that I stand before you and feel much like a pigmy before intellectual giants, but that is only the fact. I wish to state to you that I have taken the floor because no other woman has responded, and I feel that it would not be out of place for me to say in my poor way a few words about this movement.

We, the women of this country, have no ballot even if we wished to use it, and the only way that we can be represented is to take a man to represent us. You men have made such a mess of it in representing us that we have not much confidence in asking you; and I for one feel very backward in asking the men to represent me. We have no ballot, but we have our labor. I think it is August Bebel, in his "Woman in the Past, Present and Future"—a book that should be read by every woman that works for wages—I think it is Bebel that says that men have been slaves throughout all the ages, but that woman's condition has been worse, for she has been the slave of a slave. I think there was never a greater truth uttered. We are the slaves of the slaves. We are exploited more ruthlessly than men. Wherever wages are to be reduced the capitalist class use women to reduce them, and if there is anything that you men should do in the future it is to organize the women.

Source: Lucy Parsons, Address to the First Convention of the Industrial Workers of the World in *Proceedings of the First Convention of the Industrial Workers of the World* (New York: Labor News Company, 1905), 167–73.

And I tell that if the women had inaugurated a boycott of the State street stores since the teamsters' strike they would have surrendered long ago. (Applause). I do not stand before you to brag. I had no man connected with that strike to make it of interest to me to boycott the stores, but I have not bought one penny's worth there since that strike was inaugurated. I intended to boycott all of them as one individual at least, so it is important to educate the women. Now I wish to show my sisters here that we fasten the chains of slavery upon our sisters, sometimes unwittingly, when we go down to the department store and look around for cheap bargains and go home and exhibit what we have got so cheap. When we come to reflect it simply means the robbery of our sisters, for we know that the things cannot be made for such prices and give the women who made them fair wages.

I wish to say that I have attended many conventions in the twenty-seven years since I came here to Chicago, a young girl, so full of life and animation and hope. It is to youth that hope comes; it is to age that reflection comes. I have attended conventions from that day to this of one kind and another and taken part in them. I have taken part in some in which our Comrade Debs had a part. I was at the organization that he organized in this city some eight or ten years ago. Now, the point I want to make is that these conventions are full of enthusiasm. And that is right; we should sometimes mix sentiment with soberness; it is a part of life. But, as I know from experience, there are sober moments ahead of us, and when you go out of this hall, when you have laid aside your enthusiasm, then comes solid work. Are you going out with the reflection that you appreciate and grasp the situation that you are to tackle? Are you going out of here with your minds made up that the class in which we call ourselves, revolutionary Socialists so-called—that that class is organized to meet organized capital with the millions at its command? It has many weapons to fight us. First it has money. Then it has legislative tools. Then it has its judiciary; it has its army and its navy; it has its guns; it has armories; and last, it has the gallows. We call ourselves revolutionists. Do you know what the capitalists mean to do to you revolutionists? I simply throw these hints out that you young people may become reflective and know what you have to face at the first, and then it will give you strength. I am not here to cause any discouragement, but simply to encourage you to go on in your grand work.

Now, that is the solid foundation that I hope this organization will be built on; that it may be built not like a house upon the sand, that when the waves of adversity come it may go over into the ocean of oblivion; but that it shall be built upon a strong, granite, hard foundation; a foundation made up of the hearts and aspirations of the men and women of this twentieth century who have set their minds, their hands, their hearts and their heads against the past with all its miserable poverty, with its wage slavery, with its children ground into dividends, with its miners away down under the earth and with never the light of sunshine, and with its women selling the holy name of womanhood for a day's board. I hope we understand that this organization has set its face against that iniquity, and that it has set its eyes to the rising star of liberty, that means fraternity, solidarity, the universal brotherhood of man. I hope that while politics have been mentioned here—I am not one of those who, because a man or woman disagrees with me, cannot act with them—I am glad and proud to say I am too broad-minded to say they are a fakir or fool or a fraud because they disagree with me. My view may be narrow and theirs may be broad; but I do say to those who have intimated politics here as being necessary or a part of this organization, that I do not impute to them dishonesty or impure motives. But as I understand the call for this convention, politics had no place here; it was simply to be an

economic organization, and I hope for the good of this organization that when we go away from this hall, and our comrades go some to the west, some to the east, some to the north and some to the south, while some remain in Chicago, and all spread this light over this broad land and carry the message of what this convention has done, that there will be no room for politics at all. There may be room for politics; I have nothing to say about that; but it is a bread and butter question, an economic issue, upon which the fight must be made.

Now, what do we mean when we say revolutionary Socialist? We mean that the land shall belong to the landless, the tools to the toiler, and the products to the producers. (Applause.) Now, let us analyze that for just a moment, before you applaud me. First, the land belongs to the landless. Is there a single land owner in this country who owns his land by the constitutional rights given by the constitution of the United States who will allow you to vote it away from him? I am not such a fool as to believe it. We say, "The tools belong to the toiler." They are owned by the capitalist class. Do you believe they will allow you to go into the halls of the legislature and simply say, "Be it enacted that on and after a certain day the capitalist shall no longer own the tools and the factories and the places of industry, the ships that plow the ocean and our lakes?" Do you believe that they will submit? I do not. We say, "The products belong to the producers." It belongs to the capitalist class as their legal property. Do you think that they will allow you to vote them away from them by passing a law and saying, "Be it enacted that on and after a certain day Mr. Capitalist shall be dispossessed?" You may, but I do not believe it. Hence, when you roll under your tongue the expression that you are revolutionists, remember what that word means. It means a revolution that shall turn all these things over where they belong to the wealth producers. Now, how shall the wealth producers come into possession of them? I believe that if every man and every woman who works, or who toils in the mines, the mills, the workshops, the fields, the factories and the farms in our broad America should decide in their minds that they shall have that which of right belongs to them, and that no idler shall live upon their toil, and when your new organization, your economic organization, shall declare as man to man and woman to woman, as brothers and sisters, that you are determined that you will possess these things, then there is no army that is large enough to overcome you, for you yourselves constitute the army. (Applause). Now, when you have decided that you will take possession of these things, there will not need to be one gun fired or one scaffold erected. You will simply come into your own, by your own independence and your own manhood, and by asserting your own individuality, and not sending any man to any legislature in any State of the American Union to enact a law that you shall have what is your own; yours by nature and by your manhood and by your very presence upon this earth.

Nature has been lavish to her children. She has placed in this earth all the material of wealth that is necessary to make men and women happy. She has given us brains to go into her store house and bring from its recesses all that is necessary. She has given us these two hands and these brains to manufacture them suited to the wants of men and women. Our civilization stands on a parallel with all other civilizations. There is just one thing we lack, and we have only ourselves to blame if we do not become free. We simply lack the intelligence to take possession of that which we have produced. (Applause). And I believe and I hope and I feel that the men and women who constitute a convention like this can come together and organize that intelligence. I must say that I do not know whether I am saying anything that interests you or not, but I feel so delighted that I am talking to your heads and not to your hands and feet this afternoon. I feel that you will at least listen to me, and maybe you will disagree with me, but I care not; I simply want to shed the light as I see it. I wish to say that my conception of the future method of taking possession of this is that of the general strike; that is my conception of it. The trouble with all the strikes in the past has been this: the workingmen like the teamsters in our cities, these hard-working teamsters, strike and go out and

starve. Their children starve. Their wives get discouraged. Some feel that they have to go out and beg for relief, and to get a little coal to keep the children warm, or a little bread to keep the wife from starving, or a little something to keep the spark of life in them so that they can remain wage slaves. That is the way with the strikes in the past. My conception of the strike of the future is not to strike and go out and starve, but to strike and remain in and take possession of the necessary property of production. If any one is to starve—I do not say it is necessary—let it be the capitalist class. They have starved us long enough, while they have had wealth and luxury and all that is necessary. You men and women should be imbued with the spirit that is now displayed in far-off Russia and far-off Siberia where we thought the spark of manhood and womanhood had been crushed out of them. Let us take example from them. We see the capitalist class fortifying themselves to-day behind their Citizens' Associations and Employers' Associations in order that they may crush the American labor movement. Let us cast our eyes over to far-off Russia and take heart and courage from those who are fighting the battle there, and from the further fact shown in the dispatches that appear this morning in the news that carries the greatest terror to the capitalist class throughout all the world—the emblem that has been the terror of all tyrants through all the ages, and there you will see that the red flag has been raised. (Applause). According to the *Tribune*, the greatest terror is evinced in Odessa and all through Russia because the red flag has been raised. They know that where the red flag has been raised whoever enroll themselves beneath that flag recognize the universal brotherhood of man; they recognize that the red current that flows through the veins of all humanity is identical, that the ideas of all humanity are identical; that those who raise the red flag, it matters not where, whether on the sunny plains of China, or on the sun-beaten hills of Africa, or on the far-off snow-capped shores of the north, or in Russia or in America—that they all belong to the human family and have an identity of interest. (Applause). That is what they know.

So when we come to decide, let us sink such differences as nationality, religion, politics, and set our eyes eternally and forever towards the rising star of the industrial republic of labor; remembering that we have left the old behind and have set our faces toward the future. There is no power on earth that can stop men and women who are determined to be free at all hazards. There is no power on earth so great as the power of intellect. It moves the world and it moves the earth.

Now, in conclusion, I wish to say to you—and you will excuse me because of what I am going to say and only attribute it to my interest in humanity. I wish to say that nineteen years ago on the fourth of May of this year, I was one of those at a meeting at the Haymarket in this city to protest against eleven workingmen being shot to pieces at a factory in the southeastern part of this city because they had dared to strike for the eight-hour movement that was to be inaugurated in America in 1886. The Haymarket meeting was called primarily and entirely to protest against the murder of comrades at the McCormick factory. When that meeting was nearing its close some one threw a bomb. No one knows to this day who threw it except the man who threw it. Possibly he has rendered his account with nature and has passed away. But no human being alive knows who threw it. And yet in the soil of Illinois, the soil that gave a Lincoln to America, the soil in which the great, magnificent Lincoln was buried, in the State that was supposed to be the most liberal in the union, five men sleep the last sleep in Waldheim under a monument that has been raised there because they dared to raise their voices for humanity. I say to any of you who are here and who can do so, it is well worth your time to go out there and draw some inspiration around the graves of the first martyrs who fell in the great industrial struggle for liberty on American soil. (Applause). I say to you that even within the sound of my voice, only two short blocks from where we meet to-day, the scaffold was erected on which those five men paid the penalty for daring to raise their voices against the iniquities of the age in which we live. We are assembled here for the same purpose. And do any of you older men remember the telegrams that were sent out from Chicago while our comrades were not yet even cut down from the cruel gallows? "Anarchy is dead, and these miscreants have been put out of the way." Oh, friends, I am sorry that I even had to use that word, "anarchy" just now in your presence, which was not in my mind at the outset. So if any of you wish to go out there and look at this monument that has been raised by those who believed in their comrades' innocence and sincerity, I will ask you, when you have gone out and looked at the monument, that you will go to the reverse side of the monument and there read on the reverse side the words of a man, himself the purest and the noblest man who ever sat in the gubernatorial chair of the State of Illinois, John P. Altgeld. (Applause). On that monument you will read the clause of his message in which he pardoned the men who were lingering then in Joliet. I have nothing more to say. I ask you to read the words of Altgeld, who was at that time the governor, and had been a lawyer and a judge, and knew whereof he spoke, and then take out your copy books and copy the words of Altgeld when he released those who had not been slaughtered at the capitalists' behest, and then take them home and change your minds about what those men were put to death for.

Now, I have taken up your time in this because I simply feel that I have a right as a mother and as a wife of one of those sacrificed men to say whatever I can to bring the light to bear upon this conspiracy and to show you the way it was. Now, I thank you for the time that I have taken up of yours. I hope that we will meet again some time, you and I, in some hall where we can meet and organize the wage workers of America, the men and women, so that the children may not go into the factories, nor the women into the factories, unless they go under proper conditions. I hope even now to live to see the day when the first dawn of the new era of labor will have arisen, when capitalism will be a thing of the past, and the new industrial republic, the commonwealth of labor, shall be in operation. I thank you. (Applause.)

Marxism and the "Negro Question"

Ralph J. Bunche

THE FUNDAMENTAL FEATURES OF THE STATUS OF THE NEGRO IN AMERICAN SOCIETY, OF THE STRUGGLE FOR NEGRO EMANCIPATION, AND OF ITS RELATION TO THE PROLETARIAN STRUGGLE

Introduction

1. Of all questions facing the American working class and the American Communist movement, the "Negro Question" is the most specifically American of all questions, with only secondary analogies to conditions elsewhere. It is a question of first-rate importance to the American proletariat. And yet of all questions it is the one to which the least serious attention on the part of the Marxist theoreticians has been devoted; there has, in fact, not yet been made in America any serious analysis of the Negro Question from the Marxist viewpoint. The general backwardness and sterility of socialist theory in America and the traditional American Socialist "nihilism" on the Negro Question as an indirect expression of the "white supremacy" ideology ("There is no Negro question!"—"There is only an economic question of workers against bosses") are partly responsible for this condition. And, altho the Communist movement rapidly broke with the shameless white chauvinism of large sections of the prewar Socialist movement, the theoretical reorientation has been much slower. Until very recently the Communist movement remained content with vague and platitudinous phrases and, when recently a new theoretical departure

Source: Ralph Bunche, "Marxism and the 'Negro Question'" in Charles P. Henry, ed., *Ralph J. Bunche: Selected Speeches and Writings* (Ann Arbor: University of Michigan Press, 1995), 35–45.

was attempted under the stimulus of the Communist International, it went astray as a result of a fundamentally false orientation ("national minority" theory). A truly Marxist theory of the Negro question and even truly Marxist analysis of its main features still remains for the future.

2. At the same time distinct signs are not absent pointing to a definite revival of the independent social activity of the Negro masses in the North and in the South, in the urban and in the rural centers, under the stimulus of the economic crisis, the great growth in unemployment, and the incredible chaos in the cotton economy of the South. In this situation the unsatisfactory state of current Communist theory on the Negro question (especially in this country) is very serious and even dangerous.

The Status of the American Negro

3. The status of the Negro in the United States is in a very real sense specific to this country; only in the most general sense does it bear any relation to the status of colored peoples in other parts of the world, in the West Indies, in Africa, in South America, etc. Only against the background of the special course of American historical development, only in connection with the concrete relation of social forces in this country, can the status of the American Negro be understood and the problems deriving therefrom appreciated.

4. The Negro people in the United States do not constitute a colonial people under the heel of American imperialism. All of the essential characteristics of a colony (geographical separation from metropolis, the distinctness of the national economy of the

271

colony and its specific relation to the imperi-
alist economy of the metropolis, etc.) [*sic*].
But just as little do the Negro people constitute a national minority in the real sense of
the term. For the formation of a nation there
is necessary a community (and distinctness)
of language, of territory, of economic life (a
national economy), of psychic structure (culture) and tradition. Not a single one of these
conditions is characteristic of the Negroes in
the United States. The attempt to supply the
necessary community of territory by the creation of a fictitious "Negro-land" (the "Black
Belt") runs contrary to every fact of American
history and to every conception of contemporary tendencies and movements among the
Negro people. The fundamental falsity of the
"national minority" orientation comes to
erase expression in the obvious inappropri-
ateness of the slogan of "self-determination"
(the proper slogan for a people suffering
from national oppression) to the condition of
the Negroes in America. The slogan of self-
determination, in a situation where every
force of bourgeois law, custom, and public
opinion constantly operated to maintain and
widen the breach between the races, is an objective support to jim-crowism. The point of
view of the Negro people as a national minority is false in conception and dangerous in
concrete application.

5. The Negro people in the United States
constitute, in the words of Lenin, *a subject
caste on a racial basis*. The Negro people form
an integral element of the American nation
and of the American national economy; their
culture, territory, language, are all characteristically American. In the American social edi-
fice they, as a race, occupy a peculiar and
depressed status, a caste status. A close analogy would be the position of the "depressed
classes," the "untouchables," in Hindu society
in India.

6. The depressed caste status of the American Negroes is expressed primarily in the
semi-servile condition of the Negro farmer in
Southern agriculture and the inferior position of the Negro worker in industrial life.
The under-privileged state of the Negro socially (jim-crow, segregating, lynch law), and

politically, follow directly. Fundamentally, the
Negro in the United States forms a well-defined subject caste, with a distinctly inferior
economic, social, and political status.

THE HISTORICAL ROOTS OF THE CASTE STATUS OF THE NEGRO

Caste status is, as Lenin has pointed out more
than once, essentially a pre-capitalist institution, a phase or a *remnant* of a non-capitalist
social (and economic) order. How to account
for the existence of this "remnant of feudalism" in the highly developed capitalist system
of this country is the first problem of a Marxist approach to the Negro question.

8. The roots of the present subject status
of the Negro in America must be traced back
to the days of slavery, nearly three-quarters of
a century ago. Under slavery there was an immediate and obvious basis for the social subjection of the black man as such—their
economically enslaved condition as a race.
Had the American Civil War really effected
the complete emancipation of the Negro
slave, there would indeed have been no
ground for the continued existence of the
Negro as an inferior caste. But the victorious
industrial bourgeois of the North adopted a
course of action that led to quite other results. It rejected the "Radical" plan for reconstruction, a plan that envisaged the complete
destruction of the economic and political
power of the slaveocracy and the real emancipation of the Negro slaves, i. e., their transformation into free peasant-proprietors and into
free proletarians. On the contrary, the Northern bourgeois, after considerable hesitation
and vacillation, threw its support to the "Conservative" plan of Reconstruction, which aimed
at conciliating the old slave owners by abolishing chattel slavery in name but retaining it in
somewhat modified form in fact. The bourgeois democratic revolution—the essence of
the Civil War—was thereby stifled and distorted; the emancipation of the Negro was rendered incomplete, even from a consistent
bourgeois standpoint. Thus, the present economic status of the Negro was rendered in-

complete, even from a consistent economic bourgeois standpoint. Thus, the present status of the Negro farmer is essentially a survival of slavery. And when, in the course of time, the Negro farmer comes to enter industry, he naturally brings with him his caste status. The specially depressed economic position of the Negro farmer is essentially a survival of slavery. The specially depressed economic position of the Negro is the basis upon which the whole system of social, political, and cultural subjection is reared.

The caste status of the American Negro is essentially a pre-capitalist survival, a "relic of feudalism." But such pre-capitalist survivals find a welcome place in the decaying structure of capitalism in its final, imperialist-monopolistic epoch. The bourgeois is no longer, as it was in the great days of its youth, the ruthless destroyer of the obsolete and the reactionary. In its senility, "the decaying bourgeois ... supports everything that is backward, dying and medieval ..." (Lenin). The specially depressed economic status of the Negro peasant and proletarian serves as a valuable source of super-profit for monopoly-capital—in a strictly analogous manner to colonial exploitation. At the same time it serves as a point of support for the class domination of the bourgeois "Divide and rule"! For this reason the race oppression of the Negro has become an integral element of the bourgeois-imperialist stystem in this country.

10. [*sic*] It is in the specific caste status of the American Negro, and the integration of this status into the American imperialism, that race prejudice ("white chauvinism") has its roots. Class interests are directly transmuted into class ideology; this is a fundamental social mechanism. The caste status of the American Negro—so advantageous to the ruling class from the viewpoint of economic profit and class power—is transformed into the corresponding class ideology—"the theory of the inherent racial inferiority" of the Negro, race prejudice, etc. But "the ruling ideas of any age are the ideas of the ruling class" (Marx). Race prejudice thus develops into an element of the currently accepted social thought (bourgeois ideology) and is ab-sorbed by the other classes of society to the degree that they are under the ideological influence of the ruling class. It is because the white American workers and farmers are so "backward," i.e., so much under the spiritual influence of the bourgeois, that they are so afflicted with anti-Negro race prejudice. A secondary factor in the same direction is the role that the feeling of racial superiority plays as a form of psychic compensation to the backward masses of the white toilers for the incredible miseries of their everyday existence. Nor can the deliberate activities of the white ruling class in stirring up race hatred be minimized.

THE STRUCTURE OF AMERICAN NEGRO SOCIETY

11. The great Negro migrations during the last two decades, in the course of which scores of thousands of Negro farmers swarmed to the great Northern industrial centers and to the basic industries of the land, really introduced a new stage in the history of the American Negro. They effected a profound social fermentation and a basic realignment of class forces. They faced the Negro masses with a whole series of new problems arising out of the new urban and industrial environment. They really created the modern Negro proletariat. They greatly stimulated the development of the Negro bourgeois and petty bourgeois and seriously transformed the relations between these classes. They had a profound effect upon the Negro peasantry in the South, sunk in the mire of peonage and semi-reform. They also greatly influenced the relations between the two races in the North as well as in the South. All of these phenomena soon made themselves evident in their effect upon the changed structure of American Negro society.

12. The social organization of the Negro people in this country, altho, of course, closely related to and in fact integrated into American society as such, bears a characteristic aspect, especially in the relation of classes and the specific gravity of each in the whole. The

organization of Negro society bears, in certain important aspects, a significant resemblance to the organization of society in a colony or a subject nation.

13. The Negro bourgeois is rather weak numerically, absolutely and relatively, and even weaker economically. It has no hold upon or contract with basic industry; it is almost exclusively confined to certain very unimportant branches, usually organized on a small scale, or to commercial and related occupations that emerge in the large Negro sections of the big cities, South as well as North. But through the Negro bourgeois, through the more pliant elements of the petty bourgeois, and through the conservative sections of the professional "race leaders," the white American bourgeois exerts tremendous influence over the masses of the Negro people and it operates with borrowed power. The fundamental standpoint of the Negro bourgeois was theoretically formulated by Booker T. Washington in the famous "Atlanta Compromise": The Negro is to be content with his place in the bourgeois American scheme of things. He is to bend his energies toward becoming an efficient servant of the white master. Any present aspiration for social and political rights—not to speak of social equality—is a vain and dangerous delusion. In the South the Negroes are to acquiesce in their complete political disfrachisement; in the North they are to serve as blind voting cattle for the Republican Party. Lastly, an infamous flirtation with the Democratic Party (in North and South) has been initiated (the De Priest "nonpartisan" conference). Within the last year the crusade against Communism has become an important part of the services rendered by the Negro bourgeois to their white masters. The political activities of the race leaders of this class are marked by clique squabbles, gross corruption, and shameless patronage—all at the expense of the Negro masses. Of the emancipation of their people they know nothing and care less.

14. Thru the sham social power of prestige, lent it by the white ruling class, the Negro bourgeois and its professional race leaders have been able hitherto to dominate the social and political ideas of the backward Negro masses. In this work the wide-spread network of Negro social and fraternal societies (especially the churches) have played a very important role.

15. The Negro petty bourgeois and professional (most of the professionals belong to the petty bourgeois) are more enumerous altho proportionately also smaller among the Negroes than among the whites (only in the proportion clergy to the population do the Negroes show precedence) and of considerable consequence. Like the bourgeois, this class found a firm basis of existence (especially in the North) only with the great Negro migrations and the creation of the huge Negro cities in the relatively free atmosphere of the North. In the post-war "renascence," a relatively free atmosphere of the period of deepgoing fermentation and real achievement, the Negro intellectual played a brilliant role, especially in literature and fine arts.

16. As a consequence of the characteristic caste status of the Negro people in American society, the Negro petty bourgeoisie is destined to play a far more significant and progressive social role in the struggle of the Negro people for emancipation and in the general social struggle than is the white bourgeoisie in the analogous situation. As a significant factor in the life and development of the Negro race, petty bourgeoisie is second only to the Negro proletariat.

17. A large part of the Negro petty bourgeoisie is bound up, economically, organizationally, and ideologically, with the Negro bourgeoisie, which it aids in carrying out its specific role as the agency of white capitalism among Negroes. Considerable sections, however, have already gone a long way in freeing themselves, more or less, from the spiritual domination of the bourgeoisie, or at least from the greatest bourgeoisie prejudices. The social outlook of these sections of the petty bourgeoisie has hitherto been marked, quite inevitably considering their class position, by its lack of persistency and resolution, by its extravagant oscillations from one extreme to the other, by its fantastic utopianism combined with an equally fantastic "practicalism,"

but all within the framework of the basic bourgeoisie preconceptions. Especially characteristic is its strange faith in the belief that the Negro question can be solved within the framework of capitalism, perhaps with the benevolent aid of the white capitalist themselves. At one time, Garveyism, an essentially reactionary philosophy based on an inverted form of the "white supremacy" gospel of the white charlatanism, had considerable hold over the lower middle class elements of the large Negro cities. Now Garveyism is happily dead. Today the Negro intellectuals and professionals are lost in the absurd utopia of creating a self-contained Negro economy through utilizing the "organized buying power" of the race or through some equally efficacious means. The capricious and ever changing vagaries that dominate the Negro petty bourgeoisie are a certain indication of the gulf that exists between it and the masses of the Negro people, the peasants and workers, whose interests are poles apart from the unreal fantasies of the small man or professional, I to [sic] enstrangement from its own people with the consequent lack of political and social stability, is unquestionably the greatest inner weakness of the Negro petty bourgeoisie.

17. [sic] Nevertheless, from the general historical viewpoint, the Negro petty bourgeoisie still has progressive potentialities in view of the essentially democratic character of the struggle against the caste oppression of the Negro. Some sections of the Negro intellectuals are already marching leftwards, primarily as a result of the profound impression made upon them by the example of the Soviet Union. But the actual realization of its historical potentialities implies an end to reactionary and futile utopian dreaming, an organic approach to the masses, a participation in their interests and aspirations, a close alliance with the advanced sections of the proletariat, white and black.

18. As has already been pointed out the Negro farmer in the South (where the bulk of the Negro people are to be found) are not "free" farmers in the capitalist sense of the term. They occupy an intermediate position

between free farmers and slaves—a semi-serf position that is the basic element of the caste status of the Negro people in this country. There are practically no Negro agricultural capitalists and almost as few wealthy farmers. The vast majority of the Negro farmers—whether tenants (the proportion of tenancy is very high) or nominal "owners"—find themselves in the category of the rest of the poor, exploited in pre-capitalist and semi-feudal forms of exploitation (peonage, sharecropping, etc. [sic], in many cases even forced labor. The Negro agricultural worker is not a free laborer in the bourgeois sense; he also toils under semi-slave relations of exploitation. On this basis, a superstructure of caste oppression has been raised of incredible viciousness. The most elementary form of economic organization is prohibited under penalty of death (the cases of the Phillips County, Arkansas, and the Camp Hill, Alabama sharecropping unions).

19. Yet even here the wave of Negro migrations and the experiences of the World War have had an immense effect. The bleak seclusion, the dreary isolation of decades, the helpless desolation, was broken.

A vigorous breath of fresh air swept through the poisonous atmosphere of the Old South. The vision of the Negro peasant was suddenly and immensely enlarged; intimate contacts were established with migrated friends and relatives in the North; an understanding began to dawn that things must not be always—and are not everywhere—the same. The Negro peasant as a vital factor in the movement for freedom.

20. The Negro proletarian is primarily to be found in unskilled and semi-skilled capacities in large-scale basic industry. Altho he has become a proletarian he has brought his caste status with him; he occupies a position of distinct inferiority in the scheme of things in industry. He has no access to the more desirable situation; he is hindered in his approach to skilled or semi-skilled jobs; he is forced into the least paid and most menial occupations; he is discriminated against in wages and working conditions. His recent peasant background and his lack of collective experience

in the labor movement are expressed in his backwardness in class consciousness and in his indifferent or even negative attitude on many of the basic questions of class struggle. (This attitude is, of course, helped by the antagonistic attitude of the white workers and labor leaders.) The white employing class has not been slow in utilizing this backwardness of the Negro workers and the antagonism between the Negro and white workers in their attacks on the labor movement and on the working class as a whole.

21. Yet in spite of all temporary circumstances, the Negro proletariat constitutes historically the natural leadership of the Negro people in its social struggle in American society. The leading role of the proletariat within the Negro people is made inevitably by the inner processes of capitalist production, which thrust the proletariat to the fore of modern society, organizes it, stimulate its class consciousness, widen its political horizon, and give it that collective self-confidence, solidarity, and consciousness of aim which are the necessary attributes of class leadership. The emergence of the Negro proletariat as the leader of the Negro people still remains for the future but the creation of the modern Negro proletariat, thru the migrations, is certainly the most significant event in the history of the Negro since the days of Reconstruction.

THE NEGRO WORKER AND AMERICAN LABOR

22. The sudden influx of tens of thousands of black workers into Northern industry inevitably aggravated the anti-Negro prejudice of the backward. At the same time the narrow and exclusive craft structure and the opportunist [sic] philosophy of American trade unionism served from the very beginning as a most serious obstacle in the way of the black workers in industry. The conservative trade unions, in spite of occasional fine phrases, have practically closed their doors to the Negro workers and have all but invited them to throw in their lot with the white capitalists as scabs and strike-breakers—a course incessantly urged by the conservative Negro leaders as well. The darkest page in history of the American organized labor movement is its shameful record of antipathy and discrimination against the black worker.

23. But the progress of the class struggle promises to heal even this ominous breach in the ranks of the American proletariat. The white heat of the class struggle will burn out the corruption of race prejudice. The fraternization of white and colored workers in the South during the recent strikes, however hesitating, uncertain, and unstable, is a straw in the wind. The slow but inevitable deepening of the class consciousness of the white proletariat, i.e., its growing ideological liberation from the bourgeoisie, will certainly deliver the white workers from the thoroly [sic] bourgeois curse of race prejudice.

24. The submergence of national and racial differences within the proletariat in the firm ties of class solidarity is an indispensable requisite for the triumph of the revolutionary struggle against capitalism. The struggle against race prejudice of the white workers is the fundamental task of all revolutionary forces in the labor movement. In the Communist movement, in which all inner-class distinctions vanish, any open or disguised manifestations of race prejudice, which come as a result of the pressure of bourgeois ideology of the class, must be deliberately and consciously eliminated.

NEGRO EMANCIPATION AND THE PROLETARIAN REVOLUTION

25. The whole burden of the analysis of the status of the Negro people in this country goes to prove that the deliverance of the Negro people from their caste existence is in its content essentially a democratic task—the only form of an uncompleted bourgeois revolution in the United States today. In that respect it is similar to the liberation of subject nations of colonies. Only the elimination of the underlying economic conditions upon which the subjection of the American Negro is predicated can make possible any real

emancipation. The radical eradication of the semi-feudal forms of exploitation, of peonage, tenancy, sharecropping, furnishing, the shattering of the power of the Southern landlords thru the nationalization of the land and its distribution among the cultivators, the elimination of all elements of inferiority of the Negro's status in industry—these are the basic conditions upon which the social and political liberation of the colored people is conditioned. These measures represent merely the demands of consistent democracy: they are in all respects akin to the classical ideals of the bourgeois-democratic revolution, the Great French Revolution, for example. Not a single one is a specifically socialist demand— not one necessarily implies the socialization of all the means of production, etc.

26. But the democratic character of the task of the Negro liberation from caste status by no means implies that the Negro question today can be solved within the framework of the capitalist democracy. So anti-democratic has the bourgeois become in its period of decay, so organically bound up with everything that is outlived, reactionary, and decadent, that the realization of the basic democratic demands is possible only thru the overflow of capitalist "democracy" thru the concentration of political power in the hands of the proletariat. In such directional contradiction does history move that only the dictatorship of the proletariat can guarantee democracy to the masses and bring real democracy, for the first time, to the Negro people. A whole historical period has passed since the Civil War; a bourgeois revolution in the USA today is a historical impossibility— today only a proletarian revolution can accomplish what the American bourgeois revolution that was the Civil War failed to do.

27. From this viewpoint, the class differentiation, now rapidly taking place among the Negro people and destroying any possible "racial unity" of all classes, is to be regarded as a profoundly progressive and revolutionary phenomenon. The Negro bourgeoisie can only be a reactionary force in the struggle for the emancipation of its own race, so firm and numerous are the bands that tie it to white capital. The more completely and more rapidly that takes place the class separation of the popular masses of the Negro people from the Negro bourgeoisie, the better. At the opposite end of the pole stands the Negro proletariat, whose tremendous historical role as the chosen vanguard of the Negro people is only emphasized by the close organic link between the democratic emancipation of the Negro people and the socialist revolution of the proletariat in this country. Under the hegemony of and close alliance with the proletariat, the Negro peasantry and the broad sections of the Negro petty bourgeoisie can play a profoundly revolutionary role. The process of class differentiation among the Negro people lays the basis for the liberation of the Negro masses from the influence of the white bourgeoisie (transmitted through the Negro bourgeoisie) and for the achievement of the hegemony of the proletariat in the struggle for Negro emancipation.

28. It is clear that the racial, that is, caste, emancipation of the Negro cannot come as the result of any "purely racial" movement of [sic] any movement deliberately aiming to subordinate, in the name of an unreal racial unity the masses of the Negro people to the narrow interests of the Negro bourgeoisie (who work hand in glove with their white paymasters), of any movement conscientiously striving to divorce the liberation struggle of the Negro people from the chief social movement of our times, the class war of labor against capital. The racial emancipation of the American Negro, in the present historical situation, is possible only as an integral aspect and as inevitable consequence of the revolutionary overthrow of the capitalist system, of the victory of the proletariat.

THE IMMEDIATE STRUGGLE AND THE GENERAL PERSPECTIVE

29. It is clear that this far-reaching perspective can today assume vitality and general significance only if it can be shown in life itself to emerge as a natural development of a program of immediate action immediately

associated with every phase of Negro life under the caste oppression of American society. The Communist must defend and represent the basic interests of the Negro workers, of the Negro peasants, and of the Negro petty bourgeoisie, to the degree that the latter constitutes a progressive historical force. The Communists must try to weld together the masses of the Negro people (workers, peasants, city petty bourgeoisie) under the leadership of the Negro proletariat and against the white ruling class and its Negro agents (the Negro bourgeoisie). The Communists throw all energies into breaking down all barriers between the Negro and the white workers and into strengthening the bonds between the white workers and the Negro people. The Communist program must champion the abolition of peonage and the serf conditions of the Negro farmers in the South, the organization of leagues of sharecroppers and tenants and unions of farm-laborers. The Communists must stand for the complete equality of the Negro in industry, the smashing of the barriers against the Negro workers in the trade unions, the organization of the unorganized and the unskilled colored workers. The Communists must take up the struggle against lynching, jim-crowism, and discrimination. The Communists demand the complete social and political equality of the Negro race. The Communists strive to break the hold of the capitalist political parties over the Negro masses and to win these masses to the cause of labor, which is their cause as well, and to labor class political action (the labor party as the champion of the oppressed Negroes). Thru the participation of the Negro masses in these struggles (and of Negroes and whites side by side), thru the development of these struggles to ever higher and higher levels, the road will be opened for the realization of the far-reaching perspective of the final emancipation of the Negro people from their submerged caste position as a phase of the general emancipation of the toiling masses from the yoke of capitalism.

Socialism and the Negro Problem

W. E. B. DuBois

One might divide those interested in Socialism in two distinct camps: On the one hand those far-sighted thinkers who are seeking to determine from the facts of modern industrial organization just what the outcome is going to be; on the other hand, those who suffer from the present industrial situation and who are anxious that, whatever the broad outcome may be, at any rate the present suffering which they know so well shall be stopped. It is this second class of social thinkers who are interested particularly in the Negro problem. They are saying that the plight of ten million human beings in the United States predominantly of the working class, is so evil that it calls for much attention in any program of future social reform. This paper, however, is addressed not to this class, but rather to the class of theoretical Socialists; and its thesis is: In the Negro problem as it presents itself in the United States, theoretical Socialism of the twentieth century meets a critical dilemma.

There is no doubt as to the alternatives presented. On the one hand, here are 90 million white people who in their extraordinary development present a peculiar field for the application of Socialistic principles; but on the whole, these people are demanding today that just as under capitalistic organization the Negro has been the excluded (*i.e.*, exploited) class, so, too, any Socialistic program shall also exclude the ten million. Many Socialists have acquiesced in this program. No recent convention of Socialists has dared to face fairly the Negro problem and make a straight-forward declaration that they regard Negroes as men in the same sense that other persons are. The utmost that the party has

been able to do is not to rescind the declaration of an earlier convention. The general attitude of thinking members of the party has been this: We must not turn aside from the great objects of Socialism to take up this issue of the American Negro; let the question wait; when the objects of Socialism are achieved, this problem will be settled along with other problems.

That there is a logical flaw here, no one can deny. Can the problem of any group of ten million be properly considered as "aside" from any program of Socialism? Can the objects of Socialism be achieved so long as the Negro is neglected? Can any great human problem "wait"? If Socialism is going to settle the American problem of race prejudice without direct attack along these lines by Socialists, why is it necessary for Socialists to fight along other lines? Indeed, there is a kind of fatalistic attitude on the part of certain transcendental Socialists, which often assumes that the whole battle of Socialism is coming by a kind of evolution in which active individual effort on their part is hardly necessary.

As a matter of fact, the Socialists face in the problem of the American Negro this question: Can a minority of any group or country be left out of the Socialistic problem? It is, of course, agreed that a majority could not be left out. Socialists usually put great stress on the fact that the laboring class form a majority of all nations and nevertheless are unjustly treated in the distribution of wealth. Suppose, however, that this unjust distribution affected only a minority, and that only a tenth of the American nation were working under unjust economic conditions: Could a Socialistic program be carried out which acquiesced in this condition? Many American Socialists seem silently to assume that this would be possible.

Source: W. E. B. Du Bois, "Socialism and the Negro Problem," *New Review*, 1 February 1913, 138–141.

To put it concretely, they are going to carry on industry so far as the mass is concerned; they are going to get rid of the private control of capital and they are going to divide up the social income among these 90 million in accordance with some rule of reason, rather than in the present haphazard way: But at the same time, they are going to permit the continued exploitation of these ten million workers. So far as these ten million workers are concerned, there is to be no active effort to secure for them a voice in the Social Democracy, or an adequate share in the social income. The idea is that ultimately when the 90 millions come to their own, they will voluntarily share with the ten million serfs.

Does the history of the world justify us in expecting any such outcome? Frankly, I do not believe it does. The program is that of industrial aristocracy which the world has always tried; the only difference being that such Socialists are trying to include in the inner circle a much larger number than have ever been included before. Socialistic as this program may be called, it is not real Social Democracy. The essence of Social Democracy is that there shall be no excluded or exploited classes in the Socialistic state; that there shall be no man or woman so poor, ignorant or black as not to count one. Is this simply a far off ideal, or is it a possible program? I have come to believe that the test of any great movement toward social reform is the Excluded Class. Who is it that Reform does *not* propose to benefit? If you are saving dying babies, whose babies are you going to let die? If you are feeding the hungry, what folk are you (regretfully, perhaps but none the less truly) going to let starve? If you are making a juster division of wealth, what people are you going to permit at present to remain in poverty? If you are giving all men votes (not only in the "political" but also in the economic world) what class of people are you going to allow to remain disfranchised?

More than that, assuming that if you did exclude Negroes temporarily from the growing Socialistic state, the ensuing uplift of humanity would in the end repair the temporary damage, the present question is, *can* you exclude the Negro and push Socialism forward? Every tenth man in the United States is of acknowledged Negro descent; if you take those in gainful occupations, one out of every seven Americans is colored; and if you take laborers and working-men in the ordinary acceptation of the term, one out of every five is colored. The problem then is to lift four-fifths of a group on the backs of the other fifth. Even if the submerged fifth were "dull driven cattle," this program of Socialistic opportunism would not be easy. But when the program is proposed in the face of a group growing in intelligence and social power and a group made suspicious and bitter by analogous action on the part of trade unionists, what is anti-Negro Socialism doing but handing to its enemies the powerful weapon of four and one-half million men who will find it not simply to their interest, but a sacred duty to underbid the labor market, vote against labor legislation, and fight to keep their fellow laborers down. Is it not significant that Negro soldiers in the army are healthier and desert less than whites?

Nor is this all: what becomes of Socialism when it engages in such a fight for human downfall? Whither are gone its lofty aspiration and high resolve—its songs and comradeship?

The Negro Problem then is the great test of the American Socialist. Shall American Socialism strive to train for its Socialistic state ten million serfs who will serve or be exploited by the state, or shall it strive to incorporate them immediately into that body politic? Theoretically, of course, all Socialists, with few exceptions, would wish the latter program. But it happens that in the United States there is a strong local opinion in the South which violently opposed any program of any kind of reform that recognizes the Negro as a man. So strong is this body of opinion that you have in the South a most extraordinary development. The whole radical movement there represented by men like Blease and Vardaman and Tillman and Jeff. Davis and attracting such demagogues as Hoke Smith, includes in its program of radical reform a most bitter and reactionary hatred of the Negro. The average modern Socialist can scarcely grasp the extent of this hatred; even murder and torture of human beings holds a prominent place in its philosophy; the defilement of colored women is its joke, and justice toward colored men will not be listened to. The only basis on which one can even approach these people with a plea for the barest tolerance of colored folk, is that the murder and mistreatment of colored men may possibly hurt white men. Consequently the Socialist party finds itself in this predicament: if it acquiesces in race hatred, it has a chance to turn the tremendous power of Southern white radicalism toward its own party; if it does not do this, it becomes a "party of the Negro," with its growth South and North decidedly checked. There are signs that the Socialist leaders are going to accept the chance of getting hold of the radical South whatever its cost. This paper is written to ask such leaders: After you have gotten the radical South and paid the price which they demand, will the result be Socialism?

Marxism and the Negro Problem

W. E. B. Du Bois

Karl Marx was a Jew born at Treves, Germany, in March, 1818. He came of an educated family and studied at the Universities of Bonn and Berlin, planning first to become a lawyer, and then to teach philosophy. But his ideas were too radical for the government. He turned to journalism, and finally gave his life to economic reform, dying in London in 1883, after having lived in Germany, Belgium, France, and, for the last thirty-five years of his life, in England. He published in 1867, the first volume of his monumental work, *Capital*.

There are certain books in the world which every searcher for truth must know: the Bible, *Critique of Pure Reason*, *Origin of Species*, and Karl Marx's *Capital*.

Yet until the Russian Revolution, Karl Marx was little known in America. He was treated condescendingly in the universities, and regarded even by the intelligent public as a radical agitator whose curious and inconvenient theories it was easy to refute. Today, at last, we all know better, and we see in Karl Marx a colossal genius of infinite sacrifice and monumental industry, and with a mind of extraordinary logical keenness and grasp. We may disagree with many of the great books of truth that I have named, and with *Capital*, but they can never be ignored.

At a recent dinner to Einstein, another great Jew, the story was told of a professor who was criticized as having "no sense of humor" because he tried to explain the Theory of Relativity in a few simple words. Something of the same criticism must be attached to anyone who attempts similarly to indicate

Source: W.E.B. Du Bois, "Marxism and the Negro Problem," *The Crisis*, May 1933.

the relation of Marxian philosophy and the American Negro problem. And yet, with all modesty, I am essaying the task knowing that it will be but tentative and subject to much criticism, both on my own part and that of other abler students.

The task which Karl Marx set himself was to study and interpret the organization of industry in the modern world. One of Marx's earlier works, *The Communist Manifesto*, issued in 1848, on the eve of the series of democratic revolutions in Europe, laid down this fundamental proposition.

"That in every historical epoch the prevailing mode of economic production and exchange, and the social organization necessarily following from it, form the basis upon which is built up, and from which alone can be explained, the political and intellectual history of that epoch; that consequently the whole history of mankind … has been a history of class struggles, contest between exploiting and exploited, ruling and oppressed classes; that the history of these class struggles forms a series of evolution in which, now-a-days, a stage has been reached where the exploited and oppressed class (the proletariat) cannot attain its emancipation from the sway of the exploiting and ruling class (the bourgeoisie) without, at the same time, and once and for all, emancipating society at large from all exploitation, oppression, class-distinction and class-struggles."

All will notice in this manifesto, phrases which have been used so much lately and so carelessly that they have almost lost their meaning. But behind them still is living and insistent truth. The *class struggle* of exploiter and exploited is a reality. The capitalist still today owns machines, materials, and wages with which to buy labor. The laborer even in America owns little more than his ability to work. A wage contract takes place between these two and the resultant manufactured commodity or service is the property of the capitalist.

Here Marx begins his scientific analysis based on a mastery of practically all economic theory before his time and on an extraordinary, thoroughgoing personal knowledge of industrial conditions over all Europe and many other parts of the world.

His final conclusions were never all properly published. He lived only to finish the first volume of his *Capital,* and the other two volumes were completed from his papers and notes by his friend Engels. The result is an unfinished work, extraordinarily difficult to read and understand and one which the master himself would have been first to criticize as not properly representing his mature and finished thought.

Nevertheless, that first volume, together with the fairly evident meaning of the others, lay down a logical line of thought. The gist of that philosophy is that the value of products regularly exchanged in the open market depends upon the labor necessary to produce them; that capital consists of machines, materials and wages paid for labor; that out of the finished product, when materials have been paid for and the wear and tear and machinery replaced, and wages paid, there remains a surplus value. This surplus value arises from labor and is the difference between what is actually paid laborers for their wages and the market value of the commodities which the laborers produce. It represents, therefore, exploitation of the laborer, and this exploitation, inherent in the capitalistic system of production, is the cause of poverty, of industrial crises, and eventually of social revolution.

This social revolution, whether we regard it as voluntary revolt or the inevitable working of a vast cosmic law of social evolution, will be the last manifestation of the class struggle, and will come by inevitable change induced by the very nature of the conditions under which present production is carried on. It will come by the action of the great majority of men who compose the wage-earning proletariat, and it will result in common ownership of all capital, the disappearance of capitalistic exploitation, and the division of the products and services of industry according to human needs, and not according to the will of the owners of capital.

It goes without saying that every step of this reasoning and every presentation of supporting facts have been bitterly assailed. The labor theory of value has been denied; the theory of surplus value refuted; and inevitability of revolution scoffed at; while industrial crises—at least until this present one—have been defended as unusual exceptions proving the rule of modern industrial efficiency.

But with the Russian experiment and the World Depression most thoughtful men today are beginning to admit:

That the continued recurrence of industrial crises and wars based largely on economic rivalry, with persistent poverty, unemployment, disease and crime, are forcing the world to contemplate the possibilities of fundamental change in our economic methods; and that means thorough-going change, whether it be violent, as in France or Russia, or peaceful, as seems just as possible, and just as true to the Marxian formula, if it is fundamental change; in any case, Revolution seems bound to come.

Perhaps nothing illustrates this better than recent actions in the United States: our re-examination of the whole concept of Property; our banking moratorium; the extraordinary new agriculture bill; the plans to attack unemployment, and similar measures. Labor rather than gambling is the sure foundation of value and whatever we call it—exploitation, theft or business acumen—there is something radically wrong with an industrial system that turns out simultaneously paupers and millionaires and sets a world starving because it has too much food.

What now has all this to do with the Negro problem? First of all, it is manifest that the mass of Negroes in the United States belong distinctly to the working proletariat. Of every thousand working Negroes less than a hundred and fifty belong to any class that could possibly be considered bourgeois. And even this more educated and prosperous class has but small connections with the exploiters of wage and labor. Nevertheless, this black proletariat is not a part of the white proletariat. Black and white work together in many cases, and influence each other's rates of wages. They have similar complaints against capitalists, save that the grievances of the Negro worker are more fundamental and in-

defensible, ranging as they do, since the day of Karl Marx, from chattel slavery, to the worst paid, sweated, mobbed and cheated labor in any civilized land.

And while Negro labor in America suffers because of the fundamental inequities of the whole capitalistic system, the lowest and most fatal degree of its suffering comes not from the capitalists but from fellow white laborers. It is white labor that deprives the Negro of his right to vote, denies him education, denies him affiliation with trade unions, expels him from decent houses and neighborhoods, and heaps upon him the public insults of open color discrimination.

It is no sufficient answer to say that capital encourages this oppression and uses it for its own ends. This may have excused the ignorant and superstitious Russian peasants in the past and some of the poor whites of the South today. But the bulk of American white labor is neither ignorant nor fanatical. It knows exactly what it is doing and it means to do it. William Green and Mathew Woll of the A.F. of L. have no excuse of illiteracy or religion to veil their deliberate intention to keep Negroes and Mexicans and other elements of common labor, in a lower proletariat as subservient to their interests as theirs are to the interests of capital.

This large development of a petty bourgeoisie within the American laboring class is a post-Marxian phenomenon and the result of the tremendous and world-wide development of capitalism in the 20th Century. The market of capitalistic production has gained an effective world-wide organization. Industrial technique and mass production have brought possibilities in the production of goods and services which out-run even this wide market. A new class of technical engineers and managers has arisen forming a working class aristocracy between the older proletariat and the absentee owners of capital. The real owners of capital are small as well as large investors—workers who have deposits in savings banks and small holdings in stocks and bonds; families buying homes and purchasing commodities on installment; as well as the large and rich investors.

Of course, the individual laborer gets but an infinitesimal part of his income from such investments. On the other hand, such investments, in the aggregate, largely increase available capital for the exploiters, and they give investing laborers the capitalistic ideology. Between workers and owners of capital stand today the bankers and financiers who distribute capital and direct the engineers.

Thus the engineers and the saving better-paid workers, form a new petty bourgeois class, whose interests are bound up with those of the capitalists and antagonistic to those of common labor. On the other hand, common labor in America and white Europe far from being motivated by any vision of revolt against capitalism, has been blinded by the American vision of the possibility of layer after layer of the workers escaping into the wealthy class and becoming managers and employers of labor.

Thus in America we have seen a wild and ruthless scramble of labor groups over each other in order to climb to wealth on the backs of black labor and foreign immigrants. The Irish climbed on the Negroes. The Germans scrambled over the Negroes and emulated the Irish. The Scandinavians fought forward next to the Germans and the Italians and "Bohunks" are crowding up, leaving Negroes still at the bottom chained to helplessness, first by slavery, then by disfranchisement and always by the Color Bar.

The second influence on white labor both in America and Europe has been the fact that the extension of the world market by imperial expanding industry has established a worldwide new proletariat of colored workers, toiling under the worst conditions of 19th Century capitalism, herded as slaves and serfs and furnishing by the lowest paid wage in modern history a mass of raw material for industry. With this largess the capitalists have consolidated their economic power, nullified universal suffrage and bribed the white workers by high wages, visions of wealth and the opportunity to drive "niggers." Soldiers and sailors from the white workers are used to keep "darkies" in their "places" and white foremen and engineers have been established as irresponsible satraps in China and India, Africa and the West Indies, backed by the organized and centralized ownership of machines, raw materials, finished commodities and land monopoly over the whole world.

How now does the philosophy of Karl Marx apply today to colored labor? First of all colored labor has no common ground with white labor. No soviet of technocrats would do more than exploit colored labor in order to raise the status of whites. No revolt of a white proletariat could be started if its object was to make black workers their economic, political and social equals. It is for this reason that American socialism for fifty years has been dumb on the Negro problem, and the communists cannot even get a respectful hearing in America unless they begin by expelling Negroes.

On the other hand, within the Negro groups, in the United States, in West Africa, in South America and in the West Indies, petty bourgeois groups are being evolved. In South America and the West Indies such groups drain off skill and intelligence into the white group, and leave the black labor poor, ignorant and leaderless save for an occasional demagog.

In West Africa, a Negro bourgeoisie is developing with invested capital and employment of natives and is only kept from the conventional capitalistic development by the opposition and enmity of white capital, and the white managers and engineers who represent it locally and who display bitter prejudice and tyranny; and by white European labor which furnishes armies and navies and Empire "preference." African black labor and black capital are therefore driven to seek alliance and common ground.

In the United States also a petty bourgeoisie is being developed, consisting of clergymen, teachers, farm owners, professional men and retail businessmen. The position of this class, however, is peculiar: they are not the chief or even large investors in Negro labor and therefore exploit it only here and there; and they bear the brunt of color prejudice because they express in word and work the aspirations of all black folk for emancipation. The revolt of any black proletariat could not, therefore, be logically directed against this class, nor could this class join either white capital, white engineers or white workers to strengthen the color bar.

Under these circumstances, what shall we say of the Marxian philosophy and of its relation to the American Negro? We can only say, as it seems to me, that the Marxian philosophy is a true diagnosis of the situation in Europe in the middle of the 19th Century despite some of its logical difficulties. But it must be modified in the United States of America and especially so far as the Negro group is concerned. The Negro is exploited to a degree that means poverty, crime, delinquency and indigence. And that exploitation comes not from a black capitalistic class but from the white capitalists and equally from the white proletariat. His only defense is such internal organization as will protect him from both parties, and such practical economic insight as will prevent inside the race group any large development of capitalistic exploitation.

Meantime, comes the Great Depression. It levels all in mighty catastrophe. The fantastic industrial structure of America is threatened with ruin. The trade unions of skilled labor are double-tongued and helpless. Unskilled and common white labor is too frightened at Negro competition to attempt united action. It only begs a dole. The reformist program of Socialism meets no response from the white proletariat because it offers no escape to wealth and no effective bar to black labor, and a mud-sill of black labor is essential to white labor's standard of living. The shrill cry of a few communists is not even listened to, because and solely because it seeks to break down barriers between black and white. There is not at present the slightest indication that a Marxian revolution based on a united class-conscious proletariat is anywhere on the American far horizon. Rather race antagonism and labor group rivalry are still undisturbed by world catastrophe. In the hearts of black laborers alone, therefore, lie those ideals of democracy in politics and industry which may in time make the workers of the world effective dictators of civilization.

La Bourgeoisie Noire

E. Franklin Frazier

Radicals are constantly asking the question: Why does the Negro, the man farthest down in the economic as well as social scale, steadily refuse to ally himself with the radical groups in America? On the other hand, his failure so far to show sympathy to any extent with the class which *à priori* would appear to be his natural allies has brought praise from certain quarters. Southern white papers when inclined to indulge in sentimental encomiums about the Negro cite his immunity to radical doctrines as one of his most praiseworthy characteristics. Negro orators and, until lately, Negro publications, in pleading for the Negro's claim to equitable treatment, have never failed to boast of the Negro's undying devotion to the present economic order.

Source: E. Franklin Frazier, "La Bourgeoisie Noire," *Modern Quarterly* 5 (November 1928), 78–84.

Those white[s] who are always attempting to explain the Negro's social behavior in terms of hereditary qualities have declared that the Negro's temperament is hostile to radical doctrines. But the answer to what is a seeming anomaly to many is to be found in the whole social background of the Negro. One need not attribute it to any peculiar virtue (according as one regards virtue) or seek an explanation in such an incalculable factor as racial temperament.

The first mistake of those who think that the Negro of all groups in America should be in revolt against the present system is that they regard the Negro group as homogeneous. As a matter of fact, the Negro group is highly differentiated, with about the same range of interests as the whites. It is very well for white and black radicals to quote statistics to show that ninety-eight per cent of the Negroes are workers and should seek release from their economic slavery: but as a matter of fact ninety-eight per cent of the Negroes do not regard themselves as in economic slavery. Class differentiation among Negroes is reflected in their church organizations, educational institutions, private clubs, and the whole range of social life. Although these class distinctions may rest upon what would seem to outsiders flimsy and inconsequential matters, they are the social realities of Negro life, and no amount of reasoning can rid his mind of them. Recently we were informed in Dr. Herskovits' book on the Negro that color is the basis of social distinctions. To an outsider or a superficial observer this would seem true; but when one probes the tissue of the Negro's social life he finds that the Negro reacts to the same illusions that feed the vanity of white men.

What are some of the marks of distinctions which make it impossible to treat the Negro group as a homogeneous mass? They are chiefly property, education, and blood or family. If those possessing these marks of distinctions are generally mulattoes, it is because the free Negro class who first acquired these things as well as a family tradition were of mixed blood. The church in Charleston, South Carolina, which was reputed not to admit blacks did not open its doors to nameless mulatto nobodies. Not only has the distinction of blood given certain Negro groups a feeling of superiority over other Negroes, but it has made them feel superior to "poor whites." The Negro's feeling of superiority to "poor whites" who do not bear in their veins "aristocratic" blood has always created a barrier to any real sympathy between the two classes. Race consciousness to be sure has constantly effaced class feeling among Negroes. Therefore we hear on every hand Negro capitalists supporting the right of the Negro worker to organize—against white capitalists, of course. Nevertheless class consciousness has never been absent.

The Negro's attitude towards economic values has been determined by his economic position in American life. First of all, in the plantation system the Negro has found his adjustment to our economic system. The plantation system is based essentially upon enforced labor. Since emancipation the Negro has been a landless peasant without the tradition of the European peasant which binds the latter to the soil. Landownership remained relatively stationery from 1910 to 1920; while the number of landless workers increased. If this class of black workers were to espouse doctrines which aimed to change their economic status, they would be the most revolutionary group in America. From ignorant peasants who are ignorant in a fundamental sense in that they have no body of traditions even, we cannot expect revolutionary doctrines. They will continue a mobile group; while the white landlords through peonage and other forms of force will continue to hold them to the land.

Another factor of consequence in the Negro's economic life is the fact of the large number of Negroes in domestic service. One psychologist has sought to attribute this fact to the strength of the "instinct of submission" in the Negro. But it has represented an adjustment to the American environment. Nevertheless, it has left its mark on the Negro's character. To this is due the fact that he has taken over many values which have made him appear ridiculous and at the same time have robbed him of self-respect and self-reliance.

This group is no more to be expected to embrace radical doctrines than the same class was expected to join slave insurrections, concerning which Denmark Vesey warned his followers: "Don't mention it to those waiting men who receive presents of old coats, etc., from their masters, or they'll betray us."

Even this brief consideration of the social situation which has determined the Negro's attitudes towards values in American life will afford a background for our discussion of the seeming anomaly which he presents to many spectators. We shall attempt to show that, while to most observers the Negro shows an apparent indifference to changing his status, this is in fact a very real and insistent stimulus to his struggles. The Negro can only envisage those things which have meaning for him. *The radical doctrines appeal chiefly to the industrial workers, and the Negro has only begun to enter industry.* For Negroes to enter industries which are usually in the cities and escape the confinement of the plantation, they have realized a dream that is as far beyond their former condition as the New Economic Order is beyond the present condition of the wage earner. It has often been observed that the Negro subscribes to all the canons of consumption as the owning class in the present system. Even here we find the same struggle to realize a status that he can envisage and has a meaning for him. Once the Negro struggled for a literary education because he regarded it as the earmark of freedom. The relatively segregated life which the Negro lives makes him struggle to realize the values which give status within his group. An automobile, a home, a position as a teacher, or membership in a fraternity may confer a distinction in removing the possessor from an inferior social status, that could never be appreciated by one who is a stranger to Negro life. An outsider may wonder why a downtrodden, poor, despised people seem so indifferent about entering a struggle that is aimed to give all men an equal status. But if they could enter the minds of Negroes they would find that in the world in which they live they are not downtrodden and despised, but enjoy various forms of distinction.

An interesting episode in the life of the Negro which shows to what extent he is wedded to bourgeois ideals is the present attempt of the Pullman porters to organize. Some people have very superficially regarded this movement as a gesture in the direction of economic radicalism. But anyone who is intimately acquainted with the psychology of the Negro group, especially the porters, know that this is far from true. One who is connected with the white labor movement showed a better insight through his remark to the writer that the porters showed little working class psychology and showed a disposition to use their organization to enjoy the amenities of bourgeois social life. The Pullman porters do not show any disposition to overthrow bourgeois values. In fact, for years this group was better situated economically than most Negroes and carried over into their lives as far as possible the behavior patterns which are current in the middle class. In some places they regarded themselves as a sort of aristocracy, and as a colored woman said in one of their meetings recently, "Only an educated gentleman with culture could be a Pullman porter." The advent of a large and consequential professional and business class among Negroes has relegated the Pullman porters to a lower status economically as well as otherwise. Collective bargaining will help them to continue in a role in the colored group which is more in harmony with their conception of their relative status in their group. It is far from the idea of the Pullman porters to tear down the present economic order, and hardly any of them would confess any spiritual kinship with the "poor whites." The Pullman porters are emerging, on the other hand, as an aristocratic laboring group just as the Railroad Brotherhoods have done.

The Negro's lack of sympathy with the white working class is based on more than the feeling of superiority. In the South especially, the caste system which is based on color, determines the behavior of the white working class. If the Negro has fatuously claimed spiritual kinship with the white bourgeois, the white working class has taken over the tradition of the slave-holding aristocracy. When white labor in the South attempts to treat with black labor the inferior status of the latter must be conceded in practice and in theory. Moreover, white labor in the South not only has used every form of trickery to drive the Negro out of the ranks of skilled labor, but it has resorted to legislation to accomplish its aims. Experience, dating from before the Civil War, with the white group has helped to form the attitude of Negro towards white labor as well as traditional prejudices.[1]

In the February number of the *Southern Workman*, there appears an article in which the psychology of the Negro is portrayed as follows. The discovery is made by a white business in Chicago:

> The average working class Negro in Chicago earns $22 a week. His wife sends her children to the Day Nursery or leaves them with relatives or friends, and she supplements the family income by from $10 to $15 or more per week. The average white man of the same class earns $33 per week and keeps his wife at home. This colored man will rent a $65 per month aparment and buy a $50 suit of clothes while the white man will occupy a $30 per month apartment and buy a $25 suit of clothes. This average white man will come into our store to buy furniture and about $300 will be the limit of his estimated purchase, while the colored man will undertake a thousand dollar purchase without the least thought about meeting the payments from his small income.

To the writer of the article the company's new policy in using colored salesmen is a wonderful opportunity for colored men to learn the furniture business. The furniture company is going to make Negroes better citizens, according to the author of the article, by encouraging them to have better homes. This situation represents not only the extent to which the average Negro has swallowed middle class standards but the attitude of the upper class Negro towards the same values.

---

[1] E. Franklin Frazier: *The Negro in the Industrial South. The Nation*, Vol. 125, No. 3238.

There is much talk at the present time about the New Negro. He is generally thought of as the creative artist who is giving expression to all the stored-up æsthetic emotion of the race. Negro in Art Week has come to take its place beside, above, or below the other three hundred and fifty-two weeks in the American year. But the public is little aware of the Negro business man who regards himself as a new phenomenon. While the New Negro who is expressing himself in art promises in the words of one of his chief exponents not to compete with the white man either politically or economically, the Negro business man seeks the salvation of the race in economic enterprise. In the former case there is either an acceptance of the present system or an ignoring of the economic realities of life. In the case of the latter there is an acceptance of the gospel of economic success. Sometimes the New Negro of the artistic type calls the New Negro business man a Babbitt, while the latter calls the former a mystic. But the Negro business man is winning out, for he is dealing with economic realities. He can boast of the fact that he is independent of white support, while the Negro artist still seeks it. One Negro insurance company in a rather cynical acceptance of the charge of Babbittry begins a large advertisement in a Negro magazine in the words of George F. Babbitt.

A perusal of Negro newspapers will convince anyone that the Negro group does not regard itself as outcasts without status. One cannot appeal to them by telling them that they have nothing to lose but their chains. The chains which Negroes have known in the South were not figurative. Negro newspapers are a good index of the extent to which middle-class ideals have captured the imagination of Negroes. In one newspaper there is a column devoted to What Society Is Wearing. In this column the apparel of those who are socially prominent is described in detail. The parties, the cars, the homes, and the jewelry of the elite find a place in all of these papers. In fact, there is no demand on the part of Negro leaders to tear down social distinctions and create a society of equals. As the writer heard a colored editor tell a white man recently, "the white people draw the line at the wrong point and put all of us in the same class."

Negro schools in the South furnish an example of the influence of middle-class ideals which make Negroes appear in a ridiculous light. These schools give annually a public performance. Instead of giving plays such as Paul Green's folk plays of Negro life, they give fashion shows which have been popularized to boost sales. Negro students appear in all kinds of gorgeous costumes which are worn by the leisured middle class. One more often gets the impression that he has seen a Mardi Gras rather than an exhibition of correct apparel.

Even the most ardent radical cannot expect the Negro to hold himself aloof from the struggle for economic competence and only dream of his escape from his subordinate economic status in the overthrow of the present system. A Negro business man who gets out of the white man's kitchen or dining room rightly regards himself as escaping from economic slavery. Probably he will maintain himself by exploiting the Negro who remains in the kitchen, but he can always find consolation in the feeling, that if he did not exploit him a white man would. But in seeking escape from economic subordination, the Negro has generally envisaged himself as a captain of industry. In regard to group efficiency he has shown no concern. For example, a group isolated to the extent of the Negro in America could have developed cooperative enterprises. There has been no attempt in schools or otherwise to teach or encourage this type of economic organization. The ideal of the rich man has been held up to him. More than one Negro business has been wrecked because of the predatory view of economic activity.

Many of those who criticize the Negro for selecting certain values out of American life overlook the fact that the primary struggle on his part has been to acquire a culture. In spite of the efforts of those who would have him dig up his African past, the Negro is a stranger to African culture. The manner in which he has taken over the American culture has never been studied in intimate enough detail to make it comprehensible. The educated class among Negroes has been the fore-

runners in this process. Except perhaps through the church the economic basis of the civilized classes among Negroes has not been within the group. Although today the growing professional and business classes are finding support among Negroes the upper classes are subsidized chiefly from without. To some outsiders such a situation makes the Negro intellectual appear as merely an employee of the white group. At times the emasculating effect of Negro men appearing in the role of mere entertainers for the whites has appeared in all its tragic reality. But the creation of this educated class of Negroes has made possible the civilization of the Negro. It may seem conceivable to some that the Negro could have contended on the ground of abstract right for unlimited participation in American life on the basis of individual efficiency; but the Negro had to deal with realities. It is strange that today one expects this very class which represents the most civilized group to be in revolt against the system by which it was created, rather than the group of leaders who have sprung from the soil of Negro culture.

Here we are brought face to face with a fundamental dilemma of Negro life. Dean Miller at Howard University once expressed this dilemma aphoristically, namely, that the Negro pays for what he wants and begs for what he needs. The Negro pays, on the whole for his church, his lodges and fraternities, and his automobile, but he begs for his education. Even the radical movement which had vogue a few years back was subsidized by the white radical group. It did not spring out of any general movement among Negroes towards radical doctrines. Moreover, black radicals theorized about the small number of Negroes who had entered industry from the security of New York City; but none ever undertook to enter the South and teach the landless peasants any type of self-help. What began as the organ of the struggling working masses became the mouthpiece of Negro capitalists. The New Negro group which has shown a new orientation towards Negro life and the values which are supposed to spring from Negro life has restricted itself to the purely cultural in the narrow sense.

In this article the writer has attempted to set forth the social forces which have caused the Negro to have his present attitude towards the values in American life. From even this cursory glance at Negro life we are able to see to what extent bourgeois ideals are implanted in the Negro's mind. We are able to see that the Negro group is a highly differentiated group with various interests, and that it is far from sound to view the group as a homogeneous group of outcasts. There has come upon the stage a group which represents a nationalistic movement. This movement is divorced from any program of economic reconstruction. It is unlike the Garvey movement in that Garvey through schemes—phantastic to be sure—united his nationalistic aims with an economic program. This new movement differs from the program of Booker Washington which sought to place the culture of the Negro upon a sound basis by making him an efficient industrial worker. Nor does it openly ally itself with those leaders who condemn the organization of the Pullman porters and advise Negroes to pursue an opportunistic course with capitalism. It looks askance at the new rising class of black capitalism while it basks in the sun of white capitalism. It enjoys the congenial company of white radicals while shunning association with black radicals. The New Negro Movement functions in the third dimension of culture; but so far it knows nothing of the other two dimensions—Work and Wealth.

Marxist Theory and the Specificity of Afro-American Oppression

Cornel West

Will this statement be susceptible of understanding? In Europe, the black man is the symbol of Evil.... As long as one cannot understand this fact, one is doomed to talk in circles about the "black problem."

Frantz Fanon,
Black Skin, White Masks

The problem of the twentieth century is the problem of the color-line—the relation of the darker to the lighter races of men in Asia and Africa, in America and the islands of the sea.

W. E. B. Du Bois,
The Souls of Black Folk

As we approach the later years of the twentieth century, Fanon's characteristic candor and Du Bois's ominous prophecy continue to challenge the Marxist tradition. Although I intend neither to define their meaning nor defend their veracity, I do wish to highlight their implicit interrogation of Marxism. Fanon's and Du Bois's challenge constitutes the germ of what I shall call the *racial problematic:* the theoretical investigation into the materiality of racist discourses, the ideological production of African subjects, and the concrete effects of and counterhegemonic responses to the European (and specifically white) supremacist logics operative in modern Western civilization.[1]

I understand the issue of the specificity of Afro-American oppression as a particular version of the racial problematic within the context of the emergence, development, and decline of U.S. capitalist society and culture. This problematic is, in many ways, similar to contemporary philosophical discussions of "difference" that flow from the genealogical inquiries of Michel Foucault and the deconstructive analyses of Jacques Derrida.[2] Yet this problematic differs in that it presupposes a neo-Gramscian framework, one in which extradiscursive formations such as modes of production and overdetermined, antagonistic class relations are viewed as indispensable. This neo-Gramscian framework attempts to shun the discursive reductionistic elements in the works of the ex-Marxist Foucault and sidestep the textual idealist tendencies in the perennially playful performances of Derrida. But this neo-Gramscian perspective welcomes their poststructuralist efforts to dismantle the logocentric and a priori aspects of the Marxist tradition. In other words, I accent the *demystifying moment* in their genealogical and deconstructive practices which attack hegemonic Western discourses that invoke universality, scientificity, and objectivity in order to hide cultural plurality, conceal the power-laden play of differences, and preserve hierarchical class, gender, racial, and sexual orientational relations.

This effort to put forward the racial problematic within a neo-Gramscian framework occupies new discursive space on the spectrum of philosophies of difference; it also enacts an untapped potentiality within the Marxist tradition. More important, this effort constitutes a sympathetic yet biting Marxist critique of poststructuralist philosophies of difference and a supportive yet piercing critique of the Marxist tradition from the viewpoint of an Afro-American neo-Gramscian. In short, the time has passed when the so-called race question, or Negro question, can be relegated to secondary or tertiary *theoretical* significance in bourgeois or Marxist discourses. Instead, to take seriously the multileveled oppression of African peoples is to raise crucial questions regarding the conditions for the possibility of the modern West, the nature of European conceptions of rationality, and even the limited character of Marxist formulations of counterhegemonic projects against multileveled oppression.

In order to more fully understand my neo-Gramscian conception of the specificity of Afro-American oppression, it is necessary to examine briefly the history of Marxist conceptions of Afro-American oppression. Any such history is itself a *political act*—an intervention into the present state of the Afro-American freedom struggle. My own crude interpretation and bold intervention bears the stamp of my neo-Gramscian stance, which takes on practical forms in an autonomist (not micropolitical) politics (e.g., the National Black United Front) and a prefigurative (not reformist) politics (e.g., the Democratic Socialists of America).[3]

I shall argue that there are four basic conceptions of Afro-American oppression in the Marxist tradition. The first conception subsumes Afro-American oppression under the general rubric of working-class exploitation. This viewpoint is logocentric in that it elides and eludes the specificity of Afro-American oppression outside the workplace; it is reductionistic in that it explains away rather than explains this specificity. This logocentric and reductionistic approach results from vulgar and sophisticated versions of economism. I understand economism to be those forms of Marxist theory that defend either simple monodeterminist or subtle multideterminist causal relations between an evolving economic base upon a reflecting and refracting ideological superstructure, thereby giving a priori status to class subjects and modes of production as privileged explanatory variables.

In regard to Afro-American oppression, economism and its concomitant logocentric and reductionistic approach holds that African people in the United States of America are not subjected to forms of oppression distinct from general working-class exploitation. Historically, this position was put forward by the major figures of the U.S. Socialist party (notwithstanding its more adequate yet forgotten 1903 resolution on the Negro question), especially Eugene Debs. In an influential series of articles, Debs argued that Afro-American oppression was solely a class problem and that any attention to its alleged specificity "apart from the general labor problem" would constitute racism in reverse.[4] He wrote, "we [the socialists] have nothing to do with it [the race question], for it is their [the capitalists'] fight. We have simply to open the eyes of as many Negroes as we can and do battle for emancipation from wage slavery, and when the working class have triumphed in the class struggle and stand forth economic as well as political free men, the race problem will disappear." In the meantime, Debs added, "we have nothing special to offer the Negro, and we cannot make separate appeals to all races. The Socialist Party is the party of the whole working class regardless of color."[5]

My aim is not simply to castigate the U.S. Socialist party or insinuate accusative charges of racism against Debs. Needless to say, the Socialist party had many distinguished black members and Debs had a long history of fighting racism. Rather, I am concerned with the fact that the Second International economism in the U.S. Socialist party lead to a logocentric and reductionistic approach to Afro-American oppression, thereby ignoring, or at best downplaying, strategies (as opposed to personal moral duties) to struggle against racism.

The second conception of Afro-American oppression in the Marxist tradition acknowledges the specificity of Afro-American oppression beyond general working-class exploitation, yet it defines this specificity in economistic terms. This conception is antireductionistic in character yet economistic in content. This viewpoint holds that African

people in the United States of America are subjected to general working-class exploitation and specific working-class exploitation owing to racial discrimination at the workplace (at the levels of access to opportunities and relative wages received). In the U.S. Marxist past, this superexploitation thesis has been put forward by the Progressive Labor party in the late sixties and early seventies. Practically, this viewpoint accents struggle against racism yet circumscribes its concerns within an economistic orbit.

The third conception of Afro-American oppression in the Marxist tradition—the most influential, widely accepted, and hence unquestioned among Afro-American Marxists—holds the specificity of Afro-American oppression to be general working-class exploitation and national oppression: that is, it is antireductionistic and antieconomistic in character and nationalistic in content. This position claims that Afro-Americans constitute, or once constituted, an oppressed nation in the Black Belt South and an oppressed national minority in the rest of U.S. society.

There are numerous versions of the so-called Black Nation Thesis. Its classical version was put forward in the Sixth Congress of the Third International (1928), modified in its 1930 Resolution, and codified in Harry Haywood's *Negro Liberation* (1948). Subsequent versions have been put forward by the Socialist Workers party's George Breitman, the Communist Labor party's Nelson Peery, the Bolshevik League of the United States' Bob Avakian's Revolutionary Communist party, Amiri Baraka's U.S. League of Revolutionary Struggle, the Philadelphia Workers' Organizing Committee, and James Forman's recent book on *Self-Determination and the African-American People*.[6] All of these versions adhere to Joseph V. Stalin's stipulative definition of a nation as set forth in his *Marxism and the National Question* (1913): "A nation is a historically constituted, stable community of people formed on the basis of a common language, territory, economic life, and psychological make-up manifested in a common culture."[7] This formulation, despite its brevity and crudity, incorporates a crucial cultural dimension that has had tremendous attractiveness to Afro-American Marxists. In fact, the Black Nation Thesis has been and remains hegemonic on the Black Marxist Left.

Since the Garvey movement in the early twenties—the first mass movement among Afro-Americans—the Black Left has been forced to take seriously the cultural dimension of the Afro-American freedom struggle. In this limited sense, Marcus Garvey's black nationalism made proto-Gramscians out of most Afro-American Marxists.[8] Yet the expression of this cultural concern among Afro-American Marxists has, for the most part, remained straitjacketed by the Black Nation Thesis. This thesis, indeed, has promoted and encouraged impressive struggles against racism in the U.S. communist movement. But with its ahistorical racial determination of a nation, its flaccid statistical determination of national boundaries, and its allusory distinct black national economy, the Black Nation Thesis continues to serve as an honest, yet misguided, attempt by Marxist-Leninists to repudiate reductionistic views on Afro-American oppression.[9] In short, it functions as a poor excuse for the absence of a sophisticated Marxist theory of the specificity of Afro-American oppression.

The fourth and last conception of Afro-American oppression in the Marxist tradition claims that the specificity of Afro-American oppression is that of general working-class exploitation and racial oppression. This conception is put forward, on the one hand, by the Socialist Workers party's Richard Kirk (alias R. S. Fraser in reply to George Breitman), who wrote:

> The Negro Question is a racial question: a matter of discrimination because of skin color, and that's all....
>
> The dual nature of the Negro struggle arises from the fact that a *whole people* regardless of class distinction are the victims of discrimination. This problem of a whole people can be solved only through the proletarian revolution, under the leadership of the working class. The Negro struggle is therefore not the same as the class struggle, but in its independ-

ent character is allied to the working class. Because of the independent form of the Negro movement, it does not thereby become a national or separatist struggle, but draws its laws of development from its character as a racial struggle against segregation and discrimination.[10]

And on the other hand, Linda Burnham and Bob Wing wrote in *Line of March.*

> More specifically, the oppressed Black racial group in the U.S. is a unity of two interconnected but distinct aspects: Black people are a racially oppressed section of the laboring masses, as well as a distinct racially oppressed people. Between these two, the principal defining aspect of the Black racial group is that of being a racially coerced section of labor in this country. This view stems from our analysis of the connection between racial oppression and U.S. capitalism. As we have emphasized, racial oppression and class oppression are qualitatively distinct social contradictions with their own dynamics and laws of development. But they are also interconnected. In our view, the nature of this interconnection is defined by the fact that capitalism gave rise to and ultimately determines the form and content of racial oppression. In particular, the ultimate *raison d'être* of racial oppression is the need of U.S. capital accumulation for a specially oppressed, coerced section of labor.[11]

This fourth conception of Afro-American oppression in the Marxist tradition has been motivated primarily by opposition to the predominant role of the Black Nation Thesis in the American and Afro-American Left. Hence, it has been promoted by breakaway Trotskyists such as the Spartacist League, the independent Marxist-Leninist trend Line of March, the Communist party of the United States of America after 1959, and leftists in academia such as Oliver C. Cox, James A. Geschwender, and Mario Barrera.[12] These contributions have been useful in regard to broadening the theoretical discourse of Afro-American oppression within Marxist circles.

My neo-Gramscian viewpoint requires a new conception of Afro-American oppression. I suggest that certain aspects of the preceding four conceptions are indispensable for an acceptable position, though all four are inadequate. A common feature is that their analyses remain on the macrostructural level; that is, they focus on the role and function of racism within and among institutions of production and government. Any acceptable conception of Afro-American oppression, indeed, must include macrostructural analysis, which highlights the changing yet persistent forms of class exploitation and political repression of Afro-Americans. In this regard, even narrow economistic Marxist analyses of Afro-American oppression are preferable to prevailing bourgeois perspectives, such as the Weberian liberalism of William Julius Wilson, the Friedmanian conservatism of Thomas Sowell, and the Parsonsian elitism of Martin Kilson.[13]

Building upon Stanley Aronowitz's seminal though brief treatment of race,[14] my neo-Gramscian viewpoint requires not only a macrostructural approach but also a broad genealogical investigation and a detailed microinstitutional (or localized) analysis. These three moments of a neo-Gramscian perspective consist of the following:

1. aenealogical inquiry into the discursive conditions for the possibility of the hegemonic European (i.e., white) supremacist logics operative in various epochs in the West and the counterhegemonic possibilities available;

2. a microinstitutional (or localized) analysis of the mechanisms that inscribe and sustain these logics in the everyday lives of Africans, including the hegemonic ideological production of African subjects, the constitution of alien and degrading normative cultural styles, aesthetic ideals, linguistic gestures, psychosexual identities, and the counterhegemonic possibilities available;

3. a macrostructural approach that accents modes of overdetermined class exploitation and political repression of African peoples and the counterhegemonic possibilities available.

The aim of the first moment is to examine *modes of European domination* of African peoples; that of the second moment, to probe into *forms of European subjugation* of African peoples; and that of the third moment, to focus on *types of European exploitation and repression* of African peoples. These moments of theoretical inquiry—always already traversed by male supremacist and heterosexual supremacist logics—overlap and crisscross in complex ways, yet each highlights a distinctive dimension of the multi-leveled oppression of Europeans over African peoples.[15]

These three moments constitute the specificity of the European oppression of African peoples *at the level of methodology;* that is, this neo-Gramscian viewpoint should capture the crucial features of such oppression anywhere in the world. Yet the specificity of the various manifestations of European oppression of African peoples in particular countries is constituted by *detailed historical analyses* that enact the three methodological moments. Needless to say, these concrete analyses must be ensconced in the particular culture, heritage, and economic history of the Africans and the nation of which the Africans are participants and victims.

Admittedly, this neo-Gramscian project is an ambitious one, yet the complexity of the oppression of African peoples demands it. Each of the three moments requires major volumes, possibly lifetime endeavors. Given the political urgency of our times, I shall briefly sketch the contours of each moment.

In regard to the first moment—the genealogical inquiry into the conditions for the possibility of the European (i.e., white) supremacist logics operative in the West—I suggest that there are three such basic discursive logics: Judeo-Christian, scientific, and psychosexual. The Judeo-Christian racist logic emanates from the biblical account of Ham looking upon and failing to cover his father Noah's nakedness and thereby receiving divine punishment in the form of blackening his progeny. Within this logic, black skin is a divine curse owing to disrespect for and rejection of paternal authority.[16] The scientific racist logic rests upon a modern philosophical discourse guided by Greek ocular metaphors, undergirded by Cartesian notions of the primacy of the subject and the preeminence of representation, and buttressed by Baconian ideas of observation, evidence, and confirmation that promote and encourage the activities of observing, comparing, measuring, and ordering physical characteristics of human bodies. Given the renewed appreciation and appropriation of classical antiquity, these activities were regulated by classical aesthetic and cultural norms. Within this logic, the notions of black ugliness, cultural deficiency, and intellectual inferiority are legitimated by the value-laden, yet prestigious, authority of science.[17] The psychosexual racist logic arises from the phallic obsessions, Oedipal projections, and anal-sadistic orientations in European culture that endow African men and women with sexual prowess; view Africans as either cruel, revengeful fathers, frivolous, carefree children, or passive, long-suffering mothers; and identify Africans with dirt, odious smell, and feces. In short, Africans are associated with acts of bodily defecation, violation, and subordination. Within this logic, Africans are walking abstractions, inanimate things or invisible creatures.[18] For all three white supremacist logics, which operate simultaneously in the modern West, Africans personify degraded otherness, exemplify radical alterity, and embody alien difference.

The aim of neo-Gramscian genealogical inquiry is not simply to specify the discursive operations that constitute Africans as the excluded, marginal Other; it also is to show how white supremacist logics are guided by various hegemonic Western philosophies of identity that suppress difference, heterogeneity, and multiplicity. Since such discursive suppression impedes counterhegemonic practices, these philosophies of identity are not simply ideologies but rather modes of domination with their own irreducible dynamic and development. Similar to Derrida's own characterization of his work, this inquiry requires "a general determination of the conditions for the emergence and the limits of philosophy, of metaphysics, of everything that carries it on

and that it carries on."[19] Unlike Derrida's, this inquiry is but one moment in our neo-Gramscian project, leading toward microinstitutional and macrostructural analyses of oppression. I suggest this first moment is an examination of modes of European domination of African peoples because it maps the discursive modalities—for hegemonic and counterhegemonic practices—circumscribed by white supremacist logics and thereby discloses the European discursive powers over African peoples.

The second moment—the microinstitutional (or localized) analysis—examines the articulation of the white supremacist logics within the everyday lives of Africans in particular historical contexts. It focuses on the effects upon African peoples of the binary oppositions of true/false, good/evil, pure/impure within the white supremacist logics. In the complex case of Africans in the United States of America, this analysis would include the production of colored and Negro subjects principally enacted by the ideological apparatus (and enforced by the repressive apparatus) in the South, the extraordinary and equivocal role and function of evangelical Protestant Christianity (especially the Separate Baptist and Methodist denominations),[20] and the blend of African and southern Anglo-Saxon Protestants and French Catholics from which emerged distinctive Afro-American cultural styles, linguistic gestures, and counterhegemonic practices. This analysis is, in many ways, similar to Foucault's "microphysics of power"—the specifying of the power relations within the crevices and interstices of what logocentric Marxists call the superstructure. Yet, unlike Foucault's, this analysis is but one moment in my neo-Gramscian project, whose regulative ideal is not mere antibourgeois revolt but rather antihierarchical socialist transformation.[21] I suggest that this second moment is a probe into forms of European subjugation of African peoples because it shows how the various white supremacist logics shape African self-identities, influence psychosexual sensibilities, and help set the context for distinctive Afro-American cultural styles, linguistic gestures, and modes of resistance.

The third moment—the macrostructural analysis—reveals the role and function of overdetermined class exploitation and political repression upon African peoples. This traditionally Marxist focus remains as a crucial moment in my neo-Gramscian perspective, yet the nature of this focus is modified. The neo-Gramscian rejection of the base/superstructure metaphors of economism (or logocentric Marxism) entails that it is no longer sufficient or desirable to privilege the mode of production and class subjects in an a priori manner and make causal claims (whether crude or refined) about racist ideology owing to simply economic factors. Instead, following Antonio Gramsci, the metaphor of a "historical bloc" replaces those of base/superstructure. This new metaphor eschews the logocentric and a priori dimension of the old metaphors by radically historicizing them, thereby disclosing the complexity and heterogeneity suppressed by logocentric Marxism. Gramsci's rejection of vulgar economism is unequivocal: "The claim, presented as an essential postulate of historical materialism, that every fluctuation of politics and ideology can be presented and expounded as an immediate expression of the structure, must be contested in theory as primitive infantilism, and combated in practice with the authentic testimony of Marx, the author of concrete political and historical works."[22]

Gramsci's highly sophisticated investigations into the multivarious modalities of class domination serves as the springboard for my own neo-Gramscian perspective. Yet there are still significant logocentric and a priori elements in Gramsci's work, such as the primacy of class subjects and the bipolar class options for hegemony. Nevertheless, Gramsci's antireductionistic and antieconomistic metaphor "historical bloc" promotes a radically historical approach in which the economic, political, cultural, and ideological regions of a social formation are articulated and elaborated in the form of overdetermined and often contradictory class and nonclass processes.[23] Despite this rejection of forms of determinisms, this conception of social totality (or more specifically, the dynamics of particular

social formations) does not result in a mere floating crap game in that, given a historical situation, *structural constraints* impose limits upon historically constituted agents, whereas *conjunctural opportunities* can be enacted by these agents. Given the historical process, many structural constraints can become conjunctural opportunities. Yet without some notion of historical structural constraints, my neo-Gramscian perspective slides into explanatory nihilism; namely, the refusal or inability to make explanatory commitments about history and society. Economism is preferable to such explanatory impotence, but fortunately Gramsci's metaphor "historical bloc" precludes such a choice.

The controversial issue of the relation between historical context and differential intertextuality, ideological closure, and infinite dissemination serves as the major bone of contention between Marxists and poststructuralists. My neo-Gramscian viewpoint resists explanatory nihilism; that is, despite immense theoretical difficulties and practical obstacles it does not give up on explaining and transforming history and society. There is no Marxist theory without some notion of operative though transient structural constraints in particular historical conjunctures, just as there is no Marxist praxis without some notion of conjunctural opportunities. Poststructuralisms rightly dismantle the logocentric and a priori aspects of Marxist theory, yet they wrongly textualize historical constraints and political praxis into mere endless chains of signifiers. To put this issue in Ernesto Laclau's terms, the matter is not simply the impossibility of society and history but, more important, the specifying of the conditions for the possibility of the perennial process of this impossibility.[24] We must appeal to metaphors of society and history in order to account for the "impossibility" of society and history. Gramsci's metaphor of "historical bloc" performs this function. If appropriately employed, it precludes the logocentric economism of pre-Gramscian Marxisms and the labyrinthine abyss of poststructuralisms. Furthermore, my neo-Gramscian viewpoint rejects the remnant of class reductionism in

Gramsci's work. In short, my neo-Gramscian perspective yields ideological yet differential closure—provisional structural constraints and engaged political praxis—but with no guarantees.

Therefore the macrostructural analysis of the role and function of overdetermined class exploitation and political repression from my neo-Gramscian perspective goes far beyond the aforementioned four macrostructural conceptions of Afro-American oppression in the Marxist tradition. This is so, in part, because it preserves the crucial structural feature—the complex interaction of economic, political, cultural, and ideological regions in social formations—of Marxist theory, yet it does not permit a priori privileging of the economic region within this structural feature. I suggest that this third moment is an investigation into the types of European exploitation and repression of African peoples because it highlights simultaneously the relations between African slaves and white slaveholders. African workers and white capitalists, African citizens and white rulers.

In conclusion, the contemporary crisis of Marxism results, in part, from extradiscursive terrains of contestation generated from racial, feminist, gay, lesbian, and ecological social movements—movements that are historically "new" only to ostrichlike logocentric Marxists whose sight has been confined to the workplace—and from discursive terrains of contestation initiated by Gilles Deleuze and deepened by Foucault and Derrida.[25] I use Deleuze, Foucault, and Derrida (as they prefer) not as proper names but rather as tropes signifying diverse discursive forces, including Frenchified Nietzchean and Heideggerian elements, which now bombard Marxist theories. In a sense, it is unfortunate that this fierce bombardment is a thoroughly French (and more specifically Parisian) assault. It is unfortunate principally because of the national baggage that accompanies the assaults—namely, distinctively French political cynicisms and intellectual dandyisms, alien to the seemingly incurable bourgeois optimism and intellectual inferiority complexes of

North Americans in the United States, yet seductive to weary Marxist activists who have run up against walls of History and isolated Marxist intellectuals who often remain within walls of the bourgeois Academy, activists and intellectuals who have genuine antibourgeois sentiments yet possess no energizing emancipatory vision.

My neo-Gramscian conception of the multileveled oppression of Africans in the United States of America and elsewhere remains a rudimentary response to the contemporary crisis of Marxism. As racial conflicts intensify in Europe, South America, North America, Asia, and above all South Africa, the racial problematic will become more urgent on the Marxist agenda. And as the ruling classes in late capitalist societies fan and fuel the white supremacist logics deeply embedded in their cultures, a neo-Gramscian perspective on the complexity of racism is imperative if even the beginning of a "war of position" is to be mounted. In fact, the future of Marxism, at least among Afro-Americans, may well depend upon the depths of the antiracist dimension of this *theoretical* and *practical* "war of position."

NOTES

1. In this definition, "materiality" simply denotes the multiple functions of power of racist practices over Africans; by "logics" I mean the battery of tropes, metaphors, notions, and concepts employed to justify and legitimate white supremacist practices. This racial problematic is related to but not identical with other possible investigative frameworks that focus on racist practices toward other peoples of color. I do believe this problematic is useful for such endeavors, yet I deliberately confine my major focus to peoples of African descent, especially Afro-Americans. Also, this problematic does not presuppose that a nostalgic undifferentiated unity or homogeneous universality will someday emerge among black, white, red, yellow, and brown peoples. Rather, it assumes the irreducibility of racial (that is, cultural) differences. The task is not to erase such differences but rather to ensure that such differences are not employed as grounds for but-

tressing hierarchical social relations and symbolic orders.

2. The major texts I have in mind of these two prolific and profound thinkers are Michel Foucault, *Discipline and Punish: The Birth of the Prison*, trans. Alan Sheridan (New York: Vintage, 1979); and Jacques Derrida, *Of Grammatology*, trans. Gayatri Chakravorty Spivak (Baltimore: Johns Hopkins University Press, 1976). For a brilliant critique and contrast of these two texts, see Edward W. Said, *The World, the Text, and the Critic* (Cambridge: Harvard University Press, 1983), pp. 118–225.

3. My political stance is *autonomistic* in that it is existentially anchored not simply in responses to class exploitation but more immediately in cultural degradation and political oppression—as is the National Black United Front led by Rev. Herbert Daughtry. Yet this autonomistic stance does not slide into mere micropolitics because it envisions and encourages links with those movements based primarily on class exploitation. My political stance is *prefigurative* in that it is, in principle, motivated by the fundamental transformation of U.S. capitalist civilization and manifested in working within an organization (the Democratic Socialists of America) whose moral aspirations and internal mechanisms prefigure the desirable socialist society—one that is radically democratic and libertarian. This prefigurative stance does not degenerate into reformism because, following Rosa Luxemburg's formulations in *Reform or Revolution* (1900), it supports reforms yet opposes illusions about reforms.

4. Eugene Debs, "The Negro in the Class Struggle" and "The Negro and His Nemesis," *International Socialist Review*, Nov. 1903, Jan. 1904.

5. Quoted from Philip S. Foner, *American Socialism and Black Americans* (Westport, Conn.: Greenwood Press, 1977). For a noteworthy response to Debs's disappearance thesis, see Manning Marable, "The Third Reconstruction: Black Nationalism and Race Relations after the Revolution," *Blackwater: Historical Studies in Race, Class Consciousness and Revolution* (Dayton, Ohio: Black Praxis Press, 1981), pp. 187–208. For the major work of this important Afro-American Marxist figure, see *How Capitalism Underdeveloped Black America: Problems in Race, Political Economy and Society* (Boston: South End Press, 1983).

6. George Breitman, "On the Negro Struggle, etc.," *Socialist Workers Party Discussion Bulletin*, Sept. 1954; Bolshevik League, *Liberation for the Black Nation* (Bronx, 1983); Nelson Peery, *The Negro National Colonial Question* (Chicago: Workers Press, 1978); Revolutionary Union, *National Liberation and Proletarian Revolution in the United States* (Chicago, 1972); Amiri Baraka, "Black Liberation and the Question of Nationality," *Unity* 4: 12 (1981), p. 6; Amiri Baraka, "Black Struggle in the 80's," *The Black Nation: Journal of Afro-American Thought*, 1:1 (1981), pp. 2–5; Philadelphia Workers' Organizing Committee, *Black Liberation Today Against Dogmatism on the National Question* (Philadelphia, 1975); James Forman, *Self-Determination and the African-American People* (Seattle: Open Hand Publishing, 1981). To put it crudely, Breitman argues that Afro-Americans in the United States constitute an "embryonic nation"; Peery holds the "Negro Nation" to be a colony; Bob Avakian's Revolutionary Communist party claims that dispersed black communities constitute a "proletarian nation" of a new sort; Baraka, the Bolshevik League, and Forman argue for a Black Nation in the Black Belt South of the United States; and the Philadelphia Workers' Organizing Committee holds that there once was a Black Nation, but it dissolved in the fifties with vast industrialization, proletarianization, and urbanization of Afro-Americans.

7. Joseph V. Stalin, *Marxism and the National Question* (Moscow: Foreign Language Publishing House, 1954), p. 16.

8. This almost inescapable Gramscian perspective—the nearly unavoidable theoretical and practical confrontation with the problem of culture—has been a major preoccupation of the leading Marxist figures in developing nations. For brief samples of original third-world contributions to Marxist theory, see Mao Tsetung, "Report on an Investigation of the Peasant Movement in Hunan," *Selected Works*, vol. 1 (Peking: Foreign Language Press, 1966), pp. 23–59; "On the Correct Handling of Contradictions among the People," *Four Essays on Philosophy* (Peking: Foreign Language Press, 1968), pp. 79–133. See also Jose Carlos Mariategui, "People and Myth," *The Morning Spirit* (1925); and "The Religious Factor," *Seven Essays of Interpretation of the Peruvian Reality* (1927). Unfortunately, most of Mariategui's works have not yet been translated into English. For noteworthy treatments of his thought and praxis, see Geraldine Skinner, "Jose Carlos Mariategui and the Emergence of the Peruvian Socialist Movement," *Science and Society,*

43:4 (1979–80), pp. 447–71; and Jesus Chavarna, *Jose Carlos Mariategui and the Rise of Modern Peru* (Albuquerque: University of New Mexico Press, 1979). See also Kwame Nkrumah, *Consciencism: Philosophy and Ideology for Decolonization* (New York: Monthly Review Press, 1970); Frantz Fanon, *The Wretched of the Earth,* trans. Constance Farrington (New York: Grove Press, 1964); Amilcar Cabral, "Presuppositions and Objectives of National Liberation in Relation to Social Structure" and "National Liberation and Culture," *Unity and Struggle: Speeches and Writings of Amilcar Cabral,* trans. Michael Wolfers (New York: Monthly Review Press, 1979), pp. 119–37, 138–54.

9. For the most thorough and convincing critique of the Black Nation Thesis, see Linda Burnham and Bob Wing, "Toward a Communist Analysis of Black Oppression and Black Liberation, Part I: Critique of the Black Nation Thesis," *Line of March: A Marxist-Leninist Journal of Rectification,* 2:1 (1981), pp. 21–88.

10. R. S. Fraser, "For the Materialist Conception of the Negro Struggle," in *What Strategy for Black Liberation? Trotskyism vs. Black Nationalism, Marxist Bulletin* 5, rev. ed., The Spartacist League, pp. 3, 16, reprinted from *Socialist Workers Party Discussion Bulletin,* A-30 (1955).

11. Linda Burnham and Bob Wing, "Toward a Communist Analysis of Black Oppression and Black Liberation, Part II: Theoretical and Historical Framework," *Line of March: A Marxist-Leninist Journal of Rectification,* 8 (1981), p. 48.

12. For the recent pronouncements of the Afro-American freedom struggle by the Communist party of the United States, see Henry Winston, *Class, Race and Black Liberation* (New York: International Publishers, 1977), and the resolution on the Afro-American struggle—Winston's *Struggle for Afro-American Liberation*—adopted by the party's Twenty-second National Convention in August 1979. See also Oliver C. Cox, *Caste, Class, and Race: A Study in Social Dynamics* (New York: Doubleday, 1948); James A. Geschwender, *Class, Race and Worker Insurgency: The League of Revolutionary Black Workers* (Cambridge: Cambridge University Press, 1977); Mario Barrera, *Race and Class in the Southwest: A Theory of Racial Inequality* (Notre Dame: University Press of Notre Dame, 1979). Although Barrera is primarily concerned with the racial problematic as it relates to Chicanos and Chicanas, his theoretical formulations are relevant to peoples of African descent in the United States of America.

13. William Julius Wilson, *The Declining Significance of Race: Blacks and Changing American Institutions* (Chicago: University of Chicago Press, 1978); Thomas Sowell, *Race and Economics* (New York: David McKay Co., 1975); Martin Kilson, "The Black Bourgeoisie Revisited. From E. Franklin Frazier to the Present," *Dissent* (Winter 1983), pp. 85–96. This latter essay is from Kilson's forthcoming book, *Neither Insiders nor Outsiders: Blacks in American Society.*

14. Stanley Aronowitz, *The Crisis in Historical Materialism: Class, Politics, and Culture in Marxist Theory* (New York: Praeger Publications, 1981), pp. 89–112.

15. These distinctions are necessary if we are to sharpen and refine the prevailing loose usage of domination, subjugation, exploitation, repression, and oppression. In my view, domination and subjugation are discursive affairs; the former relates to racial, sexual, ethnic, or national supremacist logics, whereas the latter involves the production of subjects and subjectivities within such logics. Exploitation and repression are extradiscursive affairs in that they result from social formations and institutions such as modes of production and state apparatuses. Domination, subjugation, exploitation, and repression constitute modes of oppression, which are distinguished for analytic purposes. Needless to say, they relate to each other in complex and concrete ways. These distinctions were prompted by Michel Foucault, "The Subject and Power," *Critical Inquiry,* 8:4 (1982), pp. 775–95.

16. Winthrop Jordan, *White Over Black: American Attitudes toward the Negro, 1560–1812* (New York: Norton, 1968), pp. 18–20, 36; Thomas F. Gossett, *Race: The History of an Idea in America* (Dallas: Southern Methodist University Press, 1965), pp. 3–31.

17. For a further elaboration of this logic, see Cornel West, "A Genealogy of Modern Racism," *Prophesy Deliverance! An Afro-American Revolutionary Christianity* (Philadelphia: Westminster Press, 1982), pp. 47–65. And for the metaphilosophical motivation for this inquiry, see Cornel West, "Philosophy, Politics and Power: An Afro-American Perspective," in *Philosophy Born of Struggle: Anthology of Afro-American Philosophy from 1917,* ed. Leonard Harris (Dubuque: Kendall/Hunt Publishing Co., 1983), pp. 51–59.

18. The best exposition of this logic remains Joel Kovel's *White Racism: A Psychohistory* (New York: Pantheon, 1970). For an interesting, yet

less theoretical, treatment, see Calvin C. Hernton, *Sex and Racism in America* (New York: Grove Press, 1965).

19. Jacques Derrida, *Positions*, trans. Alan Bass (Chicago: University of Chicago Press, 1981), p. 51.

20. Primarily owing to parochial secular sensibilities, black and white Marxist thinkers—with exceptions such as Eugene Genovese in his magnum opus *Roll, Jordan, Roll: The World the Slaves Made* (New York: Random House, 1974), pp. 159–284, and Orlando Patterson's masterful *Slavery and Social Death: A Comparative Study* (Cambridge: Harvard University Press, 1982), pp. 66–76—have overlooked the tremendous impact of evangelical Protestantism on Afro-Americans in the United States, and especially the subtle ways in which Afro-Americans have employed their appropriation of this Protestantism for counter-hegemonic aims. The major legacy of this appropriation is that present-day Afro-American resistance remains under the auspices of the small, yet quite visible, prophetic wing of the black church, as exemplified by Rev. Herbert Daughtry's chairmanship of the leftist National Black United Front and the African People's Christian Organization, by Rev. Joseph Lowery's presidency of the left-liberal Southern Christian Leadership Conference (founded by Rev. Martin Luther King, Jr.), by Rev. Benjamin Hooks's executive directorship of the liberal National Association for the Advancement of Colored People, and by Rev. Jesse Jackson's leadership of the liberal People United to Save Humanity. It is no historical, political, and existential accident that, as an oppositional African intellectual and activist in the United States, I teach in a Protestant seminary and write as an Afro-American neo-Gramscian Christian! For four noteworthy texts on the religious dimension of the racial problematic in the United States, see Albert Raboteau's superb *Slave Religion: The "Invisible Institution" in the Antebellum South* (New York: Oxford University Press, 1978); James Cone and Gayraud Wilmore's indispensable *Black Theology: A Documentary History, 1966–1979* (Maryknoll, N.Y.: Orbis Books, 1979); my own provocative work, *Prophesy Deliverance! An Afro-American Revolutionary Christianity* (Philadelphia: Westminster Press, 1982); and James Washington's brilliant hundred-page introduction to *Afro-American Protestant Spirituality* (New York: Paulist Press, 1984).

21. The seductive powers of Foucault must be resisted by leftist thinkers on two fronts: the trap of discursive reductionism, which posits the absolute (as opposed to relative) autonomy of discursive practices, and the trap of full-blown (as opposed to provisional) antitotalism, which promotes revolt yet precludes revolution. The Marxist path that incorporates Foucault's insights has been blazed by the grand pioneer of cultural studies, Stuart Hall. See especially his "Cultural Studies: Two Paradigms," *Media, Culture and Society*, 2(1980), pp. 57–72, and "The Rediscovery of 'Ideology': Return of the Repressed in Media Studies," in *Culture, Society and the Media*, ed. Michael Gurevitch, Tony Bennett, James Curran, and Janet Woollacott (New York: Methuen, 1982), pp. 56–90. For subtle elaborations of this perspective on untouched frontiers, see Hazel V. Carby, "Schooling in Babylon" and "White Woman Listen! Black Feminism and the Boundaries of Sisterhood," in *The Empire Strikes Back: Race and Racism in 70s Britain*, Center for Contemporary Cultural Studies (London: Hutchinson, 1982), pp. 183–211, 212–35.

22. Antonio Gramsci, *Selections from the Prison Notebooks*, ed. and trans. Quintin Hoare and Geoffrey Nowell Smith (New York: International Publishers, 1971), p. 407. For his formulations of a "historical bloc," note pp. 136ff., 365–66. For a useful treatment of this complex issue of the relation of base and superstructure, see Raymond Williams, *Marxism and Literature* (New York: Oxford University Press, 1977), pp. 75–89.

23. The best theoretical formulation I know of this Gramscian metaphor is found in Bob Jessop's superb work *The Capitalist State: Marxist Theories and Methods* (New York: New York University Press, 1982), pp. 211–59.

24. Ernesto Laclau, "The Impossibility of Society," *Canadian Journal of Political and Social Theory*, 7:12 (1983), pp. 21–24.

25. I consider the originary text of poststructuralism to be Gilles Deleuze's *Nietzsche and Philosophy*, published in 1962 and translated into English in 1983. This provocative and often persuasive attack on Hegel and dialectics from a Nietzschean viewpoint initiated and legitimated the now familiar poststructuralist assaults on totalizing frameworks, teleological narratives, homogeneous continuities in history, and recuperative, nostalgic strategies in interpretation. The rejection of ontology left Marxists with no grounds for theorizing, given

their reliance on Hegelian dialectics. Since I agree with this rejection, the theoretical crisis of Marxism is, I believe, a serious one. Aronowitz's call—influenced by Adorno's philosophy of difference and Murray Bookchin's ecological perspective—for a new will to totality guided by ideals of workers' self-management, sexual and racial freedom, and the liberation of nature is noteworthy, as is Deleuze's and Guatarri's call—mediated by Spinoza and Nietzsche—for theoretical nomadism guided by a political metaphysics of desire. Both call for a new Marxist or materialist ethics, yet neither is forthcoming. The major alternative is to opt for a pragmatic viewpoint (informed by the work of Richard Rorty, Richard Bernstein, and others) in which dialectical modes of thinking become rhetorical strategies employed in intellectual, social, and existential warfare against dogmatic ways of thought, forms of oppression, and modes of despair. Such rhetorical Marxism or dialectical pragmatism (to use Max Eastman's term) preserves historically constituted human agency, accents the multileveled character of oppression, and demystifies poststructuralist strategies by circumscribing and thereby trivializing the radical skepticism that sustain them while accepting their powerful insights regarding the role of otherness and alterity in philosophies of identity, including most forms of dialectical thinking. Since energizing emancipatory visions are, to put it bluntly, religious visions, I see little alternative other than appropriating the subversive potential of Christianity and other religions.

FURTHER READING

Allen, Robert L. 1970. *Black Awakening in Capitalist America: An Analytic History.* Garden City, NY: Doubleday.

Ashbaugh, Carolyn. 1976. *Lucy Parsons: American Revolutionary.* Chicago: Charles H. Kerr.

Cox, Oliver C. 1948. *Caste, Class, and Race: A Study in Social Dynamics.* New York: Monthly Review Press, 1970, reprint.

Cruse, Harold. 1967. *The Crisis of the Negro Intellectual.* New York: William Morrow and Co.

Foner, Philip S. 1974. *Organized Labor and the Black Worker 1619–1973.* New York: International Publishers.

Fortune, Timothy Thomas. 1884. *Black and White: Land, Labor and Politics in the South.* New York: Arno Press, 1969, reprint.

Jacobson, Julius, ed. 1968. *The Negro and the American Labor Movement.* New York: Anchor Books.

James, Joy, ed. 1998. *Angela Y. Davis Reader.* Oxford: Blackwell Publishers.

Kelley, Robin D.G. 1990. *Hammer and Hoe: Alabama Communists During the Great Depression.* Chapel Hill: University of North Carolina Press.

Robinson, Cedric. 1980. *Black Marxism: The Making of a Radical Tradition.* London: Zed Books.

Spero, Sterling D., and Abram L. Harris. 1931. *The Black Worker: The Negro and the Labor Movement.* New York: Atheneum, reprint, 1968.

West, Cornel. 1991. *The Ethical Dimensions of Marxist Thought.* New York: Monthly Review Press.

Williams, Robert F. 1962. *Negroes with Guns.* New York: Marzani and Munsell.

CHAPTER 7

Rebellion and Radical Thought

The question of what counts as political resistance arises again in connection with the urban rebellions of the late 1960s. In this case there is a conceptual issue of whether the collective activity involved in these often spontaneous and violent outbursts constitutes social action. Unlike the well-organized strikes, sit-ins, and demonstrations of the nonviolent followers of King, urban riots involved acts of lawbreaking that exceed the limits of civil disobedience. Rather than appeal to the sense of justice and fairness of the American mainstream, the aim of rioting is often to express group frustration. Although the object of this frustration involves broader political issues that have to be addressed at the level of America's socioeconomic structure, attention by news media focusing on more volatile issues such as police abuse, or the plight of the "immigrant grocer," invariably shifts policy debates away from questions regarding the structural basis of racial inequality. Writers in the tradition of African-American radical thought that developed out of the 1960s uprisings in urban black communities have insisted upon construing urban riots as collective action. They recognize a political meaning that is denied by the construction of all aspects of the shared cooperative activity involved in these rebellions as merely individual criminal acts of looting and destroying property.

Toward the end of the 1960s King's philosophy of nonviolence began to lose ground with a younger generation of activists who were more closely aligned with the teachings of Malcolm X. The appeal of Malcolm to advocates of "black power" was due in large part to his willingness to publicly defend a role for violence in the movement. With the Declaration of Independence in mind, Malcolm proclaimed that violence is as American as apple pie. In his famous speech "The Ballot or the Bullet" he argues that the founding fathers saw political resistance as a basic human right. He appeals to this justification of the American Revolution to ground the African-American's demand for human rights.

Jill Gordon draws attention to a similarity of doctrine and language in John Locke's philosophy and the views held by Malcolm X. With reference to the specific context in which Malcolm's views were presented, she indicates the extent to which the conditions stipulated by Locke are satisfied. She maintains that at the time Malcolm wrote it was the case that the lives, liberty, and property of African-Americans were in danger. To show a connection with American founders Patrick Henry and George Washington, neither of whom represented nonviolence, Gordon cites remarks from several speeches by Malcolm to indicate the extent to which some of the political issues surrounding the American Revolution are relevant to issues African-Americans face today. One such issue is whether citizens have a right of self-defense when the government's ability to protect citizens has broken down. Malcolm argued that the denial of the ballot constitutes a failure of the government to protect the rights of its citizens. When this occurs, the people are within their rights to protect themselves "by any means necessary."

Gordon considers the worry that Malcolm's argument may be extended further than what Locke intended. She admits that Locke allows killing under certain circumstances, but neither he nor Malcolm would condone mass murder or random bombings. Given that, for Locke, rebellion applies only to tyrannical government, would he condone or reject Malcolm's statement "by any means necessary"? While Locke is not entirely clear on this matter, Gordon points out that his references to government as potentially tyrannical seem to include any magistrate, including local law enforcement as well as the registrar of voters. Gordon concludes that Locke and Malcolm X held similar views on the right to rebel, but that the racist ideological structure of the United States allows Americans to accept a white philosopher's statement of the same view expressed by a black thinker but reject the latter. Stokely Carmichael (Kwami Toure), a prominent leader of the "black power" movement that split away from the Student Nonviolent Coordinating Committee, explains the pitfalls of the earlier phase of the civil rights movement and presents the case for a future direction the movement should take, along with newly conceived goals and objectives. Drawing upon an important distinction between individual and institutional racism, Carmichael claims that the white community benefits from the existence of ghettos. The comparison of the African-American community with colonial exploitation in the Third World is not just a figure of speech—ghettos in America and South Africa are the result of identical patterns of white racism. Carmichael believes far-reaching changes in basic power relations are necessary to change this pattern.

The suggestion that so-called "integration" is the answer to the question of racial justice is rejected by Carmichael. This proposal focuses on individuals who are acceptable as minorities in middle-class communities. Carmichael questions whether the goal of the movement is to loosen up restrictions on the entry of African-Americans into the white community. He claims that the struggle for public accommodation, open housing, and job opportunity on the executive level are middle-class goals and not the concerns of a black sharecropper, dishwasher, or welfare recipient. The chief gain of the earlier phase of the civil rights movement, according to Carmichael, was to destroy the symbols of white superiority and the legally imposed limitations on black people, but the movement must now look beyond these goals to the issue of collective power.

The tactics and strategy of the earlier phase of the civil rights movement are also criticized by Carmichael. He claims that the appeal to the conscience of white institutions of power was at the expense of organizing and developing in-stitutions of community power. This encouraged black leaders to prefer forming coalitions with liberal pressure organizations, rather than to organize a base of political strength within the black community. This strategy was doomed to fail because political alliances based on appeals to conscience overlook the fact that institutions and organizations have no consciences; instead they operate in ways consistent with their own special interests. Carmichael points to the lesson of Re-construction—a case in which voting rights for African-Americans were given, then taken away—to caution that this dependency on the good will of others ren-ders the social and political rights of African-Americans "negotiable and expend-able when they conflict with the interests of our allies."

In the case of the civil rights movement Carmichael believes the long-term goals were inadequate. The goal of making the white community accessible to "qualified" black people is drawn into question by Carmichael. He claims that this decidedly middle-class aspiration must be given up in favor of developing the black community "as a functional and honorable segment of the total society with its own cultural identity, life patterns, and institutions." He cites Marx's ob-servation that the working class is the first class to want to abolish itself to point out that in similar fashion the black race is the first race that ever wished to abol-ish itself. Carmichael proposes instead that what must be abolished is not the black community but the community's dependent colonial status.

Responding to the criticism that the urban rebellions are a consequence of the black power movement's more strident orientation to social change, Carmichael points out that the riots were not produced by "black power," but by the "absence of any organization capable of giving the community the power." This is the new direction the movement will take. To avoid the abuse of poverty programs that are designed to deal only with effects not causes, Carmichael pro-poses the development of independent organizations. Only with the power to define the terms of an alliance can the black community enter into meanful re-lations when working in interracial coalitions.

One of the ardent radical voices to emerge from the urban rebellions was Huey P. Newton, cofounder and chairman of the Black Panther Party in Oak-land, California. Newton's several books include his posthumously published doctoral thesis on the political repression of the Black Panther Party. In "Func-tional Definition of Politics," Newton defines politics as war without bloodshed and war as politics with bloodshed. He discusses the failure of Reconstruction in terms of a lack of power by the black politicians of the period. They entered the political arena without power in land, economics, or the military, hence their en-deavor was doomed to fail. In the political sphere power is represented by having the ability to bring about a political consequence if one's political demands are not addressed.

Newton applies this line of thought to the situation of African-Americans to generate an argument for self-defense. According to Newton, to gain political power black political leaders must represent power in land, industry, or the mili-tary, for only by exercising power in one of these ways can black people become political in the present system. "We will make it economically non-profitable for the power structure to go on with its oppressive ways. We will then negotiate as equals. There will be a balance between the people who are economically powerful and the people who are potentially economically destructive." He identifies strategies that threaten capitalist profits as the key to changing the oppressive state policies that deny African-Americans the right to earn a living. He presents the case for the Black Panther Party's two primary objectives: to demand the right to a livelihood as a basic right to life and to transform the traditional division of police and community from the role of occupying army to a relation of police serving the interest of the community.

Speaking from the standpoint of his imprisonment, Newton argues for the idea that a prisoner can have a sense of political responsibility. In "Prison, Where is Thy Victory?" he maintains that his individual consciousness of the African-American's struggle for freedom and dignity is identical to the political consciousness that exists at the group level. To indicate the nature of this consciousness he introduces a distinction between two types of prisoners. Some prisoners wish to acquire the same goals of money, power, greed, and conspicuous consumption like most other people living in a capitalist society, but they are labeled criminal because they adopt methods society has defined as illegitimate. Newton refers to this type of prisoner as an "illegitimate capitalist." He can be distinguished from the political prisoner who rejects the assumptions upon which the present social arrangement is based. Newton employs this distinction to argue that if the people at the bottom of the society are exploited for the profit and advantage of those at the top, and there is no dignity in either exploiting or being exploited, then it is an illegitimate social arrangement. According to Newton, a political prisoner is someone who is punished for maintaining the belief that because society is illegitimate it must be overthrown.

In "Political Prisoners, Prisons and Black Liberation," written while waiting trial in the Marin County Jail, Angela Davis discusses several important issues that arise in connection with the notion of black political prisoners. She criticizes both conservative and liberal views of resistance, especially their condemnation of modes of resistance that exceed the limits of legality, by citing the fact that the existing democratic society has not fulfilled its promise of human rights for all citizens. She points out that from its inception the United States has had unjust laws expressly focused on African-Americans. Under slavery the Fugitive Slave Act necessitated the illegal Underground Railroad. Garvey's advocacy of self-defense against racist Klan violence was also illegal. Davis appeals to history to show that overt violation of law is justified when it is done to promote "the collective welfare and survival of a People." Davis distinguishes between breaking a law for one's own individual self-interest and violating it in the interests of oppressed people. Where the former counts as criminal, the latter is directed toward social change and therefore counts as political—and the persons so acting, when captured, are political prisoners.

Davis discusses several historical cases of political prisoners in America to indicate that, in the eyes of authorities, what counts most is that they sought to overthrow oppressive institutions, and not so much whether a violation occurred. She cites the fact that King was charged more with being an ememy of the Southern social arrangement than with his illegal acts of trespassing and disturbing the peace. In cases of revolt, such as Nat Turner's and John Brown's, the political prisoner is punished for opposing the state's right to maintain unjust laws. Davis presents a contemporary version of the mainstream's distorted perspective on state authority and law. Davis points to the police raid on the Los Angeles Black Panther Party office in spring 1970 to illustrate the practice of discrediting political activists who challenge the legitimacy of the present social order by construing their actions as criminal. The Panthers' armed self-defense against the police attack was grounds for a criminal assault charge against the Panthers.

Davis considers a question that arises within Marxist theory of whether criminals "who have recourse to antisocial acts are incapable of developing the discipline and collective orientation required by revolutionary struggle." She cites Marx's remarks that indicate he saw a role for the lumpenproletariat to support her claim that prisoners must be included in the tradition of the black liberation struggle. Noting that the criminal justice system is linked with poverty in a vicious cycle that also includes the activists who speak out against oppression, she urges the socialist labor movement to join ranks with oppressed minorities to resist the facist repression that is responsible for the imprisonment of political activists seeking social and economic change.

Cornel West critically examines the role of the black middle class in the civil rights movement to point out a paradox that was highlighted by the sixties' rebellions. According to West, the black middle class both propelled the civil rights movement and circumscribed its vision within limits set by liberal capitalistism. He notes the fact that King had to break with the old middle class in a fashion that portended the rift between King and the Student Nonviolent Coordinating Committee over tactics and strategy. West notes several important factors at work. The Watts riots in 1965, shortly after Birmingham and the March on Washington, signaled the close of the first stage of the movement. The urban rebellions mark a shift toward black proletarian and lumpenproletarian interests away from black middle-class liberalism. When King moved in this direction, his new focus on the urban poor led to black middle-class abandonment.

West points out that the revolt of the black masses led to a crisis. How should the black middle class respond to rebellions by the black "underclass"? He criticizes the black nationalist response as "the activity of black petit bourgeois self-congratulation and self-justification on reaching an anxiety ridden middle-class status." Although he recognizes the concrete results of organizations such as the Nation of Islam, he also notes that, as in the case of the state repression of the Black Panther Party and the internal split over nationalism in Detroit's League of Revolutionary Black Workers, there were many factors working against a successful radical movement. West believes that the black proleterian and the black middle class must be revitalized to renew this resistance. He advocates building coalitions with other progressive organizations. Along with ideas provided by intellectuals (organic and university-trained), West sees a role for black popular culture and advocates using music to provide vision.

By Any Means Necessary

John Locke and Malcolm X on the Right to Revolution

Jill Gordon

Many will ask what Harlem finds to honor in the stormy, controversial and bold young captain. And we will smile. And we will answer and say unto them: Did you ever talk to Brother Malcolm? Did he ever touch you? Did you have him smile at you? Did he ever do a mean thing? Was he ever himself associated with violence or any public disturbance? For if you did, you would know him and if you knew him you would know why we must honor him.

Ossie Davis,
Eulogy for Malcolm X, 1965

Malcolm X's claim that blacks in the United States need to bring about social change by any means necessary has been interpreted as a call to violence—and an unjustified one at that. I will demonstrate to the contrary that Malcolm X's exhortations are consistent with traditional liberal theory, in particular, a theory intimately connected to the United States Constitution, that of John Locke.[1] I will show that the content of Malcolm X's speeches and the social climate in which they were delivered match similar social and political contexts which Locke claims in the *Second Treatise on Government* warrant legitimate rebellion. In an attempt to understand better Malcolm's philosophical rejection of the non-violence movement of his time, I will also examine both his and Locke's views on the appropriate role of violence in revolution.

One of the tasks which Locke sets for himself in his *Second Treatise on Government* is the justification of legitimate rebellion.[2] But

Source: Jill Gordon, "By Any Means Necessary: John Locke and Malcolm X on the Right to Revolution," *Journal of Social Philosophy* 26.1 (Spring 1995): 53–85. © 1995 by Blackwell Publishers Journals.

this part of his political theory rests firmly on foundations laid earlier in the work. Only after laying a firm foundation of natural rights, formation of the social contract, civil rights, and government obligation, does Locke move on to address contingencies of civil life such as tyranny, dissolution of the government, and legitimate rebellion in the face of these. So while rebellion will be my eventual focus, I begin with a brief discussion of the philosophical underpinnings to Locke's views on rebellion in order to lay the groundwork for the rest of the argument. In Section II, I make the case that African Americans during Malcolm's lifetime found themselves in the kind of situation(s) which, according to Locke's theory, warranted rebellion, viz., the threat to—or loss of—life, liberty and property, and the lack of appeal in the face of that. In Section III, I quote extensively from Malcolm's speeches in order to show that his arguments for obtaining rights by any means necessary do parallel those made by Locke. I conclude in the final section that, however they are judged on the issue of revolution, Locke and Malcolm X must be judged by the same standards and that, by and large, they have not been so judged.

I

In the state of nature, Locke tells us, all men are perfectly free and equal, and no one is subject to or superior to anyone else (§4, §7).[3] Men act according to reason in nature and they formulate law from reason; this is what Locke calls the natural law (§6). The fundamental law of nature is preservation (§16) and to secure his own preservation each has the natural right to life, liberty, and property as each of these conduces to his preservation. Likewise, all are compelled by the law of nature to preserve all of mankind by not transgressing against the rights of others (§6,§7).

The rights to life, liberty, and property are accompanied by the right to judge and carry out any punishment against a transgressor of the natural law. If someone trespasses against one's natural rights, one can punish the transgressor in the interest of preservation. In this sense, we all execute the natural law. Locke justifies this right to execute the law on two grounds: as deterrent, in order to prevent the transgression from happening again, and as reparation to the injured party. One may punish, "so far as calm reason and conscience dictate, what is proportionate to (another's) transgression, which is so much as may serve for reparation and restraint" (§8). Furthermore, as executives of the law of nature, everyone again preserves doubly—preserving each individual himself and preserving the species. In our own individual cases, we may execute the law of nature and punish those who transgress against us so as to preserve ourselves and to repair the injury done. Beyond that, we can also punish in cases other than our own in order to deter further transgressions and thereby preserve the species. In cases when the punishment is on behalf of another's injury, however, the punishment can only be for deterrence—preservation of the species—and not for reparation (§7). Reparative or retributive punishment is reserved only for the injured party (§11).

In the state of nature God gives the earth in common to all men. It is through their labor, i.e., by making a bodily contribution to some project, that men transform the status of something from this initial common state into private property. While I shall not go deeply into a discussion of property, it is worth noting that life, liberty, and property are not as distinct as they appear to be. Because Locke asserts that the first and most fundamental property belonging to us is our own body, the connections to life and liberty are apparent. Property, as Locke intends to use the term,

would logically seem to include life and liberty, and Locke does come to use the term "property" in the *Treatise* to refer to the lives, persons, and possessions of individuals.[4]

In contrast to the state of nature, Locke delineates the state of war. He thus sets out to distinguish his theory from Hobbes' theory in which the state of nature *is* a state of constant war, all against all.[5] Recall that in nature, according to Locke, reason dictates that we have the right to life, liberty, and property and that, also according to reason and the natural law, we must respect those rights in others. Anyone acting contrary to the law of nature "shows that he lives by another rule than that of reason" (§8). Those who pose a threat to destroy others are not living under the dictates of reason and put themselves into a state of war with those whom they threaten. And since the fundamental law of nature is preservation, one can destroy that which threatens his own destruction (§16). Moreover, Locke makes the explicit arguments that likewise to take away someone's liberty is also to make war on him (§17) as is taking away his property (§18). In these passages, Locke is careful to point out that the state of war can also break out in civil society, not just in nature (§17, §18, §20). The social contract itself is no guarantee that the state of war will not erupt. While Locke is, at this point, focusing on the distinction between the state of nature and the state of war, it will be relevant later in the *Treatise* that the state of war can be waged after the social contract has been formed.

Whether he speaks of nature or civil society, Locke is careful to demarcate a state of war as a state in which force is used and there is no appeal. The state of war is "force, or a declared design of force, upon the person of another, where there is no common superior on earth to appeal to for relief … it is the want of such an appeal gives a man the right of war …" (§19). The appeal must not only be available, but properly functioning.

> … (W)here an appeal to the law, and constituted judges, lies open, but the remedy is denied by a manifest perverting of justice, and a

barefaced wresting of the laws to protect or in-demnify the violence or injuries of some men, or party of men, there it is hard to imagine any thing but a state of war: for where-ever violence is used, and injury done, though by hands appointed to administer justice, it is still violence and injury, however coloured with the names, pretenses, or forms of law, the end whereof being to protect and redress the innocent, by an unbiased application of it to all who are under it ... (§20).

The two elements important to demarcating and defining a state of war and distinguishing it from nature appear to be force and lack of appeal: if there is no force or threat of force, there is no state of war; and if there is a remedy or appeal open in response to the force, there is no state of war. But when one is confronted with force or the threat of force and has no available appeal, then war is being waged. Men living in nature according to reason would not use force against one another, but once that force is used, there is no appeal in the state of nature since there is no common superior (§19). It is force which initiates the state of war and the appeal which discontinues it (§21). Locke will later elaborate on what counts as force, and both the concepts of force and appeal will be key to understanding legitimate rebellion, since rebellion is legitimate in the face of waged war.

Although Locke is sure to distinguish himself from Hobbes by arguing that nature is not a state of war and that there men live peaceably according to the dictates of reason, he is eventually compelled to explain the motivation for leaving the state of nature and entering civil society. In passages where he sounds more subtly like Hobbes (§13; §124–§127), Locke explains that there are three unfortunate "inconveniences" in the state of nature which can be remedied in civil society: (1) there is no established law to which all have agreed, (2) we all tend to be partial to ourselves and there is no impartial judge to adjudicate in matters which call for it, and (3) there is no one to enforce judgment if and when it is made. Agreement to the social contract, and with it the transition

to civil society, will remedy these inconveniences.

The rights to life, liberty, and property are not lost in the move to civil society. We retain these rights by virtue of our humanity, but their protection is now transferred to the state (§89); we do lose our executive power with regard to the natural law. The entity formed by those who agree to the social contract, the society, is chiefly charged with the protection and defense of the rights of its members and the judgment and punishment of those who transgress the laws. This body of people which Locke calls the society is distinct from government, and the society has the final say, the ultimate power, sovereignty. The sovereign group in the normal course of events would appoint a government to carry out its will in which case society transfers its authority to government to act on its behalf (§106, §131, §132, §133, *et passim*). It is then the government's primary obligation to protect the life, liberty, and property of its citizens and to punish those who transgress the law. But the absolute sovereignty still remains with those who have agreed to the social contract, and the government is to carry out its will.

Now imagine scenarios in which the government can no longer or is no longer fulfilling its obligation to the people by protecting their rights. We can name two cases in particular. Either the government is not protecting the lives, liberty, or property of its citizens from the transgression of other citizens, or the government itself transgresses against citizens' rights.[6] In either case the government is culpable, and Locke provides the justification for legitimate rebellion. Two key issues are involved in understanding Locke's views on legitimate rebellion. First, in all cases one rule always applies for Locke: Force can only be used in meeting unjust and unlawful force (§204). Furthermore, Locke firmly claims that legitimate channels of appeal must be open and utilized when available.

Locke begins with a definition of tyranny. Tyranny is the exercise of power beyond right (§199), and "(w)henever (that) power ... is applied to other ends (than protection of the rights of citizens and the public good), and made use of to impoverish, harass, or subdue (the people) to the arbitrary and irregular commands of those that have it; there it presently becomes tyranny whether those that thus use it are one or many" (§201). When a magistrate of the state acts beyond the law, he ceases to be a magistrate; the magistrate is then acting without authority and "may be opposed, as any other man, who by force invades the right of another" (§202). Locke considers any magistrate acting beyond the authority granted him by law to be acting with force, and based on prior claims Locke has made, to be waging war. Herein lies the connection to Locke's previous discussion of the state of war and the first justification of the right to revolution. Locke believes that we can oppose a tyrant as we would oppose any thief regardless of whether he holds the lowest or highest office (§202). It is appropriate to infer that the right to preservation can be rightly claimed by a person who finds himself the object of force due to a magistrate's acting outside the bounds of authority granted him by law. Such being the case, one could destroy that which seeks his destruction (§16).

When a transgression first occurs, the initial response should ordinarily be an appeal to legitimate channels already in place by law. (No such established channels exist in the state of nature—one of its inconveniences, §20.) We can infer from Locke that these might include the court system, police, legal council, arbitration, or even a direct appeal to the legislature or chief executive. "For when the injured party may be relieved, and his damages repaired by appeal to the law, there can be no pretense for force, which is only to be used where a man is intercepted from appealing to the law: for nothing is to be accounted hostile force, but where it leaves not the remedy of such an appeal" (§207). Locke is quite clear that if the channels of appeal are blocked, leaving no remedy, then this is to be counted hostile force. And we know that if the people are being treated with force they may respond with force. Hence the right to revolution when legitimate channels of appeal are blocked. Locke strongly implies that

keeping the channels of appeal open is a way of ensuring political stability as well as the safety of the magistrates. Locke even wonders how the people can be kept from such resistance. If the people "are persuaded in their consciences that their laws and with them their estates, liberties, and lives are in danger, and perhaps their religion too; how they will be hindered from resisting illegal force, used against them, I cannot tell" (§209).

If the tyranny is extreme then the entire government may be in danger of dissolution. Locke carefully enumerates the various ways in which a government can dissolve (§211-§219).[7] This would not necessarily imply that the underlying, sovereign society had also been dissolved but at the point when government has already been dissolved by "oppression" and "artifice" it might be too late to save the society (§220). Therefore the people have a right not just to remedy the dissolution of government but to prevent it. "... (M)en can never be secure from tyranny if there be no means to escape it till they are perfectly under it: and therefore it is, that they have not only a right to get out of it, but to prevent it" (§220).

The citizens are warranted therefore in monitoring whether the government is acting in their interests and thereby maintaining the trust granted to them by the society to protect their rights. "There is therefore secondly, another way whereby governments are dissolved, and that is, when the legislative or prince, either of them, acts contrary to their trust" (§221). They are trusted to protect the life, liberty and fortunes (property) of the people (§221). In betraying that trust, according to Locke, they put themselves in a state of war with the people and the people "are left the common refuge which God hath provided for all men against force and violence" (§222). We can only infer from this that in such cases in which the officers of the law have betrayed the trust of the people to protect their life, liberty, and property, that the people can legitimately consider themselves at war with those officers, and proceed accordingly to meet force with force.

Against the objections that such allowances would certainly lead to political insurrection, general instability, and worse, civil war, Locke adamantly argues that people are not likely to be moved to rebellion at the slightest injustice. Rather, he argues, it would only be a long series of abuses which showed a pattern that would actually incite such behavior, and in such cases revolution would be warranted (§225).

Locke even goes so far as to say that allowing for the resistance to and prevention of tyranny would actually serve as an antidote to rebellion, and here he turns the tables with a rhetorical flair. Legitimate resistance to tyranny, as Locke considers it, "is the best fence against rebellion, and the probablest means to hinder it: for rebellion being an opposition, not to persons, but authority, which is founded only in the constitutions and laws of the government; those, whoever they be, who by force break through, and by force justify their violations of them, are truly and properly rebels …" (§226).[8] The true rebels are not those people who legitimately resist the tyranny—whether immediate or designed—but rather those who go against the law in the first place, those magistrates who betray the trust of the people and thereby wage war on them (§227).

But what really does the right to revolution mean in practical terms? Locke was attuned to the reality of violence in such political contexts and he therefore deals with the issue explicitly. Using William Barclay's views to lay the groundwork, he places himself in stark opposition to him. Even Barclay, "that great assertor of the power and sacredness of kings" (§232), must concede that resistance is sometimes necessary. But he puts two limitations on it: the resistance must be done with reverence, and one cannot exact punishment beyond the mere resistance.

> … the people have a right to resist and defend themselves from injury: but it must be with this caution, that they only defend themselves, but do not attack their prince: they may repair the damages received but must not for any provocation exceed the bounds of due reverence and respect…. The body of the people may with respect resist intolerable tyranny; for

when it is but moderate, they ought to endure it (Locke quoting Barclay, §233).

Locke responds directly to Barclay with an edge to his humor.

> How to resist force without striking again, or how to strike with reverence, will need some skill to make intelligible. He that shall oppose an assault only with a shield to receive the blows, or in any more respectful posture, without a sword in his hand, to abate the confidence and force of the assailant, will quickly be at an end of his resistance, and will find such a defense serve only to draw on himself the worse usage…. (L)et our author, or any body else, join a knock on the head, or a cut on the face, with as much reverence and respect as he thinks fit (§235).

These passages clearly indicate that Locke does endorse the use of physical force and he recognizes the violent nature of political discord under extreme circumstances. He does not balk at allowing for the possibility of deadly force being used against a magistrate or even a prince when that officer exceeds the bounds of law and wages war against a citizen.

II

Let us move, then, beyond philosophical theory to painful reality, out of the seventeenth century and into the twentieth. Throughout the history of the so-called new world, blacks have been mistreated, abused, and worse. Information regarding these abuses—both statistical and anecdotal—is overwhelmingly easy to come by, and presents us with riches which are indeed an embarrassment. Taking for granted that the abuses began early in our history and that some continue today, I will focus in particular only on the years proximal to Malcolm X's adult life, a window of time before and during the American Civil Rights Movement. One particularly graphic way to look at the treatment of blacks during this time period is through Locke's three natural rights: life, liberty and property. In systematic fashion African Americans suffered threat to and loss of property, liberty, and life. Gunnar Myrdal sums up what is in effect the argument of this section of the paper.

(I)n the south the Negro's person and property are practically subject to the whim of any white person who wishes to take advantage of him or to punish him for any real or fancied wrongdoing or "insult." A white man can steal from or maltreat a Negro in almost any way without fear of reprisal, because the Negro cannot claim the protection of the police or courts and personal vengeance on the part of the offended Negro usually results in organized retaliation in the form of bodily injury (including lynching), home burning, or banishment.[9]

I will discuss here a brief sample of abuses which represent only the most obvious cases. My discussion here then is meant to be the minimal necessary to make my case and is nothing close to exhaustive of all the civil and human rights abuses suffered by black Americans. I am aware that I speak here of natural rights but that the movement labeled itself a movement for civil rights. The two are related, however, and natural rights, by Locke's reasoning are the more fundamental. These are to be afforded to all human beings by virtue of their humanity. If I can make the case, therefore, that the rights of blacks as human beings were being abused, then *a fortiori* the case holds for their rights as citizens. It is not easy, however, to separate the abuse of natural or human rights from the civil rights abuses which were specifically targeted for redress during the 1950's and 1960's. Often the attempt to keep blacks from demanding or exercising their civil rights was accomplished by threats to or violation of life, liberty, or property. Malcolm X himself recognized this explicitly in his insistence that the United States be brought before the United Nations for *human* rights violations during the height of the Civil Rights Movement.[10]

The lives of black Americans have always been in danger to a much larger degree than any other citizens in the population. Blacks were in many cases the victims of white violence.[11] Lynching was a common practice in the United States, although statistics show that it fell off after World War II. "Efforts of civil-rights groups to secure passage of a federal anti-lynching law failed repeatedly, but effective work by white and Negro groups, many of them Southern Church organizations, virtually eliminated lynching for a time. The N.A.A.C.P. conceded the 'virtual disappearance of this form of oppression' in the early 1950's. It was to reappear later with the rise of Southern resistance to civil rights campaigns in the Deep South."[12]

Mortality rates for blacks have consistently been higher than mortality rates for whites in the United States. In 1958, for example, white men between the ages of 25-34 years had 1.6 deaths per 1000 persons; white females in that same age bracket had 0.9 deaths per 1000 persons. In that same age group nonwhite men had 4.0 deaths per 1000, and nonwhite women had a mortality rate of 2.8 per 1000.[13] To look at this kind of information from a slightly different angle, in the United States in 1970, blacks lived 7.5 years less than whites.[14] In dealing with inequality, facts about the "quantity of life have a natural priority. *Time alive* is not all that matters, but it matters very much indeed."[15] While statistics such as these could be explained by lack of access to health care, poorer living conditions, bad nutrition, or harmful work environment, all of these factors fall to the lot of blacks in a disproportionate and systematic fashion due to discrimination and exclusion throughout the entire social and economic system.

Beyond their lives, the liberty of blacks is jeopardized too. One of the most persistent and visible deprivations of liberty that blacks have suffered in the United States is the freedom to live and relocate where they wish. Despite legislation during the 1950's to counteract discrimination in education, housing and residence proved the most resistant of all areas of discrimination to the demand for equal treatment. Barriers to equal housing opportunity are among the most rigid which minority groups must face.[16]

Housing is the one commodity on the American Market that Negroes and persons belonging to certain other ethnic minorities cannot purchase freely. A complex of forces and pressures operates to exclude members of these groups from residence in the majority of the nation's urban and suburban neighborhoods. … In consequence, a minority person typically has fewer alternatives in housing than does a white homeseeker with comparable purchasing power. The latter may choose any location and compete for any available dwelling that suits his needs, tastes, and pocketbook, subject only to the general laws. The minority person, however, can compete freely only within circumscribed areas. Elsewhere he confronts formidable barriers because of his race.…

Racial restrictions on residence are an outstanding departure from the traditional American principle of freedom to move and to choose one's place of residence. Many countries do not recognize the right of free movement, but in the United States it has been so seldom challenged as to be taken for granted by most people. Exclusion from residence areas is thus, a deprivation of a traditional American freedom—a right legally denied only to paroled criminals, aliens, and, in the past, to certain minority racial groups.[17]

The 1958 *Report of the Commission on Race and Housing* states unambiguously that "no one can be said to be really free unless he can freely choose where he will live. The opportunity to compete for housing of one's choice is crucial to both equality and freedom."[18] Blacks in the United States were and still are systematically kept from exercising such freedom.

Not only are blacks limited in their freedom to live where they choose, but the areas to which they are relegated subject them to poorer living conditions. "Advanced age of the buildings, a large percentage of substandard dwellings, and high frequency of crowding are virtually standard characteristics of the housing in areas of nonwhite residence—North, South, and West."[19] While some differences in housing are due to differences in income between blacks and whites, even if we control for differences in income, the disparities exist.

If income were the only factor making for racial differences in housing quality, it would be expected that within each income class, the percentages of whites and of nonwhites occupying standard dwelling units would be substantially identical. Instead, the data show a differential unfavorable to nonwhites persisting through all the income classes. At every level of income, in every standard metropolitan area, nonwhite households occupied a smaller percentage of standard dwellings than the comparable group of white families.[20]

It is quite clear from these few examples that life, liberty, and property are linked in powerful ways. It is impossible to talk about dangers to the lives and restrictions in the liberty of blacks without seeing the immediate consequences for property. Discrimination and racism prevent blacks from sharing in the same economic opportunities as whites, excludes them from important social, political, and economic sources of well being, and perpetuates all of the concomitant disadvantages.

With such abuses taking place, one might expect, as Locke did, that citizens would have recourse to appeal for protection of their rights through existing channels. Where possible, but facing slow and unresponsive agents of the government, blacks did avail themselves to such channels. Several Supreme Court rulings since the Civil War and the Civil Rights Act of 1964 are evidence of the struggle of blacks working (paradoxically) within and against existing law. But in effect, legitimate channels of appeal were also blocked for black Americans. "The Negroes … are hurt in their trust that the law is impartial, that the court and the police are their protection, and indeed, that they belong to an orderly society which has set up this machinery for common security and welfare."[21] Three channels of appeal in particular can be shown to be blocked or, what essentially amounts to the same thing, ineffective and unresponsive for addressing the transgressions occurring against black

Americans' rights: the franchise, the judicial system, and local police.

Whites began after the Civil War to create laws that would, in effect, make it impossible for blacks to vote. Whites disenfranchised blacks "legally" through literacy tests, poll taxes, or by imposing a "grandfather clause." These laws required respectively that the voter be able to read and write, that he pay a significant poll tax, or that he have had a grandfather who had voted.

Typically the (literacy) test required the voter to be able to read and write a portion of the Constitution as a condition to register to vote. The literacy test was racially neutral on its face, but it was administered in a way which excluded blacks, but not whites, from registering. To make sure that illiterate whites were not disfranchised, alternatives to literacy were provided if the registrant could "understand and interpret" the Constitution, owned property, or was "of good character." Many states also enacted "grandfather clauses" which excused persons registered on or prior to January 1, 1866, and their descendants, from having to comply with any literacy or property requirement for registration. By definition, few Negroes could qualify for registration under the grandfather clauses, since Negroes were generally not allowed to vote prior to January 1, 1866. The poll tax was another way of limiting the franchise. The tax was, in essence, a fee for the privilege of voting and fell with disproportionate impact upon poor blacks.[22]

There were also means of keeping blacks disenfranchised that did not involve creating new laws. These illegal means included harassing or threatening with death those who registered or tried to vote. "By one means or another, including intimidation and terror, Negroes were effectively prevented from registering (to vote) even when they had the courage to try....In many Black Belt counties it was apparent that so long as voter registration and poll supervision were entrusted entirely to local (white) authority there would be little hope for significant Negro participation in the most elementary political rights."[23]

One extreme case which demonstrates the effectiveness of intimidation and terror was Lowndes County, Alabama, referred to as "Bloody Lowndes" because of the violence there. While blacks made up 80% of the county's population, they had not voted since 1865. They did finally vote in significant numbers in an election on May 3, 1966—and that, only after a concerted effort by organized civil rights groups helped black citizens to register to vote, educated them about the voting process, helped to field qualified black candidates for public office, and provided at least the semblance of safety at the polls.[24]

The judicial system has also failed to provide a channel of appeal to blacks. There is an entire history of injustice blacks have suffered in the criminal justice system. They have been arrested, convicted, and incarcerated disproportionately to their numbers; and the sentences which have been imposed against them have been harsher than sentences given to whites who have committed similar crimes.[25] Furthermore, blacks are far more likely to receive the death penalty in capital offenses than whites.[26] Sentencing practices can also be correlated to the race of the victim. Black on black crime is treated with a kind of leniency that seems to indicate that the black victims are deserving of less justice. The crimes punished most severely are those committed by blacks against whites.[27]

In some communities, the citizens as well as the police and judges have an attitude of "live and let live" as long as they "keep it among themselves." This attitude, when expressed by the assignment of fewer police officers to highly populated Negro neighborhoods, may mean that considerably less crime by Negroes is being recorded by the police than actually occurs.... (A) result of this attitude is that Negro victims often are not receiving equal protection under the law, either by police surveillance or by conviction of the guilty.[28]

Working from the other side of the criminal justice system blacks have been consistently denied the opportunity to serve on juries. Even though the Civil Rights Act of 1875 prohibited the exclusion of anyone from serving on a jury due to race, color, or previous condition of servitude, blacks were in fact systematically excluded from such service. In 1935 a watershed case came before the Supreme Court which conceded that there had been considerable discrimination in jury selection and that all white juries had unjustly convicted black citizens.[29] Evidence showed that blacks had been systematically barred from serving on juries in Alabama since the turn of the century and that this seemed contrary to the abundance of qualified blacks living there. Unfortunately, the *Norris* case, while it provided judicial grounds for the inclusion of blacks to serve on juries as well as grounds for challenging convictions of all white juries, had little practical effect. Juries would often include only one or a small minority of blacks who could have no meaningful effect on the outcome of jury deliberation.[30] Moreover, prosecutors could rely on the peremptory challenge. In fact the peremptory challenge proved to be as effective a means of striking prospective black jurors as the arbitrary disqualifications of earlier years. The effect on the racially segregated jury box between 1935–1965 was little if any.[31] Michael O. Finkelstein carried out a statistical study of the venire records of persons selected to Grand Juries in Manhattan, the Bronx, and Westchester for the years 1965–1967 with startling results.[32]

> The data revealed that Harlem districts, which are heavily populated with Negroes and Puerto Ricans, contributed less that 1 per cent of the Manhattan veniremen although they comprised 11 percent of the voting population. If veniremen were chosen at random from the registered voters lists, disparities this large would virtually never occur. (The mathematical probability, computed for the Manhattan grand jury venires in 1967, was even smaller than the probability of being dealt 24 consecutive royal flushes in an honest game of five-card draw poker.)[33]

Even before issues reach the courts, citizens normally believe that the police force is perhaps the primary channel of appeal in times of public distress. The black community, however, has had a consistently strained relationship with local police forces—for good reason in many instances—and so has felt that this channel of appeal is also obstructed. Myrdal reported that between 1920–1932, of the 479 Negroes killed by white persons in the South, 54 per cent were killed by white police officers.[34] This statistic alone says much. Working from the Lockean theoretical framework, it is not difficult to make the case that police action toward blacks often fits Locke's formal definition of tyranny, the exercise of power beyond right (§199). Myrdal argues that the police function to enforce white supremacy and to regulate customs associated with it. "To enable the policeman to carry out this function, the courts are supposed to back him even when he proceeds *far outside normal police activity*."[35] Myrdal rightly describes this behavior on the part of the police and the courts as extra-legal,[36] which fits perfectly Locke's description of tyranny. "Where-ever law ends, tyranny begins"—when "whosoever in authority exceeds the power given him by the law" (§202).

But the problem is nationwide, not simply restricted to the South. "(W)hile there are no consistent data about the extent of police brutality, studies conducted by the Crime Commission leave no doubt that such brutality exists, and not only in the South, where blacks have long been subjected to excessive police force, but in Northern cities as well."[37] When asked in a nationwide poll in 1970, "How would you rate the job done by law enforcement officials on the local level—excellent, pretty good, only fair, or poor?" 50% of blacks gave local police an unfavorable rating (the sum of "only fair" and "poor" responses combined) as compared to only 31% of whites.[38] In studies that account for income level the results still show that blacks and whites have quite different relations with police. Across four income groups males were asked in 1966, "How good a job do the police do on being respectful to people like yourself—very good, pretty good, not so good, or no opinion?" White response varied little across income groups for those who responded negatively ("not so good"). In three of the four lower income groups only 4% of white males responded "not so good," and in the highest income group, only 2% of white males responded negatively. Among non-whites, however, negative responses were 22%, 11%, 6% and 34% respectively for the four income groups.[39] Overall, studies show that blacks are more likely to be stopped by police than whites,[40] when stopped they are more likely to be searched,[41] and they are also more likely to be arrested and booked than whites.[42] And "since ... minority-group members are more likely than whites to be stopped, interrogated, searched, arrested and charged, it is reasonable to assume they also tend to experience excessive police force and abuse of authority."[43]

The 1950's and especially the 1960's were times of political unrest and sometimes the police played an active role in responding to protest against the government. While not all demonstrations were Civil Rights related, many were. Attitudes toward police reaction to political demonstration also differed across racial lines. People were asked in 1966, "There have been quite a number of political and civil rights demonstrations over the past few years. Do you think such demonstrations should be allowed no matter what, should be allowed only if the demonstrators remain peaceful, or should not be allowed at all?" Of the white male respondents, 51%, 45%, 40%, and 31% from the respective income groups responded "Allow none." The nonwhite males who responded "Allow none," comprised 4%, 2%, 3% and 0% from the respective four income groups. White females who wanted to disallow all political demonstrations, were 49%, 49%, 48%, and 36% respectively from the four income groups. Nonwhite females wanting to disallow political demonstrations completely represented 6%, 7%, 15%, and 9% respectively from the four income groups.[44]

But political demonstrations, peaceful or otherwise, were not the only matter that occupied the time of the police. There were also during this time period many urban riots, and these not only involved police action during and after the fact, but also targeted police as the cause of civil unrest.

(F)rom the beginning to the end of the rioting (during the 1960's) the police were among the principal targets. Indeed, it is impossible to conceive of the riots erupting with the same frequency or assuming the same form were it not for the ghetto's intense resentment of the police.

Many prominent blacks have attempted to explain this resentment to the United States Commission on Civil Rights, the Governor's Commission on the Los Angeles Riots, and other official investigative bodies. They have made three main points. First, that most blacks have long been and indeed still are, subjected to brutality, harassment, and other forms of police misconduct in both the North and the South. Second, that most blacks are convinced that the police enforce the law less rigorously in black ghettos than in white communities. And third, that most blacks are persuaded that they have no effective way to protest, much less to remedy, brutality, harassment, and inadequate law enforcement.[45]

In the United States there are even channels of appeal designed to address problems within the channels of appeal. Such is the function of Civilian Review Boards with respect to local police forces. Studies in Philadelphia and New York indicate that blacks are overrepresented in complaints to review boards. In New York during 1967, 36% of the 1,281 complainants appealing to New York's Civilian Complaint Review Board were Negroes who represent 20% of the city's population.[46] From 1958-1966 the Philadelphia Police Advisory Board received 64% of their complaints from nonwhites who comprised a little over 25% of the population.[47] However, blacks seem unable to obtain justice even with such backups to blockage in channels of appeal. "Much criticism has been leveled against existing review boards because so many of the cases brought before them are dismissed, and because, it is charged, disciplinary action even when taken is often not meaningful."[48] Social contract theory would preclude the legitimacy of brutality on the part of police forces, most especially when accompanied by negligence in addressing grievances. In this scenario, citizens do not receive the very protection which was the initial impetus behind the move to civil society. "(A)ny coercive practice by legal agents that constricts and endangers the freedom of the citizenry, rather than expanding and securing it, reproduces the very condition of the state of (war) that coercive legal agencies are meant to remedy. A public agency that engages in such practices literally undermines its own justification. It subjects people to precisely the sort of risks it was given special powers to prevent."[49]

III

All of the above evidence indicates that the political context in which Malcolm X and other African Americans found themselves was one in which their lives, liberty, and property were in danger, and one in which the legitimate channels of appeal were blocked. Now given this political context let us turn to Malcolm X's political philosophy. I shall let Malcolm speak for himself, as it were, for two reasons. First of all, his style and wit are worth hearing directly. Secondly, I wish to show the striking similarities between Locke and Malcolm X without leaving suspicion that the connection is manufactured on my part. Not only is the content of their thought doctrinally similar, but the language in which they chose to express themselves makes their connection even more strongly. For those not familiar with the myriad speeches which Malcolm delivered, you must take it on trust that the speeches I cite here are representative of views which Malcolm expressed often and consistently.

There is quite a bit of historical evidence as well as volumes of theoretical work which establish the connection between Locke and the Founding Fathers of the United States. Even the most cursory reading of the Declaration of Independence and Constitution show the strong influence of Locke's political theory.

The next step then is to link the Founding Fathers to Malcolm X. Malcolm himself makes this connection quite clear in several speeches.

> It's not wrong to expect equality. If Patrick Henry and all of the Founding Fathers of this country were willing to lay down their lives to get what you are enjoying today, then it's time for you to realize that a large, ever-increasing number of Black people in this country are willing to die for what we know is due us by birth (Michigan State University, 23 January 1963).[50]

> If George Washington didn't get independence for this country nonviolently, and if Patrick Henry didn't come up with a nonviolent statement, and you taught me to look upon them as patriots and heroes, then it's time for you to realize that I have studied your books well … (New York City, 8 April 1964).[51]

> You were struggling for your freedom in the Revolutionary War. Your own Patrick Henry said "liberty or death," and George Washington got the cannons out, and all the rest of them that you taught me to worship as my heroes, they were fighters, they were warriors.

> But now when the time comes for our freedom, you want to reach back in the bag and grab somebody who's nonviolent and peaceful and forgiving and long-suffering. I don't go for that—no. I say that a black man's freedom is as valuable as a white man's freedom. And I say that a black man has the right to do whatever is necessary to get his freedom that other human beings have done to get their freedom. I say that you and I will never get our freedom nonviolently and patiently and lovingly. We will never get it until we let the world know that as other human beings have laid down their lives for freedom—and also taken life for freedom—that you and I are ready and willing and equipped and qualified to do the same thing (Harlem 20 December 1964).[52]

Malcolm X is quite aware of the double standard set in the United States for issues of individual rights and freedoms. He makes the point clearly here that the issues involved in the American Revolution are analogous to ones central to the struggle of African Ameri-

cans. Rather than wanting freedom from an
external colonial force, they demand freedom from within a—some might argue, colonial—regime. Malcolm is tuned in to American ideology of freedom and uses it to his
advantage. How can white Americans fail to
concede the importance and righteousness of
the Founding Fathers' struggle? Note that in
all three passages Malcolm addresses himself
to white America directly, using the second
person, despite the fact that his audiences in
at least two of these three speeches were predominantly black. These passages also make
the link to the role of violence in rebellion to
which I will return later.

In speaking of the issues involved in the
Revolutionary War, Malcolm also makes the
astute link between rebellion and legitimate
channels for appeal and social change. Just as
Locke recognized the necessity for proper
channels for redressing injustices and for initiating social change, so did Malcolm.

> Once you get the ballot, you know what this
> means? You don't have to get out in the street
> any more and risk your health and your life
> and your limb demonstrating. All you have to
> do is organize that political power and direct
> it against anyone who's against you or direct it
> behind anyone who is for you. And in this way
> you and I will find that we're always taking
> constructive, positive action and getting some
> kind of result....
>
> So, the only way we can get them to change
> their laws is by becoming involved with the
> ballot. If the ballot won't do it, there's no al-
> ternative but the bullet. I say there's no other
> alternative but the bullet. As old Patrick
> Henry said—I always love to quote Pat because
> when I was going to their school they taught
> me to believe in it. They said he was a patriot.
> And he's the only one I quote. I don't know
> what any of the rest of them said. But I know
> what Pat said: Liberty or death. That means
> the ballot or the bullet. That's what it means
> in Harlemese, in Harlem talk (Second OAAU
> Rally, Harlem, 5 July 1964).[53]

The ballot represented for Malcolm the fundamental channel through which blacks

could work for social change and bring about
justice. It was a route of appeal for injustices.
By using the ballot effectively blacks could
theoretically vote out of office those who did
nothing to improve their lot or worse worked
against their interests; and they could use the
power of the ballot to put into office those
who would truly represent their interests.
Note that Malcolm now addresses blacks in
the audience directly and refers to whites in
the third person. Malcolm is exhorting the
black community to seize control of a legitimate and powerful political tool which is
rightfully theirs and to use it effectively. In
this speech Malcolm makes clear that if that
channel is blocked—in this case by fear, intimidation or worse for those blacks who tried
to vote, or register to vote, or enlist others to
register—then rebellion is legitimate and indeed immanent. The ballot or the bullet.

The obstacles that blocked blacks' access
to voting were to be placed among other obstacles which Malcolm considered shortcomings of the government. He further recognized that such shortcomings were really
failures of the government to fulfill its primary obligations to its citizens—protection of
their rights. Insofar as the government and its
officers had a direct role in ignoring those obstacles to blacks' rights and freedoms or in
some cases erecting them, the government
was culpable. While on one level we might
only talk about the blocking of civil rights
such as voting, natural rights were involved as
well since many blacks paid with their lives
and liberty when they tried to exercise their
civil rights. Just as did Locke, Malcolm recognized the obligation of government to protect
the rights of citizens.

> "We assert that in those areas where the gov-
> ernment is either unable or unwilling to pro-
> tect the lives and property of our people, that
> our people are within our rights to protect
> themselves by whatever means necessary." I re-
> peat, because to me this is the most important
> thing you need to know. I already know it. "We
> assert that in those areas where the govern-
> ment is either unable or unwilling to protect
> the lives and property of our people, that our

people are within our rights to protect themselves by whatever means necessary" (OAAU
Founding Rally, New York City, 28 June
1964).[54]

And so there's an increasing number of black
people in America who are absolutely ready and
willing to do whatever is necessary to see that
their lives and their own property are protected
by them (Paris, 23 November 1964).[55]

The language in these passages is particularly
significant; Malcolm has adopted a vocabulary strikingly similar to Locke's. The justification for action on the part of black Americans
lies in the failure of the United States' government—either through neglect or direct action—to protect the life and property of its
citizens.

As Locke argues, the blockage of channels of appeal, which is legitimately counted
as force against the people, is grounds for legitimate rebellion. Malcolm X's claims were
not only that blacks were denied the access to
proper channels of appeal for injustices and
avenues for social change, but that the United
States government played a role in allowing
the situation to continue at the very least, and
aided in the perpetuation of the situation at
most. Locke believed that there was potential
for violence in this situation. Malcolm agreed
as is clear from this interview.

> Les Crane: Violence or the threat of violence
> has always surrounded you. Speeches that
> you've made have been interpreted as being
> threats. You have made statements reported in
> the press about how the Negroes should go
> out and arm themselves, form militias of their
> own. I read a thing once, a statement I believe
> you made that every Negro should belong to
> the National Rifle Association—
>
> Malcolm X: No, I said this: That in areas of
> this country where the government has
> proven its—either its inability or its unwilling-
> ness to protect the lives and property of our
> people, then it's only fair to expect us to do
> whatever is necessary to protect ourselves. And
> in situations like Mississippi, places like Missis-

> sippi where the government actually has
> proven its inability to protect us—and it has
> been proven that ofttimes the police officers
> and sheriffs themselves are involved in the
> murder that takes place against our people—
> then I feel, and I say that anywhere, that our
> people should start doing what is necessary to
> protect ourselves. This doesn't mean that we
> should buy rifles and go out and initiate at-
> tacks indiscriminately against whites. But it
> does mean that we should get whatever is nec-
> essary to protect ourselves in a country or in
> an area where the governmental ability to pro-
> tect us has broken down (Interview with Les
> Crane, 2 December 1964).[56]

Malcolm accomplishes many things with this
response. To begin with, he responds to the
accusation that he advocates violence by stating clearly that blacks are re-acting to white
violence rather than indiscriminately perpetrating it themselves. He rightfully portrays
black Americans as the objects of injustice
rather than the agents of it. Secondly, he
makes clear the political justification for the
kind of self defense which he does advocate,
viz., that the usual protection which citizens
can expect to be provided by the government and its agencies has broken down.
Since all humans have the ultimate right to
preservation, and the government is failing
to protect the rights of the citizens, the
power then falls back to them to take care of
themselves.

In these dire circumstances when the
usual structure has broken down, there might
be a necessity for force to be used. This potential is recognized by both Locke and Malcolm. Furthermore, just as Locke found a
reverent reponse unintelligible and unreasonable under certain circumstances, Malcolm also speaks mockingly about the
unreasonable and unintelligent response of
not using force under certain circumstances.

> Now I'm not criticizing those here who are
> nonviolent. I think everybody should do it the
> way they feel is best, and I congratulate any-
> body who can be nonviolent in the face of all
> that kind of action in that part of the world. I

don't think that in 1965 you will find the up-coming generation of our people, especially those who have been doing some thinking, who will go along with any form of nonviolence unless nonviolence is going to be practiced all the way around.

If the leaders of the nonviolent movement can go into the white community and teach nonviolence, good. I'd go along with that. We believe in equality, and equality means that you have to put the same thing over here that you put over there. And if black people alone are going to be the ones who are nonviolent then it's not fair. We throw ourselves off guard. In fact, we disarm ourselves and make ourselves defenseless ... (Youth of McComb, Mississippi visit Harlem, 31 December 1964).[57]

I saw in the paper where they—on television where they took this Black woman down in Selma, Alabama, and knocked her right down on the ground, dragging her down the street. You saw it, you're trying to pretend like you did-n't see it because you knew you should've done something about it and didn't. It showed the sheriff and his henchmen throwing this Black woman on the ground—on the ground. And Negro men standing around doing nothing about it saying, "Well, let's overcome them with our capacity to love." What kind of phrase is that? "Overcome them with our capacity to love." (Detroit, 14 February 1965).[58]

So all we say is this: We feel we've waited long enough. And we feel that all this crawling and sitting-in and crying-in and praying-in and begging-in hasn't gotten any meaningful results (New York City, 29 May 1964).[59]

So, we are honored to have with us tonight not only a freedom fighter, but some singers on that program today—I think they're all here; I asked them to come out tonight because they sang one song that just knocked me out. I'm not one who goes for "We Shall Overcome." I just don't believe we're going to overcome, singing. If you're going to get yourself a .45 and start singing "We Shall Overcome" I'm with you. But I'm not for singing that doesn't at the same time tell you how to get something to use after you get through singing. I realize I'm saying some things that you think can get

me in trouble, but, brothers, I was born in trouble. I don't even care about trouble. I'm interested in one thing alone and that's free-dom—by any means necessary (New York City, The Audubon with Fannie Lou Hamer and the Freedom Singers, 20 December 1964).[60]

We are not for violence in any shape or form, but believe that the people who have violence committed against them should be able to defend themselves. By what they are doing to me they arouse me to violence. People should only be nonviolent as long as they are dealing with a nonviolent person. Intelligence demands the return of violence with violence. Every time you let someone stand on your head and you don't do anything about it, you are not acting with intelligence and should not be on this earth—you won't be on this earth very long either (London School of Economics, 11 February 1965).[61]

Compare the ideas and the expression Malcolm uses here with Locke's response to Barclay cited above:

How to resist force without striking again, or how to strike with reverence, will need some skill to make intelligible. He that shall oppose an assault only with a shield to receive the blows, or in any more respectful posture, without a sword in his hand, to abate the confidence and force of the assailant, will quickly be at an end of his resistance, and will find such a defense serve only to draw on himself the worse usage.... And then let our author, or any body else, join a knock on the head, or a cut on the face, with as much reverence and respect as he thinks fit (§235).

And finally, Locke was able to turn the tables and assert boldly that the tyrants were the true rebels while those who resisted tyranny were acting within their rights. Malcolm, too, recognized that in the public eye blacks were seen as rebels who needed to be contained, especially those who followed his bidding and cared less for the nonviolent movement. He sought to reverse that impression and to set aright the upside-down perspective of most whites.

I do not advocate violence. In fact the violence that exists in the United States is the violence that the Negro in American has been a victim of, and I have never advocated our people going out and initiating any acts of aggression against whites indiscriminately.

But I do say that the Negro is a continual victim of the violent actions committed by the organized elements like the Ku Klux Klan. And if the United States government has shown itself unwilling or unable to protect us and our lives and our property, I have said that it is time for our people to organize and band together and protect ourselves, to defend ourselves against this violence. Now if that is to advocate violence, then I'm shocked at the lack of proper understanding on the part of whatever elements over there that have this attitude (London, 9 February 1965).[62]

So I don't believe in violence. That's why I want to stop it.... (W)e only mean vigorous action in self-defense, and that vigorous action we feel we're justified in initiating by any means necessary.

Now for saying something like that, the press calls us racists and people of "violence in reverse." This is how they psycho you. They make you think that if you try to stop the Klan from lynching you, you're practicing violence in reverse. Pick up on this. I hear a lot of you all parrot what the man says. You say, "Well, I don't want to be a Ku Klux Klan in reverse." Well. If a criminal comes to rob your house, brother, with his gun, just because he's got a gun and he's robbing your house, and he's a robber, it doesn't make you a robber because you grab your gun and run him out. No. See, the man is using some tricky logic on you....

And when we say this, the press calls us "racist in reverse." Don't struggle only within the ground rules that the people you're struggling against have laid down. Why this is insane. But it shows you how they can do it. With skillful manipulation of the press, they're able to make the victim look like the criminal and the criminal look like the victim (Detroit, 14 February 1965).[63]

The objection might be raised that Malcolm's position is much more extreme than anything Locke might endorse, that to demand social change "by any means necessary" is to go beyond the means a classical liberal might endorse. On the contrary, my purpose here is to argue that both the means and what necessitates them are consistent with Locke's views. While Locke was himself addressing a different set of political circumstances in late seventeenth-century England, there is room in his theory to make the case that he would be compelled to support Malcolm's position. Locke faced a situation of a troubled executive and he sought to argue against absolute monarchy. While Malcolm X and black Americans faced no unstable executive, they did face the very tyrannies which Locke addresses explicitly: denial or abasement of life, liberty and property; the use of force; the use of power beyond the dictates of law; and blocking channels for appeal. It is clear that by Locke's own account a virtual war was (and is) being waged against black Americans. Since the fundamental law of nature bids them to destroy that which seeks their destruction, they can do what needs to be done to preserve themselves. Malcolm X likewise implies that the means are necessary in order to insure human rights—the lives and property of African Americans. I have already shown that Locke explicitly acknowledges the possibility of taking a human life under certain political circumstances, and this would seem to be the ultimate means of securing human rights. So, in fact, the worst case scenario is conceded by Locke. Why then would he reject "by any means necessary?"

One might object further that Locke would never, for example, condone mass murder or random bombings, and so on. To begin with, it is unclear on what basis such a claim is made. Locke allows killing under certain circumstances. To infer how much carnage he would accept is to venture beyond the text into mere speculation. But secondly, even if we could make the case that Locke would dissociate himself from such a position, this does nothing to undermine my thesis that Locke and Malcolm X argue in parallel fashion, for Malcolm X never condoned such acts either.

Two conditions in the United States during the Civil Rights Movement might seem to undermine the legitimacy of Malcolm's exhortation even judged by Lockean standards. To begin with, if we take seriously Locke's distinction between society and government, the rebellion he legitimates is that in the face of a tyrannical government, whereas the oppression experienced by blacks in the United States might better be described as societal. Secondly, the federal government, it might be argued, appears to have been responsive to grievances of African Americans as it was in the process of improving oppressive conditions during Malcolm's lifetime. In the face of these two conditions, one might object that change by any means necessary was not consistent with Locke's criteria. I do not take this to be the case.

It is true that not all oppression of blacks was fomented by the government and its agencies. It is also true that to an extent government was involved in eradicating injustices to black Americans. We must, however, reconsider government involvement and culpability in more complex and certainly more subtle ways in order to respond to such an objection. Regarding the first condition, that oppression of blacks was societal and not governmental, this is not the whole story. Government need not refer only to the federal government in general nor consist only of the supreme judiciary in particular; even Locke's discussion of legitimate rebellion implicitly refers to *any* magistrate of the government who exercises power beyond right (§199-§204). This necessitates that we examine federal, state, and local levels of government and that we hold them all to the same standards. As the statistics cited in Section II of this paper imply, the oppression of blacks could not be carried out successfully and on such a broad scale—even if only by individual citizens—were it not for the complicity of such arms of the government as local police forces, lower and higher courts, and community review boards. Beyond mere complicity, we know that officers of the government were sometimes directly involved in systematically denying both civil and human rights to African Americans as a

group. Those who registered voters or who worked at the voting polls would be another case in point.

The second condition, therefore, that the government was actively responding to the grievances of African Americans, can now be understood to be true only in a limited context. Certainly there had been recent Supreme Court rulings intended to redress oppression of blacks as a group. But in reality, government responsibility cannot be limited to the official opinions of the Supreme Court, or executive decree, or even legislation. If government's responsibility were limited only to such formalities as these, then should its responsibility have ended after the Emancipation Proclamation? After Reconstruction? After the Civil Rights Act of 1875? After *Brown v. Board of Education*? Despite these formal governmental actions at the federal level, government can still be held accountable—and indeed it was held accountable by the Civil Rights Movement during the 1950's and 1960's. While such formalities are necessary, history has shown them not to be sufficient for the protection of citizens' rights. Even in the face of Supreme Court rulings, government agents—so-called leaders—persist in defying them. George Wallace's actions in the face of desegregation laws are only one infamous example. Locke was unfortunately silent about the oppression of minority groups by the majority, and it would therefore necessitate going beyond his theory to argue strenuously that the government has the responsibility to protect a minority group of citizens from "merely" societal oppression.[64] But drawing from Locke's own reasoning, whether the denial of rights comes from government itself or from other members of society is irrelevant to whether rebellion is legitimate. The primary motivation for leaving the state of nature is the protection of rights (§123-§131; §222). Once the social contract is formed, society appoints a government to protect its rights. Not to protect the people's rights is for government to betray the trust put in them that they will do so. And betrayal of that trust is one of the grounds for legitimate rebellion (§221).

I cannot go without mentioning Locke's connection to the African slave trade since it might seem to undermine my application of his political theory to the issue I do here. It appears clear to all who address the subject that Locke himself had personal and commercial involvement in the Royal Africa Company and therefore with the slave trade, and also that he helped in drafting the Constitution of Carolina which implicitly approved of slavery by setting rules governing its practice.[65] There is little agreement, however, about what Locke's theory in the *Treatise* implies regarding the political and moral status of slaves and the institution of slavery, especially the sections in which he addresses slavery explicitly. Drawing from the same evidence, philosophers have accused Locke of being a racist,[66] an abolitionist,[67] and a hypocrite.[68] Only one conclusion seems clear to me: whether by inconsistency or incompleteness in his writing and in his life, Locke has presented philosophers with an intractable problem. I tend to be convinced by Farr that the slavery explicitly addressed in the *Treatise* is of another kind than that suffered by African Americans. Farr presents a strong argument that since Locke's only justification of slavery is by a lawful conqueror in a just war (§22, §85 et passim §175–198), that African American slavery cannot be what he is considering in the *Treatise*. "(A)t least three of the constraints (Locke) set for just-war slavery were violated in Africa or America. Slave raids were not just wars; women and children were taken captive; and the descendants of slaves were made slaves too."[69] I am willing to assert further that regardless of Locke's personal interests, actions, or commitments, there is room in his theory to argue, whether he intended it or not, against the kind of slavery suffered by African Americans on moral and political grounds.

There is one weakness in the argument here which can be attributed largely to silence on the part of both men on one important issue. In both Locke's and Malcolm's views, the initial act of force and consequent self-defense are always between individuals, even as those individuals act as agents of the larger political structure. But it is clear that one might consider as force or violence effects which are not the consequence of the actions of any individual agent. I speak here of institutionally or structurally induced violence which is a real factor in the lives of many black Americans. Malcolm might have been implicitly aware of such forces when he addressed the economic deprivations facing blacks. He recommended the need to defend against such, urging blacks to fight poverty and help the community by patronizing only black businesses. But this is only one example, and I am reading into Malcolm's view something which might not be there. A definition of "institutional violence," or "violence" for that matter, takes me too far afield here, but this is ground worth pursuing further. Given that I have chosen to speak of legitimate rebellion, considerations such as the following bear directly on the issue. Under what conditions is rebellion against institutions justified—i.e., just what kinds of institutional violence or force warrant rebellion? Furthermore, what kind of rebellion is justified, i.e., what type of response does institutional force or violence legitimate?

Locke does not treat in any satisfactory, philosophical manner issues about the actions and rights of minority groups in the liberal state.[70] The question might arise then whether legitimate rebellion must be that of a majority of the citizens, which it certainly would not have been during the United States Civil Rights Movement. This might be a plausible reading of Locke if only for his claim that rebellion may be necessary before the *government* is totally dissolved but when *society* is still intact (§220–§221) since Locke assumes that the will of the majority is representative of the will of the society initially formed by the social contract (§96, §97, §98). There are, however, passages which indicate that a legitimate rebellion need not be the will of a majority, but due to the complacency of the people generally, rebellion fomented by only a few is likely not to be successful. Such a rebellion might even be dangeros and with little hope, but legitimate nonetheless.

> ... for if (tyranny) reach no father than some private men's cases, though they have a right

to defend themselves, and to recover by force what by unlawful force is taken from them; yet the right to do so will not easily engage them in a contest, wherein they are sure to perish; it being as impossible for one, or a few oppressed men to disturb the government, where the body of the people do not think themselves concerned in it ... (§208).

One of the aims of the Civil Rights Movement must have been to urge the white majority to take seriously the oppression of blacks, to be concerned even though they "do not think themselves concerned in it." Locke seems to rely on self-interested individualism as the sole political motivation when he argues that only when the majority of people can be moved to understand that the tyranny could spread to affect even them will they be moved to join in the rebellion.

> But if either these illegal acts have extended to the majority of the people; or if the mischief and oppression has lighted only on some few, but in such cases, as the precedent, and consequences, seem to threaten all; and they are persuaded in their consciences, that their laws and with them their estates, liberties, and lives are in danger, and perhaps their religion too; how they will be hindered from resisting illegal force, used against them, I cannot tell (§209).

In a society in which racism is rampant—latent in the majority of the people—then there is little hope indeed to redress tyranny committed on the few if Locke's assumptions about political motivation for rebellion are correct. This self-interested individualism, typical of some if not many Americans, perhaps explains why race problems remain so recalcitrant today. One remains hopeful, however, that other moral considerations may go in to one's decision to recognize the righteousness of "someone else's" cause if it must be considered in that manner.

IV

So what do I wish to conclude from this? Let me begin with what I am not concluding. I am

not concluding that Malcolm was influenced by Locke directly. While he was self-educated and widely read, which might itself account for his familiarity with the content and language of liberal theory, there is no evidence to link Locke and Malcolm X directly. Secondly, I am not advocating violence as a solution to race problems which still exist today. In fact, such an inference would be a grave misunderstanding not only of my position but of Malcolm's as well, which I have tried to lay out here. Thirdly, I am not saying that we have to accept Malcolm's views, or Locke's views for that matter, uncritically. There are certainly valid philosophical objections that could be brought to bear. And finally, I am not intending by appeal to Locke's authority to legitimate Malcolm's position simply by giving him what some might think an acceptable pedigree.

What I do wish to conclude is that Malcolm X was not the violence mongering figure he was and is often portrayed as being.[71] What really follows from my thesis is that, for the most part, as we judge Locke on the right to revolution, so must we judge Malcolm. Like Locke, Malcolm X was someone who cared deeply about justice, freedom, and rights. He argued sensibly, in a manner consistent with the theoretical basis of our own Constitution, and the context in which he spoke justified the measures he recommended. The question we must ask ourselves is why two men with such political similarities are remembered so differently. The answer lies, I believe, in the very structure which Malcolm fought to change—in the racist, political, social, and ideological structure of the United States that can accept a white man's demands but not a black man's.

NOTES

I presented earlier versions of this paper in a public forum at Colby College, April 1993 and at the International Conference for Social Philosophy in Helsinki, August, 1993. I am grateful to all of my colleagues and students for their helpful questions and comments which contributed to the final version of this paper. Special thanks are due to Christine Bowditch whose insight, intelligence, and patience helped me tremendously in thinking through various parts of the paper.

1. Bill Lawson has written two interesting and relevant articles which also use Locke's contract theory as a framework for addressing issues in minority communities. In "Locke and the Legal Obligations of Black Americans," *Public Affairs Quarterly*, 3:4, July 1989, pp. 49–63, he argues that blacks are not in a state of nature with respect to the U.S. Government, and ought therefore to expect protection from it and have legal obligations to it. In "Crime, Minorities, and the Social Contract," *Criminal Justice Ethics*, 9:2, Summer-Fall 1990, pp. 16–24, he takes the position, also consistent with Locke's theory, that the victimization and lack of protection that some minorities suffer due to urban crime releases them from the obligation to obey the law under certain circumstances.

2. Ruth W. Grant defends the thesis thoroughly and convincingly that the entire purpose of Locke's *Second Treatise* was to outline legitimate and illegitimate political power; the legitimacy of rebellion is conceptually linked to the use of illegitimate power. *John Locke's Liberalism* (Chicago: University of Chicago Press, 1987).

3. All references to Locke's *Second Treatise on Government* appear in parentheses in the text and refer to section numbers. I shall retain Locke's distinctly gender specific language throughout the paper except where I make claims explicitly my own. While one would like to be able to claim that Locke meant to include women in the sharing of natural and civil rights, I believe that this remains, at the very least, in question. This, however, would have to be the focus of a different paper.

4. One can certainly also engage in complex discussions of the metaphysics of the right to liberty and life, but at their deepest level these rights must include the right to use one's body in certain ways and to have one's body free from certain kinds of abuses. Thus there is a link to the right to property. I will claim without argument that the rights to live and be free are ontologically prior to and logically entailed by the right to property.

5. *Leviathan*, Part I, Chapter 13.

6. Conquest from without is treated as a separate issue by Locke and is not particularly relevant for my purposes here. See esp. Chapter XVI "Of Conquest."

7. Specifically, when the legislative is altered, which can happen in many ways, and when the supreme executive power neglects his office so that the laws can no longer be executed.

8. For a discussion of Locke's use of "revolution," "resistance," and "rebellion," and their various connotations, see Martin Seliger, "Locke's Theory of Revolutionary Action," *Western Political Quarterly* XVI:3, September 1963, pp. 548–568, esp. pp. 563–566.

9. Gunnar Myrdal, *An American Dilemma* (New York: Harper and Brothers, 1944), p. 530.

10. Malcolm X spoke of this on many occasions. See for example one of his better known speeches, "The Ballot or the Bullet," *Malcolm X Speaks*, edited by George Breitman (New York: Pathfinder Press), 1989, see esp. pp. 34–35.

11. In the most recent years claims have been made about the particular kind of urban violence which blacks suffer, and which is in many cases black-on-black. It would be an unwarranted and horrible conclusion that this is some kind of mitigating factor! The victims involved in this kind of violence are deserving of the same protection that all citizens deserve. No kind of legitimate interpretation of contract theory could argue otherwise.

12. C. Vann Woodward, *The Strange Career of Jim Crow*, second revised edition (New York: Oxford University Press, 1966), p. 143.

13. U.S. Department of Commerce, Bureau of the Census, *Statistical Abstract of the United States*, 1960, Table Number 68, p. 62.

14. *Statistical Abstract of the United States: 1988*, as cited in Ted Honderich, *Violence For Equality, Inquiries in Political Philosophy* (New York: Routledge, 1989), p. 204, n. 2.

15. Ted Honderich, op. cit., p. 9. His emphasis.

16. *Where Shall We Live? Report of the Commision on Race and Housing* (Berkeley: University of California Press), 1958, p. 3. See also Myrdal, op. cit., p. 527.

17. *Where Shall We Live?*, op. cit., p. 1.

18. *Ibid.*, p. 3.

19. *Residence and Race, Final and Comprehensive Report to the Commission on Race and Housing* (Berkeley: University of California Pres, 1960), p. 37. See also Table 7, p. 37 and Appendix Table A-1, pp. 362–365. Information given in these tables refers to whether the number of persons per room exceeded 1.01, what the age of the building was, and whether the unit was dilapidated or lacked private bath or toilet.

20. *Ibid.*, pp. 136–137. While I am referring exclusively to blacks and these studies focused on the minority population which they label nonwhite, the difference is of little significance. At the time of these studies, blacks comprised more than 95% of the nonwhite population. See p. 9.

21. Myrdal, *op. cit.*, p. 525.

22. E. Richard Larson and Laughlin McDonald, *The Rights of Racial Minorities, An American Civil Liberties Union Handbook* (New York: Avon Books, 1980), pp. 36–37.

23. *Strange Career of Jim Crow*, op. cit., p. 142.

24. Eyes On the Prize: America's Civil Rights Years, Episode 1, "Awakenings," WGBH Boston, a Production of Blackside, Inc., and the Corporation for Public Broadcasting, 1986.

25. See Marvin E. Wolfgang and Bernard Cohen, *Crime and Race, Conceptions and Misconceptions* (New York: Institute of Human Relations Press, 1970), especially the chapter "Criminal Justice and the Courts," pp. 77–88.

26. During the years 1930 to 1966, 3,857 persons were executed in the U.S.:53.5 per cent were black; 45.4 per cent were white; and 1.1 per cent were members of other minority groups, "Executions 1930–1966," *NPS Bulletin*, Bureau of Prisons, cited in *Ibid.*, p. 85.

27. *Ibid.*, pp. 81–83. Wolfgang and Cohen specifically cite: Henry Allen Bullock, "Significance of the Racial Factor in the Length of Prison Sentences," *The Journal of Criminal Law, Criminology, and Police Science* (1961), 52:411–417; and John Dollard, *Caste and Class in a Southern Town* (New York: Harper and Brothers, 1937). For another discussion of the issues cited in this and the previous two notes, see Myrdal, op. cit., p. 526–527.

28. Wolfgang and Cohen, *op. cit.*, p. 83.

29. *Norris v. Alabama* 294 U.S. 587 (1935), cited in Douglas L. Colbert, "Challenging the Challenge: Thirteenth Amendment as a Prohibition Against the Racial Use of Peremptory Challenges," *Cornell Law Review*, Vol. 76:1, pp. 1–128; reprinted in the series, Race, Law, and American History 1700–1900, Volume 8, *Race and Criminal Justice*, edited by Paul Finkelman, pp. 29–156; p. 81. All future citations refer to pages in Finkelman's book.

30. *Ibid.*, pp. 109–118.

31. *Ibid.*, p. 121.

32. "The Application of Statistical Decision Theory to the Jury Discrimination Cases," *Harvard Law Review* (1966), 80:338, cited in Wolfgang and Cohen, *op. cit.*, p. 79.

33. Wolfgang and Cohen, p. 79. Note 8, p. 86, reveals that the actual probability computed by Finkelstein is 1.1 x 10-146.

34. Myrdal, p. 542n.

35. *Ibid.*, p. 535. My emphasis.

36. *Ibid.*, p. 536.

37. Wolfgang and Cohen, *op. cit.*, p. 70, citing *Field Surveys V, A National Survey of Police and Community Relations*, The President's Commission on Law Enforcement and Administration of Justice (Washington, D.C.: U.S. Government Printing Office, January 1967), p. 185.

38. *Sourcebook of Criminal Justice Statistics*, U.S. Department of Justice, Hindelang et al., 1973, Table 2.5, p. 134.

39. *Ibid.*, Table 2.7, p. 135. The four income groups were: 0–$2,999; $3,000–$5,999; $6,000–$9,999; and $10,000 and above. While I have used the statistics from male respondents, the differences between white females and nonwhite females reflect similar perceptions of the police. Similar data can be found in *Task Force Report, The Police*. The President's Commission on Law Enforcement and Administration of Justice (Washington, D.C.: U.S. Government Printing Office, 1967), pp. 146–147 as cited in Wolfgang and Cohen, p. 68.

40. Wolfgang and Cohen, *op. cit.*, p. 70, citing Irving Piliavin and Scott Briar, "Police Encounters with Juveniles," *American Journal of Sociology* (1964), 70, pp. 206–214.

41. Wolfgang and Cohen, *op. cit.*, p. 71, citing *Field Surveys III, Studies in Crime and Law Enforcement in Major Metropolitan Areas, Volume 2*, The President's Commission on Law Enforcement and Administration of Justice, Washington, D.C.: U.S. Government Printing Office, p. 88.

42. Wolfgang and Cohen, *op. cit.*, p. 71, citing *Field Surveys III*, p. 108.

43. *Ibid.*, p. 73.

44. *Sourcebook of Criminal Justice Statistics, op. cit.*, Table 2.11, p. 136.

45. Robert M. Fogelson, *Violence as Protest, A Study of Riots and Ghettos* (New York: Doubleday & Company, 1971), p. 55.

46. Press Release, "Civilian Complaint Review Board Report," Bureau of Public Information, Police Department, City of New York, July 1968, especially appendix F, p. 1, cited in Wolfgang and Cohen, p. 73.

47. *Field Surveys IV, The Police and the Community*, Volume 2, The President's Commission on Law Enforcement and Administration of Justice, Washington, D.C.: U.S. Government

Printing Office, 1966, p. 248, cited in Wolfgang and Cohen, p. 72–73.

48. Wolfgang and Cohen, *op. cit.*, p. 73.

49. Jeffrey H. Reiman, "The Social Contract and the Police Use of Deadly Force," in *Moral Issues in Police Work* (Totowa, New Jersey: Rowman & Allanheld, 1985), p. 240. My parenthetical; the original text here reads "... state of nature ..." because the author is using a Hobbesian framework. But remember that the very conditions that Hobbes describes as the state of nature Locke describes and differentiates as the state of war. Using either vocabulary, this claim has the same power.

50. *Malcolm X: The Last Speeches*, edited by Bruce Perry (New York: Pathfinder Press, 1989), p. 56, hereafter cited as LS.

51. *Malcolm X Speaks, op. cit.*, p. 49, hereafter cited as MXS.

52. MXS, p. 112–113.

53. *By Any Means Necessary*, edited and with a forward by George Breitman (New York: Pathfinder, 1991), p. 94, 95, hereafter cited as BAMN.

54. BAMN, p. 41.

55. *Ibid.*, p. 114.

56. LS, pp. 87–88.

57. MXS, p. 139.

58. *The Final Speeches, February 1965*, edited by Steve Clark (New York: Pathfinder Press, 1992), p. 86, hereafter cited as FS.

59. MXS, p. 70.

60. *Ibid.*, p. 134–135.

61. FS, pp. 46–47.

62. FS, p. 37. This was an interview conducted in London over the phone after Malcolm X was denied entry into France. The interview was later published in *The Militant*, 20 February 1967.

63. FS, pp. 88–89.

64. Things might, however, be moving in this direction in the United States. This seems to be the consequence of recent Supreme Court rulings and federal and state legislation regarding anti-discrimination and racial and sexual harassment laws.

65. See for example: A. Leon Higginbotham, Jr., *In The Matter of Color, Race and the American Legal Process: The Colonial Period* (New York: Oxford University Press, 1978), p. 163; John Dunn, *The Political Thought of John Locke* (Cambridge; Cambridge University Press, 1969), p. 175n; and James Farr, "'So Vile and Miserable an Estate': The Problem of Slavery in Locke's Political Thought," *Political Theory*, 14:2 May 1986, pp. 263–289.

66. H.M. Bracken, "Essence, Accident, and Race," *Hermathena* (Winter 1973), pp. 81–96, cited in Farr *op. cit.*

67. Sir Reginald Coupland, *The British Anti-Slavery Movement* (London:Cass and Co., 1933), cited in Farr *op. cit.*

68. Dunn, *op. cit.*, and Farr, *op. cit.* See also the exchange: Seymour Drescher, "On James Farr's 'So Vile and Miserable an Estate,'" *Political Theory* 16:3 August 1988, pp. 502–503; and Farr's response, "Slaves Bought With Money, A Reply to Drescher," *Political Theory* 17:3 August 1989, pp. 471–474.

69. Farr, "So Vile and Miserable an Estate ...," *op. cit.*, p. 276.

70. I am not here talking exclusively of ethnic or racial minorities, but simply those who find themselves excluded from the majority in legal or public policy matters.

71. It is noteworthy that Locke and Malcolm X differ on a point of vocabulary in particular. Locke uses the term "force" whereas Malcolm uses "violence." The two terms differ in at least their connotations. It seems at least plausible to talk convincingly about moderation in use of force or even legitimate use of force. To carry out the same discussion using the term "violence" is much more challenging. This in itself is telling. Although the issue of violence versus nonviolence did not originate with the Civil Rights Movement in the U.S., I am willing to say that it is not accidental that violence has become associated with blacks and their political struggles in the United States, and that such an association is due mostly to white prejudice and fear. Malcolm's use of the term "violence" is due to the discourse into which he was drawn, in response to accusations and labels propagated by whites. Blacks are more commonly labeled as violent and instigating rather than as forceful self-defenders or freedom fighters. Another example of this uneven treatment would be the origin and history of the Black Panther Party. Repeatedly, blacks' response to white violence, or "war" as Locke might call it, is interpreted as unprovoked, unwarranted violence against whites.

Toward Black Liberation

Stokely Carmichael

One of the most pointed illustrations of the need for Black Power, as a positive and redemptive force in a society degenerating into a form of totalitarianism, is to be made by examining the history of distortion that the concept has received in national media of publicity. In this "debate," as in everything else that affects our lives, Negroes are dependent on, and at the discretion of, forces and institutions within the white society which have little interest in representing us honestly. Our experience with the national press has been that where they have managed to escape a meretricious special interest in "Git Whitey" sensationalism and race-war-mongering, individual reporters and commentators have been conditioned by the enveloping racism of the society to the point where they are incapable even of objective observation and reporting of racial *incidents*, much less the analysis of *ideas*. But this limitation of vision and perceptions is an inevitable consequence of the dictatorship of definition, interpretation, and consciousness, along with the censorship of history that the society has inflicted upon the Negro—and itself.

Our concern for black power addresses itself directly to this problem, the necessity to reclaim our history and our identity from the cultural terrorism and depredation of self-justifying white guilt.

To do this we shall have to struggle for the right to create our own terms through which to define ourselves and our relationship to the society, and to have these terms recognized. This is the first necessity of a free people, and the first right that any oppressor must suspend. The white fathers of American

racism knew this—instinctively it seems—as is indicated by the continuous record of the distortion and omission in their dealings with the red and black men. In the same way that Southern apologists for the "Jim Crow" society have so obscured, muddied, and misrepresented the record of the reconstruction period, until it is almost impossible to tell what really happened, their contemporary counterparts are busy doing the same thing with the recent history of the civil rights movement.

In 1964, for example, the National Democratic party, led by L. B. Johnson and Hubert H. Humphrey, cynically undermined the efforts of Mississippi's black population to achieve some degree of political representation. Yet, whenever the events of that convention are recalled by the press, one sees only that aversion fabricated by the press agents of the Democratic party. A year later the House of Representatives, in an even more vulgar display of political racism, made a mockery of the political rights of Mississippi's Negroes when it failed to unseat the Mississippi Delegation to the House which had been elected through a process which methodically and systematically excluded over 450,000 voting-age Negroes, almost one half of the total electorate of the state. Whenever this event is mentioned in print it is in terms which leave one with the rather curious impression that somehow the oppressed Negro people of Mississippi are at fault for confronting the Congress with a situation in which they had no alternative but to endorse Mississippi's racist political practices.

I mention these two examples because, having been directly involved in them, I can see very clearly the discrepancies between what happened and the versions that are finding their way into general acceptance as a

Source: Stokely Carmichael, "Toward Black Liberation" *The Massachusetts Review* 7.4 (Autumn 1966).

kind of popular mythology. Thus the victimization of the Negro takes place in two phases—first it occurs in fact and deed, then, and this is equally sinister, in the official recording of those facts.

The "Black Power" program and concept which is being articulated by SNCC, CORE, and a host of community organizations in the ghettoes of the North and South has not escaped that process. The white press has been busy articulating their own analyses, their own interpretations, and criticisms of their own creations. For example, while the press had given wide and sensational dissemination to attacks made by figures in the civil rights movement—foremost among which are Roy Wilkins of the NAACP and Whitney Young of the Urban League—and to the hysterical ranting about black racism made by the political chameleon that now serves as vice-president, it has generally failed to give accounts of the reasonable and productive dialogue which is taking place in the Negro community, and in certain important areas in the white religious and intellectual community. A national committee of influential Negro churchmen affiliated with the National Council of Churches, despite their obvious respectability and responsibility, had to resort to a paid advertisement to articulate their position, while anyone shouting the hysterical yappings of "Black Racism" got ample space. Thus the American people have gotten at best a superficial and misleading account of the very terms and tenor of this debate. I wish to quote briefly from the statement by the national committee of churchmen which I suspect that the majority of Americans will not have seen. This statement appeared in *The New York Times* of July 31, 1966.

> We an informal group of Negro Churchmen in America are deeply disturbed about the crisis brought upon our country by historic distortions of important human realities in the controversy about "black power." What we see shining through the variety of rhetoric is not anything new but the same old problem of power and race which has faced our beloved country since 1619.

... The conscience of black men is corrupted because, having no power to implement the demands of conscience, the concern for justice in the absence of justice becomes a chaotic self-surrender. Powerlessness breeds a race of beggars. We are faced now with a situation where powerless conscience meets conscience-less power, threatening the very foundation of our Nation.

... We deplore the overt violence of riots, but we feel it is more important to focus on the real sources of these eruptions. These sources may be abetted inside the Ghetto, but their basic cause lies in the silent and covert violence which white middleclass America inflicts upon the victims of the inner city.... In short; the failure of American leaders to use American power to create equal opportunity *in life* as well as *law*, this is the real problem and not the anguished cry for black power.... Without the capacity to *participate with power, i.e.,* to have some organized political and economic strength to really influence people with whom one interacts—integration is not meaningful.

... America has asked its Negro citizens to fight for opportunity as *individuals*, whereas at certain points in our history what we have needed most has been opportunity for the *whole group*, not just for selected and approved Negroes.

... We must not apologize for the existence of this form of group power, for we have been oppressed as a group and not as individuals. We will not find our way out of that oppression until both we and America accept the need for Negro Americans, as well as for Jews, Italians, Poles, and white Anglo-Saxon Protestants, among others to have and to wield group power.

Traditionally, for each new ethnic group, the route to social and political integration into America's pluralistic society has been through the organization of their own institutions with which to represent their communal needs within the larger society. This is simply stating what the advocates of black power are saying. The strident outcry, *particularly* from the liberal community, that has been evoked by this proposal can only be understood by examining the historic relationship between Negro and white power in this country.

Negroes are defined by two forces, their blackness and their powerlessness. There have been traditionally two communities in America. The white community, which controlled and defined the forms that all institutions within the society would take, and the Negro community which has been excluded from participation in the power decisions that shaped the society, and has traditionally been dependent upon, and subservient to, the white community.

This has not been accidental. The history of every institution of this society indicates that a major concern in the ordering and structuring of the society has been the maintaining of the Negro community in its condition of dependence and oppression. This has not been on the level of individual acts of discrimination between individual whites against individual Negroes, but as total acts by the white community against the Negro community. This fact cannot be too strongly emphasized—that racist assumptions of white superiority have been so deeply ingrained in the structure of the society that it infuses its entire functioning, and is so much a part of the national subconscious that it is taken for granted and is frequently not even recognized.

Let me give an example of the difference between individual racism and institutionalized racism, and the society's response to both. When unidentified white terrorists bomb a Negro church and kill five children, that is an act of individual racism, widely deplored by most segments of the society. But when in that same city, Birmingham, Alabama, not five but five hundred Negro babies die each year because of a lack of proper food, shelter, and medical facilities, and thousands more are destroyed and maimed physically, emotionally, and intellectually because of conditions of poverty and deprivation in the ghetto, that is a function of institutionalized racism. But the society either pretends it doesn't know of this situation, or is incapable of doing anything meaningful about it. And this resistance to doing anything meaningful about conditions

in that ghetto comes from the fact that the ghetto is itself a product of a combination of forces and special interests in the white community, and the groups that have access to the resources and power to change that situation benefit, politically and economically, from the existence of that ghetto.

It is more than a figure of speech to say that the Negro community in America is the victim of white imperialism and colonial exploitation. This is in practical economic and political terms true. There are over twenty million black people comprising ten per cent of this nation. They for the most part live in well-defined areas of the country—in the shanty-towns and rural black belt areas of the South, and increasingly in the slums of northern and western industrial cities. If one goes into any Negro community, whether it be in Jackson, Mississippi, Cambridge, Maryland, or Harlem, New York, one will find that the same combination of political, economic, and social forces are at work. The people in the Negro community do not control the resources of that community, its political decisions, its law enforcement, its housing standards; and even the physical ownership of the land, houses, and stores *lie outside that community.*

It is white power that makes the laws, and it is violent white power in the form of armed white cops that enforces those laws with guns and nightsticks. The vast majority of Negroes in this country live in these captive communities and must endure these conditions of oppression because, and only because, *they are black and powerless.* I do not suppose that at any point the men who control the power and resources of this country ever sat down and designed these black enclaves and formally articulated the terms of their colonial and dependent status, as was done, for example, by the apartheid government of South Africa. Yet, one can not distinguish between one ghetto and another. As one moves from city to city it is as though some malignant racist planning unit had done precisely this—designed each one from the same master blueprint. And indeed, if the ghetto had been formally and deliberately planned, instead of growing spontaneously and inevitably from the racist functioning of the various institutions that combine to make the society, it would be somehow less frightening. The situation would be less frightening because, if these ghettoes were the result of design and conspiracy, one could understand their similarity as being artificial and consciously imposed, rather than the result of identical patterns of white racism which repeat themselves in cities as distant as Boston and Birmingham. Without bothering to list the historic factors which contribute to this pattern—economic exploitation, political impotence, discrimination in employment and education—one can see that to correct this pattern will require far-reaching changes in the basic power relationships and the ingrained social patterns within the society. The question is, of course, what kinds of changes are necessary, and how is it possible to bring them about?

In recent years, the answer to these questions which has been given by most articulate groups of Negroes and their white allies, the "liberals" of all stripes, has been in terms of something called "integration." According to the advocates of integration, social justice will be accomplished by "integrating the Negro into the mainstream institutions of the society from which he has been traditionally excluded." It is very significant that each time I have heard this formulation it has been in terms of "the Negro," the individual Negro, rather than in terms of the community.

This concept of integration had to be based on the assumption that there was nothing of value in the Negro community and that little of value could be created among Negroes, so the thing to do was to siphon off the "acceptable" Negroes into the surrounding middle-class white community. Thus the goal of the movement for integration was simply to loosen up the restrictions barring the entry of Negroes into the white community. Goals around which the struggle took place, such as public accommodation, open housing, job opportunity on the executive level (which is easier to deal with than the problem of semi-skilled and blue-collar jobs which involve more far-reaching economic adjustments),

are quite simply middle-class goals, articulated by a tiny group of Negroes who had middle-class aspirations. It is true that the student demonstrations in the South during the early sixties, out of which SNCC came, had a similar orientation. But while it is hardly a concern of a black sharecropper, dishwasher, or welfare recipient whether a certain fifteen-dollar-a-day motel offers accommodations to Negroes, the overt symbols of white superiority and the imposed limitations on the Negro community had to be destroyed. Now, black people must look beyond these goals, to the issue of collective power.

Such a limited class orientation was reflected not only in the program and goals of the civil rights movement, but in its tactics and organization. It is very significant that the two oldest and most "respectable" civil rights organizations have constitutions which *specifically* prohibit partisan political activity. CORE once did, but changed that clause when it changed its orientation toward black power. But this is perfectly understandable in terms of the strategy and goals of the older organizations. The civil rights movement saw its role as a kind of liaison between the powerful white community and the dependent Negro one. The dependent status of the black community apparently was unimportant since—if the movement were successful—it would blend into the white community anyway. We made no pretense of organizing and developing institutions of community power in the Negro community, but appealed to the conscience of white institutions of power. The posture of the civil rights movement was that of the dependent, the suppliant. The theory was that without attempting to create any organized base of political strength itself, the civil rights movement could, by forming coalitions with various "liberal" pressure organizations in the white community—liberal reform clubs, labor unions, church groups, progressive civic groups—and at times one or other of the major political parties—influence national legislation and national social patterns.

I think we all have seen the limitations of this approach. We have repeatedly seen that political alliances based on appeals to conscience and decency are chancy things, simply because institutions and political organizations have no consciences, outside their own special interests. The political and social rights of Negroes have been and always will be negotiable and expendable the moment they conflict with the interests of our "allies." If we do not learn from history, we are doomed to repeat it, and that is precisely the lesson of the Reconstruction. Black people were allowed to register, vote, and participate in politics because it was to the advantage of powerful white allies to promote this. But this was the result of white decision, and it was ended by other white men's decision before any political base powerful enough to challenge that decision could be established in the Southern Negro community. (Thus at this point in the struggle Negroes have no assurance—save a kind of idiot optimism and faith in a society whose history is one of racism—that if it were to become necessary, even the painfully limited gains thrown to the civil rights movement by the Congress would not be revoked as soon as a shift in political sentiments should occur.)

The major limitation of this approach was that it tended to maintain the traditional dependence of Negroes and of the movement. We depended upon the good-will and support of various groups within the white community whose interests were not always compatible with ours. To the extent that we depended on the financial support of other groups, we were vulnerable to their influence and domination.

Also, the program that evolved out of this coalition was really limited and inadequate in the long term and one which affected only a small select group of Negroes. Its goal was to make the white community accessible to "qualified" Negroes, and presumably each year a few more Negroes armed with their passports—a couple of university degrees— would escape into middle-class America and adopt the attitudes and life styles of that group; and one day the Harlems and the Wattses would stand empty, a tribute to the success of integration. This is simply neither realistic nor particularly desirable. You can integrate communities, but you assimilate individuals. Even if such a program were possible, its result would be, not to develop the black community as a functional and honorable segment of the total society, with its own cultural identity, life patterns, and institutions, but to abolish it—the final solution to the Negro problem. Marx said that the working class is the first class in history that ever wanted to abolish itself. If one listens to some of our "moderate" Negro leaders, it appears that the American Negro is the first race that ever wished to abolish itself. The fact is that what must be abolished is not the black community, but the dependent colonial status that has been inflicted upon it. The racial and cultural personality of the black community must be preserved and the community must win its freedom while preserving its cultural integrity. This is the essential difference between integration as it is currently practised and the concept of black power.

What has the movement for integration accomplished to date? The Negro graduating from M.I.T. with a doctorate will have better job opportunities available to him than to Lynda Bird Johnson. But the rate of unemployment in the Negro community is steadily increasing, while that in the white community decreases. More educated Negroes hold executive jobs in major corporations and federal agencies than ever before, but the gap between white income and Negro income has almost doubled in the last twenty years. More suburban housing is available to Negroes, but housing conditions in the ghetto are steadily declining. While the infant mortality rate of New York City is at its lowest rate ever in the city's history, the infant mortality rate of Harlem is steadily climbing. There has been an organized national resistance to the Supreme Court's order to integrate the schools, and the federal government has not acted to enforce that order. Less than fifteen per cent of black children in the South attend integrated schools, and Negro schools, which the vast majority of black children still attend, are increasingly decrepit, overcrowded, under-staffed, inadequately equipped and funded.

This explains why the rate of school drop-outs is increasing among Negro teenagers, who then express their bitterness, hopeless-ness, and alienation by the only means they have—rebellion. As long as people in the ghettoes of our large cities feel that they are victims of the misuse of white power without any way to have their needs represented—and these are frequently simple needs: to get the welfare inspectors to stop kicking down your doors in the middle of the night, the cops from beating your children, the landlord to exterminate the vermin in your home, the city to collect your garbage—we will continue to have riots. These are not the products of "black power," but of the absence of any or-ganization capable of giving the community the power, the black power, to deal with its problems.

SNCC proposes that it is now time for the black freedom movement to stop pandering to the fears and anxieties of the white middle class in the attempt to earn its "good will" and to return to the ghetto to organize these com-munities to control themselves. This organiza-tion must be attempted in northern and southern urban areas as well as in the rural black belt counties of the South. The chief an-tagonist to this organization is, in the South, the overtly racist Democratic party, and in the North, the equally corrupt big city machines.

The standard argument presented against independent political organization is "But you are only ten per cent." I cannot see the rele-vance of this observation, since no one is talk-ing about taking over the country, but taking control over our own communities.

The fact is that the Negro population, ten per cent or not, is very strategically placed be-cause—ironically—of segregation. What is also true is that Negroes have never been able to utilize the full voting potential of our num-bers. Where we could vote, the case has always been that the white political machine stacks and gerrymanders the political subdivisions in Negro neighborhoods so the true voting strength is never reflected in political strength. Would anyone looking at the distri-bution of political power in Manhattan, ever think that Negroes represented sixty per cent of the population there?

Just as often the effective political organi-zation in Negro communities is absorbed by tokenism and patronage—the time honored practice of "giving" certain offices to selected Negroes. The machine thus creates a "little machine," which is subordinate and respon-sive to it, in the Negro community. These Negro political "leaders" are really vote deliv-erers, more responsible to the white machine and the white power structure than to the community they allegedly represent. Thus the white community is able to substitute patron-age control for audacious black power in the Negro community. This is precisely what Johnson tried to do even before the Voting Rights Act of 1966 was passed. The National Democrats made it very clear that the meas-ure was intended to register Democrats, not Negroes. The President and top officials of the Democratic party called in almost one hundred selected Negro "leaders" from the Deep South. Nothing was said about chang-ing the policies of the racist state parties, nothing was said about repudiating such lead-ership figures as James Eastland and Ross Bar-nett in Mississippi or George Wallace in Alabama. What was said was simply "Go home and organize your people into the local De-mocratic party—*then* we'll see about poverty money and appointments." (Incidentally, for the most part the War on Poverty in the South is controlled by local Democratic ward heel-ers—and outspoken racists who have used the program to change the form of the Negroes' dependence. People who were afraid to regis-ter for fear of being thrown off the farm are now afraid to register for fear of losing their Head Start jobs.)

We must organize black community power to end these abuses, and to give the Negro community a chance to have its needs expressed. A leadership which is truly "re-sponsible"—not to the white press and power structure, but to the community—must be de-veloped. Such leadership will recognize that its power lies in the unified and collective strength of that community. This will make it difficult for the white leadership group to conduct its dialogue with individuals in terms of patronage and prestige, and will force them to talk to the community's representatives in terms of real power.

The single aspect of the black power program that has encountered most criticism is this concept of independent organization. This is presented as third-partyism, which has never worked, or a withdrawal into black nationalism and isolationism. If such a program is developed it will not have the effect of isolating the Negro community but the reverse. When the Negro community is able to control local office and negotiate with other groups from a position of organized strength, the possibility of meaningful political alliances on specific issues will be increased. That is a rule of politics and there is no reason why it should not operate here. The only difference is that we will have the power to define the terms of these alliances.

The next question usually is: "So—can it work, can the ghettoes in fact be organized?" The answer is that this organization must be successful, because there are no viable alternatives—not the War on Poverty, which was at its inception limited to dealing with effects rather than causes, and has become simply another source of machine patronage. And "Integration" is meaningful only to a small chosen class within the community.

The revolution in agricultural technology in the South is displacing the rural Negro community into northern urban areas. Both Washington, D.C. and Newark, New Jersey, have Negro majorities. One third of Philadelphia's population of two million people is black. "Inner city" in most major urban areas is already predominantly Negro, and, with the white rush to suburbia, Negroes will in the next three decades control the hearts of our great cities. These areas can become either concentration camps with a bitter and volatile population whose only power is the power to destroy, or organized and powerful communities able to make constructive contributions to the total society. Without the power to control their lives and their communities, without effective political institutions through which to relate to the total society, these communities will exist in a constant state of insurrection. This is a choice that the country will have to make.

Functional Definition of Politics

Huey P. Newton

Politics is war without bloodshed. War is politics with bloodshed. Politics has its particular characteristics which differentiate it from war. When the peaceful means of politics are exhausted and the people do not get what they want, politics are continued. Usually it ends up in physical conflict which is called war, which is also political.

Because we lack political power, Black people are not free. Black reconstruction failed because Black people did not have political and military power. The masses of Black people at the time were very clear on the definition of political power. It was evident in the songs of Black people at that time. In the songs it was stated that on the Day of Jubilee we'd have forty acres and two mules. This was promised Black people by the Freedman's Bureau. This was freedom as far as the Black masses were concerned.

The Talented Tenth at the time viewed freedom as operative in the political arena. Black people did operate in the political arena during reconstruction. They were more educated than most of the whites in the south. They had been educated in France, Canada and England and were very qualified to serve in the political arena. But yet, Black Reconstruction failed.

When one operates in the political arena, it is assumed that he has power or represents power; he is symbolic of a powerful force. There are approximately three areas of power in the political arena: economic power, land power (feudal power) and military power. If Black people at the time had received 40 acres and 2 mules, we would have developed a powerful force. Then we would have chosen a

Source: Huey P. Newton, "Functional Definition of Politics," *The Black Panther,* 17 January 1969. Used with the permission of Fredrika Newton.

representative to represent us in this political arena. Because Black people did not receive the 40 acres and 2 mules, it was absurd to have a representative in the political arena.

When White people send a representative into the political arena, they have a power force or power base that they represent. When White people, through their representatives, do not get what they want, there is always a political consequence. This is evident in the fact that when the farmers are not given an adequate price for their crops the economy will receive a political consequence. They will let their crops rot in the field; they will not cooperate with other sectors of the economy. To be political, you must have a political consequence when you do not receive your desires—otherwise you are nonpolitical.

When Black people send a representative, he is somewhat absurd because he represents no political power. He does not represent land power because we do not own any land. He does not represent economic or industrial power because Black people do not own the means of production. The only way he can become political is to represent what is commonly called a military power—which the Black Panther Party for Self-Defense calls Self-Defense Power. Black people can develop Self-Defense Power by arming themselves from house to house, block to block, community to community, throughout the nation. Then we will choose a political representative and he will state to the power structure the desires of the Black masses. If the desires are not met, the power structure will receive a political consequence. We will make it economically non-profitable for the power structure to go on with its oppressive ways. We will then negotiate as equals. There will be a balance between the people who are economically powerful and the people who are potentially economically destructive.

The White racist oppresses Black people not only for racist reasons, but because it is also economically profitable to do so. Black people must develop a power that will make it non-profitable for racists to go on oppressing us. If the White racist imperialists in America continue to wage war against all people of color throughout the world and also wage a civil war against Blacks here in America, it will be economically impossible for him to survive. We must develop a strategy that will make his war campaigns non-profitable. This racist United States operates with the motive of profit. He lifts the gun and escalates the war for profit reasons. We will make him lower the guns because they will no longer serve his profit motive.

Every man is born, therefore he has a right to live, a right to share in the wealth. If he is denied the right to work, then he is denied the right to live. If he can't work, he deserves a high standard of living, regardless of his education or skill. It should be up to the administrators of the economic system to design a program for providing work or livelihood for his people. To deny a man this is to deny him life. The controllers of the economic system are obligated to furnish each man with a livelihood. If they cannot do this or if they will not do this, they do not deserve the position of administrators. The means of production should be taken away from them and placed in the people's hands, so that the people can organize them in such a way as to provide themselves with a livelihood. The people will choose capable administrators, motivated by their sincere interest in the people's welfare and not the interest of private property. The people will choose managers to control the means of production and the land that is rightfully theirs. Until the people control the land and the means of production, there will be no peace. Black people must control the destiny of their community.

Because Black people desire to determine their own destiny, they are constantly inflicted with brutality from the occupying army, embodied in the police department. There is a great similarity between the occupying army in Southeast Asia and the occupation of our communities by the racist police. The armies are there not to protect the people of South Vietnam, but to brutalize and oppress them for the interests of the selfish imperial power.

The police should be the people of the community in uniform. There should be no division or conflict of interest between the people and the police. Once there is a division, then the police become the enemy of the people. The police should serve the interest of the people and be one and the same. When this principle breaks down, then the police become an occupying army. When historically one race has oppressed another and policemen are recruited from the oppressor race to patrol the communities of the oppressed people, an intolerable contradiction exists.

The racist dog policemen must withdraw immediately from our communities, cease their wanton murder and brutality and torture of Black people, or face the wrath of the armed people.

Prison, Where Is Thy Victory?

Huey P. Newton

When a person studies mathematics, he learns that there are many mathematical laws which determine the approach he must take to solving the problems presented to him. In the study of geometry, one of the first laws a person learns is that "the whole is not greater than the sum of its parts." This means simply that one cannot have a geometrical figure such as a circle or a square which in its totality, contains more than it does when broken down into smaller parts. Therefore, if all the smaller parts add up to a certain amount, the entire figure cannot add up to a larger amount. The prison cannot have a victory over the prisoner, because those in charge take the same kind of approach to the prisoner and assume if they have the whole body in a cell that they have there all that makes up the person. But a prisoner is not a geometrical figure, and an approach which is successful in mathematics, is wholly unsuccessful when dealing with human beings.

In the case of the human, we are not dealing only with the single individual, we are also dealing with the ideas and beliefs which have motivated him and which sustain him, even when his body is confined. In the case of humanity the whole is much greater than its parts, because the whole includes the body which is measurable and confineable, and also the ideas which cannot be measured and which cannot be confined. The ideas are not only within the mind of the prisoner where they cannot be seen nor controlled, the ideas are also within the people. The ideas which can and will sustain our movement for total freedom and dignity of the people, cannot be imprisoned, for they are to be found in the

people, all the people, wherever they are. As long as the people live by the ideas of freedom and dignity there will be no prison which can hold our movement down. Ideas move from one person to another in the association of brothers and sisters who recognize that a most evil system of capitalism has set us against each other, when our real enemy is the exploiter who profits from our poverty. When we realize such an idea then we come to love and appreciate our brothers and sisters who we may have seen as enemies, and those exploiters who we may have seen as friends are revealed for what they truly are to all oppressed people. The people are the idea; the respect and dignity of the people, as they move toward their freedom is the sustaining force which reaches into and out of the prison. The walls, the bars, the guns and the guards can never encircle or hold down the idea of the people. And the people must always carry forward the idea which is their dignity and their beauty.

The prison operates with the idea that when it has a person's body it has his entire being—since the whole cannot be greater than the sum of its parts. They put the body in a cell, and seem to get some sense of relief and security from that fact. The idea of prison victory then, is that when the person in jail begins to act, think, and believe the way they want him to, then they have won the battle and the person is then "rehabilitated." But this cannot be the case, because those who operate the prisons, have failed to examine their own beliefs thoroughly, and they fail to understand the types of people they attempt to control. Therefore, even when the prison thinks it has won the victory, there is no victory.

There are two types of prisoners. The largest number are those who accept the legitimacy of the assumptions upon which the

Source: Huey P. Newton, "Prison, Where Is Thy Victory?" *The Black Panther*, 3 January 1970. Used with the permission of Fredrika Newton.

society is based. They wish to acquire the same goals as everybody else, money, power, greed, and conspicuous consumption. In order to do so, however, they adopt techniques and methods which the society has defined as illegitimate. When this is discovered such people are put in jail. They may be called "illegitimate capitalists" since their aim is to acquire everything this capitalistic society defines as legitimate. The second type of prisoner, is the one who rejects the legitimacy of the assumptions upon which the society is based. He argues that the people at the bottom of the society are exploited for the profit and advantage of those at the top. Thus, the oppressed exist, and will always be used to maintain the privileged status of the exploiters. There is no sacredness, there is no dignity in either exploiting or being exploited. Although this system may make the society function at a high level of technological efficiency, it is an illegitimate system, since it rests upon the suffering of humans who are as worthy and as dignified as those who do not suffer. Thus, the second type of prisoner says that the society is corrupt and illegitimate and must be overthrown. This second type of prisoner is the political prisoner. They do not accept the legitimacy of the society and cannot participate in its corrupting exploitation, whether they are in the prison or on the block.

The prison cannot gain a victory over either type of prisoner no matter how hard it tries. The "Illegitimate capitalist" recognizes that if he plays the game the prison wants him to play, he will have his time reduced and be released to continue his activities. Therefore, he is willing to go through the prison programs and do the things he is told. He is willing to say the things the prison authorities want to hear. The prison assumes he is "reha-

bilitated" and ready for the society. The prisoner has really played the prison's game so that he can be released to resume pursuit of his capitalistic goals. There is no victory, for the prisoner [who] from the beginning accepted the idea of the society. He pretends to accept the idea of the prison as a part of the game he has always played.

The prison cannot gain a victory over the political prisoner because he has nothing to be rehabilitated from or to. He refuses to accept the legitimacy of the system and refuses to participate. To participate is to admit that the society is legitimate because of its exploitation of the oppressed. This is the idea which the political prisoner does not accept, this is the idea for which he has been imprisoned, and this is the reason why he cannot cooperate with the system. The political prisoner will, in fact, serve his time just as will the "illegitimate capitalist." Yet the idea which motivated and sustained the political prisoner rests in the people, all the prison has is a body.

The dignity and beauty of man rests in the human spirit which makes him more than simply a physical being. This spirit must never be suppressed for exploitation by others. As long as the people recognize the beauty of their human spirits and move against suppression and exploitation, they will be carrying out one of the most beautiful ideas of all time. Because the human whole is much greater than the sum of its parts, the ideas will always be among the people. The prison cannot be victorious because walls, bars and guards cannot conquer or hold down an idea.

POWER TO THE PEOPLE:
Huey P. Newton
Minister of Defense
Black Panther Party

Political Prisoners, Prisons
and Black Liberation

Angela Y. Davis

Despite a long history of exalted appeals to man's inherent right of resistance, there has seldom been agreement on how to relate *in practice* to unjust, immoral laws and the oppressive social order from which they emanate. The conservative, who does not dispute the validity of revolutions deeply buried in history, invokes visions of impending anarchy in order to legitimize his demand for absolute obedience. Law and order, with the major emphasis on order, is his watchword. The liberal articulates his sensitiveness to certain of society's intolerable details, but will almost never prescribe methods of resistance which exceed the limits of legality. Redress through electoral channels is the liberal's panacea.

In the heat of our pursuit for fundamental human rights, Black people have been continually cautioned to be patient. We are advised that as long as we remain faithful to the *existing* democratic order, the glorious moment will eventually arrive when we will come into our own as full-fledged human beings.

But having been taught by bitter experience, we know that there is a glaring incongruity between democracy and the capitalist economy which is the source of our ills. Regardless of all rhetoric to the contrary, the people are not the ultimate matrix of the laws and the system which governs them—certainly not Black people and other nationally oppressed people, but not even the mass of whites. The people do not exercise decisive control over the determining factors of their lives.

Source: Angela Y. Davis, "Political Prisoners, Prisons and Black Liberation" in Angela Y. Davis, ed., *If They Come in the Morning* (New York: New American Library, 1971), 27–52.

Official assertions that meaningful dissent is always welcome, provided it falls within the boundaries of legality are frequently a smokescreen obscuring the invitation to acquiesce in oppression. Slavery may have been unrighteous, the constitutional provision for the enslavement of Blacks may have been unjust. But conditions were not to be considered so unbearable (especially since they were profitable to a small circle) as to justify escape and other ventures proscribed by law. This was the import of the fugitive slave laws.

Needless to say, the history of the United States has been marred from its inception by an enormous quantity of unjust laws, far too many expressly bolstering the oppression of Black people. Particularized reflections of existing social inequities, these laws have repeatedly borne witness to the exploitative and racist core of the society itself. For Blacks, Chicanos, for all nationally oppressed people, the problem of opposing unjust laws and the social conditions which nourish their growth, has always had immediate practical implications. Our very survival has frequently been a direct function of our skill in forging effective channels of resistance. In resisting we have sometimes been compelled openly to violate those laws which directly or indirectly buttress our oppression. But even in containing our resistance within the orbit of legality, we have been labelled criminals and have been methodically persecuted by a racist legal apparatus.

Under the ruthless conditions of slavery, the Underground Railroad provided the framework for extra-legal anti-slavery activity pursued by vast numbers of people, both Black and white. Its functioning was in flagrant violation of the fugitive slave laws; those who were apprehended were subjected to severe penalties. Of the innumerable recorded attempts to rescue fugitive slaves from the clutches of slave-catchers, one of the most striking is the case of Anthony Burns, a slave from Virginia, captured in Boston in 1853. A team of his supporters in attempting to rescue him by force during the course of his trial, engaged the police in a fierce courtroom battle. During the gun fight a prominent abolitionist, Thomas Wentworth Higgenson, was wounded. Although the rescuers were unsuccessful in their efforts, the impact of this incident '… did more to crystalize Northern sentiment against slavery than any other except the exploit of John Brown, "and this was the last time a fugitive slave was taken from Boston. It took 22 companies of state militia, four platoons of marines, a battalion of United States artillerymen, and the city's police force … to ensure the performance of this shameful act, the cost of which, to the Federal government alone, came to $40,000.'"[1]

Throughout the era of slavery, Blacks as well as progressive whites recurrently discovered that their commitment to the anti-slavery cause frequently entailed the overt violation of the law of the land. Even as slavery faded away into a more subtle yet equally pernicious apparatus to dominate Black people, 'illegal' resistance was still on the agenda. After the Civil War, the Black Codes, successors to the old slave codes, legalized convict labour, prohibited marriage between Blacks and whites, gave white employers an excessive degree of control over the private lives of Black workers, and generally codified racism and terror. Naturally numerous individual as well as collective acts of resistance prevailed. On many occasions Blacks formed armed teams to protect themselves from white terrorists who were, in turn, protected by law enforcement agencies—if not actually identical with them.

By the second decade of the twentieth century the mass movement headed by Marcus Garvey proclaimed in its Declaration of Rights that Black people should not hesitate to disobey all discriminatory laws. Moreover, the Declaration announced, they should uti-lize all means available to them, legal or illegal, to defend themselves from legalized terror as well as Ku Klux Klan violence. During the era of intense activity around civil rights issues, systematic disobedience of oppressive laws was a primary tactic. The sit-ins were organized transgressions of racist legislation.

All these historical instances involving the overt violation of the laws of the land converge around an unmistakable common denominator. At stake has been the collective welfare and survival of a People. There is a distinct and qualitative difference between breaking a law for one's own individual self-interest and violating it in the interests of a class or a People whose oppression is expressed and particularized through that law. The former might be called criminal (though in many instances he is a victim), but the latter, as a reformist or revolutionary, is interested in universal social change. Captured, he or she is a political prisoner.

The political prisoner's words or deeds have in one form or another embodied political protests against the established order and have consequently brought him into acute conflict with the state. In the light of the political content of his act the 'crime' (which may or may not have been committed) assumes minor importance. In this country, however, where the special category of political prisoners is not officially acknowledged, the political prisoner inevitably stands trial for a specific criminal offence, not for a political act. Often the so-called crime does not even have a nominal existence. As in the 1914 murder frame-up of the IWW organizer, Joe Hill, it is a blatant fabrication, a mere excuse for silencing a militant crusader against oppression. In all instances however, the political prisoner has violated the unwritten law which prohibits disturbances and upheavals in the status quo of exploitation and racism. This unwritten law has been contested by actually and explicitly breaking a law or by utilizing constitutionally protected channels to educate, agitate and organize the masses to resist.

A deep-seated ambivalence has always characterized official response to the political prisoner. Charged and tried for a criminal act, his guilt is always political in nature. This ambivalence is perhaps best captured by Judge Webster Thayer's comment upon sentencing Bartholomew Vanzetti to 15 years for an attempted payroll robbery: 'This man, although he may not have actually committed the crime attributed to him, is nevertheless morally culpable, because he is the enemy of our existing institutions.'[2] (The very same judge incidentally, sentenced Sacco and Vanzetti to death for a robbery and murder of which they were manifestly innocent.) It is not surprising that Nazi Germany's foremost constitutional lawyer, Carl Schmitt, advanced a theory which generalized this *a priori* culpability. A thief, for example, was not necessarily one who has committed an overt act of theft, but rather one whose character renders him a thief (*wer nach seinem wesen ein Dieb ist*). Nixon's and J. Edgar Hoover's pronouncements lead one to believe that they would readily accept Schmitt's fascist legal theory. Anyone who seeks to overthrow oppressive institutions, whether or not he has engaged in an overt illegal act, is *a priori* a criminal who must be buried away in one of America's dungeons.

Even in all Martin Luther King's numerous arrests, he was not so much charged with the nominal crimes of trespassing, disturbance of the peace, etc., but rather with being an enemy of Southern society, an inveterate foe of racism. When Robert Williams was accused of a kidnapping, this charge never managed to conceal his real offence—the advocacy of Black people's incontestable right to bear arms in their own defence.

The offence of the political prisoner is his political boldness, his persistent challenging—legally or extra-legally—of fundamental social wrongs fostered and reinforced by the state. He has opposed unjust laws and exploitative, racist social conditions in general, with the ultimate aim of transforming these laws and this society into an order harmonious with the material and spiritual needs and interests of the vast majority of its members.

Nat Turner and John Brown were political prisoners in their time. The acts for which they were charged and subsequently hanged, were the practical extensions of their profound commitment to the abolition of slavery. They fearlessly bore the responsibility for their actions. The significance of their executions and the accompanying widespread repression did not so much lie in the fact that they were being punished for specific crimes nor even in the effort to use their punishment as an implicit threat to deter others from similar *armed* acts of resistance. These executions and the surrounding repression of slaves, were intended to terrorize the anti-slavery movement in general, to discourage and diminish both legal and illegal forms of abolitionist activity. As usual, the effect of repression was miscalculated and in both instances, anti-slavery activity was accelerated and intensified as a result.

Nat Turner and John Brown can be viewed as examples of the political prisoner who has actually committed an act which is defined by the state as 'criminal'. They killed and were consequently tried for murder. But did they commit murder? This raises the question of whether American revolutionaries had murdered the British in their struggle for liberation. Nat Turner and his followers killed some 65 white people, yet shortly before the Revolt had begun, Nat is reputed to have said to the other rebelling slaves: 'Remember that ours is not war for robbery nor to satisfy our passions, it is a *struggle for freedom. Ours must be deeds not words.*'[3]

The very institutions which condemned Nat Turner and reduced his struggle for freedom to a simple criminal case of murder, owed their existence to the decision, made a half century earlier, to take up arms against the British oppressor.

The battle for the liquidation of slavery had no legitimate existence in the eyes of the government and therefore the special quality of deeds carried out in the interests of freedom was deliberately ignored. There were no political prisoners, there were only criminals; just as the movement out of which these deeds flowed was largely considered criminal.

Likewise, the significance of activities which are pursued in the interests of liberation today is minimized not so much because officials are unable to *see* the collective surge against oppression, but because they have consciously set out to subvert the movement. In the Spring of 1970, L. A. Panthers took up arms to defend themselves from an assault initiated by the local police force on their office and on their persons. They were charged with criminal assault. If one believed the official propaganda, they were bandits and rogues who pathologically found pleasure in attacking policemen. It was not mentioned that their community activities—educational work, services such as free breakfast and free medical programmes—which had legitimized them in the Black community, were the immediate reason that the wrath of the police had fallen upon them in the first place. In defending themselves from the attack waged by some 600 policemen (there were only 11 Panthers in the office) they were not only defending their lives, but even more important their accomplishments in the Black community surrounding them and in the broader thrust for Black Liberation. Whenever Blacks in struggle have recourse to self-defence, particularly armed self-defence, it is twisted and distorted on official levels and ultimately rendered synonomous with criminal aggression. On the other hand, when policemen are clearly indulging in acts of criminal aggression, officially they are defending themselves through 'justifiable assault' or 'justifiable homicide.'

The ideological acrobatics characteristic of official attempts to explain away the existence of the political prisoner do not therefore stop with the equation of the individual political act with the individual criminal act. The political act is defined as criminal in order to discredit radical and revolutionary movements. A political event is reduced to a criminal event in order to affirm the absolute invulnerability of the existing order. In a revealing contradiction, the court resisted the description of the N.Y. Panther 21 trial as 'political,' yet the prosecutor entered as evidence of criminal intent literature which represent-

ed, so he alleged, the political ideology of the Black Panther Party.

The legal apparatus designates the Black liberation fighter a criminal, prompting Nixon, Agnew, Reagan et al. to proceed to mystify with their demagogy millions of Americans whose senses have been dulled and whose critical powers have been eroded by the continual onslaught of racist ideology.

As the Black Liberation Movement and other progressive struggles increase in magnitude and intensity, the judicial system and its extension, the penal system, consequently become key weapons in the state's fight to preserve the existing conditions of class domination, therefore racism, poverty and war.

In 1951, W.E.B. Du Bois, as Chairman of the Peace Information Centre, was indicted by the Federal government for 'failure to register as an agent of a foreign principle.' In assessing this ordeal which occurred in the ninth decade of his life he turned his attention to the inhabitants of the nation's jails and prisons:

> What turns me cold in all this experience is the certainty that thousands of innocent victims are in jail today because they had neither money nor friends to help them. The eyes of the world were on our trail despite the desperate efforts of press and radio to suppress the facts and cloud the real issues; the courage and money of friends and of strangers who dared stand for a principle freed me; but God only knows how many who were as innocent as I and my colleagues are today in hell. They daily stagger out of prison doors embittered, vengeful, hopeless, ruined. And of this army of the wronged, the proportion of Negroes is frightful. We protect and defend sensational cases where Negroes are involved. But the great mass of arrested or accused Black folk have no defence. There is desperate need of nationwide organizations to oppose this national racket of railroading to jails and chain gangs the poor, friendless and Black.[4]

Almost two decades passed before the realization attained by Du Bois on the occasion of his own encounter with the judicial system achieved extensive acceptance. A number of factors have combined to transform the penal system into a prominent terrain of struggle, both for the captives inside and the masses outside. The impact of large numbers of political prisoners both on prison populations and on the mass movement has been decisive. The vast majority of political prisoners have not allowed the fact of imprisonment to curtail their educational, agitational and organizing activities, which they continue behind prison walls. And in the course of developing mass movements around political prisoners, a great deal of attention has inevitably been focussed on the institutions in which they are imprisoned. Furthermore the political receptivity of prisoners—especially Black and Brown captives—has been increased and sharpened by the surge of aggressive political activity rising out of Black, Chicano and other oppressed communities. Finally, a major catalyst for intensified political action in and around prisons has emerged out of the transformation of convicts, originally found guilty of criminal offences, into exemplary political militants. Their patient educational efforts in the realm of exposing the specific oppressive structures of the penal system in their relation to the larger oppression of the social system have had a profound effect on their fellow captives.

The prison is a key component of the state's coercive apparatus, whose overriding function is to ensure social control. The etymology of the term penitentiary furnishes a clue to the controlling idea behind the 'prison system' at its inception. The penitentiary was projected as the locale for doing penitence for an offence against society, the physical and spiritual purging of proclivities to challenge rules and regulations which command total obedience. While cloaking itself with the bourgeois aura of universality—imprisonment was supposed to cut across all class lines, as crimes were to be defined by the act, not the perpetrator—the prison has actually operated as an instrument of class domination, a means of prohibiting the have-nots from encroaching upon the haves.

The occurrence of crime is inevitable in a society in which wealth is unequally distributed, as one of the constant reminders that society's productive forces are being channelled in the wrong direction. The majority of criminal offences bear a direct relationship to property. Contained in the very concept of property crimes are profound but suppressed social needs which express themselves in anti-social modes of action. Spontaneously produced by a capitalist organization of society, this type of crime is at once a protest against society and a desire to partake of its exploitative content. It challenges the symptoms of capitalism, but not its essence.

Some Marxists in recent years have tended to banish criminals and the lumpenproletariat as a whole from the arena of revolutionary struggle. Apart from the absence of any link binding the criminal to the means of production, underlying this exclusion has been the assumption that individuals who have recourse to anti-social acts are incapable of developing the discipline and collective orientation required by revolutionary struggle.

With the declassed character of lumpenproletarians in mind, Marx stated that they are capable of 'the most heroic deeds and the most exalted sacrifices, as of the basest banditry and the dirtiest corruption.' He emphasized the fact that the Provisional Government's Mobile Guards under the Paris Commune—some 24,000 troops—were largely formed out of young lumpenproletarians from 15 to 20 years of age. Too many Marxists have been inclined to overvalue the second part of Marx's observation—that the lumpenproletariat is capable of the basest banditry and the dirtiest corruption—while minimizing or indeed totally disregarding his first remark applauding the lumpen for their heroic deeds and exalted sacrifices.

Especially today when so many Black, Chicano and Puerto Rican men and women are jobless as a consequence of the internal dynamic of the capitalist system, the role of this strata of society in revolutionary struggle must be given serious thought. Increased unemployment, particularly for the nationally oppressed, will continue to be an inevitable by-product of technological development. At least 30 per cent of Black youth are presently without jobs. In the context of class exploitation and national oppression it should be clear that numerous individuals are compelled to resort to criminal acts, not as a result of conscious choice—implying other alternatives—but because society has objectively reduced their possibilities of subsistence and survival to this level. This recognition should signal the urgent need to organize the lumpenproletariat, as indeed the Black Panther Party as well as activists in prison have already begun to do.

In evaluating the susceptibility of the Black and Brown unemployed to organizing efforts, the peculiar historical features of the U.S., specifically racism and national oppression, must be taken into account. There already exists in the Black and Brown communities—the lumpenproletariat included—a long tradition of collective resistance to national oppression.

Moreover, in assessing the revolutionary potential of prisoners in America as a group, it should be borne in mind that not all prisoners have actually committed crimes. The built-in racism of the judicial system expresses itself, as Du Bois has suggested, in the railroading of countless innocent Blacks and other national minorities, into the country's coercive institutions.

One must also appreciate the effects of disproportionally long prison terms on Black and Brown inmates. The typical criminal mentality sees imprisonment as a calculated risk for a particular criminal act. One's prison term is more or less rationally predictable. The function of racism in the judicial-penal complex is to shatter that predictability. The Black burglar, anticipating a 2 to 4 year term may end up doing 10 to 15 years, while the white burglar leaves after two years.

Within the contained, coercive universe of the prison, the captive is confronted with the realities of racism, not simply as individual acts dictated by attitudinal bias; rather he is compelled to come to grips with racism as an institutional phenomenon collectively experienced by the victims. The disproportionate representation of the Black and Brown communities, the manifest racism of parole boards, the intense brutality inherent in the relationship between prison guards and Black and Brown inmates—all this and more cause the prisoner to be confronted daily, hourly, with the concentrated systematic existence of racism.

For the innocent prisoner the process of radicalization should come easy; for the 'guilty' victim an insight into the nature of racism as it manifests itself in the judicial-penal complex can lead to a questioning of his own past criminal activity and a reevaluation of the methods he has used to survive in a racist and exploitative society. Needless to say this process is not automatic, it does not occur spontaneously. The persistent educational work carried out by the prison's political activists plays a key role in developing the political potential of captive men and women.

Prisoners—especially Blacks, Chicanos, and Puerto Ricans—are increasingly advancing the proposition that they are *political* prisoners. They contend that they are political prisoners in the sense that they are largely the victims of an oppressive politico-economic order, swiftly becoming conscious of the causes underlying their victimization. The Folsom Prisoners' Manifesto of Demands and Anti-Oppression Platform attests to a lucid understanding of the structures of oppression within the prison—structures which contradict even the avowed function of the penal institution: 'The programme we are submitted to, under the ridiculous title of rehabilitation, is relative to the ancient stupidity of pouring water on the drowning man, in as much as we are treated for our hostilities by our programme administrators with their hostility as medication'. The Manifesto also reflects an awareness that the severe social crisis taking place in this country, predicated in part on the ever-increasing mass consciousness of deepening social contradictions, is forcing the political function of the prisons to surface in all its brutality. Their contention that prisons are being transformed into the 'fascist concentration camps of modern America,' should not be taken lightly, although it would be erroneous as well as defeatist in a practical sense, to maintain that fascism has irremediably established itself.

The point is this, and this is the truth which is apparent in the Manifesto: The ruling circles of America are expanding and intensifying repressive measures designed to nip revolutionary movements in the bud as well as to curtail radical-democratic tendencies, such as the movement to end the war in Indochina. The government is not hesitating to utilize an entire network of fascist tactics, including the monitoring of congressmen's telephone calls, a system of 'preventive fascism,' as Marcuse has termed it, in which the role of the judicial-penal systems looms large. The sharp edge of political repression, cutting through the heightened militancy of the masses, and bringing growing numbers of activists behind prison walls, must necessarily pour over into the contained world of the prison where it understandably acquires far more ruthless forms.

It is a relatively easy matter to persecute the captive whose life is already dominated by a network of authoritarian mechanisms. This is especially facilitated by the indeterminate sentence policies of many states, for politically conscious prisoners will incur inordinately long sentences on their original conviction. According to Louis S. Nelson, warden of San Quentin Prison, '... if the prisons of California become known as "schools for violent revolution," the Adult Authority would be remiss in their duty not to keep the inmates longer.' (*San Francisco Chronicle*, May 2, 1971). Where this is deemed inadequate, authorities have recourse to the whole spectrum of brutal corporal punishment, including out-and-out murder. At San Quentin, Fred Billingslea was teargassed to death in February, 1970. W. L. Nolan, Alvin Miller, and Cleveland Edwards were assassinated by a prison guard in January, 1970 at Soledad Prison. Strange, inexplicable suicides have occurred with incredible regularity in jails and prisons throughout the country.

It should be self-evident that the frame-up becomes a powerful weapon within the spectrum of prison repression, particularly because of the availability of informers, the broken prisoners who will do anything for a price. The Soledad Brothers and the Soledad 3 are leading examples of frame-up victims. Both cases involve militant activists who have been charged with killing Soledad prison guards. In both cases, widespread support has been kindled within the Californian prison system. They have served as occasions to link the immediate needs of the Black community with a forceful fight to break the fascist stronghold in the prisons and therefore to abolish the prison system in its present form.

Racist oppression invades the lives of Black people on an infinite variety of levels. Blacks are imprisoned in a world where our labour and toil hardly allow us to eke out a decent existence, if we are able to find jobs at all. When the economy begins to falter, we are automatically the first victims, always the most deeply wounded. When the economy is on its feet, we continue to live in a depressed state. Unemployment is generally twice as high in the ghettos as it is in the country as a whole and even higher among Black women and youth. The unemployment rate among Black youth has presently skyrocketed to 30 per cent. If one-third of America's white youth were without a means of livelihood, we would either be in the thick of revolution or else under the iron rule of fascism. Substandard schools, medical care hardly fit for animals, over-priced, delapidated housing, a welfare system based on a policy of skimpy concessions designed to degrade and divide (and even this may soon be cancelled)—this is only to begin the list of props in the overall scenery of oppression which, for the mass of Blacks, is the universe.

In Black communities, wherever they are located, there exists an ever-present reminder that our universe must remain stable in its drabness, its poverty, its brutality. From Birmingham to Harlem to Watts, Black ghettos are occupied, patrolled and often attacked by massive deployments of police. The police, domestic caretakers of violence, are the oppressor's emissaries charged with the task of containing us within the boundaries of our oppression.

The announced function of the police, 'to protect and serve the people,' becomes the grotesque caricature of protecting and preserving the interests of our oppressors and serving us nothing but injustice. They are there to intimidate Blacks, to persuade us with their violence that we are powerless to alter the conditions of our lives. Arrests are frequently based on whims. Bullets from their guns murder human beings with little or no pretext aside from the universal intimidation they are charged with carrying out. Protection for drug-pushers, and Mafia style exploiters, support for the ideologically most reactionary elements of the Black community (especially the ones who cry out for more police), are among the many functions of police forces. They encircle the community with a shield of violence, too often forcing the natural aggression of the Black community inwards. Fanon's analysis of the role of colonial police is an appropriate description of the function of the police in America's ghettos.

It goes without saying that the police would be unable to set in motion their racist machinery were they not sanctioned and supported by the judicial system. The courts not only consistently abstain from prosecuting criminal behaviour on the part of the police, but they convict, on biased police testimony, countless Black men and women. Court-appointed attorneys, acting in the twisted interests of overcrowded courts, convince 85 per cent of defendants to plead guilty. Even the manifestly innocent are advised to cop a plea so that the lengthy and expensive process of jury trials is avoided. This is the structure of the apparatus which summarily railroads Black people into jails and prisons. (During my imprisonment in the New York Women's House of Detention, I encountered numerous cases involving innocent Black women who had been advised to plead guilty. One sister had entered her white landlord's apartment for the purpose of paying rent. He attempted to rape her and in the course of the ensuing struggle, a lit candle toppled over, burning a tablecloth. The landlord ordered her to be arrested for arson. Following the advice of her court appointed attorney she entered a guilty plea, having been deceived by the attorney's insistence that the court would be more lenient. The sister was sentenced to three years.)

The vicious circle linking poverty, police, courts and prison is an integral element of ghetto existence. Unlike the mass of whites, the path which leads to jails and prisons is deeply rooted in the imposed patterns of Black existence. For this very reason an almost instinctive affinity binds the mass of Black people to the political prisoners. The vast majority of Blacks harbour a deep hatred of the police and are not deluded by official proclamations of justice through the courts.

For the Black individual contact with the law enforcement-judicial-penal network directly or through relatives and friends is inevitable because he is Black. For the activist become political prisoner the contact has occurred because he has lodged a protest, in one form or another, against the conditions which nail Blacks to this orbit of oppression.

Historically, Black people as a group have exhibited a greater potential for resistance than any other part of the population. The ironclad rule over our communities, the institutional practice of genocide, the ideology of racism have performed a strictly political as well as an economic role. The capitalists have not only extracted super profits from the underpaid labour of over 15 percent of the American population with the aid of a superstructure of terror. This terror and more subtle forms of racism have further served to thwart the flowering of a resistance, even a revolution which would spread to the working class as a whole.

In the interests of the capitalist class, consent to racism and terror has been demagogically elicited from the white population, workers included, in order more efficiently to stave off resistance. Today Nixon, Mitchell and J. Edgar Hoover are desperately attempting to persuade the population that dissidents—particularly Blacks, Chicanos, Puerto Ricans—must be punished for being members of revolutionary organizations, for advocating the overthrow of the government, for agitating and educating in the streets and behind prison walls. The political function of racist domination is surfacing with accelerated intensity. Whites who have professed their solidarity with the Black Liberation Movement and have moved in a distinctly revolutionary direction, find themselves targets of the self same repression. Even the anti-war movement, rapidly exhibiting an anti-imperialist consciousness, is falling victim to government repression.

Black people are rushing full speed ahead towards an understanding of the circumstances which give rise to exaggerated forms of political repression and thus an overabundance of political prisoners. This understanding is being forged out of the raw material of their own immediate experience with racism. Hence, the Black masses are growing conscious of their responsibility to defend those who are being persecuted for their efforts to bring about the alleviation of the most injurious immediate problems facing Black communities and ultimately to bring about total liberation through armed revolution, if it must come to this.

The Black Liberation Movement is presently at a critical juncture. Fascist methods of repression threaten physically to decapitate and obliterate the movement. More subtle yet not less dangerous ideological tendencies from within threaten to isolate the Black movement and diminish its revolutionary impact. Both menaces must be counteracted in order to ensure our survival. Revolutionary Blacks must spearhead and provide leadership for a broad anti-fascist movement.

Fascism is a process; its growth and development are cancerous in nature. While today the threat of fascism may be primarily restricted to the use of the law enforcement-judicial-penal apparatus to arrest the overt and latent revolutionary trends among nationally oppressed people, tomorrow it may attack the working class en masse and eventually even moderate democrats. Even in this period, however, the cancer has already commenced to spread. In addition to the prison army of thousands and thousands of nameless Third

World victims of political revenge, there are increasing numbers of white political prisoners—draft resistors, anti-war activists such as the Harrisburg 8, men and women who have involved themselves on all levels of revolutionary activity.

Among the further symptoms of the fascist threat are official efforts to curtail the power of organized labour, such as the attack on the manifestly conservative construction workers and the trends towards reduced welfare aid. Moreover court decision and repressive legislation augmenting police powers—as the Washington no-knock law permitting police to enter private dwellings without warning and Nixon's 'Crime Bill' in general—can eventually be used against any citizen. Indeed congressmen are already protesting the use of police-state wire-tapping to survey their activities. The fascist content of the ruthless aggression in IndoChina should be self-evident.

One of the fundamental historical lessons to be learned from past failures to prevent the rise of fascism is the decisive and indispensable character of the fight against fascism in its incipient phases. Once allowed to conquer ground its growth is facilitated in geometric proportion. Although the most unbridled expressions of the fascist menace are still tied to the racist domination of Blacks, Chicanos, Puerto Ricans, Indians, it lurks under the surface wherever there is potential resistance to the power of monopoly capital, the parasitic interests which control this society. Potentially it can profoundly worsen the conditions of existence for the average American citizen. Consequently the masses of people in this country have a real, direct and material stake in the struggle to free political prisoners, the struggle to abolish the prison system in its present form, the struggle against all dimensions of racism.

No one should fail to take heed of Georgi Dimitrov's warning: 'Whoever does not fight the growth of fascism at these preparatory stages is not in a position to prevent the victory of fascism, but, on the contrary, facilitates that victory.' (Report to the Seventh Congress of the Communist International, 1935.) The only effective guarantee against the victory of fascism is an indivisible mass movement which refuses to conduct business as usual as long as repression rages on. It is only natural that Blacks and other Third World peoples must lead this movement, for we are the first and most deeply injured victims of fascism. But it must embrace all potential victims and most important, all working class people, for the key to the triumph of fascism is its ideological victory over the entire working class. Given the eruption of a severe economic crisis, the door to such an ideological victory can be opened by the active approval or passive toleration of racism. It is essential that white workers become conscious that historically through their acquiescence in the capitalist-inspired oppression of Blacks they have only rendered themselves more vulnerable to attack.

The pivotal struggle which must be waged in the ranks of the working class is consequently the open, unreserved battle against entrenched racism. The white worker must become conscious of the threads which bind him to a James Johnson, Black auto worker, member of UAW, and a political prisoner presently facing charges for the killings of two foremen and a job setter.[6] The merciless proliferation of the power of monopoly capital may ultimately push him inexorably down the self-same path of desperation. No potential victim of the fascist terror should be without the knowledge that the greatest menace to racism and fascism is unity!

Marin County Jail,
May, 1971

NOTES

1. William Z. Foster, *The Negro People in American History*, International Publishers, New York, 1954, pp. 169-170 (quoting Herbert Aptheker).
2. Louis Adamic, *Dynamite: The History of Class Violence in America*, Peter Smith, Gloucester, Mass., 1963, p. 312.
3. Herbert Aptheker, *Nat Turner's Slave Rebellion*, Grove Press, N.Y., 1968, p. 45. According to Aptheker these are not Nat Turner's exact words.
4. *Autobiography of W.E.B. Du Bois*, International Publishers, New York, 1968, p. 390.
5. Karl Marx, *The Class Struggle in France*, New York: 1935.
6. See Part Four [of Angela Y. Davis, et al., *If They Come in the Morning*] on political prisoners for the details of James Johnson's case.

The Paradox of the
African American Rebellion

Cornel West

The distinctive feature of African American life in the sixties was the rise on the historical stage of a small yet determined petite bourgeoisie promoting liberal reforms, and the revolt of the masses, whose aspirations exceeded those of liberalism but whose containment was secured by political appeasement, cultural control and state repression. African America encountered the modern American capitalist order (in its expansionist phase)—as urban dwellers, industrial workers and franchised citizens—on a broad scale for the first time. This essay will highlight the emergence of the black parvenu petite bourgeoisie—the new, relatively privileged, middle class—and its complex relations to the black working poor and underclass. I will try to show how the political strategies, ideological struggles and cultural anxieties of this predominantly white-collar stratum both propelled the freedom movement in an unprecedented manner and circumscribed its vision, analysis and praxis within liberal capitalist perimeters.

For interpretive purposes, the sixties is not a chronological category which encompasses a decade, but rather a historical construct or heuristic rubric which renders noteworthy historical processes and events intelligible. The major historical processes that set the context for the first stage of the black freedom movement in the sixties were the modernization of southern agriculture, the

Source: "The Paradox of the African American Rebellion" in Cornel West, *Keeping Faith: Philosophy and Race in America* (New York: Routledge, 1993), 271–91. Reprinted with the permission of Routledge, Inc., a part of the Taylor and Francis Group.

judicial repudiation of certain forms of southern racism and the violent white backlash against perceived black progress. The modernization of southern agriculture made obsolete much of the traditional tenant labor force, thereby forcing large numbers of black rural folk into southern and northern urban centers in search of employment. The judicial repudiation of certain forms of southern racism, prompted by the gallant struggles of the National Association for the Advancement of Colored People (NAACP) and exemplified in the *Brown v. Board of Education* decision of 1954, was not only a legal blow against tax-supported school segregation; it also added historical momentum and political legitimacy to black struggles against racism. Yet there quickly surfaced an often violent white reaction to this momentum and legitimacy. For example, Rev. George W. Lee was fatally shot in May 1955 for refusing to take his name off the voter registration list. Sixty-three-year-old Lamar Smith was killed in broad daylight in August 1955 for trying to get out the black vote in an upcoming primary election. And most notably, Emmett L. Till, a fourteen-year-old lad from Chicago visiting his relatives, was murdered in late August 1955. These wanton acts of violence against black people in Mississippi, though part of the American southern way of life, reflected the conservative white reaction to perceived black progress. In 1955, this white reaction was met with widespread black resistance.

The greatness of Rev. Dr. Martin Luther King, Jr.—the major American prophet of this century and black leader in the sixties—was his ability to mobilize and organize this southern resistance, such that the delicate balance between the emerging "new" black petite bourgeoisie, black working poor and black underclass was maintained for a few years. The arrest of Rosa Parks on December 1, 1955 in Montgomery, Alabama—as a result of one of a series of black acts of civil disobedience against Montgomery's bus line that year—led to the creation of the Montgomery Improvement Association (MIA), the adoption of a citywide black boycott and the placement of King at the head of the movement. After nearly a year of the boycott, the U.S. Supreme Court declared Alabama's state and local bus segregation laws unconstitutional. Judicial repudiation of Southern racism again gave the black struggle for freedom momentum and legitimacy.

King is the exemplary figure of the first stage of the black freedom movement in the sixties not only because he was its gifted and courageous leader or simply because of his organizational achievements, but, more important, because he consolidated the most progressive potential available in the black Southern community at that time: the cultural potency of prophetic black churches, the skills of engaged black preachers, trade-unionists and professionals, and the spirit of rebellion and resistance of the black working poor and underclass. In this sense, King was an organic intellectual of the first order—a highly educated and informed thinker with organic links to ordinary folk. Despite his petit bourgeois origins, his deep roots in the black church gave him direct access to the life-worlds of the majority of black southerners. In addition, his education at Morehouse College, Crozier Theological Seminary and Boston University provided him with opportunities to reflect upon various anticolonial struggles around the world, especially those in India and Ghana, and also entitled him to respect and admiration in the eyes of black people, including the "old," black, middle class (composed primarily of teachers and preachers). Last, his Christian outlook and personal temperament facilitated relations with progressive nonblack people, thereby insuring openness to potential allies.

King institutionalized his sense of the social engagement of black churches, his Christian-informed techniques of nonviolence and his early liberal vision of America, with the founding in February, 1957 in New Orleans of the Southern Christian Leadership Conference (SCLC). This courageous group of prophetic black preachers from ten southern states served as the models for young black southern activists. I stress the adjective "southern" not simply because most black people in the USA at this time lived in the South, but also because the core of the first stage of the black freedom movement was a church-led movement in the belly of the violence-prone, underindustrialized, colonylike southern USA. Of course, the North was quite active—especially Harlem's Rev. Adam Clayton Powell, Jr. in Congress and the Nation of Islam's Malcolm X in the streets—but activity in the North was not the major thrust of this first stage.

Like David against Goliath, black activists openly challenged the entrenched, racist, white status quo in the South. Widespread white economic sanctions and physical attacks on black people, fueled by the so-called "Southern Manifesto" promoted in 1956 by Senator J. Strom Thurmond of South Carolina along with over a hundred congressmen, rendered both the Democratic and Republican parties relatively silent regarding the civil rights issues affecting black people. Two diluted civil rights bills (in 1957 and 1960) limped through Congress, and the Supreme Court, owing to congressional pressure, took much of the bite out of its earlier Brown decision. Black resistance intensified.

Inspired by the praxis of King, MIA and SCLC—as well as the sit-in techniques employed by the Congress of Racial Equality (CORE) in the North—four black freshmen students at North Carolina Agricultural and Technical College in Greensboro staged a sit-in at the local Woolworth's on February 1, 1960. Within a week, their day-to-day sit-in had been joined by black and white students from the Women's College of the University of North Carolina, North Carolina College and Duke University. Within two weeks, the sit-in movement had spread to fifteen other cities in Virginia, Tennessee and South Carolina. Within two months, there were sit-ins in seventy-eight cities. By the end of 1960, over fifty thousand people throughout the South had participated in sit-in demonstrations, with over twenty-five percent of the black students in predominantly black colleges participating. In short, young black people (and some progressive white people) had taken seriously King's techniques of nonviolence and the spirit of resistance.

This spontaneous rebellion of young black people against the southern taboo of black and white people eating together in public places exemplified a major component in the first stage of the black freedom movement: the emergence of politicized, black, parvenu, petit bourgeois students. These students, especially young preachers and Christian activists, prefigured the disposition and orientation of the vastly increasing number of black college students in the sixties: they would give first priority to social activism and justify their newly acquired privileges by personal risk and sacrifice. So the young black student movement was not simply a rejection of segregation in restaurants. It was also a revolt against the perceived complacency of the "old" black petite bourgeoisie. It is no accident that at the first general conference on student sit-in activity, which began Good Friday (April 15) 1960, the two keynote speakers—Rev. James Lawson and Rev. Martin Luther King, Jr.—launched devastating critiques of the NAACP and other "old" black middle-class groups. King articulated this viewpoint when he characterized the sit-in movement as "a revolt against those Negroes in the middle class who have indulged themselves in big cars and ranch-style homes rather than in joining a movement for freedom." The organization which emerged later in the year from this gathering—the Student Nonviolent Coordinating Committee—(SNCC)—epitomized this revolt against the political reticence of the "old" black middle class.

The major achievement of SNCC was, in many ways, its very existence. SNCC initiated a new style and outlook among black students

in particular and the "new" black petite bourgeoisie in general. Its activist, countercultural orientation even influenced disenchanted white students on elite university campuses. Yet SNCC's central shortcoming was discernible at its inception: if pushed far enough, the revolt against middle-class status and outlook would not only include their models but also themselves, given their privileged student status and probable upward social mobility.

The influence of SNCC's new style was seen when James Farmer departed from the program directorship of the NAACP to become National Director of CORE. Within six weeks, he announced that CORE would conduct "Freedom Rides"—modeled on the 1947 Journey of Reconciliation led by CORE—to challenge segregation in interstate bus depots and terminals. On May 4, 1961, seven black people and six white people left Washington, D.C. Within ten days, one of the buses had been burned to the ground and many riders had been viciously attacked in Birmingham and Montgomery. This "Freedom Ride" was disbanded in Montgomery on May 17. A second "Freedom Ride" was initiated by SNCC, led by Diane Nash, composed of white and black people from CORE and SNCC. Violence ensued again, with twenty-seven people arrested and given suspended two-month sentences and fines of two hundred dollars. They refused to pay and were taken to Parchman Prison.

These two "Freedom Rides"—though responsible for the desegregation of bus and train stations on September 22, 1961, by the Interstate Commerce Commission—served as a portent of the two basic realities which would help bring the initial stage of the black freedom movement to a close: first, the slow but sure rift between SNCC and King, and second, the ambiguous attitude of Democratic Party liberals to the movement. Both aspects came to the fore at the crucial August 1961 staff meeting at SNCC at the Highlander Folk School in Tennessee. It was well known that the Kennedy administration had called for a "cooling off" period, motivated primarily by its fear of alienating powerful Southern

Democratic comrades in Congress. At the meeting, Tim Jenkins, a fellow traveller of the Democratic Party, proposed that SNCC drop its emphasis on direct action and focus on voter education and registration. The majority of the SNCC staff opposed Jenkins's project, owing to its connections with the Kennedy administration and the open approval of it by King's SCLC. In the eyes of many SNCC members, the "Establishment" against which they were struggling began to encompass both the Democratic Party's liberals and the SCLC's black activist liberals. This slow rupture would result in some glaring defeats in the civil rights movement, most notably the Albany (Georgia) Movement in December 1961, and also led to the gradual breakaway of SNCC from the techniques of nonviolence.

Yet in 1963, the first stage of the black freedom movement would culminate in its most successful endeavors: Birmingham and the March on Washington. The televised confrontation between the civil rights marchers and the Commissioner of Public Safety, Eugene "Bull" Connor, as well as the dramatic arrest of King, gave the movement much sympathy and support throughout the country. And the use of hundreds of black children in the struggle reinforced this effective histrionic strategy. Despite the bombing of the black Gaston Hotel, of King's brother's home, and black spontaneous rebellions in Birmingham, the massive nonviolent direct action—including over three thousand people imprisoned—proved successful. The city of Birmingham, often referred to as the "American Johannesburg," accepted the black demands for desegregation and black employment opportunities. Furthermore, President Kennedy responded to the Birmingham campaign with a televised address to the nation in which he pledged his support for a comprehensive civil rights bill. However, the assassination of Medgar Evers, state executive secretary of the Mississippi NAACP, only hours after Kennedy's speech cast an ominous shadow over the Birmingham victory.

The famous March on Washington in August 1963—the occasion for King's powerful and poignant "I have a dream" speech—was not the zenith of the civil rights movement. The movement had peaked in Birmingham. Rather the March on Washington was the historic gathering of that coalition of liberal forces—white trade unionists, Christians, Jews and civil rights activists—whose potency was declining, whose fragile cohesion was falling apart. The central dilemma of the first stage of the black freedom movement emerged: the existence and sustenance of the civil rights movement neither needed nor required white aid or allies, yet its *success* required white liberal support in the Democratic Party, Congress and the White House.

The March on Washington exemplified this debilitating limitation of the civil rights movement. With white liberal support, the movement would achieve limited success, but slowly lose its legitimacy in the eyes of the now more politicized black petit bourgeois students, working poor and underclass. Without white liberal support, the movement could raise more fundamental issues of concern to the black working poor and underclass, yet thereby render the movement marginal to mainstream American politics and hence risk severe repression. It comes as no surprise that the March on Washington witnessed both the most powerful rhetoric and the most salient reality of the civil rights movement: King's great speech and the Kennedy administration's supervision of the March.

In summary, the first stage of the black freedom movement in the sixties—the civil rights struggle—began as a black response to white violent attacks and took the form of a critique of everyday life in the American South. This critique primarily consisted of attacking everyday cultural folkways which insulted black dignity. It was generated, in part, from the multifarious effects of the economic transformation of dispossessed southern rural peasants into down-trodden industrial workers, maids and unemployed city dwellers within the racist American South. In this regard, the civil rights movement prefigured the fundamental concerns of the American New Left: linking private troubles to public issues, accenting the relation of cultural hegemony to political control and economic exploitation.

The major achievements of the civil rights movement were noteworthy: the transformation of everyday life (especially the elimination of terror as a primary mode of social control) of central regions in the American South; the federal commitment to the civil and voting rights of African Americans; and the sense of confidence among black people that effective mobilization and organization were not only possible but imperative if the struggle for freedom was to continue. The pressing challenges were immense: transforming the power relations in the American South and North, obtaining federal support for employment and economic rights of the underprivileged, sustaining black organizational potency in the face of increasing class differentiation within the black community, and taking seriously the long-overlooked specific needs and interests of black women. The first stage came to a close principally because the civil rights struggle achieved its liberal aims, namely, absorption into mainstream American politics, reputable interest-group status in the (soon to falter) liberal coalition of the Democratic Party.

The second stage centered primarily on the issue of the legitimacy and accountability of the black political leadership. Like the first stage, this historical movement was engendered by a sense of black resistance and rebellion, and led by black petit bourgeois figures. Yet these "new," black, middle-class figures had been highly politicized and radicalized by the strengths and weaknesses of King's movement, by the rise of the New Left movement among white privileged students and by the revolutionary anticolonial struggles in the Caribbean (Cuba), Africa (Ghana and Guinea), Latin America (Chile and Bolivia) and Southeast Asia (Vietnam). The transitional events were the Mississippi Freedom Summer in 1964, the Democratic National Convention in Atlantic City, late August 1964, and the Selma campaign of 1965. The Freedom Summer brought to the surface the deep cultural and personal problems of interracial political struggle in America: white attitudes

of paternalism, guilt and sexual jealousy, and black sensibilities of one-upsmanship, manipulation and sexual adventure. The Atlantic City convention illustrated the self-serving machinery of the Democratic Party, whose support even King at this point solicited at the risk of white-controlled compromise. Finally, King's Selma campaign, initiated by SNCC years earlier, was sustained primarily by federal support, escort and legitimacy. In short, the bubble was about to burst: the vision, analysis and praxis of significant elements of the black freedom movement were to move beyond the perimeters of prevailing American bourgeois politics.

The Watts explosion in August 1965 revealed the depths of the problem of legitimacy and accountability of black political leadership. The rebellion and resistance (especially in northern urban centers) could no longer find an organizational form of expression. In the cities, it had become sheer anarchic energy and existential assertion without political direction and social vision. The Watts rebellion was a watershed event in the black freedom movement, in that it drew the line of demarcation between those who would cling to liberal rhetoric, ties to the Democratic Party and middle-class concerns, and those who would attempt to go beyond liberalism, expose the absorptive role and function of the Democratic Party and focus more on black proletarian and lumpenproletarian interests.

The pressing challenges of the second stage were taken up by Martin Luther King, Jr. His Chicago campaign in 1966—though rejected by most of his liberal black and white comrades in SCLC—pushed for the radical unionization of slum-dwellers against exploitative landlords. His aborted poor people's campaign of 1967 to 68, initiated after his break with President Johnson and the Democratic Party, which had been precipitated by his fierce opposition to the Vietnam War, was even more attuned to black, Latino and white working poor and underclass concerns. Yet, despite his immense talent, energy and courage, it became clear that King lacked the organization and support to address these concerns. Notwithstanding his 1968 murder—preceded by intense FBI harassments and threats—the widespread ideological fragmentation and increased class and strata differentiation in African America precluded King from effectively meeting the pressing challenges. His new focus on the urban poor led to black middle-class abandonment of his movement; his nonviolent approach perturbed black committed leftists who welcomed his new focus; his Christianity disturbed black secularists and Muslims already working in urban ghettoes; and his integrationist perspective met with staunch opposition from black nationalists who were quickly seizing hegemony over the black freedom movement. In other words, King was near death politically and organizationally before he was murdered, though he will never die in the hearts and minds of progressive people in the USA and abroad.

Ironically, King's later path was blazed by his early vociferous critic, Malcolm X. Even as a narrow black nationalist under the late Honorable Elijah Muhammad, Malcolm X rejected outright white liberal support and ties to the Democratic Party, and he highlighted the plight of urban black working poor and unemployed people. More than any other black figure during the first stage, Malcolm X articulated the underlying, almost visceral, feelings and sensibilities of black urban America—North and South, Christian and non-Christian, young and old. His early rhetoric was simply prescient: too honest, too candid, precisely the things black folk often felt but never said publicly due to fear of white retaliation, even in the early sixties. In fact, his piercing rhetoric had primarily a cathartic function for black people; it purged them of their deferential and defensive attitudes toward white people.

Although Malcolm X moved toward a more Marxist-informed humanist position just prior to his assassination by rival Black Muslims in February 1965, he became the major symbol for (and of) the second stage of the black freedom movement in the sixties. What were accented were neither his political successes nor his organizational achievements, but rather his rhetorical eloquence and homespun honesty. Malcolm X did not hesitate to tell black and white America "like it is," even if it resulted in little political and practical payoff. This eloquence and honesty was admired at a distance by the black working poor and underclass: it expressed their gut feelings and addressed their situation but provided little means or hope as to how to change their predicament. The "old," black, middle class was horrified; they publicly and secretly tried to discredit him. The "new" black petite bourgeoisie, especially black students, welcomed Malcolm X's rhetoric and honesty with open arms. It resonated with their own newly acquired sense of political engagement and black pride; it also spoke to a more fundamental problem they faced—the problem of becoming black leaders and elites with organic, existential and rhetorical ties to the black community.

In a complex way, Malcolm X's candid talk both fueled more protracted black rebellion and provided a means to contain it. In short, his rhetoric was double-edged and functioned in contradictory ways. On the one hand, it served as an ideological pillar for revolutionary black nationalism. On the other hand, his rhetoric was employed by manipulative black petit bourgeois politicians, professionals, administrators and students to promote their own upward social mobility. The adulation of Malcolm X in the black community is profound. Yet an often overlooked component of this adulation among the "new" black middle class was (and is) their subtle use of his truth-telling for their narrow, self-serving aims. The relative silence regarding his black sexist values and attitudes also reveals the deep patriarchal sensibilities in the black community.

The revolt of the black masses, with hundreds of rebellions throughout the country, set the framework for the second stage. The repressive state apparatus in American capitalist society jumped at this opportunity to express its contempt for black people. And the basic mechanism of pacifying the erupting black ghettoes—the drug industry—fundamentally changed the content and character of the black community. The drug industry, aided and abetted by underground capitalists, invaded black communities with intense force, police indifference and political silence. It accelerated black white-collar and solid blue-collar working-class suburban flight, and transformed black poor neighborhoods into terrains of human bondage to the commodity form, enslavement to the buying and selling of drugs. For the first time in African American history, fear and trepidation among black folk toward one another became pervasive. As crime moved toward civil terrorism, black distrust of and distance from the black poor and underclass deepened. And, of course, black presence in jails and prisons rapidly increased.

The revolt of the black masses precipitated a deep crisis—with political, intellectual and existential forms—among the "new" black petite bourgeoisie. What should be the appropriate black middle-class response be to such black working poor and underclass rebellions? This complex response is best seen in the internal dynamics of the Black Power movement. This movement, more than any other at the time, projected the aspirations and anxieties of the recently politicized and radicalized black petite bourgeoisie. From Adam Clayton Powell, Jr.'s Howard University baccalaureate address of 1966, through the Meredith March, to the Newark Black Power Conference, the message was clear: beneath the rhetoric of Black Power, black control and black self-determination was a budding, "new," black, middle class hungry for power and starving for status. Needless to say, most young black intellectuals were duped by this petit bourgeois rhetoric, primarily owing to their own identity crisis and self-interest. In contrast, the "new" black business, professional and political elites heard the bourgeois melody behind the radical rhetoric and manipulated the movement for their own benefit. The rebellious black working poor and underclass often either became dependent on growing welfare support or seduced by the drug culture.

The second stage was primarily a black nationalist affair. The veneration of "black"

symbols, rituals, styles, hairdos, values, sensibilities and flag escalated. The "Black Is Beautiful" slogan was heard throughout the black community and James Brown's "Say It Loud, I'm Black and I'm Proud" became an exemplary—and healthy—expression of the cultural reversal of alienating Anglo-American ideals of beauty and behavior. Yet this cantankerous reversal (like the black rediscovery of jazz) was principally a "new" black middle-class phenomenon.

The working poor and underclass watched as the "new" black middle class visibly grappled with its new identity, social position and radical political rhetoric. For the most part, the black underclass continued to hustle, rebel when appropriate, get high and listen to romantic proletarian love songs produced by Detroit's Motown; they remained perplexed at their idolization by the "new" black, middle class, which they sometimes envied. The black working poor persisted in their weekly church attendance, struggled to make ends meet and waited to see what the beneficial results would be after all the bourgeois "hoopla" was over. In short, the black nationalist moment, despite its powerful and progressive critique of American cultural imperialism, was principally the activity of black petit bourgeois self-congratulation and self-justification upon reaching an anxiety-ridden, middle-class status in racist American society.

To no surprise, the leading black, petit bourgeois, nationalist groups such as SNCC (after 1966), CORE, Ron Karenga's US and Imamu Amiri Baraka's Congress of African People were viewed by black proletarian and lumpenproletarian organizations as "porkchop nationalists" who confused superficial nation-talk with authentic cultural distinctiveness, middle-class guilt with working-class aspirations, and identity crises with revolutionary situations. The late Honorable Elijah Muhammad's Nation of Islam, though petit bourgeois in intent, was staunchly working poor and underclass (and especially strong in American prisons) in composition. Devoid of leading black intellectuals yet full of eloquent spokesmen, the Nation of Islam put to shame the "porkchop nationalists," not only by being "blacker than thou" in both mythology and ideology, but also by producing discernible results in the personal, organizational and financial life of its members and the black community.

The Black Panther Party (founded in Oakland, California, 1966) was the leading black lumpenproletarian revolutionary party in the sixties. It thoroughly rejected and consistently struggled against petit bourgeois nationalism from a viewpoint of strong black leftist internationalism. Yet it was overwhelmed by the undisciplined character of black underclass life, seduced by the histrionic enticements of mass media and crushed by state repression. The only other major national response of black progressives against the black petit bourgeois nationalism was George Wiley's [and] Fannie Lou Hamer's National Welfare Rights Organization (founded in August 1967). But it was unable to sustain broad membership, and thereby control encroaching bureaucratic leadership. The League of Revolutionary Black Workers (founded in Detroit, Michigan, 1969), though regional in scope, was the most important revolutionary group among black industrial workers in the country. It eventually split over the issue of the role of black nationalism in a Marxist organization.

The rift between black petit bourgeois nationalists and black revolutionary leftists was best illustrated in the American response to James Forman's historic Black Manifesto. Forman, a former executive director of SNCC, ex-minister of Foreign Affairs of the Black Panther Party, and leader of the short-lived Black Workers' Congress, proposed at the National Black Economic Development Conference in Detroit and later, more dramatically, at New York City's Riverside Church's 11:00 p.m. service, reparation funds of five hundred million dollars from white Christian churches and Jewish synagogues in order to finance the black revolutionary overthrow of the U.S. government. This "revolution" would turn into an "armed, well-disciplined, black-controlled government."

This symbolic gesture represented the peak of the black nationalist moment in the sixties, though it was enacted by a black Marxist. It also signified liberal white America's absorption and domestication of black nationalism. Despite the Manifesto's Marxist critique and demand of American capitalist society—such as the call for a black revolutionary vanguard party and even the call for white progressive people to accept this black leadership—the most salient issue became that of reparations to existing black middle-class groups.

The white American response to these demands on the eccleslastical, educational and corporate levels was widespread. Of course, the major funds were not given to Forman's group (though it received about three hundred thousand dollars), but rather to church agencies, denominational caucuses, minority-oriented programs and, above all, black businesses and banks. Regardless of Forman's naive revolutionary intent, the black petit bourgeois nationalists triumphed. Soon the federal government and even the Nixon administration would openly support such moves in the name of "black self-determination" and "black capitalism."

The hegemonic role of black petit bourgeois nationalism had four deleterious consequences for African America. First, it isolated progressive black leftists such that orthodox Marxism became the primary refuge for those concerned with class struggle and Internationalism. And even in these new Marxist formations the Black Nation Thesis—the claim that black people constitute a nation within the USA—once again became the widely accepted understanding of African American oppression. Second, the machismo lifestyles of black nationalists (of the petit bourgeois and revolutionary varieties) so marginalized black women that the black feminist movement of the seventies and eighties was often forced to sever ties with black male-dominated groups, thereby encouraging an understandable but innocuous black feminist separatism. Third, black nationalism disarmed and delimited a large number of young black intellectuals by confining them to parochial black rhetoric, pockets of "internal dialogues," which resulted in posing almost insurmountable walls of separation between progressive white, brown, red, yellow and black intellectuals. Last, black nationalist rhetoric contributed greatly to the black freedom movement's loss of meaningful anchorage and organic ties to the black community, especially the churches. In short, besides the severe state repression and the pervasive drug invasion, the black petit bourgeois nationalist perspectives and practices were primarily responsible for the radically decentered state of the black freedom movement in the seventies and eighties. This was so principally because they undergirded the needs and interests of the "new" black middle class.

The sixties in African American history witnessed an unforgettable appearance of the black masses on the historical stage, but they are quickly dragged off—killed, maimed, strung out, imprisoned or paid off. Yet history continues and the growing black petite bourgeoisie still gropes for identity, direction and vision. This black middle class is "new" not simply because significant numbers of black people recently arrived in the world of higher education, comfortable living and professional occupations, but also because they achieved such status against the backdrop of undeniable political struggle, a struggle in which many of them participated. And the relation of their unprecedented opportunities and privileges to the revolt of the black masses is quite obvious to them. This is why the "new" black middle class will more than likely refuse to opt for political complacency. Its own position hangs on some form of political participation, on resisting subtle racist practices, housing policies and educational opportunities. Only persistent pressure can ensure a managerial job at IBM, partnership in a Wall Street firm, a home in Westchester or a slot at Harvard College, whereas in the past little resistance by the "old" black middle class was required to service the black community, live in the Gold Coast of Washington, D.C. or send the kid to Howard, Fisk or Morehouse. The roots of the "new" black middle class are in political struggle, in SCLC, SNCC, CORE, in the values and sensibilities these groups generated.

The major challenge of the "new," black, petite bourgeoisie is no longer whether it will take politics seriously (as posed in E. Franklin Frazier's classic *Black Bourgeoisie* in 1957). Rather it is what kind of politics the "new" black middle class will promote in the present national context of austere economic policies, declining state support of black rights and escalating racist violence and the prevailing international context of the crisis of capitalism, the nuclear arms race and anti-imperialist struggles. Like any other petite bourgeoisie, the "new" black middle class will most likely pursue power-seeking life styles, promote black entrepreneurial growth, and perpetuate professional advancement. Yet the rampant racism in American society truncates such lifestyles, growth and advancement. The "new" black middle class can become only a "truncated" petite bourgeoisie in American society, far removed from real ownership and control over the crucial sectors of the economy and with intractable ceilings imposed upon their upward social mobility.

Presently, there are three major political options for this "truncated" black middle class: electoral politics in the bosom of the centrist Democratic Party or conservative Republican Party; social democratic and democratic socialist politics on the margin of the liberal wing of the Democratic Party (for instance, the Democratic Socialists of America) and inside grass-roots, black leftist, nationalist, preparty formations (for instance, the National Black United Front); or orthodox revolutionary politics far removed from both bourgeois American politics and black grassroots groupings. The effects of the second stage of the black freedom movement in the sixties—beneath and between the endless ideological debates about violence versus nonviolence, the viability of black-white coalitions, reform versus revolution—primarily consisted of an oscillation between the first and third options, between vulgar realpolitik and antiquated orthodoxy, bourgeois politics and utopian rhetoric, with no mediating moment, hence little acknowledgment of the historical complexity of the prevailing African American predicament.

The prospects of galvanizing and organizing renewed black resistance are open-ended. The major tasks are repoliticizing the black working poor and underclass, revitalizing progressive black proletarian and petit bourgeois organizations, retooling black organic and traditional intellectuals, and forging meaningful alliances and beneficial fusions with progressive Latino, Asian, Native American and white groups.

Despite the historical limitations of the "new" black petite bourgeoisie, the African American predicament dictates that this group play a crucial role in carrying out these tasks. This is principally because the black middle class—preachers, teachers, lawyers, doctors and politicians—possess the requisite skills and legitimacy in the eyes of the majority of African Americans for the articulation of the needs and interests of African America. This unfortunate but inescapable situation requires that the politicized progressive wing of the black petite bourgeoisie and stable working class incessantly push beyond the self-serving liberalism of major black leaders and raise issues of fundamental concern to the black working poor and underclass. In short, the "new" black middle class must not be prematurely abandoned or denigrated. Rather, black progressives must keep persistent pressure on, and radical fire under, their liberal reformism until more effective political mobilization and organization emerge among the black working poor and underclass.

The repoliticizing of the black working poor and underclass should focus primarily on the black cultural apparatus, especially the ideological form and content of black popular music. African American life is permeated by black popular music. Since black musicians play such an important role in African American life, they have a special mission and responsibility: to present beautiful music which both sustains and motivates black people and provides visions of what black people should aspire to. Despite the richness of the black musical tradition and the vitality of black contemporary music, most black musicians fall far short of this crucial mission and responsibility. There are exceptions—Gil Scott-Heron, Brian

Jackson, Stevie Wonder, Kenneth Gamble and Leon Huff—but more political black popular music is needed. Jamaican reggae music and Nigeria's Fela Anikulapo Kuti can serve as inspiring models in this regard. The radical politicization of black popular music, as best seen in Grandmaster Flash and the Furious Five's "The Message" and "New York, New York" (despite their virulent sexism) in the early years of rap is a necessary, though not sufficient, condition for the repoliticization of the black working poor and underclass. Black activists must make black musicians accountable in some way to the urgent needs and interests of the black community.

The major prerequisite for renewed organizational black resistance is the political revitalization of existing black groups—fraternities, sororities, lodges, trade unions and, especially, black churches. Without black religious participation, there can be no widespread black resistance. The prophetic wing of the black church has always been at the center of the black freedom movement. Without a strong organizational base with deep organic connections in the black community, there can be no effective renewed black resistance. Only the political revitalization of black prophetic churches can provide this broad organizational base—as Rev. Herbert Daughtry's African Peoples' Christian Organization and other such groups are attempting to do.

The role of black intellectuals—organic ones closely affiliated with the everyday operations of black organizations or traditional ones nesting in comfortable places geared toward theoretical and historical analyses, social visions and practical conclusions—is crucial for renewed black resistance. Without vision, the black freedom movement is devoid of hope. Without analysis, it lacks direction. Without protracted struggle, it ossifies. Yet the vision must be guided by profound, not provincial, conceptions of what it is to be a human being, an African human being in predominantly white, postindustrial, capitalist America, and of how human potential can be best realized in an overcoming of existing economic exploitation, racial and sexual oppression. Likewise, the analysis must be informed by the most sophisticated and cultivated, not self-serving and cathartic, tools available in order to grasp the complexity and specificity of the prevailing African American predicament on the local, regional, national and international levels. Last, the political praxis, though motivated by social vision and guided by keen analysis, must be grounded in moral convictions. Personal integrity is as important as correct analysis or desirable vision. It should be noted that while black intellectuals deserve no special privilege and treatment in the black freedom movement, the services they provide should be respected and encouraged.

It should be obvious that African Americans cannot fundamentally transform capitalist, patriarchal, racist America by themselves. If renewed black resistance is to achieve its aim, alliances and coalitions with other progressive peoples are inescapable. Without such alliances and coalitions, African Americans are doomed to unfreedom. Yet, the more consolidated the black resistance, the better the chance for meaningful and effective alliances and coalitions with others. Of course, each alliance and coalition must be made in light of the specific circumstances and the particular contexts. The important point here is that any serious form of black resistance must be open to such alliances and coalitions with progressive Latino, Asian, Native American and white peoples.

In conclusion, the legacy of the black freedom movement in the sixties still haunts us. In its positive form, it flows through our veins as blood to be spilt if necessary for the cause of human freedom, and in the visions, analyses and practices that build on, yet go beyond, those in the sixties. In its negative form, it reminds us of the tenuous status of the "new" black petite bourgeoisie—its progressive potential and its self-serving interests, its capacity to transcend its parochial past and its present white subordination. The challenge of the black freedom movement in the late twentieth century is neither a discovery of another Rev. Martin Luther King, Jr.—though it would not hurt—nor a leap of faith in a messianic black working class or underclass—though the role of both is crucial. Rather the challenge is a fusing and transforming of indigenous forms of American radicalism—of which black resistance is a central expression—into a major movement which promotes workers' self-management, cultural heterogeneity (including nonracist and non-sexist ways of life) and individual liberties.

FURTHER READING

Boxill, Bernard R. 1972. "The Morality of Reparations." *Social Theory and Practice* 11.2, 113–22.

Carmichael, Stokely, and Charles V. Hamilton. 1967. *Black Power: The Politics of Liberation in America.* New York: Random House.

Cruse, Harold. 1968. *Rebellion or Revolution.* New York: William Morrow.

Davis, Angela, Ruchell Magee, the Soledad Brothers, and Other Political Prisoners. 1971. *If They Come in the Morning: Voices of Resistance.* New York: New American Library.

Foner, Philip S., ed. 1970. *The Black Panthers Speak.* New York: Lippincott.

Forman, James. 1969. "Black Manifesto." In Arnold Schuchter. 1970. *Reparations: The Black Manifesto and Its Challenge to White America.* Philadelphia: J. B. Lippincott, pp. 191–202.

Gooding-Williams, Robert, ed. 1993. *Reading Rodney King Reading Urban Uprising.* New York: Routledge.

Jackson, George. 1970. *The Prison Letters of George Jackson.* New York: Random House.

Jackson, George. 1972. *Blood in My Eye.* New York: Random House.

Jones, Charles, ed. 1998. *The Black Panther Party Reconsidered.* Baltimore: Black Classic Press.

Manning, Marable. 1984. *Race, Reform and Rebellion.* Jackson: University Press of Mississippi.

Newton, Huey P. 1972. *To Die for the People.* New York: Writers and Readers Publishing, 1995, reprint.

Newton, Huey P. 1973. *Revolutionary Suicide.* New York: Writers and Readers Publishing, 1995, reprint.

Newton, Huey P. 1996. *War against the Panthers: A Study of Repression in America.* New York: Harlem River Press.

Scott, Joseph W. 1976. *The Black Revolts: Racial Stratification in the U.S.A.* Cambridge, MA: Schenkman Publishing.

Wagstaff, Thomas, ed. 1969. *Black Power.* Beverly Hills, CA: Glencoe Press.

CHAPTER 8

Social Activism Reconsidered

By the early 1980s the presidency of Ronald Reagan had ushered in an era of conservative social policy toward African-Americans that was supported by an outspoken group of black conservatives. Thomas Sowell, a Hoover Institute Fellow at Stanford, and Glenn Loury, a Fellow at the Kennedy School of Government at Harvard, were prominent voices among this group. The neoconservative critique of the civil rights agenda, to which their essays are devoted, has been a source of great confusion. This is due in large part to the fact that affirmative action policy, a touchstone issue, has been opposed by liberals and conservatives. As a legal remedy to a social problem, affirmative action is rejected by conservatives such as Sowell as inconsistent with principles of free-market capitalism. Sowell's libertarian perspective is not, however, the frame of reference for Shelby Steele's anxiety regarding affirmative action programs. Steele's concern regarding the impact of preferential treatment on the self-esteem of African-Americans is widely shared in black middle-class and liberal quarters. The perception of affirmative action programs as preferential treatment is an important factor influencing the adjustment of mainstream America and African-Americans as social equals. In the aftermath of an era of protest, public policy debates reflecting this concern were dominated by a conservative economic philosophy of self-help and private sector development.

To a large extent the role corporations played in promoting the liberal agenda of the nonviolent protesters has been overshadowed by the success of the civil rights movement in the judicial and legislative arenas. In "The 'Black Revolution' and the Reconstitution of Domination," Adolph Reed draws attention to the relation of the liberal social agenda of corporations and civil rights protest. While Reed is not claiming that the corporate leaders orchestrated the civil rights movement, he is claiming "that certain elements within the civil rights movement were sufficiently compatible with the social agenda of corporate elites to prompt the latter to acquiesce to and encourage them." Reed's point is that there was an important overlap of corporate interests with the goals of the civil rights movement. The reconstruction of the South would meet both interests.

The success of the campaign for voting rights and desegregation in the South did little to assuage the dissatisfaction of radicals in the civil rights movement who believed these measures were insufficient to bring about social equality. Reed charges these radicals with "a failure to develop a systematic critique of the alliance of civil rights ideology with corporate liberalism." According to Reed, the support of the corporate liberals permitted the moral egalitarian argument of the civil rights movement to fit with the goals of monopoly capitalism.

Reed cites the black power movement of the early seventies to illustrate this relationship of corporate interest and the goals of the movement. Black power was a call for indigenous control of political and economic institutions in the black community. In specific cases this meant that the administration of institutions serving the black community should have representation from the community. Reed points out that a black elite was quickly empowered by responsive corporate-state authorities. He remarks that when "community control" became "black control," President Richard Nixon's idea of "blackonomics" replaced rebellion. Reed gleans several lessons from the black power movement. The black power agenda, which equated black empowerment with black representation, allowed a black elite leverage to gain entry into mainstream political institutions but never offered anything close to popular democratization. The threat of more uprisings further rationalized a need for this elite. Indeed, the black power radicalism was itself a statement of the black elite's agenda and became "a device through which the containment of the black population was mediated."

Reed questions the employment of the term "black community" by nationalists to refer to some frozen set of "artifacts and idiosyncracies" that are used to construct "a totalizing ahistorical rhetoric of authenticity." In the black power movement this "mystification" of the black community concealed the privileged relation of the black elite to the corporate program of social reconstruction. He rejects this notion of "black culture" as a construction that became a means of legitimating the political hegemony of a black elite. Even worse, the black power movement's emphasis on "black unity" restricted the development of a black public sphere that would promote open debate on the relation of corporate interests and the interests of the black community. Reed claims that by 1974, mediated by a black political elite, corporate hegemony was total and the argument against racial discrimination in employment and education was resolved by state-sponsored democratization of access.

Thomas Sowell presents a different line of criticism of the civil rights movement. He discusses the extent to which the civil rights legislation has changed the concept of constitutional law and the role of the courts. According to Sowell, 70 percent of the American population is entitled to preferential treatment under "affirmative action" as a result of a general expansion of the principles of morality derived from the unique history of discrimination against African-Americans. Sowell questions a central premise of the civil rights argument, namely, that statistical disparities in incomes, occupations, education, and housing represent moral inequities caused by society. He insists that policies and practices of differential treatment aimed to rectify such disparities foster a belief in innate inferiority.

Sowell compares several cases of ethnic minorities who have a history of legal discrimination with the situation of African-Americans. He cites the economic success of the Chinese in Southeast Asia, Jews in England, and Italians in America to criticize the argument for affirmative action based on statistical disparities. According to Sowell the lesson to be derived from their success is that they all have studiously avoided politics in favor of economic success. He recommends against black leaders appealing to politics as a means to raise African-Americans living in poverty to greater affluence.

Glenn Loury also believes not all problems of African-Americans are due to discrimination and that it is a mistake to think some of these problems can be remedied through civil rights strategies involving racial politics. Like Sowell, Loury accuses civil rights leaders of using socioeconomic disparities to ground a charge of racial discrimination and then seeking to remedy the disparity through the courts and administrative agencies. Loury employs the example of low marriage rate among black women and white men to illustrate the misuse of statistical disparities based on race. He maintains that whatever discrimination occurred to produce this result should remain beyond the reach of law even though it is a racial inequality of opportunity with substantial costs to black women. With voluntary associations in mind, Loury distinguishes a restricted domain of personal interaction as beyond the scope of civil rights legislation.

Loury attributes the lagging economic condition of blacks to "the nature of social life with poor black communities." He cites out of wedlock parenting, crime, dropout rates, and public assistance dependency as problems that have taken on a life of their own apart from any experience of racial oppression. These problems cannot be remedied by policies advocated by civil rights leaders. He warns of greater harm resulting from redefining the problem of low SAT scores in terms of racial discrimination, for this move will destroy the educational climate of colleges. Loury rejects the idea that the low performance of black students is due to racial discrimination. He criticizes affirmative action programs for contributing to "uncertain perceptions" regarding the qualifications of minorities who benefit from them. From the standpoint of minorities this involves an issue of respect and dignity affecting one's relation with one's peers. Worse still, for Loury, affirmative action programs encourage the perpetuation of racial criteria by employers.

Shelby Steele reflects on the legacy of the civil rights movement to expore the impact of race conscious social policy on contemporary race relations in America. Like Sowell and Loury, he is concerned about the placing of too much blame for the situation of black people on society. This is not to deny that racial discrimination still exists. Steele insists that just as other oppressed groups such as Jews, West Indians, and Asians have achieved, African-Americans cannot, as victims of racial discrimination, remain "helpless" before the problems they face. Steele distinguishes the project of eliminating racial discrimination from the project of racial development. He insists that collective action is not the remedy for problems related to the development of African-Americans. His remark that, "only the individual can achieve in school" captures his point that opportunities for development must be exploited by individuals. He claims that, just as in the case of other successful minorities, racial development requires the group to assign responsibility for development to the individual. Enemy-memory inhibits group advancement by undermining the drive to achieve on equal terms.

The "Black Revolution" and the Reconstitution of Domination

Adolph Reed, Jr.

More than forty years ago Benjamin pointed out that "mass reproduction is aided especially by the reproduction of masses."[1] This statement captures the central cultural dynamic of "late" capitalism. The triumph of the commodity form over every sphere of social existence has been made possible by a profound homogenization of work, play, aspirations, and self-definition among subject populations—a condition Marcuse has characterized as one-dimensionality.[2] Ironically, while U.S. radicals in the late 1960s fantasized about a "new man" in the abstract, capital was in the process of concretely putting the finishing touches on *its new individual.* Beneath the current black-female-student-chicano-homosexual-old-young-handicapped, ad nauseam, "struggles" lies a simple truth: there is no coherent opposition to the present administrative apparatus, at least not from the left.

Certainly, repression contributed significantly to the extermination of opposition, and there is a long record of systematic corporate and state terror, from the Palmer Raids to the FBI campaign against the Black Panthers. Likewise, cooptation of individuals and programs has blunted opposition to bourgeois hegemony throughout this century, and cooptative mechanisms have become inextricable parts of strategies of containment. However, repression and cooptation can never fully explain the failure of opposi-

tion, and an exclusive focus on such external factors diverts attention from possible sources of failure within the opposition, thus paving the way for reproduction of the pattern of failure. The opposition must investigate its own complicity if it is to become a credible alternative.

During the 1960s theoretical reflexiveness was difficult because of the intensity of activism. When sharply drawn political issues demanded unambiguous responses, reflection on unintended consequences seemed treasonous. Years later, coming to terms with what happened during that period is blocked by nostalgic glorification of fallen heroes and by a surrender which Gross describes as the "ironic frame-of-mind."[3] Irony and nostalgia are two sides of the coin of resignation, the product of a cynical inwardness that makes retrospective critique seem tiresome or uncomfortable.[4]

At any rate, things have not moved in an emancipatory direction despite all claims that the protest of the 1960s has extended equalitarian democracy. In general, opportunities to determine one's destiny are no greater for most people now than before, and, more importantly, the critique of life-as-it-is has disappeared as a practical activity; i.e., an ethical and political commitment to emancipation seems no longer legitimate, reasonable, or valid. The amnestic principle which imprisons the social past also subverts any hope, which ends up seeking refuge in the predominant forms of alienation.

This is also true in the black community. Black opposition has dissolved into celebration and wish fulfillment. Today's political criticism within the black community—both Marxist-Leninist and nationalist—lacks a base

Source: Adolph Reed, Jr., "The 'Black Revolution' and the Reconstitution of Domination" in Adolph Reed, Jr., ed., *Race, Politics, and Culture: Critical Essays on the Radicalism of the 1960s* (New York: Greenwood Press, 1986), 61–95. Reprinted with the permission of Greenwood Publishing Group, Inc., Westport, CT.

and is unlikely to attract substantial constituencies. This complete collapse of political opposition among blacks, however, is anomalous. From the 1955 Montgomery bus boycott to the 1972 African Liberation Day demonstration, there was almost constant political motion among blacks. Since the early 1970s there has been a thorough pacification; or these antagonisms have been so depoliticized that they surface only in alienated forms. Moreover, few attempts have been made to explain the atrophy of opposition within the black community.[5] Theoretical reflexiveness is as rare behind Du Bois's veil as on the other side!

This critical failing is especially regrettable because black radical protests and the system's adjustments to them have served as catalysts in universalizing one-dimensionality and in moving into a new era of monopoly capitalism. In this new era, which Piccone has called the age of "artificial negativity," traditional forms of opposition have been undermined by a new pattern of social management.[6] Now, the social order legitimates itself by integrating potentially antagonistic forces into a logic of centralized administration. Once integrated, these forces regulate domination and prevent disruptive excess. Furthermore, when these internal regulatory mechanisms do not exist, the system must create them. To the extent that the black community has been pivotal in this new mode of administered domination, reconstruction of the trajectory of 1960s black activism can throw light on the current situation and the paradoxes it generates.

A common interpretation of the demise of black militance suggests that the waning of radical political activity is a result of the satisfaction of black aspirations. This satisfaction allegedly consists in: 1) extension of the social welfare apparatus; 2) elimination of legally sanctioned racial barriers to social mobility, which in turn has allowed for 3) expansion of possibilities open to blacks within the existing social system; all of which have precipitated 4) a redefinition of "appropriate" black political strategy in line with these achievements.[7] This new strategy is grounded in a pluralist orientation that construes political issues solely in terms of competition over distribution of goods and services within the bounds of fixed system priorities. These four items constitute the "gains of the 1960s."[8] Intrinsic to this interpretation is the thesis that black political activity during the 1960s became radical because blacks had been excluded from society and politics and were therefore unable effectively to solve group problems through the "normal" political process. Extraordinary actions were thus required to pave the way for regular participation.

This interpretation is not entirely untenable. With passage of the 1964 and 1965 legislation the program of the Civil Rights movement appeared to have been fulfilled. Soon, however, it became clear that the ideals of freedom and dignity had not been realized, and within a year, those ideals reasserted themselves in the demand for Black Power. A social program was elaborated, but again its underpinning ideals were not realized. The dilemma lay in translating abstract deals into concrete political goals, and it is here also that the "gains of the sixties" interpretation founders. It equates the ideals with the objectives of the programs in question.

To be sure, racial segregation has been eliminated in the South, thus removing a tremendous oppression from black life. Yet, dismantlement of the system of racial segregation only removed a fetter blocking the possibility of emancipation. In this context, computation of the "gains of the sixties" can begin only at the point where that extraordinary subjugation was eliminated. What, then, are those "gains" which followed the passage of civil rights legislation and how have they affected black life?

In 1964, the last year before the Vietnam boom (which in addition to other ways reduced black unemployment through military service) black unemployment averaged 9.6 percent; the 1971 average was 9.9 percent.[9] Moreover, among the most vulnerable groups—women and youth—unemployment rates in business cycle periods not only were not reduced in the 1960s but by 1975 were nearly twice higher than in 1957.[10] Black median income did not improve significantly in relation to white family income in the decade after passage of civil rights legislation,[11] and between 1970 and 1974 black purchasing power actually declined.[12] Moreover, blacks were still far more likely to live in inadequate housing than whites, and black male life expectancy declined, both absolutely and relative to whites between 1959 and 1961 and 1974.[13] Therefore, if the disappearance of black opposition is linked directly with the satisfaction of aspirations, the criteria of fulfillment cannot be drawn from the general level of material existence in the black community. The same can be said for categories such as "access to political decision-making." Although the number of blacks elected or appointed to public office has risen by leaps and bounds since the middle 1960s, that increase has not demonstrably improved life in the black community.

The problem is one of focus. The "gains of the sixties" thesis seems to hold only as long as the status of the "black community" is equated with that of certain specific strata. Although black life *as a whole* has not improved considerably beyond the elimination of racial segregation, in the 1970s certain strata within the black community actually have benefited. This development is a direct outcome of the 1960s activism: of the interplay of the "movement" and the integrative logic of administrative capitalism; and the "gains of the sixties" interpretation cannot spell out what "satisfaction" is because it is itself the ideology of precisely those strata which have benefited from the events of the 1960s within the black community. These "leadership" strata tend to generalize their own interests since their legitimacy and integrity are tied to a monolithic conceptualization of black life. Indeed, this conceptualization appeared in the unitarian mythology of late 1960s black nationalism. The representation of the black community as a collective subject neatly concealed the system of hierarchy which mediated the relation of the "leaders" and the "led."[14]

To analyze the genesis of the new elite is to analyze simultaneously the development of the new styles of domination in American society in general. Consequently, the following will focus on sources of the pacification of the 1970s and will expose the limitations of any oppositionist activity which proceeds uncritically from models of mass-organization politics which tend to capitulate to the predominant logic of domination.

Black resistance to oppression hardly began in Montgomery, Alabama, in 1955. Yet, it was only then that opposition to racial subjugation assumed the form of a mass movement. Why was this so? Despite many allusions to the impact of decolonization in Africa, international experiences of blacks in World War II, and so on, the reasons that black activism exploded in the late 1950s have seldom been addressed systematically.[15] Although resistance before 1955 was undoubtedly reinforced by the anticolonial movements abroad, what was significant for post-1955 growth of civil rights activity were those forces reshaping the entire American social order. An historically thorough perspective on the development of black opposition requires an understanding of the Cold War era in which it took shape.

Although popularity symbolized by "brinksmanship," "domino theory," fallout shelters, and the atmosphere of terror characterized by McCarthy, HUAC, and legions of meticulously anticommunist liberals, the Cold War was a much broader cultural phenomenon. Ultimately, it was a period of consolidation of the new mode of domination which had been developing for more than two decades. Piccone has noted that the Cold War era was the culmination of a dynamic of political and cultural adjustment to a dynamic of concentration that had attained hegemony over the American economy by the 1920s.[16] On the political front, the New Deal redefined the role of the state apparatus in terms of an aggressive, countercyclical intervention in the economy and everyday reality. At the same time, mass production required intensification of consumption. This requirement was met by the development and expansion of a manipulative culture industry and by the proliferation of an ideology of consumerism through mass communications and entertainment media.[17] Consumerism and the New Deal led to an intensification of the Taylorization of labor, which increasingly homogenized American life according to the dictates of bureaucratic-instrumental rationality. By the 1950s, Americanization had been institutionalized. Rigid political, intellectual, and cultural conformism (Riesman's "other directedness") evidenced a social integration achieved through introjection and reproduction of the imperatives of the system of domination at the level of everyday life.[18]

Pressures toward homogenization exerted for decades at work, in schools, and through the culture industry had seriously reformulated cultural particularity among ethnic groups. What remained were residues of the lost cultures—empty mannerisms and ambivalent ethnic identities mobilizable for Democratic electoral politics.[19] Moreover, the pluralist model was available for integrating the already depoliticized labor movement. In this context, the ruthless elimination of whatever opposition remained through the witchhunts was only the coup de grace in a battle already won.

For various reasons, throughout this period, one region was bypassed in the monopolistic reorganization of American life and remained unintegrated into the new social order. At the end of World War II, the South remained the only internal frontier available for large-scale capital penetration. However, even though the South could entice industry with a docile work force accustomed to low wages, full domestication of this region required certain basic adjustments.

For one thing, the castelike organization of southern society seriously inhibited development of a rational labor supply. While much has been made of the utility of the segregated work force as a depressant of general wage levels, maintenance of dual labor markets creates a barrier to labor recruitment.[20] As a pariah caste, blacks could not adequately become an industrial reserve army since they were kept out of certain jobs. Consequently, in periods of rapid expansion the suppressed black labor pool could not be fully used, nor could blacks be mobilized as a potential

strike-breaking force as readily as in other regions since employment of blacks in traditionally "white" jobs could trigger widespread disruptions.

The dual labor system was irreconcilable with the principle of reducing *all* labor to "abstract labor."[21] Scientific management has sought to reduce work processes to homogeneous and interchangeable hand and eye motions, hoping eventually to eliminate specialized labor.[22] A work force stratified on the basis of an economically irrational criterion such as race constitutes a serious impediment to realization of the ideal of a labor pool comprised of equivalent units. (Consider further the wastefulness of having to provide two sets of toilets in the plants!) In addition, the existing system of black subjugation, grounded in brutality, was intrinsically unstable. The racial order which demanded for its maintenance constant terror raised at every instant the possibility of rebellion and to that extent endangered "rational" administration. Given this state of affairs, the corporate elite's support for an antisegregationist initiative makes sense.

The relation of the corporate liberal social agenda to civil rights protest, though, is not a causal one. True, the Supreme Court had been chipping away at legal segregation for nearly twenty years, and the 1954 Brown decision finally provided the spark for intensified black protest. Yet the eruption of resistance from southern blacks had its own roots. Hence, to claim that the Civil Rights movement was a bourgeois conspiracy would be to succumb to the order's myth of its own omnipotence. Thus, the important question is not whether sectors of the corporate elite orchestrated the Civil Rights movement, but instead what elements within the Civil Rights movement were sufficiently compatible with the social agenda of corporate elites to prompt the latter to acquiesce to and encourage them. In order to answer this, it is necessary to identify both the social forces operative *within* the black community during segregation and those forces' engagement in civil rights activism. An analysis of the internal dynamic of the 1960s activism shows overlaps between the goals of the "New Deal Offensive" and the objectives of the "movement" (and, by extension, the black community).[23]

For the purposes of this analysis, the most salient aspects of the black community in the segregated South lie within a management dimension. Externally, the black population was managed by means of codified subordination, reinforced by customary dehumanization and the omnipresent spectre of terror. The abominable details of this system are well known.[24] Furthermore, blacks were excluded systematically from formal participation in public life. By extracting tax revenues without returning public services or allowing blacks to participate in public policy formation, the local political system intensified the normal exploitation in the work place. Public administration of the black community was carried out by whites. The daily indignity of the apartheidlike social organization was both a product of this political-administrative disenfranchisement as well as a motor of its reproduction. Thus, the abstract ideal of freedom spawned within the Civil Rights movement took concrete form primarily in opposition to this relation.

Despite the black population's alienation from public policymaking, an internal stratum existed which performed notable, but limited, social management functions. This elite stratum was comprised mainly of low-level state functionaries, merchants and "professionals" servicing black markets, and the clergy. While it failed to escape the general subordination, this indigenous elite succeeded, by virtue of its comparatively secure living standard and informal relations with significant whites, in avoiding the extremes of racial oppression. The importance of this stratum was that it stabilized and coordinated the adjustment of the black population to social policy imperatives formulated outside the black community.

Insofar as black public functionaries had assimilated bureaucratic rationality, the domination of fellow blacks was carried out in "doing one's job." For parts of the black elite such as the clergy, the ministerial practice of "easing community tensions" has always meant accommodation of black life to the existing forms of domination. Similarly, the independent merchants and professionals owed their relatively comfortable position within the black community to the special captive markets created by segregation. Moreover, in the role of "responsible Negro spokesmen," this sector was able to elicit considerable politesse, if not solicitousness, from "enlightened" members of the white elite. Interracial "cooperation" on policy matters was thus smoothly accomplished, and the "public interest" seemed to be met simply because opposition to white ruling group initiatives had been effectively neutralized.

The activating factor in this management relation was a notion of "Negro leadership" (later "black" or even "Black") that was generated outside the black community. A bitter observation made from time to time by the radical fringe of the movement was that the social category "leaders" seemed to apply only to the black community. No "white leaders" were assumed to represent a singular white population; but certain blacks were declared opinion-makers and carriers of the interests of an anonymous black population. These "leaders" legitimated their role through their ability to win occasional favors from powerful whites and through the status positions they already occupied in the black community.[25]

This mode of domination could not thoroughly pacify black life; only the transformation of the segregated order could begin to do that. Furthermore, the internal management strategy generated centrifugal pressures of its own. In addition to segregation, three other disruptive elements stand out within the black population in the 1950s. First, the United States' emergence from World War II as the major world power projected American culture onto an international scene. Thus, the anticolonial movements that grew in Africa and Asia amid the crumbling French and British colonial empires had a significant impact on black resistance in this country.[26] Second, the logic of one-dimensionality itself became a disruptive element. The homogenizing egalitarianism of the "New Deal" generated a sense of righteousness able to sustain a lengthy battle with southern segregation. The challenge to racial domination was justified in terms of the "American Dream" and an ideal of freedom expressed in a demand for full citizenship.[27] Thus, the same forces that since the 1880s had sought to integrate the various immigrant populations also generated an American national consciousness among blacks.

By the 1950s a sense of participation in a national society had taken root even in the South, fertilized by the mass culture industry (including black publications), schools, and a defensive Cold War ideology. In the face of this growing national consciousness "separate but equal" existence was utterly intolerable to blacks. This is not to say that a perception rooted in the nation-state was universal among southern blacks in the 1950s, especially since the chief mechanisms of cultural adjustment such as television, popular films, compulsory schooling, etc., had not fully invaded the black community. Yet, mass culture and its corollary ideologies had extensively penetrated the private sphere of the black elite: the stratum from which systematic opposition arose.[28]

Third, given the racial barrier, social mobility for the black elite was limited, relative to its white counterpart. Because of de facto proscription of black tenure in most professions, few possibilities existed for advancement. At the same time, the number of people seeking to become members of the elite had increased beyond what a segregated society could accommodate as a result of population growth and rising college attendance.[29] In addition, upward mobility was being defined by the larger national culture in a way that further weakened the capability of the black elite to integrate its youth. Where ideology demanded nuclear physics and corporate management, black upward mobility rested with mortuary service and the Elks Lodge! This disjunction between ideals and possibilities delegitimized the elite's claim to brokerage and spokesmanship. With its role in question, the entrenched black elite was no longer able effectively to perform its internal management function and lost authority with its "re-

cruits" and the black community in general. As a result, a social space was cleared within which dissatisfaction with segregation could thrive as systematic opposition.

From this social management perspective, sources of the "Freedom Movement" are identifiable within and on the periphery of its indigenous elite stratum. As soon as black opposition spilled beyond the boundaries of the black community, however, the internal management perspective became inadequate to understand further developments in the Civil Rights movement. When opposition to segregation became political rebellion, black protest required a response from white ruling elites. That response reflected congruence of the interests of blacks and corporate elites in reconstructing southern society and helped define the logic of subsequent black political activity. Both sets of interests might be met by rationalizing race relations in the South. The Civil Rights movement brought the two sets together.[30]

The alliance of corporate liberalism and black protest was evident in the aggressive endorsement of civil rights activity that was mobilized by the New Deal coalition. Major labor organizations and "enlightened" corporate elements immediately climbed aboard the freedom train through the "progressive" wing of the Democratic party and private foundations. Moreover, it was through its coverage of black resistance in the South that television developed and refined its remarkable capabilities for creating public opinion by means of "objective" news reportage (a talent that reached its acme years later with the expulsion of Richard Nixon from the presidency). However, television was not alone on the cultural front of the ideological struggle. *Life*, *Look*, the *Saturday Evening Post*, major nonsouthern newspapers, and other national publications featured an abundance of photoessays that emphasized the degradation and brutalization of black life under Jim Crow.

Even popular cinema sought to thematize black life in line with civil rights consciousness in films such as *The Defiant Ones* (1958), *All the Young Men* (1960), *Raisin in the Sun* (1961), *Band of Angels* (1957), and the instructively titled *Nothing but a Man* (1964). Those and other films were marked by an effort to portray blacks with a measure of human depth and complexity previously absent from Hollywood productions. By 1957 even the great taboo of miscegenation could be portrayed on the screen in *Island in the Sun,* and a decade later the cultural campaign had been so successful that this theme could be explored in the parlor rather than in back streets and resolved with a happy ending in *Guess Who's Coming to Dinner.* It is interesting that Dorothy Dandridge became the first black in a leading role to be nominated for an academy award for her role in *Carmen Jones* in 1954—the year of the Brown decision—and that the most productive periods of civil rights activism and Sidney Poitier's film career coincided. Poitier's lead performance in the maudlin *Lilies of the Field* won an Oscar for him in 1963, on the eve of the passage of the Public Accommodations Act! Thus endorsed by the culture industry (which affronted White Supremacy in the late 1950s by broadcasting a Perry Como show in which comedienne Molly Goldberg kissed black ballplayer Ernie Banks), the Civil Rights movement was virtually assured success.

While the civil rights coalition was made possible by the compatibility of the allies' interests in reorganizing the South, its success was facilitated by the ideals and ideologies generated in the protest. Even though there had been ties between black southern elites and corporate-liberal elements for a long time, if the civil rights program had raised fundamental questions regarding social structure, the corporate-elite response may have been suppression rather than support—especially given the Cold War context. Instead, from the very beginning the American establishment outside of Dixie supported the abolition of segregation.[31] At any rate, it is clear that the civil rights ideology fit very well with the goals of monopoly capitalism. The Civil Rights movement appealed to egalitarianism and social rationality. On both counts segregation was found wanting while nonracial features of the social order were left unquestioned.

The egalitarian argument was moral as well as constitutional. The moral argument was in the bourgeois tradition from the Reformation to the French Revolution. It claimed equal rights for all human beings as well as entitlement to equal life chances. This abstract and ahistorical moral imperative did not address the structural or systematic character of social relations and therefore could only denounce racial exclusion as an evil anomaly. The predominant form of social organization was accepted uncritically, and the moral imperative was predictably construed in terms of American constitutional law. Extension to blacks of equality before the law and equality of opportunity to participate in all areas of citizenship were projected as adequate to fulfill the promise of democracy in the backward South.

Coexisting with this egalitarian ideology was the Civil Rights movement's appeal to a functionalist conception of social rationality. To the extent that it blocked individual aspirations, segregation was seen as restricting social growth and progress artificially. Similary, by raising artificial barriers such as the constriction of blacks' consumer power through Jim Crow legislation and, indirectly, through low black wages, segregation impeded, so the argument went, the free functioning of the market. Consequently, segregation was seen not only as detrimental to blacks who suffered under it, but also to economic progress as such. Needless to say, the two lines of argument were met with approval by corporate liberals.[32]

It is apparent now that the egalitarian ideology coincided with corporate-liberalism's cultural program of homogenization. Civil rights' egalitarianism demanded that any one unit of labor be equivalent to any other, and that the Negro be thought of as "any other American." There is more than a little irony that the Civil Rights movement demanded for blacks the same "eradication of otherness" that had been forced upon immigrant populations. The demand hardly went unheard; through the blanket concept "integration" and the alliance with a corporate elite that was all too ready to help clarify issues and refine strategies and objectives, the abstract ideals of civil rights activism were concretized in a corporate elite plan for pacification and reorganization.

The elimination of segregation in the South altered the specificity of both the South as a region and blacks as a group, and the rationality in whose name the movement had appealed paved the way for reconstruction of new modes of domination of black life. The movement had begun as a result of frustrations within the black elite, and it ended with the achievement of autonomy and mobility among those elements. Public Accommodations and Voting Rights legislation officially defined new terms for the management of blacks and an expanded managerial role for the elite.

Although the Civil Rights movement did have a radical faction, that wing failed to develop a systematic critique of civil rights ideology or the alliance with corporate liberalism. Moreover, the radicals—mainly within the SNCC—never fully repudiated the leadership ideology which reinforced the movement's character as an elite brokerage relation with powerful whites outside the South. Thus, the radicals helped isolate their own position by acquiescing to a conception of the black community as a passive recipient of political symbols and directives. When the dust settled, the black "mainstream" elements and their corporate allies—who together monopolized the symbols of legitimacy—proclaimed that freedom had been achieved, and the handful of radicals could only feel uneasy that voting rights and "social equality" were somehow insufficient.[33]

Outside the South, rebellion arose from different conditions. Racial segregation was not rigidly codified, and the management subsystems in the black community were correspondingly more fluidly integrated within the local administrative apparatus. Yet, structural, generational, and ideological pressures, broadly similar to those in the South, existed within the black elite in the northern, western, and midwestern cities that had gained large black populations in the first half of the twentieth century. In nonsegregated urban contexts, formal political participation and democratized consumption had long since been achieved; there the salient political issue was the extension of the administrative purview of the elite within the black community. The centrality of the administrative nexus in the "revolt of the cities" is evident from the ideological programs it generated.[34]

Black Power came about as a call for indigenous control of economic and political institutions in the black community.[35] Because one of the early slogans of Black Power was a vague demand for "community control," the emancipatory character of the rebellion was open to considerably varied misinterpretation. Moreover, the diversity and "militance" of its rhetoric encouraged extravagance in assessing the movement's depth. It soon became clear, however, that "community control" called not for direction of pertinent institutions—schools, hospitals, police, retail businesses, etc.—by their black constituents, but for the administration of those institutions by alleged representatives in the name of a black community. Given an existing elite structure whose legitimacy had already been certified by federal social-welfare agencies, the selection of "appropriate" representatives was predictable. Indeed, as Robert Allen has shown, the empowerment of this elite was actively assisted by corporate-state elements.[36] Thus, "black liberation" quickly turned into black "equity"; "community control" became simply "black control"; and the Nixon "blackonomics" strategy was readily able to "coopt" the most rebellious tendency of 1960s black activism. Ironically, Black Power's suppression of the civil rights program led to further consolidation of the management elite's hegemony within the black community. The black elite broadened its administrative control by accepting without criticism and instrumentally deploying the inchoate elements of the Black Power agenda to gain leverage in regular political processes. Black control was by no means equivalent to popular democratization.[37]

This state of affairs remained unclear even to Black Power's radical fringe. Such a failure of political perception cannot be written off as crass opportunism or as underdeveloped consciousness. Though not altogether false, explanations of this kind only beg the question. Indeed, Black Power radicalism, which absorbed most of the floundering left wing of the Civil Rights movement and generated subsequent "nationalist" tendencies, actually blurred the roots of the new wave of rebellion. As civil rights activism exhausted itself and as spontaneous uprisings proliferated among urban blacks, the civil rights radicals sought to generate an ideology capable of unifying and politicizing these uprisings. This effort, however, was based on two mystifications that implicitly rationalized the elite's control of the movement.

First, Black Power presupposed a mass-organizational model built on the assumption of a homogeneity of black political interests embodied in community leadership. It is this notion of "black community" that had blocked development of a radical critique in the Civil Rights movement by contraposing an undifferentiated mass to a leadership stratum representing it. This understanding ruled out analysis of cleavages or particularities within the black population: "community control" and "black control" became synonymous. The implications of this ideology have already been discussed: having internalized the predominant elite-pluralist model of organization of black life, the radical wing could not develop any critical perspective. Internal critique could not go beyond banal symbols of "blackness" and thus ended up by stimulating demand for a new array of "revolutionary" consumer goods. Nothwithstanding all its bombast, Black Power formulated racial politics within the ideological universe through which the containment of the black population was mediated.

Acceptance of this model not only prevented Black Power from transcending the social program of the indigenous administrative elite, but it also indicated the extent to which, as Cruse was aware at the time,[38] Black Power radicalism was itself a frantic statement of the elite's agenda—hence the radicals' chronic ambivalence over "black bourgeoisie," capitalism, socialism, and "black unity." Their mysti-fication of the social structure of the black community was largely the result of a failure to come to terms with their own privileged relation to the corporate elite's program of social reconstruction. This state of affairs precipitated a still more profound mystification that illuminates the other side of Black Power rebellion: the reaction against massification.

The Civil Rights movement's demand for integration was superfluous outside the South, and Black Power was as much a reaction against integrationist ideology as against domination. Yet, while militant black nationalism developed as a reaction to the assimilationist approach of the Civil Rights movement, it envisioned an obsolete, folkish model of black life. This yearning was hypostatized to the level of a vague "black culture"—a romantic retrieval of a vanishing black particularity. This vision of black culture, of course, was grounded in residual features of black rural life prior to migrations to the North. They were primarily cultural patterns that had once been enmeshed in a life world knitted together by kinship, voluntary association, and production within a historical context of rural racial domination. As that life world disintegrated before urbanization and mass culture, black nationalism sought to reconstitute it.[39]

In that sense, the nationalist elaboration of Black Power was naive both in that it was not sufficiently self-conscious and that it mistook artifacts and idiosyncrasies of culture for its totality and froze them into an ahistorical rhetoric of authenticity. Two consequences followed. First, abstracted from its concrete historical context, black culture lost its dynamism and took on the commodity form (e.g., red, black, and green flags; dashikis; Afro-Sheen; "blaxploitation" films; collections of bad poetry). Second, while ostensibly politicizing culture by defining it as an arena for conflict, black nationalism actually depoliticized the movement inasmuch as the reified nationalist framework could relate to the present only through a simplistic politics of unity.[40] Hence, it forfeited hegemony over political programs to the best organized element in the black community: the administrative elite. In this fashion, black culture became a means of legitimation of the elite's political hegemony.

"Black culture" posited a functionalist, perfectly integrated black social order which was then projected backward through history as the Truth of black existence. The "natural" condition of harmony was said to have been disrupted only when divisiveness and conflict were introduced by alien forces. This myth delegitimated internal conflict and hindered critical dialogue within the black community. Correspondingly, the intellectual climate which came to pervade the "movement" was best summarized in the nationalists' exhortation to "think black," a latter-day version of "thinking with one's blood." Thus was the circle completed: the original abstract rationalism that had ignored existing social relations of domination for a mythical, unitarian, social ideal turned into a militant and self-justifying irrationalism. Truth became a function of the speaker's "blackness," i.e., validity claims were to be resolved not through discourse but by the claimant's manipulation of certain banal symbols of legitimacy. The resultant situation greatly favored the well-organized and highly visible elite.[41]

The nationalist program functioned also as a mobilization myth. In defining a collective consciousness, the idealization of folkishness was simultaneously an exhortation to collectivized practice. The folk, in its Afro-American manifestation as well as elsewhere,[42] was an ideological category of mass-organizational politics. The community was to be created and mobilized as a passively homogeneous mass, activated by a leadership elite.

While the politicized notion of black culture was a negative response to the estrangement and anomie experienced in the urban North, as a "solution" it only affirmed the negation of genuine black particularity.[43] The prescription of cohesion in the form of a mass/leadership relation revealed the movement's tacit acceptance of the black management stratum's agenda. The negativity immanent in the cultural myth soon gave way to an opportunistic appeal to unity grounded on an unspecifiable "blackness" and a commodified

idea of "soul." Black unity, elevated to an end in itself, became an ideology promoting consolidation of the management elite's expanded power over the black population. In practice, unity meant collective acceptance of a set of demands to be lobbied by a leadership elite before the corporate-state apparatus. To that extent, "radical" Black Power reproduced on a more elaborate ideological basis the old pluralist brokerage politics. Similarly, this phony unity restricted possibilities for development of a black public sphere.

To be sure, the movement stimulated widespread and lively political debate in the black community. Although it hardly approached an "ideal speech situation," various individuals and constituencies were drawn into political discourse on a considerably more democratized basis than had previously been the case. Yet, the rise of unitarian ideology, coupled with a mystified notion of "expertise," effectively reintroduced hierarchy within the newly expanded political arena.[44] At any rate, "grass roots" politics in the black community can be summarized as follows: the internal management elite claimed primacy in political discourse on the basis of its ability to project and realize a social program and then mobilized the unitarian ideal to delegitimize any divergent positions. On the other hand, the "revolutionary" opposition offered no alternative; within its ranks the ideology of expertise was never repudiated. The radicals had merely replaced the elite's pragmatism with a mandarin version of expertise founded on mastery of the holy texts of Kawaida, Nkrumaism, or "scientific socialism." By the time of the 1972 National Black Political Convention in Gary, the mainstream elite strata were well on the way to becoming the sole effective voice in the black community. By the next convention in 1974 in Little Rock—after the election of a second wave of black officials—their hegemony was total.[45]

By now the reasons for the demise of black opposition in the United States should be clear. The opposition's sources were formulated in terms of the predominant ideology and thereby were readily integrated as an affirmation of the validity of the system as a whole.

The movement "failed" because it "succeeded," and its success can be measured by its impact on the administration of the social system. The protest against racial discrimination in employment and education was answered by the middle 1970s by state-sponsored democratization of access to management and other "professional" occupations. Direct, quantifiable racial discrimination remained a pressing public issue mainly for those whose livelihood depended on finding continuous instances of racial discrimination.[46] Still, equalization of access should not be interpreted simply as a concession; it also rationalized recruitment of intermediate management personnel. In one sense the affirmative action effort can be viewed as a publicly subsidized state and corporate talent search.

Similarly, the protest against external administration of black life was met by an expansion in the scope of the black political-administrative apparatus. Through federal funding requirements of community representation, reapportionment of electoral jurisdictions, support for voter "education," and growth of the social welfare bureaucracy, the black elite was provided with broadened occupational opportunities and with official responsibility for administration of the black population. The rise of black officialdom beginning in the 1970s signals the realization of the reconstructed elite's social program and the consolidation of its hegemony over black life. No longer do preachers, funeral directors, and occasional politicos vie for the right to rationalize an externally generated agenda to the black community. Now, black officials and professional political activists represent, interact among, and legitimate themselves before an attentive public of black functionaries in public and private sectors of the social management apparatus.[47] Even the ideological reproduction of the elite is assured: not only mass-market journalists, but black academicians as well (through black "scholarly" publications, research institutes, and professional organizations) almost invariably sing the praises of the newly empowered elite.[48]

It was in the ideological sphere as well that the third major protest, that against mas-sification of the black community, was resolved. Although authentic Afro-American particularity had been undermined by the standardizing imperatives of mass capitalism, the black nationalist reaction paved the way for the constitution of an artificial particularity.[49] Residual idiomatic and physical traits, bereft of distinctive content, were injected with racial stereotypes and the ordinary petit bourgeois *Weltanschauung* to create the pretext for an apparently unique black existence. A thoroughly ideological construction of black uniqueness—which was projected universally in the mass market as black culture—fulfilled at least three major functions. First, as a marketing device it facilitated the huckstering of innumerable commodities designed to enhance, embellish, simulate, or glorify "blackness."[50] Second, artificial black particularity provided the basis for the myth of genuine black community and consequently legitimated the organization of the black population into an administrative unit—and, therefore, the black elite's claims to primacy. Finally, the otherness-without-negativity provided by the ideologized blackness can be seen as a potential antidote to the new contradictions generated by monopoly capitalism's bureaucratic rationality. By constituting an independently given sector of society responsive to administrative controls, the well-managed but recalcitrant black community justifies the existence of the administrative apparatus and legitimates existing forms of social integration.

In one sense, the decade and a half of black activism was a phenomenon vastly more significant than black activists appreciated, while in another sense it was far less significant than has been claimed.[51] As an emancipatory project for the Afro-American population, the "movement"—especially after the abolishment of segregation—had little impact beyond strengthening the existing elite strata. Yet, as part of a program of advanced capitalist reconstruction, black activism contributed to thawing the Cold War and outlined a model to replace it.

By the latter 1960s the New Deal coalition was no longer able fully to integrate recalcitrant social strata such as the black population.[52] The New Deal coalition initiated the process of social homogenization and depoliticization Marcuse described as one dimensionality. As Piccone observes, however, by the 1960s the transition to monopoly capitalism had been fully carried out, and the whole strategy had become counterproductive.[53] The drive toward homogenization and the total domination of the commodity form had deprived the system of the "otherness" required both to restrain the irrational tendencies of bureaucratic rationality and to locate lingering and potentially disruptive elements. Notwithstanding their vast differences, the ethnic "liberation struggles" and counterculture activism on the one side and the "hard hat" reaction on the other were two sides of the same rejection of homogenization. Not only did these various positions challenge the one-dimensional order, but their very existence betrayed the limitations of the administrative state.

The development of black activism from spontaneous protest through mass mobilization to system support assisted the development of a new mode of domination based on domesticating negativity by organizing spaces in which it could be legitimately expressed. Rather than suppressing opposition, the social management system now cultivates its own. The proliferation of government-generated reference groups in addition to ethnic ones (the old; the young; battered wives; the handicapped; veterans; retarded, abused, and gifted children) and the appearance of legions of "watchdog" agencies, reveal the extent to which the system manufactures and markets its own illusory opposition.[54]

This "artificial negativity" is in part a function of the overwhelming success of the process of massification undertaken since the depression and in part a response to it. Universal fragmentation of consciousness, with the corollary decline in the ability to think critically and the regimentation of an alienated everyday life set the stage for new forms of domination built in the very texture of organization.[55] In mass society, organized activity on a large scale requires hierarchization.

Along with hierarchy, however, a new social management logic also comes into being to 1) protect existing privileges by delivering realizable, if inadequate, payoffs and 2) to legitimate administrative rationality as a valid and efficient model. To the extent that organization strives to ground itself on the mass it is already integrated into the system of domination. The shibboleths which comprise its specific platform make little difference. What is important is that the mass organization reproduces the manipulative hierarchy and values typical of contemporary capitalism.[56]

Equally important for the existence of this social-managerial form is that the traditional modes of opposition to capitalism have not been able successfully to negotiate the transition from entrepreneurial to administrative capitalism. Thus, the left has not fully grasped the recent shifts in the structure of domination and continues to organize resistance along the very lines which reinforce the existing social order. As a consequence, the opposition finds itself perpetually outflanked. Unable to deliver the goods—political or otherwise—the left collapses before the cretinization of its own constituency. Once the mass model is accepted, cretinization soon follows and from that point the opposition loses any genuine negativity. The Civil Rights and Black Power movements prefigured the coming of this new age; the feminist photocopy of the black journey on a road to nowhere was its farcical rerun.

The mass culture industry in this context maintains and reproduces the new synthesis of domination. Here, again, the history of the "black revolution" is instructive. In its most radical stage Black Power lived and spread as a media event. Stokely Carmichael and H. Rap Brown entertained nightly on network news, and after ordinary black "militancy" had lost its dramatic appeal, the Black Panther Party added props and uniforms to make radical politics entirely a show business proposition. Although late 1960s black radicalism offered perhaps the most flamboyant examples of the peculiar relation of the mass media to the would-be opposition, that was only an extreme expression of a pattern at work since the early days of the Civil Rights movement.[57] Since then, political opposition has sought to propagandize its efforts through the mass media. Given the prevailing cretinization and the role of the culture industry in reproducing the fragmented, commodified consciousness, such a strategy, if pursued uncritically, could only reinforce the current modes of domination.[58]

That all forms of political opposition accepted the manipulative, mass-organization model gave the strategy a natural, uncomplicated appearance and prevented the development of a critical approach. The consequence was propagation of a model of politics which reinforced oversimplification, the reduction of ideals to banalized objects of immediate consumption—i.e., the commodity-form—and to an alienated, dehumanized hero cultishness with "revolutionary" replacing either hero or villain. In short, opposition increasingly becomes a spectacle in a society organized around reduction of all existence to a series of spectacles.[59]

So monopoly capitalism has entered a new stage typified by the extension of the administrative apparatus throughout everyday life. In this context, genuine opposition is checkmated a priori by the legitimation and projection of a partial, fragmented criticism which can be enlisted in further streamlining the predominant rationality. In cases where existing bureaucratic structures need control mechanisms to prevent excesses, diffuse uneasiness with predominant institutions ends up artificially channeled into forms of negativity able to fulfill the needed internal control function. Always a problem for opposition which seeks to sustain itself over time, under the new conditions of administered negativity, the one step backward required by organized opposition's need to broaden its constituency and conduct "positional warfare" becomes a one-way slide to affirmation of the social order. The logic of the transition to new forms of bourgeois hegemony requires adjustment of administrative rationality. The unrestrained drive to total integration now is mediated by peripheral, yet systematically controlled, loci of criticism; one-dimensional-

ity itself has been "humanized" by the cultivation of commodified facsimiles of diversity.[60]

An important question remains: what of the possibilities for genuine opposition? The picture that has been painted seems exceedingly pessimistic. Yet, this should not be understood to mean that opposition is futile. It *is* necessary, though, to examine closely the customary modes of opposition. The theory of artificial negativity historicizes the critique of the post-Cold War left and suggests at the same time some broad outlines for a reconceptualization of emancipatory strategy.

This examination of black radicalism in the wake of its integration offers a microcosmic view of the plight of the left as a whole. Having accepted an organizational model based on massification, the radicals were forced to compete with the elite on the latter's terms—an impossible proposition since the elite had access to the cultural apparatus designed for mass mobilization. Moreover, even when opposition tried to reconstruct itself, it failed to generate systematic critique of its own strategy and was therefore unable to come to terms with shifts in the structure of capitalist social relations. Instead, it remained caught within a theoretical structure adequate for an earlier, preadministrative stage of capitalist development. Thus, the failure of mysticized black nationalism was reproduced in "ideological struggles" which reached their nadir in the 1978 dispute over whether Mao Tse-tung was really dead! Still, what of emancipatory possibilities? Certain general implications follow from the preceding analysis, but they become clear only through reflection on the forces currently driving the "really existing" American corporate liberalism.

Development into a sociopolitical order pacified through administration has been realized in the political sphere mainly through the integrative mechanism of a "progrowth" coalition that has cemented linkages institutionally between national and local elites, as well as between representative elites from the various member constituencies in the coalition at both levels.[61] From the vantage point of global system logic the drive to administrative pacification reached its limits in the

1960s, as the homogenizing imperatives of mass culture were challenged by black nationalists and white counterculturists from one direction and rightist populism and white ethnic resurgence from another. Typical to such popular reactions, these challenges began with only the conceptual language of the prevailing social order in which to phrase their revolt, and before genuine alternatives could develop they were integrated into the social management apparatus as supportive appendages. They were thus reconstituted as regulators of rationality deficits in the administrative system. In this essay I have traced the operation of that dynamic in the natural history of black activism.

At the level of practical political management, the growth politics model was undermined by its own contradictions. The strategy of maintaining social peace by ensuring payoffs through the elites of potentially disruptive constituencies works only so long as the number of critical constituent groups is restricted. In this sense corporate liberalism, despite its superficial appearances and the effusions of political scientists, is exclusionist and corporativistic rather than pluralistic.[62] Incorporation of activism in the 1960s forced open the circle of privileged constituencies to include first blacks and then a steady stream of other new claimants. The increasing volume of claims, in combination with other factors, pushed the costs of social control to a point that interfered with stable corporate profit-making, the basis of the growth coalition in the first place.[63] By the early 1970s a process of gradual retrenchment had begun, largely under the aegis of the Nixon administration.

The Reaganite phenomenon of the 1980s in this regard represents an attempt to reconstitute a new growth coalition that eliminates both the claimant groups mobilized as a consequence of 1960s activism and the traditional labor component. In addition to racism, crude self-interest, and fantasies of international vigilantism, Reaganism appeals also—albeit disingenuously—to popular discontent with bureaucratic regimentation and growing administration of social life.[64] A central justification for the program of retrenchment is

that policies and programs aimed at new claimant groups have ensued primarily in creating unwarranted occupational opportunities for administrative elites.

Before such an argument, the post-Civil Rights era black elite—as principal beneficiaries of activism—is virtually helpless. As a growing segment of the black population is increasingly marginalized into a generally optionless condition, consigned to deteriorating urban areas and destined at best to low-wage, dead-end subemployment, the black managerial elite is hard-pressed to defend its claims to status and function. At the same time, this stratum—whose existence is an artifact of the old coalition—appears incapable of generating any substantive critique of the inadequacies of the Democratic model of growth politics and is left only with bankrupt demands that its own privileges be secured in the reorganization. Indeed, signs already are visible that the elite's interest-group organizations are retooling their focus away from "state interventionist" to direct "corporate interventionist" strategies that uncouple from the old coalition's social welfare focus and reformulate black interests openly and exclusively in terms of securing leverage for upper-income, professional strata.[65]

So, the wheels of corporate social reorganization turn, grinding beneath them the lives and hopes of the dispossessed and oiled by their misery. The legatees of activism, putative bearers of the principle of friction, simply cling to the wheels, hoping to go along for the ride—no matter what the outcome!

Yet, even if the current, draconian retrenchment is defeated, there will be little cause for celebration. Not only would a return to the old growth coalition be inadequate to meet the needs of large segments of American society, including a disproportionate element of the black population, but that coalition cannot be reinstated on its original basis. There is a sense, after all, in which Huntington's argument is sound. The partial success of 1960s activism in generating new status groups has intensified competition among noncorporate constituencies over the limited opportunities available for participation in the administrative distribution of privilege. Organized labor, feminists, and minority elites vie among one another in what they understand to be a zero-sum struggle for social and economic benefits. Added to these are the plethora of interest configurations arising from the maturing, upwardly mobile postwar baby boom—urban revitalization, localism, environmentalism, homosexual activism.

Not only are the agendas of these "Young Urban Professionals" often in objective conflict, if not overt antagonism, with those of minorities and organized labor, but that stratum's neo-Progressivist ideological orientation breeds fractiousness through its disposition toward the egoistic, single-issue activism of "citizen" initiative. Despite the hyper-pluralism that this orientation promotes, it often masquerades—like its early twentieth-century predecessor—as defense of the public interest.[66] However, beneath the follow "New Ideas" themes trumpeted by Anderson in 1980 and Hart in 1984 lies a "neoliberal" social agenda that at the national level would reinforce growth in the high-tech and information industries in which yuppies are concentrated and would accept decline of the old industrial base, as Hart's opposition to the Chrysler bailout indicates. At the local level this agenda endorses a model of urban redevelopment that accelerates displacement of the poor under the guise of neighborhood renewal and advocates an expanding official role for neighborhood organization in local policymaking, which automatically advantages upper-income, better-endowed—and thus more easily mobilized—neighborhoods.[67] Moreover, the national neoliberal growth agenda promises to intensify local income stratification by exacerbating tendencies to labor market segmentation; that model for growth generates for those outside language and symbol manipulating areas only service sector or other poorly remunerative, optionless employment, and not much of that.[68] The prospect of recomposition of a growth agenda along these lines, therefore, does not portend a future for the general black population that is much different from that held out by Reaganism. Indeed, the neoliberal tendency identified with Gary Hart raises the spectre of a Democratic consensus that—like Reagan's—excludes blacks and other minorities, as well as the AFL-CIO.[69]

In this context one has to strain to find emancipatory possibilities. The dangers that the present situation poses for the black population cannot even be conceptualized within the myopic and narrowly opportunistic pattern of discourse defined by the black political elite. A first step, therefore, must entail breaking this elite hegemony over ideas in the black community. The spoken-for must come to master political speech and to articulate their own interests, free of the intermediation of brokerage politicians and the antirational, antidemocratic conformism preached by charismatic authority. This mastery can develop only through a combination of unrelenting critique of the elite's program and authoritarian legitimations and practical efforts to expand the discursive arena within the Afro-American population.[70]

The very success of the post-civil rights elite in imposing its agenda of administrative management has limited the terms of black political discourse to the options thrown up within the present arrangements of domination. Yet, inadequate though they may be, those options constitute at this point the only meaningful terrain for political engagement. Creation of a sphere of black public debate on issues arising from the current tendencies in capitalist social reorganization—ranging from the ramifications of public goods allocation decisions in a local political jurisdiction to national economic and social policy—is necessary to transcend the official black posture of quiet acceptance of any initiative that includes an affirmative action component. Stimulation of political controversy within the black community would lead to recognition of the diversity of interest configurations among blacks and is therefore a precondition to formulation of genuinely collective agendas, whose adherents may or may not be coterminous with the boundaries of racial identification. This ostensibly tepid call for the development of a political liberalism within the racial community offers, under the present circumstances, the only hope for combatting the sacrifice of a growing share of the black population to permanent marginality in the American social order. The principles of "bourgeois democracy," on which the black elite has grounded its demands for participatory rights in the distributive queue of growth politics, must be applied against the hegemony of elite interests within the Afro-American group.

At stake in the short term is the specific character of the governing synthesis that ultimately replaces the New Deal coalition. The concrete form of those new arrangements, including the position of racial minorities in them, will be determined through political contention, and the black political elite—for reasons that I have adumbrated—cannot be relied upon to press the interests of a population that exists for it primarily as private capital. Beyond the immediate situation, animation of a critical-democratic black political culture constitutes a necessary, though incremental, movement toward Afro-American participation in development of a more general critical dialogue which may produce the basis for a new oppositional politics—one capable of confronting squarely the irrational logic and mechanisms that constitute the mass capitalist order of domination.

The strategic proposal that I have sketched obviously provides no blueprint; it is modest and most contingent, and—even if implemented—it hardly guarantees social transformation. Its modesty only reflects the failure of oppositional forces to develop credible alternatives in the here-and-now. Acknowledgment of that failure, however, should not be misread as pessimistic assessment; admission of failure expresses the distance between actually existing conditions and a goal that lives beyond the shortfall. Although contingent responses offer no sure exits from a bleak situation, contingency itself is the source of real hope, that which lies in recognition of the openness of history. Such hope, grounded in an unyielding vision of human emancipation, seeks its possibilities even in the darkest moments of the present; it is despair that hides its head from history and refuses to see the undesirable.[71]

NOTES

1. Walter Benjamin, "The Work of Art in the Age of Mechanical Reproduction," in *Illuminations* (New York, 1968), p. 251.
2. Herbert Marcuse, *One-Dimensional Man: Studies in the Ideology of Advanced Industrial Society* (Boston, 1964).
3. David Gross, "Irony and the 'Disorders of the Soul,'" *Telos* (Winter, 1977–1978), p. 167.
4. Possible sources of the left's failure to interpret its past meaningfully are discussed also by Christopher Lasch, "The Narcissist Society," *New York Review of Books* 23 (September 30, 1976), p. 5ff; Russell Jacoby, "The Politics of Objectivity: Notes on the U.S. Left," *Telos* (Winter, 1977–1978), pp. 74–88, and *Social Amnesia: A Critique of Conformist Psychology from Adler to Laing* (Boston, 1975), pp. 101–118; and by Andrew Feenberg, "Paths to Failure: The Dialectics of Organization and Ideology in the New Left," and David Gross, "Culture, Politics, and 'Lifestyle' in the 1960s," in *Race, Politics, and Culture*, Adolph Reed, Jr., ed. (New York: Greenwood Press, 1986).
5. The work of Alex Willingham is the most consistent and noteworthy exception. In addition to his contribution to this volume see, for example, "California Dreaming: Eldridge Cleaver's Epithet to the Activism of the Sixties," *Endarch* 1 (Winter, 1976), pp. 1–23.
6. Paul Piccone, "Beyond Critical Theory," mimeo, and "The Crisis of One-Dimensionality," *Telos* (Spring 1978), pp. 43–54. See also Tim Luke, "Culture and Politics in the Age of Artificial Negativity," ibid., pp. 55–72.
7. See, for example: Thomas R. Brooks, *Walls Come Tumbling Down: A History of the Civil Rights Movement, 1940–1970* (Englewood Cliffs, N.J., 1974), pp. 290ff; Eddie N. Williams, *From Protest to Politics: The Legacy of Martin Luther King, Jr.* (Washington, D.C., n.d.), and Robert Smith, "Black Power and the Transformation from Protest to Politics," *Political Science Quarterly* 96 (Fall, 1981), pp. 431–443.
8. This slogan first rose to prominence on the back of the black elite's voluble reaction to the Bakke case, which is said to portend reversal of those alleged "gains." One interpretation of these gains is found in Richard Freeman, "Black Economic Progress Since 1964," *Public Interest* (Summer, 1978), pp. 52–68.
9. Dorothy K. Newman, Nancy Amidei, Barbara Carter, Dawn Day, William Kruvant, Jack Rus-

sell, *Protest, Politics and Prosperity: Black Americans and White Institutions, 1940–1975* (New York, 1978), p. 64. Since 1971, of course, unemployment among blacks has averaged more than 10 percent.

10. Ibid., p. 66.

11. U.S. Department of Commerce, Bureau of the Census, *The Social and Economic Status of the Black Population in the United States: 1974* (Washington, D.C., 1975), p. 25.

12. Barbara Jones, "Black Family Income: Patterns, Sources, and Trends," paper presented at the annual meetings of the National Economic Association, American Economic Association, Atlantic City, New Jersey, September, 1976, p. 2.

13. Bureau of the Census, *Social and Economic Status*, pp. 123, 137.

14. That the leadership elite projects its interests over the entire black population is neither unique nor necessarily suggestive of insidious motives; however, it is just in the extent to which the elite's hegemony develops unconsciously that it is most important as a problem for emancipatory action. Cf. Alvin W. Gouldner's critique of intellectuals and intelligentsia, "Prologue to a Theory of Revolutionary Intellectuals," *Telos* (Winter, 1975–1976), pp. 3–36, and *The Dialectic of Ideology and Technology: The Origins, Grammar and Future of Ideology* (New York, 1976), pp. 247–248 *passim*. More recently Gouldner attempted to elaborate a systematic theory of the place of intellectuals in the modern world that concludes that they function as a "flawed universal class—a thesis that does not augur well for the emancipatory content of his theory—in *The Future of Intellectuals and the Rise of the New Class: A Frame of Reference, Theses, Conjectures, Arguments, and an Historical Perspective on the Role of Intellectuals and Intelligentsia in the International Class Context of the Modern Era* (New York, 1979). See also the critique of Gouldner's thesis in Michael Walzer's thoughtful review essay "The New Masters," *New York Review of Books* 27 (March 30, 1980), pp. 37ff.

15. John Hope Franklin does not raise the question in his standard volume, *From Slavery to Freedom: A History of Negro Americans*, third edition (New York, 1969); nor suprisingly does Harold Cruse's *The Crisis of the Negro Intellectual: From Its Origins to the Present* (New York, 1967), which is a seminal contribution to a reflexive approach to black political activity. That Cruse and Franklin fail to raise the question is perhaps because both—reflecting an aspect of the conventional wisdom—see an unbroken, if not cumulating, legacy of black activism in the twentieth century. Franklin sees the Civil Rights movement simply as the culmination of a century or more of protest. Cruse, in establishing the continuities of the poles of integrationism and nationalism, projects them back and forth from Douglass and Delany to Black Power, glossing over significant historical differences in the process. In *The Making of Black Revolutionaries* (New York, 1972), James Forman is so consumed by the movement's chronology and organizational unfoldings that he is unable to subordinate it to history. His account of the 1950s focuses entirely on his personal awakening. Louis Lomax, *The Negro Revolt*, revised edition (New York, 1971); Lewis Killian, *The Impossible Revolution? Black Power and the American Dream* (New York, 1968); and the two period volumes by Lerone Bennett, Jr., *The Negro Mood* (New York, 1964) and *Before the Mayflower: A History of the Negro in America, 1619–1964*, revised edition (Baltimore, 1969), all raise the question only to answer casually or to beg the question further. An all-too-common shortcoming exemplified by each of the writers cited and extending throughout the study of black political activity is a tendency to abstract black life from the currents of American history. The resulting scenarios of black existence suffer from superficiality. By the end of the 1970s some social scientists had begun to seek after the structural origins of black mass protest, but their accounts do not adequately consider political dynamics operating within the black community.

16. "Crisis on One-Dimensionality," pp. 45–46; "Beyond Critical Theory," p. 6.

17. John Alt observes that "The problem of legitimating industrial reorganization was solved through a new social practice and ideology structured around the pursuit of money, material comfort, and a higher standard of living through consumerism. Mass consumption, as the necessary otherness of Taylorized mass production, was itself offered as the ultimate justification for the rationalization of labor," "Beyond Class: The Decline of Industrial Labor and Leisure," *Telos* (Summer, 1976), p. 71. Stuart Ewen identifies the Cold War period as the apotheosis of consumerism, whose enshrinement during those years was aided by the continued spread of popular journalism and the "mass marketing of television ...

which carried the consumer imagery into the back corners of home life," *Captains of Consciousness: Advertising and the Social Roots of the Consumer Culture* (New York, 1976), pp. 206–215.

18. Cf. David Riesman (with Nathan Glazer and Reuel Denney), *The Lonely Crowd: A Study of the Changing American Character*, abridged edition (New Haven, 1961), pp. 19–22, and Jules Henry's perceptive and telling study of the period, *Culture Against Man* (New York, 1963). Marcuse went so far as to suggest that even the concept of introjection may not capture the extent to which the one-dimensional order is reproduced in the individual on the ground that: "Introjection implies the existence of an inner dimension distinguished from and even antagonistic to the external exigencies—an individual consciousness and an individual unconscious apart from public opinion and behavior…. (However, mass) production and mass distribution claim the entire individual…. The manifold processes of introjection seem to be ossified in almost mechanical reactions. The result is not adjustment but mimesis: an immediate identification of the individual with *his* society and, through it, with the society as a whole," *One-Dimensional Man*, p. 10.

19. The point is not that ethnicity has lost its power as a basis for self-identification or associational activity. What has been obliterated, however, is the distinctiveness of the institutional forms which were the source of group consciousness in the first place. Warner and Srole pridefully acknowledge the centrality of the prevailing order in the determination of ethnic consciousness: "The forces which are most potent both in forming and changing the ethnic groups emanate from the institutions of the dominant American social system," W. Lloyd Warner and Leo Srole, *The Social Systems of American Ethnic Groups* (New Haven, 1945), pp. 283–284. Stuart and Elizabeth Ewen, "Americanization and Consumption," *Telos* 37 (Fall, 1978), observe that the dynamic of homogenization began with integration into the system of wage labor which "created great fissures and, ultimately, gaps in people's lives. Money … rendered much of the way in which non-industrial peoples understood themselves, and the reproduction of their daily lives, useless. The money system itself was a widely disseminated mass medium which ripped the structure of peoples' needs from their customary roots, and by necessity

transplanted these needs in a soil nourished by the 'rationality' of corporate industry and the retail marketplace" (p. 47). Traditional ethnic ways of life hardly stood a chance under conditions in which the terms of survival were also those of massification! See also Maurice R. Stein, *The Eclipse of Community: An Interpretation of American Studies* (New York, 1960). Also see David Gross, "Culture, Politics and 'Lifestyle' in the 1960s."

20. See, for example: John V. Van Sickle, *Planning for the South: An Inquiry into the Economics of Regionalism* (Nashville, 1943), pp. 68–71; Gene Roberts, Jr., "The Waste of Negro Talent in a Southern State," in Alan F. Westin, ed., *Freedom Now: The Civil Rights Struggle in America* (New York, 1964), and Eli Ginzberg, "Segregation and Manpower Waste," *Phylon* 21 (December, 1960), pp. 311–316.

21. Harry Braverman, in *Labor and Monopoly Capital: The Degradation of Work in the 20th Century* (New York, 1974), notes the ironic circumstance that capital has appropriated as a conscious ideal Marx's "abstraction from the concrete forms of labor" (pp. 181–182). In the logic of monopoly capitalism—characterized in part by constant reduction of labor's share of the overall costs of production and increasing sensitivity for optimizing profits over time in a stable production environment, [cf. Andreas Papandreou, *Paternalistic Capitalism* (Minneapolis, 1972), especially pp. 80–89]—the short-term benefits likely to accrue from a dual industrial labor market situation need not be expected to hold any great attractiveness.

22. Braverman, *Labor and Monopoly Capital*, p. 319 *passim*. Also see David Noble, *America by Design: Science, Technology and the Rise of Corporate Capitalism* (New York, 1977), pp. 82, 257–320.

23. A clarification is needed concerning use of constructs "black community" and "black activism." Racial segregation and the movement against it were southern phenomena. Black Power "nationalism" was essentially a northern phenomenon for which legally sanctioned racial exclusion was not an immediate issue. Although the two historical currents of rebellion were closely related, they nevertheless were distinct. Consequently, they must be considered separately.

24. See, for example: Charles S. Johnson, *Patterns of Negro Segregation* (New York, 1943) and *Growing Up in the Black Belt* (Washington, D.C., 1941); C. Vann Woodward, *The Strange Career of Jim Crow* (New York, 1966); Wilbur J. Cash,

The Mind of the South (New York, 1941); Robert Penn Warren, *Segregation: The Inner Conflict in the South* (New York, 1956); John Dollard, *Caste and Class in a Southern Town* (New York, 1957); James W. Vander Zanden, *Race Relations in Transition* (New York, 1965); George B. Tindall, *The Emergence of the New South: 1913–1945* (Baton Rouge, 1967); Arthur Raper, *Preface to Peasantry: A Tale of Two Black Belt Counties* (Chapel Hill, 1936), and *The Tragedy of Lynching* (Chapel Hill, 1933); William L. Patterson, *We Charge Genocide* (New York, 1951); Martin Luther King, Jr., *Why We Can't Wait* (New York, 1964); Mayo Selz and C. Horace Hamilton, "The Rural Negro Population of the South in Transition," *Phylon* 24 (June, 1963), pp. 160–171; Thomas Patten, Jr., "Industrial Integration of the Negro," *Phylon* 24 (December, 1963), pp. 334ff; Donald Dewey, "Negro Employment in Southern Industry," *Journal of Political Economy* 60 (August, 1952), pp. 279–293; and Herbert R. Northrup et al., eds., *Negro Employment in Southern Industry: A Study of Racial Policies in Five Industries* (Philadelphia, 1970). (The discussion here of the South draws freely from these sources.)

25. Certainly, the bizarre notion of black leadership was not an invention of the postwar era. That strategy of pacification had been the primary nonterroristic means for subduing black opposition since Booker T. Washington's network of alliances with corporate progressives and New South Bourbon Democrats. Moreover, the notion of a leadership stratum which was supposed to speak for a monolithic black community became the ideological model and political ideal for 1960s radicalism—especially in its "nationalist" variants. Johnson (*Patterns*, pp. 65ff) discusses stratification among blacks under segregation and white responses to the different strata. Perspectives on the phenomenon of black leadership in this context can be gleaned from: Tillman C. Cothran and William Phillips, Jr., "Negro Leadership in a Crisis Situation," *Phylon* 22 (Winter, 1961), pp. 107–118; Everett Carll Ladd, Jr., *Negro Political Leadership in the South* (Ithaca, 1966); Jack Walker, "Protest and Negotiation: A Case Study of Negro Leadership in Atlanta, Georgia," *Midwest Journal of Politics* 7 (May, 1963), pp. 99–124; Daniel C. Thompson, *The Negro Leadership Class* (Englewood Cliffs, 1963); Floyd Hunter, *Community Power Structure* (Chapel Hill, 1953); and M. Elaine Burgess, *Negro Leadership in a Southern City* (Chapel Hill, 1953).

26. King's fascination with satyagraha suggests, although exaggeratedly, the influence which decolonization abroad had on the development of civil rights opposition. Cf. David L. Lewis, *King: A Critical Biography* (Baltimore, 1970), pp. 100–103, and King, "Letter from Birmingham Jail," in *Why We Can't Wait*, pp. 76–95.

27. Lomax, *The Negro Revolt*, p. 21 *passim:* Martin Luther King, Jr., "I Have a Dream," in *Speeches by the Leaders: The March on Washington for Jobs and Freedom* (New York, n.d.); Whitney Young, *To Be Equal* (New York, 1964); and Samuel DuBois Cook, "The American Liberal Democratic Tradition, the Black Revolution and Martin Luther King, Jr.," in Hanes Walton, *The Political Philosophy of Martin Luther King, Jr.* (Westport, Conn., 1971), pp. xiii–xxxviii.

28. This does not mean that *Life* magazine and "Father Knows Best" taught blacks to "dream the dream of freedom." Rather, the integrative logic of massification exacerbated disruptive tendencies already present within the black elite.

29. Enrollment in black colleges increased nearly sixfold between 1928 and 1961 and doubled between 1941 and 1950 alone, on the threshold of the Civil Rights movement. Doug McAdam, *Political Process and the Development of Black Insurgency, 1930–1970* (Chicago, 1982), pp. 101–102.

30. Concepts such as duplicity and cooptation are inadequate to shed light on why corporate and liberal interests actively supported the Civil Rights movement. Interpretations so derived cannot fully explain programs and strategies which originated in the black community. They suggest that naive and trusting blacks, committed to an ideal of global emancipation, allowed themselves to be led away from this ideal by bourgeois wolves in sheep's clothing. This kind of "false consciousness" thesis is theoretically unacceptable. Consciousness is false not so much because it is a lie forced from outside but because it does not comprehend its historical one-sidedness.

31. Of course, suppression was the reaction of certain elements, most notably within the state apparatus, whose bureaucratized priorities urged suppression of any disruptive presence in the society. Howard Zinn, *SNCC: The New Abolitionists* (Boston, 1965), as well as Forman, shows that the federal apparatus, which developed a reputation at the "grass roots" as the patron saint of equality, was at best lukewarm in response to black demands for enforcement of constitutional rights and often set out to sup-

press tendencies and distinct personalities in the movement. Nevertheless, the movement was not suppressed, and not simply because it forced its will upon history. That bit of romantic back-slapping has as little credence as the one that contends that the antiwar movement ended the Vietnam war. The state hardly was mobilized against civil rights activism; the Supreme Court had authorized its legitimacy before it even began. See also Cleveland Sellers (with Robert Terrell), *The River of No Return: The Autobiography of a Black Militant and the Life and Death of SNCC* (New York, 1973). Clayborne Carson details, though without acknowledging the ironic outcomes of the dynamic, the systematic attempts by the Kennedy administration and private foundations to steer the Civil Rights movement toward enfolding itself in the national Democratic agenda. He carefully, yet glibly, reconstructs the portentous tension this attempt generated in the movement. See his study, *In Struggle: SNCC and the Black Awakening of the 1960s* (Cambridge, 1981), pp. 35–39 *passim*.

32. John F. Kennedy picked up the line and ran it as if it were his own; see his "Message to Congress," *Congressional Record*, 88th Cong., 1st sess., Feb. 28, 1963.

33. It was out of this milieu of muddled uneasiness that the Rev. Willie Ricks gave the world the slogan, "Black Power!" on the Meredith march in 1966. A flavor of the frustration of the radicals at the time can be gotten from Julius Lester, *Look Out, Whitey! Black Power's Gon' Get Your Mama* (New York, 1968). In some respects Lester's account, though more dated, has greater value for understanding this period than either Forman's or Sellers's because *Look Out, Whitey!* is written from within Black Power, rather than retrospectively from the vantage point of new ideologies and old involvements that need to be protected. See also, Stokely Carmichael, "Who Is Qualified?" in *Stokely Speaks: Black Power Back to Pan-Africanism* (New York, 1971). Carson's account in *In Struggle* meticulously rehearses the internal ideological and programmatic tensions and debates within SNCC during this period. Unfortunately, his treatment is bereft of conscious theoretical framework.

34. This is not to suggest, however, that events in the South and outside were totally unrelated. As a practical matter, Democratic willingness to accommodate southern activism may have been influenced by increasing prominence of blacks within the urban constituencies of the party's electoral base in the Northeast and Midwest after 1930. In this context—especially after black defections from the national Democratic ticket in 1956 along with erosion of white electoral support in the South after 1948—the party was given pragmatic incentive to acknowledge a civil rights agenda. Arguments to this effect are developed in Frances Fox Piven and Richard A. Cloward, *Poor People's Movements: Why They Succeed, How They Fail* (New York, 1977), pp. 214ff, McAdam, *Political Process*, pp. 81–86, and C. Vann Woodward, *Jim Crow*, p. 129.

35. See, for example, Carmichael, "Power and Racism" in *Stokely Speaks*. This essay is perhaps the first attempt to articulate a systematic concept of the notion Black Power.

36. *Black Awakening in Capitalist America: An Analytic History* (Garden City, 1969), pp. 129–192. Allen's interpretation, however, cannot move beyond this descriptive point because he accepts a simplistic notion of cooptation to explain the black corporate/elite nexus. Julius Lester charged by 1968 that the "principal beneficiaries of Black Power have been the black middle class," *Revolutionary Notes* (New York, 1969), p. 106.

37. Piven and Cloward observe astutely that "black power" assisted in the pacification of activism by "providing a justification for the leadership stratum (and a growing black middle class more generally) to move aggressively to take advantage of … new opportunities" opened by the movement. *Poor People's Movements*, p. 253.

38. Harold Cruse, *Crisis*, pp. 544–565.

39. Jennifer Jordan notes this "nostalgic" character of 1960s culturalism and its grounding in the black elite in "Cultural Nationalism in the Sixties: Politics and Poetry," in this volume. In the most systematic and thorough critical reconstruction of black cultural nationalism to date, Jordan identifies two core nationalist tendencies: one Afro-American preservationist, the other African retrievalist. Presumably, Ron Karenga is to be seen as a bridge between those tendencies with his commitment to "creation, recreation and circulation of Afro-American culture." "From the Quotable Karenga," in Floyd Barbour, ed., *The Black Power Revolt* (Boston, 1968), p. 162.

40. Cf. Imamu Amiri Baraka (LeRoi Jones), "Toward the Creation of Political Institutions for All African Peoples," *Black World* 21 (October, 1972), pp. 54–78. "Unity will be the only method, it is part of the black value system because it is only with unity that we will get polit-

ical power," Baraka, *Raise, Race, Rays, Raze* (New York, 1971), p. 109.

41. The legacy of this ultimately depoliticizing pattern of discourse can be seen in the 1984 Jesse Jackson presidential campaign in which criticism of Jackson's effort was denounced as heresy or race treason.

42. George Mosse examines the theoretical components and historical significance of folkish ideology as a response to mass society in *The Crisis of German Ideology: Intellectual Origins of the Third Reich* (New York, 1964), pp. 13–30.

43. The fascination shared by most of the nationalists with the prospects of consciously creating a culture revealed both the loss of genuine cultural base and the extent of their acceptance of manipulation as a strategy (cf. Karenga's "seven criteria for culture," *Black Power Revolt*, p. 166). The farther away the nationalists chose to go to find their cultural referents, the more clearly they demonstrated the passage of a self-driving, spontaneous black existence from the arena of American history. The ultimate extension of escapism came with the growth of Pan-Africanism as an ideology; that turn—at least in its most aggressive manifestations—conceded as a first step the inauthenticity of all black American life. See Carmichael, *Stokely Speaks*, pp. 175–227, and Ideological Research Staff of Malcolm X Liberation University, *Understanding the African Struggle* (Greensboro, N.C., 1971).

44. In this regard expertise translates into superficial articulateness and ability to negotiate within the social management apparatus.

45. After Little Rock, Ronald Walters was able to boast that the black elected officials had become the vanguard political force in the black community. "The Black Politician: Fulfilling the Legacy of Black Power," *Current History* 67 (November, 1974), pp. 200ff. Baraka, its former chairman and a central organizer, was very nearly expelled from the National Black Assembly in 1975 by a force of elected officials put off by his newfound "Marxism." Note, however, that even he had to admit the activists' marginality and weakness compared to the mainstream elite as early as 1970 at the Congress of African Peoples. Baraka, ed., *African Congress: A Documentary of the First Modern Pan-African Congress* (New York, 1972), p. 99.

46. This is not to say that blacks no longer are oppressed, nor that the oppression no longer has racial characteristics. Nor still is it possible to agree with Wilson's claim that race is receding as a factor in the organization of American

society; as Harold Barnette notes, the integration of affirmative action programs into the social management apparatus suggests race's continuing significance. See William Julius Wilson, *The Declining Significance of Race: Blacks and Changing American Institutions* (Chicago, 1978), and Barnette's review in *Southern Exposure* 7 (Spring, 1979), pp. 121–122. With legitimation and absorption of antiracism by the social management system, race has assumed a more substantial and pervasive function than ever before in American life. Moreover, this function is often life-sustaining; controlling discrimination has become a career specialty—complete with "professional," "paraprofessional," and "subprofessional" gradations—in public and private bureaucracies. However, "racial discrimination" fails as a primary basis from which to interpret or address black oppression.

"Racism" is bound to an "equality of opportunity" ideology which can express only the interests of the elite strata among the black population; equality of access to the meaningless, fragmented and degrading jobs which comprise the bulk of work, for example, hardly is the stuff of "black liberation" and is ultimately a retrograde social demand. It is not an accident, therefore, that the only major battle produced by the struggle against racism in the 1970s was the anti-Bakke movement, whose sole objective was protection of upwardly mobile blacks' access to pursuit of professional employment status.

Racism makes its appearance in black political discourse as an opaque reification grafted onto otherwise acceptable institutions. Small wonder it is the only issue the black elite can find to contend! Not only does racism carry the elite's sole critique of U.S. society, but the claim that racism creates a bond of equivalent victimization among blacks is one of the sources of the elite's legitimation. It is interesting to recall in this context that "racism" became the orthodox explanation of black oppression when the Kerner Commission anointed it as the fundamental source of the 1964–1967 urban uprisings. *Report of the National Advisory Commission on Civil Disorders* (New York, 1968), p. 203. This document goes far toward articulating the outlines of what became the new strategy for management of the black population.

47. The most significant shift in the occupation structure of the black population in the decade after the 1964 Civil Rights Act was relative expansion of its elite component. Be-

tween 1964 and 1974 the percentage of minority males classified as "professional and technical" workers increased by half; the percentage classified as nonfarm, salaried "managers and administrators" quadrupled over that period. Similar increases were realized by minority females. See *Social and Economic Status of the Black Population*, pp. 73–74. Hefner and Kidder discuss these developments which they laud as constitutive of a new era of black opportunity, even though they express concern—appropriate to an upwardly mobile stratum—that the rate of progress could be increased. See James A. Hefner and Alice E. Kidder, "Racial Integration in Southern Management Positions," *Phylon* 33 (June, 1972), pp. 193–200.

Moreover, where in the 1960–1970 period the proportions of black low-income families decreased and high income families increased at roughly the same impressive rate, between 1970–1979 the shares of families in both categories increased. In 1970, 30.6 percent of black families earned in the low income range, and 35.2 percent were high income. In 1979, 32.5 percent were low income and 38.6 percent high income while the middle income component fell from 34.2 percent in 1970 to 28.9 percent in 1979. Between 1979–1982 the low income category rose steadily to 37.8 percent; the high income category dropped to just over 35 percent in 1981 and stabilized at that level, while middle income families continued to decline, reaching 26.9 percent in 1982. Distribution of wealth by asset category is equally instructive. While proportions of total black wealth represented by equity in homes (the largest single category) and vehicles and in financial assets declined slightly between 1967–1979, equity in rental or other property more than doubled, from 12 percent to 25 percent of the total. See William P. O'Hare, *Wealth and Economic Status: A Perspective on Racial Equality* (Washington, D.C., 1983), pp. 18, 25.

An indication of the social management apparatus' centrality for this expansion in the black elite can be gleaned from consideration of the growth of the public sector as an avenue for black middle class employment. While government consistently has been more significant for black employment than white, between 1960 and 1970 the proportion of black males in managerial or professional jobs who were employed in the government sector doubled from 18.2 percent to 37.1 percent.

Black females, whose professional opportunities had been more severely restricted to the public sector, realized more modest gains, from 57.9 percent to 63.3 percent. Despite a stabilization and slight tailing off, by 1980 nearly a third of black professional males and more than half of black professional females were employed in government. See Martin Carnoy, Derek Shearer, and Russell Rumberger, *A New Social Contract: The Economy and Government After Reagan* (New York, 1983), 133–134.

This is the context in which the Reaganite assault on public spending is most directly racial in its thrust. Indeed, the mobilization of Thomas Sowell, Walter Williams, and other ideologues of "black neo-conservatism" by the Reaganite forces is instructive. Sowell and the others seek to justify Reagan's reversal of racial palliatives and "entitlement" programs largely by pointing to the disproportionate benefits bestowed by those programs on middle class black functionaries. For critical discussion of this phenomenon see Jerry G. Watts, "The Case of the Black Conservative," *Dissent* (Summer, 1982), pp. 301–313, and Alex Willingham, "The Place of the New Black Conservatives in Black Social Thought" (unpublished).

48. The celebration of the new elite is not, as once was the case, restricted to black media. Stephen Birmingham has testified to their presence and allowed them to expose their personal habits in his characteristically gossipy style of pop journalism in *Certain People: America's Black Elite* (Boston, 1977). The *New York Times Sunday Magazine* twice at least lionized the beautiful black stratum of the 1970s. See Peter Ross Range, "Making It in Atlanta: Capital of 'Black is Bountiful,'" *New York Times Sunday Magazine*, April 7, 1974, and William Brashler, "The Black Middle Class: Making It," in the December 3, 1978, magazine. Each of these brassy accounts tends, despite occasional injections of "balance," to accept and project the elite's mystical view of itself and exaggerates its breadth and force in society. However, that the *Times* even would care to make the statement made by these two articles suggests minimally that the elite has been integrated into the corporate marketing strategy on an equal basis.

49. This distinction of "authentic" and "artificial" particularity is similar to Habermas's distinction of "living" and "objectivistically prepared and strategically employed" cultural tradi-

tions. A cultural particularity is "authentic" insofar as it: 1) reproduces itself within the institutional environment that apparently delimits the group, i.e., outside the social administrative system; and 2) is not mobilized by the mass culture industry. Cf. Jurgen Habermas, *Legitimation Crisis* (Boston, 1975), pp. 70–72. Therefore, in this usage, "authentic" particularity relates not to any notion of ethnic genuineness but to the oppositional impetus posited in a group's existence. This oppositional quality derives from the otherness that characterizes the autonomously reproductive, unintegrated group's relation to the mass capitalist social order and that necessarily: 1) demonstrates the possibility of a form of social life alternative to that decreed by the logic of administration, and 2) poses a practical negation of the order's claims to cultural hegemony. As the group is integrated into the material and cognitive frameworks of the prevailing order, the sense of alternate possibility is lost, and the negativity that had mediated the group's relation to mass capitalism is overcome in favor of a nontranscendent, system-legitimizing, and systematically authorized pluralism—which becomes the basis for what I have described as "artificial" particularity. Authenticity thus is a category of emancipatory interest rather than ethnographic integrity.

50. Jordan even contends that radical culturalism was most susceptible among all the 1960s' oppositional forms to the logic of commodification because of its tendency to reduce identity to the artifact. Cf. "Cultural Nationalism in the Sixties."

51. Compare for example: S. E. Anderson, "Black Students: Racial Consciousness and the Class Struggle, 1960–1976," *Black Scholar* 8 (January–February, 1977), pp. 35–43; Muhammad Ahmad, "On the Black Student Movement—1960–1970," *Black Scholar* 9 (May–June, 1978), pp. 2–11; and James and Grace Lee Boggs, *Revolution and Evolution in the Twentieth Century* (New York, 1974), pp. 174ff.

52. The coalition's bankruptcy was demonstrated by the defections from its electoral constituency to Nixon's "silent majority" in 1968 and wholesale collapse in the face of McGovernite and Republican challenges in 1972. Unable to end the Vietnam war and adjust to a new era of imperialism or to address the concerns of such postscarcity era advocacy centers as the student and ecology movements, the productivist liberal-labor forces who had controlled

the Democratic party for a generation also found it impossible to establish a common discursive arena with the ethnic and feminist consciousness movements of the 1960s.

53. "Future of Capitalism" in this volume; "The Changing Function of Critical Theory," *New German Critique* (Fall, 1977), pp. 35–36.

54. Habermas calls these "quasi-groups" and maintains that they perform the additional function of absorbing the "secondary effects of the averted economic crisis," *Legitimation Crisis*, p. 39.

55. Russell Jacoby, "A Falling Rate of Intelligence?" *Telos* (Spring, 1976), pp. 141–146; Stanley Aronowitz, "Mass Culture and the Eclipse of Reason: The Implications for Pedagogy," *College English* 38 (April, 1977), pp. 768–774; and *False Promises: The Shaping of American Working Class Consciousness* (New York, 1973).

56. This integrative bias in mass movements is clear from Piven and Cloward's accounts in *Poor People's Movements*. Their interpretation, however, emphasizes the structural determinants of protest movements to an extent that seems not to allow the possibility of transcendence.

57. Black Power radicals, in *The Whole World is Watching!: Mass Media in the Making and Unmaking of the New Left* (Berkeley, 1980. Also see Carson, *In Struggle.*

58. Julius Lester was one who saw the prominence of a media cult in the movement (*Revolutionary Notes*, pp. 176–180). On the peculiar media-inspired style of the Black Panthers see Earl Anthony, *Picking Up the Gun* (New York, 1970).

59. "The spectacle presents itself as an enormous unalterable and inaccessible actuality. It says nothing more than 'that which appears is good, that which is good appears.' The attitude which it demands in principle is this passive acceptance, which in fact it has already obtained by its manner of appearing without reply, by its monopoly of appearance," para. 12, Guy Debord, *Society of the Spectacle* (Detroit, 1970).

60. A shift in advertising style captures contemporary life: during the national telecast of the 1978 Miss Black America pageant, General Motors, a sponsor of the broadcast, featured a commercial in which a utilityman at a plant listed the attractions of his job. Among them were pay, fringe benefits, security, opportunity to perform various tasks (a function solely of

his particular position), congenial supervision, and a *good union*! In the metaphor of a colleague who is one of a vanishing breed of baseball fans, the bourgeoisie has a shutout going with two away in the bottom of the ninth!

61. For examination of the genesis of this growth coalition and its constituents and practices see Alan Wolfe, *America's Impasse: The Rise and Fall of the Politics of Growth* (Boston, 1981), and John H. Mollenkopf, *The Contested City* (Princeton, 1983).

62. R. Jeffrey Lustig develops this point in *Corporate Liberalism: The Origins of Modern American Political Theory, 1890–1920* (Berkeley, 1982). Samuel Huntington speaks explicitly of this characteristic of the American order and bemoans the disruptive qualities of the "democratic distemper" in *American Politics: The Promise of Disharmony* (Cambridge, 1981), and in his essay on the United States in Michel J. Crozier, Samuel P. Huntington, and Joji Watanuki, *The Crisis of Democracy: Report on the Governability of Democracies to the Trilateral Commission* (New York, 1975).

Lustig notes that the model of social management in which growth politics is embedded actually antedates the New Deal.

63. The various elements that combined to erode the efficacy of what they refer to as the "postwar corporate system" are described in Samuel Bowles, David M. Gordon, and Thomas E. Weisskopf, *Beyond the Waste Land: A Democratic Alternative to Economic Decline* (Garden City, N.Y., 1983), pp. 79–97. Barry Bluestone and Bennett Harrison emphasize the role of shortsighted corporate management strategies and capital flight in undermining the growth coalition's usefulness. See *The Deindustrialization of America* (New York, 1982).

64. Kevin P. Phillips examines this aspect of Reagan's base in *Post-Conservative America: People, Politics and Ideology in a Time of Crisis* (New York, 1982), especially pp. 193–204.

65. Earl Picard, "The New Black Economic Development Strategy," *Telos* (Summer, 1984). Picard develops this argument through a study of the current programs of the NAACP and Jesse Jackson's PUSH.

66. For a careful examination of the narcissistic style of new middle class politics and a refutation of the inherited wisdom that increased education and income produce a "public-regarding" ethos, see Clarence N. Stone, "Conflict in the Emerging Post-Industrial Community," paper given at the American Po-

litical Science Association annual meeting, Denver, Colorado, 1982.

Stone charts the coordinates of conflict through examination of the narrowly self-interested politics of the mobile middle class in Montgomery County, Maryland, a largely upper-income jurisdiction in the Washington, D.C., metropolitan area. With its skills for organization and manipulation of language and image, this "yuppie" element is naturally suited to formation of political agendas along interest group lines.

67. See for example, Mollenkopf, pp. 261–266. Organizational and ideological mechanisms through which these advantages are realized in the natural workings of the political system are discussed in Clarence N. Stone, "Systemic Power in Community Decision Making," *American Political Science Review* 74 (December, 1980), especially pp. 983–984, and David Harvey, *Social Justice and the City* (Baltimore, 1973), pp. 82–86. See also J. John Palen and Bruce London, eds., *Gentrification, Displacement and Neighborhood Revitalization* (Albany, 1984).

68. For critiques of neo-liberal, high-tech development strategies see Carnoy, Shearer, and Rumberger, pp. 150–159; and Bluestone and Harrison, pp. 210–230. Systematic statements of neo-liberal reindustrialization strategy are: Lester Thurow, *The Zero-Sum Society* (New York, 1980); Robert Reich, *The Next American Frontier* (New York, 1983); and Felix Rohatyn, *The Twenty Year Century* (New York, 1983).

69. It is instructive that the postwar baby boom voted more consistently for Reagan than did any other age cohort in 1980. One view of this group's distinctive political style is proposed in Carter A. Eskew, "Baby-Boom Voters," *New York Times* (July 15, 1984).

70. A major focus of this project must be secularization of discussion of the black political situation. Certain elements in the left buttress the foes of democratic discourse in the black community by propagating a view that blacks—unlike other groups in the American polity—are moved to action only through the intervention of charismatic spokesmen who embody collective aspirations personalistically, outside of any discursive processes. Black religiosity is adduced to validate this authoritarian politics of cathartic *volkishness*, and these leftists opportunistically endorse the confounding of church and state in the black community even as they fret over the proto-fascist characteristics of the "moral majority." See, for example,

Andrew Kopkind, "Black Power in the Age of Jackson," *The Nation* (November 26, 1983), and Cornel West, *Prophesy Deliverance!: An Afro-American Revolutionary Christianity* (Philadelphia, 1982).

I have developed critiques of these views in a review of West's book in *Telos* (Summer, 1984) and in *The Jesse Jackson Phenomenon: The Crisis of Purpose in Afro-American Politics* (New Haven, 1986).

71. "The main thing is that utopian conscience and knowledge, through the pain it suffers in facts, grows wise, yet does not grow to full wisdom. It is *rectified*—but never *refuted*—by the mere power of that which, at any particular time, *is*. On the contrary it confutes and judges the existent if it is failing, and failing inhumanly; indeed, first and foremost it provides the *standard* to measure such facticity precisely as departure from the Right," Ernst Bloch, *A Philosophy of the Future* (New York, 1970), p. 91.

The Civil Rights Vision

Thomas Sowell

May 17, 1954 was a momentous day in the history of the United States, and perhaps of the world. Something happened that afternoon that was all too rare in human history. A great nation voluntarily acknowledged and repudiated its own oppression of part of its own people. The Supreme Court decision that day was announced in an atmosphere of high drama, and some observers said that one of the black-robed Justices sat on the great bench with tears in his eyes.

Brown v. Board of Education was clearly much more than another legal case to go into the long dusty rows of volumes of court decisions. It represented a vision of man and of the world that touched many hearts across the land and around the world. The anger and rancor it immediately provoked also testified to its importance. In a larger historic context, that such an issue should reach the highest court in the land was itself remarkable. In how many places and in how many eras could an ordinary person from a despised race challenge the duly constituted authorities, force them to publicly defend their decisions, retreat, and finally capitulate?

Brown v. Board of Education may have been intended to close the door on an ugly chapter in American history, going back to slaver and including both petty and gross bigotry, blatant discrimination, and violence and terror extending all the way to brutal and sadistic lynchings. Yet it also opened a door to political, constitutional, and human crises. It was

Source: Thomas Sowell, "The Civil Rights Vision" in *Civil Rights: Rhetoric or Reality?* © 1984 by Thomas Sowell. Reprinted by permission of HarperCollins Publishers Inc.

not simply a decision but the beginning of a revolution that has not yet run its course, but which has already shown the classic symptoms of a revolution taking a very different path from that envisioned by those who set it in motion.

The civil rights revolution of the past generation has had wide ramifications among a growing variety of groups, and has changed not only the political landscape and social history of the United States, but has also altered the very concept of constitutional law and the role of courts.

Behind the many visible changes has been a change in the way the world is visualized. The civil rights vision is not only a moral vision of the way the world *should* be in the future, but also a cause-and-effect vision of the way the world *is* today. This cause-and-effect vision of the way the world works is central to understanding the particular direction of thrust of the civil rights revolution, its achievements, its disappointments, and its sharp changes in meaning that have split its supporters and confounded its critics.

It is far from incidental that the civil rights movement began among black Americans. The basic vision of what was wrong, and of what social effects would follow from what institutional changes, bore the clear imprint of the history of blacks in the United States, though the general principles arrived at were later applied successively to very different groups in American society—to women and the aged, for example, as well as to such disparate racial and ethnic groups as Asians, Hispanics, and American Indians. It is now estimated that 70 percent of the American population is entitled to preferential treatment under "affirmative action."[1] The civil rights vision has even been extended internationally to the plight of the Third World and to racial policies in other nations, such as South Africa.

Ironically, the civil rights revolution began by emphasizing precisely what was unique about the history of black Americans—slavery, Jim Crow laws, and some of the most virulent racism ever seen anywhere. But upon that very uniqueness, *general* principles

of morality and causation were established. These principles constitute the civil rights vision of the world. The extent to which that vision corresponds to reality is crucial for understanding both the successes and failures of the civil rights revolution thus far, and for assessing its future prospects and dangers.

SPECIAL CASES AND GENERAL PRINCIPLES

Because civil rights laws and civil rights concepts are applied generally—to both racial and non-racial groups—their *general* validity must be examined. The special case of blacks can then be examined precisely as a special case.

One of the most central—and most controversial—premises of the civil rights vision is that statistical disparities in incomes, occupations, education, etc., represent moral inequities, and are caused by "society." Historically, it was easy to show, for example, that segregated white schools had had several times as much money spent per pupil as in segregated black schools and that this translated into large disparities in physical plant, teacher qualifications, and other indices of educational input. Large differences in educational output, such as test scores, seemed readily attributable to these input differences. How well this model applied to other statistical disparities for other groups is another question entirely. Moreover, even for blacks, the causal link has been established by immediate plausibility rather than by systematic verification of an hypothesis.

Another central premise of the civil rights vision is that belief in innate inferiority explains policies and practices of differential treatment, whether expressed in overt hostility or in institutional policies or individual decisions that result in statistical disparities. Moral defenses or causal explanations of these statistical differences in any other terms tend themselves to fall under suspicion or denunciation as racism, sexism, etc. Again, the question must be raised as to the general validity of these premises, as well as the separate question of their applicability to the special case of blacks.

A third major premise of the civil rights vision is that political activity is the key to improving the lot of those on the short end of differences in income, "representation" in desirable occupations or institutions, or otherwise disadvantaged. Once more, it is possible to cite such things as dramatic increases in the number of black elected officials after passage of the civil rights legislation of the 1960s. But once again, the general validity of the premise for the wide variety of groups covered by civil rights policies must be examined as a separate issue. And once again, even the special case of blacks must be systematically analyzed.

Statistical Disparities

Several unspoken assumptions underlie the principle that statistical disparities imply discrimination. The first, and apparently most obvious, is that discrimination leads to adverse effects on the observable achievements of those who are discriminated against, as compared to the discriminators or to society in general. The second assumption is that the converse of this is equally true—that statistical differences signal, imply and/or measure discrimination. This assumption depends upon a third unspoken premise—that large statistical differences between groups do not usually arise and persist without discrimination. For if they do, then discrimination takes its place as only one cause among many—and inferences from statistical disparities lose their validity as evidence. Discrimination may still exist and be harmful, but the convenient statistical barometer would be lost. Even a disease that is fatal 100 percent of the time provides no automatic explanation of death if there are many other fatal diseases, along with accidents, murder, and suicide. These are the inherent pitfalls of inductive reasoning. Even if *A* is known to cause *Z*, we still cannot infer *A* whenever we find *Z*, if *B*, *C*, *D*, etc., also cause *Z*.

How important are other factors besides discrimination in producing vast statistical disparities? The civil rights vision is one of a more or less random statistical distribution of results (income, "representation," test scores, etc.) in the absence of discrimination of one sort or another. Alternative visions are also conceivable, but the crucial question here is not plausibility but how to test any given vision against observable factual evidence.

There are many decisions wholly within the discretion of those concerned, where discrimination by others is not a factor—the choice of television programs to watch, opinions to express to poll takers, or the age at which to marry, for example. All these show pronounced patterns that differ from group to group—not a random distribution.

A whole industry exists to determine the statistical profile of people who view given television programs, for the differences between the demographic and economic characteristics of the respective audiences for sports events, "soap operas," cartoon programs, news features, etc., are worth millions of dollars to advertisers and networks. Public opinion polls show similarly wide disparities on many issues by income, education, sex, age, and religion. Marital patterns also differ widely from one group to another. For example, half of all Mexican American wives were married in their teens while only 10 percent of Japanese American wives were married that young.[2]

People do not move randomly, either within a nation or between nations. The great movement of nineteenth century European immigrants to the United States was largely a movement of young adults.[3] So was the great migration of blacks out of the South, beginning in the early twentieth century.[4] Of the Chinese immigrants to the United States before the First World War, 60 percent came from only one of 98 districts in one province in southern China.[5] Among Japanese immigrants to the United States in 1935, more than 90 percent of those from Okinawa went to Hawaii, while a majority of those from the Hiroshima area went to the mainland of the United States.[6] At the same time, Japanese emigrants from the area around Nagasaki went primarily to China and southeast Asia.[7]

In post-World War II Japan, 70 percent of the emigrants from the Hidaka district settled in Canada, and of these, 90 percent from one village settled in one area of Canada.[8] Among German emigrants in the early nineteenth century, a majority went to South America, but from the 1830s to the end of the century, 90 percent went to the United States.[9] Among those Germans who emigrated to Chile in the mid-nineteenth century, most came from just one city, Hamburg.[10] Among the Jews scattered through the many countries of Latin America today, nearly half live in just one city, Buenos Aires.[11]

The sex composition of immigrants has also shown great disparities, both within groups and between groups. In the late nineteenth and early twentieth centuries, about 80 percent of all emigrants from Italy were male.[12] Among Chinese and Japanese immigrants to the United States during the same era, the men outnumbered the women by more than twenty-to-one,[13] and there were virtually no children. But among the Irish immigrants to the United States, the sex ratio was roughly even, and in some decades females outnumbered males.[14]

Statistical disparities extend into every aspect of human life. In major league baseball, for example, black players have hit home runs with significantly greater frequency than white players (in proportion to their respective times at bat) and with nearly twice the frequency of Latin players.[15] Of the five highest totals of home runs in a lifetime, three are by black players. But of the ten highest slugging averages ever achieved in a season, seven are by players of German ancestry—indeed, just two players, Babe Ruth and Lou Gehrig. Of the five times that someone has stolen 100 or more bases in a season, all were by black players.

In the toy industry, firms do not spend their annual television advertising budgets evenly—that is, 25 percent in each quarter of the year. Some of the best known toy manufacturers spend upwards of three-quarters or four-fifths of their annual television advertising budget in the last quarter.[16]

In short, statistical disparities are commonplace among human beings. Many historical and cultural reasons underlie the peculiar patterns observed. But the even "representation" of groups chosen as a baseline for measuring discrimination is a myth rather than an established fact. It is significant that those who have assumed that baseline have seldom, if ever, been challenged to produce evidence.

The civil rights vision focuses on groups *adversely* affected in statistical disparities. Here the relationship between discrimination and economic, educational, and other disadvantages is taken as virtually axiomatic. But if this apparently obvious proposition is taken as an hypothesis to be tested, rather than an axiom to be accepted, a very different picture emerges. Groups with a demonstrable history of being discriminated against have, in many countries and in many periods of history, had higher incomes, better educational performance, and more "representation" in high-level positions than those doing the discriminating.

Throughout southeast Asia, for several centuries, the Chinese minority has been—and continues to be—the target of explicit, legalized discrimination in various occupations, in admission to institutions of higher learning, and suffers bans and restrictions on land ownership and places of residence. Nowhere in Malaysia, Indonesia, Vietnam, Thailand, or the Philippines have the Chinese ever experienced equal opportunity. Yet in all these countries the Chinese minority—about 5 percent of the population of southeast Asia—owns a majority of the nation's total investments in key industries. By the middle of the twentieth century, the Chinese owned 75 percent of the rice mills in the Philippines, and between 80 and 90 percent of the rice mills in Thailand.[17] They conducted more than 70 percent of the retail trade in Thailand, Vietnam, Indonesia, Cambodia, the Philippines, and Malaysia.[18] In Malaysia, where the anti-Chinese discrimination is written into the Constitution, is embodied in preferential quotas for Malays in government and private industry alike, and extends to admissions and scholarships at the universities, the average Chinese continues to earn twice the income of the average Malay.[19]

Nor are the Chinese minorities in southeast Asia unique. Much the same story could be told of the Jews in many countries around the world and in many periods of history.[20] A similar pattern could also be found among East Indians in Africa, southeast Asia and parts of the western hemisphere, or among Armenians in the Middle East, Africa, and the United States. Italian immigrants to Argentina in the late nineteenth and early twentieth centuries also encountered discrimination, but nevertheless rose from poverty to affluence, surpassing the Argentine majority. Around the turn of the century, when Italians were 14 percent of the Argentine population, they owned more than twice as many food and drinking establishments in Buenos Aires as the native Argentines. They also owned more than three times as many shoe stores and more than ten times as many barbershops.[21] Japanese immigrants to the United States also encountered persistent and escalating discrimination, culminating in their mass internment during World War II, but by 1959 they had about equaled the income of whites and by 1969 Japanese American families were earning nearly one-third higher incomes than the average American family.[22]

In short, two key assumptions behind the civil rights vision do not stand up as general principles. The first is that discrimination leads to poverty and other adverse social consequences, and the second is the converse—that adverse statistical disparities imply discrimination. ...

Innate Inferiority

The civil rights vision tends to dichotomize the spectrum of possible reasons for group differences into (1) discrimination and (2) innate inferiority. Rejecting the latter, they are left with the former. Moreover, others who reject the former are regarded as believing the latter. Finally, institutional practices that either differentiate explicitly (as between men and women, for example) or have differential impact (test scores of blacks vs.

whites) are attributed to their proponents' overt or tacit belief in innate inferiority.

Historically, the innate inferiority doctrine has of course been most prominent in issues revolving around blacks, even though the reasoning has been extended to other contexts. But the more general question is the extent to which it explains intergroup hostility, discrimination, oppression, and violence.

It is difficult to know in what units to measure degrees of hostility or hatred, but overt violence, and especially lethal violence, leave factual records. For example, as many as 161 blacks have been lynched in one year in the United States.[23] How does this compare, historically, with violence against groups who were *not* widely viewed as innately inferior?

Many of the groups most subject to violence have not been generally viewed as innately inferior. Indeed, many have been hated precisely because of superior performances as economic competitors. That has been especially true of "middleman minorities" such as the Chinese in southeast Asia, and the Jews, East Indians, and Armenians in a number of countries around the world. All have been subjected to mass expulsions by various governments and to mass violence by the surrounding populace, sometimes aided and abetted by government. The number of Chinese killed within a few days, at various times in the history of southeast Asia, has on a number of occasions exceeded all the blacks ever lynched in the history of the United States.[24] Similarly with the massive slaughter of the Armenians in Turkey in the early twentieth century, and numerous massacres of Jews in Europe over the centuries, culminating in the Nazi Holocaust.

Even the enslavement of blacks was not the result of a doctrine of innate inferiority. On the contrary, this doctrine developed as a rationalization of slavery already in existence and under fire from both moral and political critics. Moreover, innate inferiority was not even the first rationalization used. Religious rationalizations—enslaving "heathens" for their own spiritual good—were first used and then abandoned as more slaves became Christians, and the innate inferiority doctrine was then substituted. This pattern was common both to the United States and to South Africa, though it was East Indians who were enslaved by South African whites. Moreover, in Brazil, the largest importer of slaves into the western hemisphere, the innate inferiority doctrine was rarely used.[25]

In short, belief in the innate inferiority doctrine has been neither necessary nor sufficient to explain intergroup hostility, oppression, violence, or enslavement.

Ironically, the innate inferiority doctrine and the opposite "equal representation" doctrine proceed on the same intellectual premise—that one can go from innate ability to observed result without major concern for intervening cultural factors. Unexplained residual differences between groups, after controlling for such gross differences as education or parental income, are attributed by one vision to discrimination and by the other to genetics. (As one who has opposed both doctrines,[26] it is particularly striking to me that so few have noticed their essential similarity of reasoning.)

Just how far the civil rights vision can take this line of reasoning was demonstrated by Supreme Court Justices in the *Bakke* and *Weber* cases. Alan Bakke could not have outperformed minority candidates applying to the same medical school if it were not for prior discrimination against these minority candidates, according to four of the Justices.[27] Similarly, Brian Weber would not have been able to compete successfully with black workers applying for the same training program, for "any lack of skill" on the black workers' part resulted from "purposeful discrimination in the past."[28] There are apparently no other reasons for differences in skill or capability other than discrimination, which is illegal, or innate inferiority, which is rejected. Or so it appears in the civil rights vision.

The extension of this kind of reasoning to sex differences is particularly arbitrary. In many instances, the desire to separate men from women is based on the premise that both sexes behave differently when together than when apart—regardless of whether either performs better or worse than the other. All-male and all-female schools and colleges, for example, may be established on the premise that either can be educated more effectively without the distracting or inhibiting presence of the other. The extent to which this is true, and for what kinds of students, is a separate question. The point here is simply that its basis has nothing to do with innate inferiority. Likewise, employers drawing upon a largely male labor pool may prefer an *all*-male work force, rather than one in which one or two women become the focus of male attentions to the detriment of the work, even if the women themselves are fully as productive as the men. Whatever the empirical validity or social policy implications of such employer preferences, innate inferiority is neither necessary nor sufficient to explain them.

Police departments, fire departments, the military and other organizations, where life-and-death decisions must be made, often seek a level of discipline, morale, and dedication to organizational purposes that they do not want compromised by powerful emotional attachments that can develop and cut across these organizational objectives. For this reason, such organizations may be particularly resistant to the introduction of women, as well as homosexuals, or even to members of the same family serving on active duty side by side. Again, inferiority doctrines are neither necessary nor sufficient to explain their position.

Potential hostility, as well as affinity, is among the reasons for separating various groups. Nineteenth-century American employers discovered to their loss that having Irish Protestants and Irish Catholics working together and living together on such projects as building railroads and digging canals was an open invitation to violence.[29] Later, they discovered the same to be true when the work gangs included Italians from different parts of Italy.[30] Some drinking establishments in nineteenth-century England became the exclusive domain of Irish immigrants from a given county in Ireland, because of the dangers of violence even among Irish Catholics from different counties.[31] Nor is violence necessary to cause segregation, especially in social activities. In late nineteenth-century Prague, for example, Czechs and Germans had separate pubs.[32]

In the United States, black-white separation has historically also included severe discrimination against blacks. "Separate but equal" was a transparent legal fiction. Yet discrimination cannot be *generalized* from separation. Even in the special case of blacks, the discrimination that accompanied segregation was much more prevalent and more severe in some situations than in others. At this point, however, the issue is simply whether separation necessarily implies discrimination and an innate inferiority doctrine—as general principles. It does not, either in logic or experience.

Those who dichotomize the reasons for intergroup differences into discrimination and innate inferiority not only ignore many other specific reasons, but more generally proceed as if "society" shapes groups themselves, in addition to making biased decisions about them. A series of landmark civil rights cases have declared illegal various mental tests, voting qualifications, and other standards—even when applied impartially—on the ground that society itself has made it much more difficult for some groups to acquire the skills in question, or even to stay out of jail, where employers have refused to hire people with a criminal record.[33]

Once again, the special case of blacks must be distinguished from the general principles of the civil rights vision, as it applies to 70 percent of the population. To what extent has "society" shaped groups—and in what sense? If the whole range of causal factors are dichotomized into heredity and environment, then all who are not racists or sexists are led by the logic of the argument to the view, expressed long ago by Locke, that people enter the world with their minds as blank pages on which society writes what it will. But the momentous consequences of this vision require it to be examined more closely.

What is "environment"? If it consists only of immediate surrounding circumstances, then the causal and moral responsibilities of a given society are quite different from what

they would be if environment includes behavior patterns that go back for centuries, that originated in other countries thousands of miles away, and that follow each group wherever it settles around the world. In this latter case, it would be strange indeed if merely crossing the political boundaries of the United States were to magically homogenize groups that are so different everywhere else. Blacks may have lost much of their African culture in the centuries of slavery, but the question is whether that unique history provides a general principle.

It is not a foregone conclusion but an empirical question whether the Irish, the Chinese, the Germans, etc., in various lands are more like the other peoples of those lands or more like the people in their respective countries of origins and their kinsmen elsewhere around the globe.

A number of studies over the years have shown Irish Americans to have higher rates of alcohol consumption than Americans as a whole, and correspondingly higher rates of alcohol-related diseases. Nor are these differences small. For example, one study found the rate of alcoholic psychosis among Irish Americans to be 5 times that among Italian Americans and 50 times that among Jewish Americans.[34] Those who see society as the cause of such phenomena would be hard pressed to find in the history of Irish Americans sufficient traumas *not suffered by Jewish and Italian Americans as well* to explain such differences. Moreover, high rates of alcohol consumption in Ireland go back for centuries. Today Ireland spends a higher percentage of its income on alcohol than any other nation in Europe.[35] People of Irish ancestry are only 7 percent of the population of Birmingham, England, but they constitute 60 percent of those arrested for drunkenness.[36] By contrast, both the Jewish and Italian cultures in Europe have historically featured the drinking of wine—not hard liquor, as in Ireland—and both cultures have made drunkenness taboo. These patterns existed before American society existed.

The Chinese have established reputations for working hard and long, in countries around the world, and for not being stopped by the stigma of "menial" work. In nineteenth-century Siam, the rickshaws were virtually all pulled by Chinese, for the Siamese would not stoop to such work.[37] The Chinese were also known as the first to get up in the morning in Bangkok,[38] and throughout southeast Asia they worked incredibly long hours often under exhausting conditions.[39] They did most of the hard industrial work and mining in Malaya.[40] They were imported *en masse* into South Africa for similar work, in the early twentieth century, and were later sent home after clamor by white workers who could not compete with them.[41] In the United States, Chinese immigrants were used in many arduous jobs—including building railroad tracks through the rugged Sierra mountains, a task which most white workers either abandoned shortly after being hired or else refused to do at the outset, once they were at the site and saw what was expected of them.[42]

In intellectual as well as manual work, the Chinese have been disproportionately represented in the difficult and demanding fields such as mathematics, science, and technology. In Malaysia, where Malay college students outnumber the Chinese three-to-one in liberal arts, the Chinese outnumber the Malays eight-to-one in science and fifteen-to-one in engineering.[43] In the United States, more than half of all Chinese faculty members teach engineering and the natural sciences,[44] and outside the academic profession, Chinese are similarly concentrated in the same fields.[45] Yet this has been blamed on American society's *excluding* them from other fields.[46] It is a tribute to the power of the civil rights vision that this could be said in all seriousness, even though (1) other fields are generally less well paid than science and engineering, and (2) Chinese Americans as a group earn higher incomes than white Americans.

Germans have historically been notable in the fields of family farming and of industrial technology—both in Germany and in other countries to which they immigrated. German peasants became in the United States the most successful and most numerous of American farmers.[47] They were generally self-employed family farmers, rather than either agricultural laborers or plantation owners. They achieved similarly striking success in family farming in Brazil, Australia, Ireland, and Mexico.[48] Craftsmanship, technology, and science have also been the hallmarks of Germans in Germany—and in the United States, Brazil, Australia, Czechoslovakia, and Chile, among other places.[49] Germans established the piano industry in the United States—and in Australia and in England.[50] In Brazil, the German minority came to own nearly half the industrial enterprises in the southern states, compared to only one-fifth owned by Brazilians of Portuguese ancestry, the majority of the population.[51]

The civil rights vision tends to view group characteristics as mere "stereotypes" and concentrates on changing the public's "perceptions" or raising the public's "consciousness." Yet the reality of group patterns that transcend any given society cannot be denied. Jewish peddlers followed in the wake of the Roman legions and sold goods in the conquered territories.[52] How surprising is it to find Jewish peddlers on the American frontier or on the sidewalks of New York 2,000 years later—or in many other places in between? No one needs to believe that Jews are *genetically* peddlers. But it does suggest that cultural patterns do not readily disappear, either with the passage of time or with social engineering. The very fact that there are still Jews in the world, after centuries of determined efforts to absorb them by church and state alike, implies that environmental influences extend well beyond immediate circumstances—and might better be described as cultural inheritance.

Politics

Given the civil rights premise that statistical disparities are moral inequities and are caused by social institutions, with group characteristics being derivative from the surrounding society, it follows that the solutions are basically political—changing laws and public perceptions. Political activity thus becomes crucial, with political here being broadly defined to include courts and administrative agencies as well as legislatures, and private institutional activity as well as government policy. As with so many conclusions in this area, the fact that it follows logically from the civil rights vision has largely precluded any apparent need for empirical verification.

Once more looking at this as a general principle, rather than as a projection of the special case of blacks, the question is whether political activity has generally been an important factor in the rise of groups from poverty to prosperity, or in their increased social acceptance. Again, it is an empirical question rather than a foregone conclusion.

Among the groups that have gone into other countries, begun at the bottom and later rose past the original or majority inhabitants are the Chinese in southeast Asia, the Caribbean, and the United States.[53] In all these very different settings, the Chinese have studiously avoided politics. In some countries, such as Malaysia, they have been kept out of politics, but even where political careers were possible the Chinese community leaders have opted to stay out of office-seeking or political agitation. In country after country, they have maintained their own community institutions to adjudicate disputes, care for their needy, and otherwise minimize recourse to the institutions of the surrounding society.[54] *After* achieving affluence and acceptance, some individual Chinese have gone into politics, but typically as representatives of the general population, rather than as ethnic spokesmen. But political activity has played little, if any, role in the often dramatic rises of the Chinese from poverty to affluence.

This pattern has likewise been characteristic of the Germans in the United States, Brazil and Australia. In colonial America, many Germans began as indentured servants, working for years to pay off the cost of their passage across the Atlantic. Most then worked as dirt farmers on frontier land. They were notorious for their *non*-participation in politics in colonial Pennsylvania, where they constituted one-third of the population.[55] Only *after* Germans had risen to prosperity did prominent German political leaders arise. The Muhlenbergs, Carl Schurz, and John Peter Altgeld were the best known in the eighteenth and nineteenth centuries, and Herbert Hoover and Dwight D. Eisenhower in the twentieth century. But as in the case of the Chinese, most of these leaders were by no means primarily spokesmen for German ethnic interests. More important, Germans had risen economically first. The same non-political path to economic advancement was followed by Germans in Brazil and in Australia.[56]

In Argentina, the English immigrants have historically been very successful economically and played a major role in the development of the Argentine economy—but almost no role in Argentine politics.[57]

Jews were for centuries kept out of political rule in a number of countries, either by law, by custom, or by anti-Semitic feelings in the elite or the populace. But even where political careers were at least theoretically open to them, as in the United States, Jews only belatedly sought public office, and in the United States were at first wholly subservient to Irish political bosses. While some Jewish political leaders championed special Jewish causes, the most prominent (Herbert Lehman, and Jacob Javits, for example) were basically spokesmen for more general political causes—and again, by the time that Jews developed political power, they were already well on their way economically. In South Africa, Jews are more prosperous than the ruling Afrikaners, whose policies they have generally opposed, with the result that Jews hold no important political power—certainly none such as could explain their economic advantages. Even in such a free nation as Great Britain, it was the middle of the nineteenth century before the first practicing Jew sat in Parliament, though such converted Jews as Ricardo and Disraeli had been in Parliament earlier in the same century. Yet prosperous Jews were commonplace in Britain long before then.

Until relatively recently, Italians were notorious for non-participation in American politics, and for readily supporting non-Italian candidates over Italian candidates. Even the most famous Italian American politician,

Fiorello H. La Guardia, lost the Italian vote to his Irish opponent in 1940,[58] as have other Italian candidates in Chicago, Boston, and elsewhere.[59] In Argentina as well, Italians took little part in political life during their rise from poverty to affluence, though they achieved economic dominance in a number of industries and skilled occupations.[60]

Empirically, political activity and political success have been neither necessary nor sufficient for economic advancement. Nor has eager political participation or outstanding success in politics been translated into faster group achievement. The Irish have been perhaps the most striking example of political success in an ethnic minority, but their rise from poverty was much *slower* than that of other groups who were nowhere near being their political equals. Irish-run political machines dominated many big city governments in America, beginning in the latter part of the nineteenth century, but the great bulk of the Irish populace remained unskilled laborers and domestic servants into the late nineteenth century. The Irish were fiercely loyal to each other, electing, appointing, and promoting their own kind, not only in the political arena but also in the hierarchy of the Catholic Church. This had little effect on the average Irish American, who began to reach economic prosperity in the twentieth century at about the time when the Irish political machines began to decline and when the Irish control of the Catholic Church was increasingly challenged by other ethnic groups.

It would perhaps be easier to find an *inverse* correlation between political activity and economic success than a direct correlation. Groups that have the skills for other things seldom concentrate in politics. Moreover, politics has special disadvantages for ethnic minority groups, however much it may benefit individual ethnic leaders. Public displays of ethnic solidarity and/or chauvinism are the life blood of ethnic politics. Yet chauvinism almost invariably provokes counter-chauvinism.

By the late nineteenth century, the Chinese minority in southeast Asia lived more or less at peace with the majority populations of the various countries of that region. But in the early twentieth century, a new nationalism in China reached out to the overseas Chinese, among other things offering them Chinese citizenship wherever they might live, and interceding on their behalf with the governments of their respective countries of residence. Many of these Chinese had thought of themselves for generations as Siamese, Burmese, etc., but now the resurgent nationalism of China under Sun Yat-sen became their creed as well. Within a few years, the nationalism of China provoked a counter-nationalism among its neighbors in the region, setting in motion increased discrimination and renewed persecution of their Chinese minorities. Successive Chinese governments under Chiang Kai-shek, then Mao-Tse-tung and his successors, have continued this process, provoking continued hostility to the Chinese minorities, culminating in the tragic fate of the "boat people"—most of whom were Chinese—who could find little refuge anywhere because of the general animosity toward them in southeast Asia.

The dialectic of chauvinism and counter-chauvinism was also played out in a very different setting in nineteenth-century Prague, then capital of Bohemia. Here a mixed population—mostly Czech and German—initially thought of themselves simply as Bohemians. But the rise of Czech nationalism and decades of political agitation for specifically Czech causes eventually roused the Germans to abandon their cosmopolitan view of themselves as Bohemians and to organize for specifically German causes.[61] The Czechs won out in the political struggles, especially after the creation of Czechoslovakia following World War I. But the nationalism they had aroused in the Germans came back to haunt them. The politicization and protests of the Sudeten Germans provided the pretext for Hitler's annexation of the Sudeten region of Czechoslovakia as a result of the Munich agreement, which set the stage for World War II.

Polarization by ethnic politics has proven to be easy to achieve in other settings as well, but no comparably easy way has been found to de-polarize peoples. Guyana went from an ethnic coalition government elected in 1953 to a virtually all-black government in 1969, ruling a nation that was half East Indian and only 43 percent black. The rise of counter-extremism among East Indians produced violent clashes in the streets requiring troops to restore order.[62] Blacks and East Indians in Trinidad likewise went from coalition to confrontation in a few years.[63] In the early centuries of Islam, religious minorities were much more tolerated than in later centuries, after the religious zeal of Christians had led to the persecution and expulsion of Muslim communities in Christian lands.[64] In mid-nineteenth-century Britain, the militant, paramilitary Ribbon societies of the Irish Catholic migrants flourished only in those British cities where the militant, paramilitary Orange lodges of the Irish Protestants flourished. Neither became prominent in London, for example, despite a large Irish population there.[65] Chauvinism has bred counterchauvinism in many historical contexts.

The politicization of race has proven to be explosive, in countries around the world and down through history. Sometimes it is a case of chauvinism provoking counterchauvinism. At other times, one side may go from quiescence to violence in a very short time, as history is measured. Jews in Germany were so well accepted during the 1920s that they not only achieved many high-level positions but more than half their marriages were with non-Jewish Germans.[66] Yet, just one decade later, resurgent anti-Semitism under the Nazis drove masses of Jews from the country and marked millions of others for the horrors of the Holocaust.

Nor were these merely peculiar depravities of Germans. Historically, Jews had been treated better in Germany than in most of Europe, and German Jews in other countries settled among the German minorities of those countries, where they were welcomed into the cultural and social life of German enclaves.[67] Germans in the United States were also noted historically for their ability to get along with the Indians,[68] and for their opposition to slavery[69] and even support of rights for blacks.[70] If the politicization of race could lead to barbarism and genocide among Germans, no

other peoples or society can be presumed to be immune.

However catastrophic the politicization of race may be in the long run, from the point of view of individual leaders it is a highly successful way to rise from obscurity to prominence and power. Those who promoted Czech nationalism in the nineteenth century were typically people from modest social backgrounds,[71] who achieved personal success at the long-run cost of their country's dismemberment and subjugation. Those who have stridently—and sometimes violently—promoted local group preferences in India have likewise typically been from newly educated classes on the rise.[72] Fomenting intergroup hostility has likewise raised many other obscure figures to power in many other countries, from "redneck" politicians in the American South to Idi Amin in Uganda and—the classic example—Adolf Hitler.

In short, despite the unpromising record of politics as a means of raising a group from poverty to affluence, and despite the dangers of politicizing race, there are built-in incentives for individual political leaders to do just that.

NOTES

1. George Gilder, *Wealth and Poverty* (New York: Basic Books, 1980), p. 129.
2. Peter Uhlenberg, "Demographic Correlates of Group Achievement: Contrasting Patterns of Mexican-Americans and Japanese-Americans," *Race, Creed, Color, or National Origin,* ed. Robert K. Yin (Itasca, Illinois: F. E. Peacock Publishers, Inc., 1973), p. 91.
3. Richard A. Easterlin, "Immigration: Economic and Social Characteristics," *Harvard Encyclopedia of American Ethnic Groups,* ed. Stephan Thernstrom, et al. (Cambridge, Mass.: Harvard University Press, 1980), p. 478.
4. Karl E. Taeuber and Alma F. Taeuber, "The Negro Population in the United States," *The American Negro Reference Book,* ed. John P. Davis (Englewood Cliffs, N.J.: Prentice Hall, Inc., 1970), p. 112.
5. Jack Chen, *The Chinese of America* (San Francisco: Harper & Row, 1980), p. 18.

6. Yasuo Wakatsuki, "Japanese Emigration to the United States, 1866–1924," *Perspectives in American History,* Vol. XII (1979), pp. 428, 429.

7. *Ibid.,* p. 429.

8. *Ibid.,* p. 428.

9. Wolfgang Kollmann and Peter Marschalck, "German Emigration to the United States," *Perspectives in American History,* Vol. VII (1973), pp. 518, 519.

10. George F. W. Young, *The Germans in Chile: Immigration and Colonization, 1849–1914* (New York: Center for Migration Studies, 1974), p. 30.

11. Judith Laikin Elkin, *Jews of the Latin American Republics* (Chapel Hill, N.C.: University of North Carolina Press, 1980), pp. 191, 192.

12. Robert F. Foerster, *The Italian Emigration of Our Times* (New York: Arno Press, 1969), p. 39.

13. Betty Lee Sung, *The Story of the Chinese in America* (New York: Collier Books, 1967), p. 320.

14. Robert E. Kennedy, Jr., *The Irish: Emigration, Marriage, and Fertility* (Berkeley: University of California Press, 1973), p. 78.

15. David S. Neft, Roland T. Johnson, Richard M. Cohen, *The Sports Encyclopedia: Baseball* (New York: Grosset & Dunlap, 1976), p. 493.

16. Jeannye Thornton, "Today's Toys—More Than Just Child's Play," *U.S. News and World Report,* December 20, 1982, p. 68.

17. Virginia Thompson and Richard Adloff, *Minority Problems in Southeast Asia* (New York: Russell & Russell, 1955), p. 128.

18. Yuan-li Wu and Chun-hsi Wu, *Economic Development in Southeast Asia* (Stanford: Hoover Institution Press, 1973), p. 22.

19. Robert E. Klitgaard and Ruth Katz, "Ethnic Inequalities and Public Policy: The Case of Malaysia," Mimeographed, Kennedy School of Government, Harvard University, July 1981, p. 11.

20. Thomas Sowell, *The Economics and Politics of Race* (New York: William Morrow, 1983), pp. 80–92.

21. Robert F. Foerster, *The Italian Emigration of Our Times,* p. 262.

22. Thomas Sowell, *Ethnic America* (New York: Basic Books, 1981), pp. 175, 177.

23. U.S. Bureau of the Census, *Historical Statistics of the United States: Colonial Times to 1970* (Washington, D.C.: U.S. Government Printing Office, 1975), p. 422.

24. See *Ibid.,* p. 422; Victor Purcell, *The Chinese in Southeast Asia,* 2nd edition (New York: Oxford University Press, 1980), pp. 406, 514, 519, 527; S. W. Kung, *Chinese in American Life* (Seattle: University of Washington Press, 1962), pp. 14, 15.

25. Carl Degler, *Neither Black Nor White* (New York: Macmillan Publishing Co., 1971), p. 86.

26. Thomas Sowell, "New Light on Black I.Q.," *New York Times Magazine,* March 27, 1977, pp. 57ff; *Idem.,* "Race and I.Q. Reconsidered," *Essays and Data on American Ethnic Groups* (Washington, D.C.: The Urban Institute, 1978), pp. 203–238; *Idem.,* "*Weber* and *Bakke* and the Presuppositions of 'Affirmative Action,' " *Wayne Law Review,* July 1980, pp. 1309–1336.

27. *Regents of the University of California* v. *Allan Bakke,* 438 U.S. 265, pp. 365–366.

28. *United Steelworkers of America* v. *Brian F. Weber,* 443 U.S. 193, p. 212n.

29. J. C. Furnas, *The Americans* (New York: G. P. Putnam's Sons, 1969), p. 382.

30. Robert F. Foerster, *The Italian Emigration of Our Times,* pp. 393–394.

31. Kevin O'Connor, *The Irish in Britain* (London: Sidgwick & Jackson, 1972), p. 26.

32. Gary B. Cohen, *The Politics of Ethnic Survival: Germans in Prague, 1861–1914* (Princeton University Press, 1981), p. 126.

33. Nathan Glazer, *Affirmative Discrimination* (New York: Basic Books, 1975), pp. 56–57.

34. Nathan Glazer and Daniel Patrick Moynihan, *Beyond the Melting Pot* (Cambridge, Mass.: M.I.T. Press, 1970), pp. 257–258.

35. Andrew M. Greeley, *That Most Distressful Nation* (Chicago: Quadrangle Press, 1972), p. 129.

36. Kevin O'Connor, *The Irish in Britain,* p. 137.

37. Victor Purcell, *The Chinese in Southeast Asia,* 2nd edition (Kuala Lumpur: Oxford University Press, 1980), p. 107.

38. *Ibid.*

39. Lennox A. Mills, *Southeast Asia* (University of Minnesota Press, 1964), pp. 110–111.

40. Victor Purcell, *The Chinese in Southeast Asia,* p. 284.

41. Robert Lacour-Gayet, *A History of South Africa* (New York: Hastings House, 1977), p. 230; W. H. Hutt, *The Economics of the Colour Bar* (London: The Institute of Economic Affairs, 1964), pp. 45–46.

42. Jack Chen, *The Chinese of America* (New York: Harper & Row, 1980), pp. 66–67.

43. Yuan-li Wu and Chun-hsi Wu, *Economic Development in Southeast Asia,* pp. 55–57.

44. Stanford M. Lyman, *Chinese Americans* (New York: Random House, 1974), p. 137.

45. Haitung King and Frances B. Locke, "Chinese in the United States: A Century of Occupa-

tional Transition," *International Migration Review*, Vol. 14, M.49 (Spring 1980), p. 22.

46. "In the relatively small number of occupations in which Asians were allowed to participate, they were able to attain a moderate level of economic success." U.S. Commission on Civil Rights, *Unemployment and Underemployment Among Blacks, Hispanics, and Women* (Washington, D.C.: U.S. Commission on Civil Rights, 1982), p. 58. The "deplorable" concentration of Chinese in mathematics, engineering and physics was also considered "evidence of the limited employment opportunities among Chinese intellectuals," in Haitung King and Frances B. Locke, "Chinese in the United States: A Century of Occupational Transition," *International Migration Review*, Vol. 14, No. 49 (Spring 1980), p. 22.

47. J. C. Furnas, *The Americans*, p. 86; Daniel Boorstin, *The Americans* (New York: Random House, 1958), Vol. I, p. 225.

48. Thomas H. Holloway, *Immigrants on the Land* (Chapel Hill, N.C.: University of North Carolina Press, 1980), p. 151; Harry Leonard Sawatsky, *They Sought a Country* (Berkeley: University of California Press, 1971), pp. 129, 244; Arthur Young, *A Tour in Ireland* (Shannon, Ireland: Irish University Press, 1970), Vol. I, pp. 377–379; W. D. Borrie, "Australia," *The Positive Contribution by Immigrants*, ed. Oscar Handlin, et al. (Paris: United Nations Educational, Scientific and Cultural Organization, 1955), p. 91.

49. Thomas Sowell, *Ethnic America* (New York: Basic Books, 1981), pp. 52–53, 58–59; Emilio Willems, "Brazil," *The Positive Contributions by Immigrants*, ed. Oscar Handlin, et al. (Paris: Unesco, 1955), pp. 122, 130; Charles Wagley, *An Introduction to Brazil* (New York: Columbia University Press, 1971), p. 79; W. D. Borrie, *Italians and Germans in Australia* (Melbourne: The Australian National University, 1934), pp. 93, 94; Gary R. Cohen, *The Politics of Ethnic Survival*, p. 23; Carl Solberg, *Immigration and Nationalism: Argentina and Chile, 1890–1914* (Austin: University of Texas Press, 1970), pp. 41, 101.

50. Theodore Huebner, *The Germans in America* (Radnor, Pa.: Chilton Co., 1962), p. 128; W. D. Borrie, *Italians and Germans in Australia* (Melbourne: The Australian National University, 1934), p. 94; Alfred Dolge, *Pianos and Their Makers* (Covina, Ca.: Covina Publishing Co., 1911), p. 172. Germans apparently were also pioneers in piano manufacturing in Russia. *Ibid.*, p. 264.

51. Emilio Willems, "Brazil," *The Positive Contribution by Immigrants*, ed. Oscar Handlin, et al.

(Paris: United Nations Educational, Scientific and Cultural Organization, 1955), p. 133.

52. Solomon Grayzel, *A History of the Jews* (New York: New American Library, 1968), p. 266.

53. Thomas Sowell, *The Economics and Politics of Race*, Chapter 2; David Lowenthal, *West Indian Societies* (New York: Oxford University Press, 1972), pp. 202–208.

54. Naosaku Uchido, *The Overseas Chinese* (Stanford: Hoover Institution Press, 1960), pp. 15–46; Stanford M. Lyman, *Chinese Americans* (New York: Random House, 1974), Chapter 3.

55. Albert Bernhardt Faust, *The German Element in the United States* (New York: Arno Press, 1969), Vol. II, pp. 122–124; Kathleen Neils Conzen, "Germans," *Harvard Encyclopedia of American Ethnic Groups*, ed. Stephan Thernstrom, et al. (Cambridge, Mass.: Harvard University Press, 1981), p. 421.

56. W. D. Borrie, "Australia," *The Positive Contribution by Immigrants*, ed. Oscar Handlin, pp. 90–94; Emilio Willems, "Brazil," *Ibid.*, pp. 122, 125–128.

57. J. Halcro Ferguson, *Latin America: The Balance of Race Redressed* (London: Oxford University Press, 1961), p. 56.

58. Nathan Glazer and Daniel Patrick Moynihan, *Beyond the Melting Pot*, p. 213.

59. For example, Humberto S. Nelli, *The Italians in Chicago* (New York: Oxford University Press, 1970), pp. 92–100; Herbert J. Gans, *The Urban Villagers* (New York: The Free Press, 1962), p. 174.

60. Robert F. Foerster, *The Italian Emigration of Our Times* (Cambridge, Mass.: Harvard University Press, 1924), Chapters XIII, XIV.

61. Gary B. Cohen, *The Politics of Ethnic Survival: Germans in Prague, 1861–1914* (Princeton: Princeton University Press, 1981), Chapters 1, 2.

62. Alvin Rabushka and Kenneth A. Shepsle, *Politics in Plural Societies: A Theory of Democratic Instability* (Columbus, Ohio: Charles E. Merrill Publishing Co., 1972), pp. 95, 105.

63. *Ibid.*, pp. 122–123.

64. Bernard Lewis, *The Muslim Discovery of Europe* (New York: W. W. Norton & Co., 1982), pp. 24–25, 298.

65. Lynn Hollen Lees, *Exiles of Erin* (Ithaca: Cornell University Press, 1979), p. 223.

66. Raphael Patai, *The Vanished Worlds of Jewry* (New York: Macmillan Publishing Co., Inc., 1980), p. 57.

67. Gary B. Cohen, *The Politics of Ethnic Survival*, pp. 76–83, 175–182, 260–262; Arthur A. Goren, "Jews," *Harvard Encyclopedia of American Ethnic Groups*, p. 576.

68. See, for example, Albert Bernhardt Faust, *The German Element in the United States*, Vol. I, pp. 98–99, 103, 104, 112, 213, 232; Vol. II, p. 423. This is not to claim that Germans had *no* clashes with Indians.

69. *Ibid.*, Vol. I, pp. 45–46, 182, 242, 446.

70. John Hope Franklin, *The Free Negro in North Carolina* (New York: W. W. Norton & Co., 1971), p. 26.

71. Gary B. Cohen, *The Politics of Ethnic Survival*, p. 28.

72. Myron Cohen, *Sons of the Soil: Migration and Ethnic Conflict in India* (Princeton: Princeton University Press, 1978), pp. 285–288; Mary Fainsod Katzenstein, *Ethnicity and Equality: The Shiv Sena Party and Preferential Policies in Bombay* (Ithaca: Cornell University Press, 1979), pp. 72–78.

Beyond Civil Rights

Glenn C. Loury

There is today a great deal of serious discussion among black Americans concerning the problems confronting them. Many, if not most, people now concede that not all problems of blacks are due to discrimination, and that they cannot be remedied through civil rights strategies or racial politics. I would go even further: using civil rights strategies to address problems to which they are ill-suited thwarts more direct and effective action. Indeed, the broad application of these strategies to every case of differential achievement between blacks and whites threatens to make it impossible for blacks to achieve full equality in American society.

The civil rights approach has two essential aspects: first, the cause of a particular socioeconomic disparity is identified as racial discrimination; and second, advocates seek such remedies for the disparity as the courts and administrative agencies provide under the law.

There are fundamental limitations on this approach deriving from our liberal political heritage. What can this strategy do about those important contractual relationships that profoundly affect one's social and economic status but in which racial discrimination is routinely practiced? Choice of marital partner is an obvious example. People discriminate here by race with a vengeance. A black woman does not have an opportunity equal to that of a white woman to become the wife of a given white man. Since white men are on the whole better off financially than black men, this racial inequality of opportunity has substantial monetary costs to black women. Yet surely it is to be hoped that the choice of husband or wife will always be beyond the reach of the law.

The example is not facetious. All sorts of voluntary associations—neighborhoods, friends,

Source: Glenn C. Loury, "Beyond Civil Rights" *The New Republic* 3690 (October 7, 1985): 22–25. Used with permission of *The New Republic*.

business partnerships—are the result of choices often influenced by racial criteria, but which lie beyond the reach of civil rights laws. A fair housing law cannot prevent a disgruntled white resident from moving away if his neighborhood becomes predominantly or even partly black: Busing for desegregation cannot prevent unhappy parents from sending their children to private schools. Withdrawal of university support for student clubs with discriminatory selection rules cannot prevent student cliques from forming along racial lines. And a vast majority of Americans would have it no other way.

As a result, the nondiscrimination mandate has not been allowed to interfere much with personal, private, and intimately social intercourse. Yet such exclusive social connections along group lines have important economic consequences. An extensive literature in economics and sociology documents the crucial importance of family and community background in determining a child's later success in life. Lacking the right "networks," blacks with the same innate abilities as whites wind up less successful. And the elimination of racial discrimination in the economic sphere—but not in patterns of social attachment—will probably not be enough to make up the difference. There are thus elemental limits on what one can hope to achieve through the application of civil rights strategies to what must of necessity be a restricted domain of personal interactions.

The civil rights strategy has generally been restricted to the domain of impersonal, public, and economic transactions such as jobs, credit, and housing. Even in these areas, the efficacy of this strategy can be questioned. The lagging economic condition of blacks is due in significant part to the nature of social life *within* poor black communities. After two decades of civil rights efforts, more than three-fourths of children in some inner-city ghettos are born out of wedlock; black high school dropout rates hover near 50 percent in Chicago and Detroit; two-fifths of murder victims in the country are blacks killed by other blacks; fewer black women graduate from college than give birth while in high school; more

than two in five black children are dependent on public assistance. White America's lack of respect for blacks' civil rights cannot be blamed for all these sorry facts. This is not to deny that, in some basic sense, most of these difficulties are related to our history of racial oppression, but only to say that these problems have taken on a life of their own, and cannot be effectively reversed by civil rights policies.

Higher education is a case in point. In the not too distant past, blacks, Asians, and women faced severe obstacles to attending or teaching at American colleges and universities, especially at the most prestigious institutions. Even after black scholars studied at the great institutions, their only possibilities for employment were at the historically black colleges, where they faced large teaching loads and burdensome administrative duties. Their accomplishments were often acknowledged by their white peers only grudgingly, if at all.

Today opportunities for advanced education and academic careers for blacks abound. Major universities throughout the country are constantly searching for qualified black candidates to hire as professors, or to admit to study. Most state colleges and universities near black population centers have made a concerted effort to reach those in the inner city. Almost all institutions of higher learning admit blacks with lower grades or test scores than white students. There are special programs funded by private foundations to help blacks prepare for advanced study in medicine, economics, engineering, public policy, law, and other fields.

Yet, with all these opportunities (and despite improvement in some areas), the number of blacks advancing in the academic world is distressingly low. The percentage of college students who are black, after rising throughout the 1970s, has actually begun to decline. And though the proportion of doctorates granted to blacks has risen slightly over the last decade, a majority of black doctorates are still earned in the field of education. Despite constant pressure to hire black professors and strenuous efforts to recruit them, the percentage of blacks on elite university faculties has remained constant or fallen in the past decade.

Meanwhile, other groups traditionally excluded are making impressive gains. Asian-Americans, though less than two percent of the population, make up 6.6 percent of U.S. scientists with doctorates; they constitute 7.5 percent of the students at Yale, and nine percent at Stanford. The proportion of doctorates going to women has risen from less than one-seventh to nearly one-third in the last decade. Less than two percent of Harvard professors at all ranks are black, but more than 25 percent are women.

Now, it is entirely possible that blacks experience discrimination at these institutions. But as anyone who has spent time in an elite university community knows, these institutions are not racist in character, nor do they deny opportunities to blacks with outstanding qualifications. The case can be made that just the opposite is true—that these institutions are so anxious to raise the numbers of blacks in their ranks that they overlook deficiencies when making admissions or appointment decisions involving blacks.

One obvious reason for skepticism about discrimination as the cause of the problem here is the relatively poor academic performance of black high school and college students. Black performance on standardized college admissions tests, though improving, still lags far behind whites. In 1982 there were only 205 blacks in the entire country who scored above 700 on the math component of the SAT. And, as Robert Klitgaard shows convincingly in his book *Choosing Elites*, post-admissions college performance by black students is less than that of whites, even when controlling for differences in high school grades and SAT scores. These differences in academic performance are not just limited to poor blacks, or to high school students. On the SAT exam, blacks from families with incomes in excess of $50,000 per year still scored 60 to 80 points below comparable whites. On the 1982 Graduate Record Exam, the gap between black and white students' average scores on the mathematics component of this test was 171 points. According to Klitgaard,

black students entering law school in the late 1970s had median scores on the LSAT at the eighth percentile of all students' scores.

Such substantial differences in educational results are clearly a matter of great concern. Arguably, the government should be actively seeking to attenuate them. But it seems equally clear that this is not a civil rights matter that can be reversed by seeking out and changing someone's discriminatory behavior. Moreover, it is possible that great harm will be done if the problem is defined and pursued in those terms.

Take the controversy over racial quotas at the Boston Latin School, the pride and joy of the city's public school system. It was founded before Harvard, in 1635, and it has been recognized ever since as a center of academic excellence. Boston Latin maintains its very high standards through a grueling program of study, including Latin, Greek, calculus, history, science, and the arts. Three hours of homework per night are typical. College admissions personnel acknowledge the excellence of this program; 95 percent of the class of 1985 will go to college.

The institution admits its students on the basis of their marks in primary school and performance on the Secondary School Admissions Test. In 1974, when Boston's public schools became subject to court-ordered desegregation, Judge Arthur Garrity considered closing Boston Latin, because the student population at the time was more than 90 percent white. In the end, a racial admissions quota was employed, requiring that 35 percent of the entering classes be black and Hispanic. Of the 2,245 students last year, over half were female, 57 percent white, 23 percent black, 14 percent Asian, and six percent Hispanic.

Historically the school has maintained standards through a policy of academic "survival of the fittest." Those who were unable to make it through the academic rigors simply transferred to another school. Thus, there has always been a high rate of attrition; it is now in the range of 30 percent to 40 percent. But today, unlike the pre-desegregation era, most of those who do not succeed at Boston

Latin are minority students. Indeed, though approximately 35 percent of each entering class is black and Hispanic, only 16 percent of last year's senior class was. That is, for each non-Asian minority student who graduates from Latin, there is one who did not. The failure rate for whites is about half that. Some advocates of minority student interest have complained of discrimination, saying in effect that the school is not doing enough to assist those in academic difficulty. Yet surely one reason for the poor performance of the black and Hispanic students is Judge Garrity's admissions quota. To be considered for admission, whites must score at the 70th percentile or higher on the admissions exam, while blacks and Hispanics need only score above the 50th percentile.

Recently Thomas Atkins, former general counsel of the NAACP, who has been representing the black plaintiffs in the Boston school desegregation lawsuit, which has been going on for ten years, proposed that the quota at Boston Latin be raised to roughly 50 percent black, 20 percent Hispanic and Asian, and 30 percent white—a reflection of the racial composition of the rest of Boston's public schools. Unless there were a significant increase in the size of the school, this could only be accomplished by doubling the number of blacks admitted while cutting white enrollment in half. This in turn, under plausible distributional assumptions, would require that the current difference of 20 points in the minimum test scores required of black and white students accepted be approximately doubled. Since the additional black students admitted would be less prepared than those admitted under the current quota, one would expect an even higher failure rate among minorities were this plan to be accepted. The likely consequence would be that more than three-fourths of those leaving Boston Latin without a degree would be blacks and Hispanics. It is also plausible to infer that such an action would profoundly alter, if not destroy, the academic climate in the school.

This is not simply an inappropriate use of civil rights methods, though it is surely that. It is an almost wanton moral surrender. By what logic of pedagogy can these students' difficulties be attributed to racism, in view of the fact that the school system has been run by court order for over a decade? By what calculus of fairness can those claiming to be fighting for justice argue that outstanding white students, many from poor homes themselves (80 percent of Latin graduates require financial aid in college), should be denied the opportunity for this special education so that minority students who are not prepared for it may nonetheless enroll? Is there so little faith in the aptitude of the minority young people that the highest standards should not be held out for them? It would seem that the real problem here—a dearth of academically outstanding black high school students in Boston—is not amenable to rectification by court order.

Another example from the field of education illustrates the "opportunity costs" of the civil rights strategy. In 1977 the Ann Arbor public school system was sued by public interest lawyers on behalf of a group of black parents with children in the primary grades. The school system was accused of denying equal educational opportunity to these children. The problem was that the black students were not learning how to read at an acceptable rate, though the white youngsters were. The suit alleged that by failing to take into account in the teaching of reading to these children the fact that they spoke an identifiable, distinct dialect of the English language—Black English—the black students were denied equal educational opportunity. The lawsuit was successful.

As a result, in 1979 the court ordered that reading teachers in Ann Arbor be given special "sensitivity" training so that, while teaching standard English to these children, they might take into account the youngsters' culturally distinct patterns of speech. Ann Arbors' public school system has dutifully complied. A recent discussion of this case with local educators revealed that, as of six years after the initial court order, the disparity in reading achievement between blacks and whites in Ann Arbor persists at a level comparable to the one before the lawsuit was brought. It was their opinion that, though of enormous symbolic importance, the entire process had produced little in the way of positive educational impact on the students.

This is not intended as a condemnation of those who brought the suit, nor do I offer here any opinion on whether promotion of Black English is a good idea. What is of interest is the process by which the problem was defined, and out of which a remedy was sought. In effect, the parents of these children were approached by lawyers and educators active in civil rights, and urged to help their children learn to read by bringing this action. Literally thousands of hours went into conceiving and trying this case. Yet, in the end only a hollow, symbolic victory was won.

But it is quite possible that this line of attack on the problem caused other more viable strategies not to be pursued. For example, a campaign to tutor the first and second graders might have made an impact, giving them special attention and extra hours of study through the voluntary participation of those in Ann Arbor possessing the relevant skills. With roughly 35,000 students at the University of Michigan's Ann Arbor campus (a fair number of whom are black), it would have required that only a fraction of one percent of them spare an afternoon or evening once a week for there to be sufficient numbers to provide the needed services. There were at most only a few hundred poor black students in the primary grades experiencing reading difficulties. And, more than providing this needed aid for specific kids, such an undertaking would have helped to cultivate a more healthy relationship between the university and the town. It could have contributed to building a tradition of direct services that would be of more general value. But none of this happened, in part because the civil rights approach was almost reflexively embraced by the advocating parties concerned.

The danger to blacks of too broad a reliance on civil rights strategies can be subtle. It has become quite clear that affirmative action creates uncertain perceptions about the qualifica-

tions of those minorities who benefit from it. In an employment situation, for example, if it is known that different selection criteria are used for different races, and that the quality of performance on the job depends on how one did on the criteria of selection, then in the absence of other information, it is rational to expect lower performance from persons of the race that was preferentially favored in selection. Using race as a criterion of selection in employment, in other words, creates objective incentives for customers, co-workers, and others to take race into account after the employment decision has been made.

The broad use of race preference to treat all instances of "underrepresentation" also introduces uncertainty among the beneficiaries themselves.... It undermines the ability of people confidently to assert, if only to themselves, that they are as good as their achievements would seem to suggest. It therefore undermines the extent to which the personal success of any one black can become the basis of guiding the behavior of other blacks. Fewer individuals in a group subject to such preferences return to their communities of origin to say, "I made it on my own, through hard work, self-application, and native ability, and so can you!" Moreover, it puts even the "best and brightest" of the favored group in the position of being supplicants of benevolent whites.

And this is not the end of the story. In order to defend such programs in the political arena—especially at the elite institutions—it becomes necessary to argue that almost no blacks could reach these heights without special favors. When there is internal disagreement among black intellectuals, for example, about the merits of affirmative action, critics of the policy are often attacked as being disingenuous, since (it is said) they clearly owe their own prominence to the very policy they criticize. The specific circumstances of the individual do not matter in this, for it is presumed that *all* blacks, whether directly or indirectly, are indebted to civil rights activity for their achievements. The consequence is a kind of "socialization" of the individual's success. The individual's effort to claim achievement for himself (and thus to secure the autonomy and legitimacy needed to deviate from group consensus, should that seem appropriate) is perceived as a kind of betrayal. There is nothing wrong, of course, with acknowledging the debt all blacks owe to those who fought and beat Jim Crow. There is everything wrong with a group's most accomplished persons feeling that the celebration of their personal attainments represents betrayal of their fellows.

In his recent, highly esteemed comparative history of slavery, *Slavery and Social Death,* sociologist Orlando Patterson defines slavery as the "permanent, violent domination of natally alienated and generally dishonored persons." Today's policy debates frequently focus on (or perhaps more accurately, appropriate) the American slave experience, especially the violent character of the institution, its brutalization of the Africans, and its destructive effects on social life among the slaves. Less attention is paid nowadays to the *dishonored* condition of the slave, and by extension, of the freedman. For Patterson this dishonoring was crucial. He sees as a common feature of slavery wherever it has occurred the parasitic phenomenon whereby masters derive honor and standing from their power over the slaves, and the slaves suffer an extreme marginality by virtue of having no social existence except that mediated by their masters. Patterson rejects the "property in people" definition of slavery, arguing that relations of respect and standing among persons are also crucial. But if this is so, it follows that emancipation—the ending of the master's property claim—is not of itself sufficient to convert a slave (or his descendant) into a genuinely equal citizen. There remains the intractable problem of overcoming the historically generated "lack of honor" of the freedman.

This problem, in my judgment, remains with us. Its eventual resolution is made less likely by blacks' broad, permanent reliance on racial preferences as remedies for academic or occupational under-performance. A central theme in Afro-American political and intellectual history is the demand for respect—the struggle to gain inclusion within the civic community, to become coequal participants in the national enterprise. This is, of course, a problem that all immigrant groups also faced, and that most have overcome. But here, unlike some other areas of social life, it seems that the black population's slave origins, subsequent racist exclusion, and continued dependence on special favors from the majority uniquely exacerbates the problem.

Blacks continue to seek the respect of their fellow Americans. And yet it becomes increasingly clear that, to do so, black Americans cannot substitute judicial and legislative decree for what is to be won through the outstanding achievements of individual black persons. That is, neither the pity, nor the guilt, nor the coerced acquiescence in one's demands—all of which have been amply available to blacks over the last two decades—is sufficient. *For what ultimately is being sought is the freely conveyed respect of one's peers.* Assigning prestigious positions so as to secure a proper racial balance—this as a permanent, broadly practiced policy—seems fundamentally inconsistent with the attainment of this goal. It is a truth worth noting that not everything of value can be redistributed.

If in the psychological calculus by which people determine their satisfaction such status considerations of honor, dignity, and respect are important, then this observation places basic limits on the extent to which public policy can bring about genuine equality. This is especially so with respect to the policy of racially preferential treatment, because its use to "equalize" can actually destroy the good that is being sought on behalf of those initially unequal. It would seem that, where the high regard of others is being sought, there is no substitute for what is to be won through the unaided accomplishments of individual persons.

The Memory of Enemies

Shelby Steele

One of the most time-consuming things is to have an enemy.

E. B. White

It is only human to give our enemies a distinct territory in our memory, which is why we hear the buzz of summer's first mosquito with alarm. We think only fools don't remember their enemies, because remembering is preparedness. And, conversely, what we call preparedness is often really a readiness to remember the enemy, an openness to his memory-triggering buzz. Even today, changing planes in a southern airport, the sound of a white southern accent slips right past what I know about the "New South" and finds my memory of the Old South. Recently, in line to buy a newspaper at such an airport, I found myself carefully watching the white saleswoman whose accent was particularly thick. If she was anything less than gracious to me as the lone black in line, I knew my defenses would come alive. I would think she must be of the Old South at heart, no more than a carpetbagger in the new one. And how many others down here were like her, imposters in this public-relations bromide of a New South? If she put my change on the counter rather than in my hand, I'd have all the evidence I needed to close the case against her and the New South to boot.

I could condemn this woman, or at least be willing to condemn her and even her region, not because of her racial beliefs, which I didn't know, but because her accent had suddenly made her accountable to *my* voluminous and vivid memory of a racist South. Because of this accent and my northern lack of familiarity with it, I was not encountering

the woman as much as my own memory of an extremely powerful and dreaded enemy—the Old South. A flood of emotional images accompanied the memory, constituted it, and I saw right through the woman as if into a screen of memory. Coolly I circled her with mistrust, ready for what I remembered. I thought I might take the offensive and let her glimpse the slightest disdain in the cut of my eyes. But, at the sight of this mistrustful black man, his eyes verging on disdain, might she not fall under the spell of her own enemy-memory and see before her an arrogant, hostile black against whom she must put up her own chilliness as a defense?

I think one of the heaviest weights that oppression leaves on the shoulders of its former victims is simply the memory of itself. This memory is a weight because it pulls the oppression forward out of history and into the present so that the former victim may see his world as much through the memory of his oppression as through his experience in the present. What makes this a weight is that the rememberer will gird himself against a larger and more formidable enemy than the one he is actually encountering. It was the intrusion of the enemy-memory that led me into an exaggerated and wasteful defensiveness with the saleswoman. I was willing to manufacture a little drama of one-upmanship, play it out, and then no doubt brood over it as though something was really at stake. Later I might recount it to my friends and thereby give this battle with memory even more solidity. The enemy-memory clamors to be made real, demands that we work at its realization. And in this working is its real heaviness, since scarce resources are lost in unnecessary defense. Fortunately I caught myself and did not show this woman any disdain. She sold me the newspaper, put three quarters change into

Source: Shelby Steele, "The Memory of Enemies" *Dissent* (Summer 1990): 326–32. Used with permission.

my hand, and gave me the same abbreviated, management-encouraged smile she had given everyone else before me. These little battles with memory can also be deflating.

I believe that one of the greatest problems black Americans currently face—one of the greatest barriers to our development in society—is that our memory of oppression has such power, magnitude, depth, and nuance that it constantly drains our best resources into more defense than is strictly necessary. Between defense and development, guns and butter, the enemy-memory perpetuates a costly imbalance in the distribution of energies, thoughts, and actions. None of this is to say that the real enemy has entirely disappeared. Nor is it to suggest that we should forget our oppression, assuming this was even possible. It is only to say that our oppression has left us with a dangerously powerful memory of itself that can pull us into warlike defensiveness at a time when there is more opportunity for development than ever before.

The memory of any enemy is always a pull into the past, into a preparedness against what has already happened. Some of this is necessary. But when there is a vast lake of such memory—and I can think of no group with a more powerful collective memory of its enemy than black Americans—the irresistible pull into the past can render opportunities in the present all but invisible. The look is backward rather than forward, outward rather than inward, so that the possibilities for development—education, economic initiative, job training, and so on—are only seen out of the corner of the backward-looking eye. Thus, between 1976 and 1989 middle-income blacks have endured a drop in college enrollment of between 53 and 36 percent while white enrollment increased 3.6 percent. I don't suggest that the backward pull of memory fully accounts for a statistic this dramatic. But neither does it make sense to blame so profound a drop entirely on the shift in financial aid from grants to loans that occurred in the 1980s. White enrollment increased slightly under this same shift.

I think there are many factors at work in a statistic like this. One of them is a certain un-

seeing casualness toward opportunity that itself has many sources, one being a powerful collective memory that can skew the vision of blacks away from the self-interested exploitation of opportunity and into a reenactment of past victimization that confirms our exaggerated sense of the enemy but also undermines our advancement. Not only does the enemy-memory pull us backward, it also indirectly encourages us to remain victims so as to confirm the power of the enemy we remember and believe in. It asks that we duplicate our oppression so that our remembered sense of it might be validated. I think this has something to do with the fact that so many middle-income black students decline to be admitted to colleges that woo them with preferential admissions policies. And for black students who are admitted, the national dropout rate is near 70 percent. If this is nothing less than a flight from opportunity, it is also a flight into a remembered victimization, a position we are used to, and one that makes memory into reality.

I think the literary term "objective correlative" best describes the process by which our memory of the enemy pulls the past into the present. The white southern accent I heard in the airport is an example of an objective correlative—an objective event that by association evokes a particular emotion or set of emotions. It was the savvy, musical sound of this woman's accent—an utterly random event—that evoked in me an aggregate of troublesome racial emotions. The accent was a correlative to those emotions by virtue of association alone.

The black comedian Richard Pryor does a funny bit on this. To get away from the pressures and the racism he found on the mainland, he buys a house deep in the forest on a remote Hawaiian island. But just as he settles in one night to at last enjoy his solitude, he hears from the surrounding forest the infamous cry of the southern "redneck," "YAAA-HOO!" This was the chilling cry that often preceded an escapade of mindless violence against blacks, the sort of good-ole'-boy violence that could mean anything from harassment to lynching. It correlates with and evokes the sort of terror that blacks lived with for centuries in the South, a terror that Pryor milks for great comic effect. But as far as we know, there are no real good ole' boys in his forest. The shout is by someone who does not know the meaning it carries for Pryor. It is an objective event that by correlation pulls forward a historical terror through space and time.

The enemy-memory works by correlation, by connecting events in the present to emotionally powerful memories of the enemy. In American life there are objective correlatives everywhere that evoke the painful thicket of emotions—vulnerability, self-doubt, helplessness, terror, and rage—that comes from having lived for centuries under the dominion of an enemy race. In the American language itself there are countless words and expressions that function as correlatives—"you people," "bootstraps," "reverse discrimination," "colored people" (interestingly, "people of color" is not a correlative), "black militant," "credit to his race," "one of my best friends...," "I never knew a black until college ... the Army ..."—any phrase or tone that condescends, damns with faint praise, or stereotypes either positively or negatively. Any generalization about blacks correlates with the practice of generalizing about us that led to our oppression. And then there is an entire iconography of visual correlatives covering everything from Confederate flags and pickup trucks with gun racks to black cast-iron lawn jockeys, "flesh-colored" Bandaids that are actually pink, separate black and white advertisements for the same product, and so on. Tragically, the most relentless visual correlative may be white skin itself, especially for blacks with little experience in the larger society.

Blacks grow up in America surrounded by correlatives to their collective pain. I think the recent demand on college campuses and in the workplace for more "racial sensitivity" is, among other things, a demand that whites become more sensitive to the myriad correlatives that put blacks in touch with painful emotions. White insensitivity in this area is a form of power, an unearned and unfair power, that feels to blacks like another manifestation of

their victimization. And in a sense it is, because white insensitivity in whatever form (and sometimes nothing can be more insensitive than a pained sensitivity that calls attention to itself) carries the power to diminish blacks even when unintended. On one level the push for racial sensitivity is an attempt to offset the power whites have by birthright to compromise blacks with racial anxiety by ignoring the correlatives to that anxiety.

But objective correlatives are only one part of the process by which the enemy-memory operates. They are intrusive visitations through which the objective world causes us to feel our emotional history in a way that makes us insecure in the present, and so robs us of power. But I believe this process also works in reverse, in a way that tries to restore power. That is, the enemy-memory becomes a force in its own right and actually creates correlatives for itself in the world—correlatives that reinforce its often exaggerated sense of the enemy's power so as to justify black demands for power. In this process mistrust is the transforming agent that encircles an "event" and redefines it as a correlative to the enemy's continuing intention to oppress blacks. And when the memory of the enemy is as vast and powerful as it is for black Americans, there is an abundance of mistrust available for this purpose. Correlatives created by racial mistrust are subjective rather than objective since they do not come from the outer world but rather are imposed on it. They are fabrications of racial mistrust in which current events are infused with the memory of a more powerful racism than exists today.

A recent and striking example is the claim by many blacks that the drug epidemic in black neighborhoods across the country is the result of a white conspiracy to commit genocide against black people. Here the memory of pernicious racism is being brought forward to redefine a current problem, to transform it into a correlative for what is remembered so that it cannot be seen for what it is. Even if we assume that government is not doing all it can to combat drug use in the inner city, it takes a long stretch to conclude that this is evidence of a white conspiracy to kill off blacks. I think memory and the mistrust born of it are the sources of this hyperbole. Also, once the black drug epidemic becomes a subjective correlative for black oppression, then it stands as a *racial* injustice and so entitles blacks, in the name of redress, to pursue power in relation to whites. Because subjective correlatives always make events into racial issues—by recasting them as examples of black victimization—they are used to justify the pursuit of power.

All of this, I believe, has something to do with why the civil rights leadership has lost credibility in American society since the days of Martin Luther King, Jr. Too much under the sway of their memory of the enemy, this more recent group of leaders has not always made the distinction between hyperbolic correlatives for black oppression and actual oppressive events. When the NAACP marched against the recent group of Supreme Court decisions that severely limited preferential treatment programs, it transformed this cluster of decisions into a correlative for black oppression, even though at least one decision reaffirmed for whites the same constitutional right to sue for representation that blacks demanded during the civil rights movement. None of these decisions deprived blacks of their constitutional rights, so to characterize them as antiblack is to recast them, through memory and mistrust, into symbols of the kind of oppression that blacks knew in the days of *Plessy v. Ferguson* when the principle of "separate but equal" was established. Decisions that attack *preferences* are made to correlate with decisions that deny black rights. Of course, this correlation is only suggested through the symbolism of protest marches and a rhetoric of black victimization, but its effect is to diminish the credibility of black leadership. Most Americans simply do not accept the correlation. It is an exaggeration that has the look of a power move.

The exaggeration of black victimization is always the first indication that a current event is being transformed by mistrust into a subjective correlative that sanctions the pursuit of racial power. (Victimization is a form of innocence, and innocence always entitles us to

pursue power.) The current black leadership has injured its credibility by its tendency to make so many black problems into correlatives for black oppression. The epidemic of black teen pregnancies, the weakened black family, the decline in the number of black college students, and so on are too often cast as correlatives of historic racism. About Mayor Marion Barry's arrest on drug charges, Benjamin Hooks of the NAACP said, "I don't think there's any question there's some racism involved...," despite the fact that countless other black mayors have not been hounded by such charges. Such claims are exaggerations because racism simply does not fully explain these problems. No doubt they have something to do with the historic wounds of oppression, but what the charge of racism does not explain is the giving in to these wounds more than ever before, during a twenty-five-year decline in racism and discrimination. There are more black males of college age in prison than in college even as universities across the country struggle to recruit more black students. Black leaders can solve their "credibility gap" only by distinguishing between real oppression and those correlatives that exaggerate it in the interest of narrow racial power. Without this distinction, our leaders seem always to be crying wolf. And here the point must be made that discrimination does continue to exist and we need credible leadership to resist it.

Tragically, there is a real antiblack sentiment in American life, but it is no longer as powerful as we *remember* it to be. Our memory makes us like the man who wears a heavy winter coat in springtime because he was frostbitten in winter. Every sharp spring breeze becomes a correlative for the enemy of frostbite, so that he is still actually living in winter even as flowers bloom all around him. Not only do subjective correlatives cause us to reenact the past, but they rarely bring us the power we seek through them because they are too much based on exaggeration. Worse, they cut us off from the present and its many opportunities by encouraging the sort of vision in which we look at the present only to confirm the past.

But the distortions of correlation are not the only problems that come to blacks from our enemy-memory. I think this memory has also led to one of our most serious mistakes in thinking: often to confuse the actual development of our race with the elimination of racial discrimination, somehow to see these two very different goals as synonymous. Though the elimination of discrimination clearly facilitates our development, the two goals are entirely different and require entirely different strategies. The elimination of discrimination will always be largely a collective endeavor while racial development will always be the *effect* that results from individuals within the race bettering their own lives. The former requires group solidarity, collective action, and a positive group identity while the latter demands individual initiative, challenging personal aspirations, focused hard work, and a strong individual identity. Different goals, different strategies. But I believe the powerful memory blacks have of racism and discrimination can rally us to the fight against these things at the expense of our development as a people. I think this is one of the reasons why blacks have fallen farther behind whites on many socioeconomic measures in the last twenty years even as actual discrimination has declined.

The enemy-memory distracts us from development by miring us in a very natural process of *inversion* in which we invert from negative to positive the very point of difference—our blackness—that the enemy used to justify our oppression. Inversion tries to transform the quality that made us most vulnerable into an identity of invulnerability. Blackness becomes a source of pride rather than shame, strength rather than weakness. This is a necessary and inevitable process by which any oppressed group regathers dignity and esteem from the experience of denigration.

But inversion—fueled by the visceral memory of the enemy—is also a trap. The great evil of America's oppression of blacks was the use of the collective quality of color to limit us as individuals no matter what our talents or energies—individual autonomy stifled by oppressive collectivism. When inversion drives us to make our racial collectivity positive rather than negative, it may reach for new dignity, but it also reinforces our bondage to this collectivism at the expense of individual autonomy. Whether we are struggling against shame or for pride, we are still spilling scarce energy into the pursuit of collective esteem at the expense of individual development.

Inversion draws us back into a preoccupation with our collective identity at the very moment when we most stand to gain from the initiative of individuals who are unburdened by too much collective obligation. To carry off inversion we must become self-conscious about the meaning of our race; we must redefine that meaning, invest it with an ideology and a politics, claim an essence for it, and look to it, as much as to ourselves, as a means to betterment. And, of course, this degree of racial preoccupation prepares the ground for intense factionalism within the race. Who has the best twist on blackness, the Black Muslims or the civil rights establishment, the cultural nationalists or the black Baptists, Malcolm X or Martin Luther King, Jr.? And who is the most black, who the least? Within each faction is a racial orthodoxy that must be endlessly debated and defended and that rallies the faction against other factions while imposing a censorship of thought on its own members. Even when blacks avoid factions, they must be ready to defend that choice to others and to themselves. Inversion perpetuates the fundamental imbalance of racial oppression itself by giving the collective quality of race far too much importance in the lives of individual black Americans.

One of the many advantages whites enjoy in America is a relative freedom from the draining obligation of racial inversion. Whites do not have to spend precious time fashioning an identity out of simply being white. They do not self-consciously have to imbue whiteness with an ideology, look to whiteness for some special essence, or divide up into factions and wrestle over what it means to be white. Their racial collectivism, to the extent that they feel it, creates no imbalance between the collective and the individual. This, of course, is yet another blessing of history and of power, of never having lived in the midst of an overwhelming enemy race. It is a blessing won at the expense of blacks, whose subjugation brought whites a sort of automatic racial inversion—a sense of superiority that freed them from the struggle for simple racial dignity.

It was clearly impossible for blacks to avoid inversion just as it was impossible for us to avoid our enemy. Therefore, it was also impossible for us to avoid the burden of collectivism and the preoccupation with race that goes with it. Inversion once was a survival impulse, and yet today when the oppression of blacks has greatly diminished, I believe this impulse causes our most serious strategic mistake: to put the responsibility for our racial development more in the hands of the collective than in the hands of the individuals who compose it. It is inversion that, by submerging us too deeply in collectivism, obscures the distinction mentioned above between the elimination of discrimination (societal change) and racial development. And once "collectivized," collective action seems to be the only remedy for our problems. But, although civil rights bills can be won this way, only the individual can achieve in school, master a salable skill, open a business, become an accountant or an engineer. Despite our collective oppression, opportunities for development can finally be exploited only by individuals.

Whether a stigmatized minority group develops successfully or slips into inertia has, I believe, much to do with whether the group allows its impulse toward inversion to muddy the distinction between societal change and group development. This is the distinction that allows the group to assign responsibility for development to the individual. Those groups that have somehow maintained this distinction (for historical and cultural reasons too complex to explore here) have thrived in America despite racism, anti-Semitism, and outright discrimination. Asians, Jews, West Indians, and others have found their avenues for development in the aspirations of their individuals who have approached American society with initiative, energy, and pragmatism. Certainly the point must be made here that

the civil rights movement, which won many victories against discrimination, made the road easier for the individuals within these groups. On the front of collective action against bigotry no group has made a greater contribution than black Americans. Yet I think the extremely intense memory of our enemy (along with racial vulnerability and the continuing presence of racism in America) has so absorbed us that we have overlooked the developmental power to be found in the aspirations of our individuals.

This imbalance is evident today in many areas of black life. Black college students often take a leading role in demanding change on their campuses yet as a group have the lowest grade-point average and the highest dropout rate of any student group in America—collective action over individual initiative. The national civil rights leadership relentlessly pressures the government for more and better social programs yet does not put equal pressure on blacks to achieve as individuals—one result being that we are often not developed enough to take advantage of the concessions they win, such as affirmative action. Their unconscious strategy is to transform the problems of black America into subjective correlatives. When problems like black teenage pregnancies, the drug epidemic, poor educational performance, and so on are recast as correlatives for black oppression, the primary responsibility for solving them automatically falls on the larger society. Subjective correlatives serve inversion by blame-placing, by casting blacks as victims and the society as their oppressor. But most of all they always show black problems as resulting from an oppression that can be resisted only by collective action. And here is where the distinction between societal change and racial development is lost, where the individual is subsumed by the collective.

Thus, at the 1989 NAACP convention several problems that face black America—from affirmative action to teen pregnancies—were listed on the agenda, but primarily as subjective correlatives, as evidence of society's indifference to blacks, as yet more proof of our continuing victimization and therefore our innocence. In this deterministic context the power to be found in the individual is lost amidst the exhortations for more societal change. The price blacks pay for placing too much of the blame for our problems on society is to be helpless before those problems.

Inversion also hurts our development in another way. If the memory of the enemy leads to inversion (helped along by subjective correlatives), it is also true that inversion requires us to remember the enemy. In order to invert, to make blackness positive, we must know the negative views whites have of us. In this sense, inversion not only makes the black identity itself too much a response to white racism but it also makes our identity dependent on that racism. With inversion we need a knowledge of our former oppressor's worst view of us in order to carry out the work of self-definition—a process that requires us to remember the enemy at his "worst" in order to know ourselves at our "best." In this way inversion, born of the memory of our enemy, also demands that we remember him more, thus completing a self-perpetuating cycle of obsessive and painful memory.

By exaggerating our enemy in order to define ourselves, we put ourselves in the ironic position of having to deny clearly visible opportunities in order to "be black" and claim a strong black identity. Out of this cycle of memory comes the "real black," who sees society as an oppressive withholder of black opportunities. I recently spoke with a black woman who described herself as a cultural nationalist. In her view there were virtually no opportunities for blacks to enter the mainstream of American life, which she saw as fundamentally racist. She was, as we say, the blackest of the black, yet this purified identity was achieved by an absolute denial of mainstream black opportunity. In her scheme the more opportunity one admitted to, let alone took advantage of, the less "black" one was. The power of memory and inversion had virtually called this woman back to slavery and left her no option but collective action since individual possibility was all but invisible to her. She was an extreme case, but also an extreme version of the paradigm that touches

many blacks. Even among middle-class blacks who function well in the mainstream, when the time comes to declare one's identity, to announce one's blackness, there is invariably a denial of black opportunity. This is the denial that brings one securely back inside the circle of blackness, that quite literally lets one feel black. To point to opportunity is to stand outside this circle, to be less black. Inversion is a reunion with the enemy in which we once again define ourselves as his victim.

Common wisdom sometimes tells us that it is good to have enemies. "We can learn even from our enemies," said Ovid. Probably this is true, since two other things are certainly true: we will have enemies whether they are good for us or not, and we will have a bond with them whether we wish to or not. But the quarrel I have with such wisdom is that it does not speak to the issue of degree. It is one thing to simply have an enemy; it is another thing to be inundated and sat upon by an enemy and to live in this condition over the course of centuries. The magnitude of such an enemy makes the common wisdom almost fatuous. No doubt black Americans have learned much from such an enemy, but at a price that has been absurdly punitive. Still, I think we have one thing left to learn—to discipline our memory of the enemy so that we can distinguish between that memory and the actual "enemy activity" that we may still encounter. To fail in this distinction is to remain at war with a far greater enemy than the one we actually live with.

Our greatest problem today is insufficient development—this *more* than white racism. And just as nations deplete themselves rather than develop in wartime, we can't really advance under the burden of an enemy swollen into a Goliath by memory. We must see the enemy for the mad bee that he is rather than the raging lion he used to be. If this metaphor is too charitable, then we can pick another one, but in any case we must diminish his size and scope in our minds to his actual proportions. Then we must free our individuals from the tyranny of a wartime collectivism in which they must think of themselves as victims in order to identify with their race. The challenge now is to reclaim ourselves from the exaggerations of our own memory and to go forward as the free American citizens that we are. There is no magic that will make development happen. We have to simply want more for ourselves, be willing to work for it, and not use our enemy—old or new—as an excuse not to pursue it. It doesn't really matter that southern accents in southern airports make me remember. What's important is that I can travel.

FURTHER READING

Faryna, Stan, Brad Stetson, and Joseph G. Conti, eds. 1997. *Black and Right: The Bold New Voice of Black Conservatives in America.* Westport, CT: Praeger.

Lawson, Bill, ed. 1992. *The Underclass Question.* Philadelphia: Temple University Press.

Marable, Manning. 1982. "Black Conservatives and Accommodation: Of Thomas Sowell and Others." *Negro History Bulletin* 45 (April–June): 32–5.

Meier, August. 1966. "The Dilemmas of Negro Protest Strategy." *New South* 21 (Spring 1966):1–18.

Morrison, Toni 1992. *Race-ing Justice, En-gendering Power: Essays on Anita Hill, Clarence Thomas, and the Construction of Social Reality.* New York: Pantheon Books.

Mosley, Albert G., and Nicholas Copoldi. 1996. *Affirmative Action: Social Justice or Unfair Preference?* Lanham, MD: Rowman and Littlefield.

Patterson, Orlando. 1997. *The Ordeal of Integration: Progress and Resentment in America's "Racial" Crisis.* Washington, DC: Civitas/Counterpoint.

Robinson, Cedric J. 1998. *Black Movements in America.* New York: Routledge.

Schuyler, George S. 1966. *Black and Conservative.* New Rochelle, NY: Arlington House Publishers.

Thomas, Laurence. 1989. *Living Morally: A Psychology of Moral Character.* Philadelphia: Temple University Press.

Williams, Walter. 1982. *The State Against Blacks.* New York: McGraw-Hill.

Wilson, William J. 1987. *The Truly Disadvantaged.* Chicago: University of Chicago.

CHAPTER 9

Black Women Writers on Rape

The topic of rape has long been a source of conflict among feminists. Bettina Aptheker attributes this rift to the fact that black and white women have different conceptions of rape. Commenting on Susan Brownmiller's experience conducting research on rape at the Schomberg Library in Harlem, Aptheker remarks: "For the librarian at the Schomberg the word 'rape' immediately and appropriately conjured the specter of lynching whereas for Susan Brownmiller the word conjured centuries of violence against women." Brownmiller was in search of statistical evidence to prove that black men are unusually prone to rape—a concern shared by many whites in discussions of interracial rape cases. Black feminists have not embraced Brownmiller's view. Alice Walker presents Brownmiller's concern, but with a great deal more ambivalence, given the tendency of whites to use the rape charge to justify lynching and terrorizing. She reflects on an important implication of interracial rape with regard to a conflict between racial and gender oppression.

To fully understand why rape that crosses racial boundaries is more politically charged when the suspect is a black man, the question of how rape is connected with political and economic power must be considered. Referring to lynching as "color-line murder," Ida B. Wells-Barnett relies on the statistics provided by conservative newspapers to show that lynching is a manifestation of white patriarchy—functioning to punish consensual relations between white women and black men and to terrorize black people. In her address to the National Negro Conference she comments on the 857 black victims in 1899: "No other nation, civilized or savage, burns its criminals." As a remedy she proposes federal prosecution to punish local law enforcement for failing to uphold the law. In the selection from her autobiography she reports her experience as a crusader to indicate the politics involved in pursuing this strategy. Her reputation as a tenacious fighter is well attested in her story about her campaign in Illinois to prevent the reinstatement of a sheriff who had been removed under such a law for failing to prevent a lynching met with resistance from both black and white quarters.

Alice Walker's story "Advancing Luna—And Ida B. Wells" addresses the conflict between race and gender by presenting a dilemma arising from an interracial rape. She describes being told about the rape of a white friend by a black man they both knew while working together as activists in the South in the civil rights movement. Her analysis probes the moral dimensions of choosing to speak out or to remain silent in such cases. While she believes that to speak out against the rape of Luna would violate the memory of Ida B. Wells, she wonders how black women can be expected to remain silent on this outrageous matter. Walker acknowledges her own "tangled emotions" about interracial rape but finds it difficult to remain silent about the guilty black rapist. Walker ends her story with her ambivalence unresolved. She tells us that a story that resolves her dilemma "is reserved for a society in which lynching is still reserved, at least subconsciously, as a means of racial control."

Walker's dilemma regarding interracial rape is generated by the intersection of race and gender. Valerie Smith claims that the silence Walker bemoans "speaks volumes" about the ways in which cultural anxieties about race and gender are projected. Smith criticizes Wells-Barnett's campaign against lynching on the ground that she was required "effectively to deny the veracity of any white woman's testimony against a black man." Moreover, Wells-Barnett seems to have acted in a manner counter to feminism, for the blaming of white women for the lynching of black men subordinates the sexual to the racial dimension of interracial rape. Smith focuses on the black community's need to sympathize with the accused black man as placing black women in a "particularly vexed" position. As women they share the victim's sense of violation, but unlike white women, they have an awareness of the political uses of the fraudulent rape charge. Smith points out that the unspeakability of interracial rape forces a separation between the narrator of Walker's story and Luna, but also forces a separation between the narrator and Walker.

This latter separation alludes to a conflict among black feminists over the dilemma that arises in cases involving interracial rape. Joy James disagrees with Walker's and Smith's interpretations of Wells-Barnett's strategy. James points out that Wells-Barnett did not categorically deny that black men assaulted white women, nor did she advocate that others make denials when this occurs. Instead, Wells-Barnett was concerned that "any mesalliance" was a ground for the fradulent rape charge. James maintains that it was her relentless and ruthless pursuit of an end to lynching that led to Wells-Barnett's being stigmatized as an apologist for rapists.

According to James there are important facts about the real Wells-Barnett that do not fit Walker's fictionalized characterization. Wells-Barnett operated in the women's club movement from the standpoint of black nationalism. Likewise, her antilynching activism was a defense of the entire race. James criticizes Smith's thesis that the divided loyalties of black women create their split affinities in interracial rape cases. She objects to Smith's attempt to reduce a range of views on interracial rape to one that is split over race and gender by pointing out that there is no uniform practice of subordinating gender to race by black women. She maintains instead that responses will vary in accordance with the specific circumstances. James insists that black feminism is a dual rather than a split identity. This is not to be confused with privileging black men; rather it presupposes intersectionality by acknowledging that black women identify with both the white woman survivor of a rape and the accused black man.

Lynching, Our National Crime

Ida B. Wells-Barnett

The lynching record for a quarter of a century merits the thoughtful study of the American people. It presents three salient facts:

First: Lynching is color-line murder.

Second: Crimes against women is the excuse, not the cause.

Third: It is a national crime and requires a national remedy.

Proof that lynching follows the color line is to be found in the statistics which have been kept for the past twenty-five years. During the few years preceding this period and while frontier lynch law existed, the executions showed a majority of white victims. Later, however, as law courts and authorized judiciary extended into the far West, lynch law rapidly abated, and its white victims became few and far between.

Just as the lynch-law regime came to a close in the West, a new mob movement started in the South. This was wholly political, its purpose being to suppress the colored vote by intimidation and murder. Thousands of assassins banded together under the name of Ku Klux Klans, "Midnight Raiders," "Knights of the Golden Circle," et cetera, et cetera, spread a reign of terror, by beating, shooting and killing colored people by the thousands. In a few years, the purpose was accomplished, and the black vote was suppressed. But mob murder continued.

From 1882, in which year fifty-two were lynched, down to the present, lynching has been along the color line. Mob murder increased yearly until in 1892 more than two hundred victims were lynched and statistics show that 3,284 men, women and children have been put to death in this quarter of a

Source: Ida B. Wells-Barnett, "Lynching, Our National Crime" *Proceedings of the National Negro Conference*, 1909, 174–79.

century. During the last ten years from 1899 to 1908 inclusive the number lynched was 959. Of this number 102 were white, while the colored victims numbered 857. No other nation, civilized or savage, burns its criminals; only under the Stars and Stripes is the human holocaust possible. Twenty-eight human beings burned at the stake, one of them a woman and two of them children, is the awful indictment against American civilization—the gruesome tribute which the nation pays to the color line.

Why is mob murder permitted by a Christian nation? What is the cause of this awful slaughter? This question is answered almost daily—always the same shameless falsehood that "Negroes are lynched to protect womanhood." Standing before a Chautauqua assemblage, John Temple Graves, at once champion of lynching and apologist for lynchers, said: "The mob stands today as the most potential bulwark between the women of the South and such a carnival of crime as would infuriate the world and precipitate the annihilation of the Negro race." This is the never-varying answer of lynchers and their apologists. All know that it is untrue. The cowardly lyncher revels in murder, then seeks to shield himself from public execration by claiming devotion to woman. But truth is mighty and the lynching record discloses the hypocrisy of the lyncher as well as his crime.

The Springfield, Illinois, mob rioted for two days, the militia of the entire state was called out, two men were lynched, hundreds of people driven from their homes, all because a white woman said a Negro assaulted her. A mad mob went to the jail, tried to lynch the victim of her charge and, not being able to find him, proceeded to pillage and burn the town and to lynch two innocent men. Later, after the police had found that the woman's charge was false, she published a retraction, the indictment was dismissed and the intended victim discharged. But the lynched victims were dead. Hundreds were homeless and Illinois was disgraced.

As a final and complete refutation of the charge that lynching is occasioned by crimes against women, a partial record of lynchings is cited; 285 persons were lynched for causes as follows:

Unknown cause, 92; no cause, 10; race prejudice, 49; miscegenation, 7; informing, 12; making threats, 11; keeping saloon, 3; practicing fraud, 5; practicing voodooism, 2; bad reputation, 8; unpopularity, 3; mistaken identity, 5; using improper language, 3; violation of contract, 1; writing insulting letter, 2; eloping, 2; poisoning horse, 1; poisoning well, 2; by white caps, 9; vigilantes, 14; Indians, 1; moonshining, 1; refusing evidence, 2; political causes, 5; disputing, 1; disobeying quarantine regulations, 2; slapping a child, 1; turning state's evidence, 3; protecting a Negro, 1; to prevent giving evidence, 1; knowledge of larceny, 1; writing letter to white woman, 1; asking white woman to marry, 1; jilting girl, 1; having smallpox, 1; concealing criminal, 2; threatening political exposure, 1; self-defense, 6; cruelty, 1; insulting language to woman, 5; quarreling with white man, 2; colonizing Negroes, 1; throwing stones, 1; quarreling, 1; gambling, 1.

Is there a remedy, or will the nation confess that it cannot protect its protectors at home as well as abroad? Various remedies have been suggested to abolish the lynching infamy, but year after year, the butchery of men, women and children continues in spite of plea and protest. Education is suggested as a preventive, but it is as grave a crime to murder an ignorant man as it is a scholar. True, few educated men have been lynched, but the hue and cry once started stops at no bounds, as was clearly shown by the lynchings in Atlanta, and in Springfield, Illinois.

Agitation, though helpful, will not alone stop the crime. Year after year statistics are published, meetings are held, resolutions are adopted and yet lynchings go on. Public sentiment does measurably decrease the sway of mob law, but the irresponsible bloodthirsty criminals who swept through the streets of Springfield, beating an inoffensive law-abiding citizen to death in one part of the town, and in another torturing and shooting to death a man who for threescore years had made a reputation for honesty, integrity and sobriety, had raised a family and had accumulated property, were not deterred from their heinous crimes by either education or agitation.

The only certain remedy is an appeal to law. Lawbreakers must be made to know that human life is sacred and that every citizen of this country is first a citizen of the United States and secondly a citizen of the state in which he belongs. This nation must assert itself and defend its federal citizenship at home as well as abroad. The strong arm of the government must reach across state lines whenever unbridled lawlessness defies state laws and must give to the individual citizen under the Stars and Stripes the same measure of protection which it gives to him when he travels in foreign lands.

Federal protection of American citizenship is the remedy for lynching. Foreigners are rarely lynched in America. If, by mistake, one is lynched, the national government quickly pays the damages. The recent agitation in California against the Japanese compelled this nation to recognize that federal power must yet assert itself to protect the nation from the treason of sovereign states. Thousands of American citizens have been put to death and no President has yet raised his hand in effective protest, but a simple insult to a native of Japan was quite sufficient to stir the government at Washington to prevent the threatened wrong. If the government has power to protect a foreigner from insult, certainly it has power to save a citizen's life.

The practical remedy has been more than once suggested in Congress. Senator Gallinger, of New Hampshire, in a resolution introduced in Congress called for an investigation "with the view of ascertaining whether there is a remedy for lynching which Congress may apply." The Senate Committee has under consideration a bill drawn by A. E. Pillsbury, formerly Attorney General of Massachusetts, providing for federal prosecution of lynchers in cases where the state fails to protect citizens or foreigners. Both of these resolutions indicate that the attention of the nation has been called to this phase of the lynching question.

As a final word, it would be a beginning in the right direction if this conference can see its way clear to establish a bureau for the investigation and publication of the details of every lynching, so that the public could know that an influential body of citizens has made it a duty to give the widest publicity to the facts in each case; that it will make an effort to secure expressions of opinion all over the country against lynching for the sake of the country's fair name; and lastly, but by no means least, to try to influence the daily papers of the country to refuse to become accessory to mobs either before or after the fact. Several of the greatest riots and most brutal burnt offerings of the mobs have been suggested and incited by the daily papers of the offending community. If the newspaper which suggests lynching in its accounts of an alleged crime, could be held legally as well as morally responsible for reporting that "threats of lynching were heard"; or, "it is feared that if the guilty one is caught, he will be lynched"; or, "there were cries of 'lynch him,' and the only reason the threat was not carried out was because no leader appeared," a long step toward a remedy will have been taken.

In a multitude of counsel there is wisdom. Upon the grave question presented by the slaughter of innocent men, women and children there should be an honest, courageous conference of patriotic, law-abiding citizens anxious to punish crime promptly, impartially and by due process of law, also to make life, liberty and property secure against mob rule.

Time was when lynching appeared to be sectional, but now it is national—a blight upon our nation, mocking our laws and disgracing our Christianity. "With malice toward none but with charity for all" let us undertake the work of making the "law of the land" effective and supreme upon every foot of American soil—a shield to the innocent; and to the guilty, punishment swift and sure.

Illinois Lynchings

Ida B. Wells-Barnett

Directly after the Springfield riot, at the next session of the legislature, a law was enacted which provided that any sheriff who permitted a prisoner to be taken from him and lynched should be removed from office. This bill was offered by Edward D. Green, who had been sent to Springfield to represent our race. Illinois had had not only a number of lynchings, but also a three days' riot at Springfield.

In due course of time the daily press announced that a lynching had taken place in Cairo, Illinois. The body of a white woman had been found in an alley in the residential district and, following the usual custom, the police immediately looked for a Negro. Finding a shiftless, penniless colored man known as "Frog" James, who seemed unable to give a good account of himself, according to police, this man was locked up in the police station and according to the newspapers a crowd began to gather around the station and the sheriff was sent for.

Mr. Frank Davis, the sheriff, after a brief conversation with the prisoner, took him to the railroad station, got on the train, and took him up into the woods accompanied by a single deputy. They remained there overnight. Next morning, when a mob had grown to great proportions, they too went up into the country and had no trouble in locating the sheriff and his prisoner. He was placed on a train and brought back to town, accompanied by the sheriff. The newspapers announced that as the train came to an standstill, some of the mob put a rope around "Frog's" neck and dragged him out of the train and to the most prominent corner of the town, where the rope was thrown over an electric light arch and the body hauled up above the heads of the crowd.

Five hundred bullets were fired into it, some of which cut the rope, and the body dropped to the ground. Members of the mob seized hold of the rope and dragged the body up Washington Street, followed by men, women, and children, some of the women pushing baby carriages. The body was taken near to the place where the corpse of the white girl had been found. Here they cut off his head, stuck it on a fence post, built a fire around the body and burned it to a crisp.

When the news of this horrible thing appeared in the papers, immediately a meeting was called and a telegram sent to Governor Deneen demanding that the sheriff of Alexander County be dispossessed. The newspapers had already quoted the governor as saying that he did not think it mandatory on him to displace the sheriff. But when our telegram reached him calling attention to the law, he immediately ousted him by telegram.

This same law provided that after the expiration of a short time, the sheriff would have the right to appear before the governor and show cause why he ought to be reinstated. We had a telegram from Governor Deneen informing us that on the following Wednesday the sheriff would appear before him demanding reinstatement. Mr. Barnett spent some time urging representative men of our race to appear before the governor and fight the sheriff's reinstatement.

Colonel Frank Dennison and Robert Taylor had been down in that county hunting at the time of this occurrence, and they were reported as saying they had seen signals being wigwagged between the mob which was hunting "Frog" James and the sheriff who had him

Source: Ida B. Wells-Barnett "Illinois Lynchings" in *Crusade for Justice, The Autobiography of Ida B. Wells* (Chicago: University of Chicago Press, 1970), 309–20.

in charge. Colonel Dennison was asked to appear. He refused, saying that the whole episode was going to be a whitewash and he wasn't going to have anything to do with it. When he and others were reminded that it was their duty to fight the effort to reinstate the sheriff, they still refused.

This information was given us at the dinner table by Mr. Barnett, and he wound up his recital of his fruitless efforts that Saturday afternoon to get someone to appear by saying, "And so it would seem that you will have to go to Cairo and get the facts with which to confront the sheriff next Wednesday morning. And your train leaves at eight o'clock." I objected very strongly because I had already been accused by some of our men of jumping in ahead of them and doing work without giving them a chance.

It was not very convenient for me to be leaving home at that time, and for once I was quite willing to let them attend to the job. Mr. Barnett replied that I knew it was important that somebody gather the evidence as well as he did, but if I was not willing to go, there was nothing more to be said. He picked up the evening paper and I picked up my baby and took her upstairs to bed. As usual I not only sang her to sleep but put myself to sleep lying there beside her.

I was awakened by my oldest child, who said, "Mother, Pa says it is time to go." "Go where?" I said. He said, "To take the train to Cairo." I said, "I told your father downstairs that I was not going. I don't see why I should have to go and do the work that the others refuse." My boy was only ten years old. He and the other children had been present at the dinner table when their father told the story. He stood by the bedside a little while and then said, "Mother if you don't go nobody else will."

I looked at my child standing there by the bed reminding me of my duty, and I thought of that passage of Scripture which tells of the wisdom from the mouths of babes and sucklings. I thought if my child wanted me to go that I ought not to fall by the wayside, and I said, "Tell daddy it is too late to catch the train now, that I'll go in the morning. It is bet-

ter for me to arrive in Cairo after nightfall anyway."

Next morning all four of my children accompanied my husband and me to the station and saw me start on the journey. They were intensely interested and for the first time were willing to see me leave home.

I reached Cairo after nightfall, and was driven to the home of the leading A.M.E. minister, just before he went into church for his evening service. I told him why I was there and asked if he could give me any help in getting the sentiment of the colored people and investigating facts. He said that they all believed that "Frog" James had committed that murder. I asked him if he had anything upon which to base that belief. "Well," he said, "he was a worthless sort of fellow, just about the kind of a man who would do a trick like that. Anyhow, all of the colored people believe that and many of us have written letters already to the governor asking the reinstatement of the sheriff."

I sprang to my feet and asked him if he realized what he had done in condoning the horrible lynching of a fellowman who was a member of his race. Did he not know that if they condoned the lynching of one man, the time might come when they would have to condone that of other men higher up, providing they were black?

I asked him if he could direct me to the home of some other colored persons; that I had been sent to see all of them, and it wouldn't be fair for me to accept reports from one man alone. He gave me the names of one or two others, and I withdrew. I had expected to stop at his home, but after he told me that I had no desire to do so. One of the men named was Will Taylor, a druggist, whom I had known in Chicago, and I asked to be directed to his place. The minister's wife went with me because it was dark.

Mr. Taylor greeted me very cordially and I told him what my mission was. He also secured me a stopping place with persons by the name of Lewis, whom I afterward found were teachers in the colored high schools, both the man and his wife. They welcomed me very cordially and listened to my story. I told them why I was there; they gave me a bed. The next morning Mrs. Lewis came and informed me that she had already telephoned Dr. Taylor that she was sorry she could not continue to keep me. I found afterward that after they heard the story they felt that discretion was the better part of valor.

Mr. Taylor and I spent the day talking with colored citizens and ended with a meeting that night. I was driven to the place where the body of the murdered girl had been found, where the Negro had been burned, and saw about twenty-five representative colored people of the town that day. Many of those whom I found knew nothing whatever of the action that had been taken by the citizens of Chicago.

The meeting was largely attended and in my statement to them I said I had come down to be their mouthpiece; that I correctly understood how hard it would be for those who lived there to take an active part in the movement to oust the sheriff; that we were willing to take the lead in the matter but they must give me the facts; that it would be endangering the lives of other colored people in Illinois if we did not take a stand against the all too frequent lynchings which were taking place.

I went on to say that I came because I knew that they knew of my work against lynching for fifteen years past and felt that they would talk more freely to me and trust me more fully than they would someone of whom they knew nothing. I wanted them to tell me if Mr. Frank Davis had used his great power to protect the victim of the mob; if he had at any time placed him behind bars of the county jail as the law required; and if he had sworn in any deputies to help protect his prisoner as he was obliged by law to do until such time as he could be tried by due process of law. Although the meeting lasted for two hours, and although most of those present and speaking were friends of Frank Davis, some of whom had been deputy sheriffs in his office, not one of them could honestly say that Frank Davis had put his prisoner in the county jail or had done anything to protect him. I therefore offered a resolution to that effect which was al-

most unanimously adopted. There was one single objection by the ubiquitous "Uncle Tom" Negro who seems always present. I begged the people, if they could do nothing to help the movement to punish Frank Davis for such glaring negligence of his duty, that they would do nothing to hinder us.

Next morning before taking the train I learned of a Baptist ministers' meeting that was being held there and decided to attend for the purpose of having them pass the same resolution. I was told that it would do no good to make the effort and that it would delay me until midnight getting into Springfield. But I went, got an opportunity to speak, offered the resolution, told of the men who had sent letters to the governor, showed how that would confuse his mind as to the attitude of the colored people on the subject, and stated clearly that all such action would mean that we would have other lynchings in Illinois whenever it suited the mob anywhere.

I asked the adoption of the resolution passed the night before. There was discussion pro and con, and finally the moderator arose and said, "Brethren, they say an honest confession is good for the soul. I, too, am one of those men who have written to the governor asking Frank Davis's reinstatement. I knew he was a friend of ours; that the man who had taken his place has turned out all Negro deputies and put in Democrats, and I was told that when the mob placed the rope around "Frog" James's neck the sheriff tried to prevent them and was knocked down for his pains. But now that the sister has shown us plainly the construction that would be placed upon that letter, I want her when she appears before the governor tomorrow to tell him that I take that letter back and hereby sign my name to this resolution." By this time the old man was shedding tears. Needless to say the resolution went through without any further objections.

Mr. Barnett had told me that he would prepare a brief based upon what had been gleaned from the daily press, which would be in the post office at Springfield when I got there Wednesday morning; that if I found any facts contrary to those mentioned I could easily make the correction. There had been no precedent for this procedure, but he assumed that the attorney general would be present to represent the people.

When I entered the room at ten o'clock that morning I looked around for some of my own race, thinking that perhaps they would journey to Springfield for the hearing, even though they had been unwilling to go to Cairo to get the facts. Not a Negro face was in evidence! On the other side of the room there was Frank Davis, and with him one of the biggest lawyers in southern Illinois, so I was afterward told, who was also a state senator.

There was the parish priest, the state's attorney of Alexander County, the United States land commissioner, and about half a dozen other representative white men who had journeyed from Cairo to give aid and comfort to Frank Davis in his fight for reinstatement.

The governor said that they had no precedent and that he would now hear the plea to be made by the sheriff; whereupon this big lawyer proceeded to present his petition for reinstatement and backed it up with letters and telegrams from Democrats and Republicans, bankers, lawyers, doctors, editors of both daily papers, and heads of women's clubs and of men's organizations. The whole of the white population of Cairo was evidently behind Frank Davis and his demand for reinstatement.

In addition to this there were read these letters from Negro ministers and colored politicians. Special emphasis was laid upon them. Just before reading one of them the state senator said, "Your Excellency, I have known the writer of this letter since I was a boy. He has such a standing for truth and veracity in the community that if he were to tell me that black was white I would believe him, and he, too, has written to ask that Frank Davis be reinstated."

And then he presented the names of nearly five hundred Negro men that had been signed to petitions circulated in three Negro barbershops. I had heard about these petitions while I was in Cairo and I went to

the barbershops and saw them myself. Of course, there were only a few signers present when I was there, but to the few who happened to be standing around I gave the most blistering talk that I could lay my tongue to.

When the gentlemen had finished, Governor Deneen said, "I understand Mrs. Barnett is here to represent the colored people of Illinois." Not until that moment did I realize that the burden depended upon me. It so happened that Attorney A. M. Williams, a Negro lawyer of Springfield, having heard that I was in town, came over to the Capitol to invite me to his home for dinner. Finding me by myself, he immediately camped by my side and remained with me all through the ordeal. I was indeed thankful for this help, since never before had I been confronted with a situation that called for legal knowledge.

I began by reading the brief which Mr. Barnett prepared in due legal form. I then launched out to tell of my investigation in Cairo. Before I had gotten very far the clock struck twelve, and Springfield being a country town, everything stopped so people could go home to dinner, which was served in the middle of the day. I did not go with Mr. Williams to his home but urged him to do so.

I went to his office and stayed there, getting the balance of my address in shape. At two o'clock he came for me and we went back to the Capitol. I resumed the statement of facts I had found—of the meeting held Monday night and of the resolution passed there which stated Frank Davis had not put his prisoner in the county jail or sworn in deputies to protect him although he knew there was talk of mob violence.

I was interrupted at this point by Mr. Davis's lawyer. "Who wrote that resolution?" he asked. "Don't answer him," said Mr. Williams, "he is only trying to confuse you." "Isn't it a fact," said Mr. Davis's counsel, "that you wrote that resolution?" "Yes," I said, "I wrote the resolution and presented it, but the audience adopted and passed it. It was done in the same way as the petition which you have presented here. Those petitions were signed by men, but they were typewritten and worded by somebody who was interested enough in Mr. Davis to place them where the men could reach them. But that is not all, Governor; I have here the signature of that leading Baptist minister who has been so highly praised to you. I went to his meeting yesterday and when I told him what a mistake it was to seem to condone the outrage on a human being by writing a letter asking for the reinstatement of a man who permitted it to be done, he rose and admitted he had sent the letter which has been read in your hearing, but having realized his mistake he wanted me to tell you that he endorsed the resolutions which I have here, and here is his name signed to them."

And then I wound up by saying, "Governor, the state of Illinois has had too many terrible lynchings within her borders within the last few years. If this man is sent back it will be an encouragement to those who resort to mob violence and will do so at any time, well knowing they will not be called to account for so doing. All the colored friends in Cairo are friends of Mr. Davis and they seem to feel that because his successor, a Democrat, has turned out all the Republican deputies, they owe their duty to the party to ask the return of a Republican sheriff. But not one of these, Mr. Davis's friends, would say that for one moment he had his prisoner in the county jail where the law demands that he should be placed or that he swore in a single deputy to help protect his life until he could be tried by law. It looked like encouragement to the mob to have the chief law officer in the county take that man up in the woods and keep him until the mob got big enough to come after him. I repeat, Governor, that if this man is reinstated, it will simply mean an increase of lynchings in the state of Illinois and an encouragement to mob violence."

When I had finished it was late in the afternoon, and the governor said that as he wanted to leave town next day he would suggest that both sides get together and agree upon a statement of fact. He asked that we return that evening about eight o'clock. The big lawyer was very unwilling to do this. He and his party expected to go through the form of presenting that petition and taking the afternoon train back to Cairo, arriving there in time for dinner.

Instead we had to have a night session which would necessitate their remaining over until the next day. He angrily tossed the petition across the table like a bone to a dog and insisted that there was nothing else to be considered. But the governor held firm, and I was quite willing to go home and get something to eat. I was quite surprised when the session adjourned that every one of those white men came over and shook my hand and congratulated me on what they called the wonderful speech I had made. Mr. Frank Davis himself shook hands with me and said, "I bear you no grudge for what you have done, Mrs. Barnett." The state's attorney of Alexander County wanted to know if I was not a lawyer. The United States land commissioner, a little old man, said, "Whether you are a lawyer or not you made the best speech of the day." It was he who told me that the state senator who had represented Mr. Davis, whose name I have forgotten, was the biggest lawyer in southern Illinois.

When we returned to the night session, there was all the difference in the world in the attitude of those white men. The state's attorney and the big lawyer had already drawn up what they called an agreed statement of fact and were waiting for my ratification of the same. When I picked up the pen and began to draw a line through some of the phrases which described the occurrence in Cairo, the state's attorney asked what I was doing.

I told him that although I was not a lawyer, I did know a statement of fact when I saw one, and that in the description of the things which had taken place on the day of "Frog" James's arrest, he had said that "the sheriff, fearing an outbreak by the mob, had taken 'Frog' to the railroad station." I had drawn a line through the words which said, "fearing an outbreak by the mob," because that was his opinion rather than a fact. His face grew red, but he let it ride.

By the time we had finished it was ten o'clock. The governor had been waiting in the room across the hall while we argued back and forth over this agreed statement of fact.

He then suggested that it was too late to go on, and asked that we return next morning. This we did and when I walked up the Capitol steps next morning every one of those white men with whom I had been in battle the day before swept off his hat at my approach. The big lawyer said, "Mrs. Barnett, we have decided that if you are willing we won't make another argument over this matter but will submit it all for the governor's action." I replied that whatever my lawyer advised, that I would do, and turned to Mr. Williams, who was still with me.

After scanning the papers he, too, agreed to their suggestion. We went into the governor's office and submitted the case without further argument, bade each other adieu and left for our homes. Mr. Williams said as we went down the steps, "Oh, the governor's going to send him back. I don't see how he can help it with such terrific pressure being brought to bear to have him to do so. But, by george, if I had time to dig up the law I would have furnished him so much of it that he wouldn't dare do so." I said, "We have done the best we could under the circumstances, and angels could do no more."

The following Tuesday morning Governor Deneen issued one of the finest state papers that emanated from him during his whole eight years in the Capitol. The summary of his proclamation was that Frank Davis could not be reinstated because he had not properly protected the prisoner within his keeping and that lynch law could have no place in Illinois.

That was in 1909, and from that day until the present there has been no lynching in the state. Every sheriff, whenever there seem to be any signs of the kind, immediately telegraphs the governor for troops. And to Governor Deneen belongs the credit.[1]

NOTE

1. The *Chicago Defender*, 1 January 1910, carried the following account of the manner in which Mrs. Barnett followed up the Cairo investigation: "The Bethel Literary and History Club held its first meeting under the leadership of newly elected officers last Sunday. Mrs. Ida B. Wells-Barnett gave a report of her investigation of the recent Cairo, Illinois lynching which was commendable in every detail. If we only had a few men with the backbone of Mrs. Barnett, lynching would soon come to a halt in America. A collection of $13.25 was taken and turned over to the citizens committee to apply on money spent by Mrs. Barnett in making her investigation."

Advancing Luna—And Ida B. Wells

Alice Walker

Luna and Freddie Pye are composite characters, and their names are made up. This is a fictionalized account suggested by a number of real events.

I met Luna the summer of 1965 in Atlanta where we both attended a political conference and rally. It was designed to give us the courage, as temporary civil rights workers, to penetrate the small hamlets farther South. I had taken a bus from Sarah Lawrence in New York and gone back to Georgia, my home state, to try my hand at registering voters. It had become obvious from the high spirits and sense of almost divine purpose exhibited by black people that a revolution was going on, and I did not intend to miss it. Especially not this summery, student-studded version of it. And I thought it would be fun to spend some time on my own in the South.

Luna was sitting on the back of a pickup truck, waiting for someone to take her from Faith Baptist, where the rally was held, to whatever gracious black Negro home awaited her. I remember because someone who assumed I would also be traveling by pickup introduced us. I remember her face when I said, "No, no more back of pickup trucks for me. I know Atlanta well enough, I'll walk." She assumed of course (I guess) that I did not wish to ride beside her because she was white, and I was not curious enough about what she might have thought to explain it to her. And yet I was struck by her passivity, her *patience* as she sat on the truck alone and ignored, because someone had told her to wait there quietly until it was time to go.

This look of passively waiting for something changed very little over the years I knew her. It was only four or five years in all that I did. It seems longer, perhaps because we met at such an optimistic time in our lives. John Kennedy and Malcolm X had already been assassinated, but King had not been and Bobby Kennedy had not been. Then too, the lethal, bizarre elimination by death of this militant or that, exiles, flights to Cuba, shoot-outs between former Movement friends sundered forever by lies planted by the FBI, the gunning down of Mrs. Martin Luther King, Sr., as she played the Lord's Prayer on the piano in her church (was her name Alberta?), were still in the happily unfathomable future.

We believed we could change America because we were young and bright and held ourselves *responsible* for changing it. We did not believe we would fail. That is what lent fervor (revivalist fervor, in fact; we would *revive* America!) to our songs, and lent sweetness to our friendships (in the beginning almost all interracial), and gave a wonderful fillip to our sex (which, too, in the beginning, was almost always interracial).

What first struck me about Luna when we later lived together was that she did not own a bra. This was curious to me, I suppose, because she also did not need one. Her chest was practically flat, her breasts like those of a child. Her face was round, and she suffered from acne. She carried with her always a tube of that "skin-colored" (if one's skin is pink or eggshell) medication designed to dry up pimples. At the oddest times—waiting for a light to change, listening to voter registration instructions, talking about her father's new girlfriend she would apply the stuff, holding in her other hand a small brass mirror the size of her thumb, which she also carried for just this purpose.

Source: Alice Walker, "Advancing Luna—And Ida B. Wells" in Alice Walker, *You Can't Keep a Good-Woman Down* (New York: Harcourt Brace Jovanovich, 1981).

We were assigned to work together in a small, rigidly segregated South Georgia town whose city fathers, incongruously and years ago, had named Freehold, Georgia. Luna was slightly asthmatic and when overheated or nervous she breathed through her mouth. She wore her shoulder-length black hair with bangs to her eyebrows and the rest brushed behind her ears. Her eyes were brown and rather small. She was attractive, but just barely and with effort. Had she been the slightest bit overweight, for instance, she would have gone completely unnoticed, and would have faded into the background where, even in a revolution, fat people seem destined to go. I have a photograph of her sitting on the steps of a house in South Georgia. She is wearing tiny pearl earrings, a dark sleeveless shirt with Peter Pan collar, Bermuda shorts, and a pair of those East Indian sandals that seem to adhere to nothing but a big toe.

The summer of '65 was as hot as any other in that part of the South. There was an abundance of flies and mosquitoes. Everyone complained about the heat and the flies and the hard work, but Luna complained less than the rest of us. She walked ten miles a day with me up and down those straight Georgia highways, stopping at every house that looked black (one could always tell in 1965) and asking whether anyone needed help with learning how to vote. The simple mechanics: writing one's name, or making one's "X" in the proper column. And then, though we were required to walk, everywhere, we were empowered to offer prospective registrants a car in which they might safely ride down to the county courthouse. And later to the polling places. Luna, almost overcome by the heat, breathing through her mouth like a dog, her hair plastered with sweat to her head, kept looking straight ahead, and walking as if the walking itself was her reward.

I don't know if we accomplished much that summer. In retrospect, it seems not only minor, but irrelevant. A bunch of us, black and white, lived together. The black people who took us in were unfailingly hospitable and kind. I took them for granted in a way that now amazes me. I realize that at each and every house we visited I *assumed* hospitality, I *assumed* kindness. Luna was often startled by my "boldness." If we walked up to a secluded farmhouse and half a dozen dogs ran up barking around our heels and a large black man with a shotgun could be seen whistling to himself under a tree, she would become nervous. I, on the other hand, felt free to yell at this stranger's dogs, slap a couple of them on the nose, and call over to him about his hunting.

That month with Luna of approaching new black people every day taught me something about myself I had always suspected: I thought black people superior people. Not simply superior to white people, because even without thinking about it much, I assumed almost everyone was superior to them; but to everyone. Only white people, after all, would blow up a Sunday school class and grin for television over their "victory," *i.e.*, the death of four small black girls. Any atrocity, at any time, was expected from them. On the other hand, it never occurred to me that black people *could* treat Luna and me with anything but warmth and concern. Even their curiosity about the sudden influx into their midst of rather ignorant white and black Northerners was restrained and courteous. I was treated as a relative, Luna as a much welcomed guest.

Luna and I were taken in by a middle-aged couple and their young school-age daughter. The mother worked outside the house in a local canning factory, the father worked in the paper plant in nearby Augusta. Never did they speak of the danger they were in of losing their jobs over keeping us, and never did their small daughter show any fear that her house might be attacked by racists because we were there. Again, I did not expect this family to complain, no matter what happened to them because of us. Having understood the danger, they had assumed the risk. I did not think them particularly brave, merely typical.

I think Luna liked the smallness—only four rooms—of the house. It was in this house that she ridiculed her mother's lack of taste. Her yellow-and-mauve house in Cleveland, the eleven rooms, the heated garage, the new car every year, her father's inability to remain faithful to her mother, their divorce, the fight over the property, even more so than over the children. Her mother kept the house and the children. Her father kept the car and his new girlfriend, whom he wanted Luna to meet and "approve." I could hardly imagine anyone disliking her mother so much. Everything Luna hated in her she summed up in three words: "*yellow-and-mauve.*"

I have a second photograph of Luna and a group of us being bullied by a Georgia state trooper. This member of Georgia's finest had followed us out into the deserted countryside to lecture us on how misplaced—in the South—was our energy, when "the Lord knew" the North (where he thought all of us lived, expressing disbelief that most of us were Georgians) was just as bad. (He had a point that I recognized even then, but it did not seem the point where we were.) Luna is looking up at him, her mouth slightly open as always, a somewhat dazed look on her face. I cannot detect fear on any of our faces, though we were all afraid. After all, 1965 was only a year after 1964 when three civil rights workers had been taken deep into a Mississippi forest by local officials and sadistically tortured and murdered. Luna almost always carried a flat black shoulder bag. She is standing with it against her side, her thumb in the strap.

At night we slept in the same bed. We talked about our schools, lovers, girlfriends we didn't understand or missed. She dreamed, she said, of going to Goa. I dreamed of going to Africa. My dream came true earlier than hers: an offer of a grant from an unsuspected source reached me one day as I was writing poems under a tree. I left Freehold, Georgia, in the middle of summer, without regrets, and flew from New York to London, to Cairo, to Kenya, and finally, Uganda, where I settled among black people with the same assumptions of welcome and kindness I had taken for granted in Georgia. I was taken on rides down the Nile as a matter of course, and accepted all invitations to dinner, where the best local dishes were superbly prepared in my honor. I became, in fact, a lost relative of the people, whose ancestors had foolishly strayed, long ago, to America.

I wrote to Luna at once.

But I did not see her again for almost a year. I had graduated from college, moved into a borrowed apartment in Brooklyn Heights, and was being evicted after a month. Luna, living then in a tenement on East Ninth Street, invited me to share her two-bedroom apartment. If I had seen the apartment before the day I moved in I might never have agreed to do so. Her building was between Avenues B and C and did not have a front door. Junkies, winos, and others often wandered in during the night (and occasionally during the day) to sleep underneath the stairs or to relieve themselves at the back of the first-floor hall.

Luna's apartment was on the third floor. Everything in it was painted white. The contrast between her three rooms and kitchen (with its red bathtub) and the grungy stairway was stunning. Her furniture consisted of two large brass beds inherited from a previous tenant and stripped of paint by Luna, and a long, high-backed church pew which she had managed somehow to bring up from the South. There was a simplicity about the small apartment that I liked. I also liked the notion of extreme contrast, and I do to this day. Outside our front window was the decaying neighborhood, as ugly and ill-lit as a battleground. (And allegedly as hostile, though somehow we were never threatened with bodily harm by the Hispanics who were our neighbors, and who seemed, more than anything, *bewildered* by the darkness and filth of their surroundings.) Inside was the church pew, as straight and spare as Abe Lincoln lying down, the white walls as spotless as a monastery's, and a small, unutterably pure patch of blue sky through the window of the back bedroom. (Luna did not believe in curtains, or couldn't afford them, and so we always undressed and bathed with the lights off and the rooms lit with candles, causing rather nun-shaped shadows to be cast on the walls by the long-sleeved high-necked nightgowns we both wore to bed.)

Over a period of weeks, our relationship, always marked by mutual respect, evolved into a warm and comfortable friendship which provided a stability and comfort we both needed at that time. I had taken a job at the Welfare Department during the day, and set up my typewriter permanently in the tiny living room for work after I got home. Luna worked in a kindergarten, and in the evenings taught herself Portuguese.

It was while we lived on East Ninth Street that she told me she had been raped during her summer in the South. It is hard for me, even now, to relate my feeling of horror and incredulity. This was some time before Eldridge Cleaver wrote of being a rapist/revolutionary; of "practicing" on black women before moving on to white. It was also, unless I'm mistaken, before LeRoi Jones (as he was then known; now of course Imamu Baraka, which has an even more presumptuous meaning than "the King") wrote his advice to young black male insurrectionaries (women were not told what to do with *their* rebelliousness): "Rape the white girls. Rape their fathers." It was clear that he meant this literally and also as: to rape a white girl *is* to rape her father. It was the misogynous cruelty of this latter meaning that was habitually lost on black men (on men in general, actually), but nearly always perceived and rejected by women of whatever color.

"Details?" I asked.

She shrugged. Gave his name. A name recently in the news, though in very small print.

He was not a Movement star or anyone you would know. We had met once, briefly. I had not liked him because he was coarse and spoke of black women as "our" women. (In the early Movement, it was pleasant to think of black men wanting to own us as a group; later it became clear that owning us meant exactly *that* to them.) He was physically unattractive, I had thought, with something of the hoodlum about him: a swaggering, unnecessarily mobile walk, small eyes, rough skin, a mouthful of wandering or absent teeth. He was, ironically, among the first persons to shout the slogan everyone later attributed solely to Stokeley Carmichael—Black Power! Stokeley was chosen as the originator of this idea by the media, because he was physically beautiful and photogenic and articulate. Even the name—Freddie Pye—was diminutive, I thought, in an age of giants.

"What did you do?"

"Nothing that required making a noise."

"Why didn't you scream?" I felt I would have screamed my head off.

"You know why."

I did. I had seen a photograph of Emmett Till's body just after it was pulled from the river. I had seen photographs of white folks standing in a circle roasting something that had talked to them in their own language before they tore out its tongue. I knew why, all right.

"What was he trying to prove?"

"I don't know. Do you?"

"Maybe you filled him with unendurable lust," I said.

"I don't think so," she said.

Suddenly I was embarrassed. Then angry. Very, very angry. *How dare she tell me this!* I thought.

Who knows what the black woman thinks of rape? Who has asked her? Who *cares*? Who has even properly acknowledged that *she* and not the white woman in this story is the most likely victim of rape? Whenever interracial rape is mentioned, a black woman's first thought is to protect the lives of her brothers, her father, her sons, her lover. A history of lynching has bred this reflex in her. I feel it as strongly as anyone. While writing a fictional account of such a rape in a novel, I read Ida B. Wells's autobiography three times, as a means of praying to her spirit to forgive me.

My prayer, as I turned the pages, went like this: "*Please forgive me. I am a writer.*" (this self-revealing statement alone often seems to me sufficient reason to require perpetual forgiveness; since the writer is guilty not only of always wanting to know—like Eve—but also of trying—again like Eve—to find out.) "*I cannot write contrary to what life reveals to me. I wish to malign no one. But I must struggle to understand at least my own tangled emotions about interracial rape. I know, Ida B. Wells, you spent your whole life protecting, and trying to protect, black men accused of raping white women, who were lynched by white mobs, or threatened with it. You know, better than I ever will, what it means for a whole people to live under the terror of lynching. Under the slander that their men, where white women are concerned, are creatures of uncontrollable sexual lust. You made it so clear that the black men accused of rape in the past were innocent victims of white criminals that I grew up believing black men literally did not rape white women. At all. Ever. Now it would appear that some of them, the very twisted, the terribly ill, do. What would you have me write about them?"*

Her answer was: *"Write nothing, Nothing at all. It will be used against black men and therefore against all of us. Eldridge Cleaver and LeRoi Jones don't know who they're dealing with. But you remember. You are dealing with people who brought their children to witness the murder of black human beings, falsely accused of rape. People who handed out, as trophies, black fingers and toes. Deny! Deny! Deny!"*

And yet, I have pursued it, *"some black men themselves do not seem to know what the meaning of raping someone is. Some have admitted rape in order to denounce it, but others have accepted rape as a part of rebellion, of 'paying whitey back.' They have gloried in it."*

"They know nothing of America," she says. *"And neither, apparently, do you. No matter what you think you know, no matter what you feel about it, say nothing. And to your dying breath!"*

Which, to my mind, is virtually useless advice to give to a writer.

Freddie Pye was the kind of man I would not have looked at then, not even once. (Throughout that year I was more or less into exotica: white ethnics who knew languages were a peculiar weakness; a half-white hippie singer; also a large Chinese mathematician who was a marvelous dancer and who taught me to waltz.) There was no question of belief.

But, in retrospect, there was a momentary *suspension* of belief, a kind of *hope* that perhaps it had not really happened; that Luna had made up the rape, "as white women have been wont to do." I soon realized this was unlikely. I was the only person she had told.

She looked at me as if to say: "I'm glad *that* part of my life is over." We continued our usual routine. We saw every interminable, foreign, depressing, and poorly illuminated film ever made. We learned to eat brown rice and yogurt and to tolerate kasha and odd-tasting teas. My half-black hippie singer friend (now a well-known reggae singer who says he is from "de *I*-lands" and not Sheepshead Bay) was "into" tea and kasha and Chinese vegetables.

And yet the rape, the knowledge of the rape, out in the open, admitted, pondered over, was now between us. (And I began to think that perhaps—whether Luna has been raped or not—it had always been so; that her power over my life was exactly the power *her word on rape* had over the lives of black men, over *all* black men, whether they were guilty or not, and therefore over my whole people.)

Before she told me about the rape, I think we had assumed a lifelong friendship. The kind of friendship one dreams of having with a person one has known in adversity; under heat and mosquitoes and immaturity and the threat of death. We would each travel, we would write to each other from the three edges of the world.

We would continue to have an "international list" of lovers whose amorous talents or lack of talents we would continue (giggling into our dotage) to compare. Our friendship would survive everything, be truer than everything, endure even our respective marriages, children, husbands—assuming we *did*, out of desperation and boredom someday, marry, which did not seem a probability, exactly, but more in the area of an amusing idea.

But now there was a cooling off of our affection for each other. Luna was becoming mildly interested in drugs, because everyone we knew was. I was envious of the open-endedness of her life. The financial backing to it. When she left her job at the kindergarten because she was tired of working, her errant father immediately materialized. He took her to dine on scampi at an expensive restaurant, scolded her for living on East Ninth Street, and looked at me as if to say: "Living in a slum of this magnitude must surely have been your idea." As a cullud, of course.

For me there was the welfare department every day, attempting to get the necessary food and shelter to people who would always live amid the dirty streets I knew I must soon leave. I was, after all, a Sarah Lawrence girl "with talent." It would be absurd to rot away in a building that had no front door.

I slept late one Sunday morning with a painter I had met at the welfare department. A man who looked for all the world like Gene Autry, the singing cowboy, but who painted wonderful surrealist pictures of birds and ghouls and fruit with *teeth*. The night before, three of us—me, the painter, and "an old Navy buddy" who looked like his twin and who had just arrived in town—had got high on wine and grass.

That morning the Navy buddy snored outside the bedrooms like a puppy waiting for its master. Luna got up early, made an immense racket getting breakfast, scowled at me as I emerged from my room, and left the apartment, slamming the door so hard she damaged the lock. (Luna had made it a rule to date black men almost exclusively. My insistence on dating, as she termed it "anyone," was incomprehensible to her, since in a politically diseased society to "sleep with the enemy" was to become "infected" with the enemy's "political germs." There is more than a grain of truth in this, of course, but I was having too much fun to stare at it for long. Still, coming from Luna it was amusing, since she never took into account the risk her own black lovers ran by sleeping with "the white woman," and she had apparently been convinced that a summer of relatively innocuous political work in the South had cured her of any racial, economic, or sexual political disease.)

Luna never told me what irked her so that Sunday morning, yet I remember it as the end of our relationship. It was not, as I at first feared, that she thought my bringing the two men to the apartment was inconsiderate. The way we lived allowed us to *be* inconsiderate from time to time. Our friends were varied, vital, and often strange. Her friends especially were deeper than they should have been into drugs.

The distance between us continued to grow. She talked more of going to Goa. My

guilt over my dissolute if pleasurable existence coupled with my mounting hatred of welfare work, propelled me in two directions. South, or to West Africa. When the time came to choose, I discovered that *my* summer in the South had infected me with the need to return, to try to understand, and write about, the people I'd merely lived with before.

We never discussed the rape again. We never discussed, really, Freddie Pye or Luna's remaining feelings about what had happened. One night, the last month we lived together, I noticed a man's blue denim jacket thrown across the church pew. The next morning, out of Luna's bedroom walked Freddie Pye. He barely spoke to me—possibly because as a black woman I was expected to be hostile toward his presence in a white woman's bedroom. I was too surprised to exhibit hostility, however, which was only a part of what I felt, after all. He left.

Luna and I did not discuss this. It is odd, I think now, that we didn't. It was as if he were never there; as if he and Luna had not shared the bedroom that night. A month later, Luna went alone to Goa, in her solitary way. She lived on an island and slept, she wrote, on the beach. She mentioned she'd found a lover there who protected her from the local beachcombers and pests.

Several years later, she came to visit me in the South and brought a lovely piece of pottery which my daughter much later dropped and broke, but which I glued back together in such a way that the flaw improves the beauty and fragility of the design.

AFTERWARDS, AFTERWORDS

Second Thoughts

That is the "story." It has an "unresolved" ending. That is because Freddie Pye and Luna are still alive, as am I. However, one evening while talking to a friend, I heard myself say that I had, in fact, written *two* endings. One, which follows, I considered appropriate for such a story published in a country truly committed to justice, and the one above, which is the best I can afford to offer a society in which lynching is still reserved, at least subconsciously, as a means of racial control.

I said that if we in fact lived in a society committed to the establishment of justice for everyone ("justice" in this case encompassing equal housing, education, access to work, adequate dental care, et cetera), thereby placing Luna and Freddie Pye in their correct relationship to each other, *i.e.*, that of brother and sister, *compañeros*, then the two of them would be required to struggle together over what his rape of her had meant.

Since my friend is a black man whom I love and who loves me, we spent a considerable amount of time discussing what this particular rape meant to us. Morally wrong, we said, and not to be excused. Shameful; politically corrupt. Yet, as we thought of what might have happened to an indiscriminate number of innocent young black men in Freehold, Georgia, had Luna screamed, it became clear that more than a little of Ida B. Wells's fear of probing the rape issue was running through us, too. The implications of this fear would not let me rest, so that months and years went by with most of the story written but with me incapable, or at least unwilling, to finish or to publish it.

In thinking about it over a period of years, there occurred a number of small changes, refinements, puzzles, in angle. Would these shed a wider light on the continuing subject? I do not know. In any case, I returned to my notes, hereto appended for the use of the reader.

Luna: Ida B. Wells— Discarded Notes

Additional characteristics of Luna: At a time when many in and out of the Movement considered "nigger" and "black" synonymous, and indulged in a sincere attempt to fake Southern "hip" speech, Luna resisted. She was the kind of WASP who could not easily imitate another's ethnic style, nor could she even exaggerate her own. She was what she was. A very straight, clear-eyed, coolly obser-

vant young woman with no talent for existing outside her own skin.

Imaginary Knowledge

Luna explained the visit from Freddie Pye in this way:

"He called that evening, said he was in town, and did I know the Movement was coming North? I replied that I did know that."

When could he see her? he wanted to know.

"Never," she replied.

He had burst into tears, or something that sounded like tears, over the phone. He was stranded at wherever the evening's fundraising event had been held. Not in the place itself, but outside, in the street. The "stars" had left, everyone had left. He was alone. He knew no one else in the city. Had found her number in the phone book. And had no money, no place to stay.

Could he, he asked, crash? He was tired, hungry, broke—and even in the South had had no job, other than the Movement, for months. Et cetera.

When he arrived, she had placed our only steak knife in the waistband of her jeans.

He had asked for a drink of water. She gave him orange juice, some cheese, and a couple of slices of bread. She had told him he might sleep on the church pew and he had lain down with his head on his rolled-up denim jacket. She had retired to her room, locked the door, and tried to sleep. She was amazed to discover herself worrying that the church pew was both too narrow and too hard.

At first he muttered, groaned, and cursed in his sleep. Then he fell off the narrow church pew. He kept rolling off. At two in the morning she unlocked her door, showed him her knife, and invited him to share her bed.

Nothing whatever happened except they talked. At first, only he talked. Not about the rape, but about his life.

"He was a small person physically, remember?" Luna asked me. (She was right. Over the years he had grown big and, yes, burly, in my imagination, and I'm sure in hers.) "That night he seemed tiny. A child. He was still fully dressed, except for the jacket and he, literally, hugged his side of the bed. I hugged mine. The whole bed, in fact, was between us. We were merely hanging to its edges."

At the fund-raiser—on Fifth Avenue and Seventy-first Street, as it turned out—his leaders had introduced him as the unskilled, barely literate, former Southern fieldworker that he was. They had pushed him at the rich people gathered there as an example of what "the system" did to "the little people" in the South. They asked him to tell about the 37 times he had been jailed. The 35 times he had been beaten. The one time he had lost consciousness in the "hot" box. They told him not to worry about his grammar. "Which, as you may recall," said Luna, "was horrible." Even so, he had tried to censor his "ain'ts" and his "us'es." He had been painfully aware that he was on exhibit, like Frederick Douglass had been for the Abolitionists. But unlike Douglass he had no oratorical gift, no passionate language, no silver tongue. He knew the rich people and his own leaders perceived he was nothing: a broken man, unschooled, unskilled at anything …

Yet he had spoken, trembling before so large a crowd of rich, white Northerners—who clearly thought their section of the country would never have the South's racial problems—begging, with the painful stories of his wretched life, for their money.

At the end, all of them—the black leaders, too—had gone. They left him watching the taillights of their cars, recalling the faces of the friends come to pick them up: the women dressed in African print that shone, with elaborately arranged hair, their jewelry sparkling, their perfume exotic. They were so beautiful, yet so strange. He could not imagine that one of them could comprehend his life. He did not ask for a ride, because of that, but also because he had no place to go. Then he had remembered Luna.

Soon Luna would be required to talk. She would mention her confusion over whether, in a black community surrounded by whites with a history of lynching blacks, she had a right to scream as Freddie Pye was raping her. For her, this was the crux of the matter.

And so they would continue talking through the night.

This is another ending, created from whole cloth. If I believed Luna's story about the rape, and I did (had she told anyone else I might have dismissed it), then this reconstruction of what might have happened is as probable an accounting as any is liable to be. Two people have now become "characters."

I have forced them to talk until they reached the stumbling block of the rape, *which they must remove themselves,* before proceeding to a place from which it will be possible to insist on a society in which Luna's word alone on rape can never be used to intimidate an entire people, and in which an innocent black man's protestation of innocence of rape is unprejudicially heard. Until such a society is created, relationships of affection between black men and white women will always be poisoned—from within as from without—by historical fear and the threat of violence, and solidarity among black and white women is only rarely likely to exist.

Postscript: Havana, Cuba, November, 1976

I am in Havana with a group of other black American artists. We have spent the morning apart from our Cuban hosts bringing each other up to date on the kind of work (there are no apolitical artists among us) we are doing in the United States. I have read "Luna."

High above the beautiful city of Havana I sit in the Havana Libre pavilion with the muralist/photographer in our group. He is in his mid-thirties, a handsome, brown, erect individual whom I have known casually for a number of years. During the sixties he designed and painted street murals for both SNCC and the Black Panthers, and in an earlier discussion with Cuban artists he showed impatience with their explanation of why we had seen no murals covering some of the city's rather dingy walls: Cuba, they had said, unlike Mexico, has no mural tradition. "But the point of a revolution," insisted Our Muralist, "is to make new traditions!" And he had pressed his argument with such passion for the *usefulness*, for revolutionary communication, of his craft, that the Cubans were both exasperated and impressed. They drove us around the city for a tour of their huge billboards, all advancing socialist thought and the heroism of men like Lenin, Camilo, and Che Guevara, and said, "These, *these* are our 'murals'!"

While we ate lunch, I asked Our Muralist what he'd thought of "Luna." Especially the appended section.

"Not much," was his reply. "Your view of human weakness is too biblical," he said. "You are unable to conceive of the man without conscience. The man who cares nothing about the state of his soul because he's long since sold it. In short," he said, "you do not understand that some people are simply evil, a disease on the lives of other people, and that to remove the disease altogether is preferable to trying to interpret, contain, or forgive it. Your 'Freddie Pye,'" and he laughed, "was probably raping white women on the instructions of his government."

Oh ho, I thought. Because, of course, for a second, during which I stalled my verbal reply, this comment made both very little and very much sense.

"I *am* sometimes naïve and sentimental," I offered. I am sometimes both, though frequently by design. Admission in this way is tactical, a stimulant to conversation.

"And shocked at what I've said," he said, and laughed again. "Even though," he continued, "you know by now that blacks could be hired to blow up other blacks, and could be hired *by someone* to shoot down Brother Malcolm, and hired *by someone* to provide a diagram of Fred Hampton's bedroom so the pigs could shoot him easily while he slept, you find

it hard to believe a black man could be hired *by someone* to rape white women. But think a minute, and you will see why it is the perfect disruptive act. Enough blacks raping or accused of raping enough white women and any political movement that cuts across racial lines is doomed.

"Larger forces are at work than your story would indicate," he continued. "You're still thinking of lust and rage, moving slowly into aggression and purely racial hatred. But you should be considering money—which the rapist would get, probably from your very own tax dollars, in fact—and a maintaining of the status quo; which those hiring the rapist would achieve. I know all this," he said, "because when I was broke and hungry and selling my blood to buy the food and the paint that allowed me to work, I was offered such 'other work.'"

"But you did not take it."

He frowned. "There you go again. How do you know I didn't take it? It paid, and I was starving."

"You didn't take it," I repeated.

"No," he said. "A black and white 'team' made the offer. I had enough energy left to threaten to throw them out of the room."

"But even if Freddie Pye *had been* hired *by someone* to rape Luna, that still would not explain his second visit."

"Probably nothing will explain that," said Our Muralist. "But assuming Freddie Pye *was* paid to disrupt—by raping a white woman—the black struggle in the South, he may have wised up enough later to comprehend the significance of Luna's decision not to scream."

"So you are saying he *did have* a conscience?" I asked.

"Maybe," he said, but his look clearly implied I would never understand anything about evil, power, or corrupted human beings in the modern world.

But of course he is wrong.

Split Affinities

The Case of Interracial Rape

Valerie Smith

I

Black feminism, at once imaginative, critical, and theoretical, is simultaneously deconstructive and reconstructive, reactive and proactive. Historically it has revealed ways in which the lives and cultural productions of black women have been overlooked or misrepresented within Eurocentric and androcentric discourses, yet its aims are not as fully determined by these other modes of inquiry and bodies of literature as this formulation might seem to suggest. Black feminists seek not only to dismantle the assumptions of dominant cultures, and to recover and reclaim the lives and texts of black women, but also to develop methods of analysis for interpreting the ways in which race and gender are inscribed in cultural productions.

I have argued elsewhere that black feminist criticism might be seen to have evolved in relation to Afro-Americanist criticism and Anglo-American feminist criticism.[1] Both Afro-Americanist criticism and Anglo-American feminism rely on the notion of difference, exploring, respectively, the meanings of social constructions of race and of gender. Yet in establishing themselves in opposition to hegemonic culture, Afro-Americanists and Anglo-American feminists depended historically upon totalizing formulations of race on the one hand, gender on the other. Male-authored Afro-Americanist criticism assumed a conception of blackness that concealed its masculinist presuppositions; Anglo-or Euro-

centered feminism relied upon a notion of gender that concealed its presumption of whiteness.[2] It has fallen to feminists whose work explicitly addresses issues of race, class, sexual preference, and nationality to confront the implications of difference within these modes of oppositional discourse.[3]

The critical stance that black feminism sometimes assumes in relation to other ideological modes of inquiry is from time to time regarded with disapprobation as being divisive.[4] However, it seems to me that the impetus for the development of Afro-Americanist, feminist, and other oppositional modes of inquiry depends inevitably upon our attempts to challenge and reassess our presuppositions.

In my own teaching and writing as a black feminist critic I have been drawn to those subjects around which differences both between black men and women, and between feminists are illuminated; these topics are precisely those that lend specificity to and justify the theoretical assumptions that inform my work. To borrow Mary Poovey's term, I am drawn to "border cases," issues that challenge the binary logic that governs the social and intellectual systems within which we live and work. As Poovey argues, border cases are "the site of intensive debates ... because they [threaten] to challenge *the* opposition upon which all other oppositions are claimed to be based."[5] Poovey here refers to the centrality within culture of sexual difference; I would extend her point to include the putative centrality of racial difference as well.

"Border cases" are precisely those issues that problematize easy assumptions about racial and/or sexual difference, particularly insofar as they demonstrate the interactions

Source: Valerie Smith, "Split Affinities: The Case of Interracial Rape" in Marianne Hirsh and Evelyn Fox Keller, eds., *Conflicts in Feminism* (New York: Routledge, 1990), 271–87.

between race and gender. Indeed, as Kimberlé Crenshaw has argued (drawing on work by Elizabeth V. Spelman, Barbara Smith, and others), within dominant discourses, race and gender are treated as if they are mutually exclusive categories of experience. In contrast, black feminism presumes the "intersectionality" of race and gender in the lives of black women, thereby rendering inapplicable to the lives of black women any "single-axis" theory about racism or sexism.[6]

The institution of slavery in the U.S. represents one such "border case." While feminist historians such as Catherine Clinton introduce the category of gender into the analysis of slavery, exploring the subordination of women within a system of racial oppression, they sometimes obscure the impact of race on the construction of women's place in the plantation economy. As Hazel Carby argues, the nature of the oppression of black women under slavery is vastly different from that experienced by white women within that institution. Carby shows that the primary duty of women in the planter class was to produce heirs, thereby providing the means of consolidating property through the marriages between plantation families. In contrast, black women's destiny was bound to capital accumulation; black women gave birth to property and, directly, to capital itself in the form of slaves.[7]

Given the profound and multifarious connections between racism and sexual exploitation throughout U.S. history, interracial rape constitutes another such "border case." Myths of black male and female sexual appetitiveness were constructed to enable certain white men during slavery to exert their rights over the bodies of black men and white and black women. The image of sexually inexhaustible black men was used to police relations between black men and white women and invoked in order to justify violence against black men. The myth of the promiscuity of slave women allowed white men to rape them and claim ownership of their offspring with impunity.

After slavery the slippage between racism and sexism assumed other forms and continued to victimize black men and women in related ways. Mobs of whites frequently raped black women in order to restrict the progress of black communities as a whole and black men in particular.[8] In addition, especially during the period from Reconstruction through World War II, accusations of interracial rape were used to legitimate lynching, a form of random, mob violence connected routinely to the alleged rape of a white woman by a black man, even when no evidence of sexual assault existed. Jacquelyn Dowd Hall has argued that the perceived connection between lynching and rape grows out of the construction of white women as "the forbidden fruit, the untouchable property, the ultimate symbol of white male power." This association in turn sets in motion a cultural narrative in which the rape of a frail white victim by a savage black male must be avenged by the chivalry of her white male protectors.[9]

The explosive coverage of actual or alleged cases of interracial rape (the Tawana Brawley case, the Central Park rape, the Willie Horton case, the Stuart murder case, to name but a few) and the political uses to which these incidents have been put, suggest the myriad ways in which the history of slavery and lynching informs the construction of racial and gender relations in contemporary United States culture. To explore the complex subtext of accusations of interracial rape in this essay, I consider within three contexts ways in which interracial rape operates as a site where ideologies of racial and gender difference come into tension with and interrogate each other. I analyze here representations of interracial rape in some examples of journalistic discourse and in a short story by Alice Walker entitled "Advancing Luna—and Ida B. Wells." The essay ends with a brief examination of some of the pedagogical issues that arose for me during my attempts to teach "Advancing Luna." In each context, I suggest that silences speak volumes, indicating the ways in which cultural anxieties about racial and gender differences are projected upon each other.

In her autobiography, *Crusade for Justice*, Ida B. Wells, a turn-of-the-century black woman journalist and political activist, argues that "[Lynching] really was … an excuse to get rid of Negroes who were acquiring wealth and property and thus 'keep the nigger down.'"[10] Wells's analysis acknowledges how the structure of gender relations and domination has been used to propel and facilitate racial oppression. Yet her opposition to lynching as a practice requires her effectively to deny the veracity of any white woman's testimony against a black man. Elsewhere in *Crusade* Wells discredits the testimony of an alleged rape victim even more directly. The classic situation she cites represents white women as willing participants in sexual relations with the black male victims of lynching. In one instance she argues that while white men assume the right to rape black women or consort with them, black men are killed for participating in any kind of sexual activity with white women: "these same white men lynched, burned, and tortured Negro men for doing the same thing with white women; even when the white women were willing victims" (71). The final clause, specifying the category of white women "willing victims," takes precedence over the implied "unwilling victims" to whom Wells alludes earlier in the sentence. The following sentence elaborates upon the logic of the previous one, effectively blaming white women for the lynching of black men: "It seemed horrible to me that death in its most terrible form should be meted out to the Negro who was weak enough to take chances when accepting the invitations of these white women" (71). Wells's focus on the unreliability of white rape victims may well have been strategic, if not accurate, given the structure of race relations from the mid-nineteenth until the mid-twentieth centuries; as an antecedent, however, it presents difficulties for feminist critiques of interracial rape in the late twentieth century.

Wells's formulations subordinate the sexual to the racial dimension of interracial rape, thereby dramatizing the fact that the crime can never be read solely as an offense against women's bodies. It is always represented and understood within the context of a variety of public issues, among them race, imperialism, and the law.[11] As the media coverage and public response to recent criminal cases involving the hint, the allegation, or the fact of interracial rape demonstrate, a variety of cultural narratives that historically have linked sexual violence with racial oppression continue to determine the nature of public response to them.

For example, instances of interracial rape constitute sites of struggle between black and white men that allow privileged white men to exercise their property rights over the bodies of white women. As Angela Davis has shown, in the United States and other capitalist countries, rape laws, as a rule, were framed originally for the protection of men of the upper classes whose daughters and wives might be assaulted. By this light, the bodies of women seem decidedly less significant than the interests of their male superordinates. As merely one example, this objectification of the white victim was dramatized powerfully in the recent Central Park rape case in which New York personalities and politicians issued threats against black men while the rape victim lay silent, comatose, and unnamed, in her hospital bed.[12]

The rise of feminism from the late sixties through the present has done much to construct woman-centered anti-rape positions, although these responses sometimes reveal a racist bias. In the 1970s and 1980s rape emerged as a feminist issue as control over one's body and sexuality became a major area for concern and activism. Women addressed the need to break the silence about a pervasive aspect of female experience. From that beginning derived analyses of the place and function of rape within patriarchal culture. Moreover, feminists began to develop strategies for changing the legal and medical treatment of rape victims and the prosecution of perpetrators.

Susan Brownmiller's early study of rape, *Against Our Will: Men, Women, and Rape*, contributes prominently to analyses of the historical and cultural function of rape. Yet often it risks resuscitating the myth of the black rapist. Brownmiller, for example, argues that the history of the oppression of black men makes legitimate expressions of male supremacy beyond their reach. They therefore resort to open sexual violence. In the context of her study, the wolf whistle that led to Emmett Till's lynching is read as a deliberate insult just short of physical assault.[13]

More recent feminist analyses improve upon Brownmiller's work by increasingly focusing on the interplay of issues of race and class within the context of gender relations. Susan Estrich, Angela Davis, and Catherine MacKinnon examine the implications of the fact that rape is the most underreported of all crimes and that the majority of rapes committed are intraracial.[14] Each shows in her respective argument how cultural assumptions about rapes and rapists protect privileged white men who rape white women and continue to fetishize the black male perpetrator. As MacKinnon writes:

> For every reported rape there are between two and ten unreported rapes; it is extremely important to ask not only why the ones that are reported are, but why the ones that are not reported are not.
>
> I think women report rapes when we feel we will be believed. The rapes that have been reported, as they have been reported, are the kinds of rapes women think will be believed when we report them. They have two qualities; they are by a stranger, and they are by a Black man. These two elements give you the white male archetype of rape. When the newspaper says that these rapes are unusual, they are right in a way. They are right because rapes by strangers are the least common rapes women experience. And to the extent that these are interracial, they are also the least common rapes women experience. Most rapes are by a man of the woman's race and by a man she knows: her husband, her boss, an acquaintance, or a date.[15]

Given their position within the racial and gender hierarchy in U.S. culture, it is not surprising that black Americans respond in a variety of different ways to instances of interracial rape. Within a context in which rape charges were often used to justify lynching or legal execution, black men and women often perceive an accusation of rape as a way to terrorize innocent black men. This kind of reasoning may lead to the denial of the fact that some black men do rape. To cite but one example, Alton Maddox, one of Tawana Brawley's attorneys, leaped immediately to the defense of the young men accused in the 1989 Central Park rape case and demanded proof that a rape had actually occurred.

Black women's positions in relation to cases of interracial rape are particularly vexed. As members of communities under siege, they may well sympathize with the black male who stands accused. At the same time, as women they share the victim's sense of violation. Yet that identification with white women is problematic, since black women represent the most vulnerable and least visible victims of rape. Their relative invisibility is to some degree rooted in the systematic sexual abuse to which they were subjected during slavery and upon which the institution of slavery depended. The same ideology that protected white male property rights by constructing black males as rapists, constructed black women as sexually voracious. If black women were understood always to be available and willing, then the rape of a black woman becomes a contradiction in terms.

The relative invisibility of black women victims of rape also reflects the differential value of women's bodies in capitalist societies. To the extent that rape is constructed as a crime against the property of privileged white men, crimes against less valuable women—women of color, working-class women, and lesbians, for example—mean less or mean differently than those against white women from the middle and upper classes.[16]

Given the nature of their history as rape victims, one might expect that black women would find common cause with white women in the anti-rape movement. Yet their own invisibility as victims within the movement, and a perceived indifference within the movement to the uses to which the fraudulent rape charge has been put, has qualified their support.

The reporting of and response to a variety of recent cases involving the hint, the allegation, or the fact of interracial rape demonstrate the persistent and competing claims of these various cultural narratives in the public imagination. I want here to comment briefly on the representation of the Stuart murder case and the Central Park rape, but certainly much remains to be said about many other cases, including the construction of the Tawana Brawley case, and the uses to which Willie Horton was put in the Bush-Quayle campaign.

The Stuart murder case merits consideration in the context of a discussion about race and rape precisely because no allegation of rape was made. Despite the nonsexual nature of the alleged crime, the fiction of a black male perpetrator automatically sexualized a nonsexual crime, thereby displaying the profound and unarticulated links between race and sexuality.

Initially ascribed to a black gunman in a jogging suit, the October 29, 1989 murder of Carol Stuart in Boston has subsequently been attributed to her husband, Charles, who committed suicide on January 4, 1990. The persistence and brutality of the Boston police, who terrorized working-class black communities in search of a suspect, recalls the vigilante justice of earlier decades. The specter of interracial rape hovers over this case even though no specific allegations were made; witness the sexualized ways in which at least certain black men were interrogated. As Andrew Kopkind writes: "Young black men were stopped, searched and detrousered on the street for no cause more reasonable than their skin color. The cops called the blacks "pussy" and "faggot," and sexual humiliation—white male power against black male impotence—became another disgusting tactic of the occupation."[17]

We must take note here of the sexism and homophobia inherent in the policemen's tactics for investigating a crime against a woman. In the name of the body of a woman, the white policemen sought to humiliate black men by effeminizing them. Clearly, in this case the existence and identity of the victim became secondary to the power struggle between men.

The narrative linking sexual violence to racism is evident perhaps even more powerfully in the rhetoric surrounding the incident that has come to be known as the Central Park rape. To review the details: on the night of Wednesday, April 19, 1989, a young white woman jogger was raped repeatedly and severely beaten in Central Park in Manhattan by a group of black and Puerto Rican adolescent males between the ages of 14 and 17. In the hour before they attacked the jogger, the young men were reported to have been involved in at least four other assaults: they are alleged to have robbed a 52-year-old man, obtaining a sandwich; thrown rocks at a taxicab; chased a man and a woman on a tandem bicycle; and attacked a 40-year-old male jogger, hitting him on the head with a lead pipe. The rape victim, a well-educated, 28-year-old investment banker who worked at Salomon Brothers, emerged from a coma after two weeks, but appears to have sustained some brain damage.

The inflammatory rhetoric of the journalistic accounts of the Central Park rape reveals the context within which the narrative was constructed. In and of itself the crime was certainly heinous. Yet the media coverage intensified and polarized responses in New York City and around the country, for it made the story of sexual victimization inseparable from the rhetoric of racism.

From the tabloids—*The New York Daily News* and *The New York Post*—to the putatively more respectable *New York Newsday* and *The New York Times*, journalists circulated and resuscitated myths of black male animalism and of the black male rapist. In terms that recalled lynch law at the turn of the century, a conservative Republican candidate for mayor ran prime-time television advertisements calling for the death penalty for rapists, along with cop-killers and serial murderers. Likewise, Donald Trump ran a full-page advertisement in *The New York Times* calling for the death penalty for the rapists.

News and feature stories were equally incendiary. On Friday, April 20, *The Daily News* headline announced: "Female jogger near death after savage attack by roving gang." The major story in that day's *Daily News* begins in the following manner: "A 28-year-old investment banker who regularly jogged in Central Park was repeatedly raped, viciously beaten and left for dead by a wolfpack of more than a dozen young teenagers who attacked her at the end of an escalating crime spree." The editorial in *The Daily News* that day begins:

> There was a full moon Wednesday night. A suitable backdrop for the howling of wolves. A vicious pack ran rampant through Central Park. They attacked at least five people. One is now fighting for her life. Perhaps by the time you read this, she will have lost that fight.... This was not shoplifting licorice sticks and bubble gum from a candy counter. This was bestial brutality. "Mischief" is not mugging. It is not gang rape. It is not beating someone's face to a pulp with fists and crushing someone's skull with a rock.

This imagery of the young males as subhuman is then recapitulated in articles and editorials in *The News* and the other New York dailies. Indeed, in even the ostensibly more sedate *New York Times*, and editorial dated April 26 is entitled "The Jogger and the Wolf Pack." The editorial itself is replete again with imagery of savagery and barbarity. Although the tone of the coverage is at one level appropriate for the severity of the crime, I wish to emphasize the fact that the press shaped the discourse around the event in ways that inflamed pervasive fears about the animality of black men. Further, the conventional journalistic practice of protecting the privacy of rape victims by concealing their identity—a practice that may well contribute to a climate that blames the victim—in addition to the inability of this particular woman to speak, contributed to the objectification of the victim. As a result, the young woman became a pawn in the struggle of empowered white men to seize control of their city.

The implications of the ways that journalists characterized the young men involved in the Central Park rape become powerfully clear when we juxtapose the reporting of this case with that involving the rape and sexual assault of a 17-year-old "mildly retarded" white middle-class young woman in northern New Jersey by five, middle-class white teen-age football players on March 1. This crime was first reported on March 22; formal charges were brought against the young men in mid-May. In this case, the young men were charged with having raped the young woman and penetrated her vaginally with a broomstick handle and a miniature baseball bat. Yet in this case, the rhetoric is about the effect of this crime on the community. Moreover, there is a marked emphasis on the victim's mental abilities.

My point here is not to compare the two incidents to determine which is the more savage. Rather, I mention this other case to suggest the difference that race and class make in the writing of rape. The reporting of these two cases must prompt us to ask why the rape of a brilliant, middle-class investment banker by a group of young black men is constructed to seem more heinous than the rape of a "mildly retarded" young white woman by a group of young white men. Rape here is clearly not represented as a violation of a woman's body alone. Rather, in the terms of interlocking issues of race, class, and gender, these crimes suggest that certain women's bodies are more valuable than others.

II

Unacknowledged cultural narratives such as those which link racial and gender oppression structure our lives as social subjects; the ability of some people to maintain dominance over others depends upon these narratives' remaining pervasive but unarticulated. In my teaching, both in courses that are explicitly about black feminism and those that are not, I take seriously the responsibility to teach texts by and about black women, and to develop strategies for discussing the ways in which interactions between race and gender are inscribed in narrative. However, it is to me equally important to work with my students toward the recognition of the kinds of silences that structure the social hierarchy in which we live.

The teaching of texts about "border cases" such as interracial rape, makes more explicit for students the theoretical principles of "intersectionality" that inform my courses. A story such as "Advancing Luna—and Ida B. Wells," by Alice Walker, prompts students to speak from a variety of perspectives on the issue of interracial rape. To the extent that the story foregrounds the range of positions that different women assume around the subject, it requires readers to acknowledge as well the extent to which we keep secret our responses to such cases. My goal in teaching a work such as this one is to enable students to develop a vocabulary for addressing the differences between them that necessarily exist.

I return to this particular story because of the way it confronts the issue of difference. I teach it additionally because it is representative of Walker's less well-known, but to me more interesting fiction. *The Color Purple*, which continues to be one of the most widely read and frequently taught works written by a black woman, raises knotty questions about sexual violence, and the construction of race and sexuality. Yet for me, the utopian vision with which the novel ends disappoints and undermines the complexity of narration and characterization that has gone before. In contrast, "Advancing Luna" and the other stories included in Walker's 1981 collection of stories entitled *You Can't Keep a Good Woman Down*, individually and collectively confront the inadequacy of representation and eschew easy resolutions. This story calls attention to the unspeakability of interracial rape; others in the volume address issues having to do with the representation of, for example, the female body, or the relationship between racial and gender politics.[18]

Moreover, a discussion of "Advancing Luna" seems to me to be especially pertinent in a feminist classroom because it self-consciously participates in a variety of discourses, thereby problematizing the boundaries between literature and theory, literature and "real life." By thematizing one of the central paradoxes of the black feminist enterprise, it

is simultaneously narrative and theory. It exemplifies the tendency that Barbara Christian identifies for writers of color "to theorize in narrative forms, in stories, riddles and proverbs, and in the play with language."[19] Moreover, to the extent that the narrator function breaks down and is replaced by an author figure or function who establishes a relation with narratives of the lives of "real people," the story presents itself as simultaneously fiction and fact/autobiography.

In the first two paragraphs of the story, the unnamed narrator/protagonist, a young black woman, establishes significant differences between herself and Luna, a young white woman with whom she worked in the movement and with whom she subsequently shared an apartment in New York. As the story develops, the space between them becomes increasingly resonant, charged with anger, betrayal, and the specter of sexual competitiveness.

"Advancing Luna" opens in the summer of 1965 in Atlanta at a political conference and rally. Within the context of the Civil Rights movement, the narrator is endowed with the advantages of both race and class—in this case her status as a black woman and a student. The narrator/protagonist is thus an insider among the high-spirited black people graced with a "sense of almost divine purpose."[20] An undergraduate at Sarah Lawrence College, she feels doubly at home in this "summery, student-studded" revolution (85). Luna is no doubt also a student, but the narrator represents her as an outsider, passive, and wan. While the narrator characterizes herself as bold and energetic, Luna tentatively awaits the graciousness of a Negro home. To emphasize the space between them, the narrator confidently strides through Atlanta instead of riding in the pickup truck with Luna.

The narrator's hostility to Luna is nowhere more evident than in her description of her. Here she inscribes her hostility on Luna's body in the process of anatomizing it. Moving from her breasts to the shape of her face to her acne to her asthmatic breathing, she renders Luna a configuration of inadequacies. Moreover, the idiosyncratic organization of the paragraphs of description makes it that much harder to conceive of Luna as a social or narrative subject:

> What first struck me about Luna when we later lived together was that she did not own a bra. This was curious to me, I suppose, because she also did not need one. Her chest was practically flat, her breasts like those of a child. Her face was round, and she suffered from acne. She carried with her always a tube of that "skin-colored" (if one's skin is pink or eggshell) medication designed to dry up pimples. At the oddest times—waiting for a light to change, listening to voter registration instructions, talking about her father's new girlfriend, she would apply the stuff, holding in her other hand a small brass mirror the size of a thumb, which she also carried for just this purpose. (86–87)

The narrator's hostility to Luna is evident not only in the way in which she anatomizes her, but also in less direct ways. For instance, by suggesting that Luna's skin is "skin-colored" she blames her for conforming to the image of the ideal Clearasil user. By means of the disruptive logic of the passage, the narrator caricatures her. She interrupts the order of a physical or spatial description to catch Luna, as if unawares, in the midst of the uncomplimentary, repeated activity, of applying her acne medication.

In the next paragraph, the narrator's hostility toward Luna takes the form of momentarily erasing her from her own description:

> We were assigned to work together in a small, rigidly segregated South Georgia town that the city fathers, incongruously and years ago, had named Freehold. Luna was slightly asthmatic and when overheated or nervous she breathed through her mouth. She wore her shoulderlength black hair with bangs to her eyebrows and the rest brushed behind her ears. Her eyes were brown and rather small. She was attractive, but just barely and with effort. Had she been the slightest bit overweight, for instance, she would have gone

completely unnoticed, and would have faded into the background where, even in a revolution, fat people seemed destined to go. (87)

Although Luna is not fat, the narrator says she is the sort of person who would have faded into the background if she were.

During the summer of 1965, Luna and the narrator become friends through their shared work. The story focuses primarily on their life together in New York where they shared an apartment the following year.

The first exchange between the narrator and Luna that is actually dramatized in the text is one in which Luna admits to having been raped by a black man named Freddie Pye during her summer in the South. This conversation explains the source of the narrator's retrospective hostility to her. The narrator resents Luna for having spoken of the rape; her characterization is a way of punishing her for the admission. In addition, the description might be read as an attempt to undermine Luna' testimony by denying her desirability. By sexually denigrating Luna, the narrator indirectly blames her for her own victimization. This hostility points to a thinly-veiled sexual competitiveness between the black and the white woman which may more generally problematize the discourse of interracial rape.

Immediately after Luna's revelation, the story begins to break down. The narrator is unable to position herself in relation to Luna's testimony; as a result, the trajectory of the narrative disintegrates. The narrator's first reaction is to step out of the present of the text to historicize and censure the rape—she reads it in the context of Eldridge Cleaver's and Imamu Amiri Baraka's defenses of rape. Responding to Luna's position as a silenced victim, the narrator asks why she didn't scream and says she felt she would have screamed.

As the exchange continues, almost involuntarily the narrator links the rape to the lynching of Emmett Till and other black men. Then, instead of identifying with the silenced woman victim, she locates herself in relation to the silenced black male victim of lynching:

"I had seen photographs of white folks standing in a circle roasting something that had talked to them in their own language before they tore out its tongue" (92–93). Forced to confront the implications of her split affinities, she who would have screamed her head off is now herself silenced. First embarrassed, then angry, she thinks, not says, "'How dare she tell me this!'" (93).

At this point, the narrative shifts to one of the first metatextual moments. Here it is no longer focused on the narrator/protagonist's and Luna's conversation about the rape, but rather the narrator/author's difficulty in thinking or writing about interracial rape. The narrator steps out of the story to speculate and theorize about the exclusion of black women from the discourse surrounding rape. The conversation at this juncture is not between Luna and the narrator, but between the narrator and Ida B. Wells—or rather, with an imaginary reconstruction of Wells's analysis of the relationship between rape and lynching.

The issue of rape thus forces a series of separations. Not only does it separate the narrator from Luna, but it also separates the narrator/protagonist from the narrator/author. Moreover, Luna's admission generates a series of silences. In an oddly and doubly counter-feminist move that recalls Wells's own discrediting of the testimony of white victims, the narrator wants to believe that Luna made up the rape; only Luna's failure to report the crime—her silence—convinces her that the white woman has spoken the truth. Indeed, in the final section of the main portion of the story, silences function as a refrain. Luna "never told [the narrator] what irked her" (97) the day the narrator had two male friends spend the night at their apartment, even though that event marked the ending of their relationship. The two women never discussed the rape again; they "never discussed Freddie Pye or Luna's remaining feelings about what had happened" (97). Perhaps most strikingly, they never mention Freddie Pye's subsequent visit to the apartment during which he spends the night in Luna's bedroom. It is as if the subject of interracial rape

contains within itself so many unspeakable issues that it makes communication between the black and the white woman impossible.

Near the end of the main portion of the story, the narrator mentions Freddie Pye's return visit without explicit comment. By failing to explain the relation of his visit to Luna's story, the narrator suggests that Luna's word is unreliable. Luna's position is further undermined by the anecdote with which this section ends. This portion concludes with the story of Luna's visit to the narrator's home in the South several years later. On this occasion Luna brings a piece of pottery which is later broken by the narrator's daughter. The narrator remarks that in gluing the pot back together she "improves the beauty and fragility of the design" (98). This claim yet again bestows authority upon the narrator over and above Luna's power.

What follows are four other "endings" to the story. The narrator's inability to settle on one underscores the unnarratability of the story of interracial rape. Further, each ending absents the narrator from the story, absolving her of responsibility for the account and raising issues about the possibility of representation. It is as if the conflict between her racial and her gender identity has deconstructed the function of the narrator.

The first in this series of metatextual sections, entitled "Afterwords, Afterwards Second Thoughts" emphasizes again the unresolvability of the account. Told from the perspective of a voice that suggests that of the author, it discusses her inability to conclude the story.[21] On the one hand, she would have liked to have used a conclusion, appropriate for a text produced in a just society, in which Luna and Freddie Pye would have been forced to work toward a mutual understanding of the rape. Given the contradictions around race and gender in contemporary culture, however, she is left with an open ending followed by a series of sections that problematize even that one.

The second appended section, entitled "Luna: Ida B. Wells—Discarded Notes" continues this exploration of the relationship between narrative choices and ideological context. This section acknowledges the nature of the selections that the narrator/author has made in constructing the character of Luna. In "Imaginary Knowledge," the third appended section, the narrator creates a hypothetical meeting between Luna and Freddie Pye. This ending is the one that the author figure of the "Afterwords" section says would be appropriate for a story such as this were it published "in a country truly committed to justice" (98). In this cultural context, however, she can only employ such an ending by calling attention to its fictionality: she says that two people have become "'characters'" (101). This section is called "Imaginary," but the narrator will only imagine so much. She brings Luna and Freddie to the moment when they would talk about rape and then says that they must remove that stumbling block themselves.

The story ends with a section called "Postscript: Havana, Cuba, November 1976" in which the author figure speaks with a muralist/photographer from the U.S. about "Luna." The muralist offers a nationalist reading that supplants the narrator's racial and gender analysis. In this section it becomes clear that the attention has shifted away from the narrator and the significance of her interpretation, to Freddie Pye and his motivations. The lack of closure in the story, as well as the process by which the narrator recedes from the text, all suggest that the story is unwriting itself even as it is being written.

III

I last taught "Advancing Luna" in a seminar on Black Women Writers in the United States which was evenly divided between black and white women undergraduates. In this seminar students would occasionally argue about interpretations or dispute the ascendancy of racial or gender issues in the texts under discussion, but we seemed for the most part to arrive at consentaneous readings of the texts we discussed. This particular experience of teaching this text of interracial rape dramatized within the classroom the very divisions

that operate at the level of narrative within the story itself. I found it to be a story that breaks various codes of silence even as its own narration breaks down.

The tendency toward unanimity that characterized this seminar may well have been a function of our collective response to the syllabus and to the composition of the class. As a teacher of Afro-American literature in integrated classrooms at elite white universities, I admit to foregrounding the accessibility of the texts to all students even as I articulate the strategies and components that reveal their cultural specificity. I further suspect that the students and I at some unexamined level assumed that our disagreements notwithstanding, as a community of women we would be able to contain differences within some provisional model of consensus. "Advancing Luna" forced us to confront the nature of differences that could not be resolved and to acknowledge the difficulty of speaking across them.

This story silenced a group of ordinarily talkative students in a number of ways. When I asked them where they positioned themselves in the story, no one would answer. My students then began to deconstruct the question, asking what it meant to "position" or "locate" oneself in a narrative. As our discussion progressed, they began to admit that, in fact, they did know where they positioned themselves. They were embarrassed or frightened by their affinities, however, and could not speak through that self-consciousness. For example, several white students finally admitted that they located themselves with Luna. I prompted them to discuss her motivations, and was struck by the extent to which students who are otherwise careful readers had manufactured an entire inner life for Luna. It was as if they were compensating unintentionally for the narrator's vicious representation of her character.

During the course of the conversation, it became clear that the black women students who spoke sided with Freddie Pye, the white women who spoke, with Luna.[22] Once this split became evident, then my project became to get the students to articulate their differences. My hope was that the black students would claim their divergent affinities with the black man on racial grounds and the white woman on the basis of gender, and that the students would recognize the cost of their respective identifications. For it was important to me that they acknowledge the implications of their discomfort, the extent to which they felt betrayed by their divisions from each other.

To my mind, within the space of a classroom students should be able to develop a vocabulary for speaking across differences that are initially the source of silences. Perhaps more importantly, I would hope that they would begin to develop a sense of respect for each other as the individual products of discrete cultural and historical experiences. Not surprisingly, however, I cannot claim that in my seminar I was able to achieve either of these goals. No doubt we only managed to enact the fraught and fragile nature of the issues that divide us.

The story forced the students to confront the circumstances of their own embodiment, the conditions that made them different. It perhaps also required them to confront my embodiment. The story might thus be seen as a "border case" in and of itself, for it illuminated the silences upon which our consensus depended.

The process of teaching (and then writing about the teaching) of this story has required me to confront the limits of what a class and a syllabus can accomplish. Not only were we unable to reach any kind of satisfactory closure in our discussion of "Advancing Luna," but moreover our discussions of subsequent texts did not seem to take place at a heightened level of consciousness. I can therefore only allow myself the guarded hope that in this instance, as is so often the case in teaching, a few students will comprehend the impact of our experience of this text at some point in the future.

Faced with the conundra of classroom and text, the only closure available to me (as is the case with Walker's author figure) is the metatextual. I would argue that what Walker and her narrator confront in writing "Advanc-

ing Luna" and what my students confront in discussing the story is the status of the text as a specific cultural formation that reflects and shapes their experience as social subjects. The issue of an incident of interracial rape (for our purposes here, one involving a black man and a white woman) sets in motion a variety of historical, cultural, and ideological narratives and associations. Mutually contradictory, and rooted deeply in cultural practice, these embedded narratives and associations interfere with the articulation of positions around an instance of interracial rape.

IV

During the summer of 1989 I overheard someone say that all of the talk about race and class in relation to the Central Park rape was beside the point. For this person, it was a crime about gender relations: in Central Park on April 19, a group of young men raped a young woman. Race and class had nothing to do with it.

To the extent that the crime seems not to have been racially motivated, this person's reading of the incident seems to be true at one level. Yet at another level, the comment seems strikingly naive, for neither the perpetrators nor the victim are purely gendered beings. To paraphrase Teresa de Lauretis, men and women are not purely sexual or merely racial, economic, or (sub)cultural, but all of these together and in conflict with another.[23]

From a sociological point of view, columnist Tom Wicker wrote in the April 28 issue of *The New York Times* that the crime was racial because the attackers lived surrounded by the social pathologies of the inner city and that these influences have had consequences on their attitudes and behavior. He also argued that the crime was racial to the extent that it exacerbated racial tensions in the metropolitan New York area.

I would add that to the extent that the discourses of race and rape are so deeply connected, cases of interracial rape are constituted simultaneously as crimes of race and of gender. The inescapability of cultural narratives means that instances of this sort participate in the ongoing cultural activity around ideologies of gender, race, and class. Rather than attempting to determine the primacy of race or class or gender, we ought to search for ways of articulating how these various categories of experience inflect and interrogate each other and how we as social subjects are constituted.

NOTES

I wish to thank Marianne Hirsch and Evelyn Fox Keller for their advice and patience as I prepared this essay. I am grateful also to Ruth Wilson Gilmore, Craig Gilmore, and Agnes Jackson for carefully reading this paper and suggesting revisions.

1. See Valerie Smith, "Black Feminist Theory and the Representation of the 'Other,'" in Cheryl A. Wall, ed., *Changing Our Own Words: Essays on Criticism, Theory, and Writing by Black Women* (New Brunswick, NJ: Rutgers University Press, 1989), pp. 38–57.

2. See Michèle Barrett's discussion of the construction of difference in feminist theory, "The Concept of 'Differences'," *Feminist Review*, no. 26 (July 1987), pp. 29–41.

3. See, for example, Kimberlé Crenshaw, "Demarginalizing the Intersection of Race and Sex: A Black Feminist Critique of Antidiscrimination Doctrine, Feminist Theory and Antiracist Politics," *The University of Chicago Legal Forum*, 1989, pp. 139–67.

4. See for instance Deborah McDowell's account of black male responses to black feminism in "Reading Family Matters," in Cheryl A. Wall, ed., *Changing Our Own Words*, pp. 75–97.

5. Mary Poovey, *Uneven Developments: The Ideological Work of Gender in Mid-Victorian England* (Chicago: University of Chicago Press, 1988), p. 12.

6. See Crenshaw, "Demarginalizing the Intersection of Race and Sex," p. 140.

7. Hazel V. Carby, *Reconstructing Womanhood: The Emergence of the Afro-American Woman Novelist* (New York: Oxford: University Press, 1987), pp. 20–39.

8. See Angela Y. Davis, "Rape, Racism and the Myth of the Black Rapist," in *Women, Race and Class* (New York: Random House, 1983), pp. 172–201.

9. Jacquelyn Dowd Hall, "'The Mind That Burns in Each Body': Women, Rape, and Racial Violence," in Ann Snitow, Christine Stansell, and Sharon Thompson, eds., *Powers of Desire: The Politics of Sexuality* (New York: Monthly Review Press, 1983), pp. 329–49.

10. Ida B. Wells, *Crusade for Justice: The Autobiography of Ida B. Wells* (Chicago: University of Chicago Press, 1970), p. 64.

11. Stephanie H. Jed discusses the relationship between the rape of Lucretia and the creation of republican Rome in *Chaste Thinking: The Rape of Lucretia and the Birth of Humanism* (Bloomington: Indiana University Press, 1989). See also Norman Bryson, "Two Narratives of Rape in the Visual Arts: Literature and the Visual Arts," in Sylvana Tomaselli and Roy Porter, eds., *Rape: An Historical and Social Enquiry* (New York: Basil Blackwell, 1986), pp. 152–73.

12. It seems to me that the journalistic practice of "protecting the identity" of rape victims needs to be reconsidered. I would argue that leaving victims unnamed objectifies them. Moreover, this silence contributes to the construction of rape as an experience of which the victim ought to be ashamed.

13. For a systematic analysis of the ways in which Brownmiller and some other early feminist discussions of rape use the figure of the black male rapist see Angela Y. Davis, "Rape, Racism and the Myth of the Black Rapist," pp. 178–82.

14. See Susan Estrich, *Real Rape* (Cambridge: Harvard University Press, 1987); Davis, "Rape, Racism and the Myth of the Black Rapist"; and Catherine MacKinnon, "A Rally Against Rape," in *Feminism Unmodified: Discourses on Life and Law* (Cambridge: Harvard University Press, 1987), pp. 81–84.

15. MacKinnon, "A Rally Against Rape," p. 81.

16. During the week of the Central Park rape, twenty-eight other first-degree rapes or attempted rapes were reported in New York City. Nearly all the reported rapes involved black women or Latinas. Yet, as Don Terry wrote in *The New York Times*, most went unnoticed by the public. See "A Week of Rapes: The Jogger and 28 Not in the News," *The New York Times*, May 29, 1989, p. 25.

17. Andrew Kopkind, *The Nation*, vol. 250, no. 5 (February 5, 1990), 1, p. 153.

18. See, for instance Deborah McDowell's discussion of Walker's "Source," in her essay "Reading Family Matters" in Cheryl A. Wall, ed., pp. 75–97.

19. Barbara Christian, "The Race for Theory," in

Linda Kauffman, ed., *Gender and Theory: Dialogues on Feminist Criticism* (New York: Basil Blackwell, 1989), p. 226.

20. Alice Walker, "Advancing Luna—And Ida B. Wells," in *You Can't Keep A Good Woman Down* (New York: Harcourt Brace Jovanovich, 1981), p. 85. Subsequent references will be to this edition and will be noted in the text by page number.

21. I problematize the figure of the author here to make clear that I do not intend to refer to Alice Walker, but rather to the multiplicity of narrative selves that is generated out of the disintegrating of the text.

22. This need not always be the case. See Mary Helen Washington's discussion of teaching this story in her essay "How Racial Differences Helped Us Discover Our Common Ground," in *Gendered Subjects: The Dynamics of Feminist Teaching*, ed. Margo Culley and Catherine Portuges (Boston: Routledge, Kegan Paul, 1985), pp. 221–29.

23. Teresa de Lauretis, "Feminist Studies/Critical Studies: Issues, Terms, and Contexts," in De Lauretis, ed., *Feminist Studies/Critical Studies* (Bloomington: Indiana University Press, 1986), p. 14.

Sexual Politics

An Antilynching Crusader in Revisionist Feminism

Joy James

[In] this war against Negro progress is the substitution of mob rule for courts of justice throughout the South. Judges, juries, sheriffs, and jailors ... are all white men, and thus make it impossible for a negro to escape the penalty for any crime he commits. Then whenever a black man is charged with any crime against a white person these mobs without disguise take him from the jail in broad daylight, hang, shoot or burn him as their fancy dictates.

—Ida B. Wells-Barnett,
Crusade for Justice

Source: Joy James, "Sexual Politics: An Antilynching Crusader in Revisionist Feminism" in Joy James, *Transcending the Talented Tenth: Black Leaders and American Intellectuals* (New York: Routledge, 1996), 61–81.

By waging the antilynching campaigns as resistance to both racial and sexual violence,[1] crusaders such as Ida B. Wells-Barnett established a political language to critique U.S. racial-sexual politics and the duplicity of the white press, courts, and police. Transforming the meanings of lynching, countering repressive violence, African-American women led the antilynching campaign by deconstructing the myth of the black rapist.[2] For instance, in *Southern Horrors* and *A Red Record,* Ida B. Wells-Barnett documented that the overwhelming connection between most interracial rape cases and lynching was that black women and children were raped prior to and during lynchings, as well as lynched with black males who assisted them in resisting or avenging rape by white males.[3] Women pointed out that by inverting the reality of racialized sexual violence, whites grossly exaggerated the likelihood of black male assaults on white women. A rare phenomenon for white women, interracial rape was a constant nightmare for black women. Most interracial rapes in the United States were (and remain) committed by white males.[4] Logically, if a rational connection between lynching and the prosecution of sex crimes existed, the majority of lynch victims would have been white men.

Today, using the historical, black female-led campaigns to reflect on contemporary politics surrounding (interracial) sexual violence, black feminists offer diverse responses to the campaigns and the women who led them. Conflicting depictions of antiracist activism and speech regarding charges of interracial sexual violence surround the figure of Wells-Barnett. As the icon of the antilynching crusade, she has come to represent a type of militant black womanhood immersed in controversy.

For instance, Alice Walker and Valerie Smith represent Ida B. Wells-Barnett by filtering the image of the antilynching crusader through revisionist feminism, in order to explore the racial-sexual politics of interracial rape. Walker's short story "Advancing Luna— And Ida B. Wells"[5] reconstructs Wells-Barnett's sexual politics to portray her as blinded by race-paranoia and cowed by racist violence into irrational denials concerning black males' assaults of white females. In an equally novel but harsher depiction, Smith's essay "Split Affinities"[6] represents Wells-Barnett as embittered with antiwhite resentment, a counterfeminist whose hostility toward white women reinforced moral indifference to sexual violence. In their respective portraits of Wells-Barnett, neither writer offers much in terms of historical specificity. Reconstructing Wells-Barnett, and by extension the women-led antilynching campaigns, in order to represent a form of antiracist radicalism embodied as gender regressive, Walker and Smith argue against a type of female race militancy. For each womanist/black feminist, Wells-Barnett exemplifies the race woman misled by black identity politics into reactionary sexual politics.

In the following varied portraits of Wells-Barnett—as radical activist, paranoid race woman, and antiwhite counterfeminist—her sexual politics becomes the touchstone for debates about venality, black feminist intellectualism, and radicalism regarding the intersections of race, sex, and violence.

WELLS-BARNETT THE MILITANT ACTIVIST

In the black female militancy of the antilynching crusades,[7] Wells-Barnett deconstructed the rationalizations for white terror: Negro domination of whites through the vote; Negro race riots; black male sexual assaults of white women. The last charge proved to be as specious as its predecessors but the most incendiary and tenacious. Wells-Barnett argued that although there was no record of a white female sexually assaulted by a black male during the Civil War,[8] and although the charge of rape was used in only a fraction of lynchings, this accusation became the general rationalization for racist violence. With this charge, Americans who considered themselves above the mob acquiesced to lynchings as a "necessary preventive measure" to protect white women; at the same time, they turned a blind eye to the more prevalent problem of white male sexual violence.

To demystify the belief that white men enforced written or unwritten laws for the protection of white women, Wells-Barnett's critique of lynching apologias exploded their psycho-sexual mythology and moral hypocrisy. Any chivalry toward women, writes Wells-Barnett, garners "little respect from the civilized world, when it confines itself entirely to the women who happen to be white."[9] In 1895, noting the duplicity of white men's prosecutorial performances, she wrote:

> To justify their own barbarism they assume a chivalry which they do not possess. True chivalry respects all womanhood, and no one who reads the record, as it is written in the faces of the million mulattoes in the South, will for a minute conceive that the southern

white man had a very chivalrous regard for the honor due the women of his own race or respect for the womanhood which circumstances placed in his power.[10]

During this era, whites defined voluntary sexual relationships between white women and black men as sexual assaults, reconstructing consensual relations as the rape of white women. These voluntary interracial sexual associations were punishable by the death of the black male lover or sexual partner. Although white women were ostracized, institutionalized, and beaten for such alliances, they could repudiate the relationship with the charge of rape. African-American males had no such escape clause.

African-American women activists reasoned that ending lynchings both eradicated racist terror cloaked in chivalry and diminished malfeasant prosecutions of rape. Seeing the prosecution of rape as determined by the social status of the woman assaulted and that of the accused male, they pointed out the rarity of this type of interracial sexual violence, rather than categorically, and irrationally, deny that black men assault white women.

Female crusaders demanded that society acknowledge that the lynchings of African Americans had very little to do with rape and that the barbaric murders deflected attention from the prevalence of sexual violence against black women and social contempt for their sexual safety. Late nineteenth-century African-American women recognized that the myth of black (sexual) pathology excused rape. The mythology masked sexual violence against black women, and the reality that the rapists of white women were overwhelmingly white men. As a caste, white men were the moral and legal prosecutors of sexual violence, yet were, particularly if affluent, the least prosecuted and censured for sexual violence.[11]

By demystifying the idea of lynching as rape prevention and prosecution, Wells-Barnett broadened the base of antilynching activism to establish a foundation for moral and political resistance to American violence. Discrediting the belief that white men enforced written or unwritten laws for the protection of white women, she waged a radical campaign against lynching apologias.

Her condemnations of lynchings both electrified and offended the American public. Because of white America's refusal to end lynching, the crusade became an international one. A passage from Wells-Barnett's April 9, 1894, Liverpool special correspondence for the *Inter-Ocean* typifies what some considered to be inflammatory rhetoric and others understood as antiracist militancy: "The machinery of law and politics is in the hands of those who commit the lynching," writes the author, who proceeds to argue that "it is only wealthy white men whom the law fails to reach."[12] In contrast to the virtual immunity of the white male elite, Wells-Barnett observes: "Hundreds of Negroes including women and children are lynched for trivial offenses on suspicion and in many cases when known to be guiltless of any crime … the law refused to punish the murderers because it is not considered a crime to kill a Negro."[13] She concludes the passage: "Many of the cases of 'Assault' are simply adulteries between white women and colored men."[14]

Despite her polemical writings, Wells-Barnett did not categorically deny that black men assaulted white women nor did she advocate that others make such denials. The body of her work, in which the word "many" is generally used to describe false accusations of rape, makes it clear that she makes no assertion of universal innocence. (Her memoir's reprint of an 1894 letter by Florida Ruffin Ridley, excerpted below, best reveals her position.) However, Wells-Barnett demanded that white society acknowledge that actual rape had very little to do with the lynching of African Americans: "With the Southern white man, any mesalliance existing between a white woman and a colored man is a sufficient foundation for the charge of rape."[15] She argues further that in "numerous instances where colored men have been lynched on the charge of rape, it was positively known at the time of lynching, and indisputably proven after the victim's death, that the relationship sustained between the man and woman was voluntary and clandestine, and that in no court of law could even the charge of assault have been successfully maintained."[16] Noting that the "Southern white man says that it is impossible for a voluntary alliance to exist between a white woman and a colored man, and therefore, the fact of an alliance is a proof of force,"[17] she excoriated the state and vigilantes for punishing voluntary sexual relationships between white women and black men as sexual assaults while ignoring de facto sexual violence against black women. The punishment of African-American men for real and imagined sexual violence against white women was a given while the prosecution of any male for sexual violence against African-American women was an anomaly. The myth of the black rapist and interracial rape accusations and cases increased the likelihood of, and social indifference to, lynching as well as deflected attention away from the more prevalent intraracial sexual violence. (Today, FBI statistics report that currently over ninety percent of rapes are intraracial, that is, occur within the same race or ethnic group.)[18]

Wells-Barnett's analysis of the psycho-sexual politics of lynching proved relentless and ruthless. Demystifying the rationalization of lynching as rape prevention and prosecution (for white women), she helped to make antilynching activism respectable. Her analyses influenced and shaped resistance to racist violence justified as a war to counter sexual violence. At the same time, this controversial figure was stigmatized as an apologist for rape. As Wells-Barnett's one-time colleague and later rival Mary Church Terrell noted, an "error on the subject of lynching consists of the widely circulated statement that the moral sensibilities of the best negroes in the United States are so stunted and dull, and the standard of morality among even the leaders of the race is so low, that they do not appreciate the enormity and heinousness of rape."[19] In contemporary black feminism that revisits and revises the sexual politics of Wells-Barnett, we find depictions of the antilynching militant as having been morally crippled by her antiracism.

Although mob prosecution gave way to legal executions, the most severe punishments for rape were, and are, disproportionately reserved for black males.[20] Some feminist critics argue that by focusing on the use of lynching to terrorize black men, Wells failed to note the impact of violence on women. Yet, she saw that courts which considered only interracial sexual violence against white women truly heinous enough to warrant the death penalty inevitably treated sexual assaults against black females lightly. During the lynching (and postlynching) era, the racist application of the death penalty for sex crimes reflected the different values the state and society placed on white and black lives as well as white and black sexuality. Consequently, female antilynching crusaders positioned themselves as both race leaders and (proto)feminists.

Joanne Braxton describes Wells-Barnett as such, as a radical female icon for social justice. Arguing that Wells-Barnett's activism created a matrix for "womanhood" formed by race, gender, and class, Braxton writes that her leadership in the black women's club movement created the "fusion of powerful influences: black feminism and black nationalism."[21] This fusion created "a race-centered, self-conscious womanhood" represented in the black women's club movement; consequently, Braxton argues, for women such as Ida B. Wells-Barnett, "a blow at lynching was a blow at racism and the brutally enforced sexual double standard that pervaded the South. It was a defense of the entire race."[22] Historically, the dominant society stigmatized black and white women antilynching activists as sexual deviants, expressing contempt and opprobrium for women advocating fair hearings and trials regarding interracial sexual assault cases. In spite or perhaps because of her militancy, Wells-Barnett was able to provide progressive leadership for both black and white women. Braxton writes that Wells-Barnett "forged a legitimate black feminism through the synthesis of black nationalism and the suffrage movement, providing a useful model with race, not sex, as a point of departure."[23] This model, according to Braxton, served not only the NAACP but also the antilynching activism of white women and feminists such as Jessie Daniel Ames in the Association of Southern Women for the Prevention of Lynching. Other black feminists give starkly different readings of the antilynching crusader's sexual politics.

"ADVANCING LUNA—AND IDA B. WELLS" AND THE PARANOID RACE WOMAN

Fiction and autobiography are the most noted literary forms of African-American women. When literary creativity supplants research and analysis to offer itself as political thought or political autobiographies are treated as "fiction" problems arise. In both instances, invention becomes surrogate for political substance and historical specificity. Wells-Barnett's autobiography, *Crusade for Justice,* has become a classic for understanding the life of a heroic African American and the antilynching crusades. The importance of the work is underscored by the fact that Wells-Barnett's daughter Alfreda Duster worked extensively with scholar John Hope Franklin to edit, document, and verify the accounts of this posthumously published memoir. (Duster also struggled for thirty-five years before finally finding a publisher who recognized the significance and historical accuracy of the work.) Even cursory studies of Wells-Barnett reference her memoir to legitimize their political stances.

Alice Walker references *Crusade for Justice* to historicize her narrative in "Advancing Luna—And Ida B. Wells." The story centers on the relationship between a white woman, Luna, and a black woman, the nameless narrator, and the narrator's relationship to her ancestor Ida B. Wells. Walker's story characterizes the fears shaping black women's responses to interracial rape cases and the uneasy alliances between black and white women. Throughout the story line the narrator offers unflattering observations of Luna, while recounting their friendship, which began in 1965 when they became roommates in Atlanta as civil rights activists and ended

after they left the movement and briefly roomed together in New York City. After moving into Luna's apartment, the narrator is informed by Luna that during their stay in Atlanta she was raped by Freddie Pye, a black man. The narrator immediately thinks of the "rapist-revolutionary" writings of Eldridge Cleaver and LeRoi Jones (Imamu Baraka) whose "misogynous cruelty ... was habitually lost on black men (on men in general, actually), but nearly always perceived and rejected by women of whatever color."[24] She also disdainfully recalls Pye: "He was coarse and spoke of black women as 'our' women.... He was physically unattractive ... with something of the hoodlum about him."[25] Asking Luna why she did not scream and receiving the reply, "You know why," the black woman thinks of Emmett Till, a fourteen-year old black youth lynched in Mississippi years earlier for whistling at a white woman.

Disturbed by Luna's revelation, the narrator begins to write a novel about "such a rape." In preparation, she converses with the antilynching archetype, Wells-Barnett, confiding that she has read her memoir three times "as a means of praying to her spirit to forgive me":

> My prayer, as I turned the pages, went like this: *"Please forgive me. I am a writer.... I cannot write contrary to what life reveals to me. I wish to malign no one. But I must struggle to understand at least my own tangled emotions about interracial rape. I know, Ida B. Wells, you spent your whole life protecting, and trying to protect black men accused of raping white women, who were lynched by white mobs, or threatened with it. You know, better than I ever will, what it means for a whole people to live under the terror of lynching. Under the slander that their men, where white women are concerned, are creatures of uncontrollable sexual lust.*[26]

The betrayal that weighs heavily on the narrator's conscience is truth-telling. She assumes that Wells-Barnett, feeling betrayed by writing that might contradict her own stance, will reprove the young woman for her audacious honesty.

Transferring the fearless investigation that characterized Wells-Barnett's activism onto the narrator's intellectual aspirations as a novelist, literary production supplants political deeds; now, political courage is symbolized by a literary act embodied in the narrator's allegedly transgressive fiction. Walker's narrator neatly reduces Wells-Barnett's activism to a life spent "trying to protect black men accused of raping white women" from lynching. In fact, in the most memorable historic cases around which Wells-Barnett agitated—the 1892 Memphis lynchings, the 1918 East St. Louis riots, and the 1917 executions of black soldiers at Camp Grant—sexual violence against white women was not alleged. Rather, racist fears against independent blacks, economic greed, and political ambitions motivated these attacks.

In the dialogue, the narrator shifts responsibility for her own naivete concerning racial-sexual violence onto Wells-Barnett:

"You made it so clear that the black men accused of rape in the past were innocent victims of white criminals that I grew up believing black men literally did not rape white women. At all. Ever. Now it would appear that some of them, the very twisted, the terribly ill, do. What would you have me write about them?"

Her answer was: "Write nothing. Nothing at all. It will be used against black men and therefore against all of us. Eldridge Cleaver and LeRoi Jones don't know who they're dealing with. But you remember. You are dealing with people who brought their children to witness the murder of black human beings falsely accused of rape. People who handed out, as trophies, black fingers and toes. Deny! Deny! Deny!"[27]

The theatrical exhortations uttered by Walker's Wells suggest an unrestrained emotionalism and disingenuousness among antilynching activists. Using the barbarity of white supremacy, as the argument goes, these activists excused black moral cowardliness in regard to sexual violence. The short story's Ida B. Wells is determined by a hysteria not discernible in her writings, which speak of her rage at, rather than fear of, racist violence and public acquiescence. Death threats likely contributed to Wells-Barnett's fearfulness in

probing the rape issue as a race issue; yet fear did not hinder her investigative work. Walker's story overshadows Wells's meticulous accumulation of data on lynchings with emotionalism concerning antiblack violence.

"Advancing Luna—And Ida B. Wells" thus allows the black woman writer to morally triumph over her ancestor, as the narrator rejects Wells's fictive counsel:

And yet, I have pursued it: *"Some black men themselves do not seem to know what the meaning of raping someone is. Some have admitted rape in order to denounce it, but others have accepted rape as a part of rebellion, of 'paying whitey bach.' They have gloried in it."*

"They know nothing of America," she says. *"And neither, apparently, do you. No matter what you think you know, no matter what you feel about it, say nothing. And to your dying breath!"*

Which, to my mind, is virtually useless advice to give to a writer.[28]

The narrator-writer commends herself for a sincerity and valor seemingly lacking in Wells-Barnett. Here, the antilynching crusader's moral timidity highlights in juxtaposition the narrator-writer's relentless pursuit of the truth. The narrator seems uninformed about the specificity of Wells-Barnett's praxis. Wells-Barnett was also a writer "guilty of wanting to know"; one of her mottoes was "To tell the truth—freely." She often did so at the risk of her own life as she painstakingly documented lynchings. An investigative reporter and a skilled polemicist, Wells-Barnett was adept at uncovering what "life reveals" in its most gruesome details. Walker's construction reduces this organizer to a cowering defensiveness and ignores her stance on armed self-defense for blacks, and her personal working relationships and friendships with prominent whites who likely would not have been on equal terms with Walker's semiparanoid race woman.

At the beginning of the twentieth century, most African Americans would have censored any black person who advocated sexually assaulting white women and who thereby promoted the image that antilynching activists risked their lives to dispel. Whereas at the end of the twentieth century, black Americans take multiple contradictory stances toward the image of the sexual savage, in Wells-Barnett's time such performances had deadly consequences. It is more likely that Wells-Barnett, in dialogue with a contemporary black feminist writer, would express contempt for racialist misogyny anti-thetical to black safety and beneath black dignity. She had publicly challenged or condemned prominent blacks and whites for any behavior she considered detrimental to black emancipation, and she did so irrespective of the costs to her career and safety.

Yet, Walker's revisionism allows the narrator a moral triumph over a denial-ridden, fearful Ida B. Wells who shields black rapists in order to protect black communities. Although the narrator states that she repeatedly read Wells-Barnett's autobiography, she misses the substance of the activist's political thinking. Somehow, the story appends defensive sentiments held by some contemporary black women onto the historical radicalism embodied by Wells. Walker's narrator extends her narrow representation of Wells-Barnett to black women in general: "Whenever interracial rape is mentioned, a black woman's first thought is to protect the lives of her brothers, her father, her sons, her lovers. A history of lynching has bred this reflex in her."[29] This insight is not easily generalizable today: Not every black woman considers the historical dangers of lynching, legal or extralegal, to be a contemporary problem. Not all black women perceive all black men with the protective sympathy they might extend to their brothers, father, sons, or lovers. And black women who survive sexual abuse from their brothers, fathers, or lovers may have decidedly unsympathetic responses to rightly or wrongfully accused male kin.

The short story's endings "Afterwords, Afterwards: Second Thoughts" and "Postscript: Havana, Cuba, November 1976," politicize Luna's assault to a level of state violence. In "Afterwords," the narrator and a black male friend express conflicting emotions while condemning the attack as "morally wrong" and

"politically corrupt." The narrator notes their shared concerns: "As we thought of what might have happened to an indiscriminate number of innocent young black men in Freehold, Georgia, had Luna screamed, it became clear that more than a little of Ida B. Wells's fear of probing the rape issue was running through us, too."[30] In the "Postscript," after reading "Luna" to African-American artists-activists who like herself are visiting Cuba, the narrator argues with an Afro-American muralist. As the fiction writer offers different endings for the story, the muralist discourages the one in which Pye is contrite by stating she neither understands evil nor the need to eradicate it. Evil, he continues, does not refer to Pye as an individual rapist, rather, "'Freddie Pye' … was probably raping white women on the instructions of his government."[31] Recalling the FBI's COINTELPRO, the muralist invokes the assassinations of black activists by U.S. agents, admonishing the female writer: "Even though you know by now that blacks could be hired to blow up other blacks, and could be hired *by someone* to shoot down Brother Malcolm, and hired *by someone* to provide a diagram of Fred Hampton's bedroom so the pigs could shoot him easily while he slept, you find it hard to believe a black man could be hired *by someone* to rape white women." He argues, then considers "the perfect disruptive act," noting that: "Enough blacks raping or accused of raping enough white women" would doom "any political movement that cuts across racial lines."[32] Warning that greater "forces are at work than your story would indicate," the impoverished artist reveals that such "forces"—or the government—offered him money, probably her tax dollars, to assault white women in order to disrupt civil rights organizing.[33]

Using the muralist to introduce state complicity in violence, Walker moves beyond individual motive and black male misogyny to underscore the ambiguity of the narrative and the complexities of racial-sexual violence. The postscript ends with the narrator's observation about the muralist: His look "implied I would never understand anything about evil, power, or corrupted human beings in the modern world. But of course he is wrong."[34] Walker leaves it to the reader's imagination to determine why.

Valerie Smith, on the other hand, agrees with the muralist's assessment of the narrator's ignorance, but for entirely different reasons as she retells "Advancing Luna—And Ida B. Wells" eliding the ambiguities and contradictory images of Walker's postscript and narrative. Smith's essay "Split Affinities" reviews representations of interracial rape in Walker's short story as well as "journalistic discourse" surrounding the Central Park Case in which African-American and Latino youths were convicted for the brutal assault and rape of a white woman.[35] With selective, decontextualized passages that distort Walker's story, Smith revises the historical politics of anti-lynching activism as well as Walker's fiction to reflect on black women's gender venality. "Split Affinities" uses "Advancing Luna—And Ida B. Wells" to support its thesis that the divided loyalties of black women create their split affinities in interracial rape cases. Smith, like Walker, notes that given the historical use of rape charges to justify racist violence, African Americans view accusations of rape "as a way to terrorize innocent black men." For Smith this reasoning "may lead to the denial of the fact that some black men do rape."[36] The stances of black females on interracial rape cases are "particularly vexed," according to Smith, who also notes that given society's greater indifference to violence against black women, African-American women's "indentification with white women is problematic." Smith writes that as "members of communities under siege," black women "may well sympathize with the black male who stands accused" while "as women they share the victim's sense of violation."[37] She expands this position with a historical perspective that argues that Wells-Barnett was a counterfeminist hostile to white women abused by black men. Smith uses Walker's fictitious characters as representative of historical and contemporary black women. She does so without mentioning the liabilities of using contemporary fiction, rather than historical or sociological research, to represent the politics of nonfic-

tional African Americans. Smith's argument has merit; in interracial rape cases, divided loyalties can reduce some African-American women to reactionary, counterfeminist politics leading them to pained or vindictive positions on interracial rape that support black males who rape rather than their white victims. Yet their counterprogressive politics can neither be generalized to all contemporary black women nor facilely appended to historical, black female anti-lynching radicals.

To make her generalizations plausible, Smith transforms "Advancing Luna" into a black and white polemic between a venal black counterfeminist and an equally abstract, heroic white feminist. Inconsistent with Walker's narrative, she paints political stances absent in the story to portray the narrator as determined by nationalist sensibilities. In the story, the black narrator first temporarily leaves a prestigious, white Ivy League women's college, Sarah Lawrence, for a summer commitment to civil rights activism. Then, in somewhat dilettante fashion, she departs midsummer from her organizing project in Georgia to take advantage of a travel grant to Uganda. Her writing about this African sojourn reveals a decidedly nonnationalist consciousness: "I was taken on rides down the Nile as a matter of course, and accepted all invitations to dinner, where the best local dishes were superbly prepared in my honor. I became, in fact, a lost relative of the people, whose ancestors had foolishly strayed, long ago, to America."[38] Militant, race-nationalists do not casually refer to the Middle Passage, enslavement, and genocide as hapless wandering. Smith inserts the antiwhite, black militant race woman into Walker's story, and then drapes this persona over both the fictive narrator and the historical crusader to disparage both as counterfeminists.

Smith begins three consecutive paragraphs with the phrase: "The narrator's hostility to Luna." Referring to the sexual jealousy that marks interracial relationships between some male-identified heterosexual women, she argues that the black woman's ill will "points to a thinly veiled sexual competitiveness between the black and the white woman which may more generally problematize the discourse of interracial rape."[39] Walker's story offers no evidence for Smith's interpretation of female sexual competition. Smith's story synopsis and sleight of hand in retelling the tale alter the intent of the narrative; this suggests a systemic misreading of "Advancing Luna—And Ida B. Wells" to advance the split affinities/black gender venality thesis.

The ambiguity of Walker's text seems to be reconstructed as an issue of the veracity of the rape charge. "Split Affinities" maintains that Pye, "who Luna states raped her or who raped Luna," spends the night in Luna's bedroom illustrates the "ambiguity of the story and its open ended interpretation." The ambiguity is not whether or not Pye raped Luna: The narrator recognizes Luna's account as true. The short story asserts the rape as a fact. The ambiguity lies in the responses of black and white women to the rape.

Smith's depiction of split affinities among black women implies that the narrator must choose between black men and white women in interracial rape cases. Yet Walker's narrator follows her own conscience, indentifying with rape victims as well as lynching victims. "Split Affinities" deploys a dichotomy that alters "Advancing Luna" to contend that the narrator "instead of identifying with the silenced woman victim ... locates herself in relation to the silenced black male victim of lynching."[40] It is difficult to read this position into the story. Rather than blind race loyalty or black male identification, Walker's narrator exhibits a grim determination to protect the innocent, expressing concern for nameless, unimplicated black men, rather than a guilty Freddie Pye. Presenting identification as shaped by an exclusive choice between accused black males or white female survivors, Smith ignores the possibility that the narrator might believe that black criminals should pay for their crimes, including crimes against whites; this essay fails to acknowledge the possibility that African Americans critical of racist prosecutions may still be supportive of survivors. Although African-American women's positions on interracial rape cases span from the reactionary to the radical, Smith's argu-

ment splits progressive gender and racial politics.

Having so represented the narrator's racial consciousness, Smith proceeds to illustrate the black woman's gender insensitivity. She offers as example the narrator's failure to understand why Luna is disturbed after the black woman invites two men to spend the night, one on the couch and the other in the narrator's bedroom. Without knowing the short story, and the racialized sexual preference of each woman, we might assume from Smith's essay that the men are black and be appalled by the narrator's obtuse indifference to any presence that would remind Luna of her attacker and further her emotional and psychological distress. However, Walker's protagonist is not that insensitive. Smith fails to convey that Luna and the narrator desire their ethnic opposites: The black narrator prefers white men, particularly "ethnic exotics" who look like the singing cowboy film star Gene Autry; white Luna sleeps with black men. Both men who sleep over by invitation of the black woman are white. Luna, who only has black lovers, is upset because she feels that the narrator slept with "the enemy." Cross or transracial preferences are lost to Smith's essay which provides only the line "Luna never told me what irked her so that Sunday morning [after the men had slept over], yet I remember it as the end of our relationship."[41] The lines completing Walker's paragraph, which Smith does not relay, dispel some of the mystery. Noting their "strange" assortment of friends, including Luna's friends who "especially were deeper than they should have been into drugs,"[42] the narrator expresses concern and uncertainty about their deteriorating relationship; she reflects: "It was not, as I at first feared, that she thought my bringing the two men to the apartment was inconsiderate. The way we lived allowed us to *be* inconsiderate from time to time."[43] In Walker's short story, unlike Smith's essay, the complex frailties of black-white women's relationships are not generated by black women's antiwhite sensibilities.

Building upon the image of Luna's rape, Smith recreates Luna to symbolize both white feminism and white victimization at the hands of black men and women. Depicting a traditional feminine virtue, compassion, as absent in black women's positions on interracial rape cases, "Split Affinities" applies Walker's reconstruction of Wells-Barnett as fearful, denial-ridden, and protective of black males against the narrator herself. Luna is traumatized not only by the black rapist but also by the black woman she befriends, as Smith superimposes Walker's portrait of a frightened, disingenuous Wells-Barnett onto the narrator.

WELLS-BARNETT THE COUNTERFEMINIST

The recasting of Walker's story whose first "metatextual moment," according to Smith, occurs when the narrator theorizes "about the exclusion of black women from the discourse surrounding rape," is the prelude to revising the praxis of Ida B. Wells. Rather than excluded from the discourse surrounding rape, Wells-Barnett reshaped it, through the Afro-American press, black organizations, and antilynching campaigns. With other African-American women activists, she forced public discourse on sexual violence to pursue a new agenda. Accomplishing what most whites in the United States would not do, and what black males could not do, black women created the counterdiscourse to lynching as rape prevention, changing the politics of that discourse from an apologia to a condemnation, or at least a questioning, of lynching.

"Split Affinities" severs contemporary black feminism from Wells-Barnett's analyses and black women's historical antiracist radicalism; it simplifies the complex relationships between the antilynching crusader and white as well as black female leaders. Offering no specific information about Wells-Barnett's organizing with white feminists, diagnosing Wells-Barnett as harboring a personal dislike for white women, Smith psychologizes the crusader to dismiss the antilynching campaigns as counterfeminist and antiwhite. Whereas Walker presents Wells-Barnett as reduced by anxieties of racist violence into a

paralysis of irrational disavowals, Smith depicts her as infused with both a hostility toward (female) whites and an indifference to sexual violence. Reducing Wells-Barnett's militant opposition to racist violence to a personal acrimony against women in a racially oppressive caste, she contends that Wells-Barnett bequeathed a legacy and praxis unsuitable for feminism (the essay uses this representation of Wells-Barnett as a counterfeminist to discuss the Central Park case.)

Omitting any reference to the role of white women's racism or moral reticence in false accusations of rape, Smith reminds us of "Wells's own discrediting of the testimony of white victims." Wells-Barnett's investigative reporting discredited not so much the testimony of victims but the barbaric use of the rape charge in false accusations against African-American men and the general demagoguery of using rape as a pretext for racist violence. Smith criticizes Wells-Barnett for her "focus on the unreliability of white rape victims" which she constructs as an attack on white women victims. "Victims" is somewhat of a misnomer here. Wells-Barnett did not view white women in lynchings collectively as rape victims. *A Red Record* reports that most who voluntarily or reluctantly claimed to be rape victims, to sanction lynchings, were not sexual-assault victims or were not victimized by African-American men. Smith fails to examine three vital facts concerning Wells-Barnett's era: The overwhelming number of rapes were intraracial; the charge of rape was used only in a fraction of the lynchings; and whites had defined all consensual sexual relationships between white women and black men as rape. Blurring distinctions between research and fiction (problems arise when the letter is taken as a more accurate guide for assessing the politics of this African-American antilynching activist), Smith writes that Wells-Barnett's "opposition to lynching as a practice requires her effectively to deny the veracity of any white woman's testimony against a black man."[44]

Smith claims that a logical reading of passages from *Crusade for Justice* reveals Wells-Barnett "effectively blaming white women for the lynching of black men."[45] All white women? If so, then Wells-Barnett's political and personal friendships with prominent white women—such as Susan B. Anthony and other suffragettes, "halfway house" movement leaders, British antilynching supporters, and NAACP founders—are inexplicable. If Wells-Barnett had been contemptuous of sexual violence in white women's lives or uniformly condemned all white women, as Smith implies, she would have alienated most of her white female supporters.

The progressive analyses of contemporary black feminisms are rooted in and indebted to the earlier critiques of black women antilynching crusaders who recognized the interrelatedness of racial and sexual violence. Although it would be useful to examine with specificity how, and under what conditions, African-American women choose to subordinate sex to race and vice versa, we cannot logically infer a uniform practice of subordinating sexual oppression to racial oppression in African-American women's challenges to lynching, particularly since the historical antilynching campaigns were also waged as antisexual violence campaigns.

Other problematic areas arise as Smith interchanges the terms "accusations" and "instances" when referring to interracial rape, rendering accusations synonymous with factual assaults. She also confuses the prosecution of rape with the crime of rape to write that Wells-Barnett's formulations "subordinate the sexual to the racial dimension of interracial rape, thereby dramatizing the fact that the crime can never be read solely as an offense against women's bodies."[46] Wells-Barnett's critique did not, as is asserted, "subordinate" the sexual to the racial; rather it connected the sexual to the racial to counter racist depictions of black sexuality. Wells-Barnett's journalism refers to the prevalence of white men not prosecuted for raping black women and children. The state did not perceive rape as a crime that could be "read solely as an offense against women's bodies." Nor did it prosecute it as such given that no generic woman exists under white supremacy, capitalism, and patriarchy. The prosecution of rape is, to quote

Smith, never "read solely as an offense against women's bodies," given a hierarchy of bodies based on race, class, and sexual orientation.

Unaware of the historical roots of her own feminism, Smith advocates a multitextured black feminism over a monodimensional Eurocentric one, describing the former as a more competent framework for analysis: "Black feminism presumes the 'intersectionality' of race and gender in the lives of black women, thereby rendering inapplicable to the lives of black women any 'single-axis' theory about racism or sexism."[47] This "new" analysis is in fact based on a paradigm articulated a century ago. Race and gender intersect (with class and sexuality) not only in black women's lives but also in all women's lives. Smith defines the very foundation of black feminism as one which presumes the "intersectionality" of race and gender in the lives of black women; this definition is also based on a position articulated and fought for by nineteenth-century African-American women in campaigns largely initiated by Wells-Barnett.[48] Delineating the impact of race in white women's lives and their complicity in white supremacy as well as racial-sexual violence, Wells-Barnett applied this intersectionality more consistently than Smith does in her essay. (Down-playing what Wells-Barnett underscored—white women's complicity in white supremacy and racial-sexual terror—Smith never raises the issue of white women's split affinities.)

Rather than generalize that black women's antiracism privileges males, we might note the complexities involved. Women recognize that racist violence terrorized women and children, in addition to men; women most vulnerable to violence could also prove the most vocal advocates for stiff prosecutions. Some African-American women prove highly unsympathetic to accused black males (particularly now that black males are the primary source of sexual violence against African-American females). Still others, outraged by the sexual violence as well as the racist prosecution of the accused, may identify with both survivor and defendant(s), embracing dual rather than split identities, with the understanding that just-legal prosecutions of sexual violence supersede simplistic dichotomies.[49]

CASTIGATING THE CRUSADER

Historical revisionism and historicism based in selective and skewed information concerning Wells-Barnett's sexual politics elide or distort the praxis of past radicals in order to shape perceptions and depictions of present-day race politics. Erasing the specificity of past radicalism promotes a doctrine of evolutionary leadership in which contemporary political or feminist leadership is uniformly taken to be more progressive than its predecessor. Consequently, many may assume that late twentieth-century black feminism is inherently more advanced than its nineteenth-century counterpart. Feminist revisionism regarding Ida B. Wells naturalizes that assumption. Using ahistoricism, feminist elites may diminish the contributions of historical women in order to argue for the primacy and superiority of their own gender ideologies and forms of agency.

Writers may construct contemporary womanist or black feminisms as more (gender) progressive than the views of women such as Ida B. Wells-Barnett who led the antilynching campaigns. Walker's reading of Wells-Barnett as intimidated by racist violence into fearful denials and Smith's reading of Wells-Barnett as a counterfeminist place contemporary black feminist thought above the political thought of historical activists. This evolutionary ascent toward the black feminist writer counters traditional notions of public intellectual as engage; it allows the contemporary to transcend her predecessor in progressive agency, as the writer replaces the activist. In fictional dialogues between ancestor and progeny, the contemporary heroine, as moral and political agent, consistently triumphs over her militant race-woman predecessor. In our postmovement era the postmodern, professional writer and/or academic reigns as an intellectual. Validating progressive gender and race ideology in the symbolic analyst, one may supplant the activist with the commentator-essayist as representative of ideal political leadership.

Perhaps some gender specific criticisms and caricatures found an easy target in the persona of Wells-Barnett, who unlike antilynching leaders Frederick Douglass, Du Bois, or Terrell vociferously challenged the racial-sexual apologies for lynching to trample the twin myths of white (female) sexual purity and black (male) sexual savagery. Outrage led Wells-Barnett to take risks and cross over the line of conventional antiracist rhetoric. She rejected the discourse of civility. Her abrasive militancy distanced her from those who maintained the importance of conciliatory rhetoric in resistance struggles. As her isolation grew so did her vulnerability to attack and misrepresentation. Although she transgressed the civility that the Talented Tenth were presumed to embody and was isolated by elites for her assertiveness, Wells-Barnett bequeathed a legacy of skepticism concerning state-accounts of and prosecution of racialized sexual violence through the press, police, and courts; of risk taking in investigative journalism; and of willingness to directly confront the state and elite society to stop violence. This legacy influenced later generations of women such as Rosa Parks and Ella Baker who organized in the 1930s around the Scottsboro Boys trial in which black youths were incarcerated in Alabama for raping two white women although one woman later admitted that there had never been a sexual assault.

Walker's and Smith's historiographies of Wells-Barnett, and by extension black women antilynching crusaders, argue against antiracist commitments that undermine progressive gender politics. Yet, countering black chauvinism/reactionary sexual politics with a revisionist lens distorts radical agency.

Black feminisms both illuminate and obscure radical agency and gender politics in black intellectualism. How they imagine and image historical African-American women activists-intellectuals shapes visions of contemporary antiracist radicalism and black female leadership. Some black progressives' representations of African-American leadership discredit the radical. Others alter her appearance. In both discrediting and (dis)appearing acts, we lose radical black praxis for consideration, and consequently are more likely to only validate nonradical elites, the conventional Talented Tenth, as the most viable form of leadership.

NOTES

1. Between 1889 and 1940, 3,800 black men and women were lynched in Southern border states, according to John D'Emilio and Estelle Freedman, *Intimate Matters* (New York: Harper and Row, 1988) 216. Lynch victims were often unjustly accused of crimes such as theft or the destruction of property and assault; however, African Americans were also lynched for talking back to whites, being in the wrong place at the wrong time, economic competition with whites, and exercising their political rights, such as the right to vote.
2. See: Angela Davis, "Rape, Racism and the Myth of the Black Rapist," *Women, Race, and Class* (New York: Vintage, 1983).
3. Gerder Lerner writes that generally a sexual assault against a black woman rather than against a white woman "set a lynching in motion." For instance, in 1918 in Mississippi, two African-American brothers visited a white dentist who had raped two African-American teenage girls, impregnating one; a few days later, when the dentist was found murdered, a white mob responded by lynching all four youths. In Oklahoma, whites hung Marie Scott, whose brother killed the white man who raped her. See: *Black Women in White America* ed. Gerda Lerner (New York: Vintage, 1973).
4. Reportedly the figures are five percent for black male sexual assaults against white females and eight percent for white male sexual assaults against black females.
5. See: Alice Walker "Advancing Luna—And Ida B. Wells," *You Can't Keep a Good Woman Down* (New York: Harcourt Brace Jovanovich, 1981). Because Walker offers her fiction as political commentary, rather than fantasy, the issue of historical accuracy in representation remains as relevant for her short story as it does for Smith's scholarship.
6. Valerie Smith, "Split Affinities," in *Conflicts in Feminism,* eds. Marianne Hirsh and Evelyn Fox Keller (New York: Routledge, 1990).
7. For black women, 1892 became a watershed year: The greatest number of lynchings were reported then. Among the 241 victims were 160 African Americans (five of whom were women or girls); several of the victims were friends of the young Ida B. Wells. When Negro Club women convened their largest gathering to that date for a testimonial for Wells in Brooklyn later that year, they raised $500 to publish Wells's pamphlet, *Southern Horrors,* and financed a speaking tour for her to launch antilynching campaigns in the United States and England.
8. Martha Hodes cites charges against black males for sexual violence during this time period in her essay, "The Sexualization of Reconstruction Politics," in *American Sexual Politics,* eds. John C. Fout and Maura Shaw Tantillo (Chicago: University of Chicago Press, 1990).
9. Ida B. Wells, *A Red Record* (Chicago: Donohue and Henneberry, 1895) 13.
10. *Ibid.*
11. Angela Davis, "Rape, Racism and the Capitalist Setting," *The Black Scholar* (April 1978).
12. Wells, *Crusade for Justice,* 137.
13. *Ibid.*
14. *Ibid.*
15. Wells, *A Red Record,* 11.
16. *Ibid.*
17. *Ibid.*
18. See: Loretta Ross, "Rape and Third World Women" *Aegis* (Summer, 1983).
19. Mary Church Terrell, National Association of Colored Women, 1904. Quoted in Lerner, 205.
20. "One study of sentencing found that black men convicted of raping white women received prison terms three to five times longer than those handed down in any other rape cases. Yet, at the same time that black-on-white rape evoked the most horror and outrage, it was by far the least common form of violent sexual assault. An investigation of rape cases in Philadelphia in the late 1950's found that only three percent of them involved attacks on white women by black men" (D'Emilio, 297).
21. Joanne M. Braxton, *Black Women Writing Autobiography: A Tradition Within a Tradition* (Philadelphia: Temple University Press, 1989) 122.
22. *Ibid.*
23. *Ibid.,* 137–138.
24. Walker, 92.
25. *Ibid.*

26. *Ibid.*, 93–94.
27. *Ibid.*, 94.
28. *Ibid.*
29. *Ibid.*, 93.
30. *Ibid.*, 98.
31. *Ibid.*, 103.
32. *Ibid.*
33. *Ibid.*
34. *Ibid.*, 104.
35. For a critique of Central Park Case representations, see Joy James, "Coalition Cross Fire: Antiviolence Organizing and Interracial Rape," *Resisting State Violence: Radicalism, Gender, and Race in U.S. Culture* (Minneapolis: University of Minnesota Press, 1996).
36. Smith, 275.
37. *Ibid.*
38. Walker, 90.
39. Smith, 281.
40. *Ibid.*
41. Walker, 97 quoted in Smith, 282. Smith writes: "In an oddly and doubly counter-feminist move that recalls Wells's own discrediting of the testimony of white victims, the narrator wants to believe that Luna made up the rape; only Luna's failure to report the crime—her silence—convinces her that the white woman has spoken the truth" (Smith, 281–82).
42. Walker, 97.
43. *Ibid.*
44. Smith, 273.
45. *Ibid.*, 273–274.
46. *Ibid.*, 274.
47. *Ibid.*, 272.
48. The possibility of "border-crossing" identity receives little attention in this work which misses an oppurtunity to closely scrutinize Wells-Barnett's writings.
49. Smith offers insights that could be further developed. For example, she writes that although black women are extremely vulnerable to rape, their "invisibility as victims" within the [antirape] movement and their perception that the movement was indifferent to the racist use of the rape charge mit-

igated black women's support for this movement (Smith, 276). This passage suggests a monolithic, white-led antirape movement; but in fact, African-American women independently organized and educated against rape and sexual violence. Challenging the stereotype of African-American women as sexually promiscuous and indifferent to sexual violence, Wells-Barnett worked in Chicago's Negro Women's Club movement to assist black women fleeing sexual exploitation and violence in the South only to become sexual prey in the North. Through the Negro Women's Club movement, Wells-Barnett and other African-American women later established halfway houses or safe houses for black women migrating North to escape sexual and labor exploitation in the South. The antirape movements in their plurality have historically been led by women of various ethnicities and classes.

"Split Affinities" repeats Davis's argument from the late 1970s to assert that "the relative invisibility" of black female rape victims" reflects the differential value of women's bodies in capitalist societies" (275–76). Where "rape is constructed as a crime against the property of privileged white men," writes Smith, "crimes against less valuable women—women of color, working-class women, and lesbians, for example—mean less or mean differently than those against white women from the middle and upper classes" (276). This argument could be expanded by noting that not only do some women's bodies have "greater value" than others under patriarchal, white-supremacy capitalism, some women's bodies have "greater value" than the bodies of some men. Noting the differential value of men's bodies is equally important; for such considerations point to the differing weight of prosecution and punishment. Credibility in prosecution is based upon the identity of the accused as well as the accuser.

FURTHER READING

Aptheker, Bettina. 1982. *Woman's Legacy: Essays on Race, Sex and Class.* Amherst: University of Massachusetts Press.

Brownmiller, Susan. 1975. *Against Our Will: Men, Women, and Rape.* New York: Simon & Schuster.

Carby, Hazel. 1985. "'On the Threshold of Woman's Era'; Lynching, Empire, and Sexuality in Black Feminist Theory." *Critical Inquiry* 12 (Autumn): 262–77.

Davis, Angela Y. 1981. *Women, Race and Class.* New York: Random House.

D'Emilio and Estelle Friedman. 1988. *Intimate Matters: A History of Sexuality in America.* New York: Harper and Row.

Edwards, Alison. 1979. *Rape, Racism, and the White Women's Movement.* Chicago: Sojourner Truth Organization.

Gunning, Sandra. 1996. *Race, Rape and Lynching: The Red Record of American Literature, 1890–1912.* New York: Oxford University.

Harris, Trudier. 1984. *Exorcising Blackness: Historical and Literary Lynching and Burning Rituals.* Bloomington: Indiana University Press.

Hernton, Calvin C. 1987. *The Sexual Mountain and Black Women Writers: Adventures in Sex, Literature, and Real Life.* New York: Doubleday.

Hoch Paul. 1979. *White Hero, Black Beast.* New York: Pluto Press.

Lott, Tommy L. 1999. *The Invention of Race: Black Culture and the Politics of Representation.* Oxford: Blackwell Publishers.

McKay, Nellie Y. 1991. "Alice Walker's 'Advancing Luna—And Ida B. Wells': A Struggle toward Sisterhood." In *Rape and Representation,* ed. Lynn A. Higgins and Brenda R. Silvers. New York: Columbia University Press.

Tong, Rosemarie. 1984. *Women, Sex, and the Law.* Totowa, NJ: Rowman & Allenheld.

CHAPTER 10

Alienation and Self-Respect

The earlier nonviolent phase of the civil rights movement, as well as the urban rebellions that ushered in the black power phase of this movement, were collective responses to institutional racism. The general question of how alienation and self-respect are related invites a more specific analysis of the use of various concepts of alienation and self-respect. Concepts such as those employed in the essays by Ralph Bunche and W.E.B. Du Bois have been a matter of great interest in recent discussions by philosophers. Included in the following selections are essays by several philosophers who explore, from quite different perspectives, the role of alienation and self-respect in political resistance to racial oppression.

Du Bois situates his argument for self-segregation within the context of legal segregation. He appeals to self-respect to justify his proposal that African-Americans pursue separation to avoid spiritual and physical disaster. According to Du Bois, self-separation does not preclude protest of legal segregation and racial discrimination. He tells the story of Richard Allen and Absalom Jones at St. George's Methodist Church in Philadelphia to show that the argument about being "different from other Negroes in the galleys would not have impressed the deacons." The point Du Bois seeks to establish is that racism is not an individual, but a group issue. He poses the rhetorical question: "What would you have done?" To which he replies that the only answer is self-organization.

According to Ralph Bunche, alienation is a function of racism and characterizes the relations between white and black Americans. Situating the discrimination faced by African-Americans in the context of globalized racism, he explores the concept of alienation in relation to the urban rebellions in the 1960s. He compares the anticolonial struggle in Vietnam with the black struggle in the United States but insists that assimilation is the only solution to the plight of African-Americans.

But what about racial discrimination and poverty as sources of alienation for African-Americans? In "Alienation and the African American Experience" Howard McGary critically examines the Marxist view. He is especially interested in the Marxist debate with liberals over whether the denial of rights is the source of alienation for African-Americans. McGary points out that because the liberal views of Joel Feinberg and John Rawls focus on what goes on in social institutions and practices, they overlook the alienated person who has rights, material success, and a job. McGary maintains that middle-class and wealthy African-Americans are still alienated because of the attitude of disrespect generated by the dominant society. He notes that, although this disrespect constitutes a harm, it is one for which liberals have theoretical reasons preventing them from eliminating.

McGary prefers Du Bois's concept of double-consciousness as a way to interpret the African-American experience. He presents the case of black and white workers to show that the Marxist view that the African-American experience as a function of class position is misguided. He insists that a strict reference to class divisions cannot explain racial antagonisms and criticizes the suggestion that race relations are shaped more by material conditions than by the way black and white workers think about each other. He also questions whether the lack of recognition denied African-Americans is the same as alienation.

Why is self-respect important? If the only interests the Uncle Tom or the submissive housewife sacrifice are their own, what basis do we have to complain? In "Servility and Self-Respect" Tom Hill, Jr. reflects on some of Kant's remarks regarding duties to oneself to consider whether we have a duty to avoid being servile. He points out that the Uncle Tom's feeling that he has no right to expect anything better displays a problematic attitude concerning one's rightful place in a moral community. The servile person's deferential attitude results from ignorance or a misunderstanding of one's moral rights. The willingness to place a comparative low value on one's rights is an indication that the servile person lacks self-respect. Just as the arrogant person ignores the rights of others to gain a higher status than he or she is entitled, the servile person assumes a lower status than he or she is entitled.

Hill appeals to Kant's principle that one type of respect for persons is respect for the rights which moral law accords them. He interprets Kant to have argued that the right to some minimum degree of respect from others is one formal right that cannot be waived. In this sense then the avoidance of servility is a duty to oneself rather than a duty to others. Hill concludes that duties to oneself are a *precondition* of duties to others.

Hill's claim that self-respect has more to do with rights than with merit involves an important distinction between self-respect and self-esteem. In "Rawlsian Self-Respect and the Black Consciousness Movement" Laurence Thomas charges that no adequate account of the black consciousness movement can be given in Rawls's account of self-respect. For example, we would have no reason to view Booker T. Washington as an Uncle Tom. Thomas points out that the plans of life Rawls discusses have more to do with our esteem for the achievement of others—a matter of merit. Self-respect, however, does not have to be grounded on the conviction that one's life plan is worthwhile. Thomas refers to the case of Booker T. Washington to indicate that the two conditions of Rawls's concept of self-respect are satisfied. He points out that this should settle the question of whether Washington was an Uncle Tom but doesn't. The insight Thomas gleans from this consideration is that having self-respect is a conviction of one's standing in a moral community. The black consciousness movement asserts the view that equal distribution of basic rights and liberties is required to affirm the self-respect of persons.

Washington's view raises the question of whether protesting injustice, when one can do nothing to right it oneself, is to act in accordance with self-respect. Du Bois, of course, opposed this idea with the claim that one should protest injustice and become self-reliant. In "Self-Respect and Protest" Bernard Boxill points out that Du Bois believed that if people failed to express outrage at injustice, they would lose their self-respect in the long run. According to Boxill, self-respect is not compatible with "a silent submission to cure inferiority." He argues that people ought to protest wrongs not only to stop injustice but also to know that they have self-respect.

Washington drew the conclusion that the white perpetrators of injustice are harmed more than black victims and focused on the moral salvation of America as the ground for reform. Boxill rejects this line because it shifts away from the claim that black people have rights. Washington believed that to protest the denial of one's rights is to demand help. Boxill criticizes this as a misunderstanding of the demand for rights. In the case of African-Americans this is usually a demand for noninterference with the endeavor to become self-reliant.

Washington's point that protesting the denial of one's rights may only create more problems than it will solve has to be well taken. In the face of this difficulty, why not pretend servility in order to advance one's ends? Boxill argues that self-respecting people demand respect through protest, not because they want to make others moral, for they may be satisfied if others respect them because they fear them. Washington would object to this by pointing out that this is not the best means of gaining social acknowledgment of the rights of African-Americans. Protest is not a likely way of getting a powerful group of Southern racists to agree. Indeed, Washington would point out that protest only affirms that a victim has rights; it does not persuade the racist to change. Boxill accepts this objection in order to meet it. He cites Douglass's remark that, "I cannot, however, argue. I must assert" to show that protest is not designed to persuade others; rather it aims to compel them.

Boxill distinguishes self-respect from other values. He uses several examples to illustrate divergence between being authentic and having one's rights recognized by others. He remarks that a person can have self-respect and few other good qualities. His point is that the self-respect gained through protest provides evidence of faith in one's worth. For this reason he rejects Orlando Patterson's suggestion that the "perfect" act of resistance is the Uncle Tom's behavior that appears to the slavemaster as "the ultimate act of submission." Boxill questions whether the Uncle Tom can know that he is not servile if he has no evidence. Self-respect, according to Boxill, is a manifestation of the belief that one has rights. Rather than disguise one's self-respect in servility, protesting is a means of affirming that one has rights.

Alienation and the
African-American Experience

Howard McGary

The term "alienation" evokes a variety of responses. For liberals, to be alienated signals a denial of certain basic rights, e.g., the right to equality of opportunity or the right to autonomy.[1] On the other hand, progressive thinkers believe that alienation involves estrangement from one's work, self, or others because of capitalism.[2] However, recent discussions of alienation have cast doubt on whether either of these theories totally capture the phenomenon. Drawing on the experiences of people of color, some theorists maintain that to be alienated is to be estranged in ways that cannot be accounted for by liberal and Marxist theories of alienation.[3]

The concept of alienation is often associated with Marx's conception of human beings in capitalist societies. However, non-Marxists have also used the term alienation to explain the experiences of human beings in relationship to their society, each other, their work, and themselves. But liberal theories of alienation have been criticized by Marxists for two reasons. First they see liberal theories of alienation as describing a psychological condition that is said to result from a denial of basic individual rights rather than the result of a systematic failure. Second, liberals have an account of human nature that is ahistorical, one that fails to consider the changes in human nature that result from changes in social conditions.

For the Marxist, alienation is not simply a theory of how people feel or think about themselves when their rights are violated, but an historical theory of how human beings act

and how they are treated by others in capitalist society. The Marxist theory of alienation is an explanatory social theory that places human beings at the center of the critique of socioeconomic relations. Marx's human being is not a stagnant given, but a product of an explanatory social theory. For Marx, alienation is something that all human beings experience in capitalist societies; it is not something that certain individuals undergo because they are neurotic or the victims of some unjust law or social practice.

It is clear that African-Americans have not always been recognized and treated as American citizens or as human beings by the dominant white society. Both of these forms of denial have had serious negative consequences and numerous scholars have discussed what these denials have meant to African-Americans and to the rest of society. However, it does not directly follow from the fact of these denials that African-Americans are alienated because of these things. In this paper, I shall attempt to understand this new challenge to the liberal and Marxist theories of "alienation" and its impact, if any, on the masses of African-Americans.

THE NEW ACCOUNT OF ALIENATION

According to the new account of alienation that is drawn from the experiences of people of color, alienation exists when the self is deeply divided because the hostility of the dominant groups in the society forces the self to see itself as loathsome, defective, or insignificant, and lacking the possibility of ever seeing itself in more positive terms. This type of alienation is not just estrangement from

Source: © 1993 from *African-American Perspectives and Philosophical Traditions* by John P. Pittman, ed. Reproduced by permission of Routledge, Inc., part of The Taylor and Francis Group.

one's work or a possible plan of life, but an estrangement from ever becoming a self that is not defined in the hostile terms of the dominant group.

The root idea here is not just that certain groups are forced to survive in an atmosphere in which they are not respected because of their group membership, but rather that they are required to do so in a society that is openly hostile to their very being. The hostility, according to this new account of alienation, causes the victims to become hostile toward themselves. Those who are said to be alienated in this way are thought to be incapable of shaping our common conception of reality and thus they play little, if any, role in their self-construction. The self is imposed upon them by social forces, and what is even more disturbing, no individual self can change the social forces that impose upon members of certain groups their negative and hostile self-conceptions.

Is this new account of alienation just another way of saying that people of color have had their humanity called into question? We might begin to explore this question by examining the claim that having one's humanity recognized and respected means having a say about things that matter in one's life, and having such a say means that one is unalienated. To be more specific, having opinions about things and the ability and freedom to express one's opinions is the mark of the unalienated person. This response is helpful, but it does not fully capture what recent writers have meant by alienation. It assumes that the alienated self is secure, but constrained by external forces that prevent the person from becoming fully actualized: from having one's voice recognized and respected in the moral or political process.

The above account of what it means to recognize and respect a person's humanity fails to fully appreciate that human selves result, at least in part, from social construction. How we define who we are, our interests, and our relationship with others, involves a dynamic process of social interaction. To assume that what recent writers have meant by alienation is the failure by some to be able to

express and have their opinions heard misses the mark. This view of things assumes that (1) people are clear about their interests, but have not been allowed to express them and (2) those who have power and privilege will be able to understand and fairly assess claims made by those who lack power and privilege if they were only allowed to express their opinions. Even if (1) and (2) are true, we still have not captured what recent writers have meant by alienation. This account focuses incorrectly on what the self is prevented from doing by forces external to it. However, the new account of alienation primarily concentrates on the fragility and insecurity of the self caused by the way people who are victims view and define themselves. According to this view, even if the external constraints were removed, the self would still be estranged because it has been constructed out of images that are hostile to it.

One might think that this new account of alienation is not saying anything new because Americans (including African-Americans) have always believed that people should be free to decide what kind of persons they want to be provided that in doing so they don't violate the rights of others. At least in principle, Americans have endorsed this idea. If this is so, what is new in these recent accounts of alienation? Perhaps we can gain some insight into this question by taking a closer look at the African-American experience.

African-Americans have had a paradoxical existence in the United States. On the one hand, they have rightfully responded negatively to the second-class status that they are forced to endure. On the other hand, they believe that America should have and has the potential to live up to the ideas so eloquently expressed in the Bill of Rights and in Martin Luther King, Jr.'s "I Have a Dream" speech.[4] It is clear that there was a time when African-Americans were prevented from participating in the electoral process and from having a say in the shaping of basic institutions. Many would argue that there are still barriers that prevent African-Americans from participating in meaningful ways in these areas. If this is so, does this mean that most (many) African-

Americans are alienated from themselves and the dominant society?

African-American leaders from the moderate to the militant have emphasized the importance of African-Americans' making their own decisions about what is in their interests.[5] The right to self-determination has been seen as a crucial weapon in the battle against the evils of racial discrimination. These thinkers have also recognized that one must have an adequate understanding of one's predicament if one is to devise an effective strategy for overcoming the material and psychological consequences of racial injustice. Insight into the African-American experience has come from a variety of sources. Some of these insights have been offered by social and political theorists, others have been advanced in literature and the arts.

Ralph Ellison, in his brilliant novel, *The Invisible Man*, describes what he takes to be a consuming evil of racial discrimination.[6] According to Ellison, African-Americans are not visible to the white world. They are caricatures and stereotypes, but not real human beings with complex and varied lives. In very graphic terms, Ellison reveals what it is like to be black in a world where black skin signifies what is base and superficial. Ellison skillfully describes how blacks are perceived by white society, but he also tells us a great deal about how blacks perceive themselves. It is clear that African-Americans have struggled to construct an image of themselves different from the ones perpetrated by a racist society, but this is not an easy thing to do. W. E. B. Du Bois spoke to the struggle and the dilemma that confronts African-Americans when he identified what he called "the problem of double-consciousness" in *The Souls of Black Folk*:

> It is a peculiar sensation, this double-consciousness, this sense of always looking at one's self through the eyes of others, of measuring one's soul by the tape of a world that looks on in amused contempt and pity. One ever feels his twoness—an American, a Negro; two warring ideals in one dark body, whose dogged strength alone keeps it from being torn asunder.[7]

Du Bois is pointing to what he takes to be the mistaken belief held by many blacks and whites, namely that a person cannot be both black and an American. According to Du Bois, for far too many people this was a contradiction in terms. Du Bois strongly disagreed and spent a great deal of his energy arguing against this conclusion. But why this false view was held by so many people can be traced to an inadequate conception of what it means to be "black" and what it meant to be "American." According to Du Bois, race and class exploitation contributed greatly to these false conceptions. For Du Bois, it was no surprise that African-Americans had such a difficult time identifying their true interests.

THE LIBERAL RESPONSE

Liberal political theorists rarely discuss alienation. This is in large part because alienation is seen as something that comes from within. For them alienation often is the result of injustice, but even so, it is something that can be overcome if only the individual would stand up for her rights. Liberals may realize that this might come at some serious personal cost to the individual, but they believe that the individual can and should bear these costs if they are to remain autonomous unalienated beings. For example, liberals often sympathize with white, highly educated, wealthy women who live alienated lives, but they believe that it is within the power of these women to end their estrangement or alienation even though it may be extremely difficult for them to do so. The critics of the liberal account of women's oppression have argued that liberals fail to see that capitalism and the negative stereotyping of women causes even educated and economically secure women to be at the mercy of sexist practices and traditions.

The critics of liberalism have also argued that liberalism places too much emphasis upon individuality and thus the theory fails to recognize how our conceptions of who we are and what we see as valuable are tied to our social relations. They insist that we are not alone in shaping who we are and in defining our possibilities. Society, according to these critics, plays a more extensive role than liberals are willing to admit.

Although liberals have recognized the alienation that people experience in modern society, their individual-rights framework has not readily lent itself to an in-depth analysis of this phenomenon. I disagree, however, with the critics of liberalism when they contend that the individual-rights framework is inadequate to describe the nature of alienation. I shall attempt to show that liberals can describe the nature of alienation in capitalist society even though the theory is inadequate when it comes to addressing what the liberals must admit to be a violation of important rights.

Liberal theorists might characterize this new form of alienation in terms of a denial of the rights to such things as autonomy and self-determination and claim that these denials rob persons of their freedom. Alienation on their account is just another way of saying that people are unfree and further that they don't appreciate that this is so. But if the liberal response is to be helpful, we need to know more precisely in what sense alienation is a denial of important rights, e.g., the right to be free.

In what sense is the alienated person unfree? Can a person be alienated even if she has basic constitutional rights, material success, and a job that calls upon her abilities and talents in interesting ways? Some theorists think so. If alienation is a lack of freedom as the liberal theory suggests, in what sense are the people who have constitutional rights and material well-being unfree? The liberal theorist Joel Feinberg has discussed the lack of freedom in terms of constraints.[8] If we define alienation as constraint, then alienated persons are unfairly constrained in the ways that they can conceive of themselves in a culture that defines them in stereotypical terms. But what are these constraints? To borrow Feinberg's terminology, are these constraints external or internal? According to Feinberg, "external constraints are those that come from outside a person's body-cum-mind, and

all other constraints, whether sore muscles, headaches, or refractory 'lower' desires, are internal to him."[9]

If we employ the language of constraints to understand alienation as a kind of unfreedom, should we view this unfreedom in terms of external or internal constraints or both? On a liberal reading of Du Bois's and Ellison's characterizations of the African-American experience, this experience is characterized by a denial of opportunities because of a morally irrelevant characteristic, a person's race. It is plausible to interpret them in this way because this is clearly one of the consequences of a system of racial discrimination. However, I believe that they had much more in mind. The focus on the denial of opportunities is the standard liberal way of understanding the consequences of racial injustice. This is why you find liberal writers like Feinberg discussing freedom in terms of the absence of constraints and John Rawls concentrating on designing social institutions such that offices and positions are open to all under conditions of self-respect.[10] The focus by liberals has been primarily on what goes on outside of the body-cum-mind.

This is not to say that they completely ignore such psychological harms as self-doubt and a lack of self-respect that can result from injustice. In fact, Feinberg notes that things like sickness can create internal constraints which serve to limit a person's freedom.[11] Rawls, as well, appreciates the impact that injustice can have on a person's psyche. Thus he spends some time expounding on the connection between justice and a healthy self-concept.[12] He argues that in a just society social institutions should not be designed in ways that prevent people from having the social bases for self-respect. So both Feinberg and Rawls recognize that such things as freedom and justice go beyond removing inappropriate external constraints. But nonetheless, I don't think that Feinberg and Rawls can fully capture the insight offered by Du Bois and Ellison because their emphasis on the external constraints causes them to underestimate the internal ways that people can be prevented from experiencing freedom.

Since Isaiah Berlin's distinction between positive and negative freedom, liberals have recognized that such things as ignorance and poverty can limit a person's freedom.[13] Recognition of the limitations caused by internal constraints has led some liberals to argue that a society cannot be just if it does not address internal constraints on people's freedom. Such liberals would be open to the idea that an examination of the African-American experience would reveal the obvious and subtle ways that a lack of education and material well-being can lead to a sense of estrangement, a lack of self-respect. They would argue that this is true even when formal equality of opportunity can be said to exist. On their view, the real problem is not the lack of laws that guarantee equality under the law, but finding ways to make real these guarantees. For them it is not so much how African-Americans are viewed by the rest of society, but rather that they should be treated in ways that make it possible for them to act and choose as free persons. According to this view, things are just even if people are hated by the rest of the community, provided that they are guaranteed equal protection under the law and steps are taken to ensure real equality of opportunity. These liberals insist that there is a large area of human affairs that should escape government scrutiny. In these areas, people should be able to pursue their own conceptions of the good provided that they don't cause direct harm to others. I should add that these liberals also believe that those who fail to provide such necessities as food and education to those who are in need of them cause direct harm by failing to do so.

However, some communitarian critics of liberalism have argued that this way of understanding the requirements of justice underestimates the importance of how we form a healthy self-concept in a community.[14] They emphasize the importance of being seen and treated as a full member of society as opposed to a person who must be tolerated. They question the wisdom and usefulness of attempting to find impartial norms that will guarantee each person the right to pursue his own unique conception of the good constrained by an account of the right defined by impartial reasoning. This concern has led some communitarians to reject the search for impartial ideals of justice in favor of a method of forging a consensus about justice through a process of democratically working across differences through open dialogue. According to this view, we will not be able to put aside our partialities, but we can confront them through discourse.

Communitarians would contend that African-Americans or any minority group that has been despised and subjugated will feel estranged from the dominant society if they are merely tolerated and not accepted and valued for their contributions. They believe that the liberalism of Feinberg, Rawls, and Nozick can at best produce toleration, but not acceptance. But this view, of course, assumes that we can identify some common goods (ends) to serve as the foundation for our theory of justice. This is something that liberals who give priority to the right over the good deny.

The communitarians, whether they realize it or not, have pointed to a persistent problem for African-Americans—the problem of recognition. How do African-Americans become visible in a society that refuses to see them other than through stereotypical images? One need only turn to the history of black social and political thought to see that African-Americans have wrestled with the question of what the appropriate means are for obtaining recognition and respect for a people who were enslaved and then treated as second-class citizens. Some argued that emigration was the only answer, while others maintained that less radical forms of separation from white society would do. Others contended that blacks could obtain recognition only if they assimilated or fully integrated into white society.[15] Neither of these approaches so far have been fully tested, so it is hard to say whether either approach can adequately address the problem of the lack of recognition for blacks in a white racist society.

The new alienation theorists believe that liberals cannot adequately describe or eliminate the kind of estrangement experienced by African-Americans and other oppressed racial groups. Is this so? Yes and no. I shall argue that liberals can describe the experience of estrangement using the vocabulary of rights and opportunities, but I don't think that they can eliminate this experience and stay faithful to their liberal methodology.

Typically when we think of a person being denied rights or opportunities we think of rather specific individuals and specific actions which serve as the causes of these denials. For example, we might think of a specific employer refusing to hire a person because he or she is black. The black person in this case is denied job-related rights and opportunities by a specific person. But even if we changed our example to involve groups rather than individuals, the new alienation theorists would maintain the experience of estrangement that they describe goes beyond such a description. According to their account, African-Americans who have their rights respected and don't suffer from material scarcity still are estranged in a way that their white counterparts are not.

Are these theorists correct or do prosperous and highly regarded middle-class and wealthy African-Americans serve as counterexamples to the above claim? Don't such persons enjoy their rights and opportunities? If not, what rights and opportunities are they being denied? I believe that rights and opportunities are being denied, but it is more difficult to see what they are in such cases. I think that liberals can contend that middle-class and wealthy African-Americans are still alienated because they are denied their right to equal concern and respect in a white racist society. Even though they may be able to vote, to live in the neighborhood of their choice, and to send their children to good schools, they are still perceived as less worthy because of their race. The dominant attitude in their society is that they are less worthy than whites. The pervasive attitude is not benign. It acts as an affront to the self-concept of African-Americans and it causes them to expend energy that they could expend in more constructive ways. The philosopher Laurence Thomas graphically described this experience in a letter to the *New York Times*.[16] For exam-

ple, African-Americans are too aware of the harm caused by being perceived by the typical white as thieves no matter what their economic and social standing might be. African-Americans, because of the dominant negative attitudes against them as a group, are denied equal concern and respect.

It is difficult to see that this attitude of disrespect is a denial of rights because we most often associate political rights with actions and not with attitudes. In fact, it sounds awkward to say that I have a right that you not have a certain attitude towards me. This statement seems to strike at the very heart of liberalism. However in reality it does not. Liberals can and do say that human beings should be accorded such things as dignity and respect, and they believe that this entails taking a certain attitude or having dispositions towards others as well as acting or refraining from acting in particular ways. So, it is not that they cannot account for the particular estrangement that blacks experience because of the attitude of disrespect generated by the dominant society, but that they don't seem to have the theoretical wherewithal to resolve the problem.

Since liberals assign great weight to individual liberty, they are reluctant to interfere with actions that cause indirect harm. So even though they recognize that living in a society that has an attitude of disrespect towards African-Americans can constitute a harm, and a harm caused by others, they are reluctant to interfere with people's private lives in order to eliminate these harms.

How can liberals change white attitudes in a way that is consistent with their theory? They could mount an educational program to combat false or racist beliefs. Liberals have tried this, but given their strong commitment to things like freedom of thought and expression, and the fact that power and privilege is attached to seeing nonwhites as less worthy, educational programs have only had modest success in changing white attitudes. Critics of such educational programs argue that these programs can never succeed until racism is seen as unprofitable.

Let us assume that the critics are correct. Can liberals make racism unprofitable and respect individual liberty, one of the corner-stones of their theory? There are two basic approaches available to liberals: they can place sanctions on all harmful racist attitudes or they can provide people with incentives to change their racist attitudes. But in a democracy, the will of the majority is to prevail. If the attitude of disrespect towards African-Americans is as pervasive as the new alienation theorists suggest, then it is doubtful there will be the general will to seriously take either of the approaches. I don't think that liberals can eliminate harmful racist attitudes without adopting means that would be judged by the white majority as unjustified coercion. However, they can adequately describe the alienation that African-Americans experience even if they cannot eliminate it.

THE MARXIST ACCOUNT

The Marxist explanation of the African-American condition assumes that the problems experienced by this group can be traced to their class position. Capitalism is seen as the cause of such things as black alienation. For the Marxist, a class analysis of American society and its problems provides both a necessary and sufficient understanding of these things. According to the Marxist, alienation be it black or white is grounded in the labor process. Alienated labor, in all of its forms, is based in private property and the division of labor. On this account, if we eliminate a system of private property and the division of labor, we will eliminate those things that make alienated relations possible.

The Marxist does recognize that political and ideological relations can and do exist in capitalist societies, and that these relations do appear to have the autonomy and power to shape our thinking and cause certain behaviors. But, for the Marxist, these relations only appear to be fundamental when in reality they are not. They can always be reduced or explained by reference to a particular mode of production. Racism is ideological; an idea that dominates across class lines. However class divisions explain racial antagonisms, it is

not the other way around.[17] But Marxists don't stop here. They also contend that in order to eliminate racism, we must eliminate class divisions where class is defined in terms of one's relationship to the means of production.

Classical Marxists would oppose the new account of alienation advanced by recent theorists. The classical Marxists would insist that all forms of alienation, no matter how debilitating or destructive, can be explained in terms of the mode of production in which people are required to satisfy their needs. For them, it is not a matter of changing the way blacks and whites think about each other or the way blacks think of themselves because ideas don't change our material reality, relationships with others, or our self-conceptions. Our material conditions (mode of production) shape our ideas and our behavior.

On this account, African-Americans are estranged from themselves because of their laboring activity or lack of it. They view themselves in hostile terms because they are defined by a mode of production that stultifies their truly human capacities and reduces them to human tools to be used by those who have power and influence. This all sounds good, but many black theorists (liberal and progressive) have been skeptical of this account of the causes and remedy for black alienation and oppression. They argue that the conditions of black workers and white workers are different and that this difference is not merely a difference in terms of things like income and social and political status or class position. The difference cuts much deeper. In a white racist society, blacks (workers and capitalists) are caused to have a hostile attitude towards their very being that is not found in whites. The new alienation theorists contend that the classical Marxist explanation of African-American alienation is too limiting. It fails to recognize that alienation occurs in relationships apart from the labor process. W. E. B. Du Bois, although a dedicated Marxist, claimed that the major problem of the twentieth century was race and not class. Some theorists have contended that Marxists are too quick in dismissing the significance of race consciousness.[18] I think the facts support their conclusion. In the next section, I will focus directly on this issue of African-American alienation.

AFRICAN-AMERICANS AND ALIENATION

I believe that the atmosphere of hostility created against African-Americans by our white racist society does amount to a serious assault on the material and psychological well-being of its African-American victims. I also believe that this assault can, and in some cases does, lead to the types of alienation discussed above. However, I disagree with those who conclude that most or all African-Americans suffer from a debilitating form of alienation that causes them to be estranged and divided in the ways described in the new account of alienation. I also reject the implication that most or all African-Americans are powerless, as individuals, to change their condition. The implication is that group action as opposed to individual effort is required to combat this form of alienation. There is also the implication that revolution and not reform is required in order to eliminate this form of alienation.

I don't wish to be misunderstood here. It is not my contention that capitalism is superior to socialism, but only that it is possible for African-Americans to combat or overcome this form of alienation described by recent writers without overthrowing capitalism.

Are African-Americans, as a group, alienated or estranged from themselves? I don't think so. Clearly there are some African-Americans who have experienced such alienation, but I don't think this characterizes the group as a whole. African-Americans do suffer because of a lack of recognition in American society, but a lack of recognition does not always lead to alienation. Even though African-Americans have experienced hostility, racial discrimination, and poverty, they still have been able to construct and draw upon institutions like the family, church, and community to foster and maintain a healthy sense of self in spite of the obstacles that they have faced.

Although African-Americans have been the victims of a vicious assault on their humanity and self-respect, they have been able to form their own supportive communities in the midst of a hostile environment. During the long period of slavery in this country, African-Americans were clearly in an extremely hostile environment. If there ever was a time a group could be said to be the victims of the assault caused by white racism, slavery was such a time. Slaves were denied the most basic rights because they were defined and treated as chattel. Some scholars, like Stanley Elkins, have argued that slavery did cause African-Americans as a group to become less than healthy human beings.[19] On the other hand, there is a group of scholars who argue that slaves and their descendants were able to maintain healthy self-concepts through acts of resistance and communal nourishment.[20] I tend to side with this latter group of scholars.

What is crucial for the truth of their position is the belief that supportive communities can form within a larger hostile environment that can serve to blunt the assault of a hostile racist social order. This, of course, is not to say that these communities provide their members with all that is necessary for them to flourish under conditions of justice, but only that they provide enough support to create the space necessary for them to avoid the deeply divided and estranged selves described in some recent work on alienation.

The history and literature of African-Americans is rich with examples of how communities have formed to provide the social and moral basis for African-Americans to have self-respect even though they were in the midst of a society that devalued their worth. Once again, I think it bears repeating. I don't deny that a hostile racist society creates the kind of assault that can lead to alienation, but only claim that this assault can be and has been softened by supportive African-American communities.

The sociologist Orlando Patterson disagrees. Patterson has argued that African-Americans are alienated because slavery cut them off from their African culture and heritage and denied them real participation in

American culture and heritage. He characterizes this phenomenon as "natal alienation."[21] African-Americans, on Patterson's account, feel estranged because they don't believe that they belong. They are not Africans, but they also are not Americans. One might argue that the present move from "black American" to "African-American" is an attempt to address the phenomenon of natal alienation. According to Patterson, the past provides us with crucial insight into the present psyches of African-Americans. On his view, the fact of slavery helps to explain the present condition and behavior of African-Americans, including the present underclass phenomenon.[22]

I disagree with Patterson's conclusions. He falls prey to the same shortcoming that plagues the liberal and the Marxist accounts of the African-American experience. They all fail to appreciate the role of ethnic communities in the lives of individuals and groups. Although Du Bois never played down the horrors and harms of racism, he refused to see the masses of black people as a people who were estranged or alienated from themselves. In fact, in his *Dusk of Dawn,* Du Bois describes how black people have been able to draw strength from each other as members of a community with shared traditions, values, and impulses.[23] Being anchored in a community allows people to address and not just cope with things like oppression and racism.

The work of the historian John Blassingame can also be used to call into question Patterson's natal alienation thesis and it also provides some support for the importance of community in the lives of African-Americans. Blassingame argued that even during the period of slavery, there was still a slave community that served to provide a sense of self-worth and social cohesiveness for slaves. In my own examination of slave narratives, first-hand accounts by slaves and former slaves of their slave experiences, I found that all slaves did not suffer from a form of moral and social death.[24] By moral and social death, I mean the inability to choose and act as autonomous moral and social agents. Of course this is not to deny that slavery was a brutal and dehumanizing institution, but rather that

slaves developed supportive institutions and defense mechanisms that allowed them to remain moral and social agents.

But what about the presence of today's so-called black underclass? Does this group (which has been defined as a group that is not only poor, poorly educated, and victimized by crime, but also as a group suffering from a breakdown of family and moral values) squarely raise the issue of black alienation or estrangement? Some people think so. They argue that Patterson's natal alienation thesis is extremely informative when it comes to understanding this class. Others reject the natal alienation thesis, but remain sympathetic to the idea that where there once was a black community or institutions that served to prevent the erosion of black pride and values, these structures no longer exist to the degree necessary to ward off the harms of racism and oppression.

In *The Truly Disadvantaged,* William J. Wilson argues that large urban African-American communities are lacking in the material and human resources to deal with the problems brought on by structural changes and the flight of the middle class.[25] According to Wilson, these communities, unlike communities in the past, lack the wherewithal to overcome problems that are present to an extent in all other poor communities. If Wilson is correct, the resources may not exist in present day African-American communities to ward off the assault of a hostile racist society. I am not totally convinced by Wilson's argument, but I think his work and the work of the supporters of the new account of alienation make it clear that there needs to be further work which compares African-American communities before the development of the so-called "black underclass" with urban African-American communities today.

At this juncture, I wish to distinguish my claim that supportive African-American communities have helped to combat the effects of a racist society from the claims of black neoconservatives like Shelby Steele. In *The Content of Our Characters,*[26] Steele argues that African-Americans must confront and prosper in spite of racism. Steele's recommendations have a strong individualist tone. He argues, like Booker T. Washington, that racism does exist but that African-Americans who are prudent must recognize that if they are to progress, they must prosper in spite of it. In fact, Steele even makes a stronger claim. He argues that African-Americans have become accustomed to a "victims status" and use racism as an excuse for failing to succeed even when opportunities do exist.

I reject Steele's conclusions. First, I don't think that individual blacks acting alone can overcome racism. Individual blacks who succeed in this country do so because of the struggles and sacrifices of others, and these others always extend beyond family members and friends. Next, I reject Steele's claim that the lack of progress by disadvantaged African-Americans is due in any significant way to their perception of themselves as helpless victims. Such a claim depends upon a failure to appreciate the serious obstacles that African-Americans encounter because of their race. Even if it is true that African-American advancement is contingent on African-Americans helping themselves, it does not follow that African-Americans should be criticized for failing to adopt dehumanizing means because they are necessary for their economic advancement.

African-Americans should not be viewed as inferior to other groups, but they should also not be seen as superior. Racial injustice negatively impacts the motivational levels of all people. African-Americans are not an exception. Steele makes it seem as if poor and uneducated African-Americans lack the appropriate values to succeed. He contends that the opportunities exist, but that too many African-Americans fail to take advantage of them because they cannot break out of the victim mentality. I reject this line of reasoning. As I have argued elsewhere,[27] this way of thinking erroneously assumes that most disadvantages result from a lack of motivation. In reality, it would take exceptional motivational levels to overcome the injustices that African-Americans experience. Because some African-Americans can rise to these levels, it would be unreasonable to think that all

could. Steele underestimates the work that must be done to provide real opportunities to members of the so-called black underclass who struggle with racism on a daily basis.

I would like to forestall any misunderstandings about my emphasis on the role that supportive communities play in the lives of oppressed groups. I am not maintaining that African-Americans don't experience alienation because they are able to draw strength from supportive communities. My point is that supportive communities can, in some cases, minimize the damaging effects caused by a racist society. Nor is it my intention to deny that African-Americans and other groups must constantly struggle to maintain a healthy sense of self in a hostile society that causes them to experience self-doubt and a range of other negative states.

NOTES

1. Liberal thinkers tend to argue that alienation results when human beings can no longer see themselves as being in control of or comfortable in their social environment, and they contend that this discomfort occurs when crucial rights are violated, e.g., the right to autonomy. In an interesting twist on the liberal position, Bruce A. Ackerman argues in *Social Justice and the Liberal State* (New Haven, Conn.: Yale University Press, 1980), esp. pp. 346–47, that the right to mutual dialogue is necessary to protect the autonomy of individuals in a community.

2. See, e.g., John Elster (ed.), *Karl Marx: A Reader* (Cambridge: Cambridge University Press, 1986), Chapter II; Bertell Ollman. *Alienation* (Cambridge: Cambridge University Press, 1976), Part III; Robert C. Tucker (ed.), *The Marx-Engels Reader* (New York: W. W. Norton & Co., 1978) pp. 73–75, 77–78, 252–56, 292–93.

3. See Frantz Fanon, *Black Skin/White Masks* (New York: Grove Press, 1967), Chapter 1; June Jordan, "Report from the Bahamas," *On Call* (Boston: South End Press, 1985), pp. 39–50.

4. The famous speech delivered by Martin L. King, Jr. at the March on Washington, D.C., August, 1963.

5. See Howard Brotz (ed.), *Negro Social and Political Thought 1850–1920* (New York: Basic Books, 1966).
6. Ralph Ellison, *The Invisible Man* (New York: New American Library, 1953).
7. W. E. B. Du Bois, *The Souls of Black Folk* (New York: New American Library, 1969), p. 45.
8. Joel Feinberg, *Social Philosophy* (Englewood Cliffs, N.J.: Prentice Hall, Inc., 1973), Chapter 1.
9. Feinberg, *Social Philosophy*, p. 13.
10. John Rawls, *A Theory of Justice* (Cambridge, Mass.: Harvard University Press, 1971), Section 67.
11. Feinberg, *Social Philosophy*, p. 13.
12. Rawls, *Theory of Justice*. pp. 440–46.
13. Isaiah Berlin, *Two Concepts of Liberty* (Oxford: Clarendon Press, 1961).
14. See, Alasdair MacIntyre, *After Virtue* (Notre Dame, Ind.: University of Notre Dame Press, 1981), Chapter 17; Michael Sandel, *Liberalism and the Limits of Justice* (Cambridge: Cambridge University Press, 1982), pp. 59–65, 173–75.
15. Howard McGary, Jr., "Racial Integration and Racial Separatism: Conceptual Clarifications," in Leonard Harris (ed.), *Philosophy Born of Struggle* (Dubuque, Iowa: Kendall/Hunt Publishing Co., 1983), pp. 199–211.
16. Laurence Thomas, in *The New York Times*, August 13, 1990.
17. See Bernard Boxill, "The Race-Class Question," in Harris, *Philosophy Born of Struggle*, pp. 107–16.
18. See, e.g., Howard McGary, Jr., "The Nature of Race and Class Exploitation," in A. Zegeye, L. Harris, & J. Maxted (eds.), *Exploitation and Ex-*clusion (London: Hans Zell Publishers, 1991), pp. 14–27; and Richard Schmitt, "A New Hypothesis About the Relations of Class, Race and Gender: Capitalism as a Dependent System," *Social Theory and Practice*, Vol. 14, No. 3 (1988), pp. 345–65.
19. Stanley Elkins, *Slavery: A Problem in American Institutional and Intellectual Life* (Chicago: University of Chicago Press, 1976).
20. John Blassingame, *The Slave Community: Plantation Life in the Antebellum South* (New York: Oxford University Press, 1972), esp. pp. 200–16.
21. Orlando Patterson, *Slavery and Social Death* (Cambridge, Mass.: Harvard University Press, 1982).
22. Orlando Patterson, "Towards a Future that Has No Past: Reflections on the Fate of Blacks in America," *The Public Interest*. Vol. 27, 1972.
23. W. E. B. Du Bois, *Dusk of Dawn* (New Brunswick, N.J.: Transaction Books, 1987), esp. Ch. 7.
24. See Howard McGary & Bill E. Lawson, *Between Slavery and Freedom: Philosophy and American Slavery* (Bloomington: Indiana University Press, 1992).
25. William J. Wilson, *The Truly Disadvantaged* (Chicago: University of Chicago Press, 1987).
26. Shelby Steele, *The Content of Our Characters: A New Vision of Race in America* (New York: Saint Martin's Press, 1990), especially Chapters 3 and 4.
27. Howard McGary, "The Black Underclass and the Question of Values," in William Lawson (ed.), *The Underclass Question* (Philadelphia: Temple University Press, 1992), pp. 57–70.

Race and Alienation

Ralph J. Bunche

One might wonder a bit as to why the broad theme of alienation chosen for this Fifth East-West Conference should be limited to "modern" man only. It might well have involved man's alienation experience throughout his history. True as this is, however, justification for the concentration on contemporary times is readily found in the stark fact that acute alienation in an era of unlimited nuclear destructive power direly threatens the continued existence of man on earth.

It would seem that alienation in its various manifestations has been a prime trait of man as far back as knowledge about the species goes. In all of his thousands of years here man has lived in a constant state of alienation, in his relations with nature, with his fellow men, with younger generations, with himself, his gods, his beliefs, ideas, and values. Indeed, modern man himself is now responsible for an incredible alienation of his environment by polluting it to such an extent that something akin to global suicide is in prospect if heroic measures are not soon taken.

This, however, is not at all to endorse the Hobbesian view of the natural life of man as poor, nasty, and brutish, or to say that man is innately evil or warlike and that wars are therefore inevitable. I feel sure that man will still be here thousands of years hence. For I believe that, despite so much wickedness and evil design in the world, man is essentially good, that his capacity for fellowship, for compassion, and for self-sacrifice need have no limits, and that such a conclusion can be amply documented. It is not impossible for man to achieve a life on this planet of harmony and peace rather than discord and war. The United Nations has its being in this belief; it charts the way to peace.

But the road to such a state of human affairs is long and tortuous, and the grim and grisly evidences are all around us on a constant and, indeed, increasingly extensive alienation: man's inhumanity to man (so frequently cited as to have become a cliché); his penchant for ruthlessness and disregard for human life; deep-seated prejudices and bigotries, racial and religious; the widespread disenchantment with and alienation from the established order and the establishments. I may repeat that man will survive, but he has much to overcome in himself in order to do so. The best answer to dangerous alienation, I think, is change for the good, progress.

Man's propensity for dispute and conflict is a world-wide phenomenon. It has both international and national aspects and implications.

I have chosen tonight to consider race and color as a major, possibly a preponderant, factor in alienation.

First off, may I explain that I have made this choice not because of my own racial identity, but primarily because I come from mainland United States, where the growing alienation of the black American is the outstanding domestic problem and becomes ever more severe and dangerous. The implications of this, not only for my country, but for the world, are profound and far-reaching. In my view, the increasing estrangement of one-eleventh of the American people—the black citizen—and the divisiveness and corrosiveness of the American race problem, threaten the security of the United States far more than Vietnam.

Secondly, I come from the United Nations, where it is apparent that, on the interna-

Source: Ralph J. Bunche, "Race and Alienation" (1969) in Charles P. Henry, ed., *Ralph J. Bunche: Selected Speeches and Writings* (Ann Arbor: University of Michigan Press, 1995), 305–16.

tional side, race is all-pervasive and often decisive and presents a formidable obstacle to that harmony amongst peoples that is essential to a world at peace, which is the main objective of the United Nations. To be accurate, I should say that it is not race as such that I shall talk about, but that perversion in social attitude called "racism," and the strains, hostilities, animus, and alienation which it generates.

There is, I fear, a steady tendency toward polarization of the white and non-white peoples of the world which can lead to ultimate catastrophe for all. I should explain that I use *white* and *non-white* entirely in their popular connotations. In my view, in the world today polarization of races and their alienation are virtually synonymous. The factors of race and color, directly or indirectly, figure prominently in almost all of the vital world issues and the dangerous confrontations.

There are, of course, alienations and conflicts among white people and among non-white people. The pages of history are replete with accounts of alienations between white peoples which had their most violent expressions in World Wars I and II. Among non-white peoples, conflict situations such as those in Nigeria, Malaysia, and between India and Pakistan over Kashmir have been inheritances from the colonial past. Mainland China has alienated many peoples, white and non-white alike.

Alienations of peoples, expressed in suspicions, fears, and conflicts, have led to the production of the monstrous nuclear devices. In this context, disarmament, the complete elimination of nuclear weapons and severe limitation of conventional arms, is indispensable to a secure future for mankind; "limited" nuclear disarmament is a delusion. Thus, the fateful alternative confronting mankind is alienate and perish or harmonize and survive.

Racism, certainly, is the foremost obstacle to harmonization of peoples; it is the antithesis of harmony, being alienation at its emotional worst.

The affluent peoples of the world, who are also the giants in development, trade, industry, technology, and military power, are mostly white. But the white peoples themselves are only a minority in world population, and each year they represent a smaller percentage of the whole. A 1967 United Nations estimate of the populations of the world gives a figure of 3,420,000,000 people. Of these, 1,068,000,000, or 31.2 percent, were white. A decade earlier, the white percentage had been 33 percent. The non-white percentage in 1967 thus was 68.8 percent.

Since Roman times at least, the leadership of the world, political and economic, has been controlled almost entirely by its white minority. The white nations tended to dominate the world and to have the only effective voices in its councils. But now that picture is changing markedly. The non-white nations, having for the most part only recently emerged from the suppression and subjection of colonialism, now have, numerically at least, the strongest position in world councils and their voices are ever more demanding. Wealth and military power, however, are still overwhelmingly on the white side. A majority of the member states of the United Nations, including the most populous member [*sic*], are non-white.

It is reliably estimated that on the basis of present growth rates, by the end of the twentieth century, that is within 30 years, the total population of the world will approximate 6,565,000,000 people. That explosive increase will be predominantly non-white, and the white minority, relatively, will then have become almost tiny; not to mention how diminutive it will be a century from now, in 2070, when projections foresee a world population total of 25,524,000,000 at current growth rates. One may already envisage with foreboding the prospect before long of a non-white backlash on a global scale.

Only those who have been the victims of racism can know the severity of the wounds it inflicts, and the depth of the resentment of the wounded. Such wounds—indignities, humiliations, insults, and deprivals [*sic*]—never fully heal.

I do not predict, nor do I like even to think about, the prospect of worldwide conflict between white and non-white peoples. But this cannot be excluded. In fact, there are not a few who regard war between the races as inevitable, some of whom, indeed, hold that it has already begun. Among militant black voices in my own country, for example, there are some who talk of a "third force" in the world which would be an alliance of all the non-white peoples, including the American blacks.

The threat of overpopulation is one of mankind's most critical problems. Efforts to control population growth, which is greatest among the developing peoples, mainly non-white, are handicapped to some extent by suspicions that such efforts are motivated and initiated by affluent white societies as one means of maintaining their dominance.

The world, unfortunately, is not yet nearly alert or responsive enough to the population crisis, its complexities and its dangers, nor to the prospect of increasing racial alienation implicit in that crisis.

The population explosion brings in its train a crisis of inadequate food supply. Predictions have been made in responsible quarters that, as early as 15 or 20 years from now, conditions of severe famine will develop in a number of areas of heavy population. The peoples who will suffer and die from starvation will be mainly non-white. The intolerable plight of great masses of these people, who have known for so long only misery as their way of life, may then reach the desperation stage and become unbearable to the point of violent reaction. This hostility almost inevitably would be directed in the end against the affluent white few.

There is no bigger obstacle to the building of solid foundations for secure peace than the great and dangerously widening gap between the haves and have-nots of the world. The affluent haves are few; the poverty-ridden have-nots are very many and are rapidly increasing. Here again the race factor looms prominently. The haves are very largely white; the have-nots are predominantly non-white.

Despite heroic international efforts to reverse the trend and narrow the gap by technical assistance to the developing states and by other means, the gap continues to widen ominously due to striking and continuous techno-logical advances in the highly industrialized states.

In other words, a non-white society is a poor society, with a very few exceptions, of which Japan as a developed country is the most notable. The poor or developing countries do show advances in productivity, national and per capita income. But the developed countries enjoy higher rates of growth and income and thus become ever "richer" in relation to the developing lands.

During the period 1960–67, for example, the total product of the developed countries increased by 44 percent, for an average annual rate of growth of the total product of 5.5 percent. Population in the developed countries during this period increased by 9 percent, resulting in a seven-year growth of per capita product of 52 percent for an average annual per capita increase of 5 percent.

In the developing countries, total product during the same period increased by 36 percent, for an average annual rate of growth of the total product of 4.4 percent. However, the population increase during these years in the have-not countries was 17 percent, or almost double that of the have countries. This brought down the per capita product increase for the seven-year period to 17 percent, for an average annual per capita growth rate of only 2.2 percent, or less than half the 5 percent figure of the developed group.

Both the percentage increase and the rates of growth are lower for the developing countries than for the developed ones, both in absolute and in per capita terms. Thus, the economic gap has continued to widen between the white haves and the non-white have-nots, and the relative position of the latter has continued to deteriorate. It may be noted that there have been several instances of relatively underdeveloped economies which in recent years have achieved high rates of growth, actually reducing the gap as far as they are concerned. Among these have been Romania, Pakistan, Iran, Turkey, and Mexico.

In the 15 poorest countries of the world, all of which, to be sure, are non-white, the per capita national incomes, in U.S. dollars, for the year 1967, ranged from a low of $42 for the Maldive Islands and Upper Volta, to $75 for Haiti. In this list, the figure for Ethiopia was $60, for Nigeria $72, and for India $73.

In striking contrast, the per capita national income for 1967 in the United States was $3,303; in France $1,738; in the United Kingdom $1,560; in the Federal Republic of Germany, $1,512; and in the Union of Soviet Socialist Republics $1,069.

What counts most, naturally, is how this gap between have and have-not peoples affects human needs, how it relates to the conditions of life for the individual in the less developed societies. That is to say, what chance is there for the hundreds of millions of individuals in such lands to aspire to a life that is worthy of a human being—enough to eat, have decent housing, adequate education, and medical care, a normal life expectancy, and the opportunity to make the most of individual talent and ability.

Some of the basic statistics about conditions of life in the poor lands are sobering.

Over 60 percent of the people in the poor countries are chronically undernourished, with diets containing about one-third of the protein and two-thirds of the calories which are regarded as essential to the maintenance of health and productivity in a developed or industrial society. Children, especially, are victims of the conditions of life in these societies. In many of them, half of the children will die in infancy from malnutrition, while more than half of those who survive infancy will be physically and mentally stunted throughout the rest of their lives.

In a great many developing countries, average life expectancy is 40 years or less, due in large measure to malaria, tuberculosis, cholera, bilharziasis, and many other endemic diseases.

About half of the populations of the developing countries are functionally illiterate, that is, unable to read the simplest instructional material. The odds are 2 to 1 against a child receiving any education at all, and 10 to 1 against his going to college. A majority of the teachers have themselves had no schooling beyond the elementary level.

Even in the poorest lands, of course, there are some, usually a very few, who manage in one way or another to prosper and live well.

The unhappy but inevitable conclusion from all this is that the "civilization" which characterizes the planet earth is enjoyed mainly by a white minority of its inhabitants. How long can this endure?

In the international sphere, colonialism in its various manifestations has been the major cause of alienation and of estrangement between white and non-white peoples. The colonial system in its modern version, implicitly arrogant and self-serving, was instituted and perpetuated chiefly by self-righteous and superior-minded Europeans. Its positive achievements notwithstanding, colonialism's evil legacies will bedevil the world for years to come. It has been the cause of many wars since it was instituted and is the direct source of the major conflict situations, all of them having racial aspects, now confronting the world: Vietnam, the Middle East, Nigeria, Southern Rhodesia, and Kashmir.

Division along racial lines and alienation of races is the very essence of the institution of colonialism. I doubt if this ever has been more clearly and forcefully stated than by, surprisingly enough, John Foster Dulles in the course of a speech in October 1947 to the Fourth Committee of the United Nations General Assembly. Mr. Dulles said:

> ... Now, Mr. Chairman, ... I want to make my position perfectly clear. I believe, the United States Delegation believes, that the old colonial system should be done away with—it is obsolete, if indeed it ever had justification, but it certainly has no justification for the future. It has borne some very evil fruit primarily in that it has put people of one race to rule over peoples of another race and that has been very bad for both races.... I can't find words to express myself sufficiently strongly on my belief that that system must come to an end and it must be liquidated in a prompt and orderly way....

There are no more abrasive issues in the United Nations than those involving racial injustice, and among those the colonial issue is foremost. After all, a majority of the 126 members of the United Nations—the members from Africa, Asia, and the Caribbean particularly—have had comparatively recent experience with colonial subjection.

There is a natural tendency among the member states of the United Nations to form regional blocs to represent common interest. Of these, the African and Asian blocs are numerically the largest. On racial and colonial questions, although not on others, they enjoy solidarity and unity and generally vote together. Debates at the United Nations on such issues as Southern Rhodesia, South West Africa, the Portuguese colonies, and Apartheid generate much heat and emotion. Very often, the voting on resolution on such issues is near unanimity, the dissenting members being the Union of South Africa and Portugal.

With abundant reason, non-white peoples tend to be acutely sensitive about matters of race and color. It follows that the suspicions and resentments arising from racial consciousness and experience often complicate, obstruct, and frustrate efforts of the United Nations and other bodies in political, economic, social, and assistance fields.

It bears repeating that in all international affairs today the race factor is omnipresent. For example, the question would seem entirely valid, and now and then I hear it raised, whether the People's Republic of China would not long ago have been admitted to the family of nations and seated in the United Nations if the Chinese were not "yellow" people—and so many of them. It is not in the interest of the peace of the world to refuse membership in the international community to and thus to make a maverick of a nation of more than 700 million people.

All of the other communist states, including Albania, all having white populations, have long since been taken into the community of nations. The essence of the "yellow peril" bogey survives, even if the phrase itself is now unfashionable.

The Vietnam War has very deep racial implications. There, the United States is fighting yellow men who are also considered communists. This makes it rather easy for Americans to rationalize their involvement and to broadcast daily the number of those despised little yellow men that the American and South Vietnamese forces have killed. The derogatory name Americans give to their South Vietnamese opponents is "Viet Cong," which literally means, I understand, "yellow bandits." Would the United States be engaged in that war if the North Vietnamese and the National Liberation Front were white?

In this regard, it has racial significance, no doubt, that there is no disposition on the part of the United States (or the United Kingdom) to envisage the use of force, or even to apply strong measures short of force, to liberate the overwhelming majority black population of Southern Rhodesia from the ruthless, racist tyranny of a small white minority led by an arrogant and shameless racial bigot, Ian Smith. The United Kingdom in recent years, however, has found it possible to send British troops to Kenya, Tanzania, and Anguilla.

The black Americans who have fought or are asked to fight in Vietnam find themselves in a paradoxical position. They must employ every violent means at hand to maim and kill the enemy—North Vietnamese and the South Vietnamese enrolled in the National Liberation Front. This is to protect the rights and freedom of 17 million South Vietnamese, a considerable number of whom obviously resent and resist American presence in their country. On the other hand, there are 22 million black Americans whose constitutional rights are being violated flagrantly and persistently. But the black veteran from Vietnam, like all other blacks, is not permitted to do very much about that. He cannot "disturb the peace" and must respect "law and order," although white citizens are not compelled to respect the law of the Constitution where its application to black citizens is concerned. The black veteran, along with all others, may in some places even be denied permission to demonstrate or to march peacefully in protestation against racism and racial injustice. The government requires black citizens to fight for the South Vietnamese but will not even empower the issuance of a cease and desist order to white employers who flagrantly deny employment to black men and women solely on grounds of race. That, in the eyes of the senator from Abraham Lincoln's state, Everett Dirksen, would be intolerable "harassment" of business.

The estrangement between white and black Americans intensifies and becomes increasingly disruptive and dangerous. It could reach catastrophic proportions.

The core of the problem is the glaring disparity between the theory and the practice of American democracy. The attitudes and actions of white Americans do not, and many begin to feel cannot, correspond to the ideals and promises of the American Constitution and system. This is not merely because some Americans are hard-bitten racists who oppose bitterly and openly the very idea of integration and equality in rights and opportunities for the black American. The harsh fact is that most white Americans, many without realizing it, harbor in themselves, as an inheritance from the society's history and mores, some degree of racism or bigotry. This is reflex and sub-conscious bigotry, which may become readily recognizable only in the face of some stern personal challenge. One current symptom of this is the inclination of a good many "fair-minded" Americans, including TV and radio media, to show much sympathetic interest in separatism and pro-separatist voices. Many other whites, finding their consciences whipping them, are gullible and susceptible to outlandish black demands such as the claims for "reparations."

Thus, there has been all along in the American society a built-in and comfortable complacency about the unequal status of and the injustices to the black, second-class fellow citizens. It has been enough to be able to say that equality and integration will one day be achieved here and that progress is being made. That, until recently, could always be counted upon to avert acute trouble. That is no more the case. That is no longer enough for most black Americans. These black men, however involuntarily at first, have been on the mainland shores since the beginning of the country. With far less reward than has gone to their white fellow countrymen, the blacks have given their labor, their talent, their loyalty, blood, and lives in the building and protection of the American nation. They have made also distinct and distinctive cultural contributions to the American society.

In more than 300 years in the land, nearly 300 years since the adoption of the Constitution, and more than a century after the Emancipation Proclamation, the black American is still deprived of full citizenship, is still excluded from the mainstream of American life, is still the victim of gross social injustice by a white majority in which racism is widely prevalent.

Now, after a long-enduring faith and patience without parallel, I think, in human history, the black citizen has lost his patience—and his fear—and is, I am afraid, also losing his faith in the American establishment and system insofar as their promises to him are concerned. He is demanding, not appealing, nowadays, and his demands begin to take unexpected courses—courses which could only be born out of profound frustration and complete disillusionment.

It is said by some that there is already under way in the United States a black revolution. Others deny it. Certainly, such a development springing from the obvious inadequacy of the civil rights struggle, and a feeling of futility and desperation, cannot be excluded. In any case, the insistent demands of the black American today, the growing militancy behind those demands, the increasing involvement of ordinary black men and women in them, and the radical changes in attitudes and practices and even in the structure of the society required by them, are of the nature and dimension of a revolution. Non-violence has been the traditional tactic of the black American in carrying on his struggle, but an increasing number of black people, especially in the ranks of the young, see violence as an essential weapon in desperate circumstances and scorn the non-violent, Gandhian counsel of leaders such as the late Martin Luther King. The majority of American blacks, however, still look upon integration and not separation as the desirable goal and believe in a non-violent struggle. However, last week's announcement of the national government's dismaying new policy of relaxing the deadline on school desegregation compliance by allowing "exceptions," is anything but reassuring to every black American.

Some of the leading voices in the "black revolution" seek to orient the goals and to build the future of black men on what has been the pattern of race in the United States all along—separate racial communities. The American society is, and has always been, a dualistic society—a white segment and a black segment of the population quite rigidly separated.

Ironically, despite the intensified civil rights struggle in the post-World War II years, the white and black communities are more separated—and alienated—than at any time since Emancipation. This is because of the increasing ghettoization of the black people in the urban centers, particularly of the North. Now, the majority of the 22 million Negroes live in the Northern cities, and most of them dwell in the black ghettoes of those cities. The increasing alienation of whites and blacks is reflected in Black Power on the one hand and "white backlash" on the other.

The black American in the ghetto is, by and large, confined there by the racial mores of the society, by the consequent economic and social forces, and because the ghetto understandably comes to be seen as something of a haven from an unfriendly white world. The ghettoite realizes soon enough that he is where he is because he is unwanted and rejected beyond the ghetto. He resents this as he resents his underprivilege in employment, education, health service, housing, and all other human needs. In such a situation, it is no big step to the conclusion that equality and integration are cruel mirages, to bitterness and animosity toward the white man, and to the determination that, if the white man rejects the blacks, he cannot expect also to continue to control them. The establishments are seen as white-dominated for white interests. It follows that black men begin to think of having their own establishments and controlling themselves. This readily translates into black separatism.

The depths of the despair experienced by the black American is best measured by the fact that white segregationists and black separatists now find, if for different reasons, some common ground: both reject integration and demand separation of the races; both are racist in their approaches.

Racism, white or black, is a sickness, and a society in which it is prevalent is an afflicted society.

The black American can attain no major goals in the American society except by his own determined, united, and unrelenting effort. He must believe in himself, he must know and have pride in himself, his background, and his culture. In these respects, Black Power serves a necessary purpose.

There are only two solutions: separation and integration (or, as some now prefer to say, an "open society"). Some black nationalists project a "black national community in co-existence with the white community." As I see it, separatism is based on a philosophy of defeat, of surrender to bigotry. It is unrealistic and impractical in the light of the unavoidable facts of a minority group in the world's most powerful society. It offers a false escape and is more emotional than workable.

It seems painfully clear to me that there is no possibility in the affluent, highly industrialized, and technological white-majority American society for anyone to be at once black, separate, and equal.

It follows that only the goal of integration makes practical sense. Whatever the outlook, integration and equality are worth struggling and fighting for. The black American has a huge investment, a vested interest, and a birthright in the American society.

The racial struggle will become increasingly harsh, with more frequent confrontations between whites and blacks. There will be more "hot summers" and likely hotter ones—and winters as well. There are signs of the direction the society may take which are disturbing, not alone for black Americans.

Racist backlash is widespread. The recent municipal elections in Los Angeles, Minneapolis, and New York marked triumphs for racism, reaction, and backlash. The order of the day was "law and order." President Nixon has said that the message of these election contests has come through "loud and clear": the American people are "fed up ... with violence and lawlessness." There have been a good many warning signs that very many black Americans also are "fed up" with their inferior status. But the eruptions in the ghettos, disruptions on the campuses—unhappily, some of which recently involved clashes between white and black students—and crimes in the streets, though serious breaches of the law, are not the only serious manifestations of lawlessness. The ardent protagonists of law and order rarely refer to "justice" or to that intolerable form of lawlessness which denies social justice and constitutional rights to the black one-eleventh of the nation's citizenry.

As long as racism persists in the American society, alienation will characterize the relations between the white and black sectors of the population.

More ghetto eruptions are inevitable. These outbursts thus far have been confined principally to the ghetto areas. But there is no certainty that this will continue to be the case. Ghettoization of black citizens intensifies polarization of the races and nurtures conflict between them. This, in turn, will lead to more recourse to law and order. Racial conflict in the United States could intensify to such a degree as to approach a chronic state of guerrilla warfare in the jungles of glass, steel, and concrete which are the urban centers. If that conflict should ever extend beyond the confines of the ghettos and threaten the vital communications, transportation, and industrial facilities, the reaction of the white community would be severe, the hue and cry for more and more law and order could then transform the society into something in the nature of a police state. In fact, over-action by police in some places, the too obvious readiness of some high authorities to oppose dissent with force, the shocking wire-tapping by the Federal Bureau of Investigation of the private telephone of a highly respected citizen and leader, the late Martin Luther King, give cause already for alarm.

White men, whether in the majority, as in the United States and the United Kingdom, or in the minority, as in South Africa, Southern Rhodesia, and the world at large, must find a way, if such there is, to purge themselves completely of racism or face an ultimate fateful confrontation of the races which will shake the very foundations of civilization and, indeed, threaten its continued existence and that of most of mankind as well.

The picture I have presented has been largely but unavoidably negative and gloomy. The theme of this conference requires the focus to be on alienation, which is a negative and disheartening subject. But alienation in its racial and many other forms is a bitter fact of life.

There is a brighter side of life, of course. A different topic and speech, however, would be required to elaborate on it. Suffice it now to say only that the system of colonialism, in its traditional form at least, is in its twilight. Since the United Nations came into existence in 1945, more than 800 million people have emerged from colonial rule to gain independence; 58 of the present member states of the United Nations were in colonial status at that time. The problems of overpopulation and hunger present unprecedented challenge, but they are not insoluble. The ever-widening gap between rich and poor is the most formidable of all problems. Still, astronomical sums are now being wasted in arms, nuclear and conventional, which the great military powers dare not use against each other; and for a war in Vietnam that no one can win, which makes it senseless and incomprehensible. A diversion of a substantial part of such sums and their intelligent use for and by the developing peoples to strengthen their economies and raise their living standards could at least reverse the present trend and narrow the gap. Racism is a matter of man's attitudes, and these can be changed, and, I believe, they will be changed when men come fully to realize the fatal alternative. Mankind is well-practiced at pulling back from the brink of self-extinction.

Mankind should be able to eliminate the causes of alienation, to work out reasonable and equitable solutions to all problems of human relations. The crucial question is, has man the will—the will to do what must be done to rescue the world? Can the will of man be summoned and mobilized in time, or shall the world continue to indulge in its tragically outmoded habit of futile warfare to the insane point of self-extermination?

The United Nations, I am confident, will persevere in its historic efforts to achieve [and] secure an enduring peace in the world. It seeks always to induce the parties to disputes to rely upon reasoned discussion and negotiation rather than armed force in the resolution of differences. The UN, I believe, can succeed in this effort, but only if it receives resolute support from the peoples of the world.

I like to believe, and I do believe, that despite all of his frailties and follies man will not only survive on earth through reason, common sense, and the will to live but that, through the unlimited creative capacity of his genius, he will continue to advance.

Separation and Self-Respect

W. E. B. Du Bois

What we continually face in this problem of race segregation in the United States is a paradox like this:

1. Compulsory separation of human beings by essentially artificial criteria, such as birth, nationality, language, color and race, is the cause of human hate, jealousy and war, and the destruction of talent and art.

2. Where separation of mankind into races, groups and classes is compulsory, either by law or custom, and whether that compulsion be temporary or permanent, the only effective defense that the segregated and despised group has against complete spiritual and physical disaster, is internal self-organization for self-respect and self-defense.

The dilemma is complete and there is no escape. The black man born in South Carolina has a right and a duty to complain that any public school system separated by artificial

race and class lines is needlessly expensive, socially dangerous, and spiritually degrading. And yet that black man will send his child to a Negro school, and he will see to it, if he is really a man, that this Negro school is the best possible school; that it is decently housed and effectively taught by well-trained teachers. He will demand a voice in its control, finances and curriculum, and any action of his that asks for less than this will mark him as an idiot or a coward.

A black man born in Boston has a right to oppose any separation of schools by color, race or class. He has a duty to insist that the public school attended by all kinds and conditions of people, is the best and only door to true democracy and human understanding. But this black man in Boston has no right, after he has made this academic pronouncement to send his own helpless immature child into school where white children kick, cuff or abuse him, or where teachers openly and persistently neglect or hurt or dwarf its soul. If he

Source: W. E. B. Du Bois, "Separation and Self-Respect" *The Crisis* (March 1934).

does, he must not be surprised if the boy lands in the gutter or penitentiary. Moreover, our Boston brother has no right to sneer at the "Jim-Crow" schools of South Carolina, or at the brave teachers who guide them at starvation wage; nor can he conscientiously advise the South Carolinian to move to Boston and join the bread lines.

Let the N.A.A.C.P. and every upstanding Negro pound at the closed gates of opportunity and denounce caste and segregation; but let us not punish our own children under the curious impression that we are punishing our white oppressors. Let us not affront our own self-respect by accepting a proffered equality which is not equality, or submitting to discrimination simply because it does not involve actual and open segregation; and above all, let us not sit down and do nothing for self-defense and self-organization just because we are too stupid or too distrustful of ourselves to take vigorous and decisive action.

Race segregation in the United States too often presents itself as an individual problem; a question of my admission to this church or that theater; a question as to whether I shall live and work in Mississippi or New York for my own enjoyment, emolument or convenience.

In fact this matter of segregation is a group matter with long historic roots. When Negroes were first brought to America in any numbers, their classification was economic rather than racial. They were in law and custom classed with the laborers, most of whom were brought from Europe under a contract which made them practically serfs. In this laboring class there was at first no segregation, there was some inter-marriage and when the laborer gained his freedom, he became in numbers of cases a landholder and a voter.

The first distinction arose between laborers who had come from Europe and contracted to work for a term of years, and laborers from Africa and the West Indies who had made no contract. Both classes were often held for life, but soon there arose a distinction between servants for a term of years and servants for life. Even their admission to a Christian church organization was usually considered as emancipating a servant for life,

and thus again the purely racial segregation was cut across by religious considerations.

Finally, however, slavery became a matter of racial caste, so that white laborers served for definite terms and most black workers served for life. But even here anomaly arose in the case of the small number of Negroes who were free. For a while these free Negroes were not definitely segregated from other free workers, but gradually they were forced together as a caste, holding themselves, on the one hand, strictly away from the slaves, and on the other, being excluded more and more severely from inter-course with whites of all degrees.

The result was that there grew up in the minds of the free Negro class a determination and a prejudice which has come down to our day. They fought bitterly with every means at their command against being classed with the mass of slaves. It was for this reason that they objected to being called Negroes. Negroes was synonymous with slaves. They were not slaves. They objected to being coupled with black folk by legislation or custom. Any such act threatened their own freedom. They developed, therefore, both North and South as a separate, isolated group. In large Southern cities, like New Orleans, Savannah and Charleston, they organized their own society, established schools and churches, and made themselves a complete segregated unit, except in their economic relations where they earned a living among the whites as artisans and servants, rising here and there to be semi-professional men and small merchants. The higher they rose and the more definite and effective their organization, the more they protested against being called Negroes or classed with Negroes, because Negroes were slaves.

In the North, the development differed somewhat, and yet followed mainly the same lines. The groups of free colored folk in Boston, Newport, New Haven, New York, Philadelphia, Baltimore and Cincinnati, all formed small, carefully organized groups, with their own schools and churches, with their own social life, with their own protest against being classed as Negroes. As the mass of Negroes became free in the Northern states, certain decisions were forced upon these groups. Take for instance, Philadelphia. An event happened in April 1787, which may be called by the American Negro, the Great Decision. The free colored people of Philadelphia at that time were making a desperate fight for recognition and decent social treatment.

Two of their leaders, Richard Allen and Absalom Jones, had proffered their services during the terrible epidemic in 1792, and partly at their own expense, helped bury the deserted dead of the white folk. The Mayor properly commended them. Both these men worshipped at St. George's Methodist Church, then at 4th and Vine Streets. For years they had been made welcome; but as gradual emancipation progressed in Pennsylvania, Negroes began to pour in to the city from the surrounding country, and black Christians became too numerous at St. George's. One Sunday morning during prayer, Jones and Allen were on their knees, when they were told they must get up and go to the gallery where hereafter black folk would worship. They refused to stir until the prayer was over, and then they got up and left the church. They never went back.

Under these circumstances, what would you have done, Dear Reader of 1934? There were several possibilities. You might have been able to impress it upon the authorities of the church that you were not like other Negroes; that you were different, with more wealth and intelligence, and that while it might be quite all right and even agreeable to you that other Negroes should be sent to the gallery, that you as an old and tried member of the church should be allowed to worship as you pleased. If you had said this, it probably would have had no effect upon the deacons of St. George's.

In that case, what would you have done? You could walk out of the church but whither would you walk? There were no other white churches that wanted you. Most of them would not have allowed you to cross their threshold. The others would have segregated you in the gallery or at a separate service. You might have said with full right and reason that the action of St. George's was un-Christian and despicable, and dangerous for the future of democracy in Philadelphia and in the United States. That was all quite true, and nevertheless its statement had absolutely no effect upon St. George's.

Walking out of this church, these two men formed an organization. It was called the Free African Society. Virtually it was confined to a colored membership, although some of the Quakers visited the meetings from time to time and gave advice. Probably there was some discussion of taking the group into the fellowship of the Quakers, but liberal as the Quakers were, they were not looking for Negro proselytes. They had had a few in the West Indies but not in the United States. The excluded Negroes found themselves in a dilemma. They could do one of two things: They could ask to be admitted as a segregated group in some white organization; or they could form their own organization. It was an historic decision and they did both.

Richard Allen formed from the larger part of the group, the African Methodist Episcopal Church, which today has 750,000 members and is without doubt the most powerful single Negro organization in the United States. Absalom Jones formed St. Thomas Church as a separate Negro church in the Episcopal communion, and the church has had a continuous existence down to our day.

Which of these two methods was best will be a matter of debate. There are those who think that it was saving something of principle to remain in a white church, even as a segregated body. There are others who say that this action was simply a compromise with the devil and that having been kicked out of the Methodist Church and not allowed equality in the Episcopal Church, there was nothing for a self-respecting man to do but to establish a church of his own.

No matter which solution seems to you wisest, segregation was compulsory; and the only answer to it was internal self-organization; and the answer that was inevitable in 1787, is just as inevitable in 1934.

Servility and Self-Respect

Thomas E. Hill, Jr.

Several motives underlie this paper.[1] In the first place, I am curious to see if there is a legitimate source for the increasingly common feeling that servility can be as much a vice as arrogance. There seems to be something morally defective about the Uncle Tom and the submissive housewife; and yet, on the other hand, if the only interests they sacrifice are their own, it seems that we should have no right to complain. Secondly, I have some sympathy for the now unfashionable view that each person has duties to himself as well as to others. It does seem absurd to say that a person could literally violate his own rights or owe himself a debt of gratitude, but I suspect that the classic defenders of duties to oneself had something different in mind. If there are duties to oneself, it is natural to expect that a duty to avoid being servile would have a prominent place among them. Thirdly, I am interested in making sense of Kant's puzzling, but suggestive, remarks about respect for persons and respect for the moral law. On the usual reading, these remarks seem unduly moralistic; but, viewed in another way, they suggest an argument for a kind of self-respect which is incompatible with a servile attitude.

My procedure will not be to explicate Kant directly. Instead I shall try to isolate the defect of servility and sketch an argument to show why it is objectionable, noting only in passing how this relates to Kant and the controversy about duties to oneself. What I say about self-respect is far from the whole story. In particular, it is not concerned with esteem for one's special abilities and achievements or with the self-confidence which characterizes the especially autonomous person. Nor is my concern with the psychological antecedents

and effects of self-respect. Nevertheless, my conclusions, if correct, should be of interest; for they imply that, given a common view of morality, there are nonutilitarian moral reasons for each person, regardless of his merits, to respect himself. To avoid servility to the extent that one can is not simply a right but a duty, not simply a duty to others but a duty to oneself.

I

Three examples may give a preliminary idea of what I mean by *servility*. Consider, first, an extremely deferential black, whom I shall call the *Uncle Tom*. He always steps aside for white men; he does not complain when less qualified whites take over his job; he gratefully accepts whatever benefits his all-white government and employers allot him, and he would not think of protesting its insufficiency. He displays the symbols of deference to whites, and of contempt towards blacks: he faces the former with bowed stance and a ready 'sir' and 'Ma'am'; he reserves his strongest obscenities for the latter. Imagine, too, that he is not playing a game. He is not the shrewdly prudent calculator, who knows how to make the best of a bad lot and mocks his masters behind their backs. He accepts without question the idea that, as a black, he is owed less than whites. He may believe that blacks are mentally inferior and of less social utility, but that is not the crucial point. The attitude which he displays is that what he values, aspires for, and can demand is of less importance than what whites value, aspire for, and can demand. He is far from the picture book's carefree, happy servant, but he does not feel that he has a right to expect anything better.

Source: Thomas E. Hill, Jr., "Servility and Self-Respect" *The Monist* 57.1 (January 1973): 87–104.

Another pattern of servility is illustrated by a person I shall call the *Self-Deprecator*. Like the Uncle Tom, he is reluctant to make demands. He says nothing when others take unfair advantage of him. When asked for his preferences or opinions, he tends to shrink away as if what he said should make no difference. His problem, however, is not a sense of racial inferiority but rather an acute awareness of his own inadequacies and failures as an individual. These defects are not imaginary: he has in fact done poorly by his own standards and others'. But, unlike many of us in the same situation, he acts as if his failings warrant quite unrelated maltreatment even by strangers. His sense of shame and self-contempt make him content to be the instrument of others. He feels that nothing is owed him until he has earned it and that he has earned very little. He is not simply playing a masochist's game of winning sympathy by disparaging himself. On the contrary, he assesses his individual merits with painful accuracy.

A rather different case is that of the *Deferential Wife*. This is a woman who is utterly devoted to serving her husband. She buys the clothes *he* prefers, invites the guests *he* wants to entertain, and makes love whenever *he* is in the mood. She willingly moves to a new city in order for him to have a more attractive job, counting her own friendships and geographical preferences insignificant by comparison. She loves her husband, but her conduct is not simply an expression of love. She is happy, but she does not subordinate herself as a means to happiness. She does not simply defer to her husband in certain spheres as a trade-off for his deference in other spheres. On the contrary, she tends not to form her own interests, values, and ideals; and, when she does, she counts them as less important than her husband's. When confronted by appeals from Women's Liberation she grants that women are mentally and physically equal, if not superior, to men. She just believes that the proper role for a woman is to serve her family. As a matter of fact, much of her happiness derives from her belief that she fulfills this role very well. No one is trampling on her rights, she says; for she is quite glad, and proud, to serve her husband as she does.

Each one of these cases reflects the attitude which I call servility.[2] It betrays the absence of a certain kind of self-respect. What I take this attitude to be, more specifically, will become clearer later on. It is important at the outset, however, not to confuse the three cases sketched above with other, superficially similar cases. In particular, the cases I have sketched are not simply cases in which someone refuses to press his rights, speaks disparagingly of himself, or devotes himself to another. A black, for example, is not necessarily servile because he does not demand a just wage; for, seeing that such a demand would result in his being fired, he might forbear for the sake of his children. A self-critical person is not necessarily servile by virtue of bemoaning his faults in public; for his behavior may be merely a complex way of satisfying his own inner needs quite independent of a willingness to accept abuse from others. A woman need not be servile whenever she works to make her husband happy and prosperous; for she might freely and knowingly choose to do so from love or from a desire to share the rewards of his success. If the effort did not require her to submit to humiliation or maltreatment, her choice would not mark her as servile. There may, of course, be grounds for objecting to the attitudes in these cases; but the defect is not servility of the sort I want to consider. It should also be noted that my cases of servility are not simply instances of deference to superior knowledge or judgment. To defer to an expert's judgment on matters of fact is not to be servile; to defer to his every wish and whim is. Similarly, the belief that one's talents and achievements are comparatively low does not, by itself, make one servile. It is no vice to acknowledge the truth, and one may in fact have achieved less, and have less ability, than others. To be servile is not simply to hold certain empirical beliefs but to have a certain attitude concerning one's rightful place in a moral community.

II

Are there grounds for regarding the attitudes of the Uncle Tom, the Self-Deprecator, and the Deferential Wife as morally objectionable? Are there moral arguments we could give them to show that they ought to have more self-respect? None of the more obvious replies is entirely satisfactory.

One might, in the first place, adduce utilitarian considerations. Typically the servile person will be less happy than he might be. Moreover, he may be less prone to make the best of his own socially useful abilities. He may become a nuisance to others by being overly dependent. He will, in any case, lose the special contentment that comes from standing up for one's rights. A submissive attitude encourages exploitation, and exploitation spreads misery in a variety of ways. These considerations provide a prima facie case against the attitudes of the Uncle Tom, the Deferential Wife, and the Self-Deprecator, but they are hardly conclusive. Other utilities tend to counterbalance the ones just mentioned. When people refuse to press their rights, there are usually others who profit. There are undeniable pleasures in associating with those who are devoted, understanding, and grateful for whatever we see fit to give them—as our fondness for dogs attests. Even the servile person may find his attitude a source of happiness, as the case of the Deferential Wife illustrates. There may be comfort and security in thinking that the hard choices must be made by others, that what I would say has little to do with what ought to be done. Self-condemnation may bring relief from the pangs of guilt even if it is not deliberately used for that purpose. On balance, then, utilitarian considerations may turn out to favor servility as much as they oppose it.

For those who share my moral intuitions, there is another sort of reason for not trying to rest a case against servility on utilitarian considerations. Certain utilities seem irrelevant to the issue. The utilitarian must weigh them along with others, but to do so seems morally inappropriate. Suppose, for example, that the submissive attitudes of the Uncle Tom and the Deferential Wife result in positive utilities for those who dominate and exploit them. Do we need to tabulate *these* utilities before conceding that servility is objectionable? The Uncle Tom, it seems, is making an error, a moral error, quite apart from consideration of how much others in fact profit from his attitude. The Deferential Wife may be quite happy; but if her happiness turns out to be contingent on her distorted view of her own rights and worth as a person, then it carries little moral weight against the contention that she ought to change that view. Suppose I could cause a woman to find her happiness in denying all her rights and serving my every wish. No doubt I could do so only by nonrational manipulative techniques, which I ought not to use. But is this the only objection? My efforts would be wrong, it seems, not only because of the techniques they require but also because the resultant attitude is itself objectionable. When a person's happiness stems from a morally objectionable attitude, it ought to be discounted. That a sadist gets pleasure from seeing others suffer should not count even as a partial justification for his attitude. That a servile person derives pleasure from denying her moral status, for similar reasons, cannot make her attitude acceptable. These brief intuitive remarks are not intended as a refutation of utilitarianism, with all its many varieties; but they do suggest that it is well to look elsewhere for adequate grounds for rejecting the attitudes of the Uncle Tom, the Self-Deprecator, and the Deferential Wife.

One might try to appeal to meritarian considerations. That is, one might argue that the servile person *deserves* more than he allows himself. This line of argument, however, is no more adequate than the utilitarian one. It may be wrong to deny others what they deserve, but it is not so obviously wrong to demand less for oneself than one deserves. In any case, the Self-Deprecator's problem is not that he underestimates his merits. By hypothesis, he assesses his merits quite accurately. We cannot reasonably tell him to have more respect for himself because he *deserves* more respect; he knows that he has not *earned* better treatment. His problem, in fact, is that he thinks of his moral status with regard to others as entirely dependent upon his merits. His interests and choices are important, he feels, only if he has earned the right to make demands; or if he had rights by birth, they were forfeited by his subsequent failures and misdeeds. My Self-Deprecator is no doubt an atypical person, but nevertheless he illustrates an important point. Normally when we find a self-contemptuous person, we can plausibly argue that he is not so bad as he thinks, that his self-contempt is an overreaction prompted more by inner needs than by objective assessment of his merits. Because this argument cannot work with the Self-Deprecator, his case draws attention to a distinction, applicable in other cases as well, between saying that someone deserves respect for his merits and saying that he is owed respect as a person. On meritarian grounds we can only say 'You deserve better than this,' but the defect of the servile person is not merely failure to recognize his merits.

Other common arguments against the Uncle Tom, et al., may have some force but seem not to strike to the heart of the problem. For example, philosophers sometimes appeal to the value of human potentialities. As a human being, it is said, one at least has a capacity for rationality, morality, excellence, or autonomy, and this capacity is worthy of respect. Although such arguments have the merit of making respect independent of a person's actual deserts, they seem quite misplaced in some cases. There comes a time when we have sufficient evidence that a person is not ever going to *be* rational, moral, excellent, or autonomous even if he still has a capacity, in some sense, for being so. As a person approaches death with an atrocious record so far, the chances of his realizing his diminishing capacities become increasingly slim. To make these capacities the basis of his self-respect is to rest it on a shifting and unstable ground. We do, of course, respect persons for capacities which they are not exercising at the moment; for example, I might respect a person as a good philosopher even though he is just now blundering into gross confusion.

In these cases, however, we respect the person for an active capacity, a ready disposition, which he has displayed on many occasions. On this analogy, a person should have respect for himself only when his capacities are developed and ready, needing only to be triggered by an appropriate occasion or the removal of some temporary obstacle. The Uncle Tom and the Deferential Wife, however, may in fact have quite limited capacities of this sort, and, since the Self-Deprecator is already overly concerned with his own inadequacies, drawing attention to his capacities seems a poor way to increase his self-respect. In any case, setting aside the Kantian nonempirical capacity for autonomy, the capacities of different persons vary widely; but what the servile person seems to overlook is something by virtue of which he is equal with every other person.

III

Why, then, is servility a moral defect? There is, I think, another sort of answer which is worth exploring. The first part of this answer must be an attempt to isolate the objectionable features of the servile person; later we can ask why these features are objectionable. As a step in this direction, let us examine again our three paradigm cases. The moral defect in each case, I suggest, is a failure to understand and acknowledge one's own moral rights. I assume, without argument here, that each person has moral rights.[3] Some of these rights may be basic human rights; that it, rights for which a person needs only to be human to qualify. Other rights will be derivative and contingent upon his special commitments, institutional affiliations, etc. Most rights will be prima facie ones; some may be absolute. Most can be waived under appropriate conditions; perhaps some cannot. Many rights can be forfeited; but some, presumably, cannot. The servile person does not, strictly speaking, violate his own rights. At least in our paradigm cases he fails to acknowledge fully his own moral status because he does not fully understand what his rights are, how they can be waived, and when they can be forfeited.

The defect of the Uncle Tom, for example, is that he displays an attitude that denies his moral equality with whites. He does not realize, or apprehend in an effective way, that he has as much right to a decent wage and a share of political power as any comparable white. His gratitude is misplaced; he accepts benefits which are his by right as if they were gifts. The Self-Deprecator is servile in a more complex way. He acts as if he has forfeited many important rights which in fact he has not. He does not understand, or fully realize in his own case, that certain rights to fair and decent treatment do not have to be earned. He sees his merits clearly enough, but he fails to see that what he can expect from others is not merely a function of his merits. The Deferential Wife *says* that she understands her rights vis-à-vis her husband, but what she fails to appreciate is that her consent to serve him is a valid waiver of her rights only under certain conditions. If her consent is coerced, say, by the lack of viable options for women in her society, then her consent is worth little. If socially fostered ignorance of her own talents and alternatives is responsible for her consent, then her consent should not count as a fully legitimate waiver of her right to equal consideration within the marriage. All the more, her consent to defer constantly to her husband is not a legitimate setting aside of her rights if it results from her mistaken belief that she has a moral duty to do so. (Recall: "The *proper* role for a woman is to serve her family.") If she believes that she has a *duty* to defer to her husband, then, whatever she may say, she cannot fully understand that she has a *right* not to defer to him. When she says that she freely gives up such a right, she is confused. Her confusion is rather like that of a person who has been persuaded by an unscrupulous lawyer that it is legally incumbent on him to refuse a jury trial but who nevertheless tells the judge that he understands that he has a right to a jury trial and freely waives it. He does not really understand what it is to have and freely give up the right if he thinks that it would be an offense for him to exercise it.

Insofar as servility results from moral ignorance or confusion, it need not be something for which a person is to blame. Even self-reproach may be inappropriate; for at the time a person is in ignorance he cannot feel guilty about his servility, and later he may conclude that his ignorance was unavoidable. In some cases, however, a person might reasonably believe that he should have known better. If, for example, the Deferential Wife's confusion about her rights resulted from a motivated resistance to drawing the implications of her own basic moral principles, then later she might find some ground for self-reproach. Whether blameworthy or not, servility could still be morally objectionable at least in the sense that it ought to be discouraged, that social conditions which nourish it should be reformed, and the like. Not all morally undesirable features of a person are ones for which he is responsible, but that does not mean that they are defects merely from an esthetic or prudential point of view.

In our paradigm cases, I have suggested, servility is a kind of deferential attitude towards others resulting from ignorance or misunderstanding of one's moral rights. A sufficient remedy, one might think, would be moral enlightenment. Suppose, however, that our servile persons come to know their rights but do not substantially alter their behavior. Are they not still servile in an objectionable way? One might even think that reproach is more appropriate now because they know what they are doing.

The problem, unfortunately, is not as simple as it may appear. Much depends on what they tolerate and why. Let us set aside cases in which a person merely refuses to *fight* for his rights, chooses not to exercise certain rights, or freely waives many rights which he might have insisted upon. Our problem concerns the previously servile person who continues to display the same marks of deference even after he fully knows his rights. Imagine, for example, that even after enlightenment our Uncle Tom persists in his old pattern of behavior, giving all the typical signs of believing that the injustices done to him are not really wrong. Suppose, too, that the newly enlightened Deferential Wife continues to defer to her husband, refusing to disturb the old way of life by introducing her new ideas. She acts as if she accepts the idea that she is merely doing her duty though actually she no longer believes it. Let us suppose, further, that the Uncle Tom and the Deferential Wife are not merely generous with their time and property; they also accept without protest, and even appear to sanction, treatment which is humiliating and degrading. That is, they do not simply consent to waive mutually acknowledged rights; they tolerate violations of their rights with apparent approval. They pretend to give their permission for subtle humiliations which they really believe no permission can make legitimate. Are such persons still servile despite their moral knowledge?

The answer, I think, should depend upon why the deferential role is played. If the motive is a morally commendable one, or a desire to avert dire consequences to oneself, or even an ambition to set an oppressor up for a later fall, then I would not count the role player as servile. The Uncle Tom, for instance, is not servile in my sense if he shuffles and bows to keep the Klan from killing his children, to save his own skin, or even to buy time while he plans the revolution. Similarly, the Deferential Wife is not servile if she tolerates an abusive husband because he is so ill that further strain would kill him, because protesting would deprive her of her only means of survival, or because she is collecting atrocity stories for her book against marriage. If there is fault in these situations, it seems inappropriate to call it *servility*. The story is quite different, however, if a person continues in his deferential role just from laziness, timidity, or a desire for some minor advantage. He shows too little concern for his moral status as a person, one is tempted to say, if he is willing to deny it for a small profit or simply because it requires some effort and courage to affirm it openly. A black who plays the Uncle Tom merely to gain an advantage over other blacks is harming them, of course; but he is also displaying disregard for his own moral position as an equal among human beings. Similarly, a woman throws away her rights too lightly if

she continues to play the subservient role because she is used to it or is too timid to risk a change. A Self-Deprecator who readily accepts what he knows are violations of his rights may be indulging his peculiar need for punishment at the expense of denying something more valuable. In these cases, I suggest, we have a kind of servility independent of any ignorance or confusion about one's rights. The person who has it may or may not be blameworthy, depending on many factors; and the line between servile and nonservile role playing will often be hard to draw. Nevertheless, the objectionable feature is perhaps clear enough for present purposes: it is a willingness to disavow one's moral status, publicly and systematically, in the absence of any strong reason to do so.

My proposal, then, is that there are at least two types of servility: one resulting from misunderstanding of one's rights and the other from placing a comparatively low value on them. In either case, servility manifests the absence of a certain kind of self-respect. The respect which is missing is not respect for one's merits but respect for one's rights. The servile person displays this absence of respect not directly by acting contrary to his own rights but indirectly by acting as if his rights were nonexistent or insignificant. An arrogant person ignores the rights of others, thereby arrogating for himself a higher status than he is entitled to; a servile person denies his own rights, thereby assuming a lower position than he is entitled to. Whether rooted in ignorance or simply lack of concern for moral rights, the attitudes in both cases may be incompatible with a proper regard for morality. That this is so is obvious in the case of arrogance; but to see it in the case of servility requires some further argument.

IV

The objectionable feature of the servile person, as I have described him, is his tendency to disavow his own moral rights either because he misunderstands them or because he cares little for them. The question remains: why should anyone regard this as a moral defect? After all, the rights which he denies are his own. He may be unfortunate, foolish, or even distasteful; but why *morally* deficient? One sort of answer, quite different from those reviewed earlier, is suggested by some of Kant's remarks. Kant held that servility is contrary to a perfect nonjuridical duty to oneself.[4] To say that the duty is perfect is roughly to say that it is stringent, never overridden by other considerations (e.g., beneficence). To say that the duty is nonjuridical is to say that a person cannot legitimately be coerced to comply. Although Kant did not develop an explicit argument for this view, an argument can easily be constructed from materials which reflect the spirit, if not the letter, of his moral theory. The argument which I have in mind is prompted by Kant's contention that respect for persons, strictly speaking, is respect for moral law.[5] If taken as a claim about all sorts of respect, this seems quite implausible. If it means that we respect persons only for their moral character, their capacity for moral conduct, or their status as "authors" of the moral law, then it seems unduly moralistic. My strategy is to construe the remark as saying that at least one sort of respect for persons is respect for the rights which the moral law accords them. If one respects the moral law, then one must respect one's own moral rights; and this amounts to having a kind of self-respect incompatible with servility.

The premises for the Kantian argument, which are all admittedly vague, can be sketched as follows:

First, let us assume, as Kant did, that all human beings have equal basic human rights. Specific rights vary with different conditions, but all must be justified from a point of view under which all are equal. Not all rights need to be earned, and some cannot be forfeited. Many rights can be waived but only under certain conditions of knowledge and freedom. These conditions are complex and difficult to state; but they include something like the condition that a person's consent releases others from obligation only if it is autonomously given, and consent resulting from underestimation of one's moral status is not autonomously given. Rights can be objects of knowledge, but also of ignorance, misunderstanding, deception, and the like.

Second, let us assume that my account of servility is correct; or, if one prefers, we can take it as a definition. That is, in brief, a servile person is one who tends to deny or disavow his own moral rights because he does not understand them or has little concern for the status they give him.

Third, we need one formal premise concerning moral duty, namely, that each person ought, as far as possible, to respect the moral law. In less Kantian language, the point is that everyone should approximate, to the extent that he can, the ideal of a person who fully adopts the moral point of view. Roughly, this means not only that each person ought to do what is morally required and refrain from what is morally wrong but also that each person should treat all the provisions of morality as valuable—worth preserving and prizing as well as obeying. One must, so to speak, take up the spirit of morality as well as meet the letter of its requirements. To keep one's promises, avoid hurting others, and the like, is not sufficient; one should also take an attitude of respect towards the principles, ideals, and goals of morality. A respectful attitude towards a system of rights and duties consists of more than a disposition to conform to its definite rules of behavior; it also involves holding the system in esteem, being unwilling to ridicule it, and being reluctant to give up one's place in it. The essentially Kantian idea here is that morality, as a system of equal fundamental rights and duties, is worthy of respect, and hence a completely moral person would respect it in word and manner as well as in deed. And what a completely moral person would do, in Kant's view, is our duty to do so far as we can.

The assumptions here are, of course, strong ones, and I make no attempt to justify them. They are, I suspect, widely held though rarely articulated. In any case, my present purpose is not to evaluate them but to see how, if granted, they constitute a case against servility. The objection to the servile person, given our premises, is that he does not satisfy the basic requirement to respect morality. A person who fully respected a system of moral rights would be disposed to learn his proper place in it, to affirm it proudly, and not to tolerate abuses of it lightly. This is just the sort of disposition that the servile person lacks. If he does not understand the system, he is in no position to respect it adequately. This lack of respect may be no fault of his own, but it is still a way in which he falls short of a moral ideal. If, on the other hand, the servile person knowingly disavows his moral rights by pretending to approve of violations of them, then, barring special explanations, he shows an indifference to whether the provisions of morality are honored and publicly acknowledged. This avoidable display of indifference, by our Kantian premises, is contrary to the duty to respect morality. The disrespect in this second case is somewhat like the disrespect a religious believer might show towards his religion if, to avoid embarrassment, he laughed congenially while nonbelievers were mocking the beliefs which he secretly held. In any case, the servile person, as such, does not express disrespect for the system of moral rights in the obvious way by violating the rights of others. His lack of respect is more subtly manifested by his acting before others as if he did not know or care about his position of equality under that system.

The central idea here may be illustrated by an analogy. Imagine a club, say, an old German dueling fraternity. By the rules of the club, each member has certain rights and responsibilities. These are the same for each member regardless of what titles he may hold outside the club. Each has, for example, a right to be heard at meetings, a right not to be shouted down by the others. Some rights cannot be forfeited: for example, each may vote regardless of whether he has paid his dues and satisfied other rules. Some rights cannot be waived: for example, the right to be defended when attacked by several members of the rival fraternity. The members show respect for each other by respecting the status which the rules confer on each member. Now one new member is careful always to allow the others to speak at meetings; but when they

shout him down, he does nothing. He just shrugs as if to say, 'Who am I to complain?' When he fails to stand up in defense of a fellow member, he feels ashamed and refuses to vote. He does not deserve to vote, he says. As the only commoner among illustrious barons, he feels that it is his place to serve them and defer to their decisions. When attackers from the rival fraternity come at him with swords drawn, he tells his companions to run and save themselves. When they defend him, he expresses immense gratitude—as if they had done him a gratuitous favor. Now one might argue that our new member fails to show respect for the fraternity and its rules. He does not actually violate any of the rules by refusing to vote, asking others not to defend him, and deferring to the barons, but he symbolically disavows the equal status which the rules confer on him. If he ought to have respect for the fraternity, he ought to change his attitude. Our servile person, then, is like the new member of the dueling fraternity in having insufficient respect for a system of rules and ideals. The difference is that everyone ought to respect morality whereas there is no comparable moral requirement to respect the fraternity.

The conclusion here is, of course, a limited one. Self-sacrifice is not always a sign of servility. It is not a duty always to press one's rights. Whether a given act is evidence of servility will depend not only on the attitude of the agent but also on the specific nature of his moral rights, a matter not considered here. Moreover, the extent to which a person is responsible, or blameworthy, for his defect remains an open question. Nevertheless, the conclusion should not be minimized. In order to avoid servility, a person who gives up his rights must do so with a full appreciation for what they are. A woman, for example, may devote herself to her husband if she is uncoerced, knows what she is doing, and does not pretend that she has no decent alternative. A self-contemptuous person may decide not to press various unforfeited rights but only if he does not take the attitude that he is too rotten to deserve them. A black may demand less than is due to him provided he is prepared to acknowledge that no one has a right to expect this of him. Sacrifices of this sort, I suspect, are extremely rare. Most people, if they fully acknowledged their rights, would not autonomously refuse to press them.

An even stronger conclusion would emerge if we could assume that some basic rights cannot be waived. That is, if there are some rights that others are bound to respect regardless of what we say, then, barring special explanation, we would be obliged not only to acknowledge these rights but also to avoid any appearance of consenting to give them up. To act as if we could release others from their obligation to grant these rights, apart from special circumstances, would be to fail to respect morality. Rousseau held, for example, that at least a minimal right to liberty cannot be waived. A man who consents to be enslaved, giving up liberty without *quid pro quo*, thereby displays a conditioned slavish mentality that renders his consent worthless. Similarly, a Kantian might argue that a person cannot release others from the obligation to refrain from killing him: consent is no defense against the charge of murder. To accept principles of this sort is to hold that rights to life and liberty are, as Kant believed, rather like a trustee's rights to preserve something valuable entrusted to him: he has not only a right but a duty to preserve it.

Even if there are no specific rights which cannot be waived, there might be at least one formal right of this sort. This is the right to some minimum degree of respect from others. No matter how willing a person is to submit to humiliation by others, they ought to show him some respect as a person. By analogy with self-respect, as presented here, this respect owed by others would consist of a willingness to acknowledge fully, in word as well as action, the person's basically equal moral status as defined by his other rights. To the extent that a person gives even tacit consent to humiliations incompatible with this respect, he will be acting as if he waives a right which he cannot in fact give up. To do this, barring special explanations, would mark one as servile.

V

Kant held that the avoidance of servility is a duty to oneself rather than a duty to others. Recent philosophers, however, tend to discard the idea of a duty to oneself as a conceptual confusion. Although admittedly the analogy between a duty to oneself and a duty to others is not perfect, I suggest that something important is reflected in Kant's contention.

Let us consider briefly the function of saying that a duty is *to* someone. *First*, to say that a duty is *to* a given person sometimes merely indicates who is the object of that duty. That is, it tells us that the duty is concerned with how that person is to be treated, how his interests and wishes are to be taken into account, and the like. Here we might as well say that we have a duty *towards*, or *regarding* that person. Typically the person in question is the beneficiary of the fulfillment of the duty. For example, in this sense I have a duty to my children and even a duty to a distant stranger if I promised a third party that I would help that stranger. Clearly a duty to avoid servility would be a duty to oneself at least in this minimal sense, for it is a duty to avoid, so far as possible, the denial of one's own moral status. The duty is concerned with understanding and affirming one's rights, which are, at least as a rule, for one's own benefit.

Second, when we say that a duty is *to* a certain person, we often indicate thereby the person especially entitled to complain in case the duty is not fulfilled. For example, if I fail in my duty to my colleagues, then it is they who can most appropriately reproach me. Others may sometimes speak up on their behalf, but, for the most part, it is not the business of strangers to set me straight. Analogously, to say that the duty to avoid servility is a duty to oneself would indicate that, though sometimes a person may justifiably reproach himself for being servile, others are not generally in the appropriate position to complain. Outside encouragement is sometimes necessary, but, if any blame is called for, it is primarily self-recrimination and not the censure of others.

Third, mention of the person to whom a duty is owed often tells us something about the source of that duty. For example, to say that I have a duty to another person may indicate that the argument to show that I have such a duty turns upon a promise to that person, his authority over me, my having accepted special benefits from him, or, more generally, his rights. Accordingly, to say that the duty to avoid servility is a duty to oneself would at least imply that it is not entirely based upon promises to others, their authority, their beneficence, or an obligation to respect their rights. More positively, the assertion might serve to indicate that the source of the duty is one's own rights rather than the rights of others, etc. That is, one ought not to be servile because, in some broad sense, one ought to respect one's own rights as a person. There is, to be sure, an asymmetry: one has certain duties to others because one ought not to violate their rights, and one has a duty to oneself because one ought to affirm one's own rights. Nevertheless, to dismiss duties to oneself out of hand is to overlook significant similarities.

Some familiar objections to duties to oneself, moreover, seem irrelevant in the case of servility. For example, some place much stock in the idea that a person would have no duties if alone on a desert island. This can be doubted, but in any case is irrelevant here. The duty to avoid servility is a duty to take a certain stance towards others and hence would be inapplicable if one were isolated on a desert island. Again, some suggest that if there were duties to oneself then one could make promises to oneself or owe oneself a debt of gratitude. Their paradigms are familiar ones. Someone remarks, 'I promised myself a vacation this year' or 'I have been such a good boy I owe myself a treat.' Concentration on these facetious cases tends to confuse the issue. In any case the duty to avoid servility, as presented here, does not presuppose promises to oneself or debts of gratitude to oneself. Other objections stem from the intuition that a person has no duty to promote his own happiness. A duty to oneself, it is sometimes assumed, must be a duty to promote one's own happiness. From a utilitarian point of view, in fact, this is what a duty to oneself would most likely be. The problems with such alleged duties, however, are irrelevant to the duty to avoid servility. This is a duty to understand and affirm one's rights, not to promote one's own welfare. While it is usually in the interest of a person to affirm his rights, our Kantian argument against servility was not based upon this premise. Finally, a more subtle line of objection turns on the idea that, given that rights and duties are correlative, a person who acted contrary to a duty to oneself would have to be violating his own rights, which seems absurd.[6] This objection raises issues too complex to examine here. One should note, however, that I have tried to give a sense to saying that servility is contrary to a duty to oneself without presupposing that the servile person violates his own rights. If acts contrary to duties to others are always violations of their rights, then duties to oneself are not parallel with duties to others to that extent. But this does not mean that it is empty or pointless to say that a duty is to oneself.

My argument against servility may prompt some to say that the duty is "to morality" rather than "to oneself." All this means, however, is that the duty is derived from a basic requirement to respect the provisions of morality; and in this sense every duty is a duty "to morality." My duties to my children are also derivative from a general requirement to respect moral principles, but they are still duties *to* them.

Kant suggests that duties to oneself are a precondition of duties to others. On our account of servility, there is at least one sense in which this is so. Insofar as the servile person is ignorant of his own rights, he is not in an adequate position to appreciate the rights of others. Misunderstanding the moral basis for his equal status with others, he is necessarily liable to underestimate the rights of those with whom he classifies himself. On the other hand, if he plays the servile role knowingly, then, barring special explanation, he displays a lack of concern to see the principles of morality acknowledged and respected and thus the absence of one motive which can move a moral person to respect the rights of others. In either case, the servile person's lack of self-respect necessarily puts him in a less than ideal position to respect others. Failure to fulfill one's duty to oneself, then, renders a person liable to violate duties to others. This, however, is a consequence of our argument against servility, not a presupposition of it.

NOTES

1. An earlier version of this paper was presented at the meetings of the American Philosophical Association, Pacific Division. A number of revisions have been made as a result of the helpful comments of others, especially Norman Dahl, Sharon Hill, Herbert Morris, and Mary Mothersill.
2. Each of the cases is intended to represent only one possible pattern of servility. I make no claims about how often these patterns are exemplified, nor do I mean to imply that only these patterns could warrant the labels "Deferential Wife", "Uncle Tom", etc. All the more, I do not mean to imply any comparative judgments about the causes or relative magnitude of the problems of racial and sexual discrimination. One person, e.g. a self-contemptuous woman with a sense of racial inferiority, might exemplify features of several patterns at once;

and, of course, a person might view her being a woman the way an Uncle Tom views his being black, etc.
3. As will become evident, I am also presupposing some form of cognitive or "naturalistic" interpretation of rights. If, to accommodate an emotivist or prescriptivist, we set aside talk of moral knowledge and ignorance, we might construct a somewhat analogous case against servility from the point of view of those who adopt principles ascribing rights to all; but the argument, I suspect, would be more complex and less persuasive.
4. See Immanuel Kant, *The Doctrine of Virtue*, Part II of *The Metaphysics of Morals*, ed. by M. J. Gregor (New York: Harper & Row, 1964), pp. 99–103; Prussian Academy edition, Vol. VI, pp. 434–37.
5. Immanuel Kant, *Groundwork of the Metaphysics of Morals*, ed. by H. J. Paton (New York: Harper & Row, 1964), p. 69; Prussian Academy edition, Vol. IV, p. 401; *The Critique of Practical Reason*, ed. by Lewis W. Beck (New York: Bobbs-Merrill, 1956), pp. 81, 84; Prussian Academy edition, Vol. V, pp. 78, 81. My purpose here is not to interpret what Kant meant but to give a sense to his remark.
6. This, I take it, is part of M. G. Singer's objection to duties to oneself in *Generalization in Ethics* (New York: Alfred A. Knopf, 1961), pp. 311–318. I have attempted to examine Singer's arguments in detail elsewhere.

Rawlsian Self-Respect and the Black Consciousness Movement

Laurence M. Thomas

One of the most important effects of what is called the Black Consciousness Movement is thought to be the enhancement of the self-respect of blacks. But surprisingly enough, the analysis of self-respect which we find in John Rawls' book, *A Theory of Justice,* cannot account for the fact that this is so.[1] And consider the case of the famed black educator Booker T. Washington. Although it is undoubtedly true that few blacks of his time ever attained his prominence, it is not, however, a *foregone* conclusion that he was not an uncle tom, and so that he failed to have self-respect.[2] But according to the Rawlsian analysis of self-respect, we could have no reason to suppose that Washington lacked self-respect, given his prominence. As these brief remarks would suggest, I think that Rawls' analysis of self-respect is defective. And as I hope to show, this is so because Rawls has failed to distinguish between self-respect and self-esteem.

Now the distinction between self-respect and self-esteem, while often overlooked by philosophers, is one which psychologists frequently make and which, to some extent, is reflected in ordinary discourse.[3] For instance, the distinguishing characteristic of an uncle tom, or servile persons generally, is said to be a lack of self-respect, and not self-esteem. And we do not say "No self-esteeming person would do such-and-such," but rather "No self-respecting person would do such-and-such." To be noted, also, is that we can esteem persons only for (what we take to be) their accomplishments or abilities. There is no such thing as esteeming a person just because he or she is a person. But we can respect persons just because they are persons. There seems to be a sense in which we can respect all persons equally—the rich, the poor, the talented, and so on.

At any rate, I suspect that one reason why the distinction between self-respect and self-esteem often escapes us is that both concepts have to do with a person's sense of worth: a person with self-respect has a sense of worth, and so has a person with self-esteem. What is the nature of the difference between these two senses of worth? I hope to provide a satisfactory answer to this question as I attempt to show that what we have in *A Theory of Justice* is not an account of self-respect, but self-esteem instead.

Rawls defines self-respect (self-esteem) as having the conviction that one's plan of life is worthwhile (178, 440). And according to Rawls, one comes to have this conviction in two ways: (1) by having a rational plan of life which satisfies the Aristotelian Principle, and (2) by finding one's person and deeds appreciated and confirmed by people whose association one enjoys and who are likewise esteemed (440). A rational plan of life is to be understood in the way that rational planning is traditionally thought of. For Rawls remarks that it is "... the plan that would be decided upon as the outcome of careful reflection in which the agent reviewed, in the light of all the relevant facts, what it would be like to carry out these plans and thereby ascertained the course of action that would best realize his more fundamental desires" (417).

The Aristotelian Principle reads as follows:

Source: Laurence M. Thomas, "Rawlsian Self-Respect and the Black Consciousness Movement," Used with the permission of the author.

other things equal, human beings enjoy the exercise of their realized capabilities (their innate or trained abilities), and this enjoyment increases the more the capacity is realized, or the greater its complexity (426).

And the Aristotelian Principle has what Rawls refers to as the companion effect which is that

As we witness the exercise of well-trained abilities of others, these displays are enjoyed by us and arouse a desire that we should be able to do the same things ourselves. We want to be like those persons who can exercise the abilities that we find latent in nature (428).

Now the important things to bear in mind regarding Rawls' (so-called) theory of self-respect is that (1) and (2) are not independent of each other. Rather, (2) holds true of a person only if (1) holds true of that person's plan of life. Although Rawls does not say this explicitly, it seems clear that we should understand (1) and (2) in this way, given the various remarks which he makes throughout *A Theory of Justice*.

Our self-respect, Rawls maintains, depends upon the respect of those with whom we associate (178, 441f). If this is so, then the obvious question to ask is "When are those with whom we associate disposed to respect us?" The answer, it appears, is that our associates are disposed to respect us when they see that our plan of life satisfies the Aristotelian Principle, that is, when they witness the well-trained abilities which our plan of life displays. For as the companion effect would suggest, when others witness these abilities, they come to judge that our plan of life is worthwhile. And for others, in particular our associates, to judge that our plan of life is worthwhile is for them to respect us. For Rawls thinks of a person as a human life lived according to a plan (408). These considerations would seem to indicate that, as I have remarked, (1) and (2) are not independent of one another. What is more, it should be obvious, given just these considerations, that the Aristotelian Principle and its companion effect are the backbone of what Rawls presents as a theory of self-respect.

Now the Aristotelian Principle is relative to the abilities of persons. Thus for any two persons S and N, it does not follow from the fact that S and N have similar plans of life, that their plans equally satisfy the Aristotelian Principle. For if the abilities and talents of S far exceed those of N, then although they are in pursuit of similar plans of life, S's plan will satisfy the Aristotelian Principle to a lesser extent than N's plan. For S's plan will not realize the abilities of S to the fullest extent.

Since the Aristotelian Principle is relative to the abilities of persons, Rawls seems to think that all persons can have the secure conviction that their plan of life is worthwhile. But not so. Consider two plans of life K and J. And suppose that K, on the one hand, is such that all persons have the ability, and know that they have it, to pursue K. On the other hand, suppose that J is a plan of life which most lack, and know that they lack, the ability to pursue. Given the Aristotelian Principle and its companion effect, only persons who successfully pursue the J plan of life are the ones who should have a more secure conviction of the worth of their plan of life. For they are the ones whose plan of life will exhibit the well-trained abilities which others lack, and so have their plan judged to be more worthwhile by others. For by hypothesis, the K plan of life is such that everyone knows that they could successfully pursue it if only they should try. Thus, in contrast to the J plan of life, the K plan will appear less attractive to persons.

Now Rawls would like to think that it does not matter that some persons are able to pursue plans of life which are beyond the reach of others, so long as each person can find an association of persons which affirms the plan of life that he or she pursue (441). But as Rawls' further explanatory remarks make clear, what is meant is this: It does not matter that some persons are able to pursue plans of life which are beyond the reach of others, so long as each person associates with those whose abilities are similar to their own[4] For in so doing, a person does not, so Rawls would like to think, see the plan which she pursues as lacking in worth. But is Rawls' contention here sound? I think not.[5]

For we are not oblivious to the abilities of people around us. We can see that others have abilities which we and those with whom we associate lack. And although each person amongst a group of associates may feel, given his or [her] plan of life, that her abilities equal those of any other member of the group, it may be symptomatic of the group itself that each member, in contrast to the plans of life of non-members, views her abilities to be very minimal. Moreover, what about persons whose abilities are extremely minimal? Is the answer to their having a secure conviction of the worth of their plan of life, and so their self-respect, that they associate with only those whose abilities are equally minimal? Surely not!

Now as my discussion of Rawls' account of self-respect should make clear, it is mere wishful thinking to suppose that the self-respect of all persons can be equal, if self-respect consists in having the conviction that one's plan of life is worthwhile. But is the sense of worth thus grounded that which we should want to call self-respect? As I think the case of Booker T. Washington and the Black Consciousness Movement will show, the answer to this question is a negative one.

As I have already remarked, few blacks ever attained the prominence of Booker T. Washington, who lived during his life time. As a black who founded an educational institution, the Tuskegee Institute, and who was consulted by virtually everyone concerning monetary appropriations to blacks,[6] Washington surely had to have the conviction that his plan of life was worthwhile. For he was universally esteemed for his accomplishments. Few blacks, and for that matter, few whites could boast of similar accomplishments for which they also were universally esteemed. And so if (1) in finding our person and deeds appreciated by those with whom we associate we come to have the conviction that our plan of life is worthwhile, and (2) in having this conviction we thereby have the sense of worth which constitutes self-respect, then it should be a settled question that Washington was not an uncle tom, and so failed to have self-respect, since on any one's account Washington stands as one of the most esteemed blacks of

his time. But it is not a settled question as to whether or not Washington was an uncle tom. For his famed "Atlanta Exposition Address" renders Washington vulnerable to the view that he was an uncle tom.[7]

Of course, I do not mean to say that Washington was an uncle tom. Rather, I claim only that it is not a *foregone* conclusion that he was not one. And if this is so, then either (1) or (2) of the preceding paragraph is false. (1) is surely not false, thus it follows that (2) is false.

Turning now to the Black Consciousness Movement (BCM), one of the most important changes which came about as a result of this movement was a change in blacks' self-description from "colored" or "Negro" to "black". Of course, there were other changes as well.[8] But I shall take the change in blacks' self-description as indicative of the fact that the self-respect of blacks was enhanced as a result of the BCM. But is this so because blacks came to pursue more worthwhile plans of life, as Rawls' account of self-respect would have us to say? Clearly not.

The change from "colored" or "Negro" to "black" has a significance which cannot be fully explained by the fact that blacks came to pursue more worthwhile plans of life. To be sure, many blacks did come to pursue more worthwhile plans as the governmental, educational, and business institutions of America began to hire blacks for their more status positions. And there is no question but that the increased appreciation of many aspects of the black culture by the American society has made it possible for many blacks to pursue more worthwhile plans. The increased appreciation of music generally characterized as "soul" music proves to be the most striking example of this.[9] But the plans of many blacks remained unchanged with respect to their worth. That is to say, many blacks who pursued a plan of life of little worth proper to the BCM did not come to pursue a plan of greater worth as a result of the BCM. Yet one thing seems clear: The BCM enhanced the self-respect of not only those blacks who came to pursue a more worthwhile plan of life, but of those who did not as well.

The change in blacks' self-description, then, was not indicative of the fact that they came to pursue more worthwhile plans of life, though many in fact did. Rather, it indicated a more fundamental change, namely, a change in the way blacks came to view themselves as persons *qua* persons. For the BCM was a rejection of a conception of persons according to which to have a certain pigmentation of the skin was *ipso facto* to be less worthy of the rights and liberties to which other members of the American society had been so long accustomed. The adoption of the self-description of "black" serves to indicate that blacks came to view themselves in this way. And it is in so coming to view themselves that, as a result of the BCM, the self-respect of blacks was enhanced.

Together, the case of Booker T. Washington and the BCM show that having a plan of life which is worthwhile, and hence one that satisfies the Aristotelian Principle, is neither a necessary nor sufficient condition for having self-respect. And if this is right, then the sense of worth which Rawls calls self-respect is not that at all. As I remarked earlier, I want to say that what Rawls calls self-respect is self-esteem instead. And to say this is not simply to make a dogmatic assertion. For as I have noted, we esteem persons for their accomplishments and abilities. And it should be clear from my discussion of Rawls that, in the last analysis, his account of self-respect turns upon persons being esteemed for just these things. For to have the conviction that one's plan of life is worthwhile is to have a sense of worth with respect to one's accomplishments and abilities. Given that the sense of worth thus grounded is that which is properly called self-esteem, this much is evident: Self-esteem is not a sense of worth which we are justified in having in virtue of the fact that we are persons.[10]

Turning now to self-respect, it is perhaps obvious from my remarks concerning the BCM that I want to say that self-respect is a sense of worth which we are justified in having in virtue of the fact that we are persons. Moreover, though, I want to say that it is a sense of worth which should be equal among persons. But what aspect of persons can serve as the basis for this sense of worth? The answer, I believe, is the moral status of persons.

An obvious, though far from trivial, fact about the world is that not every thing in the world has the same moral status. The moral status of some things, most notably those which are inorganic, is nil. One can do no moral wrong to a book lying on the side of the road. It has no rights, nor are there duties or obligations owed to it. To be sure, a moral wrong is done when, in the absence of permission to do so, a person wilfully destroys a book knowing that it belongs to someone else. But the moral wrong done in this case is to the person to whom the book belongs, and not to the book itself.

Sentient animals which are non-human have, so it would appear, partial moral status. For at the very minimum, it may be said that persons have a moral duty not to treat such animals cruelly. Some, in fact, would want to say that such animals have a moral right not to be treated cruelly. I shall not enter the dispute as to whether or not animals have moral rights. Suffice it to note, however, that the so-called moral rights of animals are conceptually predicated upon the fact that persons exist. For it is all but absurd to speak of non-human animals as exercising or acting within their rights. Consider also that if, as happened during the Mesozioc era, there were animals but not persons, it would certainly be out of place to speak of animals as having a right not to be treated cruelly. And even though animals are said to violate the territorial space of others or defend their own, we do not countenance these activities as the violation or defense of rights of any kind.

Finally, there are those living things, namely persons, which have full moral status. Their full moral status is evidenced by the following: First, the moral rights of persons and the duties which persons have towards one another are not conceptually predicated upon the existence of any other *form of life*; and secondly, the moral duties which persons have toward any other living things are a subset of the moral duties which persons have towards one another. And this remark holds *mutatis mutandis* with respect to non-human animals having moral rights, if indeed this is so.

Now it is clear that the moral status of a thing determines, in part at least, the modes of conduct towards it which are proper. It is precisely the fact that a piece of wood has no moral status at all that one can do no moral wrong to it, however one treats it. Similarly, it is because sentient but non-human animals have some moral status that it is not morally wrong to kill them for the purposes of food, although it is morally wrong to inflict needless pain upon them. And, finally, it is just the difference between the moral status of non-human animals and that of persons in virtue of which it is morally wrong to treat persons as mere property which can be bought and sold for labor, but not non-human animals.

Now on my view the sense of worth which is properly called self-respect is grounded in the fact that persons have full moral status. Self-respect, I want to say, consists in having the belief that one has and is worthy of full moral status. And to believe this is to believe that one is as worthy as any other person of the set of moral rights to the the recognition of which persons are entitled. At this point there are two questions which immediately arise: (1) In virtue of what is it that persons are worthy of full moral status? And (2) What are the moral rights of which persons are worthy? I shall discuss these questions in turn.

To our first question, the answer, I believe, is that persons are worthy of full moral status in virtue of the fact that they are self-conscious beings. I shall not attempt to fully vindicate this reply here; instead, I shall offer a few considerations which indicate that it points in the right direction. We may think of a self-conscious being as one which has a concept of itself as a continuing subject of experiences and other mental status, along with the belief that it is such a being. It is one which as the capacity (a) to identify with the past, present, and future stages of itself, and (b) to formulate and execute long-term plans of action.[11]

Now it seems that moral systems can address themselves only to beings who have this capacity, since a fundamental characteristic of moral systems is what we may refer to as temporal indifference: If at time t, R is a moral reason for doing act A in circumstances C, then (other things being equal) (i) R is also a moral reason for doing A in C at some future time, and (ii) R was also a moral reason for doing A in C in times past.[12]

Accordingly, a being with full moral status must be one who has the capacity (a) to recognize that a reason which presently applies to it for doing act A in circumstances C can be, as in the case of moral systems it is (other things equal) a reason which will apply to it in the future for doing A in C, and (b) to formulate and execute long-term plans of action accordingly. This is something that self-conscious beings can do. But what is more, it seems that it is precisely among self-conscious beings that morality is possible. These considerations do not, of course, show that self-consciousness is a sufficient ground for having full moral status. But in offering these considerations my aim has been only to indicate that as a sufficient ground for having full moral status, self-consciousness points in the right direction. I should like to think that at least this much has been accomplished.

I now take up the issue of the moral rights of which persons are worthy in virtue of the fact that they are persons. To begin with, it should be clear that such rights are not, to adopt H.L.A. Hart's terminology, special moral rights.[13] For these are rights which rise out of special transactions between individuals, as in the case of promising; and so they cannot be the sort of rights which we have in virtue of the fact that we are persons. But needless to say, it would hardly be informative to say simply that the moral rights of which persons are worthy *qua* person are non-special rights, in the absence of an enumeration of such rights. Yet, aside from the so-called natural rights, it is anything but obvious as to what a complete list of such rights would look like. Fortunately, though, my view of self-respect is in no way affected by this difficulty.

True enough, I want to say that self-respect consists in having the belief that one is worthy of one's moral rights in virtue of the fact that one is a person. But from this it does not follow that a person has self-respect if and only if he knows what all the moral rights of persons are, and therefore his own moral rights. For having self-respect is not so much the ability to give a run down of what one's moral rights happen to be, as it is a conviction of one's standing in the moral community.[14] Differently put, then, we may say that to have self-respect is to have the belief that one is a member of good standing in the moral community in virtue of the fact that one is a person. And although this belief entails the belief that for any non-special moral right M, one is worthy of M, it does not call for knowing what all the non-special moral rights happen to be.

I want now to bring into sharper focus the connection between my view of self-respect and the BCM. Although self-respect pertains to our moral status, we must not lose sight of the fact that it is amongst social institutions that we live, that we are members of a society. And as others have noted, the view that we have of ourselves is fundamentally influenced by these institutions. This is no less so in regard to our moral status. The social institutions in which we live can either sustain or undermine the view that we have full moral status, that we are members of good standing in the moral community, in virtue of the fact that we are persons. As one might suspect, I want to say that a society does the former when and only when the grounds for being a member of good standing in that society are co-extensive with the grounds for being a member of good standing in the moral community, which is that one is a person. This means, then, that the basic rights and liberties of society are to be distributed equally.

Now as one has no doubt noted, the very claim which Rawls makes in *A Theory of Justice* is that the equal distribution of basic rights and liberties sustain the self-respect of persons (sec. 82). But he thinks that this is so because such a distribution affirms the worth of each person's plan of life. For what he should like to think is that the self-respect of each person is secured in virtue of the fact that each has the conviction that she is free to pursue her plan of life, whatever its end may be.[15]

But the equal distribution of rights and liberties does not affirm the worth of the plans of life which persons pursue. That is to say, the knowledge that one is free to pursue one's plan of life whatever its end may be is not sufficient for one to also have the conviction that one's plan of life is worthwhile. If all that one can do well is sweep floors, the knowledge that one is guaranteed the freedom to do this will not in itself result in one also having the conviction that one's plan of life—that of floor sweeping—is worthwhile. At least this is so in societies of the Western Culture, where ends such as the arts and sciences and the high forms of culture are more highly valued. Moreover, as I have already shown, it is a consequence of the Aristotelian Principle and its companion effect that a person whose plan of life exhibits the greater and more subtle number of well-trained abilities is the person who will have a more secure conviction of the worth of his plan of life. And between a floor sweeper and a symphony conductor, say, it is clear whose plan of life is more subtle and calls for the greater number of well-trained abilities. Presumably any (healthy) person could be an excellent floor sweeper, if only they should try; though not so with symphony conducting.

What is more, if (1) the equal distribution of rights and liberties were to suffice for persons to have the conviction that their plan of life is worthwhile, then why is (2) having a plan of life which satisfies the Aristotelian Principle a necessary condition for having a plan of life which is worthwhile? Either (1) or (2) is true, but not both. It is obvious, I believe, that (2) is true, at least in general.

The equal distribution of basic rights and liberties does indeed affirm the self-respect of persons. For, as I should like to think, it is the only way in which society can affirm the fact that each person is a being with full moral status in virtue of the fact that he or she is a person. The Black Consciousness Movement supports this view.

For slavery and racism in America has been a deliberate and systematic denial to blacks the rights and liberties to which others in America have been so long accustomed. As a result of the Black Consciousness Movement, we did not all come to regard ourselves as brilliant. Nor, again, did we all suddenly discover talents which were hitherto latent in us. These things could never have been accomplished by the Black Consciousness Movement as such. Rather, we came to believe that, our blackness to the contrary notwithstanding, we were worthy of first-class citizenship in the American society. And on my view, to believe this is, in part, what it means to have self-respect.[16]

NOTES

1. Belknap Press, 1971. All parenthetical page references are to this text. I give an account of the Black Consciousness Movement later on in the essay.

   This paper is an attempt to spell out some of the practical implications of the distinction between self-respect and self-esteem as I have drawn it in my "Morality and Our Self-Concept," *The Journal of Value Inquiry*, v. 12 (1978). For implications of a different sort, see my "Marxism versus Capitalism: A Psychological Discussion," *Studies in Soviet Thought* 20 (1979).
2. See Booker T. Washington's *Up From Slavery: An Autobiography*, (Doubleday and Co., 1901). It is Washington's Atlanta address which makes him so vulnerable to the label uncle tom. See note 7 below.
3. For example, see Stanley Coopersmith, *The Antecedents of Self-Esteem*, (W.H. Freeman and Co., 1967), p. 26; Karen Horney, *New Ways in Psychoanalysis*, (W. W. Norton and Co., 1939), ch. 5 especially;————, *Self-Analysis*, (W.W. Norton and Co., 1942), pp. 43f.; Robert W. White, "Ego and Reality in Psychoanalytic Theory," *Psychological Issues*, v. 3 (1963), Monograph 11; and Albert Bandura, "Self-efficacy: Toward a Unifying Theory of Behavioral Change," *Psychological Review*, v. 84 (1977).
4. Rawls writes: "It is our plan of life that determines what we feel ashamed of, and so feelings of shame are relative to our aspirations, to what we try to do and with whom we wish to associate. Those with no musical ability do not strive to be musicians and feel no shame for this lack. Indeed it is no lack at all, not at least if satisfying associations can be formed by doing other things" (444).

5. This criticism of Rawls' account of self-respect is developed more fully in the "Morality and Our Self-Concept" paper mentioned in note 1 above, See Section I.
6. On this point, see John Hope Franklin, *From Slavery to Freedom*, (Vintage Books, 1947), ch. 21, and Charles E. Silberman, *Crisis in Black and White*, (Vintage Books, 1964), pp. 125ff.
7. In his "Atlanta Exposition Address," Washington emphasized the importance of industrial education for blacks, rather than their obtaining the suffrage. Thus for him, the political and civil status of blacks were, on the face of it at any rate, of secondary importance. Indeed, in this address, Washington implies that the suffrage was something of which blacks should have to become worthy. Consider the following passages:

   No race can prosper till it learns that there is as much dignity in tilling a field as in writing a poem. It is at the bottom of life we must begin, and not at the top.... In all things that are purely social we can be as separate as the fingers, yet one as the hand in all things essential to mutual progress.... It is important and right that all privileges of the law be ours, but it is *vastly more important* that we be prepared for the exercises of these privileges.

   Of course, as John Hope Franklin observes, *op. cit.*, p. 395, weaknesses in Washington's views may seem more obvious today than they were then. All the same, it should be noted that not all of Washington's black contemporaries viewed his Atlanta speech favorably. Most notably, W.E.B. Du Bois thought Washington's speech to be a call for compromise and submission. See Du Bois' *The Soul of Black Folks*, (A.C. McClurgh, 1903), pp. 41–59.
8. As the expressions "I'm black and I'm proud" and "Black is beautiful" would indicate, from the standpoint of physical appearance, blacks no longer thought of their not possessing white features as a lack on their part. The standards of white beauty simply no longer applied. And as blacks, we came to take greater pride in various aspects of our culture.
9. See, for example, Maureen Orth, "Stevie, The Wonder Man," *Newsweek*, (October 28, 1974), pp. 59–65. She writes: "It was American black music that provided the inspiration—and often the music itself—for the explosion of white-dominated rock in the '50s and '60s. But with the rare exception... , it was white stars who got the big money and the white audiences. Now the sheer creative power of black

music has pushed it into the mainstream...
Today the color line is almost completely
erased, and the record charts are studded with
black names and groups."
10. The concept of self-esteem is far more complex than my remarks would indicate. Aside
from our abilities and accomplishments, another factor is the ends which we value. The
successful pursuit of a given end will be a
source of self-esteem to us only if we value that
end itself. And as I have remarked in my "Capitalism versus Marxism" essay, cited in note 1
above, there is also the factor of what I have
called derivative self-esteem. Suppose that 0 is
an end which is valued by society at large, and
that as it happens persons most successful at
pursuing 0 are of kind K. If the association of
end 0 with people of kind K becomes strong
enough, then being of kind K can itself suffice
to enhance one's self-esteem. The most striking example of derivative self-esteem is the
self-esteem which often stems from being a
member of a high socio-economic class. See S.
Coopersmith, *op. cit.*, pp. 82f.; and M.D. Vernon, *Human Motivation*, (Cambridge University Press, 1969), pp. 132f. This is the point
which I believe Thomas Nagel to be making in
his "Rawls on Justice," *The Philosophical Review*,
v. 82 (1973), note 6.

11. For a fuller account of self-respect, see my
"Morality and Our Self-Concept," Section II.
12. Here I borrow from Thomas Nagel, *The Possibility of Altruism*, (Clarendon Press, 1970), p.
58, and Michael Tooley, "Abortion and Infanticide," (Princeton University Press, 1973), pp.
52–84. Against Tooley, though, I want to say
that a being's having the potential for these
capacities *is* a morally relevant consideration.
See my "Human Potentiality: Its Moral Relevance," *The Personalist*, v. 59 (1978).
13. Henry Sidgwick makes this point in *The
Method of Ethics*, 7th ed., pp. 31, 207, 379. Each
in section 3 of their respective books and
chapters.
14. "Are There Any Natural Rights," *The Philosophical Review,* v. 64 (1955).
15. Here I am much indebted to the essays of
Thomas E. Hill Jr., "Servility and Self-Respect," *The Monist*, v. 57 (1973), and Gregory
Vlastos, "Justice and Equality," in ed. Richard
B. Brandt, *Social Justice*, (Prentice Hall, Inc.
1962), pp. 31–72.
16. The proviso is that a person's plan of life conform to the principles of justice as fairness.
17. I wish to thank Irving Thalberg and Newton
Garver for commenting upon the penultimate
draft of this essay.

Self-Respect and Protest

Bernard R. Boxill

Must a person protest his wrongs? Booker T. Washington and W.E.B. Du Bois debated this question at the turn of the century. They did not disagree over whether protesting injustice was an effective way to right it, but over whether protesting injustice, when one could do nothing to right it oneself, was self-respecting. Washington felt that it was not. Thus, he did not deny that protest could help ameliorate conditions or that it was sometimes justified; what he did deny was that a person should keep protesting wrongs committed against him when he could not take decisive steps to end them. By insisting on "advertising his wrongs" in such cases, he argued, a person betrayed a weakness for relying, not on his "own efforts" but on the "sympathy" of others. Washington's position was that if a person felt wronged, he should do something about it; if he could do nothing he should hold his tongue and wait his opportunity; protest in such cases is only a servile appeal for sympathy; stoicism, by implication, is better. Du Bois strongly contested these views. Not only did he deny that protest is an appeal for sympathy, he maintained that if a person failed to express openly his outrage at injustice, however assiduously he worked against it, he would in the long run lose his self-respect. Thus, he asserted that Washington faced a "paradox" by insisting both on "self-respect" and on "a silent submission to civic inferiority,"[1] and he declared that "only in a ... persistent demand for essential equality ... can any people show ... a decent self-respect."[2] Like Frederick Douglass, he concluded that people should protest their wrongs. In this essay I shall expand upon and defend Du Bois' side of the

debate. I shall argue that persons have reason to protest their wrongs not only to stop injustice but also to show self-respect and to know themselves as self-respecting.

Washington's detractors charge that his depreciation of protest was appeasement; his defenders maintain that it was prudence. Detractors and defenders therefore agree that black protest would have been a provocation to the white South. A provocation arouses an individual's resentment because it challenges his moral claim to a status he enjoys and wants to preserve, thus black protest would have challenged the white South's justification of the superior status it claimed. Washington did not disapprove of every attempt to effect greater justice, he rejected protest in particular. Thus his frequent efforts to urge America to reform were consistent with his position. Since his remonstrations were received considerately, and not at all as provocation or protest, they must have avoided making the kind of challenge protest presumably presents. Therefore, an analysis of them should suggest what protest is.

Washington always failed to press the claim that black people are victims of America's racial injustice. He frequently implied, and sometimes stated explicitly, that the white perpetrators of injustice were economically and, especially, morally the people most hurt and maimed by racial injustice and that, by comparison, the black victims of injustice suffered only "temporary inconvenience."[3] From this kind of reasoning it is easy to conclude that the morally compelling ground for reform is to save, not so much the victims of injustice, but its perpetrators because their "degradation" places them in greatest need.

The notion that because it implies guilt and ultimately moral degradation, inflicting injustice is a greater evil than suffering it is, of course, part of the Christian tradition and be-

Source: Bernard R. Boxill, "Self-Respect and Protest," © 1976 by Princeton University Press. Reprinted by permission.

fore that, the Socratic. Washington seems, however, to be one of the few to use it as an argument for social reform. Whether he really believed it is completely irrelevant. What is pertinent is that this was the consideration he thought prudent to present to America and that he hoped would be efficacious in motivating reform. This consideration, though urged insistently, did not arouse resentment. America, apparently did not mind being accused of degradation—as long as its affairs, its advancement, and its moral salvation remained the center of moral concern. For, as I have indicated, Washington did explicitly draw the conclusion that the morally compelling ground for reform was the moral salvation of white America.[4]

The idea that being a perpetrator is worse than being a victim is, of course, true in the sense that the person guilty of perpetrating injustice is morally worse than the person who must endure it. But, it does not follow from this that the perpetrator of injustice suffers greater evil than his victim or that the ground for seeking justice is to save the unjust man. As I have argued in another essay, such a position can be maintained only if the victim has no rights. For, if the victim has rights then the perpetrator's duty is not to avoid degrading himself but to respect those rights. To claim that the victim of injustice has rights is thus to challenge the transgressor's arrogant assumption that his own advancement, economic or moral, is the sole legitimate object of social policy. Washington never challenged white America's assumption that its advancement justified the reform he advocated, because he never claimed that black Americans had rights. Black protest would have affirmed that they do.

Because protest emphasizes the wrongs of the victim and declares that redress is a matter of the highest urgency, a person who insistently protests against his own condition may seem to be self-centered and self-pitying. He appears to dwell self-indulgently on his grievances and to be seeking the commiseration of others. Washington, for example, criticized Frederick Douglass for constantly reminding black people of "their sufferings"[5] and sus-

pected that persistent protesters relied on "the special sympathy of the world" rather than on "their own efforts."[6] This is an important charge since the self-respecting person is self-reliant and avoids self-pity. It is not answered by the claim that people have rights, for having rights does not necessarily justify constant reiteration that one has them. The charge is answered, however, by a closer consideration of what is involved in claiming a right. The idea that the protester seeks sympathy is unlikely, since in claiming his rights he affirms that he is claiming what he can demand and exact, and sympathy cannot be demanded and exacted. The idea that the protester is self-pitying is likewise implausible, since a person who feels pity for himself typically believes that his condition is deplorable and unavoidable, and this is not all what the protester affirms. On the contrary, he affirms that his condition is avoidable, he insists that what he protests is precisely the illegitimate, and hence avoidable, interference by others in the exercise of his rights, and he expresses the sentiment, not of self-pity, but of resentment. Protest could be self-indulgent if it were a demand for help, and it could show a lack of self-reliance if it claimed powerlessness. But, in insisting on his rights, the protestor neither demands help nor claims powerlessness. He demands only noninterference. What Frederick Douglass protested against, for example, was interference. He scorned supererogatory help. "Do nothing with us," he exclaimed, "And, if the Negro cannot stand on his own legs, let him fall."[7]

It follows from the above that when a person protests his wrongs, he expresses a righteous and self-respecting concern for himself. If, as we assume, the self-respecting person has such a concern for himself, it follows that he will naturally be inclined to protest his injuries. Would he always have good reason actually to give vent to his indignation? Protest, it seems, is the response of the weak. It is not a warning of retaliation. The strong man does not waste too much time protesting his injuries; he prevents them. Why then should the weak, but self-respecting, person protest his wrongs? Surely if either protest or whining will prevent injury, the self-respecting person will protest rather than whine. For protest is self-respecting. Though it cannot compel the transgressor to reform, it tells him that he should be compelled to reform and that he is being asked no favors. But, if as Washington's defenders aver, protest often provokes persecution, why should a weak and vulnerable people protest? What good could it do? If it will help, why can't a self-respecting people pretend servility? But it seems that people do protest their wrongs, even when it is clear that this will bring no respite and, instead, cause them further injury. W.E.B. Du Bois exhorted black people, "even when bending to the inevitable," to "bend with unabated protest."[8] Is this mere bravado? Or does a person with self-respect have a reason to protest over and above the hope that it will bring relief?

It may be argued that he does; that he should protest to make others recognize that he has rights. But, though a person who believes he has a right not to be unjustly injured also believes that others wrong him if they injure him unjustly and that they should be restrained from doing so, it is not clear that he must want them to share his conviction that he has this right. Why should he care what they believe? Why, just because he believes that he has a right, should he desire that others share his belief? There is no reason to suppose that the self-respecting person must want others to believe what he believes. Though he believes that the morally respectable ground for not injuring him is that he has a right not to be injured, it does not follow that he must want others to act on morally respectable grounds. Self-respect is a morally desirable quality but the self-respecting person need not be a saint. He need not want to make others moral. To this it may be objected that he nevertheless has a good reason to convince others of his rights, because the surest and most stable protection from unjust injury is for others to be restrained by solid moral convictions. This may be true. But it does not show that a person will want others to respect him just because he respects himself. Even the person who fails to respect himself may want the surest and most stable protection from unjust injury, and thus may want others to respect him. And, in general, for the protection of his rights, the self-respecting person cannot depend too heavily on the moral restraint of others. His self-reliance impels him to seek the means of self-defense. Secure in the conviction that it is legitimate to defend himself, he is satisfied if others respect him because they fear him.

Alternately, it may be proposed that the self-respecting person will want others to respect him because he wants to remain self-respecting. For unopposed injustice invites its victims to believe that they have no value and are without rights. This confident invitation may make even the self-respecting fear that their sense of their own value is only prejudiced self-love. It may therefore be argued that since protest is an affirmation of the rights of the victim, the self-respecting victim of injustice will protest to make others recognize, and in that way reassure him, that he has rights. Frederick Douglass, for example, once referred to this acknowledgment as the "all important confession."[9] But, though the self-respecting need to reassure themselves that they have rights, they would disdain this kind of reassurance. It is inappropriate because unanimous acknowledgment of a proposition does not imply its truth but only that everyone avows it. It is not self-respecting because it shows a lack of self-reliance. The self-respecting person cannot be satisfied to depend on the opinions of others. This is not to question the proposition that it is difficult to believe what everyone denies and easy to believe what everyone affirms. It is to say that, even while he concedes this, the self-respecting person will want to have his conviction of his worth rationally based.

But it is not clear that the self-respecting person has good reason to protest, even if he does want others to respect him. Washington, for example, understood that social acknowledgment was important but condemned protest. He argued that to be acknowledged as worthy citizens black people would do better to develop the qualities and virtues that would make them economically valuable members of society. Washington was right.

For though protest is an uncompromising claim that the victim of some injury has a right not to be injured, it does not follow that protest is therefore a likely way of getting others to agree. To affirm something, no matter how sincerely and passionately, may be an indifferent way of persuading others of it. And protest is, essentially, an affirmation that a victim of injury has rights. It is not an argument for that position. Typically, people protest when the time for argument and persuasion is past. They insist, as Du Bois put it, that the claim they protest is "an outrageous falsehood,"[10] and that it would be demeaning to argue and cajole for what is so plain. Responding to a newspaper article that claimed "The Negro" was "Not a Man," Frederick Douglass disdainfully declared, "I cannot, however, argue, I must assert."[11]

It may be objected that though protest is not plausibly designed to persuade others that the victim of some injury has value or rights, it is designed to compel them to acknowledge that he is a moral being. This issue is raised by Orlando Patterson in his essay "Toward a Future that has no Past."[12] Speaking of a slave's stealing as "an assertion of moral worth"—that is, as protest—Patterson points out that by screaming, "You are a thief," the master admits that the slave is a moral being, since it is in the act of punishing him as a thief that the master most emphatically avows the slave to be a moral being. If the slave's stealing is indeed an act of protest then, as I have indicated, protest need not be designed to promote conciliation. Further, since what the slave wants to hear is that he is a thief, his aim is surely not to be acknowledged as an economically valuable asset but as a being who is responsible for his acts. Finally, though this concession is made loudly and publicly and, by all accounts, sincerely, it is nevertheless absurd and paradoxical. For though the master calls the slave a thief, and thus a moral being, he continues to treat him as a piece of property. Still, it may seem that the slave wins a victory. At least, even if it is painful, he enjoys the satisfaction of forcing a most unwilling agent to treat him as a moral being. This argument has considerable force.

For a self-respecting person no doubt desires to be treated as a moral being. But it is not clear that a master must, in consistency, deny that a slave is a moral being. If he wants to justify himself, what he must deny is that the slave has rights. And, even if to be consistent he must deny that the slave is a moral being, it is not clear that the slave can always get the master to call him "thief." Or, even if he does, it is not clear that the master must admit that he uses the word in any but an analogical sense. And, it is not true that property cannot be punished without absurdity. Animals, for example, are routinely punished without absurdity and with no implication that they are anything but property.

It may finally be argued that affirming one's rights may be necessary to keeping the sense of one's value simply because doing so is an essential part of having self-respect. This must first be qualified. It may be false that one believes that one has rights. Thus, since lying cannot be an essential part of anything valuable, merely affirming that one has rights cannot, without qualification, be essential to keeping the sense of one's value. The argument must therefore be that protest is necessary to keeping the sense of one's value if one believes that one has rights. But why should one affirm what one believes, however deeply and firmly one believes it? To this it may be proposed that the self-respecting person wishes to seem to be what he is; he is, we may say, authentic. But, though authenticity may be a virtue, it is not clear why the self-respecting person must be authentic. To say that someone has self-respect is certainly not to say that he has all the virtues. Further, it is not evident that authenticity is necessarily one of the qualities that the self-respecting person believes to be valuable about himself. Neither is it clear, without further argument, that the self-respecting person's authenticity can be derived from the fact that he is convinced he has rights. Secret convictions seem possible. In the second place, even if the self-respecting person is authentic and wishes to seem to be what he is, it does not follow that he has to say what he is, unless saying what he is, is part of what he is. But this latter proposition is just what is at issue. The self-respecting person may protest because he believes he has rights. He does not believe he has value only if he protests.

Besides meting out injury incommensurate with the victim's worth and rights, uncontested and unopposed injustice invites witnesses to believe that he is injured just because he is wicked or inferior. Oppressors, no doubt, desire to be justified. They want to believe more than that their treatment of others is fitting; they want those they mistreat to condone their mistreatment as proper, and therefore offer inducements and rewards toward that end. Thus, even the self-respecting person may be tempted at least to pretend servility for some relief. But he will find that such pretense has its dangers; it shakes his confidence in his self-respect. I shall argue that the self-respecting person in such straits must, in some way, protest to assure himself that he has self-respect.

Since self-respect is valuable, it contributes to an individual's worth. But a person can have self-respect and few other good qualities. Since all men have inalienable rights, there is always a rational basis for self-respect, but a person may have an inflated and false sense of his worth. He may be utterly convinced, on what he falsely believes to be rational grounds, that he is much better than he really is. He may be mean and cowardly and cut an absurd figure, but insofar as he has faith in himself, he has self-respect. Consequently, when an individual desires to know whether he has self-respect, what he needs is not evidence of his worth in general but evidence of his faith in his worth. I argued earlier that protest is an indifferent way of getting others to acknowledge and thus to confirm that one has worth. But it may be an excellent way of confirming that one has faith in one's worth. For, as the preceding discussion should suggest, evidence of faith in one's worth is different from evidence of one's worth in general.

A person with a secure sense of his value has self-respect. This does not mean that he cannot lose it. It is a contradiction in terms, however, to suppose that anyone with self-respect would want to lose it. A person would want to lose his self-respect only if he feared that his belief in his worth was false or irrational, or, for some other reason, undesirable. But a person cannot be securely convinced of what he fears is false or irrational. And if a person believes that something has worth, he cannot believe that it is desirable to be ignorant of it. Hence, the person with self-respect cannot want to lose it.

Moreover, the self-respecting person cannot be oblivious to, or unconcerned about, the question of his self-respect. He must be aware that he believes he has value and that this is important. A person can have a belief and be unaware of having it, or have a sense of security and be unable to specify what he feels secure about. But the self-respecting person does not merely believe in his worth or have a vague sense of security. He feels secure about his belief in his worth. Thus, since a person cannot feel certain about something and be unaware of what he feels certain about, the self-respecting person must be aware that he believes he has value. And, for reasons already stated, he must believe that this belief is desirable. This does not mean that a person with self-respect must be continuously agitated by the fear of losing it. But it would be a mistake to urge further that only the confident, self-assured person who can take his self-respect for granted really does have self-respect. This would be to confuse self-respect with self-confidence. People sometimes do lose their self-respect. Thus to the extent that he is reflective, the person with self-respect will concede the possibility of losing it. And, though he may be confident of retaining it, he need not be. For, what he is sure of is that he has worth; not that he will always be sure of this. Whether he has this confidence depends on matters other than his self-respect. Though he may not be servile, a person may properly fear that, because of what he is doing or because of what is happening to him, he will become servile.

He may also fear that he is already servile. If he has self-respect he will be aware that he entertains the belief that he has worth and that he should be convinced of it, though he need not be sure that he is convinced of it. For he will probably also know that servile people too can value and persuade themselves that they have the self-respect which they lack. Thus, not only may a person with self-respect fear losing it; he may fear not having it. And this is not untypical. The early Christian may have had faith but doubt that he had it; to abolish his doubt he often sought the test of martyrdom. The courageous man may test his courage in order to know it. Though such tests may incidentally develop qualities they are meant to test, their main function is to discover to the agent a faith he may have, but of which he is not certain.

In sum, a person with self-respect may lose it. He may not be confident of always having it. He may not even be sure that he really has it. But if he does have self-respect, he will never be unconcerned about the question of his self-respect. Necessarily he will want to retain it. But no one will be satisfied that he has something unless he knows that he has it. Hence, the self-respecting person wants to know that he is self-respecting.

To know this he needs evidence. The need for such evidence must be especially poignant to the self-respecting person when, to prevent injury, he pretends servility. Observers often cannot agree on how to interpret such behavior. The "Sambo" personality, for example, is supposed to typify the good humored, ostensibly servile black slave. Sambo was apparently very convincing. In *Slavery: A Problem in American Institutional Life*, Stanley Elkins suggests that Sambo's "docility" and "humility" reflected true servility. On the other hand, other historians suspect that Sambo was a fraud. Patterson, for example, argues that Sambo's fawning laziness and dishonesty was his way of hitting back at the master's system without penalty. Thus, Patterson sees Sambo's "clowning" as a mask, "to salvage his dignity," a "deadly serious game," in which "the perfect stroke of rebellion must ideally appear to the master as the ultimate act of submission." Patterson is persuasive, but true servility is possible. Sambo could have been genuinely servile. Certainly every effort was made to make him so. There is therefore

room for uncertainty. Further, it is not clear that Sambo can himself definitively settle the question. The master could have reason to suspect that Sambo's antics were a pretense only if he had evidence that they were. But if he is to know that he is not servile, Sambo too needs such evidence.

It may be pointed out that if Sambo's ostensible servility was his way of "hitting back," he was providing evidence of self-respect all along. But this must be qualified. Unless it is already known to be pretense, apparent servility is evidence of servility. If Sambo gave a perfect imitation of servility, neither he nor his master could have any reason to think he was anything but servile. If his pretense is to provide him with evidence of his self-respect it must, to some discernible extent, betray him. Patterson may be right that the "perfect stroke of rebellion must seem to the master as the ultimate act of submission,"[13] but the deception must succeed, not because it is undetectable, but because the master is so blinded by his own arrogance that he cannot see that what is presented as abasement is really thinly disguised affront.

If the above argument is sound, only consummate artistry can permit a person continuously and elaborately to pretend servility and still know that he is self-respecting. Unless it is executed by a master, the evidence of servility will seem overwhelming and the evidence of self-respect too ambiguous. But, as I have argued, the self-respecting person wants to know he is self-respecting. He hates deception and pretense because he sees them as obstacles to the knowledge of himself as self-respecting. If only occasionally, he must shed his mask.

This may not be so easy. It is not only that shedding the mask of servility may take courage, but that if a person is powerless it will not be easy for him to make others believe that he is taking off a mask. People do not take the powerless seriously. Because he wants to know himself as self-respecting, the powerless but self-respecting person is driven to make others take him seriously. He is driven to make his claim to self-respect unmistakable. Therefore, since nothing as unequivocally expresses what a person thinks he be-lieves as his own emphatic statement, the powerless but self-respecting person will de-clare his self-respect. He will protest. His protest affirms that he has rights. More im-portant, it tells everyone that he believes he has rights and that he therefore claims self-re-spect. When he has to endure wrongs he can-not repel and feels his self-respect threat-ened, he will publicly claim it in order to reassure himself that he has it. His reassur-ance does not come from persuading others that he has self-respect. It comes from using his claim to self-respect as a challenge.

Thus, even when transgressors will not desist, protest is nevertheless directed at them. For the strongest challenge to a claim to self-respect and one which can consequent-ly most surely establish it as true will most like-ly come from those most anxious to deny that it has any basis. Protest in such straits is often unaccompanied by argument showing that the protester has rights, for what is relevant to his claim to self-respect is not whether he has rights but whether he believes he has them.[14]

NOTES

I am grateful to Tom Hill and Jan Boxill for helpful discussions and to the editors of *Philosophy & Public Affairs* for valuable comments and criticisms.

1. W.E.B. Du Bois, "Of Mr. Booker T. Washing-ton and Others," in *Negro Social and Political Thought 1850–1920*, ed. Howard Brotz (New York, 1966), p. 514. Hereafter cited as Brotz.
2. *W.E.B. Du Bois*, ed. William M. Tuttle, Jr. (New Jersey, 1973), p. 48.
3. Booker T. Washington, "Democracy and Edu-cation," in Brotz, p. 37c.
4. Ibid.
5. Booker T. Washington, "The Intellectuals and The Boston Mob," in Brotz, p. 425.
6. Ibid., p. 429.
7. Frederick Douglass, "What the Black Man Wants," in Brotz, p. 283.
8. *W.E.B. Du Bois*, p. 43.
9. Frederick Douglass, "What are the Colored People Doing For Themselves?" in Brotz, p. 208.
10. W.E.B. Du Bois, "The Evolution of the Race Problem," in Brotz, p. 549.
11. Frederick Douglass, "The Claims of the Negro Ethnologically Considered," in Brotz, p. 228.
12. Orlando Patterson, "Toward a Future That Has No Past—Reflections on the Fate of Blacks in the Americas," in *The Public Interest*, no. 27 (Spring 1972), p. 43.
13. Ibid.
14. I have argued that the person with self-respect has a special reason to protest wrongs commit-ted against him. It may be asked whether he also has a special reason to protest wrongs committed against others. As I have indicated, though he possesses one important quality—self-respect itself—he need not possess all or most of the other morally desirable qualities. He need not, for example, be altruistic or care much about others. If he does conceive of himself as having duties to aid others, howev-er, he will want to defend his right to be that sort of person and will accordingly protest in-terferences with that right. Typically, he will have occasion to do this when his efforts to prevent wrongful injury to others are inter-fered with.

FURTHER READING

Gordon, Lewis. 1992. *Bad Faith and Antiblack Racism*. Atlantic Highlands, NJ: Humanities Press.
Hill, Thomas, Jr. "Self-Respect Reconsidered." In O. H. Green, ed., *Respect for Persons*. New Orleans, LA: Tulane University, Tulane Studies in Philosophy.
McGary, Howard. 1999. "Reparations, Self-Respect, and Public Policy." In Howard Mc-Gary, Jr., *Race and Social Justice*. Oxford: Blackwell Publishers.

Moody-Adams, Michelle. 1992. "The Social Construction of Self-Respect." *Philosophical Forum* 24.

Sachs, David. 1981. "How to Distinguish Self-Respect from Self-Esteem." *Philosophy & Public Affairs* 10.4.

Thomas, Laurence. 1983. "Self-Respect in Theory and Practice." In Leonard Harris, ed., *Philosophy Born of Struggle: An Anthology of Afro-American Philosophy from 1917.* Dubuque, IA: Kendall-Hunt Publishing Company.